VALUING A BUSINESS
The Analysis and Appraisal of Closely Held Companies

VALUING A BUSINESS
The Analysis and Appraisal of Closely Held Companies

Second Edition

Shannon P. Pratt, DBA, CFA, FASA
President
Willamette Management Associates, Inc.

BUSINESS ONE IRWIN Homewood, Illinois 60430

© RICHARD D. IRWIN, INC., 1981 and 1989

Project editor: *Jean Roberts*
Production manager: *Irene H. Sotiroff*
Jacket Designer: *Ray Machura*
Compositor: *Weimer Typesetting Company, Inc.*
Typeface: *11/13 Century Schoolbook*
Printer: *Von Hoffmann Press, Inc.*

Library of Congress Cataloging-in-Publication Data

Pratt, Shannon P.
    Valuing a business: the analysis and appraisal of closely held companies/Shannon P. Pratt—2nd ed.
        p.   cm.
    Bibliography: p.
    Includes index.
    ISBN 1-556-23127-X
    1. Corporations—Valuation. 2. Corporations—Valuation—Law and legislation—United States. I. Title.
    HG4028. V3P7 1989   88-28308
    657′.73—dc19   CIP

Printed in the United States of America

3 4 5 6 7 8 9 0   VH   5 4 3 2 1 0

To the staff of Willamette Management Associates, Inc.,
who have demonstrated dedicated professionalism
and who have contributed immeasurably to this book

About the Author

Shannon P. Pratt is president of Willamette Management Associates, Inc., a national business valuation firm headquartered in Portland, Oregon, with a branch office in Washington, D.C. Over the past 20 years, Dr. Pratt and his staff of business valuation analysts have become widely recognized and respected as leading contributors to the conceptual development of the business appraisal profession. Having completed thousands of appraisal assignments, Dr. Pratt and his professional associates are frequently called upon to testify in state and federal courts as expert witnesses in business valuation disputes.

Sometimes characterized as the "quintessential researcher" for his endeavor to keep abreast of the issues in the business appraisal profession, Dr. Pratt has been instrumental in developing within his firm one of the most extensive business valuation research libraries in existence, with a constantly updated collection of hundreds of books, articles, transaction data sources, and court cases involving business valuation issues. This book draws heavily on that resource.

Dr. Pratt holds a Doctorate in Finance from Indiana University. He is a Fellow of the American Society of Appraisers in Business Valuation (the highest designation awarded by the Society for outstanding contribution to his field). He also holds the professional designations of Chartered Financial Analyst, Certified Review Appraiser, Certified Business Counselor, Certified Financial Planner, and Senior Certified Valuer.

Dr. Pratt has been a member of the American Society of Appraisers Business Valuation Committee since its inception in 1980; he currently serves as Chairman of The ESOP Association Valuation Advisory Committee and is a member of its Legislative and Regulatory Advisory Committee.

Author of numerous articles on business valuation topics, published in a variety of national professional and trade journals, Dr. Pratt is a frequent speaker at professional appraisal meetings, as well as bar and CPA meetings, industry associations, and financial and estate planning groups. He is also the author of the first edition of this book, *Valuing a Business* (1981), and *Valuing Small Businesses and Professional Practices* (1986), (see outside back cover), both published by Dow Jones-Irwin.

Preface

As my professional colleagues are well aware, I thoroughly enjoy the challenge of keeping abreast of developments in the rapidly evolving business valuation profession and sharing the knowledge and insights with others. This book is the core of that ongoing effort.

Intended Audience

I have developed this book primarily for the use of business and professional people who must deal with business valuation matters in one way or another. This audience includes business appraisers, attorneys, CPAs, bankers, fiduciaries, and, of course, owners of businesses and business interests. The book is also suitable as a text for a course in business valuation at the graduate or senior undergraduate level.

Objective and Scope

The book is a primer on the theory and practice of determining the value of a business or business interest. Its purpose is twofold:

- To provide a complete, self-contained educational tool for those seeking a comprehensive introduction to the basics of business valuation.
- To serve as reference manual for those needing information or direction on some specific aspect of business valuation.

Each aspect of business valuation is described in fundamental terms, with no prior knowledge on the reader's part assumed. Each possibly esoteric term or reference is defined or otherwise identified the first time it is used. Extensive use of examples is made where appropriate. For those who must go beyond the scope of a single-volume text, extensive bibliographical and court case citations are included.

I have attempted to identify, where appropriate, those valuation matters on which there is general consensus among practitioners and those subject to controversy at the time of this writing. Any personal opinions are clearly identified as such.

Changes Since the First Edition

The preparation of this second edition was a humbling experience. The research involved in making it as comprehensive as possible revealed several hundred new laws, regulations, court cases, books, articles, and information sources in the eight years since the first edition. Also, during these eight years I have gained greater appreciation for the current relevance of some earlier classic works and have incorporated their highlights as additional background in this edition.

I have included more excerpts from the wisdom of long-established valuation theory, such as James Bonbright's *Valuation of Property*. The theory section also includes more material from modern financial theory, particularly the capital asset pricing model. This strengthened theoretical underpinning is followed up with greatly expanded attention to methods and sources for developing required rates of return and capitalization rates.

In keeping with the needs of business valuation and related professionals in this litigious age, the edition devotes far more attention to valuation law; Part VII dedicates three entire chapters to litigation. The chapters on estate planning and ESOPs have been greatly revised and expanded. Several chapters on important topics that the original edition did not address have been added, including a four-chapter section on valuing partial interests.

Chapters and appendixes that are new to this edition are:

Chapter 8	Data on Required Rates of Return
Chapter 15	Valuing Minority Interests
Chapter 16	Valuing Debt Securities
Chapter 17	Valuing Preferred Stocks
Chapter 18	Valuing Stock Options
Chapter 24	Court Cases Involving ESOP Valuation Issues
Chapter 25	Divorces, Dissolutions, Dissenting-Stockholder Suits, and Damages
Chapter 26	Going Public
Chapter 27	Litigation Support
Chapter 28	Expert Testimony
Chapter 29	Arbitration
Appendix B	Uniform Standards of Professional Appraisal Practice—Excerpts Applicable to Business Appraisals
Appendix C	Definitions of Terms Adopted by the Business Valuation Committee of the American Society of Appraisers.

Organization of the Book

Chapter 1 addresses the foundation of any appraisal exercise: defining the assignment. From there, the book moves from the general theory and practice of business valuation through a step-by-step application of the theory and principles to the final product in the form of a complete written valuation report. The second half of the book is divided into three parts: Part V, "Valuing Partial Interests"; Part VI, "Valuations for Specific Purposes"; and Part VII, "Litigation."

Eight chapters contain bibliographies on their subject matter. In addition, an extensive general bibliography at the end of the book covers both general and specific topics. I have attempted to exclude from the bibliographies material that is proprietary, obscure, or very difficult to find and include only material that is available for purchase and/or can be found in major libraries.

Finally, the book is comprehensively indexed to assist readers in locating references to a specific topic, author, source, regulation, or court case. I have attempted to present the material in a form as comprehensive and easy to use as possible within the constraints of a single volume. As always, I welcome readers' comments and discussion on anything from errata to conceptual issues.

Shannon Pratt
Portland, Oregon
September 1988

Acknowledgments

This work has benefited immensely from the unstinting efforts of many of the leading intellects in the business valuation profession, as well as of several eminent attorneys and other professionals who interface regularly with business valuation practitioners. Two valuation experts willingly donated their time to review and comment on all or most of the manuscript and provided invaluable input from their unique perspectives:

Mike Bolotsky
American Appraisal Associates, Inc.

Jay Fishman
Financial Research, Inc.

In addition, the entire professional staff of Willamette Management Associates reviewed the full manuscript and provided critiques in a series of 15 two- to three-hour intensive give-and-take sessions. These included Ralph Arnold, Kathryn Aschwald, Jacie Daschel, Richard Dole, Todd Henne, John Hunter, Curt Kimball, Christy Kolbye, Steve Krug, Pam Mastroleo, Mary McCarter, Ed McReynolds, Lou Paone, Jeff Patterson, Phil Smith, and Donna Walker. Kathie Martin, our administrative vice president, and Charlene Cottingham, my secretary, also made valuable contributions to these sessions. Jan Bear, our valuation report editor, meticulously and thoughtfully edited the manuscript and also participated in the critique sessions.

Others reviewed anywhere from one to several chapters and provided very valuable comments:

John Bakken
Business Appraisal Associates

Bill Berg
Paulson Investment Company

Barnes Ellis
Stoel, Rives, Boley, Jones & Grey

John Emory
Robert W. Baird & Company, Inc.

Don Erickson
Arthur Young

Robert Howard
Houlihan, Lokey, Howard & Zukin, Inc.

Yale Kramer
Reiss Corporation

Ron Ludwig
Ludwig & Curtis

Bob Oliver
Phillip Osborne
Management Planning, Inc.

Eugene Ritti   Willis Snell
Hawley, Troxell, Ennis &   Steuart Thomsen
Hawley   *Sutherland, Asbill & Brennan*

Several members of my professional staff prepared the initial drafts of various chapters or portions of chapters. Christy Kolbye, Ed McReynolds, and Todd Henne, all CPAs, contributed their accounting expertise to the revision of Chapter 5, "Company Data—Written Information." Jacie Daschel revised Chapter 6, "Company Data—Field Trips and Interviews"; Chapter 7, "Economic and Industry Data"; and Chapter 9, "Comparative Transaction Data." Jeff Patterson was responsible for updating Chapter 11, "Analyzing and Adjusting Financial Statements." Phil Smith revised the text in Chapter 12, "Comparative Ratio Analysis" and designed the formulas, tables, and exhibits presented there. A team effort by Mary McCarter, Kathryn Aschwald, and Jacie Daschel created the sample report in Chapter 14.

Part V is completely new to this book. Members of my professional staff responsible for drafting the initial chapters were Jeff Patterson (Chapter 16, "Valuing Debt Securities"), Kathryn Aschwald (Chapter 17, "Valuing Preferred Stocks"), and Phil Smith (Chapter 18, "Valuing Stock Options"). Chapter 19, "Estate Planning and Tax Valuations," and Chapter 22, "Other Federal Gift and Estate Tax Cases," were substantially updated by Curt Kimball, whose extensive knowledge in this area was particularly helpful in light of the sweeping tax reform in recent years. Mary McCarter was responsible for the initial draft of Chapter 23, "Employee Stock Ownership Plans," another area that has undergone considerable change. Another new chapter to this book is Chapter 25, "Divorces, Dissolutions, Dissenting-Stockholder Suits, and Damages." The initial draft for this chapter was the result of a joint effort by Ralph Arnold and Jacie Daschel.

In addition to either revising or writing the initial drafts, these individuals contributed their unique talents and expertise to the creation of the exhibits included in the respective chapters.

For permission to use material, I wish to thank AMACOM, American Institute of Certified Public Accountants, American Institute of Real Estate Appraisal, American Society of Appraisers, Appraisal Foundation, *Business Week,* Callaghan & Company, Commerce Clearing House, CPA Services, Inc., Disclosure, Inc., Dow Jones-Irwin, The Dryden Press, The ESOP Association, *The Financial Planner, Harvard Business Review,* Ibbotson & Associates, *Illinois Bar Journal, Journal of the American Society of CLU,* Leopold Bernstein, McGraw-Hill Book Company, *Mergers & Acquisitions,* Merrill Lynch, Pierce, Fenner & Smith, Inc., The Miche Company, *Oklahoma Law Review,* Panel Publications, Para Publishing, Prentice-Hall, Reston Publishing (a division of Simon & Schuster), Robert Morris Associates, Standard & Poor's Corporation, University of Southern California Institute on Federal Taxation, *Value Line Investment Survey,* W. T. Grimm & Company, Inc., and Warren, Gorham & Lamont.

Typesetting and artwork for the exhibits were done by our graphic artist, Leah Firth, to whom we are very grateful. The entire manuscript was typed by Suzette Sparks, who somehow maintained her good humor throughout—a feat appreciated by all. Last but not least, responsibility for coordination of the entire project rested on the shoulders of our librarian, Pam Mastroleo, who also created the very comprehensive bibliographies. She maintained her composure through months of intensive effort, for which I am at once both incredulous and very thankful.

My deep gratitude goes to all of the above contributors of time, effort, and talent and to many others who extended their help somewhere along the way. Final responsibility for all judgments and content rests, of course, with the author.

Contents

for Lack of Marketability. Sum of Parts Not Necessarily Equal to Whole. Other Qualitative Factors Affecting Value: *Private versus Public Ownership. Qualitative Company Characteristics.* Summary of Business Valuation Principles.

Extraordinary or Nonrecurring Items: *Ordinary versus Extraordinary Items. Other Nonrecurring Items. Discontinued Operations.* Operating versus Nonoperating Items. Management Compensation and Perquisites. Transactions Involving Company Insiders. Contingent Assets and Liabilities. Adjustments to Asset Valuations: *Marketable Securities. Other Assets.* Computation of Earnings per Share: *Weighted-Average Basis. Primary versus Fully Diluted Earnings.* Computation of Book Value per Share. An Example of the Effect of Alternative Accounting Methods. Adjusting the Balance Sheet to Current Values. Summary.

Economic Outlook: *Overview. Consumer Spending and Retail Sales. Outlook.* Economic Outlook for the Metropolitan Areas of Baltimore, Maryland; Washington, D.C.; and Norfolk, Virginia. Consumer Electronics Industry: *Overview. The Superstore Concept. Products. Dependence on Imports. Outlook.* Fundamental Position of the Company: *Background. Operations. Employees and Management. Marketing. Suppliers. Competition. Facilities. Expansion Plans. Summary of Positive and Negative Factors. Prior Transactions in the Stock.* The Search for Comparatives: *Selection of Comparative Companies. Description of Comparative Companies.* Financial Statement Analysis: *Adjustments to Income Statements. Trend Analysis. Analysis of Comparative Publicly Traded Companies.* Appraisal of Fair Market Value: *Valuation Approaches. Approaches Considered but Not Used. Capitalization of Earnings. Price/Revenues Approach. Price/Book Value Approach. Valuation Summary. Discount for Lack of Marketability. Prior Transaction.* Conclusion.

ESOPs. Criteria for Establishing an ESOP. Special Issues in Valuing ESOP Stock: *Requirement of Independent Annual Stock Appraisal. Proximity of Appraisal to Transaction Date. Formula Appraisals. Accounting for Dilution. Effect of ESOP on Earnings Base to Capitalize. Treatment of Excess Management Compensation. Control versus Minority Basis for Valuation. Discount for Lack of Marketability. Valuations in Leveraged ESOPs.* ESOP Valuation Problems. Summary. Bibliography: Employee Stock Ownership Plans.

Damage Cases. The Arbitration Agreement: *Factors Specified in the Arbitration Agreement. Factors Left to the Arbitrators' Discretion. Other Factors to Address.* Procedure for Selecting Arbitrators. Criteria for Selecting Arbitrators: *Qualifications. Independence. Availability and Compensation.* Engagement of Arbitrators. The Arbitration Process: *Review of the Arbitration Document. Initial Communication among Arbitrators. Field Visit. Hearings. The Valuation Meeting.* Reporting the Results of the Arbitration. Summary: The Most Critical Elements.

Code of Abbreviations

acq., acquiesed
aff'd sub nom., affirmed sub nominee
A.F.T.R., American Federal Tax Reports
A.L.R., American Law Reports
Am. Juris., American Jurisprudence
Am. Juris. P.O.F., American Jurisprudence Proof of Facts
app. dism'd, appeal dismissed
A.2d, Atlantic Reporter 2d
B.T.A., Board of Tax Appeals
cert. den., Certificate denied
C.L.U., Chartered Life Underwriter
C.F.R., Code of Federal Regulations
C.J.S., Corpus Juris Secundum
C.B., Cumulative Bulletin
ERISA, Employee Retirement Income Security Act
F.2d, Federal Reporter 2d
F. Supp., Federal Supplement
I.R.C., Internal Revenue Code
P.2d, Pacific Reporter 2d
reh. den., rehearing denied
rev'd, reviewed
S.E.C., Securities and Exchange Commission
S. Ct., Supreme Court Reports
T.C., Tax Court
T.C.M., Tax Court Memorandum (Commerce Clearing House)
U.S.C., United States Code
U.S., United States Reports
U.S.T.C., United States Tax Cases
vac'd & rem'd, vacated and remanded

List of Exhibits

Introduction: The State of the Art of the Business Appraisal Profession

Default in Academia
Professionalization of the Practitioners
    Canadians Lead the Way
    The ESOP Association Valuation Advisory Committee
    Business Valuation Committee of the American Society of Appraisers
"Beware of Amateur Hour"
Uniform Standards of Professional Appraisal Practice
Summary

As this second edition is written, the profession of business appraisal is still in an embryonic state, but it is growing rapidly.

According to the U.S. Small Business Administration, there were over 17 million businesses in the United States in the 1980s:

Over 2.8 million corporations.

Almost 1.5 million partnerships.

More than 13 million sole proprietorships.

Every year, hundreds of thousands of businesses completely change ownership. Millions of partial changes of ownership also occur. Moreover, hundreds of millions of dollars in payments based on decisions about the values of businesses are made every year. Such payments arise from gift, estate, and inheritance taxes, ad valorem (property) taxes, matrimonial property settlements, amounts of relief in damage cases, and many other matters. Considering the economic importance to millions of people of the proper appraisal of businesses and business interests, it seems almost incredible that it is only in the last few years that business appraisal has begun to emerge as a unified discipline in the United States.

In the last few years, the emergence and growth of the business valuation discipline have been led by a core of dedicated professionals who have conducted and disseminated a large amount of research and education on the subject. The discipline's development benefited from the availability of many new data sources on relevant subjects such as merger and acquisition prices, rates of return on equity, and measurement of risk. Most of these data bases did not even exist in the 1970s. Their usefulness in a broad variety of business valuation applications has been vitally enhanced by the communication and computer capabilities for searching out, retrieving, and analyzing data that meet almost any set of criteria the analyst may choose to specify.

Default in Academia

The typical finance professor at most business schools still is not even aware of business appraisal as a career option for students. This is especially unfortunate because business appraisal offers one of the most challenging and intellectually rewarding career opportunities for the brightest students of finance, applying as it does the full gamut of financial theory and principles.

Economists and business school professors teach us in no uncertain terms that the most important objective of the owner, or head, of a business enterprise—one who is economically motivated by the "invisible hand" of Adam Smith—should be to maximize the value of the firm. However, in 1987 the closest most business schools got to teaching students how to determine a firm's value was through a theoretical chapter or two in a general finance or investments text. Only about a dozen business schools offered even a single course in how to value a business. The number appears to be growing, albeit slowly.

Courses in the closely related subjects of security analysis and investment portfolio management abound. But such courses are narrowly focused, dealing almost entirely with minority interests in large corporations in the form of publicly traded stocks and bonds. Such courses do not, for the most part, deal directly with the question of the value of the total firm. Furthermore, they do not cover the values of either total or partial interests in closely held firms.

Business schools also offer courses in corporate finance, whose content tends to focus on obtaining and managing funds and making investment decisions in regard to capital budgeting. Capital budgeting decisions have much in common with decisions on a reasonable price to pay for an existing business. However, business schools generally fail to point out this important connection.

The analytical skills germane to the disciplines of security analysis and corporate finance are essential to the discipline of business appraisal. But business schools have left a major gap by failing to undertake the logical step of applying these skills to the valuation of closely held companies and interests in them. The result is that the conceptual leadership in the development of the business appraisal discipline has arisen from collaborative efforts on the part of professional practitioners rather than from the academic community.

Professionalization of the Practitioners

Canadians Lead the Way

Canada led the United States in an organized effort toward conceptual development of the business appraisal discipline. Not surprisingly, a specific catalyst spurred the discipline's earlier organized development. That catalyst was called *Valuation Day,* December 31, 1971 (Valuation Day for publicly traded companies was December 22, 1971).

The significance of Valuation Day was that it set a base valuation date from which all capital appreciation was measured for capital gains taxes and estate taxes. Consequently, the valuation of all property, including all businesses and business interests, as of that date became a considerably significant matter. Since there were no market quotations for the values of closely held businesses and business interests, there suddenly was a need to develop values as of one specific date for a large number of entities.

The Canadian Institute of Chartered Business Valuators (CICBV), originally called the Canadian Association of Business Valuators, was born on January 6, 1971. Since then it has held biennial meetings, with the proceedings published as *The Journal of Business Valuation.*

The CICBV holds educational meetings for its members at varying intervals.

The CICBV has developed a rigorous examination for testing a candidate's professional skills in business valuation. It awards the professional designation of CBV (chartered business valuator) to those who demonstrate three years of full-time experience in business appraisal, five years of part-time experience, or two years and a required course of study, pass the exam, and meet certain other requirements. Information on the CICBV may be obtained from the Canadian Institute of Chartered Business Valuators, 150 Bloor Street West, second floor, Toronto, Ontario M5S 2Y2.

The ESOP Association Valuation Advisory Committee

The first organized national effort in the United States toward some unification among leading business appraisers also resulted largely from certain tax legislation. Although the United States has had income taxes since 1913, the catalyst that spurred a group of business appraisers to come together in an organized manner was the portion of the 1974 Tax Act that granted especially favorable tax treatment to companies with employee stock ownership plans (ESOPs). This advantageous tax treatment prompted the development of thousands of ESOPs, the large majority of which were in privately held companies.

Each private company with an ESOP must have its stock valued annually, and the nature of an ESOP poses certain unique valuation problems. In order to address these valuation problems in a unified manner, a group was formed consisting of business appraisers who were active in the valuation of ESOP shares throughout the country. This group became an advisory committee of The ESOP Association, an organization of companies that have ESOPs.

The ESOP Association Valuation Advisory Committee meets twice a year, primarily to discuss issues concerning the valuation of ESOP shares in privately held companies. The committee has worked toward developing of valuation guidelines and in 1985 developed a 75-page booklet titled *Valuing ESOP Shares*.[1] Committee members also conduct educational sessions for ESOP Association members and companies considering ESOPs.

While The ESOP Association is contributing a worthwhile effort to the refinement and sophistication of ESOP stock valuation, it should be understood that it neither certifies nor endorses business appraisers or any other specialists. There are no requirements for membership in the Association except the payment of dues.

Information on The ESOP Association may be obtained from The ESOP Association, 1100 17th Street, N.W., Suite 310, Washington, D.C. 20036.

---

[1] *Valuing ESOP Shares* (Washington, D.C.: The ESOP Association, 1985).

Business Valuation Committee of the American Society of Appraisers

The need for a broad program of education and professional accreditation in the discipline of business valuation finally was met with the formation in 1981 of the Business Valuation Committee of the American Society of Appraisers (ASA). The ASA is a long-standing, multidisciplinary organization that offers education and professional accreditation in many appraisal disciplines, including real property, machinery and equipment, personal property, and public utilities.

Prior to the formation of the Business Valuation Committee, the ASA had for many years offered accreditation in "Intangible Property," which included stocks or other interests in businesses as well as patents, copyrights, and other intangible property. However, there were few candidates for accreditation under that designation. Under the auspices of the Business Valuation Committee, the name of the accreditation category was changed from "Intangible Property" to "Business Valuation" and the content of the examinations was revised to include a heavy emphasis on current techniques for appraising businesses of all sizes, professional practices, and partial interests in them. The Business Valuation Committee now has the support of almost all the leading U.S. business appraisal firms, and from 1984 through 1988 the business valuation discipline was the fastest-growing category of accreditation in the American Society of Appraisers.

The professional designation ASA stands for *Accredited Senior Appraiser.* In order to acquire it, one needs the following: five years of experience in the discipline in which the designation is granted; passing the relevant examinations; and submitting two appraisal reports that meet the examining committee's standards.

The American Society of Appraisers offers a series of four three-day basic courses in business valuation, each presented several times per year at various locations around the United States. In addition, the ASA holds an annual meeting for members from all appraisal disciplines. In recent years, this event has included two days of educational meetings on business appraisal topics. Also, the Business Valuation Committee sponsors a two-day Advanced Business Valuation Seminar each fall. Local chapters or regional groups of chapters of the ASA occasionally sponsor educational programs.

The Business Valuation Committee also publishes a quarterly journal, *Business Valuation Review,* and the ASA publishes a multidisciplinary appraisal journal, *Valuation.*

The society's code of ethics requires an appraiser using the professional designation of ASA as a credential in connection with a valuation report to set forth the discipline in which certification was achieved in the statement of qualifications and/or limiting conditions presented to, or received by, clients (e.g., "Peter Plausible, ASA, Business Valuation"). It would be a breach of ethics for someone accredited in machinery and equipment appraisal, for example, to write a business valuation report and be identified only as "Sandy Shoveler, ASA," which might mislead the reader to think that the author is accredited in business valuation when in fact the accreditation is in a different appraisal discipline.

Information on the American Society of Appraisers, its courses, and a list of senior members accredited in Business Valuation may be obtained from the ASA National Headquarters, P.O. Box 17265, Washington, D.C. 20041.

"Beware of Amateur Hour"

The growth in the recognition and use of business appraisers has attracted literally thousands of people to practice business valuation around the fringes of the profession, a bit akin to practicing law without ever going to law school. A 1987 article in *Business Week* titled "Business Appraising: Beware of Amateur Hour " made the following observations:

> . . . the explosive growth is spawning an alarming number of amateurs, unqualified part-timers, and conflicts of interest. . . .
>
> . . . there is general agreement that the business-appraisal profession needs tighter standards. Since 1980, the number of practitioners has grown from a few hundred to perhaps 25,000, including part-timers. Yet only about 400 are certified by the American Society of Appraisers, a professional organization whose members must have five years' experience, pass a rigorous examination, and submit a series of reports to a review committee.[2]

An article in *Inc.* recognized "a sharp upward swing in both the quantity and the quality of practitioners" but also sounded a cautionary alarm:

> Credentials? Maybe. The ASA's testing and practice requirements for certification do establish a quality floor. But assuring a business owner that he is hiring neither a neophyte nor a fool is far from saying he has bought the best service.
>
> Experience? I'd say . . . essential, maybe, but no guarantee. Some of the charlatans have been at it for years.[3]

Given ambiguous directions through uncharted territory, a business could use a simple word of advice. Sherwin Simmons (senior tax and estate-planning lawyer with the Tampa law firm of Trenam, Simmons, Kemker, Scharf, Barkin, Frye & O'Neill) has it:

> Network. . . . Ask around, and then ask around some more. Talk to people in your geographical area, even if their businesses aren't just like yours; talk to people with similar businesses, even if they're not in your geographical area. Appraisal is a fraternity, and once you know who's in the fraternity, who's respected, you'll know who to go to. And very impor-

---

[2] Stuart Weiss, "Business Appraising: Beware of Amateur Hour," *Business Week*, February 9, 1987, p. 74.
[3] Nell Margolis, "Something of Value," *Inc.* January 1986, p. 104.

tantly, if the reason you're looking for a valuation has anything to do with taxes, or is likely to somewhere down the line, find out who's respected by the Internal Revenue Service—who do they use to do their valuation work? You've got to remember at all times why you're doing this in the first place: sooner or later, there's a player on the other side, and if the other side doesn't buy your valuation, then you wasted your money.[4]

Uniform Standards of Professional Appraisal Practice

In 1987, nine of the leading U.S. professional appraisal organizations adopted a landmark document titled "Uniform Standards of Professional Appraisal Practice." Eight of the nine groups are composed entirely of real estate appraisers; one, the American Society of Appraisers, is multidisciplinary.

Standards 9 and 10 establish guidelines for developing and communicating business appraisals. Appendix B of this book presents the Preamble, Competency Provision, Definitions, and Standards 9 and 10 in their entirety. Although broad, the standards represent an important initial step in setting some minimum requirements to which all professional appraisals are expected to conform.

The Uniform Standards of Professional Appraisal Practice are being promulgated and administered through the Appraisal Foundation, whose salient history and plans are as follows:

1. In November 1987, the Appraisal Foundation was approved by the participating appraisal societies.
2. The Appraisal Foundation is the parent entity for an Appraisal Standards Board and an Appraiser Qualifications Board.
3. The Standards Board will continue to develop and promulgate the Uniform Standards of Professional Appraisal Practice.
4. The Qualifications Board will establish guidelines for certifying qualified appraisers and promote and disseminate this information to the states, government agencies, and other users of appraisal services for adoption as uniform certification requirements.
5. The self-regulatory organization will provide a mechanism for promulgating these consensus standards that could be adopted by states and other government entities and enforced through a state-level licensing or certification procedure.

Summary

Every year, billions of dollars' worth of decisions are made on the basis of values of businesses or business interests as determined by owners, buyers, financial intermediaries, regulatory agencies, and courts. Yet,

---

[4] Ibid.

amazingly, business appraisal was in most respects a neglected discipline until the early 1980s.

Today the discipline of business appraisal is rapidly achieving recognition among buyers and sellers, fiduciaries, attorneys, regulatory agencies, and courts. More and more parties to transactions involving business valuations are demanding that the value be based on thorough and informed analysis by a professional business valuation specialist. A small but rapidly growing number of such professionals are emerging to fill this demand.

The appraisal of businesses may well be the most complex of all appraisal disciplines. The theoretical framework and standards of practice for business valuation, and especially the tools for implementation, have undergone extensive development during the 1980s. Such tools include affordable computers that are becoming increasingly powerful in their computational capabilities and data storage and manipulation; large data bases relevant to business valuation; and increasingly rapid and inexpensive communications capabilities, both in North America and worldwide. A growing breed of sophisticated business valuation practitioners are putting these tools to good work, providing decision makers with ever more rigorously conceived and executed business appraisals. This book offers the reader an overview of the state of the art of the business appraisal discipline as it stands at the end of the 1980s.

Part I

Principles of Business Valuation

Chapter 1

Defining the Appraisal Assignment

Basic Elements of the Appraisal Assignment
Definition of Who Made and Who Accepted the Assignment
Definition of the Interest or Interests to Be Appraised
    Definition of the Entity
    Definition of the Interest Relative to the Entity
Date or Dates of the Valuation
Purpose or Purposes of the Appraisal
    Gift, Estate, and Inheritance Taxes and Estate Planning
    Employee Stock Ownership Plans (ESOPs) and Other Employee Benefit
      Plans
    Ad Valorem Taxes
    Selling Out, Merging, Acquiring, or Divesting
    Going Public
    Buy-Sell Agreements
    Marital, Partnership, and Corporate Dissolutions
    Damage Cases
    Bankruptcy Reorganizations
Applicable Standard of Value
    Fair Market Value
    Fair Value
    Investment Value
    Intrinsic or Fundamental Value
    Going-Concern Value
    Liquidation Value
    Book Value
Form and Extent of the Written and/or Verbal Report(s)
Schedule
Fee Arrangements
Summary

It is impossible to intelligently discuss methods of valuation without reference to some assumed definition of value[1] . . .

Basic Elements of the Appraisal Assignment

I cannot overemphasize the importance of clearly defining the elements of the appraisal assignment *at the outset of a business appraisal.* It may seem obvious that the first step is to define the task. However, it is my own experience—-undoubtedly shared by most other professional business appraisers—that most initial assignments are incomplete, misstated, or both. The reason may be that the client lacks sufficient experience to realize all the details that should be included in the appraisal assignment or has not thought through the implications of some aspects of the appraisal. The professional appraiser should guide the client in these details. Regardless of why the shortcomings occur, failure to be thorough and explicit in the appraisal assignment is one of the greatest sources of errors, delays, excess costs, and misunderstandings between client and appraiser in business valuations.

The basic elements of the appraisal assignment are:

1. Name of client retaining appraiser.
2. Name of appraiser.
3. Definition of the interest or interests to be appraised.
4. Date or dates of the valuation.
5. Purpose or purposes of the appraisal.
6. Applicable standard of value.
7. Form and extent of written and/or verbal report.
8. Schedule.
9. Fee arrangements.
10. Any special requirements.

Often it is impossible to define at the outset all the relevant details of the appraisal assignment. In those cases, the appraiser should list the elements remaining to be filled in and see that such questions are answered as soon as possible. Making the list clarifies the unknown aspects and thus helps prevent a material factor from being overlooked or misconstrued.

As the appraisal assignment develops, the file containing information on it will grow. As the missing details from the original appraisal assignment are filled in, the appraiser notes them by memoranda to the file. Formerly overlooked questions should be answered by memoranda to the file as they are discovered. Similarly, any subsequent changes in the assignment should be documented by memoranda to the file.

---

[1] James C. Bonbright, *Valuation of Property,* vol. I (Charlottesville, Va.: The Miche Company, 1965 [reprint of 1937 ed.]), p. 128.

Definition of Who Made and Who Accepted the Assignment

For a number of reasons, the statement of the assignment should specify who the client is and who the appraiser is. The most obvious reason is the need to know who is responsible for providing and who for paying for the services. Another reason is that the appraiser has a fiduciary responsibility to release information about the appraisal only to the client and to others only with the client's permission. If the case involves pending or potential litigation, the attorney may prefer to have his law firm retain the appraiser, rather than have the client retain the appraiser directly. This relationship may better protect the appraiser's working papers and files from subpoena by the opposing attorney.

If a business transaction is likely to be the ultimate outcome, it may be important to specify whom the appraiser represents, such as the board of directors of the buying or selling company, the employee stock ownership plan, or one or more individual stockholders of the buying or selling company. The appraiser's relationship to the parties involved should be clear, since the appraiser may be considered to be in a position of advocacy.

In specifying who is to provide the appraisal services, the important distinction is whether the client is retaining the person primarily responsible for the appraisal directly or the appraisal firm that employs that person. Among professional appraisers, as among certified public accountants who perform audits, the common practice is to retain the firm rather than the individual appraiser. This procedure protects the client, since the firm is responsible for completing the job regardless of impairments to the individual's ability to perform the work. The practice also tends to provide continuity in the working papers and related records, making them accessible if they're needed months or years later, as they frequently are.

Definition of the Interest or Interests to Be Appraised

Definition of the Entity

If the entity at issue is incorporated, both the official name and the state of incorporation are necessary to an adequate definition of it. The state of incorporation is necessary because two or more corporations that are incorporated in different states may have identical names. Furthermore, the laws of the state of incorporation may have a bearing on the value of a particular business interest.

If, on the other hand, the business is not a corporation but some other structure, the form as well as the name must be specified. Some of the most common forms of business organization are sole proprietorships, general and limited partnerships, and cooperatives. By the same token, if the entity's structure gives rise to special legal or tax considerations, that structure should be specified. Some of these forms include Subchapter S corporations (corporations that are taxed in the same manner as partnerships; that is, the shareholder's interests in the company's earnings are taxed at an individual rather than a corporate rate), professional corporations, real estate investment trusts (REITs), investment companies registered under the Investment Company Act of 1940, and personal holding companies. Some businesses, especially sole proprietorships, have one formal name for the company and another name—d.b.a. ("doing business as")—by which the public knows the company. In such cases, it is wise to identify the entity in the appraisal assignment by both names.

If the business to be appraised is only a portion of the entire entity, such as a division or branch, it is necessary to state explicitly which aspects of the total company are included in the appraisal. Correspondingly, if the appraisal requires that the value attributable to a parent corporation be broken out from the value attributable to interests in one or more subsidiaries, this fact and the relationship between the parent and the subsidiaries must be specified.

Definition of the Interest Relative to the Entity

A critical question in defining the assignment is whether the appraisal is of the assets that make up the business or of stock or some other interest, such as a partnership interest, in the entity. In the sale of a business, for example, noteworthy tax, legal, and financial ramifications arise from the decision to consider the transaction either a transfer of assets or a transfer of an interest (whether stock or partnership) in the entity. Moreover, for many purposes, such as gift or estate taxes, it can make a considerable difference whether one is valuing a direct interest in the assets comprising the business or a corporation, partnership, or some other entity intervenes between the investment assets and the owner of the business interest.[2]

If the interest is a partnership or joint-venture interest, the appraisal assignment should indicate the percentage being valued. If a limited partnership, it should specify the respective percentage interests of the limited and general partners.

If the business is incorporated, the appraisal assignment must indicate the number of shares to be valued. It may also be helpful to indicate the number of shares outstanding. (Treasury stock, which is stock once issued and subsequently reacquired by the corporation, is *not* outstanding and must be subtracted from the shares issued in determining the number of shares outstanding.) If there is more than one class of stock, such as preferred and common, or voting and nonvoting common, the appraisal assignment should indicate which class of stock is being valued. It may also help to indicate the proportion of

---

[2] See, for example, *Edwin A. Gallun* v. *Comm.*, 33 T.C.M. 284 (1974).

the number of shares being valued to the total equity capitalization as well as to the respective classes of stock.

Any special restrictions pertaining to the shares being valued should also be included in the description of the interest being valued, since these restrictions normally have a negative effect on value, all other things being equal. The most common category of such restrictions, which may or may not apply to all the securities of the class being valued, is restrictions on transferability. Public companies, for example, commonly issue restricted stock (also called *investment letter stock*) in connection with acquisitions or in order to raise capital through private placements. Closely held companies may restrict transferability by having all or part of their shares subject to some form of buy-sell or repurchase agreement.

Other provisions of the shares being valued may have a positive effect on value, such as the owner having a put option to sell the shares to the corporation under certain circumstances. A *put* is an option to sell, exercisable at the owner's discretion, under certain prescribed terms and conditions. Technically, a put option is a separate security with its own value that serves to increase the *combined* value of the put option and the share of stock, and the put would only enhance the value of the share itself if it were nonseverable from the share of stock. However, in many instances, valuation practitioners and the users of their services accept, by consensus, that the put should be treated as an enhancement of the shares' value rather than as a separate security. For example, various forms of put options exist in employee stock ownership plans. In such a case, a share of stock owned by the ESOP, or by a beneficiary who has received a distribution of stock from the ESOP, may be worth more than another share of the same company that is not subject to the ESOP privileges.

The appraisal assignment may also need to indicate who owns the interest in question, who owns the other interests (and in what proportion), or whether it is to be a newly created interest. Sometimes the relationship of the owner of the interest to other members of the control group has a bearing on the value. The value per share of stock in an ESOP usually is less if it is newly issued stock than if it has been acquired from an existing shareholder, since there is dilution in the former case and not in the latter.

Date or Dates of the Valuation

The specific valuation date or dates are critical variables that must be determined at the outset. The value will vary from one date to another for various reasons, and sometimes it will change drastically within a short time as a result of certain events. Every day, observers of the public stock markets see sudden and substantial changes in the value of a particular company's stock. In many court cases, especially those involving tax litigation, significant changes in value over very short time spans have been justified because of changes in relevant circumstances.[3]

Many events both within and outside the individual company's control can cause changes in the value of an interest in a company—events that at first glance may seem to have little to do with value. Obviously, a sudden change in a company's earnings, especially if unanticipated, can have a substantial effect on value. Also, the value of a business interest varies inversely with the cost of capital to businesses, a factor over which individual businesses have little control. Key agreements, such as the signing or termination of a major customer contract, can raise or lower value significantly. Other major events, such as the sale of a portion of the company or a public offering of its stock, can also have a dramatic, immediate impact on value. These are just a few examples of variables that can cause significant and sometimes abrupt changes in value from one date to another.

In most business valuations, the opinion of value will be based at least partly on other, similar transactions, such as the prices at which stocks in the same or a related industry are trading in the public market relative to their earnings, assets, dividends, or other relevant variables. It is important to know the valuation date when using comparative companies in the appraisal so that the comparative transaction data can be compiled for the valuation date, or as near to it as is practically possible.

Sometimes there is more than one valuation date, such as in a series of gifts of stock. Unless the dates are quite close together and relevant circumstances have not changed materially, a separate set of data for each date must be gathered and analyzed.

Alternatively, the valuation date may be the undetermined date of some as yet unscheduled event such as the sale of the company, a public offering of stock, or a trial that hinges on the business interest's value on the trial date. Having a moving target for a valuation date challenges the appraiser to keep the relevant data as current as possible.

If the valuation must satisfy Securities and Exchange Commission (SEC) requirements, the usual rule is that the data must be current to within 90 days of the relevant event, such as an offering of stock. This rule stems from the fact that most public companies report earnings and other relevant data on a quarterly basis. The SEC's "current-within-90-days" requirement can serve as a rough guideline for other situations lacking hard and fast rules, provided that no significant pertinent events have occurred during the intervening time.

In some litigated valuations, the valuation date itself is an issue to be resolved by the court. In such situations, the appraiser must be prepared to address the valuation as of several dates, sometimes without knowing until after the judgment is rendered which date the court determined to be relevant. Since the choice of valuation date in such

---

[3] See, for example, *Morris M. Messing*, 48 T.C. 502 (1967), acq. 1968-1 C.B. 2. Even though the company made a public offering at over $36 shortly after a gift of stock, the court upheld a value of $13 for gift tax purposes as of the date of the gift.

cases will be a legal matter, the attorney for whom the expert appraiser will be testifying should take the responsibility, as part of giving the appraiser the assignment, of considering all the potentially applicable valuation dates and instructing the appraiser to be prepared to address the value as of each date.

Purpose or Purposes of the Appraisal

Perhaps the most important point to establish in this chapter is that no single methodology is universally applicable to all appraisal purposes. Different statutory, regulatory, and case precedent standards govern valuations of businesses and business interests under various jurisdictions for diverse purposes. Also, there are many practical business reasons for valuation criteria to vary from one situation to another.

I have seen literally hundreds of business appraisals that missed the target because the appraiser failed to match the appraisal methodology to the purpose for which it was being done, or because the client attempted to use the appraisal for some purpose other than the intended one. Most professional business appraisal reports contain a set of limiting conditions, such as the following:

> This appraisal is valid only for the appraisal date or dates specified herein and only for the appraisal purpose or purposes specified herein. The client warrants that any reports, analysis, or other documents prepared for it by the appraiser will be used only in compliance with all applicable laws and regulations.

It is essential that the above condition be accorded the utmost respect.

This book devotes three chapters to litigation, because litigation over business valuation issues has become very prevalent. Most such litigation has arisen because someone failed to use proper valuation methodology within the valuation's specific legal or business context. I emphasize this point in this initial chapter in the hope that it will make users of the book conscious of the need to match the valuation methodology to the appraisal's intended purpose, especially when there are applicable legal standards of value, and thus *avoid* litigation or other problems later on.

The professional literature on business appraisals indicates a wide consensus that the methods appropriate for a particular valuation depend at least partly on the valuation's purpose. For example, as the *Harvard Law Review* has pointed out:

> Some appraisers and courts tend to assume that accounting valuations of corporations and of stock for other purposes can serve as models for appraisal valuation. Although this may sometimes be true, more often *the method should depend on the reason for the valuation* [Emphasis supplied]. [4]

---

[4] "Valuation of Dissenters' Stock under Appraisal Statutes," *Harvard Law Review* (May 1966), p. 1454.

Victor I. Eber, a CPA and former chairman of the Business Management Institute, explains the critical importance of defining the purpose of the appraisal:

> Appraisal techniques for income, estate, and gift tax purposes can substantially differ from methods used to appraise a business for purposes of acquisition, merger, liquidation, divestiture, split-up and spin-offs. . . . [T]he typical appraisal for commercial purposes will frequently deal with factors of concern to prospective purchasers, liquidators, or merger partners, as distinguished from a determination of an IRS-acceptable value of the business as a free-standing going concern.[5]

Eber elaborates with an example:

> Many principals and their advisers in buy-sell situations consciously consider a limited number of variables in establishing a value. For example, a small loan holding company negotiating for the purchase of an additional office would concentrate almost entirely on the origin and condition of receivables, with minimum regard for the organization structure, the condition of the office, book values, or the past earnings of the business under existing management. Such truncated appraisal is based on the assumption that the acquiring company can supply those things. Thus, it appears that many essential factors are being ignored, on the recognized assumption that the principals expect to overcome the business deficiencies.
>
> For estate and gift tax appraisals, such shortcuts are not taken because the appraiser is typically valuing a business in a noncommercial, nonacquisition setting. Further it is a situation in which the appraiser must follow requirements.[6]

Valuation methods for different purposes may vary significantly in their degree of reliance on forward projections rather than on historical data. Professional business appraisers unanimously agree that the present value of a business interest involves a prophecy about the future. However, it is often difficult or impossible to agree on such a prophecy. Many differences in valuation approaches and methods, then, involve differing emphasis on forecasted future financial results in proportion to current and historical results and circumstances.

Chapter 3 presents the discounted future returns method of valuing a business (discounting either future earnings or future cash flow to a present worth). Students and practitioners of business appraisal generally agree that this method is theoretically the most correct one for determining the value of a business investment. This approach is widely used for making business decisions, such as the price to offer for a potential acquisition. Nevertheless, however theoretically correct some version of the discounted future returns method may be, the validity of the result depends on the accuracy of estimates of earnings, cash flow, or other variables for several years into the future. Courts tend to range from reluctant to totally unwilling to rely on such estimates in arriving at a business's value. Therefore, in most valuations

---

[5] Victor I. Eber, "How to Establish Value for Close Corporation Stock That Will Withstand an IRS Audit," *Estate Planning* (Autumn 1976), pp. 28–29.
[6] Ibid., p. 28.

involving existing or potential litigation, the appraiser must emphasize the valuation approaches based on historical and current data. Chapter 4 discusses such appraisals, and several chapters in Part VI detail valuations for some of the most common valuation purposes. The following subsections comment briefly on various valuation purposes. The next main section defines and discusses the most frequently encountered standards of value.

Gift, Estate, and Inheritance Taxes and Estate Planning

Guidelines for the valuation of businesses and business interests for gift, estate, and inheritance taxes are more clear-cut and extensive than those available for most other valuation purposes. The legally mandated standard of value is *fair market value* as defined later in this chapter. Basic guidelines are found in Revenue Ruling 59-60, which, at this writing, has stood almost a 30-year test of time. Further, both case law and literature abound. Valuations for all types of estate purposes, including gifting, estate taxes, and charitable contributions, are discussed in Chapter 19, "Estate Planning and Tax Valuations," and Chapter 22, "Other Federal Gift and Estate Tax Cases."

Employee Stock Ownership Plans (ESOPs) and Other Employee Benefit Plans

ESOP valuations are subject to the same guidelines as valuations for federal gift and estate taxes, plus those imposed by the Employee Retirement Income Security Act (ERISA), as administered through the Department of Labor. At this writing, major controversy still surrounds certain aspects of stock valuation for ESOPs, as well as for stock held in other types of employee benefit plans. Valuations for ESOPs and other employee benefit plans, along with the limited case law to date, are discussed in Chapter 23, "Employee Stock Ownership Plans," and Chapter 24, "Court Cases Involving ESOP Valuation Issues."

Ad Valorem Taxes

Ad valorem is a Latin expression meaning "according to value." The term is used in conjunction with state and local property taxes, which are levied as a percentage of the assessed value of the property being taxed. Properties subject to ad valorem taxation include such diverse entities as railroads, utilities, manufacturing plants, shopping centers, and other industrial and commercial enterprises. Fair market value is the universal standard for determining assessed values for property taxes. However, the regulations and case law for interpreting that standard for the purpose of levying ad valorem taxes vary widely from one jurisdiction to another.

In the past, appraisals of industrial and commercial operations for property tax purposes have been largely within the province of physical asset appraisers, such as real estate and machinery and equipment appraisers, with much emphasis on cost approaches to appraisal. In recent years, however, it has become apparent that, when valued by a discounted future returns method, many properties do not nearly measure up to values indicated by a depreciated replacement cost approach. As a result, many companies owning commercial, industrial, and utility properties have retained business appraisers to assist in dealing with tax-assessing authorities. By shifting more emphasis to rigorously researched income and comparative market transaction approaches, companies have pared many millions of dollars from their tax bills.

Selling Out, Merging, Acquiring, or Divesting

The majority of businesses tend to grow in value over time. To the extent that a thorough capitalization of current or historical earnings approach (based on comparative companies or other empirical data) reflects the future growth prospects in the choice of a multiple or capitalization rate, the value indicated by a historical approach should not differ significantly from the value indicated by a discounted future returns approach. However, it is often difficult to subjectively assess the impact of future growth in choosing a multiple or capitalization rate to apply to historical earnings, particularly in a fast-growing business. Thus, the forward-looking appraisal may result in a higher concluded value than an appraisal based primarily on past and current data. Sellers of businesses should try to get all they can for the speculative value of future opportunities in their businesses. To some extent, buyers are willing to pay for opportunities that promise good business risks.

Consequently, valuations for the transfer of ownership of an entire business tend to rely more on projections of the future than do valuations set in a stricter legal context, such as for litigation or tax purposes. Buyers tend to look at *investment value* as defined later in this chapter. On the other hand, most states' statutes give minority stockholders in a selling company the right to be paid off in cash at *fair value* as discussed later in this chapter. Therefore, if there are minority stockholders in the selling company, the appraiser should be aware of the dissenting-stockholder statutes and relevant case law in the state of incorporation. Dissenting-stockholder actions are discussed in Chapter 25.

Going Public

Valuations for initial public offerings of a company's stock are more oriented toward short-term market conditions than are valuations for any other purpose. Within weeks or even days, the price at which the underwriter believes the public market will accept the stock may move up or down by 25 percent or more. Furthermore, changing conditions over very short periods can determine whether or not the public market will absorb a particular company's stock at any price. Valuation and other considerations for going public are discussed in Chapter 26.

Buy-Sell Agreements

At the time of drafting a buy-sell agreement, the provisions for valuing the stock or partnership interest can be virtually anything the parties desire. It is extremely important, however, that the parties to a buy-sell agreement, as well as their respective attorneys, have a good understanding of the valuation implications of language used in such agreements in order to avoid disagreeable surprises when an event triggers valuation under the agreement. Buy-sell agreements are the subject of Chapter 20.

Marital, Partnership, and Corporate Dissolutions

Generally, guidelines for valuation of businesses and business interests for divorces are the least clearly defined category of business valuation. There are virtually no statutory standards, and most of the court decisions are not cases that are written up in the various legal reporting services. Divorce situations frequently involve emotionalism, distrust, and/or naiveté on the parts of either or both parties involved. This helps to explain why so many valuations for marital property distributions in divorces end up going to court rather than being settled.

The same is often true for partnership and corporate dissolutions, unless they are subject to a well-written buy-sell agreement. Valuations for divorces and dissolutions are discussed in Chapter 25.

Damage Cases

Business valuations become the focal point of many types of damage cases. Some of the most common damage claims are based on breach of contract, antitrust, condemnation, lost profits, or lost business opportunity. The legally acceptable criteria for valuation vary widely from one type of case to another and across jurisdictions. Valuation for damage cases is discussed in Chapter 25.

Bankruptcy Reorganizations

Valuation for reorganization in bankruptcy is essentially a forward-looking exercise, since the company's history led it to its bankrupt condition. Generally, the potential for reorganizing the company and continuing its operations depends on whether or not the value as a going concern exceeds the liquidation value.

As noted in an excellent article in the *Temple Law Quarterly,* a bankruptcy reorganization almost always involves restructuring of interests:

> The firm's capital structure may be altered under chapter 11 in several significant ways, including stretching out principal payments on outstanding loans, lowering interest charges, reducing outstanding claims, or converting fixed charges into contingent obligations by exchanging old debt for new equity. In other words, chapter 11 generally involves exchanging the old participations in a firm's value for new participations. A reorganization plan is fundamentally concerned with determining which parties can share in the value of the reorganized firm and the extent of that party's share.[7]

As a consequence, the role of the valuation expert in a bankruptcy reorganization usually is broader than just the appraisal of the entity. The valuation expert's assignment typically includes participating in designing the classes of interests and allocating the total value among them, much as in a multi-investor leveraged-buyout situation.

Applicable Standard of Value

Books, articles, court decisions, and other sources use many terms to describe various notions of value, but, unfortunately, such terms mean different things to different people. As one experienced attorney put it:

> Many terms are used to define value . . . Only a few of these terms have some definition. Others have the definition which the parties choose to place upon them.[8]

This section discusses the concepts of value most widely encountered in business valuation. Each of the concepts of value discussed could be applicable to the valuation of either a control or a minority interest.

Fair Market Value

The most widely recognized and accepted standard of value is *fair market value.* It is the standard that applies to all federal and state tax matters, such as estate, gift, inheritance, income, and ad valorem taxes. It is also the legal standard of value in many other—though not all—valuation situations. The definition of fair market value is almost universally accepted as the cash, or cash-equivalent, price at which

---

[7] Richard H. Fearon and Mitchell R. Julis, "The Role of Modern Finance in Bankruptcy Reorganizations," *Temple Law Quarterly* 56 (1983), pp. 1–2.

[8] John E. Moye, *Buying and Selling Businesses* (Minneapolis: National Practice Institute for Continuing Legal Education, 1983), p. 25.

property would change hands between a willing buyer and a willing seller, both being adequately informed of the relevant facts and neither being compelled to buy or to sell. There is also general agreement that the definition implies that the parties have the ability as well as the willingness to buy or to sell. The *market* in this definition can be thought of as all the potential buyers and sellers of like businesses or practices.

In legal interpretations of fair market value, the willing buyer and willing seller are hypothetical persons dealing at arm's length rather than any "particular" buyer or seller. In other words, a price would not be considered representative of fair market value if influenced by motivations not characteristic of a typical buyer or seller.

The concept of fair market value also assumes prevalent economic and market conditions at the date of the particular valuation. You probably have often heard someone say, "I couldn't get anywhere near the value of my house if I put it on the market today" or "The value of XYZ Company stock is really much more (or less) than the price it's selling for on the New York Stock Exchange today." The standard of value implied in these statements is some standard *other than* fair market value, since the concept of fair market value means the cash-equivalent price at which a transaction could be expected to take place under *conditions existing at the valuation date.* Also, one important aspect of the definition of fair market value is that it is denominated in cash or cash equivalents, not some combination of cash and non-marketable notes.

The terms *market value* and *cash value* frequently are used interchangeably with the term *fair market value.*[9]

Fair Value

The expression *fair value* is an excellent example of ambiguous terminology used in the field of commercial appraisal. In order to understand what the expression means, you must know the context of its use. The accepted definition of fair value in real estate appraisal terminology differs substantially from the interpretation the courts have given to fair value as a statutory standard of value applicable to a business appraisal.

A leading authority on real estate terminology states that fair value is synonymous with market value or fair market value.[10] However, in most states fair value is the statutory standard of value applicable in cases of dissenting stockholders' appraisal rights. In these states, if a corporation merges, sells out, or takes certain other major actions and the owner of a minority interest believes that he or she is

---

[9] Byrl N. Boyce, ed., *Real Estate Appraisal Terminology,* rev. ed. (Cambridge, Mass.: Ballinger, 1982), p. 98. Richard M. Wise, a prominent Canadian business appraiser draws a slight distinction between the two terms: "*Fair* in *fair market value* means that the market (and the price) must have some consistency and cannot be affected by a transient boom or sudden panic; that is, the word *fair* qualifies the market on which the valuation is based." See Richard M. Wise, "The CA's Role in Valuations: An Inside-Out Perspective," *CA Magazine,* September 28, 1984, pp. 28-40.

[10] Boyce, *Real Estate Appraisal Terminology,* p. 98.

being forced to accept inadequate consideration for the stock, that owner has the right to have the shares appraised and to receive fair value in cash. There is no clearly recognized consensus on the definition of fair value in this context; but precedents established in the various state courts certainly have not equated it to fair market value. I have served as an adviser or expert witness for one side or the other in many dissenting stockholder suits, and I can say that when a situation of actual or potential stockholder dissent arises one must carefully research the legal precedents applicable to each case.

Since fair value is the statutory standard that generally applies in dissenting-stockholder suits and sometimes in corporate dissolutions, shares being valued under this standard almost always are minority shares. My study of the case law suggests that the major distinction in courts' interpretations of the fair value standard from one jurisdiction to another is the extent to which the shares are valued as minority interests, as a proportionate share of what a third-party buyer might pay for controlling interest, or at some standard of value between these two extremes.

Representative of one extreme in the case law interpretation of fair value is *Brown* v. *Allied Corrugated Box Co., Inc.* under California Corporation Code 2000, in which the court held that "plaintiffs were entitled here to their proportionate share of the entire corporation."[11]

Representative of the minority-interest value side of the issue is a 1988 Idaho decision, the first under Idaho Code Section 30-1-81(h)(4), which specifies fair value as the statutory standard of value for dissenting-stockholder suits. I was appointed by the court to appraise the shares of Silver Syndicate, Inc., immediately before the effectuation of a merger with Sunshine Mining Company and was asked to submit a value on a minority interest basis and also on a proportionate share of a controlling interest basis. The court found that the fair value was the value that represented a minority interest.[12]

The distinction between minority interest and controlling interest value is discussed in Chapter 2, "Principles of Business Valuation— Theory and Practice," and Chapter 15, "Valuing Minority Interests." Case law pursuant to the fair value standard is discussed in Chapter 25, "Divorces, Dissolutions, Dissenting-Stockholder Suits, and Damages."

One typical distinction between *fair value* and *fair market value* is that most court decisions do not reflect a discount for lack of marketability for a closely held stock under the fair value standard, while a discount for lack of marketability is virtually universally recognized for closely held minority interests under the fair market value standard. The concept of discounts for lack of marketability is discussed in Chapter 2, "Principles of Business Valuation—Theory and Practice," and data to quantify the discount for lack of marketability are discussed in Chapter 10, "Data on Discounts for Lack of Marketability."

---

[11] *Brown* v. *Allied Corrugated Box Co., Inc.*, 91 Cal. App. 3d 477, 154 Cal. Rptr. 170 (1979).

[12] *Sunshine Mining Co.* v. *Barbara Engstrom, et al.*, Dissenters Rights Appraisal Suit Pursuant to Section 30-1-81 Idaho Code, Case No. 24265 (District Court Idaho) (1987).

Investment Value

In my 1986 book *Valuing Small Businesses and Professional Practices*, I used the terms *investment value, intrinsic value,* and *fundamental value* interchangeably, as many people do.[13] I noted, however, that "some writers make certain distinctions among these standards of value." After studying several score more books, articles, and court cases that use these terms, I decided that the distinctions in their typical usage should be brought to readers' attention. Therefore, I am treating *intrinsic* or *fundamental value* separately from *investment value.*

In real estate terminology, investment value is defined as "value to a particular investor based on individual investment requirements, as distinguished from the concept of market value, which is impersonal and detached."[14] In real estate appraisal, calculations of investment value conventionally involve discounting an anticipated income stream. One of the leading real estate appraisal texts makes the following comments regarding the distinction between market value and investment value:

> Market value can be called "the value of the marketplace"; *investment value is the specific value of goods or services to a particular investor (or class of investors) for individual investment reasons.* Market value and investment value are different concepts, although the values estimated for each may or may not be numerically equal depending on the circumstances. In addition, market value estimates are commonly made without reference to investment value, but investment value estimates are frequently accompanied by a market value estimate to facilitate decision making.
>
> Market value estimates assume no specific buyer or seller. Rather, the appraiser considers a hypothetical transaction in which both the buyer and the seller have the understanding, perceptions, and motivations that are typical of the market for the property or interests being valued. Appraisers must distinguish between their own knowledge, perceptions, and attitudes and those of the market or markets for the property in question. The special considerations of a given client are irrelevant to a market value estimate.[15]

In their well-received text *The Stock Market: Theories and Evidence,* Lorie and Hamilton discuss investment value by reference to the classic work of John Burr Williams:[16]

> He considers the appropriate rate of discounting, the effects of stock rights and assessments, risk premiums, the effect of the capital structure of the firm, and the marketability of the security. His treatment of these various subjects leads to the grand conclusion that the investment value

---

[13] For example, in his classic *Valuation of Property,* James Bonbright describes the concept of *intrinsic value* as including both *value to the owner* (which other authors refer to as *investment value*) and *justified price* (the general notion that other authors ascribe to *intrinsic value*), Chapter II.

[14] Boyce, *Real Estate Appraisal Terminology,* p. 140.

[15] *The Appraisal of Real Estate,* 9th ed. (Chicago: American Institute of Real Estate Appraisers, 1987), p. 596. [Reprinted by permission from The Appraisal of Real Estate, 9th ed., © 1987 by the American Institute of Real Estate Appraisers, Chicago.]

[16] John Burr Williams, *The Theory of Investment Value* (Cambridge, Mass.: Harvard University Press, 1938 [reprinted in Amsterdam by North Holland Publishing Company, 1956]).

of a stock is determined by discounting the "expected" [authors' term] stream of dividends at the discount rate appropriate for the individual investor . . .[17]

There can be many valid reasons for the investment value to one particular owner or prospective owner to differ from the fair market value. Among these reasons are:

1. Differences in estimates of future earning power.
2. Differences in perception of the degree of risk.
3. Differences in tax status.
4. Synergies with other operations owned or controlled.

The discounted future returns valuation method (see Chapter 3) is essentially oriented toward developing an investment value. Whether or not the value thus developed also represents fair market value depends on whether the assumptions used would be accepted by a consensus of market participants.

If sound analysis leads to a valid conclusion that the investment value to a particular owner exceeded market value at a given time, the rational economic decision for that owner would be to not sell at that time unless a particular buyer could be found to whom investment value would be higher than the consensus of value among a broader group of typical buyers.

Of course, the concept of investment value as described above is not completely divorced from the concept of fair market value, since it is the actions of many specific investors, acting in the manner just described, that eventually lead to a balancing of supply and demand through the establishment of an equilibrium market price that represents the consensus value of the collective investors.

Finally, the term *investment value* has a slightly different meaning when used in the context of dissenting stockholder suits. In this context it means a value based on earning power, as described above except that the appropriate discount or capitalization rate usually is considered to be a consensus rate rather than a rate peculiarly appropriate for any specific investor.

Intrinsic or Fundamental Value

Intrinsic value (sometimes called *fundamental value*) differs from *investment value* in that it represents an analytical judgment of value based on the perceived characteristics inherent in the investment, not tempered by characteristics peculiar to any one investor, but rather tempered by how these perceived characteristics are interpreted by one analyst versus another.

Financial Decision Making defines *intrinsic value* as follows:

---

[17] James H. Lorie and Mary T. Hamilton, *The Stock Market: Theories and Evidence* (Homewood, Ill.: Richard D. Irwin, 1973), pp. 116–17.

Value, intrinsic of common stock. The price that is justified for a share when the primary factors of value are considered. In other words, it is the real worth of the stock, as distinguished from the current market price of the stock. It is a subjective value in the sense that the analyst must apply his own individual background and skills to determine it, and estimates of intrinsic value will vary from one analyst to the next.

The financial manager estimates intrinsic value by carefully appraising the following fundamental factors that affect common stock values:

1. *Value of the firm's assets.* The physical assets held by the firm have some market value. In liquidation approaches to valuation, assets can be quite important. In techniques of going-concern valuation, assets are usually omitted.
2. *Likely future earnings.* The expected future earnings of the firm are the most important single factor affecting the common stock's intrinsic value.
3. *Likely future dividends.* The firm may pay out its earnings as dividends or may retain them to finance growth and expansion. The firm's policies with respect to dividends will affect the intrinsic value of its stock.
4. *Likely future growth rate.* A firm's prospects for future growth are carefully evaluated by investors and are a factor influencing intrinsic value.[18]

Further concurrence on the meanings of intrinsic value and fundamental value is found in the following definitions from an authoritative reference in the accounting field:

Intrinsic value. The amount that an investor considers, on the basis of an evaluation of available facts, to be the "true" or "real" worth of an item, usually an *equity security.* The value that will become the market value when other investors reach the same conclusions. The various approaches to determining intrinsic value of the *finance* literature are based on expectations and discounted cash flows. See *expected value; fundamental analysis; discounted cash flow method.*[19]

Fundamental analysis. An approach in security analysis which assumes that a security has an "intrinsic value" that can be determined through a rigorous evaluation of relevant variables. Expected earnings is usually the most important variable in this analysis, but many other variables, such as dividends, capital structure, management quality, and so on, may also be studied. An analyst estimates the "intrinsic value" of a security on the basis of those fundamental variables and compares this value with the

---

[18] John J. Hampton, *Financial Decision Making: Concepts, Problems and Cases*, 3rd ed. (Englewood Cliffs, N.J.: Prentice Hall, Inc., 1983), pp. 429–30. Reprinted by permission of Prentice-Hall, Inc., Englewood Cliffs, New Jersey.

[19] W. W. Cooper and Yuri Ijiri, eds., *Kohler's Dictionary for Accountants*, 6th ed. (Englewood Cliffs, N.J.: Prentice-Hall, 1983), p. 285. Reprinted by permission of Prentice-Hall, Inc., Englewood Cliffs, New Jersey.

current market price of this security to arrive at an investment decision.[20]

In the analysis of stocks, intrinsic value generally is considered the appropriate price for a stock according to a security analyst who has completed a fundamental analysis of the company's assets, earning power, and other factors. Lorie and Hamilton comment on the notion of intrinsic value as follows:

> The purpose of security analysis is to detect differences between the value of a security as determined by the market and a security's "intrinsic value"—that is, the value that the security *ought* to have and will have when other investors have the same insight and knowledge as the analyst.[21]

If the market value is below what the analyst concludes is the intrinsic value, the analyst considers the stock a "buy." If the market value is above the assumed intrinsic value, the analyst suggests selling the stock.

It is important to note that the concept of intrinsic value also cannot be entirely divorced from the concept of fair market value, since it is the actions of buyers and sellers based on their *specific* perceptions of intrinsic value that eventually leads to the *general* consensus market value and the constant and dynamic changes in market value over time.

Case law often refers to the term *intrinsic value*. However, almost universally, such references do not define the term other than by reference to the language in the context in which it appears. Such references to *intrinsic value* can be found both in cases where there is no statutory standard of value and in cases where the statutory standard of value is specified as *fair value* or even *fair market value*. When references to *intrinsic value* appear in the relevant case law, the analyst should heed the notions ascribed to that term as discussed in this section.

Going-Concern Value

The concept of *going-concern value* is not a standard of value but an assumption about the business's status. It merely means that the business or practice is being valued as a viable operating entity; that is, it has its assets and inventory in place, its work force established, and its doors open for business, with no imminent threat of discontinuance as a going concern.

As noted earlier, fair market value, fair value, and investment value are examples of standards of value. Thus, in many instances it would be correct to characterize the value being estimated as *fair market value on a going-concern basis, fair value on a going-concern basis,*

---

[20] Ibid., p. 228.
[21] Lorie and Hamilton, *The Stock Market*, p. 114.

or *investment value on a going-concern basis*. Unless otherwise noted, we will assume in this book that we are dealing with values of businesses or practices on a going-concern basis.

In most cases, the phrase *going-concern value* is used to mean the total value of the entity as a going concern. However, in a context most often applicable to court cases involving disputed purchase price allocations, the term has been interpreted to mean a class of intangible assets (in the aggregate or specific intangibles) that relate to the incremental value of a going business in excess of the value of the tangible assets, but excluding the value of certain specific intangibles, such as goodwill or intangibles for which a specific income stream can be identified.[22]

Liquidation Value

Liquidation value is, in essence, the antithesis of going-concern value. *Liquidation value* means the net amount the owner can realize if the business is terminated and the assets sold off piecemeal. The term *orderly liquidation* means that the assets are sold over a reasonable time period in an attempt to get the best available price for each. The term *forced liquidation* means that the assets are sold as quickly as possible, frequently all at one time at an auction sale.

When computing liquidation value, it is essential to recognize all costs associated with the enterprise's liquidation. These costs normally include commissions, the administrative cost of keeping the company alive until the liquidation is completed, taxes, and legal and accounting costs. Also, in computing the present value of a business on a liquidation basis, it is necessary to discount the estimated net proceeds, at a rate reflecting the risk involved, from the time the net proceeds are expected to be received back to the valuation date. For these reasons, the liquidation value of the business as a whole normally is less than the sum of the liquidation proceeds of the underlying assets.

Book Value

Book value is something of a misnomer, because *it represents no standard of value; it is an accounting term, not an appraisal term.* The term *book value* means the sum of the asset accounts, net of depreciation and amortization, less the liability accounts, as shown on a balance sheet.

Assets usually are accounted for at historical cost, less depreciation, which may be computed by one of various methods. Some assets may be completely written off the books. Liabilities usually are shown at face value. Intangible assets normally do not appear on the balance

---

[22] For a more complete discussion of the phrase *going-concern value* in this latter context, see Benjamin N. Henszey, "Going Concern Value after *Concord Control, Inc.*," *Taxes* (November 1983), p. 699.

sheet unless they were purchased or the actual cost of development was recorded. Neither contingent assets nor contingent liabilities are recorded on the books.

The longer an individual asset or liability item remains on the books, the less likely is that item's book value to bear an identifiable relationship to any standard of value for it, much less for the entity as a whole.

Form and Extent of the Written and/or Verbal Report(s)

The purpose of the assignment will largely determine the form of the report. In cases involving taxes or tax implications, such as gift or estate tax valuations, ESOPs, or recapitalizations, the appraiser should prepare a formal written report that scrupulously satisfies the requirements of Revenue Ruling 59-60, which contains the guidelines for implementing Treasury Regulation 20.2031. Such a report also satisfies most state inheritance tax requirements.

If a written report is for presentation to prospective buyers for the purpose of selling the company, it usually will focus heavily on projections, studies of markets for the company's existing and prospective products and services, and other factors to help convince a buyer that an attractive business opportunity exists. The report's language and documentation normally will be much more informal than a report for tax purposes.

For litigation, the appropriate balance between written report and oral testimony will depend on the preferences of the court, the attorney involved, and the appraiser who will have to present his or her findings as expert testimony. A judge might enter a pretrial order requiring each side's experts to prepare and exchange complete written reports prior to the trial, with copies to the court, and then limit verbal testimony to selected issues of significant disagreement.

In many cases—including most involving the SEC, such as an offer to the stockholders to take a public company private—the only formal written output required is a letter expressing an opinion on the transaction's fairness. This may be as brief as a page and may or may not reveal any significant details of the basis for the opinion.

Frequently, the client requires only an oral report. This practice is common in estate planning, especially when the purpose of the exercise is to help the client get an approximate idea of the business's value in order to decide what to do. When the client ultimately makes a decision to make stock gifts, form an ESOP, attempt to sell the business, or whatever, a timely and complete report appropriate to the situation is in order.

Often, the appraiser gives a very brief written or oral opinion in the early stages of potential litigation, discussing existing or potential valuation disputes. The appraiser may take a cursory look at a situation and offer a preliminary range of potential values, usually qualified by the stipulation that he or she is not bound by the preliminary conclusion if a more in-depth examination indicates otherwise. This preliminary opinion letter or oral report frequently provides the basis for a negotiated settlement between the parties. If the initial appraisal assignment is limited to this kind of report, the parties usually will also agree to the appraiser conducting a complete valuation study and testifying about the findings in court if that becomes necessary.

In any case, the appraisal assignment should specify as clearly as possible the expected form and extent of the written and/or oral report.

Schedule

One of the most common practical problems in conducting a business valuation thoroughly and on a timely basis is the lack of proper scheduling, a problem that usually can be avoided with appropriate planning. Scheduling problems often arise because the client delays making the appraisal assignment (perhaps hoping that the valuation problem will go away) until there is no time left for anything but a crash assignment. In other cases, once the assignment is made, the person responsible for getting information to the appraiser fails to do so in a timely manner. Still another common source of scheduling problems is a major change in some aspect of the assignment midway through the project—another good reason for the client and the appraiser to think through and agree on the details of the appraisal assignment as thoroughly as possible at the outset.

The client, or his or her attorney or CPA, may procrastinate in making the appraisal assignment and thus delay its start partly because of failure to define the client's needs and objectives in the appraisal and partly because of failure to anticipate the lead time required for a thorough valuation. Once brought into the case, the appraiser can help the client avoid delays by clearly spelling out the steps to be taken and explaining why adequate lead time is necessary.

I hope that the reader will gain a better appreciation of the necessity of having adequate time to get the job done well. In addressing the problem of defining the appraisal assignment, the client can call in an appraiser early in the decision process, without committing to the expense of a complete appraisal, and perhaps cut down professional fees in the long run.

I also hope that this book—especially the checklist of documents and information to be used presented in Chapters 5 and 6—will help those contemplating the need for an appraisal to gather the material needed on a timely basis so that they can avoid last-minute scrambles for data and attendant delays in the appraisal work.

The appraisal assignment should specify when the work is expected to be completed. But it should also make it clear that the appraiser's ability to meet the proposed schedule depends on getting the necessary material on a timely basis and that changes midway through the assignment will likely cause changes in the schedule if the schedule is already tight. One safety valve available in some tight scheduling situations, such as filing a gift or estate tax return by a certain date, is to specify that the appraiser will arrive at a figure by the required filing date and that the formal, written, documented report will follow within a reasonable time.

Business appraisal situations vary so much that it is very difficult to generalize about reasonable scheduling. My firm has done an appraisal in a week and some appraisals have stretched over a year. If there is such a thing as a "typical" business valuation—say, an initial valuation of stock in conjunction with the formation of an ESOP for a relatively uncomplicated business with a few million dollars in sales—a reasonable time schedule might be to allow for a period of about 90 days to complete the work comfortably and thoroughly.

Fee Arrangements

The appraisal budget can be either a fixed price, on a straight hourly basis, or some combination of the two. To the extent that the appraisal assignment is clearly and thoroughly defined, it is reasonable to expect the parties to agree to a fixed fee. As with contracting for construction, changes in specifications after the work has started usually result in increased costs—another good reason to specify the appraisal assignment as completely as possible at the outset. If third-party independence of judgment is required of the appraiser—as in any case involving expert testimony in pending or potential litigation—the appraiser's fees must be fixed, hourly, or set in some manner totally independent of the outcome of any litigation or the appraiser's independent third-party status will be jeopardized. In any case, the amount of or basis for determining the appraiser's fees should be considered at the outset of the appraisal assignment.

Summary

As this chapter shows, the exact specification of the appraisal assignment may be both more complicated and more important than most people realize, unless they have had a considerable amount of business valuation experience in a variety of contexts. A clear understanding between the client and the appraiser of the assignment's details should focus the work and help avoid misdirected efforts. Exhibit 1–1 is a simple form on which one might capture the essential elements of the appraisal assignment.

As Chapter 13 will discuss, a typical report may start with a statement of the appraisal assignment. Exhibit 1–2 gives three examples of statements of the appraisal assignment, each in the context of a different appraisal situation.

EXHIBIT 1-1

ABC Appraisal Company
Specification of Appraisal Assignment

Name of party retaining appraiser

Name(s) of entity or entities to be appraised

Form of ownership
    [ ] Regular corporation
    [ ] Subchapter S corporation
    [ ] General partnership
    [ ] Limited partnership
    [ ] Sole proprietorship
    [ ] Other (please specify)

State in which incorporated or registered

_____

Exact description of financial interest to be appraised

Any special rights or restrictions on shares or interest being appraised

Date or dates as of which the property is to be appraised

Purpose or purposes of the appraisal

Applicable standard of value

Schedule

Fee arrangements

Above information provided or verified by

    Name

    Signature

    Date

EXHIBIT 1-2

Sample Statements
of the Appraisal Assignment

Value for a divorce

ABC Appraisal Company was retained by George Randolph to determine the fair market value of a 20 percent interest in Gotham Insurance Agency (Gotham), a New York general partnership, as of the present time, for the purpose of a property settlement in the marital dissolution of Mr. and Mrs. Randolph.

Value for ESOP transactions

ABC Appraisal Company was retained by the trust department of First Universal Bank, as trustees of the Employee Stock Ownership Plan and Trust of Gotham Insurance Agency, Inc. (Gotham), a Delaware corporation, to determine the fair market value of minority shares of Gotham's common stock owned by Gotham's ESOP as of April 30, 1988, for the purpose of ESOP stock transactions.

Value for a dissenting stockholder action

ABC Appraisal Company was retained by Mr. and Mrs. George Randolph to determine the fair value of 500 shares of common stock of Gotham Insurance Agency, Inc. (Gotham), a Delaware corporation, as of April 30, 1988, pursuant to Del. Code Ann. tit. Section 8 262(a) - 262(d), for the purpose of a dissenting stockholder action.

Chapter 2

Principles of Business Valuation—Theory and Practice

Value, like beauty, is in the mind of the beholder.

It is no wonder then, that there is so much controversy about the criteria by which to determine the value of a business or business interest. To quote a popular phrase of the younger generation, "It depends on where you're coming from." James C. Bonbright, a widely recognized valuation authority, offers the following insight on this point:

> One of the frequent sources of legal confusion between cost and value is the tendency of courts, in common with other persons, to think of value as something inherent in the thing valued, rather than as an attitude of persons toward that thing in view of its estimated capacity to perform a service. Whether or not, as a matter of abstract philosophy, a thing has value except to people *to whom* it has value, is a question that need not be answered for the sake of appraisal theory. Certainly, for the purpose of a monetary valuation, property has no value unless there is a prospect that it can be exploited by human beings.[1]

Generally Accepted Theory

A generally accepted theoretical structure underlies the process of valuing a business interest. In theory, the value of an interest in a business depends on the future benefits that will accrue to it, with the value of the future benefits discounted back to a present value at some appropriate discount (capitalization) rate. Thus, the theoretically correct approach is to project the future benefits (usually earnings, cash flow, or dividends) and discount the projected stream back to a present value.

However, while there is general acceptance of a theoretical framework for business valuation, translating it into practice in an uncertain world poses one of the most complex challenges of economic and financial theory and practice. Deviations from the theoretically correct approach to business valuation, however, are not necessarily, or even usually, inconsistent with the underlying theory.

Since the value of a business interest depends on its future benefits, direct implementation of the correct theoretical approach to valuation requires a quantified forecast of the benefits considered relevant in the case, be they earnings, cash flows, dividends, or some other form of return. The discounted future returns approach is applicable in practice only to the extent that the projections and assumptions used are acceptable to the decision maker for whom the business valuation is being prepared.

Such projections may be difficult to make—and even more difficult to get two or more parties with different economic and business expectations to agree on. Therefore, business valuation practitioners have

---

[1] **James C. Bonbright,** *The Valuation of Property,* vol. I (Charlottesville, Va.: The Miche Company, 1965 [reprint of 1937 ed.]), p. 21.

developed various approaches that use historical rather than projected data to arrive at a valuation. In some cases, approaches using historical data tend to be carried out in a somewhat more conservative manner than the discounted future returns approach with respect to reflection of potential future growth. In general, however, approaches using historical data, if properly carried out, should yield a result that is reasonably reconcilable with what a well-implemented discounted future returns approach would derive.

Reliance on Projected versus Historical Data

In the real world of business valuation practice, the situations that most closely approach using a theoretical discounted future benefits model to arrive at a value are in the merger market and, to a lesser extent, in the markets for publicly traded securities. In applying the discounted future returns approach, one must make estimates of the future returns that are sufficiently credible to make someone else willing to act on them. Businesspeople are trained to make and evaluate business and economic forecasts and use them as a basis for daily decision making. Thus, many merger and stock transaction decisions are made in this manner. As a practical matter, however, because of the lack of a set of projections and assumptions acceptable to all parties, many business valuations tend to end up relying on historical data, which are evaluated to reflect reasonable expectations about foreseeable future changes.

Of course, in many cases it is not at all unreasonable to go through the valuation exercise based on projected data and also do a valuation based on historical data. The choice of which to rely on, or the relative weights to be assigned in reaching the final valuation conclusion, will depend on the circumstances of the particular case and the appraiser's judgment.

In any business valuation involving existing or potential litigation, the courts must rely on evidence. Historical facts usually make more credible evidence in the eyes of the court than forward projections of what somebody thinks will happen. Therefore, when legal evidence is required the focus tends to be on the past record, tempered by any evidence about predictable future changes indicating that the historical record is inadequate as a basis for current valuation.

The extent to which a court will rely on projections as evidence in a valuation case probably is a function of its degree of confidence in the validity of those projections or at least in their general acceptability on the valuation date. It is not surprising that a prospective buyer in a merger situation, who probably has an intimate knowledge of the industry involved, finds it easier to assess the validity of the company's projections than does a judge in a courtroom.

A good example of a court's unwillingness to rely on future projections to arrive at a business valuation is provided in an Oregon Supreme Court opinion. Georgia-Pacific Corporation (GP) was the defendant in a case involving an alleged breach of contract, and the issue at hand was the value on a particular date of an interest in a corporation called Montana Pacific International (MPI). The court's opinion included the following statement:

> As evidence of the appropriate value plaintiffs point to a "pro forma" projection of MPI's anticipated profits over a ten-year period, prepared by GP in support of an application for bank financing. *We find these projected profits far too speculative to provide the basis for relief in this case.*[2]

In this case, the court stated that it was unwilling to rely on the projections as a basis for determining the business value for the purpose of assessing the amount of damages for which the defendant could be liable, even though it stated that the projections were actually prepared by the defendant itself.

Discussing dissenting-stockholder suits, Warren Banks, an attorney involved in valuation litigation, stated that: "It seems fair to say that the Delaware courts have been reluctant to base their valuations on a projection of future earnings. . . ." [3]

For example, in one case decided in the Supreme Court of Delaware, the opinion stated: "As between the valuation based on a forecast of the future and one based on actual figures, the latter method seems preferable."[4] In another Delaware case, the court opinion's discussion of the matter of estimated earnings included the following language: ". . . his estimate was based principally on long-range projections, a technique which has not met with approval in Delaware. . . ."[5] More recently, however, a landmark Delaware decision said that projections, if available, should be considered as a relevant factor rather than being totally ignored.[6]

There are certain major categories of exceptions in the historical versus forward-looking basis for judicial valuation decisions. Courts usually rely on capitalization of anticipated future earnings in business valuations in conjunction with reorganization proceedings under bankruptcy statutes.[7] It would seem almost essential that it do so, since, unless there was a reasonable expectation that the future would be more economically rewarding than the past, the reorganization would appear to be a fruitless effort. Other categories in which projections usually are necessary are antitrust, lost business opportunity, and certain other types of damage cases that need to address the amount of value lost as a result of the damage.

In summary, this difference in focus between the historical record and future projections is dictated by what the respective decision makers are willing to rely on. There is a big difference in this respect between an investment decision in the market and a judicial decision in a court (other than bankruptcy and certain kinds of damage cases).

---

[2] *Delaney v. Georgia-Pacific Corp.*, 42 OR App. 439, 601 P 2d 475 (1979).
[3] Warren E. Banks, "A Selective Inquiry into Judicial Stock Valuation," *Indiana Law Review* (1972), p. 23.
[4] *Cottrell v. Pawcatuck Company*, 128 A.2d 224 (Del. S.C. 1956), p. 231.
[5] *Levin v. Midland Ross Corp.*, 194 A.2d 50 (Del. Ch. 1963), p. 57
[6] *Weinberger v. UOP, Inc.*, 457 A.2d 701 (Del. Supr. 1963).
[7] Banks, "A Selective Inquiry," pp. 33–37.

Businesspeople can and should use their knowledge and experience in allocating resources entrusted to them for the purpose of taking business risks, and accept calculated risks inherent in decision making based on forecasts of an uncertain future. The court typically acknowledges that it lacks such expertise and that its mandate should be to reduce the element of uncertainty or risk to the greatest possible extent in its decision-making process. To be practically useful, the business valuation procedure selected must conform to the criteria acceptable to those who ultimately decide what action to take as a result of the valuation process.

The summary of this age-old controversy of focusing on historical versus projected earnings offered by Bonbright half a century ago is well worth reviewing today:

> *Realized Earnings versus Prophesied Earnings.* In the valuation of entire business enterprises or of shareholdings in these enterprises, one of the most sharply contested questions has concerned the relative weight to be given to the earnings actually realized, as shown by the companies' financial statements after proper auditing, and the future earnings as estimated by the witnesses for the two parties to the controversy. Sometimes, indeed, the controversy arises from a denial by one of the parties that prophesied earnings should even be admitted as competent evidence. It is alleged that these prophecies are necessarily too highly speculative to merit consideration; that they are based on guesses as to future business conditions and as to managerial efficiency, the validity of which cannot adequately be checked by cross-examination or by the countervailing testimony of opposing experts. Hence, it is argued, only the realized earnings, whose amount can be approximately established by a careful audit, should be brought to the attention of the tribunal for such weight as it sees fit to give this type of data. Lawyers who take this position generally concede that facts having a general bearing on the immediate prospects of the business may be brought to the attention of the court. They object, however, to the false appearance of precision which is given by any estimate, in monetary amounts, of future net earnings. Their objection is likely to be even more strenuous if the case is being tried by a jury or by any other unsophisticated tribunal. Such bodies are in danger of taking the prophecies at their face value, without applying those drastic discounts for risk of nonoccurrence which cautious appraisal experts would apply.
>
> These practical objections to the admission of prophesied gross and net earnings are well taken. Indeed, the courts have shown a wholesome tendency to belittle the significance of the prophecies, and even on occasion to refuse to let them get into the record. But the language by which they have justified their treatment of this type of evidence has not always been acceptable to appraisal theory and has sometimes been very confusing. At times the courts have come close to stating that, as a matter of principle, the *present* value of a business property depends on *present* earnings, and that future earnings are irrelevant because they will determine merely future value. More frequently they have stated that present value depends on both present *and* future earnings, but with the implication that the present earnings have the more direct bearing on the worth of the property as it exists today.

In fact, neither of these two statements correctly expresses the relevance of realized earnings and of prospective earnings. The truth is that, when earnings have once been "realized," so that they can be expressed with some approach to accuracy in the company's accounts, they are already water under the mill and have no direct bearing on what the property in question is now worth. Value, under any plausible theory of capitalized earning power, is necessarily forward looking. It is an expression of the advantage that an owner of the property may expect to secure from the ownership in the future. The past earnings are therefore beside the point, save as a possible index of future earnings.[8]

. . . .

In a litigated appraisal, a more convincing argument for the capitalization of realized earnings, rather than of prophesied earnings, can be found in the possibility. . . . of capitalizing the realized earnings at a rate objectively determined by rates established on the marketplace. Assume, for example, that the case at bar requires the valuation of a railroad enterprise, the net earnings of which have averaged $10 million per year. Assume also that the securities issued by this particular railroad have no established market value, since they are closely held. If the various securities of other, comparable railroad companies are quoted at prices which average twenty times current annual net earnings, a rate of 5 per cent suggests itself as the appropriate rate at which the current earnings of the instant railroad company may fairly be capitalized. Of course, any such conclusion involves a number of highly shaky assumptions—assumptions, not only as to the comparability of the various railroad enterprises, but also as to the relevance of quoted security prices as bearing on the value of an entire enterprise. But the errors implicit in this method of arriving at a proper rate of capitalization are probably far less serious than are the errors implicit in any other method available to an inexpert tribunal.[9]

Chapter 3 addresses the procedure for valuing a business using the discounted future returns method. Chapter 4 addresses general procedures for a business valuation relying on historical data.

Financial Variables Affecting Value

Whether one actually attempts to make future projections or relies on historical data to derive some proxy for reasonable future expectations, there are certain key variables on which the business valuation will focus. Their relative importance will vary in different types of situations. Theorists will continue to argue for longer than this book remains in print about which variables are the most appropriate ones on which to focus in various valuation situations.

One way or another, the financial benefits from ownership of an interest in a business enterprise must come from the following sources:

---

[8]Bonbright, *The Valuation of Property*, pp. 249–50.
[9]Ibid., p. 263.

1. Earnings or cash flow:
   a. From operations.
   b. From investments (e.g., interest and/or dividends received).
2. Liquidation or hypothecation of assets.
3. Sale of the interest.

Therefore, any valuation approach—at least from a financial point of view—must focus on quantifying the ability of the business interest to provide benefits to its owner from one or some combination of the above sources.

The primary financial variables (internal variables) to be considered (though not necessarily all in every case) are:

1. Earnings.
2. Cash flow.
3. Dividends or dividend-paying capacity.
4. Gross revenues.
5. Assets (broadly construed to include analysis of the balance sheet).

In many instances, a conclusion as to value may be tempered by other internal variables, such as:

1. Size of interest being valued (control or minority interest).
2. Voting rights.
3. Marketability.
4. Restrictive provisions affecting ownership rights.
5. Special ownership or management perquisites.

The key external variable in the valuation process is *cost of capital*—the amount of expected return required for attracting investment—which depends on the general level of interest rates and the amount of premium for risk the market demands. The cost of capital is discussed in a later section.

Relative Importance of Financial Statement Variables

There is no universal answer concerning which variable among the future benefits deserves the greatest attention in the valuation. However, there is general consensus within the business valuation discipline that earning power is the most important internal variable affecting the going-concern value of most operating companies, such as manufacturers, merchandisers, and service firms.

Earnings

One of the difficulties in determining the most important variable or variables on which to focus in any particular situation is the elusiveness of the definition and measurement of "earnings" within the broad scope of generally accepted accounting principles (GAAP). Therefore, if anticipated future earnings is to play a significant part in the valuation process, it is important that the parties involved in the analysis thoroughly understand of how they are defining and measuring earnings. If earnings are defined such that they offer some reasonable approximation of economic income accruing to the business interest before dividend payouts, I am inclined to agree with the consensus that earnings are the best variable on which to focus for valuation purposes.

Cash Flow

Cash flow also can be defined in a number of ways. The typical accounting definition of *cash flow* is *net earnings plus book charges such as depreciation and amortization.* On the other hand, cash flow can be defined to include or exclude several other account classifications considered appropriate for the particular valuation purpose. For example, in deriving "net cash flow" to use in a discounted cash flow form of income approach, capital expenditures and other required investments necessary to fund the projected level of revenues would be deducted from the projected flows.

Focusing on cash flow is particularly appealing in situations where cash flow provides a better measurement of earnings in an economic sense than do earnings as reported according to accounting principles. This generally applies, for example, for companies whose main business is holding improved real estate that they lease or rent out. In inflationary times, most well-maintained buildings hold their value or appreciate in terms of current dollars, and the depreciation charged against earnings for such companies does not really represent a decrement to the enterprise value. Thus, in valuing companies such as real estate investment trusts (REITs), analysts tend to focus more on cash earnings than on net earnings.

The cash flow measure also applies to capital-intensive companies in which the timing and magnitude of capital expenditures and depreciation policy can have a material effect on earnings. These effects are more clearly reflected in cash flow, since depreciation is incorporated into the cash flow measure.

The basic arithmetic for valuing a company by the discounted cash flow (DCF) method is exactly the same as that for the discounted future earnings (DFE) method. The two approaches just use different variables, including a carefully selected discount rate that is appropriate for the future benefit stream being measured.

Dividends

One of the earliest and most frequently cited works on the theory of stock valuation asserted the proposition that the value of a share is based entirely on its future stream of dividend payments, discounted back to a present value at an appropriate discount rate.[10] Despite John Burr William's classic pioneering work in this regard, contemporary business valuation theory and practice tends to put less weight on

---

[10] John Burr Williams, *The Theory of Investment Value* (Cambridge, Mass.: Harvard University Press, 1938). Reprinted in Amsterdam by North Holland Publishing Company, 1956.

dividend-paying capacity than on earning power in arriving at the value of a controlling interest in a business. This is largely because dividend-paying capacity stems primarily from earning capacity. Once the company achieves earning capacity, it becomes a discretionary decision on the directors' part whether to use available funds for dividends or for retained earnings and further pursuit of the company's business opportunities. In some cases, however, the dividend-paying capacity of a closely held company may be severely constrained by the need to retain earnings for capital expenditures or other purposes.

The emphasis on discounting a dividend stream might be considered most appropriate in cases where the buyers of the stock attribute value to it primarily because of its dividends. Utility stocks are probably the industry group most commonly regarded in this manner. Also, it is generally recognized that dividends or lack of them should assume relatively greater importance in valuing a minority interest than in valuing a controlling interest, since the minority holder has no power to exercise discretion to pay dividends even if the firm has adequate dividend-paying capacity. However, care must be exercised with respect to the dividend variable. A lack of dividend payments does not always detract from the minority interest's value. Analysis of retained earnings utilization and the incremental return generated therefrom provides insight into the rationale and impact on value of a company's dividend policy.

An alternative to valuing a stock by estimating its dividends in perpetuity and discounting them at an appropriate discount rate is to discount a stream of anticipated dividends for some finite number of years, plus some estimated terminal value, also discounted to a present value. Determining the terminal value (the price at which the interest presumably could be sold at some specified future time) is the obvious problem with this approach.

Revenues

Revenues may be the primary focus of the valuation process in certain situations—usually service businesses—and especially in connection with a sellout or merger. Even if earnings are depressed or negligible, either from mismanagement or from management's expense and compensation policies, a buyer frequently is willing to pay some multiple of revenues for the established market share and hence accept the risk in making the operation satisfactorily profitable.

The valuation emphasis frequently tends to be on revenues when buying or selling various commission-type service agencies, such as advertising or insurance, or professional practices, such as medical or accounting. Sometimes emphasis on revenues is found in transactions in the publishing field. Occasionally units of output or productive capacity rather than actual revenues are considered, on the theory that a certain amount of capacity *should* be able to generate a desired level of revenue. Examples would be the number of beds in a nursing home and the number of cars operated by an auto rental franchise.

It is unusual, however, for revenue to be the sole value criterion even when heavy weight is accorded to it in the valuation. In comparing two similar service businesses with the same level of revenues, most people would pay more for the one with the better underlying level of and growth in earnings, cash flow, and asset base.

Assets

It is important to dispel the popular misconception that ownership of a share of stock represents rights to a proportionate share of the underlying assets. That simply is not true. The importance of assets in the valuation process depends on the extent to which they can be utilized to generate the other benefits, such as earnings, cash flows, or dividends, either through operations or through liquidation.[11] As George Lasry explains it,

> A share of common stock does not represent a share in the ownership of the assets of a business. It represents a claim on the income derived from these assets by the people entrusted with their management.[12]
>
> . . . .
>
> [A] share of common stock is simply a share in the title to a claim on the income of the corporation. This title encompasses a claim on the residual income, the retained earnings and original capital, and the expected income produced by the assets of the corporation. Only the corporation itself holds title to all its assets and liabilities. A shareholder only owns a claim on income and not a share in the corporate title to its net property. A thirsty shareholder of a brewery cannot walk into "his" company and demand that a case of beer be charged to his equity account.[13]

The U.S. Supreme Court firmly established the principle that ownership of stock was not tantamount to ownership of a company's assets clear back in 1925:

> "The capital stock of a corporation, its net assets, and its shares of stock are entirely different things. . . . The value of one bears no fixed or necessary relation to the value of the other."[14]

Of course, if liquidation is contemplated, asset values assume a major role in the valuation. In most operating companies, however, asset values are considered in a supporting role, providing the means for continuing the earning power and some defense against the magnitude of downside risk in the enterprise's future value in the event of periods of low earnings or losses.

One type of enterprise in which assets typically would take on a relatively greater emphasis is a firm that is primarily a holding company rather than an operating company. In a company whose primary business is holding a portfolio of real estate, securities, or, in some cases, even operating subsidiaries, the underlying asset value, defined as the holding company's investment in the *holdings,* but *not* in the underlying assets of the holdings when the holdings are operating subsidiaries or securities, usually takes on more weight than earnings, dividends, or cash flow.

---

[11] Examples of this point appear in the courts' opinions on the *Gallun* and *U.S. News & World Report* cases discussed in later chapters.

[12] George Lasry, *Valuing Common Stock* (New York: AMACOM, 1979), p.1.

[13] Ibid., p. 15.

[14] *Ray Consol. Copper Co.* v. *United States,* 45 S. Ct. 526 (1925).

Some companies are hybrids, that is, combinations of operating and holding companies. In such cases, it may be appropriate to value the company in two parts, with greater emphasis on earnings for the operating portion of the company and greater emphasis on asset values for the nonoperating portion.

Sometimes, if an operating company owns certain nonoperating assets—especially if they are nonoperating assets not contributing to the present or foreseeable earnings stream in any way—the assets' liquidating value, or some portion of it, may be added to the value that is otherwise determined on a capitalization-of-earnings basis. However, the appraiser must be careful to adjust the earnings base to exclude nonoperating income and/or expenses before capitalizing the operating earnings.

Another type of enterprise in which asset values predominate is one that can readily be started by simply buying and assembling the necessary assets rather than buying an existing business. Repair and construction companies that generate their business primarily by competitive bid are examples of companies in this category.

Chapter 11 addresses analysis of the balance sheet to arrive at a total or per share adjusted net asset value. The essential point to keep in mind in according weight to any asset value approach in valuing a business interest is that the corporate entity intervenes between the assets and the shareholder. Even when an asset value approach is used, a share of stock may be worth either more or less than the underlying asset value, since the shareholder does not have the direct ability to withdraw assets from the corporation. The techniques for translating underlying asset values into their implications for the value of a share of stock are discussed in later chapters.

Impact of Risk and the Cost of Capital

The appraiser must be sure to consider the expected returns in two dimensions: the magnitude of the expected returns and the risk that these returns will or will not be realized. For the purpose of discussion in this book, we will define *risk* as *the degree of certainty or uncertainty as to the realization of expected future returns.* For a given level of expected future returns, the market will pay more to the extent that a realization of those returns is more certain or less to the extent that their realization is less certain. In other words, for a given level of expected future earnings (or cash flow, dividends, and the like), the lower the risk, the higher the present value or, conversely, the higher the risk, the lower the present value.

The appraiser can handle the element of risk in the valuation exercise in one of two ways. The first is to make a downward adjustment to the expected future stream (earnings, cash flow, dividends, and so on) to reflect the uncertainty. The second is to reflect the risk by using an increased discount rate in valuing the expected stream. Sometimes the appraiser (either consciously or unconsciously), uses a combination of these methods.

Bierman and Smidt, two Cornell professors, make a convincing argument that the theoretically most correct way to handle the element of risk is to adjust the future expectations stream to what they call a *certainty adjusted equivalent.* They adjust the expectations downward by some factor that reflects the probability that the expectations will be achieved. They then apply the same cost of capital to the valuation of all alternative investment choices. They do quite a good job, in my opinion, of explaining the rationale for this approach.[15]

Notwithstanding Bierman and Smidt's fine presentation, the more commonly used approach to incorporating risk in the valuation of a business is to reflect it in the cost of capital. For the purpose of discussion in this book, we will adopt a commonly used definition of *cost of capital* as *the rate of return available in the marketplace on investments comparable both in terms of risk and other investment characteristics,* such as marketability and other qualitative factors. We could paraphrase the definition to say that the cost of capital is the expected rate of return an investor would require to be induced to purchase the rights to future streams of income, as reflected in the business interest under consideration. As the cost of capital goes up, the present value of a given stream of future expected dollars goes down, and vice versa.

Thus, the cost of capital, one of the most important variables in the valuation of the business, is determined by the market and is almost totally outside the control of the business's owners. The market determines a basic risk-free required rate of return and the amount of premium required for assuming various levels of risk. Of course, one thing the owners can do to lower their cost of capital, and thus increase the value of their enterprise, is lower the degree of risk associated with it. The lower the evaluators perceive the risk to be, the lower will be the cost of capital considered applicable in the valuation and, thus, the higher will be the resulting value.

While ultimately, as noted above, the cost of capital must reflect the investment's degree of marketability (liquidity) or lack of it, the marketability factor often is handled separately from the discount rate in the valuation process. This is because most of the available empirical data for determining discount rates comes from highly liquid publicly traded securities. The lack of marketability for a closely held security can be reflected either by adding some amount to the discount rate applicable to otherwise comparable but readily marketable securities or by taking a discount for lack of marketability from the net present value of the future benefits as a separate step.

The Capital Asset Pricing Model

One of the most widely discussed developments in modern financial theory is the *capital asset pricing model (CAPM)*. This model is predicated on the fact that investors in risky assets require some addi-

---

[15]Harold Bierman, Jr., and Seymour Smidt, *The Capital Budgeting Decision,* 4th ed. (New York: Macmillan, 1975).

tional expected return above the risk-free rate as compensation for bearing the risk of holding those assets. The technical term for this behavior is *risk aversion*. Risk-averse investors do not necessarily *avoid* risk, but they require compensation, in the form of an additional expected return, for assuming the risk of an investment that lacks a guaranteed payoff. In simple terms, the CAPM hypothesizes that the return on a risky asset is a function of some risk-free return plus a risk "premium," which is a function of the amount of risk associated with the asset. The risk premium is developed as a function of the volatility of the price of the asset over time relative to the volatility of the market as a whole over the same time period. Thus, the CAPM addresses the most important external variable in the valuation of businesses by providing a theoretical framework for determining the appropriate required rate of return.

The CAPM is part of a larger theory known as *capital market theory (CMT)*. CMT also includes *portfolio management theory,* a *normative* theory that describes how investors should behave in choosing common stocks for their portfolios under a given set of assumptions. In contrast, the CAPM is a *positive* theory, meaning that it describes the market relationships that will result *if* investors behave in the manner prescribed by portfolio theory.

The capital asset pricing model is the cornerstone of modern capital market theory. Its relevance to business valuations is that businesses are a subset of the investment opportunities available in the total capital market; thus, determination of the prices of businesses theoretically should be subject to the same economic forces and relationships that determine the prices of other investment assets.

Modern capital market theory suggests that prices of investment assets are determined by two variables: risk and expected return. Although capital market theory is based on complex mathematics, it lends itself to intuitive explanations, which will be our focus in the following sections.

Rate of Return

The capital asset pricing model seeks to determine required rates of return for investment assets with various degrees of risk. As noted earlier, investors view risk as the uncertainty of receiving expected returns. Risk for a particular company can arise from a variety of sources, including the nature of the business and its degree of operating and financial leverage. Theoretically, the rate of return means the *total* rate of return, reflecting all interest, dividends, or other cash received, plus or minus any realized or unrealized appreciation or depreciation in the asset's value. The rate of return on an investment for a given time period is as follows:

Formula 2–1

$$R = \frac{\text{Ending price - Beginning price + Cash distributions}}{\text{Beginning price}}$$

This formula says simply that the rate of return is equal to the ending price of an investment, minus the beginning price, plus any cash flows received from holding that investment, divided by the initial price. For example, if Paola Pizza Parlours stock started the year at $10 per share, paid $.50 in cash dividends during the year, and ended the year at $11.50 per share, the total rate of return for the year would be computed as follows:

Formula 2–2

$$R = \frac{\$11.50 - \$10.00 + \$.50}{\$10.00} = \underline{\underline{.20}}$$

Given a series of prices for a particular investment and the cash flows received by the owner of that investment, it is possible to calculate the rate of return over any time period or over any number of subperiods.

Systematic and Unsystematic Risk

In the previous section, we defined risk conceptually as *the degree of certainty or uncertainty as to the realization of expected future returns.* Capital market theory divides risk into two components: systematic risk and unsystematic risk. Stated in nontechnical terms, *systematic risk* is the uncertainty of future returns due to the sensitivity of the return on the subject investment to movements in the return for the market as a whole. *Unsystematic risk* is a function of characteristics of the industry, the individual firm, and the type of investment interest. Firm characteristics could include, for example, management's ability to weather economic conditions, relations between labor and management, the possibility of strikes, the success or failure of a particular marketing program, or any other factor specific to the firm. Total risk, therefore, depends on these systematic and unsystematic factors.

The fundamental assumption of the capital asset pricing model is that the risk premium portion of the expected return of a security is a function of that security's systematic risk. This is because capital market theory assumes that investors hold or have the ability to hold common stocks in large, well-diversified portfolios. Under that assumption, the unsystematic risk attaching to a particular company's stock is eliminated because of the portfolio's diversification. Therefore, the only risk pertinent to a study of capital asset pricing theory is systematic risk.

Beta: The Measure of Systematic Risk

Systematic risk is measured in the capital asset pricing model by a factor called *beta*. Beta is a function of the relationship between the return on an individual security and the return on the market as measured by the return on some market index such as the Standard

& Poor's 500 Composite Stock Price Index. In general, we can think of beta as *the covariance of the rate of return on the subject security with the rate of return on the market.*

The notion of beta as a measure of systematic risk can perhaps best be illustrated by example. If a stock tended to have an increase in return of about 10 percent when the market had an increase in return of about 10 percent, and vice versa, when the market return decreased, the volatility of return on the stock would be equal to the volatility of return on the market. That stock's beta would be equal to 1. If the stock tended to have an increase in rate of return of 12 percent when the market had an increase rate of return of 10 percent, the volatility of return on the stock would be 1.2 times the volatility of return on the market; hence, the beta of that stock would be 1.2. If the stock tended to have an increase in rate of return of 8 percent when the market had an increase in return of 10 percent, the volatility of return on the stock would be .8 times the volatility of return on the market; hence, the beta of the stock would be .8.

In other words, beta measures the volatility of the individual security relative to the market. Securities that have betas greater than 1 are characterized as aggressive securities and are more risky than the market. Securities that have betas of less than 1 are characterized as defensive securities and have risks lower than the market.

The steps for calculating beta are illustrated in Exhibit 2–1. (The computation usually is done by regressing the stock return on the market return.)

Using Beta to Determine Expected Rate of Return

The capital asset pricing model hypothesizes that the expected return on an individual security is equal to the risk-free return plus beta (the measure of risk) times a benchmark risk premium, usually calculated as the excess return of some broad market index over the risk-free rate. The following formula shows this relationship in notational terms:

Formula 2–3

$$E(R_i) = R_f + B\,[E(R_m) \text{ - } R_f]$$

where

$$E(R_i) = \text{Expected return on an individual security}$$
$$R_f = \text{Rate of return on a risk-free security}$$
$$B = \text{Beta}$$
$$E(R_m) \text{ - } R_f = \text{Risk premium of the market}$$

The linear relationship in notational form above is shown graphically in what is called the *security market line* in Exhibit 2–2. According to capital asset pricing theory, if the combination of the expected rate of return on a given security and its risk, as measured by beta, places it below the security market line, such as security X in Exhibit 2–2, that security (or that common stock) is mispriced. It is mispriced

EXHIBIT 2-1

Calculation of Beta

Month End, t^a	Return on Security A^b	Return on S&P Index^c	Calculated Covariance^d	Calculated Variance^f
1/78	(.038)	(.080)	.0046	.00757
2/78	.076	.048	.0025	.00168
3/78	.062	.008	.0005	.00001
.				
.				
.				
9/87	(.004)	.040	(.0063)	.01090
10/87	.091	.016	.0068	.00080
11/87	.174	.109	.1622	.10400
12/87	.083	(.030)	.0363	.01370
Sum	1.800	.840	.20952	.23374
Average	.015	.007	.00175^e	.00194^g

$$\text{beta} = \frac{\text{Covariance (Security A, S\&P Index)}}{\text{Variance of S\&P Index}} = \frac{.00175}{.00194} = .90$$

[a] 10 years or 120 months.

[b] Returns based on end-of-month prices and dividend payments.

[c] Returns based on end-of-month S&P 500 Index.

[d] Values in this column are calculated as:

(Observed return on security A — Avg. return on sec. A) X (Observed return on S&P Index — Avg. return on S&P Index)

$0.0046 = [(0.038) — 0.015]$ X $[(0.080) — 0.007]$

[e] The average of this column is the covariance between Security A and the S&P Index.

[f] Values in this column are calculated as:

(Observed Return on S&P Index — Avg. Return on S&P Index)^2

$0.00757 = [(0.080) — 0.007]^2$

[g] The average of this column is the variance of return on the S&P Index.

in the sense that the return on that security is less than what it would be if the security were correctly priced, assuming fully efficient capital markets.

In order for the return on a security to be appropriate for that security's risk, the price of the common stock must decline, allowing the rate of return to increase until it is just sufficient to compensate the investor for bearing the security's risk. All common stocks in the market, in equilibrium, adjust in price until the rate of return on each is sufficient to compensate investors for holding them. In that situation, the risk/rate of return characteristics of all those securities will place them on the security market line.

The application of the capital asset pricing model to the choice of an appropriate discount rate can be illustrated using our previous example of stocks with betas of 1.0, 1.2, and .8, which we will call stocks A, B, and C, respectively. We will assume that a return of 8 percent is available on risk-free securities (such as Treasury bills) and that the

EXHIBIT 2-2

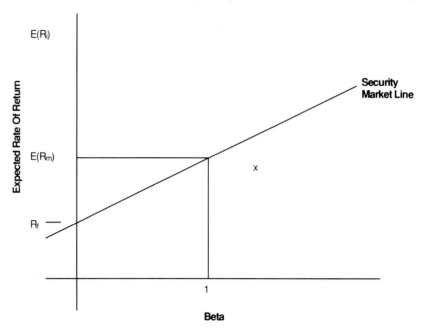

Security Market Line

consensus estimate of the expected market return for stocks is 15 percent. Substituting in the above formula, we get:

Formula 2–4

$$E(R_A) = .08 + 1.0(.15 - .08) = .15 = 15 \text{ percent}$$
$$E(R_B) = .08 + 1.2(.15 - .08) = .164 = 16.4 \text{ percent}$$
$$E(R_C) = .08 + .8(.15 - .08) = .136 = 13.6 \text{ percent}$$

Assumptions Underlying the Capital Asset Pricing Model

The assumptions underlying the capital asset pricing model are as follows:

1. Investors are risk averse.
2. Rational investors seek to hold efficient portfolios, that is, portfolios that are fully diversified.
3. All investors have identical investment time horizons (expected holding periods).
4. All investors have identical expectations about such variables as expected rates of return and how capitalization rates are generated.
5. There are no transaction costs.
6. There are no taxes.
7. The rate received from lending money is the same as the cost of borrowing money.
8. The market has perfect divisibility and liquidity.

Obviously, the extent to which the above assumptions are or are not met in the real world will have a bearing on the application of the CAPM for valuation of closely held businesses.

Pertinent Differences between the Markets for Closely Held and Publicly Traded Companies

Two differences between the market for closely held companies and the market for publicly traded stocks are particularly worth noting with respect to the assumptions of the capital asset pricing model enumerated above. These differences pertain to the assumptions of all investors holding fully diversified portfolios and having identical time horizons. These differences suggest certain possible modifications to the capital asset pricing model when using it for valuing closely held companies.

Degree of Portfolio Diversification. Most owners of closely held businesses or interests in closely held businesses do not diversify their portfolios of such interests nearly to the extent to which investors diversify their holdings of publicly traded stocks. Thus, since the unsystematic portion of total risk is unlikely to be diversified away to the same extent as in the case for a portfolio of public stocks, it is worth considering reflecting at least some part of unsystematic risk as well as systematic risk in determining an appropriate expected rate of return.

Differences in Time Horizon. I think it is fair to assume that the typical buyer of a closely held company or an interest in one approaches the investment with a longer time horizon in mind than does the typical buyer of publicly traded stocks. This implies that investors in closely held companies are likely to be less than fully responsive to short-term swings in the public stock market's expected rate of return. In other words, they may be more likely to base their expected rate of return on the public market's average or normalized rate of return over some time period than on its expected rate of return as of any specific date or short-term period. In fact, market evidence bears this out, as demonstrated later in the chapter.

Arbitrage Pricing Theory

The notion of *arbitrage pricing theory (APT)* was introduced by academicians in 1976,[16] but it was not until 1988 that data in a commercially usable form became generally available to permit applying the theory to estimation of required rates of return in day-to-day practice.

As noted in the previous section, the CAPM recognizes only one risk factor—systematic risk. In a sense, APT is an extension of the CAPM in that it recognizes a variety of risk factors that may bear on an investment's required rate of return, one of these being systematic risk. However, in another sense it may be argued that the CAPM and

[16]Stephen A. Ross, "The Arbitrage Theory of Capital Asset Pricing," *Journal of Economic Theory* (December 1976), pp. 341–60, and Stephen A. Ross, "Return, Risk, and Arbitrage," in *Risk and Return in Finance,* ed. Irwin I. Friend and J. Bicksler (Cambridge, Mass.: Ballinger, 1977), pp. 189–218.

APT might not be mutually exclusive nor of greater or lesser scope than one another, since it can be argued that the CAPM beta implicitly reflects the information included separately in each of the APT "factor betas." Under APT, the required rate of return for an investment varies according to that investment's sensitivity to each risk factor. The APT model takes the following form:

Formula 2–5

$$E(R_i) = R_f + (B_{i1}K_1) + (B_{i2}K_2) + \ldots + (B_{iN}K_N)$$

where

$$E(R)_i = \text{Expected return on an individual security}$$
$$R_f = \text{Rate of return on a risk-free security}$$
$$K_1 \ldots K_N = \text{Risk premium associated with factor K for the average asset}$$
$$B_{i1} \ldots B_{iN} = \text{Sensitivity of security i to each risk factor relative to the market average sensitivity to that factor}$$

The risk factors considered in current APT applications are economic variables such as changes in the inflation rate, changes in industrial production, and the differential in returns between long-term and short-term bonds. Like the CAPM, APT ignores risk factors unique to a particular company, since investors theoretically could avoid such risks through diversification.

A recent book makes the following observations regarding APT:

> In theory, a specific asset has some number of units of each risk; those units are each multiplied by the appropriate risk premium. Thus, APT shows that the equilibrium expected return is the risk-free rate plus the sum of a series of risk premiums.
>
> . . . .
>
> APT is more realistic than CAPM because investors can consider other characteristics besides the beta of assets as they select their investment portfolios. While neither the CAPM nor APT is a perfectly realistic model, each is beginning to be widely employed to test and predict the relationship between expected return and various risk factors.[17]

A source of data for required rates of return using APT is included in Chapter 8.

Approaches to Value

Beware the appraiser who makes a pedantic, blanket statement such as "There are three approaches to valuing a business" or "There are seven approaches to valuing a business." Trying to force the approaches to the appraisal of all businesses under all circum-

---

[17]Roger G. Ibbotson and Gary P. Brinson, *Investment Markets* (New York: McGraw-Hill, 1987), p. 52. For a more extensive discussion of APT, see Frank K. Reilly, *Investment Analysis and Portfolio Management*, 2nd ed. (Hinsdale, Ill.: Dryden Press, 1985), pp. 637–47.

stances into a fixed number of labeled categories is an exercise in spurious taxonomy. The following two sections discuss the categorizations of approaches traditionally used in the real estate appraisal that are sometimes adapted to business appraisals, followed by other categorizations of approaches commonly used in business appraisals.

Categorization by Income, Cost, and Market

Many people are certain that they "know," as a result of decades of real estate appraisal doctrine, that there are three approaches to appraisal: income, cost, and market. It is *possible* to subsume the approaches to valuing of a business under these categories, and some authors propound doing so. For example:

> While there is no universally agreed upon taxonomy of valuation methods, most financial analysts would probably agree that, generally speaking, there are three main approaches to valuation:
> 1. The discounted income approach.
> 2. The asset appraisal approach.
> 3. The comparative appraisal approach.
>
> As will be seen below, the three methods are not mutually exclusive, but are somewhat interrelated. It should also be noted that each procedure is conceptually analogous to one of the three classic approaches used in valuing real estate: the income, cost, and market data approaches, respectively.[18]

The key phrase in the above passage is *the three methods are not mutually exclusive but are interrelated*. The discounted income approach (discounted future returns approach) requires a discount rate, which by definition, is the expected rate of return applicable to the stream being discounted that is generally available from comparable investments in the market. Asset appraisal approaches usually are based on some measure of market values of assets. All comparative appraisal approaches relate some market value observation either to some measure that is somehow indicative of a company's ability to produce income, to some measure of its asset values, or to some combination of the two. Barring the possible expectation of selling the investment at a higher price to a greater fool, companies' values are driven by earning power and/or prospective liquidation of assets, and the values attributable to those two factors are determined by market forces and measured to the best of the valuation analyst's ability by observation of comparable market data.

The American Institute of Real Estate Appraisers (AIREA) refers to the income, cost, and market approaches as the *income capitalization approach, cost approach, and sales comparison approach*.[19] It recognizes full well, however, that these "approaches" are not mutually exclusive but, in fact, are quite interdependent:

---

[18]W. Terrance Schreier and O. Maurice Joy, "Judicial Valuation of 'Close' Corporation Stock: *Alice in Wonderland* Revisited," *Oklahoma Law Review* 31 (1978), p. 858.

[19]*The Appraisal of Real Estate,* 9th ed. (Chicago: American Institute of Real Estate Appraisers, 1987).

The income capitalization approach is one of the three traditional approaches an appraiser may use in the valuation process. However, it is not an independent system of valuation that is unrelated to the other approaches. The valuation process considered as a whole is composed of integrated, interrelated, and inseparable techniques and procedures designed to produce a convincing and reliable estimate of value, usually market value. The analysis of cost and sales data is often an integral part of the income capitalization approach, but capitalization techniques may be frequently employed in the cost and sales comparison approaches as well. For example, capitalization techniques are commonly used to analyze and adjust sales data in the sales comparison approach; in the cost approach, obsolescence is often measured by capitalizing an estimated rental loss.[20]

Real estate appraisers consider the cost approach particularly applicable in valuing new or relatively new construction when improvements represent the highest and best use of the site, land value is well supported, and no functional or external obsolescence is evident.[21] The AIREA makes the basic point that

> The cost approach is based on a comparison between the cost to develop a property and the value of the existing developed property. Because the market relates value to cost, the cost approach reflects market thinking. Buyers tend to compare the value of existing structures with the prices and rents obtained for similar buildings and with the cost to create new buildings with optimal physical and functional utility. Buyers adjust the prices they are willing to pay by estimating the cost to bring an existing structure up to desired levels of physical and functional utility.[22]

The cost approach thus can be viewed as an approach to an *upper limit of value*. The notion could be applied to appraisal of a business provided all elements of the business—intangible as well as tangible—are reflected, since it would not be prudent to purchase an existing business for more than it would cost to create a comparable new business.

Other Commonly Accepted Categorizations

Business appraisal approaches tend to fit less neatly than real estate appraisal approaches into a triumvirate of definitive categories. The most commonly used approaches to the valuation of a business generally can be subsumed under the following categories:

Discounted future earnings or discounted cash flow.

Capitalization of current, normalized, or historical earnings.

Capitalization of current, normalized, or historical cash flow.

Capitalization of dividends or dividend-paying capacity.

Multiple of gross revenue or physical volume.

---

[20]Ibid., p. 407 (Reprinted by permission from *The Appraisal of Real Estate*, 9th ed., © 1987 by the American Institute of Real Estate Appraisers, Chicago.)

[21]Ibid., p. 354.

[22]Ibid., pp. 353–54.

Excess earnings approach.

Adjusted net asset value.

Ratio of price to book value or to adjusted net asset value.

Prior transactions in or offers for the stock adjusted to current conditions.

Discount rates, capitalization rates, or multiples to be used in the above categories of approaches may be derived through analyzing specific comparative transactions or through analyzing the generic rate or multiple that the market or the investor may require for the variable being capitalized for some broad investment category of similar characteristics. Furthermore, most of the above categories of approaches are susceptible to being applied assuming that either the company's capital structure remains at its present or some other given configuration or is adjusted to a "debt-free" basis. Moreover, since comparative transaction data for the valuation of businesses often are drawn from minority interest transactions in the public stock market, approaches sometimes are categorized on the basis of the source of the data, that is, the public stock market or mergers and acquisitions.

Exhibit 2–3 illustrates two possible ways to categorize a set of approaches to the value of the business. Note that only the outline differs; the same 18 approaches are included in both lists. Neither is "right" nor "wrong"; each is just one way of organizing and viewing the same data. It would be unusual, of course, to find this many approaches in a single appraisal, but the list by no means exhausts all the possibilities.

As noted earlier, Chapter 3 addresses the discounted future earnings or cash flow approach and Chapter 4 covers valuation approaches that rely on current or historical data.

Impact of Controlling versus Minority Interest

Degree of Control

One of the most important variables affecting value is the degree of control rights, if any, inherent in the interest being valued.

Whether an interest is a controlling or a minority interest is not necessarily a cut-and-dried distinction, but it may well be a matter of degree. The value of control depends on the ability to exercise any or all of a variety of rights typically associated with control. Consequently, if control is an issue in the valuation, the analyst should assess the extent to which the various elements of control do or do not exist in the particular situation and consider the impact of each element on the value of control. Following is a checklist of some of the more common prerogatives of control:

1. Elect directors and appoint management.
2. Determine management compensation and perquisites.

EXHIBIT 2-3

Different Classifications of Approaches to Value

Approaches grouped into three classifications	Approaches grouped into seven classifications
The income capitalization approach	**Discounted future returns**
Discounted future earnings	Discounted future earnings
Discounted future cash flow	Discounted future cash flow
Capitalization of normalized earnings	
Capitalization of normalized cash flow	**Capitalization of earning power**
The excess earnings method	Capitalization of normalized earnings
	Capitalization of normalized cash flow
The cost approach--adjusted net asset value	
	The excess earnings method
The sales comparison approach	**Current market value indicators**
Price/current earnings	Price/current earnings
MVIC/debt-free earnings	Price/current cash flow
Price/current cash flow	Price/current revenues
MVIC/debt-free cash flow	Price per subscriber
Price/current revenues	Capitalized dividend-paying capacity
MVIC/revenues on debt-free basis	Price/tangible book value
Price per subscriber	
Capitalized dividend-paying capacity	**Debt-free approaches**
Price/tangible book value	MVIC/debt-free earnings
MVIC/tangible total capital	MVIC/debt-free cash flow
Past transactions in company stock	MVIC/revenues on debt-free basis
Offer to purchase company	MVIC/tangible total capital
	Adjusted net asset value
	Past transactions
	Past transactions in company stock
	Offer to purchase company

MVIC = Market value of invested capital

3. Set policy and change the course of business.
4. Acquire or liquidate assets.
5. Select people with whom to do business and award contracts.
6. Make acquisitions.
7. Liquidate, dissolve, sell out, or recapitalize the company.
8. Sell or acquire treasury shares.
9. Register the company's stock for a public offering.
10. Declare and pay dividends.
11. Change the articles of incorporation or bylaws.

From the above list, it is apparent that the owner of a controlling interest in an enterprise enjoys some very valuable rights that an owner not in such a position does not. However, many factors may limit a majority owner's right or ability to exercise many of the prerogatives normally associated with control, thus limiting the value accruing to the control position. On the other hand, minority interests may not be totally bereft of control factors. For example, a minority holder may be in a position to cast crucial swing votes and, in some measure, influence important business policies.

Cumulative versus Noncumulative Voting.[23] In the case of election of directors, if the company has noncumulative voting, the whole pie belongs to the majority. If the company has cumulative voting, some of the value attributable to the ability to elect directors will shift from the majority holder with less than enough to elect the whole board to the minority stockholders.

Contractual Restrictions. Many typical control rights may be denied to a company through contractual restrictions. For example, indenture provisions in conjunction with debt obligations frequently prevent dividend payments, increased management compensation, liquidation of assets, acquisitions, or changes in the direction of the business.

Effect of Regulation. Government regulation of operations may preempt the usual prerogatives of control. For example, it is a lengthy and sometimes even impossible process to liquidate companies in such regulated industries as insurance and utilities. Government regulation may prevent certain acquisitions and, similarly, prevent a company from selling out to certain other companies or investors.

Financial Condition of Business. Many of the rights associated with control are rendered economically empty or of little value simply because of the company's financial condition. These could include the right to decide on management compensation, dividends, stock or asset purchases, or acquisition of other companies.

Effect of State Statutes. Statutes affecting the respective rights of controlling and minority stockholders vary from state to state. In about half the states, a simple majority can approve major actions such as a merger, sale, liquidation, or recapitalization of the company. Other states require a two-thirds or greater majority to approve such actions, which means that a minority of just over one-third (or less in a few states) has the power to block such actions. Under California statutes, minority stockholders enjoy certain rights under some circumstances that those in other states do not.[24] The variations in state law concerning which rights are given to what proportion of ownership can have an important bearing on the valuation of certain percentage interests in some cases.

Effect of Distribution of Ownership. If one person owns 49 percent of the stock and another 51 percent, the 49 percent holder has little or no positive control and in many states may not even have the "negative control" of being able to block certain actions. However, if two stockholders own 49 percent each and a third owns 2 percent, the

---

[23] *Cumulative voting* is a system of voting in proportional representation in which each voter is given as many votes as there are positions to be filled and allowed to cast those votes for one candidate or distribute them in any way among the candidates.

[24] California Corporations Code §2000 allows a minority interest shareholder to seek dissolution of the corporation and also authorizes the purchase by the other shareholders of the shares of the "moving parties" at "fair value."

49 percent stockholders may be on a par with each other depending on who owns the other 2 percent. The 2 percent stockholder may be able to command a considerable premium for that particular block of stock over a pro rata portion of the value of the total company because of its swing vote power.

If each of three stockholders or partners owns a one-third interest, no one has complete control. However, no one is in a relatively inferior position unless two of the three have close ties with each other that the third does not share. Equal individual interests normally are each worth less than a pro rata portion of what the total enterprise would be worth. Thus, the sum of the values of the individual interests usually is less than what the total enterprise could be sold for to a single buyer. However, the percentage discount from pro rata value for each equal interest normally will be lower than that for a minority interest that has no control whatsoever.

In summary, each situation must be analyzed individually with respect to the degree of control or lack of it. When any of the control elements are lacking in a particular case, any value attributable to control must be diminished accordingly. If there is any significant element of control present in a minority interest, that value also should be recognized. Chapter 15 addresses the valuation of minority interests.

Voting Rights

Closely related to the matter of a controlling versus a minority interest is the matter of voting rights or lack thereof. Voting rights constitute one of the most difficult variables to quantify in terms of impact on value. In general, the greater the extent to which the issue of control is involved, the greater the importance of voting rights in terms of value. For extremely small minority interests, the market accords very little value to voting rights. Where swing votes or majority interests are involved, the impact on value can be significant. In fact, a majority block of nonvoting stock may actually be worth less per share than a small block of nonvoting stock, since there are fewer potential buyers for the large block and this factor is not balanced by the access to voting control that would occur if the majority block had voting rights.

Marketability

Ready marketability definitely adds value to a security, or, conversely, lack of marketability detracts from the security's value vis-à-vis one that is otherwise comparable but readily marketable. In other words, the market pays a premium for liquidity, or, conversely, exacts a discount for lack of it. For two given investments identical in all other valuation criteria, the market will accord a considerable premium to the one that can be instantly liquidated into cash, especially without risk of loss of value, relative to the one that cannot be so liquidated.

Since interests in closely held businesses do not, by definition, enjoy the ready market of a publicly traded stock, a share in a privately held company usually is worth less than an otherwise comparable share in a publicly held one. Many factors affect the relative marketability of different business interests. The size of the interest can have a bearing too. In some cases, a smaller block would be easier to market than a larger block, and in other cases the reverse would be true. The importance of the marketability factor in business valuation has been gaining increasing recognition over the years. There is considerable evidence suggesting that the discount for the lack-of-marketability factor alone for a closely held stock compared with a publicly traded counterpart should average between 35 and 50 percent.

Chapter 10 is devoted to analysis of data that can be used to help quantify appropriate discounts for lack of marketability.

Restrictive Provisions Affecting Ownership Rights

As correctly noted in at least one authoritative article, the presence of practically any type of restrictive agreement tends to reduce the appraised market value established for a closely held company's stock.[25] Such restrictive agreements include, for example, mandatory buy-sell agreements, first rights of refusal, requirement of consent to sell, pooling agreements, and voting trusts.

Distinction between Discount for Minority Interest and Discount for Lack of Marketability

Much confusion exists because some writers and appraisers fail to distinguish between a minority interest discount and a discount for lack of marketability. These are two separate concepts, although they are somewhat interrelated.

The concept of *minority interest* deals with the relationship between the interest being valued and the total enterprise based on the factors discussed in the first two sections of this chapter. The primary factor bearing on the value of the minority interest in relation to the value of the total entity is the degree of control the minority interest does or does not have over the particular entity. The concept of *marketability* deals with the liquidity of the interest, that is, how quickly and certainly it can be converted to cash at the owner's discretion.

People sometimes overlook the fact that discounts are meaningless until the bases from which they are to be taken have been defined. Since a minority interest discount reflects lack of control, the base from which the minority interest discount is subtracted is its proportionate share in the total-entity value, including all rights of control. Since a discount for lack of marketability reflects lack of liquidity, the

---

[25]W. Terrance Schreier and O. Maurice Joy, "Judicial Valuation of 'Close' Corporation Stock: *Alice in Wonderland* Revisited," *Oklahoma Law Review* 31 (1978), p. 865.

base from which the discount is subtracted is the value of an entity or interest that is otherwise comparable but enjoys higher liquidity.

Even controlling interests suffer to some extent from lack of marketability. It usually takes at least a few months to sell a company, and sometimes considerably longer. The relationship between the discount for lack of marketability and that for minority interest lies in the fact that even after discounting a minority interest for its lack of control, it is still usually much harder to sell a minority interest than to sell a controlling interest in a closely held business.

Many court decisions, especially those involving valuations for gift and estate tax purposes, have taken a single lump sum discount to reflect marketability, minority, and sometimes still other factors. However, conceptual thinking in the valuation exercise usually can be more precise to the extent that it is possible to isolate and separately quantify the various valuation factors, especially the more important ones. Fortunately, in recent years both valuation practitioners and courts increasingly have been giving separate recognition to the impact of minority interest and marketability factors. A 1982 estate tax decision articulated the distinction between the minority and marketability discounts very clearly:

> In their arguments, neither petitioner nor respondent clearly focuses on the fact that two conceptually distinct discounts are involved here, one for lack of marketability and the other for lack of control. The minority shareholder discount is designed to reflect the decreased value of shares that do not convey control of a closely held corporation. The lack of marketability discount, on the other hand, is designed to reflect the fact that there is no ready market for shares in a closely held corporation. Although there may be some overlap between these two discounts in that lack of control may reduce marketability, it should be borne in mind that even controlling shares in a nonpublic corporation suffer from lack of marketability because of the absence of a ready private placement market and the fact that flotation costs would have to be incurred if the corporation were to publicly offer its stock.[26]

If a minority interest in a closely held business is valued by reference to day-to-day trading prices of publicly held stocks, minority interests are being compared with other minority interests. The closely held stock value should be discounted for marketability with respect to the public stock, as discussed in the previous section, but not for minority interest.

If a minority interest in a closely held business is being valued by capitalization of earnings, book value, adjusted book value, or some other approach but without comparison to daily trading prices of public stocks, and if the capitalization rates or multiples employed are applicable to controlling interests, discounts may be appropriate in order to reflect *both* the lack of marketability and the minority interest. It is not uncommon to find a minority interest valued at 35 percent or less of the stock's underlying net asset value, reflecting both the minority interest and lack-of-marketability factors.

---

[26]*Estate of Woodbury G. Andrews,* 79 T.C. 938 (1982).

Conversely, if a controlling interest in a closely held business is being valued with reference to day-to-day trading prices of public stocks, which are minority interests, it may be appropriate to add a premium for control to the price that otherwise would appear to be indicated. In valuing controlling interests in closely held companies by reference to prices of publicly traded stocks, it occasionally works out that the discount for lack of marketability and the premium for control just about offset each other. One possible explanation for this is that public companies acquiring private ones tend to be reluctant to incur dilution by paying a higher price/earnings ratio than the price at which their own stock is selling. In effect, a controlling stockholder of a closely held company who sells to a public company is giving up control but gaining liquidity.[27] Apart from other valuation factors, in some cases these two factors by themselves have the net effect of canceling each other out. In cases where the value of control versus the disadvantage of lack of liquidity do not offset each other, the scale usually tips in favor of the former when the interest being valued has all the benefits of control. However, when the interest being valued holds a small majority but does not have all the rights of control, the scale may very well be tipped in favor of the disadvantage of lack of liquidity. Sources of data for quantifying premiums for control over publicly traded market values are found in Chapter 9. Chapter 15 deals with valuing minority interests.

Sum of Parts Not Necessarily Equal to Whole

As the previous analysis suggests, the sum of the values of partial interests may or may not add up to the value of the entity taken as a whole. In most cases, the sum of the values of the partial interests taken individually is less than what might be received if a single buyer purchased the entire entity. The company in its entirety has a different value because it conveys different rights and interests than the sum of all the interests taken on a minority basis. This economic fact, of course, is one of the catalysts in the cauldron of merger and acquisition activity.

Other Qualitative Factors Affecting Value

Certain qualitative factors bear on value yet defy quantification on the basis of empirical data within the framework of the valuation factors discussed up to this point. Such factors may influence the analyst's judgment as to the relative weight to accord various approaches. In some cases, such factors may be reflected in a specific adjustment in arriving at the value conclusion.

---

[27]The degree of liquidity gained will depend, of course, on the extent to which the seller gets cash, freely tradable public securities, restricted securities, or some other consideration.

Private versus Public Ownership

Much of the comparative market data used for valuing closely held companies come from public market data. This is appropriate because of the large amounts of available data reflecting prices determined in a free, competitive, and relatively efficient market system. Nevertheless, it is also important to recognize the differences between private and public ownership and their implications for the ways in which values are determined in the respective markets.

As noted in the section on the capital asset pricing model, I believe it is reasonable to assume that the average investment in a closely held company is made on the basis of a longer time horizon than the average investment in a publicly traded stock. Also, it is far less practically possible to hold an efficient, fully diversified portfolio of closely held company investments than to hold a comparable portfolio of publicly traded stocks. The typical investor in a closely held company does not have enough discretionary funds to hold a portfolio of closely held interests that would diversify away the unsystematic risk. It is also reasonable to assume that private-company investments probably depart more than publicly traded stock investments from certain other assumptions of the capital asset pricing model. These assumptions would include identical expectations regarding rate of return, no transaction costs, ability to borrow money at the same rate as that at which it can be loaned, and perfect divisibility and liquidity of the investment.

These factors are somewhat interrelated, and all tend to support the notion of a longer time horizon for investments in closely held companies than for publicly traded stocks. Also, market evidence very strongly supports this belief. The merger and acquisition market is considerably less volatile over time, as measured by fundamental value measures such as price/earnings and price/book value ratios, than is the public stock market, as several studies have borne out.

Exhibits 2–4 and 2–5 present evidence demonstrating less volatility in the merger and acquisition market than in the public stock market. Note that P/E ratios in the merger market are less volatile than those in the public stock market and that acquisition premiums over public trading prices diminish when public market P/Es are high, and vice versa.

The implications of the data shown in Exhibits 2–4 and 2–5 similar studies seem clear. The factors that impact on the prices of publicly traded stocks also affect the values of mergers and acquisitions. However, the magnitude of the volatility is smaller in the merger and acquisition market than in the public stock market.

Qualitative Company Characteristics

The list of qualitative factors that can affect value is endless. This section mentions just a few of the most common ones.

Key Management Personnel. Perhaps the most important qualitative factor characteristic of many closely held companies is reliance

EXHIBIT 2-4

Comparison between S&P 500 P/E Ratios and Acquisition P/E Ratios 1968-1986

| Year | S&P 500 Composite Index | | | Acquisitions | | |
	Avg. P/E Ratio[a]	4-Year Moving Avg.[b]	% Difference between Cur. Yr. P/E and Avg. P/E	Avg. P/E Ratio[c]	4-Year Moving Avg.	% Difference between Cur. Yr. P/E and Avg. P/E
1968	18.1			24.6		
1969	15.1			21.0		
1970	16.7			23.1		
1971	18.3	17.1	7.3	24.3	23.3	4.5
1972	19.1	17.3	10.4	21.4	22.5	(4.7)
1973	12.2	16.6	(26.4)	18.9	21.9	(13.8)
1974	7.3	14.2	(48.7)	13.5	19.5	(30.9)
1975	11.7	12.6	(7.0)	13.3	16.8	(20.7)
1976	11.0	10.6	4.3	15.1	15.2	(.7)
1977	8.8	9.7	(9.3)	13.8	13.9	(.9)
1978	8.3	10.0	(16.6)	14.3	14.1	1.2
1979	7.4	8.9	(16.7)	14.3	14.4	(.6)
1980	9.1	8.4	8.3	15.2	14.4	5.6
1981	8.1	8.2	(1.6)	15.6	14.9	5.1
1982	10.2	8.7	17.2	13.9	14.8	(5.8)
1983	12.4	10.0	24.6	16.7	15.4	8.8
1984	10.8	10.4	4.1	17.2	15.9	8.5
1985	11.5	11.2	2.4	18.0	16.5	9.4
1986	16.0	12.7	26.2	22.2	18.5	19.8
Mean	12.2			17.7		
Standard Deviation	3.78			3.81		
Coefficient of Variation	30.9%			21.5%		

[a] Based upon an average of weekly prices and quarterly earnings.

[b] Average of the current and three prior years' P/E ratios.

[c] Based upon prices paid in all transactions where earnings information was available.

Source: W.T. Grimm's *Mergerstat Review* 1986 and Willamette Management Associates, Inc. calculations.

on one or a few key management personnel. The analyst may incorporate this factor in choosing valuation multiples or capitalization rates. However, in some cases it may be an important enough factor to warrant a separate, specific adjustment to value.

Lack of Product Diversity. Many closely held companies have very limited product lines, which can increase their risks and/or limit their opportunities relative to other firms. Limited product diversity can restrict both the categories of potential customers and the number of potential customers within a category. It can also increase risks arising from shortages of critical supplies or competitive product innovation.

Lack of Vertical Integration. Another frequently encountered problem is a competitive disadvantage compared with other companies that benefit from vertical integration. Some companies—especially, for example, original-equipment component manufacturers—face virtual annihilation if their customers decide to make the products instead of buying them. The risk of a sudden cessation of the income stream for this or any other reason obviously has a bearing on value.

EXHIBIT 2-5

Acquisition Premium over S&P 500 P/E Ratio and Public Stock Trading Prices 1976-1985

Year	S&P 500 Average P/E Ratio	Acquisitions Average P/E Ratio	Acquisition Premium Over S&P 500 %	Premium Over Market Trading Price[a] %
1976	11.0	15.1	37.2	31.1
1977	8.8	13.8	56.8	36.2
1978	8.3	14.3	72.2	41.5
1979	7.4	13.3	93.2	47.6
1980	9.1	15.2	67.0	44.6
1981	8.1	15.6	92.6	41.9
1982	10.2	13.9	36.3	43.5
1983	12.4	16.7	34.7	34.0
1984	10.8	17.2	59.3	34.4
1985	11.5	18.0	56.5	27.7
1986	16.0	22.2	39.0	29.9

[a] Premium based on market price of stock two days prior to announcement 1976-1978; five days prior to announcement 1979-1986.

Source: W.T. Grimm's *Mergerstat Review,* 1985 and 1986, and computations by Ray Klaris, senior valuation analyst, Marshall & Stevens.

Other Qualitative Factors. Other factors to consider in various cases include the company's degree and nature of research and development efforts, industry position, quantity and quality of asset base relative to other companies, and education and training programs. Analysis of qualitative factors and assessment of their impact on value require the best in the valuation analyst's skill and judgment, which develop through long years of study and experience.

Summary of Business Valuation Principles

Although specific procedures for valuing a business or business interest vary greatly from one situation to another, several basic principles are fundamental to the business valuation discipline:

1. It is generally accepted theory that from a financial point of view, the value of a business or business interest is the sum of the expected future benefits to its owner, each discounted back to a present value at an appropriate discount rate for the length of time remaining until each benefit is expected to be received.
2. The market determines the appropriate discount rate for calculating fair market value. This rate is the expected rate of return (applicable to the stream being discounted) required for attracting capital to the investment, which is considered as being the expected rate of return available in the market from other investments of comparable risk and other factors as of the applicable valuation date.

3. Recognizing the difficulties inherent both in projecting future benefits and in agreeing on an appropriate discount rate, business valuation analysts have developed accepted procedures for estimating value based on current or historical rather than projected financial data. The primary variables used in such procedures are revenues, various measures of earning power (including measures of cash flow), dividends or dividend-paying capacity, and asset values. These procedures reflect the economic fact that the possible sources of future benefits to the owners arise from earnings from operations, earnings from investments, liquidation of assets, and/or sale of the business or business interest to another party. Values estimated from such procedures should not be expected to be inconsistent with estimates of value from a discounted future benefits approach provided that the latter approach was based on reasonable estimates of benefits and an appropriate discount rate.

4. A shareholder has no direct claim on a corporation's assets, because a corporate entity intervenes between the assets and the shareholder. Therefore, the value of a share of stock may be either more or less than a proportionate share of the underlying net asset value and sometimes bears little relationship to the underlying net asset value.

5. When relying on specific comparative market transactions for guidance in estimating the value of a subject business or interest, investors' specific expectations regarding future returns and risk that are incorporated into capitalization rates, multipliers, and other valuation parameters are not known. This makes it imperative that financial variables utilized in the valuation be defined on a consistent basis between the comparative and subject companies and that measurements for estimating variables be taken as of the same point in time or over the same time period relative to the valuation date for the comparative companies and the subject company.

6. Because of their lack of control over various decisions affecting the business enterprise, minority interests may be worth considerably less than a pro rata portion of the business's value if it were valued as a single 100 percent interest.

7. The market pays a premium for liquidity, or, conversely, demands a discount for lack of liquidity. This is most applicable to equity investments in businesses, although some restricted and/or nonpublic bonds and preferred stocks do seem to sell at a yield premium, and hence, at a lower price due to their lack of liquidity. Consequently, businesses and business interests that lack ready marketability generally are worth less than otherwise comparable businesses or business interests that are readily marketable.

8. Minority interest and marketability are distinct concepts, although they are related. Both controlling and minority interests, suffer somewhat from lack of marketability.

9. The sum of the values of individual fractional interests in a business is not necessarily, or even usually, equal to the value of a

100 percent ownership interest in the business taken in its entirety.

10. Within the scope of these business valuation principles, different standards of value apply for different valuation purposes and within different legal contexts. The respective standards may bear on both the valuation procedures to be utilized and the final determination of value. The appraiser should understand the applicable standard of value and its implications for each valuation assignment.

The above principles, though broad, are rigid enough to provide a much-needed framework for consistency in the practice of the business appraisal discipline. If appraisers understand and adhere to them carefully, they will avoid many errors leading to unreasonable appraisal conclusions. The principles provide the business appraisal user with a basic perspective from which to review and evaluate a business appraisal work product.

Chapter 3

The Discounted Future Returns Approach to Valuation[1]

---

[1]This chapter was partially adapted from Shannon P. Pratt and Craig S. Hugo, "Pricing a Company by the Discounted Future Earnings Method," *Mergers & Acquisitions* 7 (Spring 1972), pp. 18–32.

The value of an asset is the present value of the expected returns from the asset during the holding period.[2]

What is someone who buys a company or an interest in a company really buying? Management? Markets? Technological skills? Products? Although each of these may be involved, what is actually being bought is a stream of future returns. Thus, the problem in valuing a business for acquisition as well as many other purposes becomes one of predicting future returns and discounting them to a present worth.

The future returns to be estimated and discounted to a present value can be defined in any of several ways. The most conventional are some measure of either earnings (in which case the discounting techniques are referred to as the *discounted future earnings (DFE) method*) or cash flow (in which case the discounting techniques are called the *discounted cash flow (DCF) method*). *In any event, it is essential that the return stream to be discounted be clearly defined and a discount rate appropriate for that return stream chosen.*

The discounted future returns (DFR) approach to valuation probably is most often used in the context of mergers and acquisitions. However, as discussed in Chapter 2, it is the theoretically most correct approach to valuation and serves a wide variety of valuation purposes, including the valuation of both controlling and minority interests in many cases, provided that the future return stream to be discounted is credible and that the discount rate chosen is appropriate for that return stream and for the particular valuation purpose.

The Discounted Future Returns Concept

Remember Miss Grundy, the fourth grade teacher? "Invest $1 at 6 percent interest, and it will be $2 in 12.4 years." With those words, she drilled the idea of compound interest into you and me and all of us. Unfortunately, however, she forgot to teach the corollary: that $2 paid out 12.4 years from now is worth only $1 today. That's *discounting,* as opposed to compounding, and Jones's *Fourth Grade Arithmetic Reader* never covered that subject.

Yet for the merger maker, discounting is as important as compounding—perhaps even more so—for any acquisition, whether paid in stock, cash, or debt, is an investment that represents payment *today* for a stream of future returns. Thus, the same discounting model historically used in evaluating equipment purchases, plant additions, marketing programs, and other capital investment projects is equally applicable in buying a company.

This chapter demonstrates the technique of discounting expected future returns to present value. Proper understanding and application of this technique can be worth millions of dollars in a merger decision.

---

[2]Frank K. Reilly, *Investment Analysis and Portfolio Management,* 2nd ed. (Hinsdale, Ill.: Dryden Press, 1985), p. 273.

To turn the discounting process into concrete numbers, one must quantify two things: (1) the amounts of the expected future cash flow or earnings stream and (2) the appropriate discount rate. If the discount rate is held constant, then the higher the expected future cash flow or earnings stream, the higher the present value. On the other hand, if the future return stream is held constant, then the higher the discount rate (determined primarily by the cost of capital), the lower the present value.

Exhibit 3–1 shows the arithmetic of present value computations. Tables for use in calculating present value are included as Appendix Tables A–1 and A–2 at the back of the book. Many inexpensive pocket calculators that work present value problems simply and virtually instantly are available today. Exhibit 3–2 shows how to apply the arithmetic from Exhibit 3–1 to a hypothetical case problem.

Forecasting Future Cash Flow and/or Earnings

The cash flow and/or earnings forecast is the heart of the entire valuation process and requires a thorough knowledge of the complex factors influencing an investment venture. As a preliminary step, a company being considered for purchase should have an operating plan for at least five years into the future, even if it must retain an outside consultant to prepare it. In merger analysis, the best method for gaining reasonably reliable forecasts depends somewhat on the type of activity of the company being investigated. If its activity is closely related to that of the buying company, the buyer obviously is in a much better position to both make and evaluate forecasts for the target company.

Even in the best of circumstances, forecasting a range of possible future returns for an investment is one of the most difficult aspects of the discounted future returns model. However, the process is invaluable because it forces the buying company to take into account the many variables that will influence the acquired concern's earnings, thus facilitating a wiser investment decision.

Evaluation of the various elements involved—sales volume, wholesale and retail prices, costs of materials, operating expenses, the competition's strength, to mention only a few—must be undertaken by those executives best prepared to do so, which usually means that salespeople estimate sales, production people provide production figures, and so on. The financial analyst's role is primarily to initiate and coordinate the various segments of the analysis.

No matter how much care is taken in producing an earnings forecast, it can never be more than an estimate. As Edward G. Bennion states:

> It is impossible to make an economic forecast in which full confidence can be placed. No matter what refinements of techniques are employed, there still remain at least some exogenous variables. It is thus not even possible to say with certainty how likely our forecast is to be right. We must be

EXHIBIT 3-1

Arithmetic of Present Value

ARITHMETIC OF PRESENT VALUE

Discounting future values back to present value is just the opposite of taking a present value and determining what its value will be at some time in the future at some given compound rate of return. The formula for determining the future amount of some present value growing at some compound rate is as follows:

$$FV_i = PV(1+r)^n$$

where:

FV_i = Amount at some future time (i)

PV = Present value

r = Rate of return (In varying contexts, this may appropriately be called the discount rate, the interest rate, the capitalization rate or the opportunity cost rate.)

n = Number of periods into the future for which the compounding is being computed (usually designated in years)

Problem: Assume that $1,000 is invested for three years at a 10% rate of return, what is the value of this investment at the end of the time period?

Using the formula: $FV_i = PV(1+r)^n$

Substituting: $FV_i = \$1000(1+.10)^3 = \$1331$

When we know or have a workable estimate of what some future amount "FV" (a projected earnings stream, for example) will be and we want to determine its present value, we work the above formula into a "present value" formula:

$$PV = \frac{FV_i}{(1+r)^n}$$

Problem: Assume that an investment has a value certain of $1,331 at the end of three years, and you want to know what you should pay for it today in order for the compound rate of return on today's investment to be equal to 10%:

Using the formula: $PV = \dfrac{FV_i}{(1+r)^n}$

Substituting: $PV = \dfrac{\$1331}{(1+.10)^3} = \underline{\$1000}$

(Use Appendix A-1 to simplify this calculation.)

There is just one more wrinkle, and that is the fact that the return on most investments (certainly including acquired companies) is not just one lump sum at a single future time, but a series of sums over a number of future times. To account for this we need to introduce into our formula the standard mathematical notation "Σ," pronounced Sigma, which simply means to sum up all the numbers or expressions which directly follow it. Then the formula appears as:

$$PV = \Sigma \frac{FV_i}{(1+r)^n}$$

Problem: Assume that you are considering buying a $1,000 bond, issued several years ago and bearing an annual interest rate of 5½%, with three years remaining until maturity. Assume that, because of rising interest rates, comparable bonds now sell in the market to yield 10%. What would the present value of this bond be in the marketplace?

Using the formula: $PV = \Sigma \dfrac{FV_i}{(1+r)^i}$

Substituting: $FV_1 = \$55$ (Interest at end of first year)

$FV_2 = \$55$ (Interest at end of second year)

$FV_3 = \$1055$ (Interest at end of third year plus repayment of face value at maturity)

$$PV = \frac{\$55}{(1+.10)^1} + \frac{\$55}{(1+.10)^2} + \frac{\$1055}{(1+.10)^3}$$

1st Yr.   2nd Yr.   3rd Yr.

(from Appendix A-1)

= $50 + $45.45 + $792.64

= $888.09

The following case is slightly simplified by the fact that the amounts of the expected cash flows are the same for each of the future years.

Problem: Assume that you are considering the purchase of a $3000 equipment contract that pays $1000 at the end of each year for three years. What would you be willing to pay for this contract if you required a 10% rate of return on your investment?

Using the formula $PV = \Sigma \dfrac{FV_i}{(1+r)^i}$

Substituting:

$$PV = \frac{\$1000}{(1+.10)^1} + \frac{\$1000}{(1+.10)^2} + \frac{\$1000}{(1+.10)^3}$$

= $909.09 + $826.45 + $751.31

= $2486.85

In each of the above cases, the present value of each of a series of future cash flows has been computed and then summed together to determine the present value of the total investment. This general approach can be applied to determine the present value of an acquisition, as well as to most other investments.

Note that if a DFE return on a project is 20%, it is implicitly assumed that the earnings generated in each period will be reinvested at a rate of 20%. If periodically generated earnings don't earn 20% return, the DFE return on the original investment will not be 20%.

---

brash enough to label a forecast as "most probable," but this implies an ability on our part to pin an approximate probability coefficient on a forecast: 1.0 if it is virtual certainty, 0.0 if it is next to an impossibility, or some other coefficient between these extremes. But, again, since we have no precise way of measuring the probability of our exogenous variables behaving as we assume them to do, there is no assurance that the

EXHIBIT 3-2

Analysis of Present Value of Firm as of January 1, 1988 by the Discounted Future Earnings Approach

Assume that we have carefully projected a merger candidate's earnings for each of the first five years. In addition we have assumed an annual compound growth rate in earnings of 6% per year for the sixth through eleventh years, and no growth in future earnings thereafter. The projected earnings thus derived are as follows:

1988	$ 20,000	
1989	40,000	
1990	70,000	
1991	90,000	
1992	100,000	
1993	106,000	$(100,000 \times 1.06^1)$
1994	112,000	$(100,000 \times 1.06^2)$
1995	119,000	$(100,000 \times 1.06^3)$
1996	126,000	$(100,000 \times 1.06^4)$
1997	134,000	$(100,000 \times 1.06^5)$
1998 and after	142,000	$(100,000 \times 1.06^6)$ per year

Beginning in the eleventh year, we have what is, in effect, a net level annuity in perpetuity. The value of such an annuity can be calculated simply by dividing the annual amount by the capitalization rate. Take, for example, a straight high-grade preferred stock with a $5 dividend. If the going market rate of return on such a security is 8%, the present value is found simply by dividing the amount, $5, by the rate, .08, giving a present value of $62.50. In the above problem, the same valuation procedure is applied to the assumed annuity in perpetuity starting with the eleventh year. Dividing the $142,000 by an assumed required rate of return of 20%, or 0.20, we value this annuity as of the beginning of the eleventh year at $710,000 ($142,000 ÷ 0.20 = $710,000). But note that this is the value as of the end of the tenth year, and we still have to discount that value back for ten years in order to arrive at its present value.

$$\text{Present Value} = \Sigma \; \frac{E_i}{(1+r)^i}$$

where:

- E_i = Earnings in the ith year in the future
- i = The year in the future in which the earnings are achieved
- r = The discount rate or required rate of return at which the future earnings are to be capitalized

Thus, substituting the assumed figures in our present value formula, the equation appears as follows:

$$PV = \frac{\$\,20,000}{(1+.20)^1} + \frac{\$\,40,000}{(1+.20)^2} + \frac{\$\,70,000}{(1+.20)^3} + \frac{\$\,90,000}{(1+.20)^4}$$

$$+ \frac{\$100,000}{(1+.20)^5} + \frac{\$106,000}{(1+.20)^6} + \frac{\$112,000}{(1+.20)^7} + \frac{\$119,000}{(1+.20)^8}$$

$$+ \frac{\$126,000}{(1+.20)^9} + \frac{\$134,000}{(1+.20)^{10}} + \frac{\$142,000/.20}{(1+.20)^{10}}$$

Using the present value tables (Appendix A), or any handy pocket financial calculator, this seemingly complex problem is easily solved:

$$PV = \$16,666.67 + \$27,777.78 + \$40,509.26$$

$$+ \$43,402.78 + \$40,187.76 + \$35,499.19$$

$$+ \$31,257.14 + \$27,675.60 + \$24,419.64$$

$$+ \$21,641.75 + \$114,668.96$$

$$= \$423,706.53$$

Note: As long as the year-to-year percentage increase in the assumed earnings is greater than the discount rate, the present value of each subsequent annual increment increases; but when the annual rate of growth is less than the discount rate, the present value of each additional year's increment decreases.

Using the same procedures and varying the discount rate applied from 14% to 26% in 2% increments, the range of present values for our merger candidate's projected future earnings would work out as follows:

Capitalization Rate	Present Value
14%	$684,049
16%	573,250
18%	489,050
20%	423,707
22%	371,432
24%	328,946
26%	293,872

Typically, an analyst could "pin down" an appropriate discount rate within a much narrower range than shown above, resulting in a much narrower range of relevant values. The wider range is shown above to illustrate the extent of the effect of varying the discount rate.

estimated probability coefficient for our forecast is anything like 100 percent correct.[3]

A decision maker armed with only a single "most-probable" forecast is in no position to make a wise investment decision unless the

---

[3]Edward G. Bennion, "Capital Budgeting and Game Theory," *Harvard Business Review* (November–December 1956), pp. 115–23.

forecast is 100 percent correct—an impossibility without an all-know-ing crystal ball. To account for the fact that the forecasts for a given period may not materialize as anticipated, the analyst should obtain a range of possible outcomes.

One relatively simple approach for considering a range of earnings forecasts for any future year is for forecasters to give their most opti-mistic estimate (in this case, the most they think the company could earn under the most favorable conditions), their most likely estimate (the amount they think has the highest probability of occurring), and their most pessimistic estimate (how much they think the firm would earn or lose under the worst circumstances they can envision). With these estimates in hand, forecasters can then calculate a weighted average expected return for each year using one of the following for-mulas.

In the first equation, each possible outcome is assigned a numerical probability (see Table 3–1):

TABLE 3-1

	Probability		Outcome		Expected value
Low	0.25	x	$ 800,000	=	$ 200,000
Probable	0.50	x	1,000,000	=	500,000
High	0.25	x	1,400,000	=	350,000
Weighted average	1.00				$1,050,000

An alternative for calculating a weighted estimated earnings figure is this:

Formula 3–1

$$E = \frac{a + 4m + b}{6}$$

where

E = Estimated earnings (weighted)
a = Most pessimistic estimate
m = Most likely estimate
b = Most optimistic estimate

Using the same example as above, the formula would work out as:

Formula 3–2:

$$E = \frac{\$800,000 + 4(\$1,000,000) + \$1,400,000}{6} = \$1,033,333$$

However, either of these weightings is arbitrary and may be too sim-plistic for many situations. More exhaustive treatments of the subject of making and evaluating earnings forecasts appear in the bibliog-raphy.

It is common to attempt specific forecasts for five years and then assume a percentage growth rate for five more years and a flat stream of earnings in perpetuity after the tenth year. It is also common to assume a constant, albeit perhaps conservative, growth rate after the fifth year. Some people think it is realistic to make specific forecasts for only three years and then apply a percentage growth component. The percentage growth assumption need not be the same for all years. Although it probably is more realistic to carry some growth projections out for 15 or 20 years instead of only 10, the effect of the difference is relatively small when using the high discount rates appropriate for equity analysis and projecting many years into the future.

The assumptions underlying the terminal value may have a significant impact on the present value, especially if the period of specific year-by-year forecasts is relatively short. If doing an earnings model, many analysts simply assume that the terminal year P/E ratio will be the same as the current P/E ratio. However, if a lower level of growth is expected from that point forward, a lower P/E ratio would be warranted. In a cash flow model, if growth will be at a lower rate in later years, then requirements for capital expenditures and additions to working capital also are likely to be lower. In general, when assumptions regarding one variable change, it is essential that the analyst reflect the effect of that change on all other variables that are affected by it.

Treating the Element of Risk

In discounted future returns analysis, *risk* may be defined as *the estimated degree of uncertainty with respect to the realization of expected future returns*. Risk, then, is in the mind of the beholder. What seems very risky to one person may seem less risky to another depending on his or her confidence in the predictions and attitudes toward risk aversion. This is perfectly appropriate in discounted future returns analysis for merger and acquisition purposes and will result in evaluators with less certainty placing a lower present value on a company than will those who regard the same company's future with more certainty. Optimally, this desirable bias will lead acquirers to favor companies whose businesses they know and understand best and to lean away from those further outside their fields of expertise. Generally speaking, the wider the range of expected future returns around the "best estimate," the more risky the investment.

These different expectations of future returns and various perceptions of risk obviously tend to lead to different conclusions as to value. To the extent that the projected returns and discount rate reflect a particular investor's unique circumstances and perceptions, the value indicated by this exercise would conform to the definition of *investment value*, as discussed in Chapter 1. To the extent that the projected earnings and discount rate reflect a consensus of perceptions among market participants, the value so derived could be considered an indication of *fair market value*, also discussed in Chapter 1.

There are two basic ways (each with many variants) to handle risk in the discounted future returns analysis. One is to reduce the expected value of the future returns to a "confidence-adjusted equivalent," using a larger reduction factor to indicate greater risk. A more common method is to vary the rate at which the expected future returns stream is discounted, using a higher discount rate to reflect greater risk. Whatever the method used, the main point in risk analysis is that a company with a given level of expected returns that is highly uncertain has a lower present value than a company with the same expected returns level but one that is more certain. The objective of risk analysis is to quantify this difference.

Setting the Discount Rate

"Don't count your future returns before they are discounted" paraphrases an old adage. The question is: At what rate should future returns be discounted? Volumes of material have been written on the subject, yet it is still difficult to generalize.

Broadly speaking, the discount rate should be the expected rate of return available on alternative investment opportunities with comparable risk. In other words, the appropriate discount rate can be regarded as an *opportunity cost,* which is the rate of return available from other, comparable investment media. This would be the rate that investors expect their investments to earn on equity to induce them to make the investments. If the capital markets are operating efficiently, this opportunity cost establishes the cost of capital for businesses with a degree of risk comparable to that of the subject company.

This notion was explained in the previous chapter in terms of the capital asset pricing model. Generally, the indicated discount rate derived from the CAPM is applicable to a projection of net cash flow, while the indicated discount rate derived from an earnings growth model (discussed later) is applicable to a projection of earnings. As noted there, the capital asset pricing model provides a framework for deriving an expected rate of return from the market, usually defined in terms of some broad common stock index such as the S&P 500. It also provides a mechanism for adjusting the expected rate of return based on differences in systematic risk between the average stock in the market index and the subject stock. This, then, leaves us with three questions we must answer in order to implement the derivation of an appropriate discount rate within the framework of the capital asset pricing model:

1. Should the market rate be based on historical data or current expectations?
2. How will one estimate a beta for a closely held stock with no trading history?

3. Since the market rate in the CAPM is based entirely on systematic risk, what, if anything, should be done to reflect nonsystematic risk?

Estimating the Market Required Rate of Return on Equity

One can estimate the market's required rate of return at any given time on the basis of either historical rate-of-return data or the rate-of-return expectations implied from current stock prices and analysts' estimates of the expected total returns (dividends plus appreciation) on those stocks.

If the analyst uses historical data, the procedure is to start with a risk-free rate, such as the current rate of return available on Treasury bills or Treasury bonds, and add the premium for risk that the market actually has provided to holders of stocks over some representative long-term period. Sources of data for these figures are discussed in Chapter 8, "Data on Required Rates of Return."

If the analyst uses market expectation data, the starting point is a single figure for total expected return with no breakdown as to the risk-free and risk premium components. Expected market return data are also available, or can be developed, for industry groups and individual stocks as well as for a defined market index. Sources of data on returns expected by the market are discussed in Chapter 8.

The presumption in using historical data is that they will provide a reasonable guide as to future return expectations. The presumption in using market expectation data for implied expected rates of return is that the forecasted returns on which the implied rates are based are reasonably accurate. Merrill Lynch commented on this presumption as of late 1987:

> Based on analysts' combined estimates for companies comprising the S&P 500, stocks offer an implied return of 12.6 percent with the S&P 500 selling at 250. Those returns, however, are based on estimates that individual companies' growth rates will total 9.7 percent a year for the next five years. The risk is, of course, that in a sluggish low-growth environment, particularly one in which the consumer and financial sectors are as heavily leveraged as they are at present, such growth rates may ultimately prove to be unattainable, and expectations must be revised downward. [4]

There is no right or wrong answer to the question of whether to use historical market risk premium data or implied return expectations based on analysts' current estimates. At least up until the time of this writing, I have seen more valuation practitioners using historical data than the returns implied from analysts' estimates, but that may reflect the relative availability of the data more than conceptual preferences.

---

[4]*Quantitative Analysis* (Washington, D.C.: Merrill Lynch, November-December 1987), p. 1.

Estimating Beta for Closely Held Stocks

As explained in the previous chapter, beta is a means of quantifying that portion of the risk known as *systematic risk,* that is, that portion of the risk that is related to movements in the general market rather than to industry- or company-specific factors. Specifically, beta is measured as the covariance between the excess return portion of the total return on the subject investment and the excess return portion of the total return on the market index, the total return being composed of dividends plus changes in the stock's market price, as discussed in Chapter 2.

With closely held firms, since a historical price series rarely exists, it usually is necessary to employ comparative analysis, using companies that are sufficiently comparable to the subject company. An investigation of the systematic risk, or betas, of those comparative companies will give the appraiser an indication of the appropriate measure of risk, or the appropriate beta, for the subject company. A discussion of ratios to be considered in comparative analysis for risk assessment appears in Chapter 12, "Comparative Ratio Analysis."

Treatment of "Unsystematic" Risk

As noted in the previous chapter, the idea that all unsystematic risk (risk specific to the particular industry and company as opposed to the general market) can be diversified away is less valid for most investors in closely held companies than for most investors in publicly traded stocks. Therefore, it is reasonable to expect that investors in closely held companies will be more concerned with unsystematic risk than investors in public stocks. In addition, some studies show that even the public market is concerned to some extent with unsystematic risk.[5]

Consequently, it seems prudent to analyze factors that provide evidence of the business and financial risk for the subject company. Such factors would include variability of earnings, variability of return on equity, leverage ratios, ratios of coverage of fixed charges, and so on. To some extent, these factors are correlated with, rather than independent of, systematic risk. Therefore, it must be a matter of the analyst's judgment as to whether analysis of internal risk factors indicate the need for any additional required rate of return over that indicated by the estimate of systematic risk.

An Alternative to Beta

Fortunately, there is available a data series that shows average historical risk premiums for "small stocks" (defined as companies the size of the 20 percent of stocks on the New York Stock Exchange with the

---

[5] See, for example, G.W. Douglas, "Risk in the Equity Markets: An Empirical Appraisal of Market Efficiency," *Yale Economic Essays* 9, no. 1 (1969), pp. 3–48.

smallest market value of equity) over and above the equity risk premium for S&P 500 stocks.[6]

If the analyst starts with a risk-free rate and adds the "equity risk premium" for the S&P 500 stocks, he or she may then add the "small-stock" premium. It can be argued that this provides an alternative to multiplying the equity risk premium by an estimated beta, avoiding the need to estimate a beta, as long as the analyst analyzes the subject company's risk factors to make a judgment as to whether the firm's risk premium should be equal to, greater than, or less than the publicly traded small-stock premium. Another school of thought holds that the equity risk premium for the S&P 500 would still be multiplied by the average beta for a group of comparative, public companies and the result would be augmented by the small-stock risk premium.

The sources and applications of the small-stock risk premium are discussed in Chapter 8, "Data on Required Rates of Return."

Discount Rate for Overall Capital

In the foregoing discussion, we have assumed that what is being valued is the company's common equity and that the cost of capital with which we are concerned is the cost of common equity capital.

If the desired discount rate is the one that is applicable to total capital, it will be determined by a weighted average of the rate applicable to equity, as discussed above, and the cost of debt, weighted in the proportions that would be normal for a company of the type being valued.

Sample Application of Discounted Future Returns Analysis

Assume that the corporate planner of Ace Widget Company, a large manufacturing concern, is responsible for completing a discounted future returns analysis in connection with the possible acquisition of a small manufacturing company that produces a limited line of specialty items and that he decides to use a DFE approach rather than a DCF approach. (The general points in the following example are equally applicable to either DFE or DCF.)

As the coordinator of the analysis, the planner's first step is to instruct other company executives responsible for such areas as marketing, production, and finance to make forecasts for the candidate company. The marketing executive supplies forecasts on future expected unit sales, prices, advertising volume, and selling expenditures. The production executive uses these sales forecasts to estimate future plant requirements and additional production costs. Someone from finance incorporates the estimates from the various departments into

---

[6]*Stocks, Bonds, Bills, and Inflation: 1988 Yearbook* (Chicago: Ibbotson Associates, annual).

projected earnings statements for future years. (If the candidate company already has pro forma statements prepared, the team doing the analysis for the acquirer probably will evaluate the available projections rather than build their own from scratch.) The analyst must then determine the discount rate that the company should use, taking into consideration the acquiring company's cost of capital, plus any amount to be added for special risks entailed in the acquisition.

Since the entire discounted future earnings approach is based on valuing future events, which are uncertain at best, the analyst may want to derive a range of reasonable values for the subject company rather than a single value. The greater the uncertainty regarding future expectations, the wider this range will be, and vice versa. More pessimistic estimates of future earnings will result in lower present values, as will application of a higher discount rate. Therefore, the lowest reasonable price to be paid for a company will be determined by applying a relatively high discount rate to a relatively conservative estimate of future earnings. Conversely, the highest price to be paid will be that calculated by applying the lowest reasonable discount rate to optimistic earnings projections.

The real value in a DFE analysis is that it lets any statement about a company's future earnings stream and the chances of attaining a predicted earnings level be converted into a dollar price. "I think we have a damn good chance to make $1 million after tax in two years" can be converted into a reasonable price estimation when "damn good chance" is converted to "80 percent."

Exhibit 3–3 shows how the different values can be compared when using various discount rates and applying them to "pessimistic," "most-likely," and "optimistic" earnings forecasts. Note that in this case earnings estimates are shown for 11 years and it is assumed that there will be a flat earnings stream in perpetuity from the end of the tenth year onward. The pessimistic projection shows the company at $75,000 earnings in the fifth year and assumes about a 7 percent annual growth rate for the next five years. The most-likely projection brings the company to $90,000 earnings in the fifth year and assumes about a 10 percent growth rate for the next five years. The optimistic forecast has the company at $95,000 in the fifth year and assumes about a 15 percent annual growth rate for the next five years.

Exhibit 3–3 suggests that a case can be made for pricing Ace Widget Company anywhere from $224,000 to $512,000, depending on future earnings expectations and the choice of appropriate discount rate. Although this range seems wide, it places some upper and lower boundaries on what might be considered reasonable, along with the appropriate conclusion for each set of assumptions.

Note the phenomenon that each annual earnings increment increases in present value to the extent that its growth rate over the previous year exceeds the discount rate and decreases to the extent that it does not. Looking at the most-likely forecast in the 20 percent discount rate column, note that the present value of each year's earnings increases through year 4 because the growth rate each year is

EXHIBIT 3-3

Present Value of Ace Widget Company
(by the Discounted Future Earnings Approach)

Pessimistic Earnings Forecast

Year	Projected Earnings	Present Value Discounted at 20%	22%	24%	26%	28%
1	$ 36,000	$ 30,000	$ 29,508	$ 29,032	$ 28,571	$ 28,125
2	44,000	30,556	29,962	28,616	27,715	26,855
3	54,000	31,250	30,323	28,322	26,995	25,749
4	65,000	31,346	29,341	27,493	25,789	24,214
5	75,000	30,141	27,750	25,583	23,616	21,828
6	80,000	26,792	24,262	22,007	19,992	18,190
7	86,000	24,001	21,379	19,079	17,057	15,277
8	92,000	21,396	18,746	16,459	14,482	12,768
9	98,000	18,993	16,368	14,139	12,243	10,625
10	105,000	16,958	14,374	12,217	10,411	8,894
11	on 105,000	84,790	65,338	50,905	40,042	31,764
Total Value		$346,223	$307,621	$273,852	$246,913	$224,289

Most Likely Earnings Forecast

Year	Projected Earnings	Present Value Discounted at 20%	22%	24%	26%	28%
1	$ 40,000	$ 33,333	$ 32,787	$ 32,258	$ 31,746	$ 31,250
2	50,000	34,722	33,593	32,518	31,494	30,518
3	62,000	35,880	34,144	32,518	30,994	29,564
4	75,000	36,169	33,855	31,723	29,756	27,940
5	90,000	36,169	33,300	30,670	28,339	26,193
6	99,000	33,155	30,025	27,234	24,741	22,510
7	109,000	30,420	27,096	24,181	21,619	19,362
8	120,000	27,900	24,451	21,469	18,889	16,693
9	132,000	25,582	22,046	19,045	16,491	14,311
10	145,000	23,418	19,850	16,871	14,377	12,282
11	on 145,000	117,092	90,229	70,298	55,295	43,864
Total Value		$433,840	$381,376	$338,785	$306,741	$274,487

Optimistic Earnings Forecast

Year	Projected Earnings	Present Value Discounted at 20%	22%	24%	26%	28%
1	$ 44,000	$ 36,667	$ 36,066	$ 35,484	$ 34,921	$ 34,375
2	55,000	38,194	36,952	35,770	34,643	33,569
3	67,000	38,773	36,897	35,141	33,494	31,948
4	80,000	38,588	36,112	33,838	31,740	29,802
5	95,000	38,178	35,150	32,405	29,914	27,649
6	109,000	36,504	33,057	29,984	27,240	24,784
7	127,000	35,443	31,571	28,174	25,189	22,560
8	145,000	33,722	29,545	25,941	22,825	20,123
9	166,000	32,172	27,725	23,950	20,738	17,998
10	190,000	30,686	26,011	22,107	18,839	16,094
11	on 190,000	153,430	118,231	92,114	72,456	57,477
Total Value		$512,357	$447,317	$394,908	$351,999	$320,379

greater than the 20 percent discount rate applied. The present value of the fifth year's earnings is exactly the same as that of the fourth year's earnings, because the year-to-year growth is exactly 20 percent (from $75,000 to $90,000), precisely the same as the discount rate. From year 6 onward, the present value of each year's earnings decreases, because the assumed growth of about 10 percent per year is less than the 20 percent discount rate. Moving over to the 28 percent discount rate column in the most-likely forecast, we see that the present value of each year's earnings is less than the previous year's, because there is no year in which the percentage growth rate is assumed to be as high as the 28 percent discount rate applied.

Another phenomenon worth noting is the extent to which the choice of discount rate magnifies the value conclusion, because the future earnings to be discounted are farther out in time. Again looking at the most-likely forecast, we see that the present value of the earnings in the sixth year is $33,155 discounted at 20 percent or $22,510 discounted at 28 percent, a difference of slightly less than one-third. But the earnings for year 11 onward, discounted at 20 percent, have a present value of $117,092 compared with only $43,864 discounted at 28 percent, or 62 percent less for the higher discount rate. This demonstrates the critical difference that the choice of discount rate can make in applying the discounted future returns approach in valuation practice.

The Myth of Dilution

Almost everyone who has been involved in mergers has heard (or said), "We can't pay a price/earnings multiple for an acquisition higher than the P/E multiple our own stock sells at, because that will dilute our earnings per share." This myth has deadlocked many potentially sound merger negotiations.

An acquiring company can pay a higher multiple for an acquisition than its own stock commands and still come out ahead in the long run—provided that the company being acquired has a higher expected future growth rate than the acquirer. Although it is true that some dilution in earnings will occur in the short run, it can be more than overcome very quickly if the differential in earnings growth between the two companies is substantial. The premium price paid in terms of a higher price/earnings multiple should be regarded as an investment that will be repaid over the years, and, as with any other investment, a cost-versus-benefits comparison will determine whether it is justified.

One way to analyze how much of a premium is justifiable is to apply the DFE technique specifically to the *difference* between the two companies' expected earnings growth. This will provide a present value for only that part of the expected earnings that is over and above the earnings the acquired company would have were they to grow at the same rate as those of the acquirer.

Exhibit 3–4 shows the computation of the present value of the growth component of an acquired concern's expected future earnings and illustrates how quickly initial dilution can be overcome when the growth differential is substantial. Even though company A, which is selling at 10 times earnings, pays 13 times company B's earnings, the dilution is fully overcome in the third year. From that time on, the excess earnings are available for discretionary investments or dividend payout.

In the case shown in Exhibit 3–4, it is assumed that the acquirer's price/earnings ratio remains constant. However, because of the increased rate of earnings growth resulting from the acquisition, one can reasonably assume that the acquirer stands a good chance of benefiting further by some increase in its own P/E ratio.

Capital Base Must Support Projected Growth

One error I have often seen in applying the discounted future returns method is projecting growth that could not possibly be achieved with the existing capital base and projected retained earnings. James C. Bonbright called attention to this complication 50 years ago:

> With an expanding business, the anticipated increase in earnings cannot be credited entirely to the present capital investment. This increase will be attainable only if more funds are invested in the business. But the necessity of investing these funds is a factor adverse to the present value of the enterprise, and it must be allowed for if the appraiser includes the higher anticipated earning power in his estimate of capitalizable earnings.[7]

If the projected return stream will require additional investment (that is, greater than the amount obtainable from projected retained earnings), the amount of that investment must be accounted for in computing the net present value of the present investment on the basis of the discounted future returns approach. There are many ways to recognize the impact of the additional investment on the current investment's present value, depending on the form and timing of the former and whether one is using DCF or DFE analysis. In the DCF, the additional investment is explicitly recognized in the net cash flow equation. On the other hand, in a DFE, the additional investment must be recognized in other ways. One of the simplest is to reflect the percentage dilution resulting from the additional investment. For example, if the projected returns will require additional equity that is expected to result in 20 percent dilution to the existing equity, the existing equity should be worth 80 percent of the total net present value of the discounted future returns that would be attributable to the combination of the existing and incremental investments.

---

[7]James C. Bonbright, *Valuation of Property*, vol. 1 (Charlotte, Va.: The Miche Company, 1965 [reprint of 1937 ed.]), p. 262.

EXHIBIT 3-4

The Myth of Dilution

	Acquiring Company A		Acquired Company B
Market Price	$ 10.00	Market Price	—
Total Earnings	400,000	Total Earnings	$100,000
Shares Outstanding	400,000	Shares Outstanding	100,000
Earnings Per Share	$ 1.00	Earnings Per Share	$ 1.00
Assumed Growth	None	Assumed Growth	12% per year

Company A stock is selling at 10 times earnings, but Company A pays 130,000 shares — or 13 times Company B's earnings — to acquire Company B. Company A now has 530,000 shares outstanding and $500,000 earnings, resulting in an immediate dilution in earnings per share from $1.00 to $.94/share. This dilution is soon recovered, however, as shown below:

	Company A Earnings	Company B Earnings	Earnings Per Share
Time of Merger	$400,000	$100,000	$500,000/530,000 = $ .94/share
End of Year 1	400,000	112,000	512,000/530,000 = $ .97/share
End of Year 2	400,000	125,440	525,440/530,000 = $ .99/share
End of Year 3	400,000	140,490	540,490/530,000 = $1.02/share

The "premium" paid can be regarded as 30,000 shares at $10.00 or $300,000. What Company A is buying is the extra earnings resulting from Company B's earnings growth (total earnings less $100,000). Discounted at 15%, this future growth is worth $660,268:

$$\frac{\$12,000}{(1.15)^1} + \frac{25,440}{(1.15)^2} + \frac{40,490}{(1.15)^3} + \frac{57,352}{(1.15)^4} + \ldots\ldots + \frac{121,068}{(1.15)^7} + \frac{147,596}{(1.15)^8} + \frac{177,307}{(1.15)^9} + \frac{210,584}{(1.15)^{10}} + \frac{210,584/.15}{(1.15)^{10}} = \$660,268$$

It is assumed that after 10 years, Company B's earnings will be constant and will experience no further growth. The extra earnings in year 10 are treated as an annuity in perpetuity having a value of $210,584/.15 or $1,403,893 at the end of the tenth year — resulting in a present value of $347,014.

Result: Company A has paid a "premium" of $300,000 for Company B over what it would pay for B's earnings if valued at A's price-earnings multiple. This was justified by Company B's projected future growth in earnings, the present value of which, discounted at 15%, is over twice the "premium" paid by Company A.

SOURCE: Shannon P. Pratt and Craig S. Hugo, "Pricing a Company by the Discounted Future Earnings Method," *Mergers & Acquisitions* (Spring 1972), p. 26. Reprinted with permission from Mergers & Acquisitions (Spring 1972), © 1972 Mergers & Acquisitions, 229 S. 18th Street, Philadelphia, Pennsylvania 19103. All rights reserved.

DCF or DFE? Matching the Return Stream with the Discount Rate

If the discount rate is derived through the capital asset pricing model (CAPM), the arbitrage pricing theory (APT), or the traditional *dividend growth model*[8] (dividend yield plus expected annually compounded percentage growth in dividends), the returns from which the discount rate is derived represent money available to the investor in the form of dividends plus capital appreciation. Such returns are after corporate income taxes, but would be taxable to the investor at the time that the investor actually realized the return. As such, they represent cash flows (or potential cash flows), and the discount rates thus derived would be applicable to cash flows in a DCF model. The question then becomes, "To what definition of cash flow should this discount rate be applied?" In practice, I find considerable variation in the answer to this question. Some theorists have suggested that cash flow for this purpose be defined as what some call *net free cash flow:*

> Net income (after taxes)
> + Noncash charges
> − Capital expenditures (the net changes in
>   fixed and other noncurrent assets)*
> − Changes in working capital*
> + Net changes in long-term debt*
> = Net free cash flow

> *Assumes amounts are those necessary to support projected operations.

If there are preferred dividends, they would have to be subtracted, of course, if the objective is to determine cash flow available to common equity.

If the discount rate derived from CAPM, APT, or the dividend growth model is applied to a projection of earnings (the DFE approach) rather than to a projection of cash flow (the DCF approach), the assumption is implicit that internally generated funds from noncash sources (depreciation and so forth) plus net new debt will finance net new additions to working capital and fixed and other noncurrent assets.

An alternative method to derive a discount rate to apply to a projection of earnings (the DFE approach) rather than to cash flow (the DCF approach) is to use an *earnings growth model* (earnings yield

---

[8]The dividend growth model is generally specified as follows:

$$PV = \frac{D_o\,(1\,+\,g)}{r\,-\,g}$$

where:

PV = Present value of the stock
D_o = Latest 12 months' dividends
 g = Expected annually compounded rate of growth
   in dividends
 r = Required total rate of return

plus expected annually compounded percentage growth in earnings). The model is in the same form as the dividend growth model, except that earnings is the variable in the numerator instead of dividends, and the growth is the expected growth in earnings rather than the expected growth in dividends:

$$P_o = \frac{E_o (1 + g)}{r - g}$$

where:

P_o = Price of the stock
E_o = Latest 12 months earnings
 g = Expected annually compounded rate of growth in earnings
 r = Required total rate of return in terms of earnings

To solve for the discount rate applicable to earnings, the above formula would be rewritten as follows:

$$r = \frac{E_o (1 + g)}{P_o} + g$$

The data for this approach to derive a required rate of return applicable to a DFE model are found primarily in publications such as *Value Line* or Merrill Lynch's *Quantitative Analysis*, as discussed in Chapter 8, "Data on Required Rates of Return."

Garbage in, Garbage out

Like all mathematical models, the discounted future returns model is only as good as the inputs to it; it will produce a correct answer for any type of input. The relevant question, then, is not how correct the resulting answer is but how correct was the input data that produced the answer. For investment decisions involving large capital outlays, it is far better to be approximately right than precisely wrong. And if used improperly, the discounted future returns model will produce just that: a precise answer that is completely wrong.

Making Money with the Discounted Future Returns Approach

It costs money to do discounted future returns analysis or to have it done. As a matter of fact, it's very expensive—and it's hard work. Some companies may need outside consultants because they lack the know-how to do it properly themselves. (Also, outside consultants may be more objective.) Using DCF or DFE analysis also requires working with numbers and fitting them into one or more formulas, a process most businesspeople find disconcerting. Some of the best executives suffer from "symbol shock" when faced with an algebraic formula.

But in many merger situations, the discounted future returns method is the most valid and accurate approach available for valuing a company. The exercise clearly establishes a reasonable price range within which to confine negotiations. For the buyer, the discipline of working through the exercise may save money when rampant enthusiasm and overoptimism about a proposed acquisition may otherwise preclude sound judgment about its value. For the seller, a good presentation using sound discounted future returns analysis can easily make a difference of 20 percent in the price for which the company sells. With a company that otherwise might go for $5 million, that's a cool $1 million!

There is no business decision bigger than that final one—the price at which to sell a company. With such high stakes, few expenditures can be more worthwhile than those that will get it valued properly.

Chapter 4

Approaches Using Current or Historical Data

Because of the frequent difficulties in making future projections with enough reliability to get a meaningful result by applying a discounted future earnings or discounted cash flow approach, a number of valuation approaches using historical data have found general acceptance in the discipline of business appraisal. It should be remembered, however, that historical data are used as a proxy for future expectations. Therefore, if the past history is not reasonably representative of current or foreseeable future conditions, appropriate modifications should be made. If the various approaches are applied properly, results of those using historical data generally should be reconcilable with results using discounted future returns.

Virtually all the conventional approaches to valuation using historical data can be grouped into four categories:

1. Capitalization of earning power or cash flow.
2. Capitalization of dividends.
3. Multiple of gross revenues or units of output or capacity.
4. Asset value approaches.

In some cases, one of these factors may be used solely or primarily in reaching a value conclusion. In others, two or more may be combined in some manner to reach a conclusion.

In addition to using some measurement of one or more of the above factors, the valuation conclusion may be modified by any of the following factors:

1. History of past transactions in the securities.
2. Degree of marketability, or lack thereof, including effects of any specific restrictions on transfer.
3. Extent of control or minority position represented, including the effect of voting rights.
4. Other contractual rights or obligations connected to the securities.
5. Other qualitative factors.

Capitalization of Earnings

A basic *capitalization of earnings approach* means applying one divisor or multiplier to one earnings figure, with the result being an indication of value derived from that single multiplication or division. Thus, capitalization of earning power is conceptually a simple, two-variable approach, requiring a figure for the company's earning power and a figure for the appropriate capitalization rate or multiple. As one might expect, however, the complexities in arriving at these two numbers pose intriguing challenges for the valuation analyst's knowledge and ingenuity.

In order to use historical reported earnings data to determine a company's earning capacity, one must analyze the data and adjust for any items not representative of the company's earning capacity. The types of items that most commonly require some adjustment are discussed in Chapter 11, "Analyzing and Adjusting Financial Statements."

The income stream to be capitalized can come either before or after any or all of several items, such as interest, depreciation, allowance for replacements, owners' compensation, taxes, and principal payments on debt. The income stream can be the latest year's, a straight or weighted average of past years', a trend line value, a normalized income stream, a forecast of the coming year's, or some other variation. *The key is that the income stream being capitalized must be clearly defined and the capitalization rate or multiple chosen must be a rate that is appropriate for the particular income stream as defined.* The analyst cannot use a single formula in all situations, because the appropriate analysis will vary considerably from one set of circumstances to another.

Defining the Earnings Base

The *earnings base* can be defined in many ways, especially if the term *earnings* is broadened to include any or all of the many definitions associated with the term *cash flow.* The term *cash flow* is used by different people in different contexts to mean an earnings base before or after a wide variety of items, including depreciation, interest, taxes, capital expenditures, changes in working capital, and/or principal repayments. Some such items affect the balance sheet but not the income statement.

The most commonly used definition of earnings is *net income* in the accounting sense, which is the bottom line after all expenses, including owners' compensation, depreciation, interest, and taxes, but before any capital expenditures or payments of principal on any debt owed. There can be many valid reasons for using some definition of earnings other than net income as the base to be capitalized. Criteria to be considered in choosing an earnings base to be capitalized include the following:

1. Is it representative of income in an economic sense?
2. Can it be measured accurately for the subject company?
3. Can it be measured accurately (and/or comparably) for comparative companies from which P/E ratios or capitalization rates might be derived?
4. Is it an earnings base on which buyers and sellers tend to focus in determining market prices?

These criteria often conflict. For example, one definition of earnings may provide a conceptually preferable measurement of true economic income, while another may have more and/or better comparative company data available. Consequently, analysts often use more than one definition of earnings to develop indications of value from a capitalization of earnings approach.

From the viewpoint of availability of data, for medium-size and larger companies the earnings figure usually most readily available for comparative companies is net income (after taxes). For small companies, comparative data on pretax income often are more readily available. Generally, the most accessible data for cash flow are for the accounting definition—net income plus all noncash charges (such as depreciation and amortization).

The best conceptual definition of earnings in terms of representing true income in an economic sense depends substantially on the nature of the asset mix. For a company that owns primarily improved real estate that is depreciating on the books but not actually declining in value, some measure of cash flow usually would be more relevant than an accounting definition of earnings. On the other hand, for a company with equipment that is rapidly wearing out or becoming obsolete, the standard accounting definition of earnings probably is a more relevant earnings base than the standard accounting definition of cash flow.

Measuring the Earnings Base

In measuring earnings, certain adjustments to the financial statements may be appropriate, as discussed in Chapter 11. If comparative companies are used, it is important to measure earnings by the same criteria for the subject and comparative companies, which in some cases may require some adjustments to financial data as reported by the latter.

Besides the adjustments to the financial statements, two decisions are necessary in order to measure an earnings base from current or historical data: (1) the duration of time to be covered and (2) if more than one accounting period, the method of averaging or weighting the various periods.

Choice of Time Period.   The most commonly selected historical period for evaluation of earning capacity is five years. The general idea is that for many companies, analysis of five years' results goes back far enough to demonstrate some type of continuum but not so far that the past results have no relevance to today's conditions or operations. The analyst, then, should vary from the conventional five-year historical period to the extent that this underlying assumption is not valid.

If, for example, the company drastically changed its operations three years ago, it might be more appropriate to consider data for only the three years in which it operated in its current mode. On the other hand, if the company is in an industry subject to fairly lengthy business cycles, five years may be heavily weighted to a depressed or buoyant period for the company and may be too short to be representative of the company's reasonable long-term fortunes. The analyst should consider the circumstances and exercise reasonable judgment in selecting the historical period on which to rely.

Analysts often encounter problems in choosing a time period when the valuation date is several months after the end of the subject company's fiscal year. In that case, the analyst must decide what use, if any, to make of the interim data in order to bring the historical period over which earnings are measured as close to the valuation date as possible. The decision will depend on several factors, two of the most important of which are the quality of the interim earnings data and the extent to which the recent interim period is or is not significantly more representative of future expectations for the company than the results of the last fiscal year. The use of interim data is far too complex to lend itself to a set of automatic decision rules; it is a matter that the analyst must resolve by applying experience and careful judgment of the circumstances of each case.

Of course, if the analyst is using comparative companies, the time period over which earnings are measured for the comparative and subject companies should be either the same or as close as feasibly possible.

Unweighted, Weighted, or Trend Line Values.   If there is no apparent pattern to the past earnings analyzed, or if what appears to be a pattern may not reasonably be expected to continue, a simple average of the historical earnings might be an adequate representation of earning capacity. If there appears to be a pattern that may be extrapolated into the future, it may be appropriate to accord more weight to the more recent earnings than to the earlier years'.

One simple and thus commonly used technique for weighting the historical earnings is the weighted average. It is computed in the same manner as the sum-of-the-years'-digits method of computing depreciation. If, for example, five years' earnings are being used, the most recent year is accorded 5/15 of the total weight, the next most recent year 4/15, and on back to the earliest year, which is weighted 1/15.

If the company's past earnings trend is expected to continue, a trend line analysis may be appropriate. The trend line would be preferable to the weighted average if the most recent year took an unusual upswing or downswing and, for that reason, should not be given the greatest weight in the earning power evaluation. Note, however, that a span of five years' data is a relatively short period over which to compute a statistical trend line, especially if the data are erratic. The statistical validity of a trend line increases with the number of points or "observations" and the extent to which the data are reasonably consistent, that is, not highly volatile from period to period.

For a company with the seven-year earnings record shown in Exhibit 4–1, the earning power by the simple average, weighted average, and trend line methods would be computed as:

Formula 4–1

Simple average method:

$$\frac{\$1.00 + \$1.15 + \$1.25 + \$1.50 + \$1.60 + \$2.00 + \$2.50}{7} = \$1.57$$

Weighted average method:

$$
\begin{array}{rcl}
\$\ 1.00 \times 1 &=& \$\ 1.00 \\
1.15 \times 2 &=& 2.30 \\
1.25 \times 3 &=& 3.75 \\
1.50 \times 4 &=& 6.00 \\
1.60 \times 5 &=& 8.00 \\
2.00 \times 6 &=& 12.00 \\
2.50 \times \underline{\ 7\ } &=& \underline{17.50} \\
28 && \$50.55 \\
\$50.55 \div 28 &=& \underline{\underline{\$\ 1.80}}
\end{array}
$$

Trend line method: The formula to be solved is

$$Y = a + bX$$

where:

$$b = \frac{N(\Sigma XY) - (\Sigma X)(\Sigma Y)}{N(\Sigma X^2) - (\Sigma X)^2}$$

$$a = \frac{\Sigma Y - b(\Sigma X)}{N}$$

X_i = The ith year and weighting to be accorded the ith year
Y_i = Earnings in ith year
N = Number of observations
Σ = Sum of the variables, X_i; Y_i; X^2_i; X_iY_i

In order to solve the formula, the following format is suggested:

X	Y	X²	XY	
1	1.00	1	1.00	N = 7 Observations
2	1.15	4	2.30	
3	1.25	9	3.75	
4	1.50	16	6.00	
5	1.60	25	8.00	
6	2.00	36	12.00	
7	2.50	49	17.50	
Σ = 28	ΣY = 11.00	ΣX^2 = 140	ΣXY = 50.55	

$Y = a + bx$

$$b = \frac{7(50.55) - [(28)(11)]}{7(140) - (28)^2} = \frac{353.85 - 308}{980 - 784} = \frac{45.85}{196} = .234$$

$$a = \frac{11 - .234(28)}{7} = \frac{4.45}{7} = .636$$

Substituting:

$$Y = .636 + .234(X)$$

To calculate the trendline value for years 7 and 8:

$$
\begin{array}{ll}
Y = .636 + .234(7) & Y = .636 + .234(8) \\
Y = .636 + 1.64 & Y = .636 + 1.87 \\
Y = 2.28 & Y = 2.51
\end{array}
$$

Fortunately, the arithmetic shown in the trend line example need not discourage use of the method, since many modern business pocket cal-

EXHIBIT 4-1

Seven Years' Earnings for Reliable Company

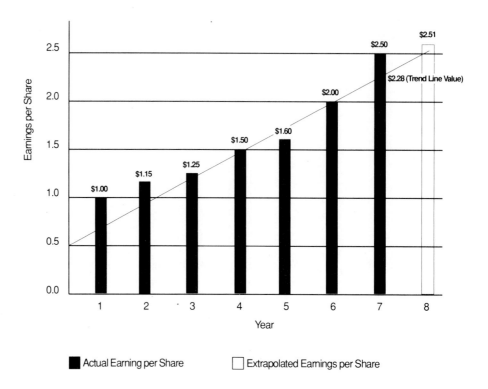

■ Actual Earning per Share   □ Extrapolated Earnings per Share

culators are programmed to compute regression coefficients and trend line values in seconds.

As this example shows, when the earnings progression is very stable, the weighted average method computes a higher value than does the average method and the trend line method a higher value yet. Even so, none of the methods computes a value as high as the latest year's earnings, which benefited from an unusual jump. Most people would intuitively agree that in this example the weighted average and trend line methods present a fairer estimation of the company's earning power than a simple average of past years' earnings. However, few companies exhibit as stable a pattern as that in the example. The less stable the pattern, the less reliable are the weighted average or trend line methods as estimators of earning power.

Obviously, the selection of the most appropriate earnings base is a matter of judgment. Sometimes it is useful for comparative purposes to work out the valuation exercises using two or more methods of calculating the earnings base, even occasionally using more than one historical time period and/or method of weighting for comparison.

Determining the Appropriate Price/Earnings Ratio

Definition of Price/Earnings Ratio. The definition of the *price/ earnings ratio* is, exactly as its name implies, the *price divided by the earnings*. Although it seems simple and straightforward at first blush, in practice the analyst must define precisely what price and what earnings to use in computing it. The ratio can be computed on either a total company basis or a per share basis. Usually the latter is more convenient. However, it should be noted that if the shares outstanding have changed from year to year, the ratios may differ on an aggregate basis from those on a per share basis when using weighted shares outstanding to calculate earnings per share.

The key factor in defining what price and what earnings base to use in the ratio is comparability. For the purpose of valuing a business or business interest as discussed in this book, we are interested in a price on a particular valuation date as defined in the description of the valuation assignment. Therefore, if we plan to use price/earnings ratios for shares of comparative companies as a guide to determining an appropriate price/earnings ratio for the subject company, the prices we use for the comparative companies should be on our valuation date or as close to it as possible.

The figure to use for earnings usually is derived in one of the manners described in the previous section. The key factor again is comparability; that is, if we define the price/earnings ratio a certain way for our subject company and plan to use P/E ratios of comparative companies to determine what our P/E ratio should be, we must define the ratio's components the same way for the comparative companies as for our subject company. For example, if we use the latest five years' average earnings as the earnings base for the subject company, we should use the average of the same latest five years' earnings as the base for each comparative company. If we exclude extraordinary and nonrecurring items from the subject company's earnings base, we should exclude extraordinary and nonrecurring items from the comparative companies' earnings.

In other words, in defining prices and earnings to be used in computing comparative price/earnings ratios, as in defining any other variables to be used in the valuation, the measurement of the variables must be done on a consistent basis throughout the exercise. Furthermore, the definitions of the prices and earnings used should be stated clearly in the valuation report to leave no room for ambiguity in the reader's mind. The foregoing discussion implies that *the earnings base used for the subject company should bear a relationship to earnings capacity somewhat similar to the comparative companies' earnings bases to their respective earning capacities*. The analyst should adjust the earnings base for any abnormal factors that would result in noncomparability. Some of the possible adjustments are discussed in Chapter 11.

Sources of Price/Earnings Ratios. Usually the best guidance on what multiple is appropriate for a given stream of earnings lies in what other people are willing to pay for comparable earnings streams. The two most important criteria of comparability are the relative degree of risk and the expected growth rate associated with the earnings stream. The various participants in a given industry are subject to at least a partially common set of risk factors and factors influencing expected growth. Thus, the starting point for calculating an appropriate price/earnings ratio for a particular company is to find out the P/E ratios at which other companies or shares of other companies in the same or similar industries are selling.

The most commonly used data for this exercise are the prices at which the stocks of companies in the subject company's industry sell in the open market on a day-to-day basis. If possible, at least when valuing a controlling interest, it also is desirable to obtain data on prices at which companies in the subject company's industry were acquired by other companies. Chapter 9, "Comparative Transaction Data," is devoted to the mechanics of gathering and analyzing data on comparative companies.

Naturally, the more comparatives and the better the comparatives one is able to find, the more confidence one will likely have in this approach to determining an appropriate price/earnings multiple. Also, one intuitively tends to have more confidence in relying on such data to the extent that the comparative companies' P/E ratios are grouped in a reasonable range rather than being widely disparate unless one is able to explain the disparity from the application of fundamental factors that can be used to explain the appropriate P/E for the subject company as well. The degree of applicability of the resulting P/E ratios to the subject company will vary considerably from one case to another depending on how many comparatives one is able to find and how comparable they really are. In most cases, an appropriate P/E ratio for the subject company can be postulated somewhere within the range of the price/earnings ratios found for the comparative companies. However, it is important to note that the appropriate P/E may lie outside the range of the comparatives, if there are justifiable fundamental factors that explain this disparity. The appraiser must use caution if applying a P/E outside of the range, and the reasons must be clearly and cogently stated. In any case, the appraiser must carefully compare the subject company's relevant strengths and weaknesses with those of the comparative companies. Only in this way can he arrive at an informed and supportable judgment about where the subject company should fall.

Relationship among Price/Earnings Ratio, Capitalization Rate, and Discount Rate

Unfortunately, the term *capitalization rate* is a source of widespread confusion, because it is used profusely in the literature and practice of finance with different meanings in different contexts. To *capitalize* means to *convert the income stream into an indication of value by di-*

viding or multiplying the selected definition of the stream by some fac-tor, called a capitalization rate. Thus, when we have applied an appropriate price/earnings multiple to a stream of earnings, we have capitalized that earnings stream. Thus, one properly might say, "We have chosen to capitalize the earnings at a multiple of 7."

The ambiguity lies in the term *capitalization rate.* Some people use it interchangeably with *price/earnings ratio* and *price/earnings multi-ple.* Others use the term to mean the reciprocal of the price/earnings ratio (e.g., if the P/E ratio is 5, the capitalization rate is 1/5, or .20). Still others use *capitalization rate* interchangeably with *discount rate,* that is, as used in the denominator of the present value formula pre-sented in the preceding chapter on pricing the company by the dis-counted future returns approach. For the purpose of this book we will use the terms *discount rate* and *capitalization rate* as follows:

> *Discount rate: A rate of return used to convert a series of future income amounts into present value.* This is the sense in which the term is used in the discounted future earnings or discounted cash flow model and represents the cost of capital for comparably risky investments, as discussed in Chapter 3.

> *Capitalization rate: A divisor used to convert a defined stream of income to an indicated value.* For example, if an income stream of $10,000 per year were to be capitalized at 25 percent, the calcula-tion would be $10,000 divided by .25, which equals a capitalized value of $40,000. The income stream to be capitalized can be de-fined in an almost infinite variety of ways, and it is essential that the capitalization rate chosen be appropriate for the particular def-inition of that income stream.

For example, if a company expects to earn $10,000 the first year, $11,000 the second year, $12,000 the third year, and $13,500 in the fourth and all subsequent years, and the earnings stream is to be discounted at a discount rate of 30 percent, the calculation will be as follows:

Formula 4–2: Present Value Application

$$PV = \frac{\$10,000}{1 + .30} + \frac{\$11,000}{(1 + .30)^2} + \frac{\$12,000}{(1 + .30)^3} + \frac{\$13,500/.30}{(1 + .30)^3}$$
$$= \$40,145 \cong \$40,000$$

In both of these examples, a company with a first year's income stream of $10,000 was found to be worth about $40,000. In the first case, only the first year's earnings were considered explicitly and capitalized at a *capitalization rate* of 25 percent. In the second case, the future in-comes were projected and discounted at a *discount rate* of 30 percent.

In the unique case where the earnings stream is considered to be flat, that is, a more or less constant level of earnings in perpetuity with no clearly discernable growth or decline projected, the capitali-zation rate and the price/earnings ratio are reciprocals of each other and the capitalization rate equals the discount rate. If A is a reciprocal of B, this means that A is 1 divided by B. If the price/earnings ratio is the reciprocal of the capitalization rate, the P/E ratio is 1 divided by the capitalization rate. For example, if the capitalization rate is 20 percent, then:

Formula 4–3: P/E Ratio

$$\text{P/E ratio} = \frac{1}{\text{Capitalization rate}} = \frac{1}{.20} = 5.0$$

Remember, however, that the notion that the discount rate (the rate of return that the market requires) and the P/E ratio are reciprocals of each other is valid only to the extent that no appreciable growth or decline is anticipated from the earnings base being capitalized. If *no* growth is expected and the price/earnings ratio is 4, the implied discount rate is .25 ($1/4 = .25$).

If the expectation of future earnings growth is impounded in the price/earnings ratio, that ratio will be higher than the reciprocal of the discount rate. Take, for example, a stock selling at 20 times current earnings. The reciprocal of this P/E ratio would be .05 ($1/20 = .05$). Obviously, no one has any interest in investing for a 5 percent expected return on equity. The notion that the discount rate applicable to the company's equity, or the company's implied cost of equity capital, would be 5 percent is nonsense. The ratio of the market price of the company's shares to its current earnings in effect reflects two variables in one, that is, the discount rate and the market's expectations regarding the company's future earnings growth.

To illustrate this point with an example, we will refer to Exhibit 3–3 in the previous chapter, the present value of Ace Widget Company determined by the discounted future returns approach. As can be seen from even the pessimistic earnings forecast, Ace Widget Company is expected to achieve quite substantial earnings growth. If we are willing to accept the most likely earnings forecast and discount that earnings stream at a 24 percent discount rate, the present value of the company works out to $338,785. The table provides no data on the latest year's earnings, but the current year's earnings on this most likely estimate are projected at $40,000. On this basis, the appropriate price/earnings ratio for the company using the current year's projected earnings as the earnings base is:

Formula 4–4

$$\frac{\$338,785}{\$40,000} = 8.5$$

The reciprocal of 8.5 is .118, but the company's required rate of return on equity certainly is not 11.8 percent. The price/earnings ratio of 8.5 times projected current earnings reflects a combination of the required total rate of return of 24 percent and acceptance of the most likely forecast of future earnings growth.

In the same example, if one is willing to accept the same set of earnings projections but a discount rate of only 20 percent, the appropriate P/E ratio for the company using the current year's projected earnings as the earnings base is:

Formula 4–5

$$\frac{\$433,840}{\$40,000} = 10.8$$

Note that for a company with a projected earnings growth pattern such as this, a change in the discount rate has a more than proportional effect on the ratio of price to current earnings. As noted earlier, when the earnings are projected to be flat, a change in the discount rate has an exactly proportional, inverse effect on the ratio of price to current earnings.

Thus, we can see that the price/earnings ratios at which publicly traded stocks sell in the market impound two variables into a single figure: the discount rate the market applies to the company's earnings and the market's expectations about the prospective changes in the company's earnings. The analyst should explicitly recognize that these two factors are the components determining price/earnings ratios when using P/E ratios of public companies as a guide for determining an appropriate P/E ratio for a closely held company. To the extent that the subject company's earnings growth prospects are greater or smaller than the average for the public company comparatives, the ratio of price to current or historical earnings should be greater or less than the average for its industry. To the extent that the subject company's risk factors and, consequently, appropriate discount rate are greater or less than the average for the comparative public companies, the ratio of price to current or historical earnings should be less or greater than the average for its industry.

The discounted future earnings approach specifically identifies the relative impact of differences in the discount rate and differences in the assumptions regarding future earnings. Although price/earnings ratios reflect these two factors, their relative impacts are not identified separately. The analyst must compare the subject company to the public companies and use his or her best judgment to arrive at a P/E multiple that reflects both an appropriate discount rate and the earnings prospects for the subject company.

The No-Growth or Constant-Growth Assumption

If it is reasonable to assume that there will be no growth from the historical or current earnings base, or that earnings can be expected to grow at a constant rate into perpetuity, the analyst can use a special version of the direct capitalization method.

No-Growth Case. As noted in the previous section, if it is assumed that there will be no change in the earnings base, the capitalization rate is equal to the discount rate.

Constant-Growth Case. If one makes the simplifying assumption that the subject company's earnings will grow at a constant rate into perpetuity, one can use a simplified direct capitalization of earnings formula that is conceptually equivalent to the discounted future earnings method discussed in the previous chapter.[1] This formula, sometimes referred to as the *earnings growth model,* is as follows:

Formula 4–6

$$PV = \frac{E_0 (1 + g)}{R - g}$$

where

> PV = Present value
> E_0 = Base level of earnings from which the constant level of growth is expected to proceed as of the valuation date
> g = Annually compounded rate of growth in earnings
> R = Discount rate (required total rate of return)

A little experimentation with this formula will quickly demonstrate that it is extremely sensitive to changes in the assumed growth rate and becomes increasingly so as the assumed growth rate approaches the discount rate. This formula is most useful for companies whose expected earnings growth rates are relatively modest and predictable. A common error in applying this formula is to assume a growth rate that could be achieved only if additional capital were invested, thus overstating the present value of the current investment.

Capitalization of Dividends or Dividend-Paying Capacity

Dividends ultimately are possible only as a result of earnings and adequate available cash flow. Therefore, capitalization of dividends or dividend-paying capacity may or may not be analyzed as a valuation approach separate from capitalization of earnings and/or cash flow, depending on the circumstances and the valuation's purpose. Revenue Ruling 59-60 states that dividends or dividend-paying capacity should be one of the factors in the valuation of a business interest for federal estate or gift tax purposes. In court cases involving valuations of shares under dissenting stockholder appraisal rights, capitalization of dividends has been a factor specifically recognized in the courts' determinations of value in only a minority of cases. Most potential acquirers are not specifically interested in the acquiree's dividend-paying capacity, since the acquiree will not continue to operate as an independent entity.

---

[1]For a discussion of the use of this formula in the context of real estate appraisal, see Gale Graham, "Use 'EQUIVALENCY--Keep Your Lender Solvent," *The Real Estate Appraiser and Analyst* (Winter 1985), pp. 19–22. For discussion of other variations of the formula, see Frank K. Reilly, *Investment Analysis and Portfolio Management,* 2nd ed. (Hinsdale, Ill.: Dryden Press, 1985), Chapter 10, "The Process and Theory of Valuation," and Chapter 15, "Analysis of Growth Companies."

If the valuation is of a controlling interest, dividend-paying capacity is more important than actual dividends paid, since the controlling stockholder has the discretion to pay or not pay dividends as long as the company has the capacity to do so. In valuing a minority interest, however, the actual dividends the company pays usually are more important than the dividend-paying capacity, since the minority stockholder generally cannot force the company to pay dividends even if it unquestionably has the capacity to do so.

When the capitalization of dividends approach is used as an element in the valuation, it usually is by reference to dividend yields on comparative publicly traded companies. For example, if comparative publicly traded companies were found to have an average dividend yield (market price per share divided by annual dividends per share) of 5 percent and the subject company paid dividends or was determined to have a dividend-paying capacity of $1 per share, the capitalization of dividends approach would be to simply divide the dividend-paying capacity per share by the appropriate capitalization rate or dividend yield—in this case, $1.05, which implies a $20-per-share value by the capitalization of dividends approach.

An estimate of dividend-paying capacity may be based in part on typical payout ratios of publicly traded companies in the subject company's industry. For example, if public companies in that industry typically pay out 30 percent of their earnings in dividends, 30 percent of earnings might be a good starting point from which to estimate the subject company's dividend-paying capacity. However, the typical closely held company is less well capitalized than its publicly traded counterpart and may have less dividend-paying capacity per dollar of earnings capacity than most of the publicly traded companies with which it might be compared. This factor must be considered in estimating the subject company's dividend-paying capacity.

Multiple of Revenues or Physical Volume

In some situations, capitalization of gross revenues is an appropriate approach to valuation. It can be one of several approaches considered in a particular valuation and, in some instances, may even be the most highly relied on approach.[2] The capitalization of gross revenues approach is applied most frequently to service businesses, such as advertising agencies, insurance agencies, mortuaries, professional practices, and some types of publishing operations. In a way, a capitalization of gross revenues approach can be considered a shortcut to a capitalization of earnings approach, since generally there is an implicit assumption that a certain level of revenues should be able to generate a specific earnings level in a given type of business. The analyst may

---

[2]For an interesting book that focuses on price/revenues multiples as a starting place for analysis, see Kenneth L. Fisher.*Super Stocks* (Homewood, Ill.: Dow Jones-Irwin, 1985). Fisher does not, however, advocate using multiples of revenue as a measure of value without also doing other analysis.

prefer to try to derive an appropriate multiple of gross revenues as the valuation criterion rather than attempt to adjust the company's income statements to arrive at an estimate of earning power or may at least want to consider a multiple of gross revenues approach as a check against a valuation result based on an adjusted earnings approach.

The valuation's purpose assumes even more than its normal significance when one is deciding whether or how much to rely on a capitalization of gross revenues approach. Probably the most valid use of the multiple of gross revenues approach occurs when selling or acquiring a service business. The acquirer can eliminate discretionary expenditures, may be able to improve earnings through tried and proven management techniques, and may create efficiencies by centralizing some of the functions in its home office. Therefore, the acquirer may have reasonably reliable guidelines regarding the worth of a given level of revenue production regardless of the earnings that an independent entity may or may not be achieving with that level of revenue production.

Of course, if the acquirer is to rely on this approach, it must make a very careful assessment of the future continuity of the revenue production. It is not uncommon for an acquirer to pay top dollar to establish a branch by buying a strong, independent company only to experience a mass exodus of the sales force within a year or two (or sooner) because they found working for the acquirer less attractive than working for the former independent entity.

On the other hand, if the service business is not going to sell out but the stock is being valued for gift, ESOP, or other purposes, the earnings may assume a greater weight in the valuation process, since changes that an acquirer might impose are not in prospect. Naturally, if the valuation is for estate tax purposes, the analyst must assess the effect that the owner's death might have on the company's future prospects. In many service businesses, the death of a key person may reduce the business's value to the net scrap value, if any, of the assets.

One can find guidance in arriving at an appropriate multiple of gross revenues for a particular business in both public stock market data and merger and acquisition data. There are quite a few publicly traded companies in most service business categories, such as insurance agencies, advertising and public relations firms, and securities brokers. For most categories of service establishments, there are trade associations or periodicals that publish data on prices of recent acquisitions.[3]

Logically, the multiplier of revenues at which a company should sell would be the company's profits expressed as a percentage of sales, divided by the applicable rate at which its earnings should be capitalized. For example, suppose a manufacturing company earned an average of 5 percent on its sales and buyers of companies in that industry demanded a 20 percent return on their investment. The buyers would be willing to pay:

---

[3]See, for example, Shannon P. Pratt, *Valuing a Property Management Company* (Chicago: Institute of Real Estate Management Foundation, 1988).

Formula 4–7

$$\frac{.05}{.20} = .25, \text{ or 25 percent of sales}$$

To put the above in dollar terms, assume that a company with $1 million in sales earns $50,000 (5 percent of sales). If the capitalization rate is 20 percent, the company should be worth about $250,000 ($50,000/.20 = $250,000). The $250,000 is equal to 25 percent of sales ($250,000/$1 million = .25); thus, the gross revenue multiplier in this case is .25.

If someone proposes to price a company or group of companies in an industry on the basis of a gross revenue multiplier, the average return on sales for the industry can be looked up in sources discussed in Chapter 7, "Economic and Industry Data," or from trade association statistics, if available. If the average profit on sales divided by a satisfactory capitalization rate comes out somewhere near the proffered gross revenue multiplier, the multiplier will appear to be fairly accurate.

As one would expect, the multiples of gross sales at which companies sell normally are highly correlated with their respective profit margins on sales. If the subject company's true return on sales is known, an estimate of a reasonable price/sales ratio can be derived by simple regression analysis using comparative companies' price/sales ratios and returns on sales. The procedure for doing this is the same as that for deriving an appropriate price/book value by regression analysis which is described in a later section.

Valuations by mutiples of gross revenue are particularly susceptible to distortion because of differences in capital structure between subject and comparative companies. Therefore, this approach is often done on a debt-free basis as discussed in a later section.

One step removed from a multiple of gross revenues is a multiple of some measure of unit volume or capacity. Examples would include nursing homes at so much per bed, forest products plants at so much per thousand board feet of production, service stations and fuel distributors at so much per gallon sold per month, and so on. The implication of this approach, of course, is that so much volume can be expected to translate into some anticipated amount of sales and profits.

The Excess Earnings Method[4]

Another version of a capitalized earnings approach is the *excess earnings method,* sometimes called the *Treasury method* because it originally appeared in a 1920 publication of the U.S. Treasury Department, "Appeals and Review Memorandum Number 34" (*ARM 34*). It was

---

[4]This section draws on a more extended discussion in Shannon P. Pratt, *Valuing Small Businesses and Professional Practices* (Homewood, Ill.: Dow Jones-Irwin, 1986) Chapter 12, "The Excess Earnings Method."

adopted to compute the value of goodwill that breweries and distilleries lost because of Prohibition. Since then, both taxpayers and IRS agents have widely used (and misused) it in connection with business valuations for gift and estate taxes. Also, perhaps partly because of its wide publicity and partly because its apparent simplicity is appealing, it has been widely adopted in one form or another for pricing small businesses and professional practices.

In 1968, the Internal Revenue Service updated and restated the ARM 34 method with the publication of Revenue Ruling 68-609, which is reproduced in Exhibit 4–2. This ruling is still in effect.[5]

Description of the Method

The steps in the excess earnings method can be summarized as follows:

1. Determine a net tangible asset value. (Note that this value is for net tangible assets only and would not include intangible items such as leaseholds, patents, copyrights, and so on.)
2. Determine a normalized earnings level.
3. Determine an appropriate percentage rate of return or, in the parlance of this book, a capitalization rate applicable to that portion of the expected total return, as determined in Step 2, that is based on or supported by net tangible assets. Multiply the net tangible asset value from Step 1 by that rate to determine the amount of earnings attributable to the tangible assets. Subtract that amount from the normalized earnings developed in Step 2. The result of this step is called the *excess earnings*, that is, the amount of earnings above a fair return on the net tangible asset value.
4. Determine an appropriate capitalization rate to apply to the excess earnings, which presumably are the earnings attributable to goodwill and all other intangible assets as opposed to tangible assets. Capitalize the excess earnings into an indication of total intangible asset value at that rate.
5. Add the values from Steps 1 and 4.[6]

The excess earnings approach may be done either on an equity basis or on a "debt-free" basis as discussed for other approaches later in the chapter.

An Example.   Let's suppose that a small business has a net tangible asset value of $20,000. Let's also suppose that after allowance for a reasonable salary for the owner, the business earns about $8,000 per year. For the purpose of this example, we will use a 15 percent rate of return on the tangible assets and capitalize the excess earnings at

---

[5]It is worth noting that Revenue Ruling 68-609 is specifically stated to be applicable to the valuation of the total intangible assets of a business, and is nowhere indicated to be applicable to the valuation of the business as a whole.

[6]As an alternative to using the present net tangible asset value and normalized earnings, some appraisers base the computations of the value of excess earnings on average net tangible assets and average earnings for some time period, usually five years. This procedure is satisfactory if the period used is representative of reasonable future expectations. If this procedure is used, the value of excess earnings is still added to the present net tangible asset value to arrive at the value for the total entity.

EXHIBIT 4-2

Revenue Ruling 68-609

REVENUE Ruling 68-609 (formula method)

The "formula" approach may be used in determining the fair market value of intangible assets of a business only if there is not better basis available for making the determination; A.R.M. 34, A.R.M. 68, O.D. 937, and Revenue Ruling 65-192 superseded. (1968-2, C.B., 327).

Revenue Ruling 68-609

The purpose of this Revenue Ruling is to update and restate, under the current statute and regulations, the currently outstanding portions of A.R.M. 34, C.B. 2, 31 (1920), A.R.M. 68, C.B. 3, 43 (1920), and O.D. 937, C.B. 4, 43 (1921).

The question presented is whether the "formula" approach, the capitalization of earnings in excess of a fair rate of return on net tangible assets, may be used to determine the fair market value of the intangible assets of a business.

The "formula" approach may be stated as follows:

A percentage return on the average annual value of the tangible assets used in a business is determined, using a period of years (preferably not less than five) immediately prior to the valuation date. The amount of the percentage return on tangible assets, thus determined, is deducted from the average earnings of the business for such period and the remainder, if any, is considered to be the amount of the average annual earnings from the intangible assets of the business for the period. This amount (considered as the average annual earnings from intangibles), capitalized at a percentage of, say 15 to 20 percent, is the value of the intangible assets of the business determined under the "formula" approach.

The percentage of return on the average annual value of the tangible assets used should be the percentage prevailing in the industry involved at the date of valuation, or (when the industry percentage is not available) a percentage of 8 to 10 percent may be used.

The 8 percent rate of return and the 15 percent rate of capitalization are applied to tangibles and intangibles, respectively, of businesses with a small risk factor and stable and regular earnings; the 10 percent rate of return and 20 percent rate of capitalization are applied to businesses in which the hazards of business are relatively high.

The above rates are used as examples and are not appropriate in all cases. In applying the "formula"

approach, the average earnings period and the capitalization rates are dependent upon the facts pertinent thereto in each case.

The past earnings to which the formula is applied should fairly reflect the probable future earnings. Ordinarily, the period should not be less than five years, and abnormal years, whether above or below the average, should be eliminated. If the business is a sole proprietorship or partnership, there should be deducted from the earnings of the business a reasonable amount for services performed by the owner or partners engaged in the business. See Lloyd B. Sanderson Estate v. Commissioner, 42 F 2d 160 (1930). Further, only the tangible assets entering into net worth, including accounts and bills receivable in excess of accounts and bills payable, are used for determining earnings on the tangible assets. Factors that influence the capitalization rate include (1) the nature of the business, (2) the risk involved, and (3) the stability or irregularity of earnings.

The "formula" approach should not be used if there is better evidence available from which the value of intangibles can be determined. If the assets of a going business are sold upon the basis of a rate of capitalization that can be substantiated as being realistic, though it is not within the range of figures indicated here as the ones ordinarily to be adopted, the same rate of capitalization should be used in determining the value of the intangibles.

Accordingly, the "formula" approach may be used for determining the fair market value of intangible assets of a business only if there is no better basis therefor available.

See also Revenue Ruling 59-60, C.B. 1959-1, 237, as modified by Revenue Ruling 65-193, C.B. 1965-2, 370, which sets forth the proper approach to use in the valuation of closely-held corporate stocks for estate and gift tax purposes. The general approach, methods, and factors, outlined in Revenue Ruling 59-60, as modified, are equally applicable to valuations of corporate stocks for income and other tax purposes as well as for estate and gift tax purposes. They apply also to problems involving the determination of the fair market value of business interests of any type, including partnerships and proprietorships, and of intangible assets for all tax purposes.

A.R.M. 34, A.R.M. 68, and O.D. 937 are superseded, since the positions set forth therein are restated to the extent applicable under current law in this Revenue Ruling. Revenue Ruling 65-192, C.B. 1965-2, 259, which contained restatements of A.R.M. 34 and A.R.M. 68, is also superseded.

SOURCE: 1968-2, C.B. 327

33⅓ percent. In this scenario, the value of the business would be computed as follows:

Formula 4–8

Net tangible asset value		$20,000
Normalized earnings	$8,000	
Earnings attributable to tangible assets ($20,000 × .15) =	3,000	
Excess earnings	$5,000	
Value of excess earnings ($5,000 ÷ .333) =		15,000
Total value		$35,000

Denunciation by the IRS

The IRS Appellate Conferee Valuation Training Program uses colorful language to denounce the use of ARM 34, or the excess earnings method of valuation. Following are some pertinent excerpts:

> One of the most frequently encountered errors in appraisal is the use of a formula to determine a question of fact, which on a reasonable basis must be resolved in view of all pertinent circumstances . . . ARM 34 has been applied indiscriminately by tax practitioners and by members of the Internal Revenue Service since it was published. On occasion the Tax Court has recognized ARM 34 as a means of arriving at a fair market value. The latest and most controlling decisions on valuation, however, relegate the use of a formula to a position of being a last resort. ARM 34 was published in 1920, but since that time it has continually appeared in the annals of tax valuation and resulted in many improper appraisals. . . .
>
> The basic defect is apparent; the rates of return which are applied to tangibles and to intangibles are completely arbitrary and have no foundation in fact. . . .
>
> If there were a somewhat comparable business which had earned $50,000 per year as an average for five years and which had been sold for $400,000 cash it could be said that there was a 12½ percent indicated rate of return on total investment but no one could ascertain what has been the rates of return on the tangible and intangible assets. All that can be said for ARM 34, or a similar formula method of capitalization using two rates of interest, is that you hope to get a good answer based on two bad guesses. It is difficult enough to get one reasonably accurate rate of capitalization using normal appraisal methods . . . To get two fairly accurate rates, one for tangibles and the other for intangibles, other than by the use of pure guesswork, is impossible . . .
>
> To attempt to segregate value based on earnings as between normal income and that induced by whatever goodwill or other intangible assets the business may possess is to aspire to a higher degree of clairvoyance than has yet been demonstrated as obtainable by mere man.[7]

---

[7]U.S. Internal Revenue Service, *IRS Appellate Conferee Valuation Training Program* (Chicago: Commerce Clearing House, 1978), pp. 82–86. The section was repeated with no substantive changes in the 1980 revision.

Common Errors in Applying the Excess Earnings Method

A method that has been so thoroughly denounced by its own promulgators and yet is one of the most widely used methods in existence today certainly deserves some analysis. However, since the method is used primarily for small businesses, discussion here will be limited.[8]

A few brief comments about some of the most commonly encountered errors in attempting to use the method may help alert readers to identify a misuse of it when they see it.

"Negative Goodwill." If the method fails to demonstrate positive "excess earnings," some people simply conclude that the company has no goodwill and is worth only its tangible asset value. If a company's earnings do not support its tangible asset value, a better conclusion might be that the company is worth somewhat less than the computed tangible asset value.

Failure to Allow for Owner's Salary. As noted in Revenue Ruling 68-609 (Exhibit 4–2), "If the business is a sole proprietorship or partnership, there should be deducted from the earnings of the business a reasonable amount for services performed by the owner or partners engaged in the business." I have often seen valuations done by the excess earnings method that did not include a reasonable allowance for compensation to the owner or owners for services performed. This error results in an overstatement of the true economic earnings, which in turn leads to an overstatement of the business's value.

Failure to Use Realistic Normalized Earnings. The validity of the method depends on a reasonable estimate of normalized earnings. As noted in Revenue Ruling 68-609, "The past earnings to which the formula is applied should fairly reflect the probable future earnings." I frequently have seen the method applied blindly to the latest year's earnings, or to some simple or weighted average of recent years' earnings, without regard to whether or not the earnings base used fairly reflects the probable future earnings. Such uninformed use of some historical earnings base usually results in an under- or overvaluation.

Errors in Choosing Appropriate Rates. The choice of the two capitalization rates is critical to the validity of the outcome of the excess earnings method. One recurring clearly erroneous practice is using the rates suggested in Revenue Ruling 68-609.

The ruling, written in 1968, suggests rates of 8 to 10 percent on tangible assets, with 15 to 20 percent applied to the excess earnings. However, the ruling states,

> The percentage of return . . . should be the percentage prevailing in the industry involved at the date of the valuation. . . . The above rates are

---

[8]For a more complete analysis and critique of the method, see Pratt, *Valuing Small Businesses,* Chapter 12.

used as examples and are not appropriate in all cases. . . . The capitalization rates are dependent upon the facts pertinent thereto in each case.[9]

Both the wording of the ruling and common sense indicate that the specific rates mentioned in the ruling are examples and the appropriate rates to use depend on the facts at the time. In spite of that, we find people using the rates for the excess earnings method suggested in 1968, when prevailing rates were much lower. Using capitalization rates that are too low inevitably results in overstating the entity's value.

Asset Value Approaches

Asset value approaches to valuing a business interest tend to carry more weight with respect to holding companies than operating companies, such as manufacturers, merchandisers, or service companies. Also, asset value approaches are more relevant to the extent that a significant portion of the assets are of a nature that could be liquidated readily if so desired, such as a portfolio of notes or contracts receivable for which there might be a ready market.

Nevertheless, the notion that a business interest is worth the value of its underlying assets is basically fallacious in most instances, at least for an operating company.[10] Unless liquidation of the assets is a reasonable prospect, the assets' value lies in their ability to generate earnings rather than being an element of value that is distinct from the company's value based on its earning power. A strong asset base also contributes value in that it enhances a company's ability to survive periods of low or negligible earnings or losses.

Apart from the question about the degree of weight to attribute to an asset valuation approach versus other approaches, the asset value approach can be regarded as a two-step function. The first step is to arrive at the appropriate value of the net assets that relate to the business interest. The second step is to determine an appropriate ratio of the value of the business interest itself (i.e., the share of stock, the partnership interest, and so forth) to the underlying net asset value. Thus, a properly applied asset value approach is really a type of capitalization approach, drawing a multiple to apply to asset value from prices of comparative companies.

Determining the Appropriate Asset Value

All serious practitioners of business valuation agree that book value is not necessarily an adequate proxy for representing the underlying net asset value of a business for valuation purposes, much less for representing the value of the business itself. However, book value is a figure that is available for almost all businesses. Furthermore, it is a

---

[9]Revenue Ruling 68-609 (1968-2 C.B. 327).

[10]As noted in Chapter 2, the Supreme Court stated that "the capital stock of a corporation, its net assets, and its shares of stock are entirely different things . . . The value of one bears no fixed or necessary relation to the other." *Ray Consol. Copper Co.* v. *United States*, 45 S. Ct. 526 (1925).

value that different businesses have arrived at by some more or less common set of rules, usually some variation within the scope of generally accepted accounting principles (GAAP). Also, each asset or liability number that is a component of book value as shown in the financial statements represents a specific set of assets or obligations that can be identified in detail by referring to the company's records, assuming that the bookkeeping is complete and accurate. Therefore, book value usually provides the most convenient starting point for an asset value approach to the valuation of a business interest.

The nature and extent of adjustments that should be made to book value for the business valuation depend on many factors. One, of course, is the valuation's purpose. Another, which is frequently a limiting factor, is the availability of reliable data on which to base the adjustments both for the subject company and for other companies with which it might be compared in the course of the valuation.

Revenue Ruling 59-60 quite specifically states that the asset values to be adjusted if the valuation is for gift or estate tax purposes are the nonoperating assets, or assets of the investment type. The ruling states:

> Consideration also should be given to any assets not essential to the operation of the business, such as investments in securities, real estate, etc. In general, such nonoperating assets will command a lower rate of return than do the operating assets, although in exceptional cases the reverse may be true. In computing the book value per share of stock, assets of the investment type should be revalued on the basis of their market price and the book value adjusted accordingly.[11]

However, when using the comparative company approach, the analyst must be careful to analyze the asset structure of the comparative companies before making any adjustments to the subject company's book value for nonoperating assets. For example, the analyst might determine that the subject company holds investments (such as marketable securities) that are unrelated to the company's primary operations. If an analysis of the comparative companies reveals that they too hold similar investments unrelated to their primary operations, adjusting the subject company's assets without also adjusting the comparative publicly traded companies' assets would result in rendering the latter no longer comparable.

Revenue Ruling 59-60 also applies to valuations for ESOPs and for recapitalizations and other situations governed by the Internal Revenue Code.

To adjust values of publicly traded stocks and bonds owned, the analyst can use readily available market quotations. Guidance for adjusting non-publicly-traded debt securities and preferred stocks is contained in Chapters 16 and 17, respectively.

In adjusting real estate values, it may be quite expensive to obtain real estate appraisals. If using real estate appraisals, the analyst should realize that appraised values of real estate may vary considerably depending on the appraisal purpose. Tax assessment values, al-

---

[11]Revenue Ruling 59-60 (1959-1 C.B. 237).

though they do not constitute appraisals, may in some cases be a suitable basis for making adjustments to book values of real estate.

If it is considered appropriate to adjust operating plant and equipment values, the most common standard used in an asset value approach to a going-concern value of the business is the depreciated replacement cost value. This means that the analyst must estimate the present cost of replacing the facilities and their useful life. *Depreciated replacement cost* is defined as the *current replacement cost reduced by both the percentage of the useful life over which the existing facilities already have been in service and any degree of obsolescence present in the facilities.*

Part II of this book, especially Chapters 5 and 6 on company data, suggests information to collect that can help in analyzing asset values. Chapter 11, "Analyzing and Adjusting Financial Statements," discusses many adjustments to the balance sheet that might appropriately be made in an asset approach to valuation. The result of the exercise should be an adjusted book value or adjusted net asset value suitable as an input for subsequent steps in the valuation process.

Ratio of Stock Value to Asset Value

When the analyst has determined that book value or some adjusted book value figure provides a useful representation of the company's underlying net asset values, the next step is to translate that figure into its implication for the value of the shares of stock or partnership interest being valued. This usually is done by referring to the relationship of the prices of comparative companies' stocks to their respective underlying net asset values. The data for the comparative companies may be based on prices of stocks traded on the open market, prices paid in acquisitions, or both, depending on several factors, including the percentage ownership interest being valued.

As in any aspect of valuation based on comparisons with other companies, the analyst must use full expertise to ensure that the comparisons are as valid as possible within the limitations of data availability. It may be possible to compute the ratio of market price to book value for a group of comparative companies that have stock trading in the public market and apply a ratio somewhere within the range of such ratios to the subject company's book value. If the book values of the subject and comparative companies were computed on comparable bases, and if the assets' composition is comparable, this procedure may provide a reasonably realistic figure for the value of the business interest using the asset value approach.

If accounting methods for the subject and comparative companies significantly differed, the analyst must make appropriate adjustments before computing the market price/book value ratios and applying them to the valuation. There can be additional significant differences, such as in asset mix, that challenge the validity of using one company's price to book value ratio in valuing another's stock.

Obviously, if one wants to use a ratio of market prices to book values adjusted for depreciated replacement costs of the relevant assets, one must have the depreciated replacement cost data for the comparative companies as well as for the subject company. Such information is not readily available for most public companies; but to the extent that they are, this can enhance the usefulness of the asset value approach in valuing a business interest.

If the subject company's return on equity is high relative to the comparatives', the appropriate price to asset value ratio probably should be in the upper end of the relevant range, and vice versa. As common sense would suggest, empirical tests indicate a significant degree of correlation between price/book value ratios and return on equity for both publicly traded stocks and acquisition prices in most industries. Exhibit 4–3 illustrates this relationship for the trucking industry. As a consequence, an analysis of the relationship between price/book value ratios and return on equity for the comparative companies often can provide objective guidance in deciding on an appropriate price/book value ratio for the subject company. If the correlation between the price/book value ratios and return on equity for the comparative companies is reasonably good, the analyst might use a simple linear regression to compute an indicated price/book value ratio for the subject company based on market data. Exhibit 4–3 illustrates such a computation, and Exhibit 4–4 demonstrates it graphically.

As with capitalization of earnings or other general categories of approaches to the business valuation, it may be fruitful to work out the results of two or more variations of asset value approaches. As with most approaches, the work will result in a range of possible values.

Debt-Free Valuation Methods

Sometimes it is useful to develop market valuation parameters (price/earnings, price/cash flow, price/revenues, price/book value ratios, and so on) on a *debt-free* basis, that is, assuming that the company has no financial leverage. These methods can be useful in either or both of two situations:

1. When the appraiser wants to reach a value for the total equity and/or total invested capital (defined as the sum of equity plus either all interest-bearing or long-term debt), especially when valuing a controlling interest in a company whose capital structure may be changed by the controlling party.
2. When the capital structures of the comparative companies and the subject company differ significantly and the analyst wishes to compare them without the distortions that might be introduced as a result of the substantially different leverage.

EXHIBIT 4-3

Correlation Between Price/Book Ratio
and Return on Equity

Company	July 1987	
	ROE	Price/Book
Yellow Freight Systems	15.6	2.56
Arkansas Best Corp.	13.5	1.67
Carolina Freight Corp.	13.3	1.79
Roadway Services, Inc.	10.9	2.26
Viking Freight Inc.	10.3	1.27
American Carriers, Inc.	.6.1	.77
Preston Corp.	.5.4	1.04
U.S. Truck Lines	(4.0)	.77
Transcon Incorporated	(4.1)	.46

$$r^2 = .72$$

The regression formula to be solved is

$y = a + bx$

Price/book value ratio = $a + b$ (return on equity)

where:

a = Price/book value ratio (y) intercept

b = Slope of the line

Using a calculator capable of linear regression analysis, the analyst can calculate the y intercept (a) and slope of the line (b) using return on equity and price/book value ratio data from the comparative companies.

Using the returns on equity and price/book ratio data for July 1987 we calculate:

$a = .779$

$b = .083$

(See Formula 4-1 in this chapter for the arithmetic of linear regression analysis.)

$y = .779 + .083(x)$

Substituting in the subject company's return on equity, 9.81%, we compute an indicated price/book value ratio:

$y = .779 + .083(9.8)$

$y = .779 + .813$

$y = 1.59$

Outline of Steps in Debt-Free Analysis

In debt-free analysis, the procedure is to compute market value ratios made up of the companies' market value of invested capital as the numerators and the pro forma values of relevant variables, as though the companies had no interest-bearing debt, as denominators. The steps in carrying out valuation approaches on a debt-free basis are as follows:

1. Adjust the earnings and/or cash flow (before preferred stock dividends) for the subject and each comparative company to the pro forma earnings that would be available if the company had no debt. This involves adding to the earnings and/or cash flow the amount of interest expense incurred, net of the tax effect (assuming that the interest incurred would have been a tax-deductible expense).

2. Compute the market value of the invested capital for each comparative company. This involves adding together the market value of all the equity and the relevent interest-bearing debt. If there is no public market for part or all of the comparative companies' preferred stock and/or debt, the analyst should estimate the market values on the basis of the best available evidence. Occasionally, there will be no readily available data on which to base an estimate of the market value of the debt and/or the benefits to be gained are significantly outweighed by the cost to do so. In these

EXHIBIT 4-4

Price/Book Value Compared to
Return on Equity

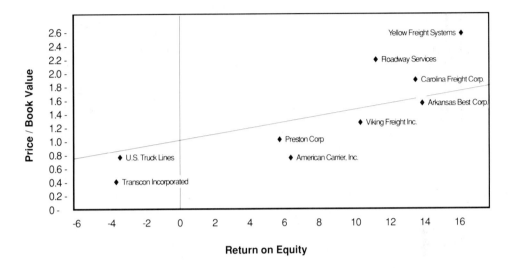

cases and only as a last resort, the analyst might use the book value of the debt as a proxy for market value, if the resulting distortion is not material. (See Chapter 16, "Valuing Debt Securities," and Chapter 17, "Valuing Preferred Stocks.")

3. Adjust the book values for the subject and each comparative company to their respective pro-forma book values assuming no interest-bearing debt. Book value of invested capital involves adding the debt's book value to the equity's book value (including preferred stocks).

4. Compute the ratio of each comparative company's market value of invested capital to the debt-free amounts for each variable (earnings, cash flow, book value, and so on).

5. Out of the array of ratios for each variable for the comparative companies, decide where the subject company's ratio should fall (mean, median, upper or lower quartile, etc.), based on an analysis of the same types of fundamental factors for the subject company relative to the comparatives that would be used in a normal (i.e., non-debt-free) analysis.

6. Multiply the value for each of the subject company's debt-free variables (earnings, cash flow, book value, and so on) by the ratio selected as appropriate for that variable. This will indicate the market value of invested capital for the subject company based on each variable analyzed.

7. If the subject company has interest-bearing debt, subtract the market value of that debt from the indicated market value of the invested capital. If the subject company has preferred stock outstanding, deduct the market value of the preferred stock from the

indicated market value of invested capital. This will indicate the market value of the subject company's common equity.

Following is a simple illustration of the foregoing steps. Let's say that our objective is to determine appropriate market value ratios for company A, a closely held company, for the purpose of valuing its shares for an ESOP. The only guidance we have found is company B, whose shares are publicly traded. Our analysis indicates that company B is an excellent comparative except for one major difference: company A (our subject company) has no long-term debt outstanding, while company B's capital structure is leveraged with long-term bonds, which also are publicly traded. Table 4–1 shows condensed balance sheets and operating statements for companies A and B.

With the above steps in mind, we will turn to valuing a company using debt-free price/earnings ratio, price revenues ratio, and price/book value ratio approaches.

Price/Earnings Ratio on a Debt-Free Basis

Looking at the data in Table 4–1—especially just examining the earnings without taking into account the difference in capital structure—one's initial reaction might be to use company B's P/E multiple of 4.5 to price company A's shares, which would result in (4.5 × $3.20) = $14.40 per share. But the earnings on company B's shares, being leveraged with long-term debt, are more risky than the earnings on company A's shares. This difference should call for a higher capitalization

TABLE 4-1

	A	B
Condensed balance sheet	*(Private)*	*(Public)*
Assets	$2,000,000	$2,000,000
Current liabilities	500,000	500,000
Long-term debt (12%)	0	500,000
Stockholders' equity	1,500,000	1,000,000
Shares outstanding	150,000	100,000
Book value per share	10.00	10.00
Condensed operating statement		
Sales	$5,000,000	$5,000,000
Operating expenses	4,200,000	4,200,000
Earnings before interest and taxes	$ 800,000	$ 800,000
Interest expense	0	60,000
Net income before taxes	$ 800,000	$ 740,000
Income taxes	320,000	296,000
Net income	$ 480,000	$ 444,000
Earnings per share	$ 3.20	$ 4 .44
Market price per share		$ 20.00
Price/earnings ratio		4.5

rate for company B or a lower P/E ratio for company B's earnings than for company A's to reflect company B's higher risk arising from the leverage. Of course, the effect on the P/E multiple of the higher risk for company B's earnings could be offset by a higher expected growth rate in earnings per share for company B.

In our example, we will assume that company B's bonds are selling at a discount from par value and have a market value of $400,000. The market value of company B's common stock is $2 million (100,000 shares × $20). Therefore, the aggregate market value of company B's outstanding capital is $2.4 million ($400,000 + $2,000,000).

If company B had no debt outstanding, it would have no interest expense. However, the higher pretax earnings would be subject to income tax, which we will assume to be at 40 percent. Adjusting for elimination of the interest expense net of the tax effect, company B's earnings would be $480,000 on a debt-free basis. Dividing the market value of invested capital by its debt-free earning capacity gives a debt-free equivalent P/E ratio of 5.0 ($2,400,000/$480,000). Applying this P/E ratio to company A's shares would result in $16 per share (5.0 × $3.20) , compared with $14.40 per share using company B's P/E ratio on an unadjusted basis. (If the subject company has long-term debt, one must subtract the debt from the value arrived at by applying a debt-free equivalent P/E ratio to the company's debt-free earnings. This applies to all debt-free approaches.) Most practitioners would agree that the adjusted figures provide a better comparison between the two companies.

In some instances, the analyst might go a step further and compare price/earnings ratios adjusted not only to a debt-free basis but to a debt-free *pretax* basis. Generally, such a comparison would be applicable if the subject of the valuation would not remain in its present independent form, such as in a comparative valuation of acquisition candidates. In this situation, any acquired company would end up being subject to the acquirer's tax rate. If the potential acquiree had a significantly lower independent tax rate than the acquirer, the difference in the effect on value could be enough to make it more attractive to remain independent than to sell for what the potential acquirer would be willing to pay!

Price/Revenues Ratio on a Debt-Free Basis

Continuing with the same example, company B's stock price/revenues ratio is 1.0 based on a $2 million market value of stock and $2 million in revenues. Using that ratio to develop an indication of market value for company A's shares results in $13.33 per share ($2,000,000/ 150,000). But the capital being used to generate company B's earnings includes debt as well as equity, and the debt was not reflected in the above ratio.

Company B's ratio of market value of invested capital to revenues is .48 based on a $2.4 million market value of total capital and $5 million revenues. If we apply the ratio of 1.2 in company A's case, the result is $16 per share (.48 × $5,000,000)/150,000.

Price/Book Value Ratio on a Debt-Free Basis

Using the same example, company B (the public company) has a market price per share of $20 and a book value of $10 for a ratio of market price to book value of 2:1 ($20/$10). If we apply this ratio to company A (the private company), which also happens to have a book value of $10 per share, the result will be $20 per share (2 × $10). But note that company A also has half again as many shares outstanding as company B. Is it justifiable that the market value/book value per share ratio be the same for both companies despite such a considerable difference in their respective capital structures? Probably not.

We previously computed the aggregate market value of company B's capital to be $400,000 for its bonds and $2 million for its stock, or a total of $2.4 million. The book value of the bonds and the stocks taken together is $500,000 for the bonds and $1 million for the stock, or a total of $1.5 million. Therefore, the ratio of the aggregate market value of the company's total capital to the book value of its capital is 1.6 ($2,400,000/$1,500,000). Applying this market value/book value ratio to company A's book value per share results in $16 per share (1.6 × $10), compared with $20 per share using company B's market price/book value per share ratio on an unadjusted basis.

Incidentally, the fact that the aggregate market value to earnings, revenues, and book value approaches each produce an identical value of $16 per share for company A stock occurs only because the figures for company B and company A were drawn to be identical except for the leverage factor to demonstrate the technique. It is interesting to note that in this case the distortion introduced by using company B's unadjusted ratios in valuing company A's shares was downwardly biased in valuing company A's shares on the basis of the earnings and revenue approaches and upwardly biased in valuing company A's shares on an asset value approach basis, because company B's market value ratios reflect its leveraged position.

Choosing Which Debt to Include in Total Capital

One complication in applying the debt-free techniques is the choice of whether to use just long-term debt or all interest-bearing debt in computing the market value of total capital (and, of course, the related interest adjustment to earnings). Total capital normally is defined as equity plus long-term debt (including current portion of long-term debt). However, many businesses, especially smaller ones, use short-term debt as if it were long-term debt. Neither version is necessarily right or wrong, but much confusion may arise unless the appraiser clearly specifies whether the total capital is being defined to include only long-term debt or all interest-bearing debt. In any case, it is necessary to ensure that the amount used for total capital represents the amount of debt outstanding during the time period for which the interest is being added back to the earnings base.

As a practical matter, in many cases the choice of definition of capital used may end up being more dependent on the availability of comparative data and how they are reported than on the analyst's preference on conceptual grounds. For example, it often is not possible to obtain the amount of interest on long-term debt only; rather, only the amount of total interest is available. In that case, to be consistent, the analyst must include *all* interest-bearing debt in the balance-sheet adjustments. When all interest-bearing debt as well as all interest expense are used in the analysis and when the subject company or the comparatives make use of seasonal borrowing that is reduced to zero at the end of the fiscal year, the analyst is presented with a particularly vexing problem. On the one hand, if the actual balance of year-end debt is used in conjunction with total annual interest expense, the apparent interest rate on the company's debt will be far higher than the actual rates charged. In other words, the analyst will be overstating the interest return relative to the amount of debt used in the analysis, and this may cause an overvaluation of the market value of the debt. On the other hand, if the analyst adds to the year-end long-term debt balance the average monthly or quarterly balance of short-term financing, he or she will be factoring in to the analysis an amount that the company was legitimately able to pay down to zero at least one point during the year, and an argument can be made that the analyst is overvaluing the invested capital. While there is no consensus on this issue, most practitioners seem to favor adding back the average annual balance of short-term financing when total after-tax interest expense is added to earnings, even if the year-end balance of the short-term financing might be different from the average balance or equal to zero. Finally, the analyst should note that, even in the case of long-term debt, an argument can be made that the average balance should be used, since it was the average balance, not the year-end balance, that generated the reported level of interest expense.

Premiums and Discounts in Debt-Free Analysis

A common error in valuation of controlling interests is to apply a full premium for control, based on comparative premiums paid for purchases of 100% of the common equity, to the subject company's total invested capital on a minority basis. This will very often result in an overvaluation of the subject company's total capital, and, if the subject is heavily leveraged, the percentage error may be magnified into an extremely large percentage error relative to the equity value when the debt is subtracted. Clearly, an acquirer of corporate control would not be favorably inclined to pay a premium over the market value of the target's debt, except possibly to the extent of the avoidance of new debt placement costs, and the debt should therefore not have an implicit premium to the total capital number on a minority basis. To correct this error, the preferred approach is to reduce the percentage premiums paid in the comparative transactions to their "debt-free equivalent" percentage premiums, and then to select an appropriate premium to apply to the subject's total capital, based on these adjusted premiums for the comparatives. A less desirable but simpler alternative is to value the subject company on a debt-free minority interest basis, subtract the debt to obtain an indication of minority interest equity value, and then apply a full premium for control to this equity number, based on the unadjusted comparative company transactions for full control of the equity.

A similar error, in reverse, is often made in the application of a discount for lack of marketability. In the case of the discount for lack of marketablility, applying the full discount to the debt-free value may result in a significant undervaluation or complete obliteration of equity value after subtraction of the debt. In the case of the discount for lack of marketability, the preferred approach is to apply the discount *after* the debt has been subtracted from the total capital value, rather than attempting to adjust the discount to a "debt-free equivalent" basis. It is rare that data will exist to make this adjustment.

Combination Approaches

Sometimes different aspects of a single company are dissimilar enough that one part of the company should be valued differently than another part. Such may be the case if the company has operations in two or more dissimilar industries or has a significant amount of nonoperating assets.

Different Types of Operations

When a company has two or more separate and different operations, and if the financial information can be adequately segregated between them, the valuation of the total company might be approached as if it were virtually two or more separate and independent valuations using the approach or approaches most applicable in each case. In some cases, it may be appropriate to discount the value of the total somewhat from the sum of the parts to reflect the unattractiveness to some buyers of the particular combination of operations. This discount is sometimes referred to as a *portfolio discount*.

Treatment of Nonoperating Assets

If a company has nonoperating assets, they may be valued separate from the operations, especially if valuing a controlling interest that has the power to liquidate the assets. Perhaps the operations would be valued by relying primarily on a capitalization of earnings approach and then attributing some value to the nonoperating assets. Of course, if the valuation is to be divided in this way, any earnings generated by the nonoperating assets would have to be subtracted from the earnings base that would be capitalized in valuing the company's operations; otherwise there would be a double-counting of values.

The theory of valuing nonoperating assets separate from operating assets rests on the assumption that the nonoperating assets could be liquidated without impairing operations. Thus, if the market value of nonoperating assets is higher than their book value and the analyst is going to mark the nonoperating assets up to the market value to make the valuation, the analyst should also consider offsetting factors. These factors might include the capital gains or ordinary income tax, as the case might be, that the company would have to pay if it liquidated the assets, any costs of liquidation, and any discounts that might be appropriate in reflecting the estimated time required to liquidate and the risk that the actual amounts realized might be less than the market values as of the valuation date.

Treatment of Asset Deficiencies

It is also common to find the reverse situation, that is, one in which it might be appropriate to value the company by a capitalization of earnings approach but then subtract an amount reflecting the inadequacy of operating assets. This can easily be the case if net working capital is inadequate to support the level of business or if certain plant and equipment are in imminent need of replacement or major repair. Evaluating such inadequacies may require more subjective judgment than would assessing excess or nonoperating assets, but the potential problem of measurement does not render recognition of the concept of asset inadequacy any less important.

Analysis of Past Transactions

The analyst should consider past transactions in the securities being valued for whatever past period might provide a reasonable guide to current value. Past transactions carry more weight in determining the current value if they are many, involve large blocks or numbers of shares, and are closer to the valuation date than otherwise.

However, by far the most important criterion to consider in assessing the weight of past transactions is the extent to which they were on an arm's-length basis among fully informed and sophisticated parties. Transactions among family members or other closely related parties may be accorded little or no weight in arriving at a fair current value on the basis that they may not be arm's length.

In fact, however, there is no love lost among members of some families. In one fairly typical case, one family member had purchased some shares from another a few months prior to an intrafamily gift of some shares. There was considerable animosity between the family member who had bought the shares and the one who had sold them, and the price bargaining had been every bit as intense as any arm's-length transaction. Nevertheless, the IRS agent handling the case was unwilling to accord any weight at all to the price of the intrafamily sale in arriving at a value for the gift tax.

In some cases, bona fide offers to buy or sell that did not result in a transaction could carry some weight as an indicator of value. To be seriously considered such an offer normally would have to be documented in writing, legally binding if accepted, and made on an arm's-length basis.

Other Factors to Consider

Marketability

Ready marketability definitely adds value to a security—or, conversely, lack of marketability detracts from the value of the security—vis-à-vis one that is otherwise comparable but readily marketable. Since interests in closely held businesses do not, by definition, enjoy the ready market of a publicly traded stock, this difference must be considered when valuing an interest in a closely held business by reference to prices of publicly traded stocks.

The importance of marketability in the valuation has been gaining increasing recognition over the years. There is considerable evidence to suggest that the discount for lack of marketability alone for a closely held stock compared with its publicly traded counterpart should be at least 35 percent and, in most cases, probably more.

Chapter 10 covers analysis of data that can be used to help quantify appropriate discounts for lack of marketability.

Extent of "Elements of Control" versus Minority Position

If a minority interest in a closely held business is valued by reference to day-to-day trading prices of publicly held stocks, minority interests are being compared with minority interests, and the resulting value for the subject company shares is a "value as if publicly traded." This value should be discounted for marketability relative to the public stock, as discussed in the previous section, but not for minority interest, since the value as if publicly traded already represents a minority interest value.

If a minority interest in a closely held business is being valued by a capitalization of earnings, book value, adjusted book value, or any other approach on a controlling-interest basis, but without comparison to daily trading prices of public stocks, discounts must be taken to reflect *both* the lack of marketability and the minority interest. However, a strong word of caution is in order regarding use of the discounted future returns approach. Most published equity return data used to develop an appropriate capitalization rate is derived from return data developed from minority shares of publicly traded securities. Therefore, in this situation a discount for minority interest would *not* be appropriate. It is not uncommon to find a minority interest discounted at 65 percent or more below the stock's indicated 100% controlling interest value, with the total discount reflecting both the minority interest and lack of marketability factors.

Conversely, if a controlling interest in a closely held business is being valued with reference to day-to-day trading prices of public stocks, which are minority interests, it may be appropriate to add a premium for control to the price that otherwise would be indicated. In valuing controlling interests in closely held companies by reference to prices of publicly traded stocks, it sometimes works out that the discount for lack of marketability and the premium for control just about offset each other. Intuitively this seems reasonable at least by one way of looking at it; that is, public companies acquiring private ones tend to be reluctant to incur dilution by paying a higher price/earnings ratio than the P/E's at which their own stock is selling. In effect, a controlling stockholder who sells to a public company is giving up control but gaining liquidity. Apart from other valuation factors, in some cases these two factors by themselves end up canceling each other. When the value of control versus the disadvantage of lack of liquidity do not offset each other, which may be the case in many situations, the scale is usually tipped in favor of the former. The notion that purchases of private companies are, on average, effected at a premium over minority value as if publicly traded, but not as high a premium as is paid for public companies, is further supported by the fact that consistently over the past several years, the average P/E ratio paid in purchases of private companies is lower than that paid in tender offers for public companies, but somewhat higher than the average P/E of the public companies based on their public market price. Sources of data for quantifying premiums for control over publicly traded market values are found in Chapter 9, "Comparative Transaction Data."

Voting Rights. The matter of voting rights, of course, is inseparable from the whole matter of control. There is very little empirical transaction data—and scant guidance from court decisions—that are helpful in quantifying the value of voting rights in various circumstances.

For small minority interests, what little market data exist suggest that voting rights are accorded little or no value unless they are significant. It seems reasonable that the value of voting rights should increase to the extent that those rights become meaningful. For example, in one ESOP whose shares my company values annually, we have used a 5 to 7 percent difference in the value between voting and nonvoting shares. In that particular case, no single stockholder has voting control, so certain combinations of voting could result in specific minority interests constituting the swing votes.

Of course, if only a small percentage of a company's outstanding shares are of a voting class, and they can exercise wide discretionary powers over a substantial amount of resources, the voting rights could have significant value. Since little guidance is available, the quantification of such value will have to be made with a large dose of informed judgment.

Elements of Control.   Control versus minority positions are not necessarily cut-and-dried differences but may be matters of degree. In about half the states, a simple majority in a corporation can approve such major actions such as a merger, sale, liquidation, or recapitalization of the company. Other states generally require a vote of two thirds or more to liquidate or take certain other major corporate actions. Also, many other factors may limit the exercise of prerogatives normally associated with control. On the other hand, minority interests may not be totally bereft of control factors, as we just discussed, for example, in connection with potential swing votes.

The value of control depends on the stockholder's ability to exercise any or all of a variety of rights typically associated with control. Consequently, if control is an issue in the valuation, the analyst should assess the extent to which the various elements of control do or do not exist in the particular situation, and determine the impact of each element on the value of control. Following is a checklist of some of the more common prerogatives of control:

1. Elect directors and appoint managers.
2. Determine management compensation and perquisites.
3. Declare and pay dividends.
4. Sell or acquire treasury shares.
5. Acquire or liquidate assets.
6. Set policy and change the course of business.
7. Make acquisitions.
8. Select people with whom to do business and award contracts.
9. Change the articles of incorporation or bylaws.
10. Liquidate, dissolve, sell out, or recapitalize the company.

In the case of election of directors, if the company has noncumulative voting, the whole pie belongs to the majority. If the company has cumulative voting, some of the value that is attributable to the ability to elect directors will shift from the majority stockholder with less than enough to elect the whole board to the minority stockholders.

Many of the rights associated with control simply are rendered economically empty or of little value because of the company's financial condition. These could include the rights to decide on management compensation, dividends, stock or asset purchases, and acquisition of other companies.

Many typical control rights may be denied to a company through contractual restrictions. For example, indenture provisions in conjunction with debt obligations frequently prevent dividend payments, increased management compensation, liquidation of assets, acquisitions, or changes in the direction of the business.

Government regulation of operations may preempt the usual prerogatives of control. For example, it is a lengthy and sometimes even impossible process to liquidate companies in such regulated industries as insurance and utilities. Government regulation may prevent certain acquisitions and, similarly, prohibit a company from selling out to certain other companies.

In certain cases—especially in merger and acquisition situations with the objective of vertical integration—the element of selecting people with whom to do business and award contracts can have a considerable value. For example, a wholesaler or retailer that is only marginally profitable might become an attractive acquisition candidate for a manufacturer seeking to lock up assured channels of distribution.

When any of the elements of control are lacking in a particular case, any value attributable to control will be diminished accordingly, all other things being equal.

In summary, control, or lack of it, is not all black and white. Its impact on valuation must be analyzed on the basis of all the relevant circumstances of the particular case.

Other Contractual Rights or Obligations

There can be such a variety of contractual rights or obligations affecting value that it is hard to generalize except to say that the analyst should attempt to identify and evaluate any existing rights or obligations that could affect the value.

The most common right or obligation connected with an interest in a closely held company would arise from a buy-sell agreement. (Chapter 20 is entirely devoted to the subject.) Certain rights or obligations also could be written into the company's bylaws. If, for example, a stockholder must offer his or her shares back to the company at book value before selling them to anyone else, and if the company has the financial capability to make the redemption, it becomes difficult to value the shares much above book value, even though they might be worth much more in the absence of such a provision.

In valuing a general partner's interest, the potential costs resulting from unlimited liability could have a severely negative impact on the value of the general partnership interest.

Analyzing and Balancing the Valuation Factors

When all the relevant factors have been individually analyzed and assessed, they must be brought together to arrive at a final number that represents the valuation conclusion. Sometimes it will be obvious that the analyst should rely on a single approach, such as a capitalization of earnings approach where the asset base is negligible compared with the earnings or an asset value multiple approach, if earnings are negligible or nonexistent. In other cases, two or more valuation approaches may yield such similar results that it matters little how much weight one approach receives. However, the real world of business valuations is fraught with apparent inconsistencies, with different approaches to the valuation leading to markedly different results, which must be reconciled into a single number to be used for the valuation at hand.

An intuitively appealing method of dealing with this dilemma is for the analyst to use subjective but informed judgment and decide on a percentage weight to assign the results of each relevant valuation approach used and base the final valuation on a weighted average of the results of the various factors. Suppose, for example, that the analyst is valuing a minority interest in a closely held manufacturing company by comparing the publicly traded stocks in the same industry. Since it is an operating company but has a substantial asset base, the analyst thinks the appropriate capitalization of earnings approach should be accorded 60 percent of the total weight, the capitalization of dividends approach 10 percent, and the asset value approach 30 percent. We will assume in this case that the company has been unable to generate a good rate of return on its asset base; thus, the result would be that shown in Table 4–2.

TABLE 4-2

	Value per share	Weight	Total
Capitalization of earnings:			
$2.00 per share x 5.0	$10.00	.6	$ 6.00
Capitalization of dividends:			
$0.60 per share ÷ .05	12.00	.1	1.20
Asset value approach:			
$20.00 book value x .8	16.00	.3	4.80
			$12.00
Less discount for lack of marketability:			
(.35 x 12.00)			4.20
Value per share			$ 7.80

In the case shown in Table 4–2, although companies in the same industry generally are selling below book value, the subject company is valued at a larger discount from book value than the average in its industry because of poorer earnings. However, the asset base is accorded some weight, and the company is valued at a lower discount from book value than it would be if it were valued strictly on a capitalization of earnings basis. As it turns out, in this case, the effect of the capitalization of dividends is neutral.

The main weakness of the above method is that no acceptable mathematical model is available for use in deriving the weights to assign to the results of each valuation approach. The relative weights to assign each approach depend on the analyst's judgment; however, it forces the analyst to present his or her thinking in clearly quantified terms. The method also has the appeal of being clear and simple to understand. If someone evaluating the results disagrees with some aspect of the analyst's judgment, the point of departure is readily identifiable and it is easy to apply an alternate set of numbers and quickly recompute the result.

Court cases in which values of stocks must be determined under dissenting stockholders' appraisal rights have tended to rely on this method. However, the wording of Revenue Ruling 59-60 does not embrace the method. The ruling states:

> Because valuations cannot be made on the basis of a prescribed formula, there is no means whereby the various applicable factors in a particular case can be assigned mathematical weights in deriving the fair market value. For this reason, no useful purpose is served by taking an average of several factors (for example, book value, capitalized earnings and capitalized dividends) and basing the valuation on the result. Such a process excludes active consideration of other pertinent factors, and the end result cannot be supported by a realistic application of the significant facts in the case except by mere chance.[12]

In spite of this wording, the method has been used successfully in many gift and estate tax cases both in dealing with the IRS and in cases decided in court. The wording of Revenue Ruling 59-60 indicates concern that the averaging or weighted average method leaves room for omission of pertinent factors. However, it is possible to use the basic weighted average of factors method and still, at one stage or another, incorporate consideration of all the pertinent factors mentioned in Revenue Ruling 59-60. For several years I directed my staff to avoid using this method of resolving differences in results of various approaches in tax cases because of the wording of 59-60. However, the method has obvious appeal for the reasons discussed. We have started using it for some tax cases and, at least so far, have not had it rejected. Of course, we have been careful to demonstrate in each case that all other pertinent factors were actively considered and reflected in the result to the appropriate extent.

---

[12]Ibid., Sec. 7.

Part II

Gathering Data

Chapter 5

Company Data—Written Information

Planning the Data-Gathering Process
Generalized Company Information Checklist
Financial Statements
    Balance Sheets
    Income Statements
    Statement of Cash Flows
    Statements of Changes in Financial Position
    Statements of Stockholders' Equity
    Statements of Partners' Capital Accounts
    Interim Statements
Levels of Financial Statement Preparation
    Audited Statements
    Reviewed Statements
    Compiled Statements
Federal Tax Returns
Other Financial Schedules
    Aged Receivables List
    Aged Payables List
    Stockholder List
    Dividend Schedule
    Real Estate and Equipment Lists and Depreciation Schedules
    Inventory List
    Officers' and Directors' Compensation Schedule
    Related Party Transaction Information
Miscellaneous Financial Information
    Schedule of Key-Man Life Insurance
    List of Past Transactions in the Stock or Offers to Buy
    Budgets
    Capital Requirements
    Order Backlog
    Customer Base
    Supplier List
    Accountants' Workpapers and Company Books
Evidence of Real and Personal Property Values
    Real and Personal Property Tax Assessments
    Insurance Appraisals
    Independent Appraisal Reports
Contractual Agreements and Obligations
    Lease Agreements
    Loan Agreements

Planning the Data-Gathering Process

The data needed for valuing a business or business interest can be roughly categorized into four groups:

1. Data on the subject company.
2. Relevant economic and industry data, including data on interest rates and required rates of return relative to risk.
3. Comparative transaction data.
4. Other relevant information, such as data for use in quantifying appropriate discounts and/or premiums.

This chapter and Chapter 6 deal with company data and Chapters 7 through 10 with other applicable information. This and the next chapter overlap somewhat, since some companies may supply information in written form while others may provide similar information during interviews or facility visits.

The information one needs for the valuation need not be gathered in the order shown above; in fact, the data usually are gathered more or less simultaneously, either by one analyst or a team of analysts. For example, supporting analysts may be collecting industry, economic, rate-of-return, and comparative transaction information at the same time that the analyst managing the assignment is working directly with the subject company. For that reason, it is important to get a sufficient overview of the company at an early meeting with company representatives (by telephone or in person) so that the analysts will get a sense of what information will be relevant and can begin collecting it right away.

If time allows, the analyst should request financial statements and other readily available company information before visiting the company. The analyst can use this information to prepare questions and topics for discussion and thus maximize the productivity of visits to facilities and interviews with management.

Generalized Company Information Checklist

Exhibit 5–1 presents a checklist of documents and information commonly used in appraisals. Not every item on the list will necessarily be required for every appraisal, and in many instances special circumstances will require the analyst to review documents not listed. Nevertheless, the analyst can work from the list shown in Exhibit 5–1 and the discussion in this chapter to develop a list applicable to the business being valued.

Having requested whatever documents seem likely to be available, the appraiser should be flexible enough to work within the limits of the documentation that the company is able to provide. It would be unusual and fortuitous to find every item on the checklist readily available; therefore, the analyst usually will need to obtain some of the information through interviews. Often it would be cumbersome for the company to copy all the documents; in these cases, the analyst may inspect the documents on the company's premises during the field trip. As the valuation progresses, the appraiser can review the written information and supplement it, when necessary, by requesting more documents through interviews with management and visits to facilities and by reference to written information from outside the company.

Financial Statements

According to the American Institute of Certified Public Accountants (AICPA), the term *financial statement* refers to a presentation of financial data, including accompanying notes, derived from accounting records and intended to communicate an entity's economic resources or obligations at a point in time or the changes therein for a period of time in accordance with a comprehensive basis of accounting.[1] The basic financial statements, which, along with footnotes, comprise a complete set of financial statements, are:

1. Balance sheet.
2. Income statement.
3. Statement of stockholders' equity.
4. Statement of cash flows (formerly Statement of changes in financial position).

Other, supplementary schedules often provide useful information for specific valuation situations. Any of the statements or schedules can be prepared either as of the end of a fiscal year or as of any interim date within the fiscal year.

---

[1]American Institute of Certified Public Accountants, *AICPA Professional Standards,* vol. A (Chicago: Commerce Clearing House, 1985), p. 1072.

EXHIBIT 5-1

Generalized Documents and Information Checklist
for Valuation of a Business or Business Interest

Financial statements

Balance sheets, income statements, statements of changes in financial position or statement of cash flows, and statements of stockholders' equity or partners' capital accounts for up to the last five fiscal years, if available

Income tax returns for the same years

Latest interim statements if valuation date is three months or more beyond end of last fiscal year and interim statement for the comparable period the year before

List of subsidiaries and/or financial interests in other companies, with relevant financial statements

Other financial data

Equipment list and depreciation schedule

Aged accounts receivable list

Aged accounts payable list

List of prepaid expenses

Inventory list, with any necessary information on inventory accounting policies (including work in progress, if applicable)

Lease or leases (if lease does not exist or is not transferable, determine what new lease or rental terms will be)

Any other existing contracts (employment agreements, covenants not to compete, supplier and franchise agreements, customer agreements, royalty agreements, equipment lease or rental contracts, loan agreements, labor contracts, employee benefit plans, and so on)

List of stockholders or partners, with number of shares owned by each or percentage of each partner's interest in earnings and capital

Compensation schedule for owners, including all benefits and personal expenses

Copies or descriptions of employee benefit plans

Schedule of insurance in force (key-man life, property and casualty, liability)

Budgets or projections, if available

Company and other documents relating to rights of owners

If a corporation, articles of incorporation, by-laws, any amendments to either, and corporate minutes

If a partnership, articles of partnership, with any amendments

Any existing buy/sell agreements, options to purchase stock or partnership interest, rights of first refusal, trust agreements, or other documents affecting the ownership rights of the interest being valued

Other information

Brief history, including how long in business and details of any changes in ownership and/or bona-fide offers received

Brief description of business, including position relative to competition and any factors that make the business unique

Organization chart, if one exists

Information on related-party transactions

Marketing literature (catalogs, brochures, advertisements, and so on)

List of locations where company operates, with size, and whether owned or leased

List of states in which licensed to do business

If customer or supplier base concentrated, list of major accounts, with annual dollar volume for each

List of competitors, with location, relative size, any other relevant factors

Resumes of, or list of, key personnel, with age, position, compensation, length of service, education, and prior experience

Trade associations to which company belongs or would be eligible for membership

Relevant trade or government publications

Any existing indicators of asset values, including latest property tax assessments and any appraisals that have been done

List of patents, copyrights, trademarks, and other intangible assets

Any contingent or off-balance-sheet assets or liabilities (pending lawsuits, compliance requirements, warranty or other product liability, and so on)

Any filings or correspondence with regulatory agencies

Information on prior transactions

SOURCE: Willamette Management Associates, Inc.

One critical question is how many years of annual statements will be needed. While there may be no rule-of-thumb answer, the most commonly used period is five years. Conceptually, however, the answer must be that the statements should cover a *relevant period,* that is, a period over which the statements represent the company's general operations, leading up to and including the valuation date. If the company significantly changed its operations a few years before the valuation date, only the last three or four years' statements may be relevant to the valuation. But if the business has a long history and some or all recent years were abnormal in some way (such as during a cyclical peak or trough in the company's industry), statements for the past seven, ten, or more years may constitute a relevant period for valuing it.

Balance Sheets

The *balance sheet* shows the amounts of a company's assets, liabilities, and equity as of a point in time. Exhibit 5–2 shows a sample balance sheet with typical headings. However, specific line items for real companies are likely to differ greatly. Usually the appraiser focuses on the current balance sheet, but it is useful to present a spread of several years' balance sheets, with each line item shown as a percentage of total assets (*common-size balance sheets*) in order to demonstrate changes over time. Examples of common-size balance sheets and income statements are shown in Chapter 12, "Comparative Ratio Analysis." Since the balance sheet details assets, liabilities, and owners' equity, the emphasis it will receive in valuing the business depends on the importance of asset-related approaches to the valuation.

Income Statements

The *income statement,* in contrast, presents a financial summary of a company's operating results for a certain time period. Its two main components are revenues and expenses. Exhibit 5–3 shows a sample income statement. Like the line items on the sample balance sheet, the income statement's line items are likely to differ greatly from company to company. Valuations usually focus on a series of income statements rather than on just the most recent statement; thus, the analyst can review and reflect operating results under varying conditions. Like the balance sheet, the income statement often appears in common-size format, with each line item shown as a percentage of total revenues. The common-size statements help the analyst see the relative proportions of line items under differing conditions, as well as any trends that may emerge over time. In valuing most operating businesses, the analyst gives considerable attention to the income statements in order to arrive at an estimate of operating results that the company may reasonably expect in the future.

Statement of Cash Flows

Statement of Financial Accounting Standards No. 95, "Statement of Cash Flows," became effective for all financial statements issued after July 15, 1988. The statement of cash flows replaced the statement of changes in financial position.

The *statement of cash flows* is designed to provide information about the cash receipts and cash payments generated by the business's operations over a specified time period. In addition, the statement details information about the company's financing and investing activities during the same period. Cash flows from operating activities are those not associated with financing or investment activities. Financing activities include obtaining resources from owners and providing them with a return on, and a return of, their investment; borrowing money and repaying amounts borrowed or otherwise settling the obligation; and obtaining and paying for other resources obtained from creditors

EXHIBIT 5-2

Sample Balance Sheet

CONSOLIDATED BALANCE SHEET
Alaska Air Group, Inc.

ASSETS

As of December 31 (In Thousands)	1985	1986
Current Assets		
Cash and short-term investments (Note 3)	$147,982	$ 66,215
Receivables—less allowance for doubtful accounts		
($1,421,000–1985; $2,603,000–1986)	37,883	40,380
Expendable and spare parts	5,109	14,193
Prepaid expenses	6,666	8,887
Total Current Assets	197,640	129,675
Property and Equipment (Note 4)		
Flight equipment	245,757	398,713
Other property and equipment	85,151	97,134
	330,908	495,847
Less accumulated depreciation and amortization	73,350	92,527
	257,558	403,320
Purchase deposits for flight equipment	26,254	3,400
	283,812	406,720
Capital leases (Note 5)		
Flight equipment	43,200	43,200
Other equipment	1,825	2,326
	45,025	45,526
Less accumulated amortization	1,071	3,581
	43,954	41,945
Total Property and Equipment—Net	327,766	448,665
Intangible Assets—Subsidiaries (Note 1)	–	80,407
Other Assets	11,643	13,142
Total Assets	$537,049	$671,889

LIABILITIES AND SHAREHOLDERS' EQUITY

As of December 31 (In Thousands)	1985	1986
Current Liabilities		
Accounts payable and accrued liabilities	$ 37,962	$ 62,626
Accrued wages, vacation pay and payroll taxes	15,128	20,118
Accrued income taxes	2,646	1,038
Air traffic liability	28,407	35,463
Current portion of long-term debt and lease obligations	10,354	19,241
Total Current Liabilities	94,497	138,486
Long-Term Debt (Note 4)	190,795	248,677
Long-Term Capital Lease Obligations (Note 5)	43,232	42,974
Other Liabilities		
Deferred income taxes (Note 9)	37,250	46,812
Other deferred credits and liabilities	10,264	17,761
	47,514	64,573
Commitments (Note 5)		
Shareholders' Equity (Note 6)		
Common stock, par value $1 per share		
Authorized: 30,000,000 shares		
Issued: 1985–12,334,803 shares; 1986–12,383,805 shares	12,335	12,384
Capital in excess of par value	66,784	67,169
Retained earnings	81,892	97,626
	161,011	177,179
Total Liabilities and Shareholders' Equity	$537,049	$671,889

Note: Accountant's notes to financial statements not included in exhibit.
SOURCE: Alaska Air Group, Inc. 1986 Annual Report.

EXHIBIT 5-3

Sample Income Statement

CONSOLIDATED STATEMENT OF INCOME
Alaska Air Group, Inc.

Year Ended December 31 (In Thousands)	1984	1985	1986
Operating Revenues			
Passenger	$314,244	$377,195	$412,387
Freight and mail	32,387	39,892	39,917
Contract service and other–net	15,011	16,100	15,960
Total Operating Revenues	361,642	433,187	468,264
Operating Expenses			
Wages and benefits	105,949	119,754	134,166
Aircraft fuel	87,196	96,318	73,730
Aircraft maintenance	13,685	18,846	17,239
Aircraft rent	17,263	24,524	29,072
Commissions	24,381	29,936	34,667
Depreciation and amortization	12,098	16,260	25,491
Other	67,069	96,383	116,124
Total Operating Expenses	327,641	402,021	430,489
Operating Income	34,001	31,166	37,775
Other Income (Expense)			
Interest income	5,780	10,523	9,137
Interest expense	(9,264)	(17,110)	(22,520)
Interest capitalized	3,926	4,200	957
Gain (loss) on disposition of assets (Note 8)	(187)	5,120	2,264
Other–net	(226)	(113)	305
	29	2,620	(9,857)
Income before income tax expense	34,030	33,786	27,918
Income tax expense (Note 9)	10,122	7,851	10,205
Net Income	$ 23,908	$ 25,935	$ 17,713
Earnings Per Share Calculations: (Note 2)			
Primary–			
Net income	$ 23,908	$ 25,935	$ 17,713
Average shares outstanding	10,907	12,361	12,566
Earnings per share	$ 2.19	$ 2.10	$ 1.41
Fully diluted–			
Net income	$ 24,803	$ 27,973	$ 20,801
Average shares outstanding	12,852	15,141	15,977
Earnings per share	$ 1.93	$ 1.85	$ 1.30

Note: Accountant's notes to financial statements not included in exhibit.
SOURCE: Alaska Air Group, Inc. 1986 Annual Report.

on long-term credit.[2] Investing activities include making and collecting loans and acquiring and disposing of debt or equity instruments and property, plant, and equipment and other productive assets—that is, assets held for or used in the production of goods or services (other than materials that are part of the enterprise's inventory).[3] The statement of cash flows can give good insight into a company's cash flow. It is especially useful in analyzing the company's liquidity and assessing its potential capital needs.

Exhibit 5–4 illustrates a sample statement of cash flows, using the indirect method. It is not related to the financial statements of Alaska Air Group, since *SFAS No. 95* was not in effect when the company published its 1986 financial statements.

---

[2]*Statement of Financial Accounting Standards No. 95*, "Statement of Cash Flows," *Journal of Accountancy* (February 1988), p. 141.
[3]Ibid., p. 141.

EXHIBIT 5-4

Sample Statement of Cash Flows

For Year Ended December 31, 19XX

Cash flows from operating activities		
Net income		$ 250,000
Add (deduct) items not affecting cash:		
Depreciation expense	$ 31,000	
Gain on sale of equipment	(6,000)	
Increase in deferred income taxes	5,000	
Decrease in accounts receivable	12,000	
Increase in inventory	(37,000)	
Increase in prepaid expenses	(3,000)	
Increase in accounts payable	4,000	
Increase in accrued liabilities	9,000	15,000
Net cash provided by operating activities		265,000
Cash flows from investing activities:		
Purchase of land	(65,000)	
Purchase of building	(245,000)	
Purchase of equipment	(180,000)	
Sale of equipment	34,000	
Net cash used by investing activities		(456,000)
Cash flows from financing activities:		
Issuance of long-term debt	250,000	
Payment of cash dividends	(50,000)	
Issuance of common stock	60,000	
Net cash provided by financing activities		260,000
Net increase in cash		69,000
Cash at January 1, 19XX		76,000
Cash at December 31, 19XX		$145,000

Statements of Changes in Financial Position

Financial statements issued prior to July 15, 1988, include the statement of changes in financial position rather than the statement of cash flows. The *statement of changes in financial position* was prepared as a broad concept to include all the important changes in financial position that took place during the accounting period. As typically presented, the statement was a product of *Accounting Principles Board Opinion No. 19 (APB Opinion 19)*. *Opinion 19* permitted, but did not require, reporting of cash flow information in the statement of changes in financial position.

The working capital basis was the most common and preferred form of presentation. The statement was presented in two main sections. The first illustrated the amount of funds generated from or used in operations during the period and summarized all the major financing and investing transactions. Such transactions included the issuance of long-term debt or stock to acquire fixed assets or the conversion of preferred stock or a convertible bond into common stock. The second main section showed the net changes in each element of working capital (defined as current assets minus current liabilities) for the period. Exhibit 5–5 is a sample statement of changes in financial position.

Many appraisers fail to give the statement of cash flows and statement of changes in financial position the attention they deserve. I suggest that these statements be given careful scrutiny in the valuation process.

Statements of Stockholders' Equity

The *statement of stockholders' equity* (sometimes called *statement of shareholders' equity*) shows amounts flowing into and out of the equity section of the balance sheet during the year, including earnings, dividends, and changes in shares outstanding. It reconciles the equity amount shown on the balance sheet from one year to the next. The statement enables the analyst to take proper account of changes in equity and the related shares from period to period. This is especially important in computing such figures as book value per share and earnings per share when changes in the number of shares outstanding have occurred. Exhibit 5–6 is a sample statement of stockholders' equity.

Many closely held companies do not bother to prepare separate statements of stockholders' equity as part of their financial statements. If there are any complications regarding the equity accounts, the analyst preparing the materials for the company's valuation should make up such a statement so that all changes in the equity accounts will be clearly presented.

Statements of Partners' Capital Accounts

The partnership counterpart of the statement of stockholders' equity is the *statement of partners' capital accounts*. In a corporation, each holder of a class of stock is treated identically in the equity section of the balance sheet; thus, changes in equity need to be broken down only by class of stock rather than by owner. In a partnership, however, changes in each partner's capital account must be identified separately, because different partners may be treated differently for various reasons. In effect, each partnership interest must be treated as a separate class of stock. Exhibit 5–7 is a sample statement of partners' capital accounts.

In a corporation, if a stockholder deposits or withdraws assets in exchange for cash rather than stock, the transaction is recorded as if the transaction were with some outside party, not in the equity section of the financial statements. If stockholders receive cash as dividends, all holders of a class of stock participate in proportion to their stock ownership. In a partnership, however, transactions involving deposits or withdrawals of partnership assets may be posted directly to a part-

EXHIBIT 5-5

Sample Statement of Changes in Financial Position

CONSOLIDATED STATEMENT OF CHANGES IN FINANCIAL POSITION
Alaska Air Group, Inc.

Year Ended December 31 (In Thousands)	1984	1985	1986
Financial Resources Were Provided By:			
Net income	$ 23,908	$ 25,935	$ 17,713
Add (deduct) income items not affecting working capital—			
Depreciation, overhaul and other amortization	15,966	21,463	33,362
Loss (gain) on disposition of property and equipment	211	(5,120)	(2,264)
Deferred income taxes	10,347	3,017	9,662
Interest capitalized	(3,926)	(4,200)	(957)
Other	516	737	2,412
Working Capital Provided by Operations	47,022	41,832	59,928
Disposition of property and equipment	43,623	17,829	5,432
Employee benefit trust fund—net	(3,101)	10,816	3,358
Revenue bond construction fund—net	(13,593)	11,237	2,356
Long-term debt issued	35,065	100,000	30,000
Long-term capital lease obligations incurred	–	42,075	–
Common stock issued	198	27,781	434
Other	922	6,304	6,745
	110,136	257,874	108,253
Financial Resources Were Used For:			
Property and equipment purchases and deposits	104,589	161,920	73,774
Reduction in long-term debt and lease obligations	7,045	9,623	32,993
Acquisition of subsidiaries' noncurrent net assets	–	–	109,611
Cash dividends	1,508	1,911	1,979
Other	1,137	4,229	1,850
	114,279	177,683	220,207
Increase (Decrease) In Working Capital	$ (4,143)	$ 80,191	$(111,954)
Summary Of Changes In Components Of Working Capital			
Increase (decrease) in current assets—			
Cash and short-term investments	$ 5,695	$ 86,992	$ (81,767)
Receivables	5,328	6,411	2,497
Expendable and spare parts	611	1,392	9,084
Prepaid expenses	1,388	2,963	2,221
Net change in current assets	13,022	97,758	(67,965)
Increase (decrease) in current liabilities—			
Accounts payable and accrued liabilities	7,368	12,408	28,046
Air traffic liability	9,805	1,975	7,056
Current portion of long-term debt and lease obligations	(8)	3,184	8,887
Net change in current liabilities	17,165	17,567	43,989
Increase (Decrease) In Working Capital	$ (4,143)	$ 80,191	$(111,954)

SOURCE: Alaska Air Group, Inc. 1986 Annual Report.

ner's capital account, thus changing that partner's ownership status in relation to the other partners. Also, frequently the partners do not share the earnings (or losses) in the same proportion as what their shares in the partnership assets would be on liquidation. For this reason too, then, holdings in the partnership may shift among partners' capital accounts from period to period as those accounts are credited with different proportions of the partnership's earnings and losses.

The analyst valuing a partnership interest subject to any such complications probably will need to read the partnership agreement to be sure that he or she completely understands each partner's rights. If one partner owns a 20 percent interest in the capital account of a

EXHIBIT 5-6

Sample Statement of Stockholders' Equity

CONSOLIDATED STATEMENT OF SHAREHOLDERS' EQUITY
Alaska Air Group, Inc.

| | Common Stock | | | |
| | $1 Par Value | Capital in Excess of Par Value | Treasury Stock at Cost | Retained Earnings |
(In Thousands)				
Balances at December 31, 1983	$10,866	$40,789	$(515)	$35,468
Net income for 1984				23,908
Cash dividends ($.14 per share)				(1,508)
Stock issued under stock plans	33	165		
Balances at December 31, 1984	10,899	40,954	(515)	57,868
Net income for 1985				25,935
Cash dividends ($.155 per share)				(1,911)
Issuance of 1,521,900 shares of common stock	1,522	26,174		
Stock issued under stock plans	17	68		
Cancellation of treasury stock	(103)	(412)	515	
Balances at December 31, 1985	12,335	66,784	–	81,892
Net income for 1986				17,713
Cash dividends ($.16 per share)				(1,979)
Stock issued under stock plans	49	385		
Balances at December 31, 1986	$12,384	$67,169	$ –	$97,626

SOURCE: Alaska Air Group, Inc. 1986 Annual Report.

very profitable partnership but is entitled to 60 percent of the earnings, that interest is not necessarily equal in value to another 20 percent interest that is entitled to a lesser participation in the earnings.

Interim Statements

Interim statements are those prepared as of some time other than the last day of the fiscal year. For valuation purposes, they are most commonly used when the valuation date is so distant from the company's prior fiscal year-end—usually three months or more—that the year-end statements lose some of their relevance. They are also used to

EXHIBIT 5-7

Sample Statement of Partners' Capital Accounts

For Year Ended December 31, 19XX

	Able	Baker	Total
Balance, January 1, 19XX	$300,000	$120,000	$420,000
Add capital investments	0	30,000	30,000
	$300,000	$150,000	$450,000
Add net income	60,000	36,000	96,000
	$360,000	$186,000	$556,000
Less personal drawings	50,000	30,000	80,000
Balance, December 31, 19XX	$310,000	$156,000	$476,000

facilitate more detailed analysis of variables such as cash flow, inventory turnover, and interest-bearing debt outstanding. Such analysis often provides a better understanding of businesses with highly seasonal operations whose trends the analyst may want to track on a monthly or quarterly basis.

Some closely held companies prepare interim statements regularly—every quarter or even every month. Others are more casual about it, preparing them on an as-needed basis or even not at all. Therefore, it is important that the analyst have an idea of these statements' usefulness before launching the client's accounting department on such a task. Several factors influence the usefulness of interim statements, particularly:

1. The proximity of the valuation date to the fiscal year-end.
2. The quality of the interim statement data.
3. The importance of seasonality to the company being valued.
4. The extent to which interim statements are likely to affect the valuation.

Having decided that interim statements are necessary, the analyst must also request interim statements for the corresponding period of the prior fiscal year so that the two periods can be compared on a consistent accounting basis. It is important to remember that interim statements usually do not contain certain adjustments typically made when closing the books at year-end, such as those for physical inventory count, prepaid expenses, and a variety of accrual items. Therefore, to interpret interim statements and use them as if they were comparable to year-end statements, the analyst probably will need to obtain additional information with which to approximate such adjustments.

Levels of Financial Statement Preparation

Since 1979, the accounting profession has offered three levels of service in connection with financial statement preparation:

1. Audited statements.
2. Reviewed statements.
3. Compiled statements.

Many people simply assume that all statements prepared by CPA firms or statements with reports from CPA firms are audited. On the contrary, a CPA firm will issue a report regardless of the level of services it performs. The report's wording differs according to the level of service; examples are presented later in the chapter.

Valuation analysts prefer to work with audited statements because of the statements' completeness and reliability, but the large majority of closely held businesses do *not* go to the expense of having statements audited. It is important for both the valuation analyst and persons using the valuation report to appreciate the various levels of scrutiny represented by audited, reviewed, and compiled statements of different companies or of one company for different years.

Audited Statements

Regarding an audit of financial statements, the AICPA advises:

> The objective of the ordinary examination of financial statements by the independent auditor is the expression of an opinion on the fairness with which they present financial position, results of operations, and changes in financial position in conformity with generally accepted accounting principles. The auditor's report is the medium through which he expresses his opinion or, if circumstances require, disclaims an opinion. In either case, he states whether his examination has been made in accordance with generally accepted auditing standards. These standards require him to state whether, in his opinion, the financial statements are presented in conformity with generally accepted accounting principles and whether such principles have been consistently applied in the preparation of the financial statements of the current period in relation to those of the preceding period.[4]

If a company has its statements audited, the auditor's opinion becomes a part of the completed set of financial statements.

Unqualified Opinions. An *unqualified opinion,* commonly known as a *clean opinion,* consists of two paragraphs. The first states the scope of the audit, what basic financial statements were audited, and for what dates or periods. The second states that the figures are presented fairly in accordance with generally accepted accounting principles (GAAP). An example of an unqualified opinion, Arthur Andersen & Company's opinion on the statements of Alaska Air Group for 1986, is shown in Exhibit 5–8.

Qualified Opinions. There are three main reasons for an auditor to give a *qualified opinion:*

1. The scope of the examination was limited in some way, either by client's choice or by availability of data.
2. The figures do not fairly present the company's financial position, either because of inadequate disclosure or because the accounting used was not in accordance with GAAP.
3. There are uncertainties about future events that the auditors consider material enough to warrant a qualification.

If the auditor's opinion is qualified, one or more paragraphs are added between the beginning and concluding paragraphs, explaining the nature of the qualification or qualifications.

---

[4]*AICPA Professional Standards,* vol. A, p. 61.

EXHIBIT 5-8

Example of Unqualified Opinion

REPORT OF INDEPENDENT PUBLIC ACCOUNTANTS

To the Board of Directors and Shareholders of Alaska Air Group, Inc.

We have examined the consolidated balance sheet of Alaska Air Group, Inc. (a Delaware corporation) and subsidiaries as of December 31, 1985 and 1986 and the related consolidated statements of income, shareholders' equity and changes in financial position for each of the three years in the period ended December 31, 1986. Our examinations were made in accordance with generally accepted auditing standards and, accordingly, included such tests of the accounting records and such other auditing procedures as we considered necessary in the circumstances.

In our opinion, the financial statements referred to above present fairly the financial position of Alaska Air Group, Inc. and subsidiaries as of December 31, 1985 and 1986 and the results of their operations and the changes in their financial position for each of the three years in the period ended December 31, 1986, in conformity with generally accepted accounting principles applied on a consistent basis.

Arthur Andersen + Co.

ARTHUR ANDERSEN & CO.

Seattle, Washington,
January 23, 1987

SOURCE: Alaska Air Group, Inc. 1986 Annual Report.

If the opinion is qualified because of limited scope, the analyst is basically in the same position as would be the case if the available statements were not audited, at least with respect to that portion of the statements that were not able to be audited. (In some cases, for example, the balance sheet may be audited but not the income statement for the period ended as of the balance-sheet date.) This qualification should be only a minor disappointment to the analyst accustomed to valuing closely held companies, since most closely held companies lack the luxury of audited statements anyway.

If the figures do not fairly present the company's position, the analyst must investigate the inadequacy and make whatever adjustments or allowances are necessary to get what is needed for analysis. The most commonly encountered departure from GAAP is the presentation of one or more items (or the whole set of statements) on a cash rather than accrual basis.

The real befuddlement to the valuation analyst is a qualification "because of future uncertainties." Since the value of a company depends on the outlook for its economic future, any uncertainty about that future significant enough to warrant a qualification in the auditor's opinion must complicate the valuation. The most common future uncertainties that give rise to a qualification in the auditor's opinion are existing or potential litigation and financial instability, which cause the auditor to question the company's viability as a going concern. In cases where existing or possible litigation is involved, the appraiser must study the situation as thoroughly as possible and make an ultimately subjective judgment. If $1 million is at stake and the appraiser concludes that there is a 30 percent probability that the company will lose, he or she probably will deduct more than $300,000 (0.3 × $1,000,000) from the determined value because of the risk.[5] The appraiser also will be very cautious if there is doubt about the company's viability as a going concern. In any case, if such extreme uncertainties exist, the appraiser should include a qualification to that effect in his or her own appraisal report.

To give a widely publicized example, in December 1985 a jury rendered a verdict against Texaco (*Pennzoil Company* v. *Texaco, Inc.*) that, if upheld, could have forced Texaco into liquidation or bankruptcy. Since Texaco was in the process of appealing the verdict and the ultimate outcome of the litigation could not be determined but could have a material adverse effect, Arthur Andersen & Company qualified its opinion on the 1986 financial statements (see Exhibit 5–9). It should be recognized, of course, that it does not require an event nearly this dramatic in order for an auditor to feel compelled to issue a qualified opinion under normal auditing standards.

Reviewed Statements

The AICPA defines and discusses reviewed financial statements as follows:

> *Review of financial statements.* Performing inquiry and analytical procedures that provide the accountant with a reasonable basis for expressing limited assurance that there are no material modifications that should be made to the statements in order for them to be in conformity with generally accepted accounting principles or, if applicable, with another comprehensive basis of accounting. . . .
>
> . . . .
>
> The objective of a review also differs significantly from the objective of an examination of financial statements in accordance with generally accepted auditing standards. The objective of an audit is to provide a reasonable basis for expressing an opinion regarding the financial statements taken as a whole. A review does not provide a basis for the expression of such an opinion because a review does not contemplate a study and evaluation of internal accounting control, tests of accounting records and responses to inquiries by obtaining corroborating evidential matter through inspection, observation or confirmation, and certain other

---

[5]One reviewer of the manuscript suggested that this was analogous to assessing an insurance premium to account for the risk.

EXHIBIT 5-9

Example of Qualified Opinion

Auditors' report

Arthur Andersen & Co.
New York, N.Y.

To the Stockholders, Texaco Inc.:

We have examined the consolidated balance sheet of Texaco Inc. (a Delaware corporation) and subsidiary companies as of December 31, 1986 and 1985, and the related statements of consolidated income, retained earnings and changes in financial position for each of the three years in the period ended December 31, 1986. Our examinations were made in accordance with generally accepted auditing standards and, accordingly, included such tests of the accounting records and such other auditing procedures as we considered necessary in the circumstances.

A judgment against Texaco Inc. has been rendered by the District Court of Harris County, Texas and substantially affirmed by the Court of Appeals for the First Supreme Judicial District of Texas. The Federal courts have granted a preliminary injunction which enjoins the Texas plaintiff from taking any action to enforce or attempt to enforce the judgment during the appeals process. A United States Supreme Court decision is pending regarding the Texas plaintiff's appeal to have the preliminary injunction overturned. Certain developments, as more fully explained in Note 17 to the Consolidated Financial Statements, could cause Texaco Inc. to face prospects such as having to seek protection of its assets and business pursuant to the bankruptcy and reorganization provisions of Chapter 11 of Title 11 of the United States Code and being subject to liquidation of significant assets. While Texaco Inc. intends to pursue all available remedies to set aside or to reverse the judgment entered by the Texas District Court, the ultimate outcome of this litigation is not presently determinable.

In our opinion, subject to the effect on the 1986 and 1985 financial statements of such adjustments, if any, that might have been required had the outcome of the litigation mentioned in the preceding paragraph been known, the financial statements referred to above present fairly the financial position of Texaco Inc. and subsidiary companies as of December 31, 1986 and 1985, and the results of their operations and the changes in their financial position for each of the three years in the period ended December 31, 1986, in conformity with generally accepted accounting principles applied on a consistent basis.

February 26, 1987

SOURCE: Texaco, Inc. 1986 Annual Report

procedures ordinarily performed during an audit. A review may bring to the accountant's attention significant matters affecting the financial statements, but it does not provide assurance that the accountant will become aware of all significant matters that would be disclosed in an audit.[6]

Exhibit 5–10 shows illustrative wording for accountants' reports on reviewed statements.

Compiled Statements

The AICPA defines the compilation of financial statements as:

> Presenting in the form of financial statements information that is the representation of management (owners) without undertaking to express any assurance on the statements.[7]

Exhibit 5–11 shows illustrative wording for accountants' reports on compiled statements.

---

[6]American Institute of Certified Public Accountants, *AICPA Professional Standards,* vol. B (Chicago: Commerce Clearing House, 1985), p. 3313.
[7]Ibid.

EXHIBIT 5-10

Illustrative Wording for Accountants' Reports
on Reviewed Statements

Review report

I (we) have reviewed the accompanying balance sheet of XYZ Company as of December 31, 19XX, and the related statements of income, retained earnings, and changes in financial position for the year then ended, in accordance with standards established by the American Institute of Certified Public Accountants. All information included in these financial statements is the representation of the management (owners) of XYZ Company.

A review consists principally of inquiries of company personnel and analytical procedures applied to financial data. It is substantially less in scope than an examination in accordance with generally accepted auditing standards, the objective of which is the expression of an opinion regarding the financial statements taken as a whole. Accordingly, I (we) do not express such an opinion.

Based on my (our) review, with the exception of the matter(s) described in the following paragraph(s), I am (we are) not aware of any material modifications that should be made to the accompanying financial statements in order for them to be in conformity with generally accepted accounting principles.

SOURCE: *AICPA Professional Standards*, Vol. B, American Institute of Certified Public Accountants, Inc., New York, As of June 1, 1985, p. 3323. Copyright ©1985 by the American Institute of Certified Public Accountants, Inc.

EXHIBIT 5-11

Illustrative Wording for Accountants' Reports
on Compiled Statements

Compilation report

I (we) have compiled the accompanying balance sheet of XYZ Company as of December 31, 19XX, and the related statements of income, retained earnings, and changes in financial position for the year then ended, in accordance with standards established by the American Institute of Certified Public Accountants.

A compilation is limited to presenting in the form of financial statements information that is the representation of management (owners). I (we) have not audited or reviewed the accompanying financial statements and, accordingly, do not express an opinion or any other form of assurance on them. However, I (we) did become aware of a departure (certain departures) from generally accepted accounting principles that is (are) described in the following paragraph(s).

SOURCE: *AICPA Professional Standards*, Vol. B, American Institute of Certified Public Accountants, Inc., New York, As of June 1, 1985, pp. 3322-3323. Copyright © 1985 by the American Institute of Certified Public Accountants, Inc.

According to the AICPA, the objective of a compilation differs significantly from that of a review. The inquiry and analytical procedures performed in a review should provide the accountant with a reasonable basis for expressing limited assurance that there are no material modifications to be made to the financial statements. On the other hand, no expression of assurance is contemplated in a compilation.

Statements may be compiled internally rather than by outside CPAs. In such cases, the analyst will have to make extensive inquiries and use judgment as to the quality of information presented.

Federal Tax Returns

There can be many fully justifiable differences between amounts and items reported on federal income tax returns and those reported on financial statements. Discrepancies between tax returns and financial statements usually result from timing differences. Common discrepancies include different methods of revenue recognition, differences in depreciation methods, and capitalizing costs for book purposes while expensing them on the tax return. For corporations filing Form 1120, "U.S. Corporate Income Tax Return," a convenient summary of differences between tax return and income statement reporting is found in Schedule M-1, "Reconciliation of Income per Books with Income per Return."

If such differences exist, the analyst must use his or her professional judgment to determine which figures will provide the most appropriate basis for appraisal purposes. In general, the statements that most closely conform to industry practices would most fairly represent the company's financial position and earning power. The financial data and ratios derived from tax return data normally would *not* be relied on when comparing the subject company to the price/earnings or price/book value ratios derived from publicly traded comparatives.

Some small closely held companies prepare no financial statements at all, leaving the analyst with only tax returns as a basis for financial statements. In such cases, the analyst usually recasts the information from the tax returns into conventional financial statement format to facilitate further analysis.

Discussion of all the many federal tax forms that may be relevant for a particular valuation would be much too detailed to fit within the scope of this book. Sample forms, along with their respective instructions, are found in the Internal Revenue Service's "Package X," which recently was published in two volumes.

Other Financial Schedules

Aged Receivables List

The *aged receivables list* (aged list) can yield insight into the company's profitability, and even viability. However, many relatively small companies do not prepare them. Because the aged list gives the appraiser a useful means for recognizing situations that could affect the firm's value, the analyst should have either the client's accounting department or a member of his or her own staff prepare one, if necessary. The statement lists the accounts alphabetically, sometimes categorized into customer groups. The spreadsheet is laid out with columns for the total amount due, the current portion, and the portions over 30 days, over 60 days, over 90 days, and over 120 days past due. Unusual circumstances regarding a specific account should be noted somewhere on the statement, perhaps as footnotes. Any notes or other receivables besides normal trade receivables should be listed separately, with enough detail to permit evaluation. The statement date should be as of the latest annual or interim financial statement so that the total on the balance sheet will reconcile with the amount on the aged list.

Aged Payables List

The *aged payables list* usually takes the same format as the receivables list. Again the purpose is to alert the analyst to special situations that could affect the valuation.

Stockholder List

The *stockholder list* should include each stockholder's name and number of shares held. If there is more than one class of stock, it should show the stockholders' holdings in each class. It should also identify any family or other relationships among the stockholders. This list will be examined by the IRS and the courts if they are involved.

Dividend Schedule

The *dividend schedule* normally should cover the same time period that the financial statements do. It should show the date of each dividend payment and the per share amount for each class of stock.

Real Estate and Equipment Lists and Depreciation Schedules

Lists of property owned should include the acquisition date, a description adequate for identifying each piece or group, the original cost, the depreciation method and life used, and the net depreciated value. The totals of such schedules should reconcile with line items in the financial statements. For real estate, the schedule should show the size (acres of land and dimensions and square feet of floor space of buildings), with a brief description of the construction and any special features. It should also indicate the dates and costs of additions and remodeling.

Inventory List

The amount of detail desired in the *inventory list* will vary greatly from one appraisal to another, depending on the inventory's importance in the valuation and the extent to which inventory accounting methods tend to differ within the particular industry. In any case, the total should be reconcilable with the inventory as shown on the financial statements, using whatever adjustments conform to the company's method of inventory valuation. The analyst should examine the company's write-down policy and, occasionally, make a market value adjustment.

Officers' and Directors' Compensation Schedule

An *officers' and directors' compensation schedule* usually should be prepared for the same number of years as the financial statements. It may provide a basis for adjustments to the income statements, offering evidence of the company's earning capacity.

The compensation schedule should show for each applicable year all payments made to or for the benefit of each upper-level manager and owner or person related to an owner. These benefits would include base salary; bonuses or commissions; amount paid into pension, profit-sharing, or other employee benefit funds; and other employee benefits. It also should include compensation other than cash, such as stock or options, company cars, or other property used, and any significant expenses paid or reimbursed for business activities performed by the employee. The appraiser should be mindful at all times that the IRS sometimes attempts to depict compensation to owners of closely held businesses as excessive so as to get dividend tax treatment for a portion of it. In order to avoid involvement in such a disagreement, the appraiser should carefully phrase the description of any adjustment to owners' compensation.

Related Party Transaction Information

As the Financial Accounting Standards Board (FASB) states in its *Statement No. 57* regarding *related party transactions:*

> Related party[8] transactions may be controlled entirely by one of the parties so that those transactions may be affected significantly by considerations other than those in arm's length transactions with unrelated parties.[9]
>
> Without disclosure to the contrary, there is a general presumption that the transactions reflected in the financial statements have been consummated on an arm's-length basis between independent parties. . . . Because it is possible for related party transactions to be arranged to obtain certain results desired by the related parties, the resulting accounting measures may not represent what they usually would be expected to represent.[10]

It is important that the analyst obtain any and all information on related party transactions in order to determine their nature and propriety.

Audited financial statements will include this information in their accompanying notes. In the absence of audited financial statements, the analyst must ask management to prepare a listing of such transactions and the terms at which they were transacted. Transactions could include loans to and from related parties, sales, leases, or purchases from or sales to related parties, guarantees to or for related parties, and so on.

---

[8]Defined in *Financial Accounting Standards Board (FASB) Statement No. 57*, Appendix B (f).
[9]*FASB No. 57*, Appendix A, para. 13 (1982).
[10]Ibid., para. 15.

Miscellaneous Financial Information

Schedule of Key-Man Life Insurance

In many closely held companies, the loss of a single key man can have a significant impact on the company's operations. It is always desirable to know how much of this risk is covered by life insurance. This insurance may have to be considered as part of the company's value.

List of Past Transactions in the Stock or Offers to Buy

To the extent that past transactions in the stock were at arm's length, they provide objective evidence of value. Even if not accepted, a bona fide offer, particularly if submitted in writing, can at least corroborate the value. In preparing the record of past transactions or offers, it is important to list any relationships among the parties in order to determine whether each transaction was at arm's length. The transaction record usually should go as far back as the number of years of financial statements used. On this basis, past transaction prices can be compared with then current book values, earnings, or other relevant variables.

Budgets

The budgets closely held companies prepare vary widely from no budget at all to fairly detailed and accurate ones. Since the value of a business interest ultimately depends on what the business will accomplish in the future, reasonable estimates of future expectations should help in arriving at a value. A good way to test the quality of a company's budgeting process is to compare past budgets to actual results.

The extent to which the appraiser can rely on budgets in deriving the business's current value also varies greatly. It depends on both the quality of the company's budgets and the purpose of the valuation. For existing or potential litigation, the appraiser should not rely on budgets too heavily. The court may decide that since the budget looks into an inherently uncertain future, the entire exercise is too speculative for use as a basis for valuation. On the other hand, budgets are widely used in determining value for mergers. In most cases, a company that produces convincing budgets will command a higher selling price than one that does not.

Capital Requirements

Capital requirements can arise from many sources, including catching up on deferred maintenance (a common need in small and medium-size companies), increasing working capital needs, or making capital expenditures. Dividend-paying capacity, one criterion of the value of a business interest, represents a competing use of capital, and each company must decide whether to retain cash with which to carry out needed purchases or distribute its earnings to stockholders. A prospective buyer of a company must be aware that if the company will require any immediate cash infusions, such outlays should be considered as part of the business's total cost, so that the proper amount paid to the seller would be the total value of a properly financed business less the amount of the acquired cash infusion. If cash infusions are known or reasonably expected to be required in the future to support the expected earnings, they must be reflected as a cash outflow, the present value of which should represent a decrease in the value of the business as otherwise determined.

Order Backlog

If the company's order backlog (customer orders that are yet to be filled) is significant, the analyst should compare the backlog on the valuation date with that on one or more past dates. Such comparison, especially with the backlog a year prior to the valuation date, is one indication of the company's future prospects that is solidly based on its past record.

Customer Base

The fewer customers the company relies on for its market, the more important an analysis of the customer base becomes. A convenient way to compile the customer base information is in simple tabular form. The analyst should list, in order of size of billings, the 10 to 20 largest customers in the latest year or fiscal period and the dollar amounts of billings and the percentage of total billings for each. This information should be shown for several periods in the past as well as for the latest period. The columns for the past years should also show any customers that accounted for a significant proportion of the billings at that time, even if they are not current customers. A budgeted figure for each customer for the current or forthcoming year is helpful if available.

Exhibit 5–12 presents a sample format for showing the customer base using the ten largest customers based on their budgets for the current year and any others that have accounted for over 10 percent of revenues in any of the past four years. Of course, the analyst will use this information, along with information developed in interviews, in assessing the potential for customer turnover.

Supplier List

Like the customer base, the supplier list becomes more important with fewer suppliers. It also becomes more important if the future availability of certain supplies is uncertain enough to increase the company's risk. If future sources of supply are a critical factor, the

EXHIBIT 5-12

Western Advertising Agency
Analysis of Customer Base

(Dollars in 000s)

Customer	1988 (Budget)	%	1987	%	1986	%	1985	%	1984	%
Agency Total	$9,863	100.0	$8,160	100.0	$6,943	100.0	$5,961	100.0	$4,820	100.0
Runwell Sport Shoes	3,350	34.0	2,520	30.9	1,900	27.4	1,025	17.2	570	13.8
Pacific Cruises	2,500	25.3	1,750	21.4	750	10.8	---	---	---	---
Rainier Airline	1,100	11.2	639	7.8	---	---	---	---	---	---
Thunderegg Motels	800	8.1	---	---	---	---	---	---	---	---
Top-Flite Personnel	600	6.1	480	5.9	321	4.6	268	4.5	122	2.5
Henry's Hemlock Homes	400	4.1	768	9.4	1,123	16.2	822	13.8	630	13.1
Growling Grizzly Pizza	325	3.3	278	3.4	257	3.7	210	3.5	115	2.4
Grand Pine Furniture	250	2.5	280	3.4	350	5.0	267	4.5	180	3.7
Coast Resorts Assn.	100	1.0	50	0.6	---	---	---	---	---	---
Siskiyou Ski School	50	0.5	35	0.4	---	---	---	---	---	---
Schludwiller Beer	---	---	112	1.4	381	5.5	732	12.3	1,223	25.4
Big Joe's Supermarkets	---	---	---	---	1,340	19.3	1,112	18.7	980	20.3
Leaping Leopard Air Freight	---	---	---	---	---	---	1,130	19.0	750	15.6

Overall, total customer base has increased from 12 clients in 1984 to 19 clients in 1988.

appraiser should compile a list of sources other than those currently being used. The supplier list could take the same format as the customer base.

Accountants' Work Papers and Company Books

The appraiser's basic function is not to audit, but to express an opinion of value on the basis of available financial information. Nevertheless, in some situations the accountants' work papers and/or company books may provide additional insight that is relevant to the appraisal, and the appraiser may request to see such information.

Evidence of Real and Personal Property Values

Real and Personal Property Tax Assessments

Tax assessments may not be the best yardstick of asset values, but they are almost always readily available. Most tax-assessed values are lower than replacement costs, although they may be well above liquidating value, especially those for personal property.

The analyst usually can obtain local information on the broad relationship between tax-assessed values and market values for a particular jurisdiction. In many jurisdictions, the tax-assessed value purports to represent not market value but some fixed percentage of market value, such as 30 percent. Of course, in those instances the analyst must adjust the figures upward to the market value directly implied by the tax-assessed value before making further adjustments, if any, for whatever systematic biases are perceived as prevailing in the particular jurisdiction.

Insurance Appraisals

Unlike tax appraisals, insurance appraisals have some tendency to overvalue property, primarily to ensure that the insurance will be adequate to cover any potential loss. The reason is that following a casualty, if it is demonstrated that a company's insurance was far less than the value of the property insured, the company may recover only that portion of its policy's face value equal to the percentage of the value of the lost property to the total property value. Also, insurance appraisals tend to be based on replacement value rather than on used values. Therefore, the analyst should not rely on insurance appraisals, since replacement cost is not always equivalent to depreciated value or to market value.

Independent Appraisal Reports

An independent appraisal by a qualified practitioner, if available, usually is a more reliable guide to asset value than either a tax assessment or insurance appraisal. Such appraisals generally specify the approach taken, the assumptions made, and some guidance for appropriate interpretation and use of the appraisal. A replacement cost or depreciated replacement cost appraisal, for example, normally will differ significantly from a liquidation value appraisal, and none of those may be appropriate for appraising assets being used in a specific ongoing business situation.

Contractual Agreements and Obligations

The appraiser must evaluate all significant contractual obligations for their potential positive or negative effect on the company's value. Contracts that may be significant for the value of a business or business interest can cover a wide variety of subjects.

Lease Agreements

It is important that the appraiser look not only at real estate leases but at any important equipment leases. A lease may be favorable or unfavorable. A long-term lease costing the company less than the current market value could add to the company's value; on the other hand, being saddled with a long-term lease on inadequate quarters for which the company cannot find an alternative tenant is anything but favorable. Renewal terms of a lease about to expire also can come into play, particularly if the lease is not renewable or renewable only at a significantly increased cost. For companies that have many leased outlets, such as retail chains, the appraiser may want to prepare a list of leases with a summary of their provisions.

If a sale of the business is being contemplated, the question as to whether or not the lease(s) are transferable is of paramount importance. If a below-market lease would be subject to a 50 percent increase in the event of a sale of the business, the impact on the business's value could be significant.

It should be noted that since rent is an expense in the financial statement, the benefit or drawback associated with a favorable or unfavorable lease is already captured in the reported income. Therefore, it would constitute a form of double-counting to capitalize the earnings and to separately account for the favorable or unfavorable leasehold value. Since leases are typically of a limited life, while capitalizing income assumes an ongoing level of revenue and expense, the preferable approach if data are available is to restate the income with an imputed rental payment at market, and then to separately add or subtract the value of the favorable or unfavorable lease.

Loan Agreements

Most loan agreements contain various requirements and restrictive covenants. One reason for reading the loan agreements is to check whether the company is in danger of defaulting on any requirement. Another consideration is the effect of any loan agreement restrictions on the company's ability to pay dividends and/or transfer stock ownership.

Franchise or Distributorship Agreements

One of the key things to look for in franchise or distributorship agreements is the rights the business owns under the agreement. It is common to find that such agreements are cancelable on relatively short notice, such as 30 days. Sometimes the rights under such agreements rest with an individual rather than with the corporation being valued. It also is common to find that whatever rights might exist under such agreements are nontransferable. The analyst should also determine future mutual obligations and costs.

Customer Contracts

Customer contracts are significant items for some companies, such as a manufacturer whose customers lease rather than buy its equipment. Contracts to obtain key raw materials may be significant for some firms. An analysis of the terms and strengths of such contracts can be an important consideration in valuing the business.

Buy-Sell and ESOP Agreements

Buy-sell or repurchase agreements with major stockholders may contain provisions that can affect the company's shares to which they apply and, in many cases, all the outstanding stock as well. Provisions in such agreements may address the question of value directly or may impose restrictions on transferability, which may bear on the value of the affected shares. If the company has an employee stock ownership plan (ESOP), the terms of the buy-back provisions have a major bearing on the marketability of the shares involved and thus must be considered when valuing ESOP shares.

Employment and Noncompete Agreements

Employment agreements with key personnel may affect the company's value, as may important agreements not to compete. These agreements could have either a positive or negative effect on value depending on the relationship between the cost and the value to the company.

Other Contractual Matters

The variety of contractual matters that can bear significantly on the value of a business is nearly infinite. The analyst should draw on personal experience to inquire about contracts that typically occur in certain lines of business and ask management whether any other significant contracts exist.

Off-Balance-Sheet Assets or Liabilities

There are many financial items that can significantly affect the business's value that do not appear as line items on the balance sheet, usually because they are of a contingent nature. Such items may or may not be referenced in footnotes.

One of the most common "off-balance-sheet" assets or liabilities is a prospective award or payment arising from a lawsuit. The appraiser should inquire about any pending or potential suits and note the details. Following the extended stock market rise in the mid-1980s, many companies accumulated hidden assets in the form of overfunded defined-benefit plans, which were not shown on the balance sheet but generally could be found in the footnotes to the financial statements.[11]

---

[11]Pension accounting is complicated and, although beyond the scope of this book, is important to the valuation analyst. In December 1985, *Financial Accounting Standards Board Statement No. 87*, "Employees' Accounting for Pensions," superseded *Accounting Principles Board Opinion No. 8*, "Accounting for the Cost of Pension Plans." For an extended discussion of this topic, see Paul B. W. Miller, "The New Pension Accounting," *Journal of Accountancy*, parts I and II (January–February 1987), pp. 98–108, 86–94.

An important category of off-balance-sheet liabilities for many companies these days is the potential cost of compliance with environmental, OSHA, or other government requirements.

Product liability and liability for warranties are other significant items for some companies.

Corporate or Partnership Records

The official documents of a corporation or partnership often hold facts that significantly affect the entity's valuation. The articles of incorporation, along with any amendments, and documents specifying rights attaching to each class of stock outstanding provide information that is particularly important for companies with more than one class of stock. There may be other information in the articles or bylaws relevant to the value. Certain items in the board of directors' and stockholders' minute books may be important, especially if transactions with parties related to the company have occurred. In a partnership, the partners' rights and obligations should be contained in the articles of partnership.

Company History

The appraiser must set the stage for placing the company in the context of its industry, especially its competition, as well as in the general economy. A relatively brief history will suffice in most cases. The history should indicate how long the company has been in business and some chronology of major changes, such as form of organization, controlling ownership, location of operations, and lines of business. Sometimes predecessor companies are a relevant part of the background. Some companies have relatively complex histories, requiring detailed explanations of transactions that have fundamentally contributed to the company's composition as of the valuation date.

Brochures, Catalogs, and Price Lists

The company should furnish the analyst with a set of its sales materials, such as brochures, catalogs, and price lists. These items will enable the analyst to become familiar with the company's products, services, and pricing and to evaluate the written sales materials. As with many of the written items furnished, these will help the analyst get an overview of the company and prepare relevant questions for the visit to the company's facilities and inquiries of company personnel.

Key-Personnel List

Key personnel include directors and officers, heads of departments or divisions, and anyone else who the analyst believes plays an important role in the company's operation. The list should include, at minimum, the person's age, position, tenure with the company, and educational and professional credentials. It is desirable to include a description of present and past duties with the company and background prior to joining it.

Patents, Copyrights, and Trademarks

A list of patents, copyrights, and trademarks should include the items covered and relevant issue and/or expiration dates. It should have at least a brief description and enough information to permit understanding of the items. The importance of these items and the degree of detail necessary vary greatly from one situation to another.

Trade Associations and Industry Sources

It is helpful to have the company furnish a list of trade associations to which it belongs, or is eligible to belong, along with the name and address of the executive director of each. The analyst can then contact the trade association for industry information. Many industries have other trade sources, such as trade journals or sources of composite data. The company usually can furnish a list of such sources and often can supply copies of relevant publications.

Conclusion

Gathering and analyzing the foregoing information will give the analyst the groundwork on which to base the company interview and pinpoint still-needed details that are relevant to the valuation. The specific material needed will vary with the particular valuation and is a matter of the analyst's judgment. Following the guidelines in this chapter will help the analyst to avoid the all-to-common pitfall of overlooking certain company data that may have a significant bearing on the value of the business or interest being appraised.

Chapter 6

Company Data—Field Trips and Interviews

The need for the valuation analyst to visit company facilities and have personal contact with company personnel and other related people varies greatly from one valuation situation to another. The extent of the necessary field work depends on many things, including the purpose of the valuation, the nature of the operation, and the size and complexity of the case. Another factor is how extensively the written material discussed in the previous chapter covers the many subjects.

The objectives of the field work range from gaining a broad, general perspective on the company and its operations to filling in necessary minutiae. My experience has been that a visit to the company's headquarters to observe operations provides substantial insight beyond what is gleaned solely from financial statements and other written material. Seeing operations firsthand and participating in face-to-face interviews make a company come alive for an analyst. Also, the analyst can fill in many details more easily and productively through conversation than with written material.

The analyst can get the most out of the field trip and interview process by thinking and planning in terms of accomplishing three objectives: (1) to gain a better overall understanding of the company; (2) to better understand the implications of the company's financial statements and other written information for the valuation; and (3) to identify current or potential changes that might cause the company's future to differ from that indicated by a mere extrapolation of historical data.

In trying to establish the value of a business interest at some specified time, the analyst recognizes the necessity of going beyond the financial statements. Financial statements are based on historical costs, varying depreciation methods, and accounting conventions that often leave much room for discretion as to their application and may or may not bear a significant relationship to current economic realities and values. The field trip and interviews should focus on establishing the relationship between the financial statements or other information gathered and the current economic values.

Furthermore, in only a small minority of cases is pure extrapolation of the past trend a valid indicator of the future results for any business enterprise. Therefore, the third focus of the field trip and interviews is to identify and evaluate the internal and external forces that will generate a set of future results that differ from the past pattern.

Since the analyst usually is trying to assess the company on a going-concern basis, one area of inquiry is identification of patterns or deviations therefrom that will help clarify what does and does not represent ongoing expectations for the company.

Scheduling the Sequence of Steps

Scheduling the sequence of reading and analyzing various aspects of the written material, seeing the company's operations, and conducting interviews are matters that must be worked out to suit each case. Scheduling the various steps should be a priority at the beginning of the valuation, along with defining the valuation assignment, and the schedule should be reviewed and changed as necessary throughout the process.

Generally, it is advisable to prepare in advance a thorough list of questions to ask during the field work. While the specific issues pertinent to the valuation will vary from case to case, it is often useful to review a standard laundry list of questions in preparing a list for a specific valuation to ensure that an important question is not overlooked.

Usually, it is best to intersperse the field work with analysis of the written material. By studying the financial statements and other basic information, the analyst can gain an overview of the company and prepare a list of specific questions that will make the field work more meaningful and productive. Also, after seeing the operation and talking with management, the analyst will be able to read and analyze the written material with greater insight.

The field work also helps identify other steps to take. Among the myriad written materials discussed in the previous chapter, the field trip can resolve whether the analyst needs certain documentation. Some items may be dismissed as irrelevant. Some may be examined at the company offices, without making copies for the analyst's files. In other cases, the field work may turn up circumstances suggesting the need for additional documentation. The field trip to the company also helps identify other sources of information to consult, such as trade associations, periodicals, government agencies, customers, suppliers, and competitors. The analyst can ask many questions that will help in analyzing the financial statements, as discussed in Part III.

The initial screening process for identifying comparative companies can start at the beginning of the valuation process. However, seeing the subject company's facilities and talking with its management generally helps in making the final decision about which companies are most comparable. The field work also may bring to mind certain companies or categories of companies considered similar but overlooked in the comparative company search process conducted at the analyst's office.

For these reasons, it usually is best to visit company facilities and interview management fairly early in the valuation process—after getting and reviewing enough preliminary information to get a general overview of the company. The analyst can then conduct follow-up interviews, if needed, either in person or by telephone.

The following sections present a generalized discussion of interview topics. Naturally, the actual topics and sequence of coverage will vary considerably from one situation to another.

History

The company's history, although rarely the most exciting or important part of the interview process, might be an appropriate beginning. This will give the analyst a perspective on how the business got where it is.

The history should cover when the business, or any of its predecessors, was founded, any acquisitions or divestitures along the way, any changes in the basic form of organization, any major changes in lines of business, and any changes in the geographical areas served. It should also cover major changes in ownership and how they came about, that is, whether from new outside owners buying into the business or from one generation succeeding another.

Although the business's total history should be sketched briefly, the parts most relevant to the valuation analysis usually will be the most recent past. A chronology of major events will help the analyst decide how many years of the company's financial data are relevant to the current valuation and identify any major changes in the business or special circumstances to consider in analyzing the financial statements.

Overview of Company Position and Objectives

The analyst might well begin the discussion of the company's present position by asking for the chief executive officer's perception of the company's economic contribution—in other words, what does the company do, why does it need to be done, and what makes this company particularly well qualified to do it? What is the company's perception of the economic niche into which it fits, and how does it try to do the best job of fitting there? These questions should lead to a general discussion of the company's industry, its particular role within that industry, and its lines of products or services.

The analyst should try to gain an understanding of how the company perceives the industry and the particular aspect of it within which it operates: What are the nature and rate of technological change, and how does this help or hinder the company? What developments or trends are expected in the industry in the foreseeable future, and how will they impact the company? What special industry factors have a bearing on this particular company?

Some other points to include are how the company perceives its own major strengths and weaknesses and the key factors that enable it to operate profitably, such as a unique product or product line, brand name acceptance, marketing strength, and reputation for service. Also, to what extent is the company the master of its own destiny, and how much are its fortunes subject to outside forces over which it has no control?

If the company has relatively new operations, this might be a good place in the interview to inquire how management views their fit in the total picture and how the operations are working out. This should include the progress and prognosis for new products or services, locations, channels of distribution, and other aspects of the operation that may be in a developmental or transitional stage.

The analyst should explore with top management the company's program for capital expenditures, acquisitions, divestitures, and research and development. These inquiries should cover how much is being spent, for what, and how it is being financed. The analyst will want to know the company's program for corporate development, including further development of existing and/or new products or markets.

The analyst should evaluate the advantages of various prospective expenditures and their effect on the company's value. In the case of debt, the cost can be both the direct expense and the cost of the additional risk incurred by increasing the company's financial leverage. If expansion or acquisitions are to be financed by issuing additional stock, the analyst must assess the effect of the potential dilution.

Present management's intention for major aspects of future company policy is much more critical if a minority rather than a controlling interest is being valued. Nevertheless, even in the case of a controlling interest, most prospective buyers would want to know how management sees the major opportunities and problems facing the company and how it plans to deal with them.

The analyst should try to gain a context within which to assess the strength of the company's intangible assets, whether or not they may be carried on the company's books. Does the company have proprietary products or services? If so, what characteristics do they contribute to their market to give them comparative value over the competition? To what extent does the company benefit from brand names, trademarks, copyrights, or patents? How well protected are they, and when do any important ones expire? Does the company enjoy goodwill arising from location, personnel, or other factors?

This Pandora's box of inquiries obviously has such broad potential implications for the valuation and will vary so much from one company to another that only the most general discussion of these topics is possible within the scope of this chapter. In essence, the analyst at this stage of the interviewing is trying to gain an understanding of what moves this machine—at least as those in the driver's seat see it—and what could accelerate it, slow it down, or bring it to a halt.

When the analyst is certain of having obtained a sufficiently broad overview, the logical next step is a more detailed study of the company's markets and marketing.

Markets and Marketing

The interview on marketing should enable the analyst to identify and describe the company's markets and its program for and degree of success in reaching them.

A major part of the marketing aspect of the interview should focus on competition. The analyst should make a list of the firms that the company considers competitors for each product or service and in each market segment it serves. The analyst should attempt to quantify the market share for each segment held by the company and by each major competitor and try to estimate the trends in these market shares.

In such interviews, it is common for the marketing manager to understate the company's competition, usually by defining too narrowly the groups of competing companies or products or by giving inadequate credit to the product acceptability or marketing ability of one or more competitors. Many companies, especially smaller ones, tend to be blind-sided by potential competition that has not yet surfaced. The analyst should conduct the interview to obtain hints of these situations and, in some cases, augment the analysis with interviews of customers, suppliers, and competitors.

One of the most important aspects of the marketing interview is determining how the company competes. Is it through product differentiation, either by uniqueness or quality? Is it heavily based on providing superior service? Is it a matter of providing the customer with wider selections or other conveniences? What is the company's pricing policy, and how is it forced to meet price competition?

It is equally important to identify potential competition. Might another company usurp a portion of the market by opening a competitive location or developing and introducing a technologically comparable or superior product?

Who currently uses and might use the company's products and services, and why? The market should be defined both geographically and by category of customer. What is the economic outlook for the markets the company serves? What are the forces that determine the demand and changes in demand for the company's products or services? Does the market have identifiable seasonal, cyclical, or secular characteristics? Are there technological changes in progress or in prospect that will alter the shape of the market? What does the company do to anticipate and cope with market change, and how effective are its efforts?

Still another consideration is how the company reaches its market both in promotional programs and channels of distribution. To what extent does this conform to or differ from industry norms?

As discussed in Chapter 5, the analyst should try to assess the breadth and stability of the company's market. To what extent can the company rely on repeat business and customer continuity?

The interview should also cover marketing personnel. What is the degree of turnover? Where do the marketing people come from, and where do the departing ones go? What are the structure and level of compensation for marketing people, and how do they compare with the competition?

The marketing interview is a logical time for the analyst to inquire about the order backlog on the valuation date and how it compares with the previous year's level.

The analyst should ask about any changes in the marketing program that are in progress or anticipated. If the company apparently is doing less well than it should in certain respects, what is it doing about that? If the company sees further opportunities, how does it plan to capitalize on them? If competitive forces or other problems are building up, what is the company doing to protect itself?

By the conclusion of the marketing discussion, the analyst should have a good grasp of the company's markets, competition, and marketing program.

Management

Analyzing the ability of management is one of the most subjective aspects of a company valuation; yet in many companies it is a critical or even the most critical factor. Therefore, assessment of management should be a constant and conscious objective of the analyst throughout the field trip and interview process, regardless of the subject being discussed.

The analyst should make a list or organization chart of the key management and analyze their competence, breadth, and depth. An important item to evaluate in most closely held companies is the adequacy of provision for management succession, which often runs from somewhat lacking to nonexistent.

As mentioned in Chapter 5, the analyst should inquire about age, health, and qualifications for each key person. Qualifications will include education and professional credentials, experience, background before joining the company, and history with the company.

The analyst should note each person's compensation package and level of compensation. This includes participation in all employee benefit plans, fringe benefits, expense allowances, and other perquisites. Part of the purpose of this inquiry is to help the analyst judge whether key people are being compensated well enough to keep them from being lured to greener pastures. Another purpose is to judge whether there may be excess compensation that the company could reduce if it fell on hard times, either by direct reductions or by replacement of certain personnel with others who could do a comparable job at a lower cost.

The analyst should also inquire about the time and effort devoted by each key person and what the true contribution is to the company's well-being. Many companies carry people—usually family members—at full salary even though they have only a figurehead role and work only occasionally. On the other hand, some senior people who devote only limited hours per month may make a significant contribution because of experience and acumen.

Operations

Obviously, the appropriate line of questioning about operations depends on the type of company, whether manufacturing, merchandising, services, or whatever. The purpose in any case is to learn what operations the company carries out, how efficiently and effectively it does so, and the prospects for either improvement or deterioration.

Supplies

Supplies are vital to the operations of any business enterprise. The analyst should obtain answers to the following questions in the interview process.

To what extent does the company fabricate versus assemble, and how much flexibility does it have in this respect? What are the key supplies and sources of those supplies? How much is the make-or-buy decision within the company's control as conditions change?

Continuity of availability and of pricing are the two key factors the analyst should pursue in questioning about the company's supply situation. The extreme—which is less rare than one might think—is the existence of a single source for a critical supply that if cut off could shut down the company's operations. Most distributorships, for example, can be terminated on 30 days' notice. For many manufacturing companies, one or more raw materials with limited sources of supply are essential to the operation.

The analyst should list key suppliers and alternates, including names of individuals with whom the company deals. He or she also should inquire about supplier contracts or agreements and terms. The analyst may wish to contact suppliers directly, either for additional information about the present or potential supply situation or for references concerning the company's credit, reputation, or other attributes.

Energy

While energy is itself a form of supply, it is important enough in some company situations, especially manufacturing, to be discussed separately. As with other supplies, the critical factors are availability and price. What types of energy does the company use, how much (both in units and cost) does it use, and where do the energy supplies come from? What conservation efforts are being made? Is the company subject to temporary interruption of operations because of energy curtailment? If so, how severe could they be? Is there any possibility that lack of energy will cause permanent shutdown? What impact will future changes in energy costs have on the company's overall cost structure?

Labor

The analyst must be concerned with the continuity of labor availability and cost as well as with the efficiency and effectiveness of the labor force. In taking the facilities tour, the analyst should be alert to clues about labor morale and efficiency in addition to seeing the physical plant and operation.

To what extent is the company unionized? If it is not unionized, have there been attempts to unionize it? To what degree is it unionized compared to others in the industry? What is the history of strikes? What contracts presently exist, when do they expire, and what are the prospects for satisfactory renewal in terms of both acceptable costs and conditions and risks of work stoppage? How do company compensation levels compare with other firms in the industry? Is there an adequate pool of skilled labor in the area? What is the company's experience with personnel turnover, and how does this compare with industry norms?

Regulatory Climate

The analyst should inquire about government regulations that may impinge on the company's operations. To what extent does the company face costs associated with environmental protection or with OSHA? The analyst may wish to examine government inspection sheets and question the costs of compliance. Also, the industry might impose restrictions that affect the company's value. These would be in the form of quality standards or pricing pressures.

To what extent is the company subject to industry regulations? Are there prescribed quality standards in effect? If so, does the company have a problem meeting them? Are there restrictions on pricing, promotional activities, geographical or other expansion, product innovation, or other phases of the company's operations? What is the impact of these regulations on the company's earning capacity, flexibility, and other aspects affecting the company's value?

Plant and Equipment

Usually a company representative will take the analyst on a tour of company facilities. How extensive and detailed this must be varies. One objective of the tour is to give the analyst a better idea of the company's operations from a physical viewpoint. Another is to permit some evaluation of the physical plant's adequacy. The business enterprise appraiser makes such an evaluation only in a general sense. Any real estate or equipment appraisals needed usually are made by appraisers who specialize in those areas.

If the analyst will need to communicate some description of the operations, facilities, or both to someone lacking the opportunity to visit the facilities, such as a judge in a court case, it may be desirable to take a set of pictures while on tour.

The analyst usually will want to include at least a brief description of the facilities in the report. For this purpose, it may help to inquire about sizes, such as acres or square feet, of various sites or buildings. The analyst also should make some notes of the type of construction.

The analyst will want to observe the efficiency of the location and layout and the condition of the facilities. Are they cramped? What is the schedule of use? How much unused capacity is available? What are the opportunities for expanding capacity? Is the equipment modern? Is it well maintained? In general, will the plant be adaptable to future cost savings, or will it be a source of increasing operating costs? The analyst should also discuss these points with management.

Inventory

While touring the facilities, the analyst will have the opportunity to observe inventories on hand. This can be any combination of raw materials, work in progress, or goods available for sale or shipment. The analyst is interested in how much inventory is obsolete, damaged, excessive, or inadequate. The analyst should ask for assistance in interpreting the status of inventory. The facilities tour offers a good time to inquire about inventory turnover and quality.

As discussed elsewhere in this book, there may be a significant amount of near worthless inventory carried on the books or of valuable inventory in stock that has been written off. Since this variable can have a large effect on reported earnings and net worth in some types of companies, it is a subject worth considerable attention.

Financial Analysis

As an aid in financial analysis, the analyst may conduct interviews with the chief financial officer, controller, other company personnel, or the firm's outside accountant or attorney. For suggestions to accomplish the most comprehensive results in conducting this stage of the interview process, the reader is referred to Part III, "Analyzing Financial Statements," especially Chapter 11, which suggests many possible adjustments to the financial statements. Many of the questions suggested in that chapter are not referred to separately in this section.

Exhibit 6–1 lists illustrative inquiries to be made in reviewing financial statements. Such a list can be a useful reference and help prevent the analyst from inadvertently missing important questions. While this list of inquiries was designed for accountants, it is applicable for the business appraiser as well.

Financial Position

Interviews can contribute a great deal toward genuine understanding of a company's financial position beyond simply what the financial statements show, and the depth of inquiry will be beneficial.

Current Assets.   The reliability of the accounts receivable depends on the collectibility of the individual accounts. The analyst should go over the aging of accounts receivable with a financial officer, covering specific overdue accounts. One indicator of the receivables' worth is the amount of bad-debt write-offs during the previous couple of years. What is the policy for bad-debt write-offs? Are there doubtful or disputed accounts beyond those reflected in the Allowance (or Reserve) for Doubtful Accounts? Are there accounts written off that probably will be collected? What is the average collection period? In other

EXHIBIT 6-1

Illustrative Inquiries to be Made in Review of Financial Statements

The inquiries to be made in review of financial statements are a matter of the accountant's judgment. In determining his inquiries, an accountant may consider (a) the nature and materiality of the items, (b) the likelihood of misstatement, (c) knowledge obtained during current and previous engagements, (d) the stated qualifications of the entity's accounting personnel, (e) the extent to which a particular item is affected by management's judgment, and (f) inadequacies in the entity's underlying financial data. The following list of inquiries is for illustrative purposes only. The inquiries do not necessarily apply to every engagement, nor are they meant to be all-inclusive. This list is not intended to serve as a program or checklist in the conduct of a review; rather it describes the general areas in which inquiries might be made. For example, the accountant may feel it is necessary to make several inquiries to answer one of the questions listed below, such as item 3(a).

(1) General
  (a) What are the procedures for recording, classifying, and summarizing transactions (relates to each section discussed below)?
  (b) Do the general ledger control accounts agree with subsidiary records (for example, receivables, inventories, investments, property and equipment, accounts payable, accrued expenses, non-current liabilities)?
  (c) Have accounting principles been applied on a consistent basis?

(2) Cash
  (a) Have bank balances been reconciled with book balances?
  (b) Have old or unusual reconciling items between bank balances and book balances been reviewed and adjustments made where necessary?
  (c) Has a proper cutoff of cash transactions been made?
  (d) Are there any restrictions on the availability of cash balances?
  (e) Have cash funds been counted and reconciled with control accounts?

(3) Receivables
  (a) Has an adequate allowance been made for doubtful accounts?
  (b) Have receivables considered uncollectible been written off?
  (c) If appropriate, has interest been reflected?
  (d) Has a property cutoff of sales transactions been made?
  (e) Are there any receivables from employees and related criteria?
  (f) Are any receivables pledged, discounted, or factored?
  (g) Have receivables been properly classified between current and non-current?

(4) Inventories
  (a) Have inventories been physically counted? If not, how have inventories been determined?
  (b) Have general ledger control accounts been adjusted to agree with physical?
  (c) If physical inventories are taken at a date other than the balance sheet date, what procedures were used to record changes in inventory between the date of the physical inventory and the balance sheet date?
  (d) Were consignments in or out considered in taking physical inventories?
  (e) What is the basis for valuation?
  (f) Does inventory cost include material, labor, and overhead where applicable?
  (g) Have write-downs for obsolescence or cost in excess of net realizable value been made?
  (h) Have proper cutoffs of purchases, goods in transit, and returned goods been made?
  (i) Are there any inventory encumbrances?

(5) Prepaid expenses
  (a) What is the nature of the amounts included in prepaid expenses?
  (b) How are these amounts amortized?

(6) Investments, including loans, mortgages, and intercorporate investments
  (a) Have gains and losses on disposal been reflected?
  (b) Has investment income been reflected?
  (c) Has appropriate consideration been given to the classification of investments between current and noncurrent, and the difference between the cost and market value of investments?
  (d) Have consolidation or equity accounting requirements been considered?
  (e) What is the basis of valuation of marketable equity securities?
  (f) Are investments unencumbered?

(7) Property and equipment
  (a) Have gains or losses on disposal of property or equipment been reflected?
  (b) What are the criteria for capitalization of prop-erty and equipment? Have such criteria been applied during the fiscal period?
  (c) Does the repairs and maintenance account only include items of an expense nature?
  (d) Are property and equipment stated at cost?
  (e) What are the depreciation methods and rates? Are they appropriate and consistent?
  (f) Are there any unrecorded additions, retirements, abandonments, sales, or trade-ins?
  (g) Does the entity have material lease agreements? Have they been properly reflected?
  (h) Is any property or equipment mortgaged or otherwise encumbered?

(8) Other assets
  (a) What is the nature of the amounts included in other assets?
  (b) Do these assets represent costs that will benefit future periods? What is the amortization policy? Is it appropriate?
  (c) Have other assets been properly classified between current and non-current?
  (d) Are any of these assets mortgaged or otherwise encumbered?

(9) Accounts and notes payable and accrued liabilities
  (a) Have all significant payables been reflected?
  (b) Are all bank and other short-term liabilities properly classified?
  (c) Have all significant accruals, such as payroll, interest, and provisions for pension and profit-sharing plans been reflected?
  (d) Are there any collateralized liabilities?
  (e) Are there any payables to employees and related parties?

(10) Long-term liabilities
  (a) What are the terms and other provisions of long-term liability agreements?
  (b) Have liabilities been properly classified between current and noncurrent?
  (c) Has interest expense been reflected?
  (d) Has there been compliance with restrictive covenants of loan agreements?
  (e) Are any long-term liabilities collateralized or subordinated?

(11) Income and other taxes
  (a) Has provision been made for current and prior-year federal income taxes payable?
  (b) Have any assessments or reassessments been received? Are there tax examinations in process?
  (c) Are there timing differences? If so, have deferred taxes been reflected?
  (d) Has provision been made for state and local income, franchise, sales, and other taxes payable?

EXHIBIT 6-1

Illustrative Inquiries to be Made in Review of Financial Statements
(Continued)

(12) **Other liabilities, contingencies, and commitments**
  (a) What is the nature of the amounts included in other liabilities?
  (b) Have other liabilities been properly classified between current and non-current?
  (c) Are there any contingent liabilities, such as discounted notes, drafts, endorsements, warranties, litigation, and unsettled asserted claims? Are there any unasserted potential claims?
  (d) Are there any material contractual obligations for construction or purchase of real property and equipment any commitments or options to purchase or sell company securities?

(13) **Equity**
  (a) What is the nature of any changes in equity accounts?
  (b) What classes of capital stock have been authorized?
  (c) What is the par or stated value of the various classes of stock?
  (d) Do amounts of outstanding shares of capital stock agree with subsidiary records?
  (e) Have capital stock preferences, if any, been disclosed?
  (f) Have stock options been granted?

  (g) Has the entity made any acquisitions of its own capital stock?
  (h) Are there any restrictions on retained earnings or other capital?

(14) **Revenue and expenses**
  (a) Are revenues from the sale of major products and services recognized in the appropriate period?
  (b) Are purchases and expenses recognized in the appropriate period and properly classified?
  (c) Do the financial statements include discontinued operations or items that might be considered extraordinary?

(15) **Other**
  (a) Are there any events that occurred after the end of the fiscal period that have a significant effect on the financial statements?
  (b) Have actions taken at stockholder, board of directors, or comparable meetings that affect the financial statements been reflected?
  (c) Has there been any material transactions between related parties?
  (d) Are there any material uncertainties? Is there any change in the status of material uncertainties previously disclosed?

SOURCE: *Statements on Standards for Accounting and Revenues Services No. 1,* Compilation and Review of Financial Statements, issued by the Accounting and Review Services Committee, American Institute of Certified Public Accountants, Inc., New York, December 1978, pp. 24-25. Copyright©1979 by the American Institute of Certified Public Accountants, Inc.

words, to what extent does the net accounts receivable figure represent an amount that is genuinely collectible, and how long will it take to collect it? What is the prognosis for collection of any notes or other receivables? The analyst should explore the company's cash management techniques.

How is inventory accounted for? How does physical flow relate to the accounting flow? To what extent does the inventory figure represent the value of the inventory in a going-concern context? What is the company's write-off policy?

Fixed Assets.   One objective of inquiry about fixed assets is to get some feeling for the extent to which the company's carrying values of fixed assets compare with those of other companies in the industry owning similar assets. This can be especially relevant if an asset value or comparative price-to-book value approach will be a factor in the valuation.

How do the depreciation lives and methods compare with industry norms? What is happening to replacement costs of the kind of assets used in the business?

The analyst should discuss the probable time and cost of liquidating all or any part of the assets, as well as the potential net realizable value if possible liquidation is another factor to consider in the valuation.

Other Assets.   Intangible assets, such as goodwill, patents and trademarks, or copyrights, should be discussed to get management's perception, to determine accounting practices, and to gain an appreciation for the legal protection of the intangible rights.

Current Liabilities.   Usually the most important purpose of inquiry regarding current liabilities is to get an understanding of the company's banking relationship. Does it have a line of credit? What are the costs and terms? Does the company have unused credit, or is it under pressure to pay down on a bank line?

An important current liability is accounts payable. Practices for aging accounts payable should be determined. What are the company's relationships with creditors? What are its suppliers terms? Does the company have slack, or is it under pressure on its use of accounts payable? What are the terms, conditions, and expectations regarding other current liability items?

Capital Structure.   Questions to ask about the capital structure will vary greatly. If there is long-term debt maturing in the foreseeable future, what are the company's options and intentions about rolling it over? How much more term debt, if needed or wanted, is available to the company, and from what sources and on what terms? Are personal guarantees on company loans necessary? If so, by whom and to what extent? Are the guarantors adequately compensated for these guarantees?

In order to investigate potential dilution, the analyst should ascertain the prognosis concerning exercise of any convertible notes, puts, calls, warrants, or options. What changes in the capital structure might be anticipated? Will there be equity financing or debt financing?

In virtually every case, the analyst will want to discuss who owns the shares currently outstanding and what are the shareholders' relationships to one another.

Off-Balance-Sheet Items.   This category may include both potential liability and potential asset items which should be investigated. Is there potential legal liability, such as for compliance with environmental protection, OSHA, or other government regulations? Is there product liability? Liability for service under warranties? Unfunded pension liability or an overfunded pension? Is the company a co-signer or guarantor on any debt? Is there any potential tax liability or refund? Are any tax losses carried forward? Are there leases on real or personal property, and if so, what are the terms? Is litigation pending? What is its substance, and are there any pending judgments that might be either favorable or unfavorable?

Analysis of Profitability

Budgeting is an important area of inquiry. To what extent does the company do profitability or cash flow budgeting or both? How far into the future, in how much detail, and how often is the budget reviewed? How accurate have been the company's past budgets? A review of past and current budgets can be a good starting point from which to gain greater insight into the company's profit history and potential. Does the company use budgeted versus actual comparisons? As discussed in

Chapter 7, "Economic and Industry Data," the analyst may wish to evaluate the reasonableness of the budget forecasting in light of the economic and industry outlook data developed.

In analyzing the company's sales, the analyst should attempt to distinguish between changes in unit sales and price changes. Such a distinction should help the analyst in evaluating the company's outlook.

If the company is involved in multiple products or product lines, it is desirable to try to identify which are most profitable and why. What is the outlook for maintaining profitability of the good ones and improving that of the poor ones?

A useful area of discussion is the company's fixed and variable costs and their elements—that is, the degree of operating leverage. *Operating leverage* refers to the existence of fixed costs in a company's cost structure (see Chapter 12, "Comparative Ratio Analysis," for a more complete discussion). To what extent can increased or decreased volume be expected to affect the company's operating margins?

What elements have determined the company's effective tax rate in the past, and to what extent might the effective tax rate differ in the future?

What can be done to make the company more profitable? What will it cost? What are the risks?

Identification of Changes or Aberrations

To what extent are changes more or less predictable, such as seasonal, cyclical, or secular patterns? If accounts receivable, accounts payable, inventory, or other variables are abnormally high or low, why is this so and what does it imply?

Should any special circumstance be taken into account on the valuation date, such as unusual present or imminent competitive pressure, supply problems, or labor problems?

In analyzing past operations, what is reflected in the statements for various periods that are not representative of the company's current and prospective operations? Such items could include results of discontinued operations or results that occurred under unusual conditions.

Were there any changes in accounting policy during the time under review?

Insurance

Whether the company carries insurance can be significant for its viability. An uninsured catastrophe could wipe out the business. How adequate is the company's insurance coverage, if any? The questions about insurance should investigate the adequacy of key-man life insurance, product and other liability insurance, and all forms of casualty insurance, including fire, theft, and business interruption. If no insurance is carried, the analyst should determine adequacy of reserves.

Management Emoluments

Many expenses that are of a management emolument nature may not be thought of as employee benefits or compensation to the closely held company that has incurred such expenses as a matter of routine for a generation or more. The analyst, therefore, may have to do some probing to identify all such items and their magnitude.

The analyst should find out about the company's fleets of vehicles, including cars, boats, and airplanes. To what extent are they dispensable? What is the company supporting in terms of condominiums or recreational locations or activities? How big is the travel and entertainment budget, and how much could be trimmed? What salaries, bonuses, profit-sharing arrangements, or other benefits could be reduced or eliminated if necessary?

Dividend Policy

What is the company's dividend-paying policy? The analyst should try to obtain a complete record of past dividend payments. Beyond that, the analyst should assess both the company's dividend-paying capacity and intentions with regard to dividends if dividend-paying capacity exists.

Prior Transactions or Offers

The previous chapter suggested that the written material include a list of prior transactions in the stock. It might be a good idea to verify whether the record so furnished is complete. It is somewhat easy to overlook one or more past transactions. What price was paid for stock, or was it bonus stock at no cost to the recipient?

Catch-All Question

If the person doing the field work for a business valuation reviews this chapter and collects the questions applicable to the particular company into a supplementary list, the result should be a reasonably comprehensive facility visit and set of interviews. This will be especially true if the person is an experienced interviewer, because the ramifications of many interview subjects and techniques are not conducive to explanation in a single book, much less in one chapter.

Nevertheless, even the most experienced interviewer may fail to ask just the right questions to elicit responses on every aspect bearing on the valuation. Therefore, somewhere near the end of each interview the analyst might ask each interviewee a catch-all question. This can be something like: "Is there any information that you know of that hasn't been covered and that could have a bearing on the valuation of the company?" This should help protect the analyst against material omissions in the questioning process and place the burden on company management if they are deliberately withholding material information.

Interviewing Professionals Related to the Company

It may not be necessary to interview outside professionals related to the company, but it usually is a good idea to get their names during the company interview in the event it might be desirable. It may be necessary to have management contact those individuals to grant them permission to release pertinent information or discuss company issues. Sometimes interviews with the company's outside professionals are helpful not only for specific technical information but for independent viewpoints on certain aspects of the company.

Attorney

The most common reason for interviewing the company's attorney arises from the need for a legal interpretation of a company document or contract or for an assessment of a pending lawsuit or potential litigation.

There are times when the analyst may work very closely with the company's attorney. If, for example, the company is structuring a recapitalization, buy-sell agreement, or ESOP, the wording of the legal documents may have a considerable bearing on the valuation. In such cases, the attorney may want the analyst's opinion about the impact of certain prospective provisions on the valuation.

Independent Accountant

It may be necessary for the analyst to interview the company's outside independent accountant, usually to get an explanation or interpretation of something in the financial statements, consult working papers, or obtain other details with which to augment the statements. This is most likely to be necessary if the statements are not audited and do not contain all the footnote information normally found in audited statements. If there is a qualification to the statement, the analyst may seek further amplification of details.

Banker

If the company's banking relationship is important, or in jeopardy, it is a good idea to hear first hand how the banker perceives it. The banker also may be a good source of general information about the company and the industry.

Other Outside Interviews

Considerable discretion is called for in conducting certain outside interviews.

Customers

In some circumstances, the company's customers can be a good source of information. They can tell why they use the company's products and discuss the outlook for their own businesses to help the analyst evaluate the continuing demand for the products or services.

The customers may be a much better source of information about the competition than the company itself. They can describe their own perceptions of differences in product design, quality, service, and pricing and explain their own purchase decision criteria.

It may also be desirable, if possible, to contact former customers to find out why they no longer patronize the company.

Suppliers

Suppliers may be good sources of information about the company and may also be helpful in identifying and evaluating the competition. Particularly if the company deals in a technological area, the suppliers may be able to explain technology changes in the industry and, in some cases, make some evaluation of the company's expertise.

Competitors

Often it is possible to interview competitors. In the majority of cases, this has to be done without disclosing the purpose of the interview to avoid violating confidentiality. If a competitor is a publicly held company, it is accustomed to being interviewed by analysts, and the interview should be no problem. If the company is private, it will probably be necessary to explain the purpose of the interview in a general sense, being careful not to divulge any confidences. It will be up to the private company, of course, to choose to cooperate or not cooperate.

The analyst may ask the competitor many of the same questions asked of the subject company. For instance, demand, supply, and pricing factors, technological change in the industry, and relative merits of the products and services of the various companies in the industry might be discussed, including, of course, the subject company.

Former Employees

Sometimes former employees may be useful as information sources— about why they left and other aspects of the company as seen in hindsight and from an objective viewpoint.

Conclusion

A good analyst can gain a great deal of insight into a company through the field trip and management interview process. The preceding queries should provide the analyst with a perspective on the company being valued and yield a multitude of details relevant to the valuation assignment. What the analyst gets from the process will depend partly on the thoroughness of preparation and partly on the degree of cooperation provided by the subject company and those being interviewed.

Chapter 7

Economic and Industry Data

It is hard to overemphasize the importance of thorough and relevant economic and industry research for a well-prepared valuation. First, Revenue Ruling 59-60 requires consideration of "the economic outlook in general and the condition and outlook of the specific industry in particular." Second, an understanding of the economic and industry outlook is fundamental to developing reasonable expectations about the subject company's prospects. This chapter introduces some of the most useful sources of economic and industry information that can bear on a company valuation.

This chapter is organized in a top-down fashion. Because the general economic outlook exerts some influence on all industries and all companies, this chapter starts off with a discussion of general economic research, highlighting useful sources for researching both the national and regional economies. The chapter then turns to the topic of industry research for both general industry information and composite company statistics. Since the potential sources are so numerous, the chapter concludes with references to several indexes of economic and industry data sources.

Before discussing the data sources themselves, I would like to emphasize one point. All too often, I have seen appraisal reports include economic and industry outlooks for no other apparent reason than to take up space—outlooks that are obviously boilerplate. Economic and industry outlooks included in appraisal reports should be clearly tied to the company being valued. It is particlularly important to point out how the outlooks will affect the subject company and to focus on those issues most relevant to a thorough understanding of the company's competitive position in its market. As a corollary to this issue, it is important to understand the subject company's relationship to the structure of the industry as a whole. Each segment of an industry or an economy may be affected differently by a particular trend or development. Therefore, it is important to focus on the logical impact of each relevant factor on the subject company, whether positive or negative. This last—and most critical—step of applying economic and industry research to the valuation of the subject company is too often given short shrift.

National Economic Data

Generally, economic outlooks should include a discussion of each of the most important leading economic indicators. For example, it typically is appropriate for appraisal reports to discuss such variables as economic growth—usually measured by real gross national product (GNP) on a national level or real gross state product (GSP) on a state level—inflation, employment, consumer spending, business investment, construction, interest rates, and population trends. The following sections outline some of the most useful sources of economic information for both national and regional economic research.

In addition to the economic indicators discussed above, the economic outlook should include the most relevant national economic issues at the time of the valuation. In the economic environment of the late 1980s, for example, such issues would include the U.S. budget deficit, the U.S. foreign trade deficit, and tax reform. Because of the huge variety of national economic data available, I can mention only a few of the most generally useful sources. Beyond that, I refer the reader to the section at the end of the chapter on indexing services that can lead to the specific types of economic data sought.

U.S. Government Publications

The plethora of U.S. government publications containing some kind of economic data is mind-boggling. Four of the most widely used monthly publications are the *Federal Reserve Bulletin, Survey of Current Business, Business Conditions Digest,* and *Monthly Labor Review.* Two widely used annuals are the *Statistical Abstract of the United States* and the *Economic Report of the President.*

Each monthly issue of the *Federal Reserve Bulletin,* published by the Board of Governors of the Federal Reserve System, contains articles relating to monetary policy and issues that affect the monetary climate, plus many tables of domestic and international financial and nonfinancial statistics. In addition, the February or March issue usually includes lengthy articles on how the national economy fared in the previous year and what is expected for the current year. One of the most useful aspects of the *Federal Reserve Bulletin* for business valuations is that it provides insight into many financial components of the economy that directly bear on companies' cost of capital, especially various categories of current interest rates. Series include interest rates on various maturities of U.S. government obligations, new issues of AAA utility bonds, various grades of seasoned corporate bond issues, mortgages, bank prime rates, other short-term rates, preferred and common stock yields, various stock price indexes, housing permits, starts and completions, various consumer and producer price indexes, and other economic series, such as gross national product and personal income. Most of the statistics are quoted monthly, going back for several months, and annually, dating back a few years; some are quoted on a quarterly basis.

In addition to the *Federal Reserve Bulletin,* each of the 12 district Federal Reserve banks puts out a monthly publication, with varying emphasis on national versus regional information. The Federal Reserve Bank of Cleveland's *Economic Trends,* published monthly, is a particularly useful source of historical statistical data and narrative as well as forward-looking information. This publication is quite comprehensive in its coverage of the U.S. economy and also includes information on foreign exchange markets and international trade.

The *Survey of Current Business,* produced monthly by the U.S. Bureau of Economic Analysis, is considered by some to be the most important single source for current business statistics. It covers a broad range of business indicators, price series, employment figures, and business activity data. A biennial supplement, *Business Statistics,* presents definitions and sources for the many statistical series, plus a historical record of the statistics.

Business Conditions Digest, also produced monthly by the U.S. Bureau of Economic Analysis, emphasizes the so-called cyclical indicators. These are classified by leading, coincident, and lagging indicators and by the type of economic process that each represents, such as employment, production, consumption, capital investment, inventory changes, prices and profits, and money and credit. All together, some 300 statistical series are tracked each month. The information is presented on a monthly or quarterly basis for the most recent three years, with annual data going back as far as 1948.

The *Monthly Labor Review* is the premier journal of the U.S. Bureau of Labor Statistics. In addition to articles on labor topics, the *Monthly Labor Review* includes statistics on employment, unemployment, price indexes, wages and other compensation, and labor productivity. The data in the *Monthly Labor Review* are accumulated in the *Handbook of Labor Statistics.* This publication is intended to be an annual compilation but has been done less frequently in recent years.

The *Statistical Abstract of the United States* is published annually by the U.S. Bureau of the Census. The 32 sections of this volume run to almost 1,000 pages and include data on virtually every conceivable subject. Some topics potentially of interest include the labor force, employment, and earnings; income, expenditures, and wealth; prices; banking, finance, and insurance; business enterprise; energy; transportation; agriculture, forests, and forest products; fisheries; mining and mineral products; construction and housing; and manufacturers. The *Abstract* is also valuable as a reference for additional sources.

The *Economic Report of the President,* prepared annually by the U.S. Council of Economic Advisers, is another valuable source of summary data on the U.S. economy. Released each year in January or February, the document is essentially a report from the executive branch to Congress on the state of the economy. About two thirds of the report consists of narrative analysis of the economy, with the remainder devoted to statistical tables. An important feature of the narrative section is a five-year outlook for the U.S. economy, including projections for GNP and other key indicators. This annual report is updated monthly in *Economic Indicators.*

An additional resource, which is not published by the U.S. government, is the *American Statistics Index.* Published by Congressional Information Service, it provides monthly, quarterly, and annual indexes and abstracts covering all statistical data published by U.S. government departments, agencies, and offices.

Business Periodicals and Statistical Services

Business periodicals such as *Business Week, Forbes, Fortune, Barron's, Business Month,* and *The Wall Street Journal* are good sources of timely information on the national economy, as well as other types of information. In every issue, both *Business Week* and *Fortune* include forecasts for certain segments of the economy and articles on recent economic developments. They and other magazines also publish extensive economic forecasts in their January issues. *The Wall Street Journal* is a particularly valuable source for the most current national economic information, since it is published daily. In addition to frequent articles on the most recent economic developments, *The Wall Street Journal* includes a great deal of information on the financial markets. By using *The Wall Street Journal/Barron's Index,* which lists articles by subject and by company, the analyst can also find historical economic information in both *The Wall Street Journal* and *Barron's.*

Standard & Poor's (S&P) *Statistical Service,* which is updated monthly, is one of the best sources of summary economic data. The S&P *Statistical Service* consists of two parts: a *Current Statistics* volume, issued monthly, and a set of *Basic Statistics* volumes that provide historical data. Each current issue provides monthly data for the past three years, together with annual averages or totals for each year. *Current Statistics* includes a wide range of economic indicators, heavily weighted toward banking and investment statistics. *Basic Statistics* is published in 10 volumes by topic, ranging from "Building and Building Materials" to "Agricultural Products." It also provides the annual *Security Price Index Record,* which lists daily stock and bond averages for industry groups. S&P's *Trends & Projections* is a valuable source for more information on the economic outlook. This monthly publication includes concise analyses of the current economic situation as well as the expected outlook for the near future. The back page of *Trends & Projections* offers quarterly and annual projections for GNP, components of GNP, income and profits, prices, interest rates, and other key indicators.

The *Handbook of Basic Economic Statistics* is another commercial publication offering comprehensive coverage of general economic data. It is published monthly by the Economic Statistics Bureau, a private company in Washington, D.C.

Banks, Utilities, and Private Companies

Many companies that serve a broad cross section of the population compile economic data for various purposes, much of which is available in published form. Because of the almost universal nature of the populations they serve, banks and utilities tend to publish most of these data. Most large stock brokerage firms also have one or more staff economists and generally have available published analyses of the economic outlook and its various aspects.

One of the advantages of bank, utility, and other privately compiled data over many government sources is that they tend to be more up to date. A particularly important advantage to the valuation analyst is that private company sources tend to be more forward looking than government sources. This characteristic is especially valuable because any business valuation has at least implicit future expectations; thus, the more explicit the available data on future expectations, the better the valuation will be.

Summary of Key National Economic Series

For the convenience of its analysts, my firm publishes internally a summary of the national economic series to which we refer most frequently. A sample of that summary, along with the specific source for each item, appears in Exhibit 7–1.

Regional Economic Data

In addition to data on the national economic outlook, it is sometimes appropriate to gather data on the outlook for the region or regions in which the subject company operates. The regional economic outlook is more relevant in some cases than in others. More often than not, however, the outlook for a specific city, county, or group of counties, cities, or states is relevant to the valuation of a particular company. For example, in Chapter 14, "A Sample Report," the outlook for Baltimore, Maryland; Washington, D.C.; and Norfolk, Virginia, particularly in terms of personal income and retail sales, is very relevant to the valuation of JMK, a consumer electronics retailer. It is crucial to recognize the importance of properly defining the region to be researched for a particular valuation. Even within the same state, the economic outlook can differ dramatically in different locales.

There are several possible sources of regional economic data. However, the quality of data the various sources provide may vary by location. State and city agencies, such as a state employment division, a regional planning council, or an economic development commission, regional or local banks, local publications (magazines and newspapers), and city chambers of commerce are valuable starting points for regional economic research. The chamber of commerce is particularly good because it generally has both economic and demographic information, such as population, sources of employment, income, age distribution, and so on, and may provide additional sources of information for the area. State and regional agencies generally are good sources for population and employment projections, which are often very useful since they are forward looking.

Another useful source of regional economic information is *Sales and Marketing Management Annual Survey of Buying Power,* published annually by Sales and Marketing Management. This periodical is an excellent source of information on retail sales, personal income, population, and demographics for all 50 states, broken down by metropolitan areas and counties. Retail sales are broken down by store group and merchandise line. This periodical also forecasts population and retail sales by metropolitan area and county.

EXHIBIT 7-1

Willamette Management Associates, Inc., Economic Indicators and Investment Trends

	1983 1st Q	1983 2nd Q	1983 3rd Q	1983 4th Q	1984 1st Q	1984 2nd Q	1984 3rd Q	1984 4th Q	1985 1st Q	1985 2nd Q	1985 3rd Q	1985 4th Q	1986 1st Q	1986 2nd Q	1986 3rd Q	1986 4th Q	1987 1st Q	1987 2nd Q
Economic Indicators																		
1. Real GNP Growth (1% increase)[a]	2.6	8.7	7.6	4.8	10.1	7.1	2.7	3.9	0.3	1.9	3.0	0.7	3.7	0.6	2.2	3.3	4.4	2.6
2. GNP Implicit Price Deflator[a]	5.5	4.5	3.6	4.2	4.4	3.3	3.6	2.4	5.4	2.6	2.9	3.3	2.5	2.0	2.8	1.7	4.2	3.8
3. Consumer Price Index[a]	(0.4)	4.2	4.8	4.8	5.0	3.7	3.6	3.9	3.3	4.2	2.6	4.3	1.4	(1.7)	2.5	2.9	5.3	4.3
4. National Unemployment Rate[b]	10.4	10.1	9.4	8.5	7.9	7.5	7.5	7.2	7.3	7.3	7.2	7.0	7.1	7.2	6.9	7.0	6.6	6.1
5. Housing Starts (000s)[c]	1,592	1,743	1,679	1,666	1,948	1,826	1,638	1,630	1,849	1,693	1,653	1,882	1,960	1,852	1,652	1,621	1,749	1,590
Interest Rates																		
6. Prime Rate[d]	10.50	10.50	11.00	11.00	11.50	13.00	12.75	10.75	10.50	9.50	9.50	9.50	9.00	8.50	7.50	7.50	7.75	8.25
7. 13-Week T-Bill[e]	8.30	8.82	9.05	8.96	9.44	9.94	10.41	8.16	8.57	7.01	7.08	7.07	6.59	6.21	5.19	5.42	5.48	5.81
8. 1-Year T-Note[e]	9.82	10.21	10.49	10.85	11.50	13.19	11.98	10.38	10.66	8.81	8.74	8.11	7.24	7.26	6.72	6.51	6.69	7.35
9. 7-Year T-Note[e]	10.25	10.72	11.11	11.53	12.21	13.56	12.47	11.65	11.89	10.11	10.11	8.86	7.71	7.66	7.52	7.14	7.40	8.23
10. 30-Year T-Bond[e]	10.60	10.86	11.21	11.76	12.37	13.56	12.28	11.65	11.77	10.44	10.51	9.24	8.00	7.91	8.16	7.79	7.99	8.75
Investment Trends																		
11. Merrill Lynch Ready Asset Trust Money Market Fund[e]	NA	8.22	8.79	8.94	9.15	10.21	10.49	8.31	8.03	7.09	7.11	7.22	6.88	6.17	5.30	5.46	5.44	5.46
12. 1-Month Commercial Paper[f]	8.48	9.03	9.28	9.50	9.86	11.23	10.94	8.55	9.23	7.38	7.86	7.62	7.08	6.63	5.61	5.88	6.40	6.85
13. Municipal Bonds (Average Yield)[e]	9.35	9.51	9.47	9.80	9.92	10.73	10.47	9.99	9.77	8.91	9.53	8.41	7.25	7.69	7.17	6.91	7.01	7.91
14. Corporate Bonds (Composite)[e]																		
aa	11.53	11.83	11.91	12.50	12.06	14.03	12.87	12.04	12.48	11.10	11.20	10.07	9.21	9.36	9.37	8.06	9.00	9.57
a	11.81	11.99	12.22	12.70	13.42	14.34	13.21	12.32	12.61	11.37	11.52	10.43	9.36	9.57	9.57	9.29	9.05	9.74
bbb	12.45	12.65	12.91	13.41	13.95	15.22	14.03	13.03	13.14	11.74	11.93	11.03	10.13	10.22	10.01	9.67	9.55	10.26
Corporate Bonds (Industrials)																		
aa	11.39	11.63	11.10	12.29	12.91	13.83	12.66	11.95	12.34	11.19	11.22	10.13	9.35	9.46	9.52	9.31	9.15	9.64
a	11.10	11.80	12.13	12.45	13.29	14.15	13.06	12.24	12.27	11.34	11.41	10.33	9.04	9.63	9.65	9.45	9.04	9.66
bbb	12.46	12.72	12.89	13.07	13.64	14.97	14.15	13.18	12.91	11.75	11.90	11.13	10.46	10.36	10.08	9.81	9.67	10.16
15. Dow Jones Industrial Average[g]	1130.15	1216.90	1233.75	1255.95	1162.00	1110.35	1217.70	1218.09	1266.78	1335.46	1320.79	1513.53	1739.22	1885.26	1774.18	1895.95	2390.34	2436.86
16. S&P 400 Industrials[h]																		
Price Index	171.68	189.98	187.38	186.24	180.14	174.73	187.41	186.36	201.67	211.92	203.67	234.56	263.51	279.78	258.51	335.53	330.17	352.98
Price/Earnings Multiple	13.32	14.63	13.60	12.64	12.64	10.02	10.52	10.38	11.44	12.97	13.09	15.39	17.56	18.05	18.40	18.73	21.97	21.76
Dividend Yield (%)	4.19	3.79	3.88	3.96	4.09	4.24	3.93	3.99	3.75	3.60	3.79	3.30	2.98	2.84	3.16	3.02	2.43	2.38
Yearly Total Return on S&P 400 (%)	44	61	43	23	9	(4)	4	4	16	26	13	30	35	36	31	42	23	25
17. S&P 500 Composite[h]																		
Price Index	152.96	168.11	164.40	164.93	159.18	153.18	166.1	166.09	180.66	191.85	182.08	211.28	238.90	250.84	233.60	291.70	284.57	304.00
Price/Earnings Multiple	12.32	13.35	12.52	11.76	10.44	9.45	10.26	10.26	11.02	12.29	11.96	14.46	16.45	17.03		16.72	19.23	21.07
Dividend Yield (%)	4.52	4.13	4.22	4.30	4.51	4.77	4.44	4.44	4.24	4.03	4.31	3.74	3.36	3.23	3.56	3.42	2.86	2.80
Yearly Total Return on S&P 500 (%)	43	60	42	22	9	(5)	4	6	18	30	14	31	37	35	33	46	28	29
18. NASDAQ (OTC) Ind. Price Index[i]	323.52	392.9	353.52	323.68	283.34	270.65	275.16	260.73	297.37	303.82	284.39	330.17	374.65	407.88	345.08	350.19	465.16	452.98
19. Preferred Stock Yields (%)[j]																		
aa	11.17	11.34	11.70	12.18	12.40	13.28	12.31	12.25	11.62	10.25	10.60	10.00	8.61	8.54	8.09	7.98	7.82	8.66
a	11.79	12.05	12.15	12.61	13.12	14.22	13.13	12.97	12.32	10.83	11.05	10.28	9.05	9.32	8.76	8.64	8.36	9.13
bbb	12.51	12.47	12.72	13.34	13.55	14.85	14.28	13.71	12.98	11.97	12.52	11.09	9.78	9.89	9.36	9.27	8.90	9.75
20. Gold (Price for 1 troy oz.)[k]	419.70	412.80	411.50	388.00	394.70	378.10	341.30	319.50	340.40	316.80	322.90	322.80	363.40	343.10	419.40	369.60	409.90	449.75
21. Silver (Price for 1 troy oz.)[k]	10.61	11.75	11.92	8.84	9.65	8.75	7.26	6.69	6.01	6.17	6.06	5.89	5.64	5.15	5.69	5.37	5.71	7.07

Sources:

[a] S&P Trends & Projections. Wall Street Journal
[b] Oregon Labor Trends
[c] Barron's. Wall Street Journal
[d] S&P Outlook and Wall Street Journal
[e] S&P Outlook
[f] S&P Statistical Service. Wall Street Journal
[g] S&P Statistical Service
[h] S&P Statistical Service & WMA calculations
[i] Barron's
[j] Moody's Bond Record
[k] S&P Statistical Service. Wall Street Journal (Handy & Harman)

Industry Data

This section is divided into three parts. The first focuses on the process of researching the industry outlook and briefly discusses some of the most useful sources for industry research. The second covers the various sources of composite financial statistics that can be used for comparison with the subject company. The third overviews sources of information on management compensation.

After reviewing the standard industry sources and while gathering more detailed information on the industry, the analyst should begin developing an outline of the relevant factors and events influencing the industry outlook. It is also advisable to keep a thorough bibliography of all information gathered, including the full name of the source and the date of the publication or meeting. The analyst should also comb through sources as they are found for additional sources of information. Many articles cite individuals or other sources that will provide more informative and authoritative information.

In addition, the analyst must begin analyzing the information to evaluate how the subject company is and will be affected by the various industry trends. For example, how will it be affected by price increases for key commodities? How will it be affected by shifts in demand, changes in technology, or shifts in the competitiveness of the industry? The analyst must consider the possible answers to these questions in the analysis and valuation of the subject company. The industry section of the report should include the analyst's conclusion as to the impact of the industry outlook on the valuation of the subject company, particularly as to how the subject company may respond differently or to a different degree than the comparative companies, as well as provide an overview of the industry outlook at the time of the valuation.

General Industry Data

The first step in conducting industry research is to get a *general overview* of the industry. This will allow the analyst to get a firm grasp on where the subject company fits into the industry and which industry factors or events are most relevant to the subject company. This general overview will also provide enough information about the overall industry to assist the analyst in searching for additional information and analyzing the relevance of new information as it is gathered. Several standard industry sources provide this general overview for most industries.

Standard Industry Sources.   Two standard sources that provide a very good overview of most industries are the *U.S. Industrial Outlook* and Standard & Poor's *Industry Surveys*.

The *U.S. Industrial Outlook* is produced annually by the U.S. Bureau of Industrial Economics. It provides information on the prospects for over 350 industries, focusing on the structure of the industry and the most significant factors influencing it. The *Outlook* usually includes forecasts for industries' revenue growth for the coming year as well as the long term. In addition, this publication provides a very useful list of additional references for each industry covered.

Standard & Poor's *Industry Surveys* is also a useful starting point in researching an industry. It is organized into 36 broad industry groups and indexed for reference into about 500 subgroups. It gives each industry group a reasonably comprehensive background analysis about once a year, with occasional updates in the form of a shorter current analysis. *Industry Surveys* generally includes discussion of the industry's structure, trends, and outlook and a section with financial statistics on publicly traded companies in the industry.

Trade Associations and Trade Magazines.   Perhaps the most valuable source of authoritative information on a particular industry is that industry's trade association(s). Trade associations often collect financial statements from their members and compile composite financial data. More often, though, trade associations publish general industry information and may include annual industry reports or articles in their trade magazines. Generally, the executives of the subject company have information on the industry's trade associations and whether or not such data are available.

The *National Trade & Professional Associations of the United States,* published annually, has a comprehensive directory of existing trade and professional associations. The associations are categorized by industry, by geographic location, and alphabetically. This publication gives the association's address, phone number, and a brief description of its activities and publications. By using this publication, the analyst can develop a list of potential trade associations to call. If a trade association is unwilling to send certain information to nonmembers, the analyst might check with the subject company's management to see if they have the information or can get it directly from the association.

While trade associations often have their own publications, most industries have at least one or two trade magazines as well. If the subject company's management cannot furnish information on relevant trade magazines, the analyst can turn to one of several directories of trade publications. One directory we have found useful is the *Guide to Special Issues and Indexes of Periodicals,* published by the Special Libraries Association in Washington, D.C. This directory classifies periodicals into general industry categories and provides information on each periodical, including the publisher's phone number. An even more comprehensive source is *Business Publication Rates and Data.* While this publication is designed for the magazine advertising industry, it is useful as a directory of industry information sources because it lists periodicals by industry.

After identifying the appropriate periodicals, the analyst can usually obtain them directly from the publishers or a local business library. Often it is worthwhile to phone the publisher and ask if any articles on the industry were published over a time period relevant to the valuation date in order to avoid ordering a year's worth of back issues with no relevant information. While not always successful, it is generally worth trying. Many valuation firms maintain extensive research libraries on various industries.

Government Agencies and Government Publications. Federal and state agencies compile astronomical amounts of data, most of which is indexed in some form or another. However, one disadvantage of government publications is that they often are somewhat outdated by the time they are published. The *Statistical Abstract of the United States* can help direct the analyst to various federal agencies, state agencies, and other sources of industry information. Regulatory agencies are often good sources of data on industries that are or used to be regulated, such as communications, trucking, airlines, food, and drugs. One of the best ways to find relevant government publications is to work with a local business librarian.

Business Press. A wide variety of business publications cover companies and industries on an intermittent basis. *The Wall Street Journal, Fortune, Barron's,* and *Forbes* are but a few of the publications that frequently include industry articles. The two best ways to find these articles are to use a standard reference source such as the *Business Periodicals Index* or *The Wall Street Journal/Barron's Index* or to use an on-line reference copy service such as *NEXIS*. Often, articles in the business press will provide valuable leads to authoritative sources or important industry observers.

Brokerage House Reports and Private Industry Studies. Research reports written by security analysts for publication by brokerage houses generally are very useful sources of information on industries with several publicly traded companies.

One valuable source of brokerage reports is *Corporate and Industry Research Reports* (CIRR). This service consists of a set of microfiche, which in 1986 included the full text of 23,000 research reports issued during 1985 by 62 investment firms. The index, updated quarterly, arranges companies alphabetically by name and by industry and includes a brief abstract of each report. *The Wall Street Transcript* is another important source of announcements and abstracts of brokerage house reports. Some industries are regularly reviewed in extensive industry studies by specialized research or consulting firms, such as Frost and Sullivan, Arthur D. Little, and the Stanford Research Institute. However, for the most part these are extremely expensive and may not be justifiable in all cases.

Contacting Industry Observers Directly. In addition to gathering published data, it is often necessary to contact various types of industry observers directly to get a comprehensive outlook on the particular industry. Often it is useful to talk with security analysts who follow companies in the industry, trade association officials, or other people familiar with the industry in addition to the subject company's management. One source we have found very helpful in locating names and phone numbers for security analysts who follow a particular company or industry is *Nelson's Directory of Wall Street Research,* published annually by W. R. Nelson & Company.

Composite Company Data

The Business Source Books, prepared annually by the Statistics of Income Division, Internal Revenue Service, are by far the most comprehensive set of composite company statistics. However, they generally are about three to four years out of date. They include the *Corporation Source Book, Partnership Source Book,* and *Sole Proprietorship Source Book.* A sample page from the *Corporation Source Book of Statistics of Income* is shown in Exhibit 7–2.

The *Almanac of Business and Industrial Financial Ratios* profiles over 181 industries, showing two tables for each industry. One reports the operating and financial information for corporations with and without net income; the other provides the same information for only those corporations that operated at a profit. Beginning with the 1985 edition, the *Almanac* provides an appendix cross-referencing the industries included by SIC code. All the information in this publication is from corporate income tax returns filed with the Internal Revenue Service. As a result, the *Almanac* has one significant weakness: The data generally are three to four years out of date when published. For example, the 1988 edition covers income tax returns filed for tax years between July 1984 and June 1985.

RMA Annual Statement Studies, published by Robert Morris Associates, offers common-size balance sheets and income statements, plus 16 ratios, for over 340 SIC groups broken down into four size categories based on total assets. This source is especially useful for comparisons with smaller companies. RMA gathers data from approximately 1,500 commercial lending banks across the country that belong to the National Association of Bank Loan and Credit Officers. Data for contractor industries are shown in a separate section in a slightly different format. There is also a finance industry supplement that shows a variety of ratios for several types of finance companies. Also, a bibliography lists additional sources of composite financial data, especially sources that may specialize in data for a particular industry. A sample page from *RMA Annual Statement Studies* is shown in Exhibit 7–3.

One of the primary sources of composite financial information on the larger publicly traded companies is the *Standard & Poor's Analyst's Handbook.* The handbook is published annually, with statement and balance sheet items and related ratios grouped by industry. Approximately 90 industry groups are included, with data going back 30 years. A sample page from the *Standard & Poor's Analyst's Handbook* is shown in Exhibit 7–4.

EXHIBIT 7-2

Sample Page from *Corporation Source Book of Statistics of Income*

1984 CORPORATION SOURCE BOOK OF STATISTICS OF INCOME, WHOLESALE AND RETAIL TRADE:
INCOME TAX RETURNS OF ACTIVE CORPORATIONS WITH ACCOUNTING PERIODS ENDED JULY 1984 THROUGH JUNE 1985-- RETAIL TRADE: FOOD STORES
BALANCE SHEET, INCOME STATEMENT, AND SELECTED ITEMS, BY MINOR INDUSTRY, BY SIZE OF TOTAL ASSETS
(ALL FIGURES ARE ESTIMATES BASED ON SAMPLE--MONEY AMOUNTS AND SIZE OF TOTAL ASSETS ARE IN THOUSANDS OF DOLLARS)

	MAJOR GROUP 38 RETURNS WITH AND WITHOUT NET INCOME		SIZE OF TOTAL ASSETS											
		TOTAL	ZERO ASSETS	1 UNDER 100	100 UNDER 250	250 UNDER 500	500 UNDER 1,000	1,000 UNDER 5,000	5,000 UNDER 10,000	10,000 UNDER 25,000	25,000 UNDER 50,000	50,000 UNDER 100,000	100,000 UNDER 250,000	250,000 OR MORE
1	NUMBER OF RETURNS	50594	3258	23614	11364	6267	3264	2284	242	166	57	29	24	25
2	TOTAL ASSETS	50341942	-	999262	1752056	2201984	2283179	4310066	1666051	2552619	1908408	2117880	3612136	26938302
3	CASH	3843843	-	140217	258904	310324	325718	532426	153412	297639	183192	159807	273018	1209188
4	NOTES AND ACCOUNTS RECEIVABLE	4138413	-	58953	96629	125374	180977	389624	161461	170169	145139	136481	248580	2425027
5	LESS: ALLOWANCE FOR BAD DEBTS	49329	-	*5	5	*807	*1028	10684	1426	2449	1077	1188	8881	21780
6	INVENTORIES	13756194	-	309468	590081	706691	652074	1106921	372436	621345	509952	515191	1003577	7368456
	INVESTMENTS IN GOVT. OBLIGATIONS:													
7	TOTAL	390085	-	-	-	*2115	*6403	*6623	*2817	*14437	*14014	11755	2000	329920
8	OTHER CURRENT ASSETS	1629181	-	21111	30039	81168	87673	100093	48614	122165	70406	80979	92938	893996
9	LOANS TO STOCKHOLDERS	313099	-	12755	33526	50835	42886	62995	11480	17305	*7893	-0	7345	66079
10	MORTGAGE AND REAL ESTATE LOANS	140795	-	*4184	*680	*26308	*3768	29077	*1504	6549	*8278	37890	1222	21334
11	OTHER INVESTMENTS	4003834	-	*3741	41124	106291	115798	306831	164704	161166	144328	88590	176158	269510[illegible]
12	DEPRECIABLE ASSETS	32248251	-	859327	1135947	1285331	1425158	2908910	1081288	1784561	1178842	1572527	2302110	16714250
13	LESS: ACCUMULATED DEPRECIATION	14540313	-	507379	650208	720151	746499	1433695	499245	836430	528837	677088	843854	7096926
14	DEPLETABLE ASSETS	233219	-	-	-	*14465	*4022	*99	-	*155	77	-	7426	206974
15	LESS: ACCUMULATED DEPLETION	*11647	-	-	-	*11528	*68	-	-	*45	5	-	-	-
16	LAND	1883188	-	*24315	29603	43194	79066	150284	73098	106531	82136	87195	151140	1056624
17	INTANGIBLE ASSETS (AMORTIZABLE)	744031	-	25431	100443	28726	17809	39179	32283	20087	66206	81209	101764	230894
18	LESS: ACCUMULATED AMORTIZATION	249066	-	7369	31106	12482	5974	8607	11545	7302	31764	20027	35023	77867
19	OTHER ASSETS	1868163	-	54512	116400	166133	95394	129991	75171	76735	59627	44558	132614	917028
20	TOTAL LIABILITIES	50341942	-	999262	1752056	2201984	2283179	4310066	1666051	2552619	1908408	2117880	3612136	26938302
21	ACCOUNTS PAYABLE	11168327	-	151469	303421	437963	421194	954261	360034	621189	400968	458839	696450	6362538
22	MORT, NOTES, AND BONDS UNDER 1 YR.	2169475	-	136925	132618	133479	155379	322068	120768	112126	183324	95996	182616	594175
23	OTHER CURRENT LIABILITIES	4648880	-	70134	108492	196232	178371	315391	142027	220487	182733	179334	340586	2715094
24	LOANS FROM STOCKHOLDERS	1390731	-	448288	295476	233046	108865	120600	13895	15216	*26156	339	29581	99270
25	MORT, NOTES, BONDS, 1 YR OR MORE	11120132	-	315452	468828	463098	504818	1042852	364449	535844	413323	424584	948009	5638877
26	OTHER LIABILITIES	2207261	-	9546	33642	48633	21502	69808	47649	53581	67119	84675	258972	1512134
27	CAPITAL STOCK	2796249	-	256638	269926	180293	152458	254445	56538	126001	96670	102458	209228	1091595
28	PAID-IN OR CAPITAL SURPLUS	3866029	-	60653	89198	79795	69623	126336	20449	40780	113965	76753	336683	2851795
29	RETAINED EARNINGS, APPROPRIATED	83280	-	*416	*6135	*5082	-	*17691	3089	532	*18399	-	8089	23849
30	RETAINED EARNINGS, UNAPPROPRIATED	11663779	-	-365841	96709	499004	723263	1173368	560841	891240	417114	718725	670741	6278616
31	LESS: COST OF TREASURY STOCK	772202	-	84418	*52388	74641	52294	86753	23689	64377	11361	23822	68820	229640
32	TOTAL RECEIPTS	231671006	1310323	6461033	9747551	13193326	14421627	26099917	8650161	13942092	9416259	10669055	17359726	100399936
33	BUSINESS RECEIPTS	228353145	1242984	6403421	9669018	13094986	14295305	25779557	8531332	13705971	9311435	10513132	17066660	98739344
34	INTEREST	479867	*3821	3073	8682	20461	26089	58628	15699	30637	18315	22218	25312	246932
	INTEREST ON GOVT. OBLIGATIONS:													
35	STATE AND LOCAL	19740	-	-	*72	*530	*33	*8	*31	3110	*478	438	171	14870
	NONQUALIFYING INTEREST & DIVIDENDS													
36	FORMS 1120S	18203	*5	1297	896	*1490	*1446	5650	*1408	*5060	951	-	-	-
37	RENTS	504046	*4298	*6840	*3540	4784	20977	55231	12653	37904	19183	18794	58347	261495
38	ROYALTIES	14625	-	*431	*43	*1743	*472	*3625	*1396	*836	-	123	3569	2308
39	NET S-T CAP GAIN LESS NET L-T LOSS	27011	-	-	-	*319	*156	*473	*46	*242	*110	1303	994	23368
40	NET L-T CAP GAIN LESS NET S-T LOSS	173584	*13895	*2	*12718	*2284	7763	15631	10417	16382	3593	1843	31660	57397
41	NET GAIN, NONCAPITAL ASSETS	123242	38734	*4314	*14364	*895	5392	11071	2794	2276	1304	3014	4582	34504
42	DIVIDENDS, DOMESTIC CORPORATIONS	76969	*3	*10	*47	734	1235	4159	*5685	4118	1772	3703	2464	53039
43	DIVIDENDS, FOREIGN CORPORATIONS	58957	-	-	-	-	-	-	-	-	-	-	258	58697
44	OTHER RECEIPTS	1821616	6582	41646	38170	65101	62758	165887	68700	135556	59119	104487	165709	907903
45	TOTAL DEDUCTIONS	229135685	1291710	6583917	9725630	13127354	14327361	25970968	8564109	13768807	9324508	10538058	17190466	98722798
46	COST OF SALES AND OPERATIONS	177170189	982396	4561254	7350442	10374576	11381140	20577639	6738880	10792783	7451281	8011171	13647477	75301152
47	COMPENSATION OF OFFICERS	1563625	34668	234923	266991	231547	212642	289312	60902	58593	27947	25668	32414	88018
48	REPAIRS	1186560	8148	38351	54861	70617	73906	141991	42722	69066	52917	62961	94440	476583
49	BAD DEBTS	126521	*972	6255	4681	4347	8561	17829	7403	5214	4103	2198	7504	57453
50	RENT PAID ON BUSINESS PROPERTY	3511375	21826	215403	203799	214635	165397	333443	110686	211063	126708	173761	261603	1473052
51	TAXES PAID	3068854	20128	166249	168877	189567	169600	312140	111598	185479	136167	159723	210393	1238932
52	INTEREST PAID	1351586	12339	58603	70782	72163	73189	142737	52675	68573	52067	38120	105576	604763
53	CONTRIBUTIONS OR GIFTS	53851	*79	240	884	1518	1429	4019	1863	5157	2190	2640	4792	29041
54	AMORTIZATION	71492	*642	4058	9242	5240	4362	8059	2912	5668	1874	3331	2307	23797
55	DEPRECIATION	3363400	19459	113611	127650	143335	151727	302095	113054	179599	115663	151147	226382	1719679
56	DEPLETION	3675	1	*68	-	*224	*365	-	-	-	*829	1	-	2187
57	ADVERTISING	2435331	16061	60501	87980	150785	193292	292008	78156	132453	68847	126292	142131	1086825
58	PENSION, PROF SH, STOCK, ANNUITY	596595	*1208	*573	*2473	9400	27996	52507	24581	34152	23096	26861	44271	349477
59	EMPLOYEE BENEFIT PROGRAMS	1903221	*5486	8453	15659	43801	48107	110989	43650	67806	52434	97996	139440	1269399
60	NET LOSS, NONCAPITAL ASSETS	44295	*1190	*16835	*688	*443	*422	8021	2273	1600	3058	2092	4235	3439
61	OTHER DEDUCTIONS	32685118	167107	1098541	1360621	1615155	1815227	3378180	1172755	1951601	1205327	1654097	2267502	14999004
62	TOTAL RECEIPTS LESS TOTAL DEDUCTS	2535320	18614	-122884	21921	65972	94267	128949	86052	173285	91751	130997	169259	1677138
63	CONST TAXABLE INC FRM REL FRN CORPS.	78788	-	-	-	-	-	-	-	-	-	-	-	78788
64	NET INCOME (LESS DEFICIT), TOTAL	2594367	18614	-122884	21849	65442	94234	128942	86021	170175	91273	130558	169088	1741056
65	NET INCOME TOTAL	3355744	68859	75423	113070	160483	133277	266222	102767	209129	117675	138607	175061	1795172
66	DEFICIT, TOTAL	761377	50245	198307	91221	95040	39043	137280	16746	38954	*26402	8048	5973	54116
67	NET INCOME (LESS DEFICIT), F 1120S	-34005	*-25735	-67408	3966	-8221	31324	5976	*11762	*22535	-8204	-	-	-
68	NET INCOME (LESS DEF), 1120-DISC	4299	-	-	-	-	-	4299	-	-	-	-	-	-
69	STATUTORY SPECIAL DEDUCTIONS, TOTAL.	462942	*5620	22044	13737	11683	3506	25396	9280	3827	3856	3145	5333	355515
70	NET OPERATING LOSS DEDUCTION	402839	*5617	22035	13710	11059	*2456	22036	*4446	*309	*2352	-	3239	315580
71	DIVIDENDS RECEIVED DEDUCTION	60103	*3	*8	*28	624	1050	3360	*4834	3517	1507	3145	2094	39934
72	PUBLIC UTILITY DIV PAID DEDUCTION.	-	-	-	-	-	-	-	-	-	-	-	-	-
73	INCOME SUBJECT TO TAX, TOTAL	3545152	52130	34000	69745	124813	97479	212279	82151	180886	110818	135931	169770	2275151
74	NET L-T CAP GN TAXED AT ALT RATES.	122921	-	-	*4781	-	*2657	11444	*5903	14508	3030	1366	29749	49483
75	INC TAX (BEFORE CRED), TOTAL	1126192	21758	5207	12707	23761	23061	73158	35001	79889	50524	62514	74082	664559
76	REG AND ALTERNATIVE TAX	1108852	19389	5147	12658	23690	22742	71775	34155	79014	49855	62151	72596	655680
77	TAX FRM RECOMP PRIOR YR INV CR.	16498	*2369	*60	*49	*71	320	1307	815	663	502	364	1369	8608
78	ADDITIONAL TAX FOR TAX PREFS	843	-	-	-	-	-	*76	*31	*211	*167	-	87	271
79	FOREIGN TAX CREDIT	60368	-	-	-	-	-	-	-	-	-	-	379	59989
80	U.S. POSSESSIONS TAX CREDIT	1005	-	-	-	-	-	-	-	-	-	-	1005	-
81	ORPHAN DRUG CREDIT	-	-	-	-	-	-	-	-	-	-	-	-	-
82	NONCONVENTIONAL SOURCE FUEL CREDIT	-	-	-	-	-	-	-	-	-	-	-	-	-
83	RESEARCH ACTIVITES CREDIT	2827	-	-	-	-	-	*141	-	11	15	140	**	2520
84	GENERAL BUSINESS CREDIT	271103	*415	1190	3686	6696	7334	17214	6736	12658	12081	12649	20083	170361
	DISTRIBUTIONS TO STOCKHOLDERS:													
85	CASH AND PROPERTY EXCEPT OWN STOCK	681893	623	*1760	*2319	2657	4308	14147	6489	9527	6849	18199	22068	592962
86	CORPORATION'S OWN STOCK	55731	-	-	-	-	-	-	*2190	-	*16618	24119	18169	2635
87	INVEST CREDIT: COST OF PROPERTY	3141452	*7872	68558	115424	123734	155255	249535	110743	178912	110947	141713	196168	1690409
88	INVESTMENT QUALIFIED FOR CREDIT	2594968	*6581	28481	71458	85693	109178	194742	82332	148704	95195	121056	155255	1496170

SOURCE: U.S. Internal Revenue Service, *Corporation Source Book of Statistics of Income*, 1984–85 (Washington, D.C.: U.S. Government Printing Office, 1987), p. 167.

Information on Management Compensation

As discussed later in this book, management compensation often must be adjusted when valuing a company on a control basis. Following is a brief overview of some of the sources of comparative information on management compensation.

RMA Annual Statement Studies, the *Corporation Source Book of Statistics of Income,* and the *Almanac of Business and Industrial Financial Ratios,* described earlier, provide information on management compensation as a percentage of revenues.

The *Growth Resources Officer Compensation Report* is a valuable source of information on officer or management compensation. It is a comprehensive study of officer compensation at over 1,400 companies with annual revenues of under $60 million. Compensation data are broken down by such categories as officer position, company size, profit performance, and general industry group (manufacturing, technology, general products manufacturing, or service). The survey reports the compensation in effect early in the year in which the report is published; therefore, the results are very timely.

The proxy statements of comparative publicly traded companies are another useful source, since they generally present detailed information on the compensation of companies' top executives. Trade associations are another frequent source of information on management compensation, depending on the industry. For particularly small businesses, *Financial Statement Studies of the Small Business,* published annually, is a useful source.

Helpful Telephone Tips

In many cases, the gathering of industry information requires a series of telephone calls to existing or potential sources of the desired information. Often the analyst must locate those people who can either send the necessary information or answer questions on the phone. This process requires good telephone techniques. There are a few things to keep in mind when calling for information, particularly when one is unsure whether the other party will cooperate or exactly what helpful information it has.

It is important to be as clear as possible about the type of information being sought. When calling for economic information, it is helpful to specify the type of information wanted, for example, information on population trends, employment trends, recent events in the area that would affect the economic outlook, personal income growth, new construction and development, the area's economy and demographics in general, and so on. If the valuation date is several years back, it is important to specify the relevant time period.

One should speak in a friendly, polite tone of voice and emphasize that it is important to receive the information as soon as possible. When calling someone who may not immediately perceive any self-benefit or obligation to talk, it is important to find an "in," either by asking the person to verify the accuracy of a quote found in an article

EXHIBIT 7-3

Sample Page from *RMA Annual Statement Studies*

RETAILERS · GROCERIES & MEATS SIC# 5411

Current Data					Type of Statement	Comparative Historical Data				
24	40	49	16	129	Unqualified			129	138	129
3	10	2		15	Qualified			8	10	15
43	59	14		116	Reviewed	DATA NOT AVAILABLE		106	112	116
182	73	4		259	Compiled			168	197	259
90	50	13	1	154	Other			124	135	154
302(6/30-9/30/86)		371(10/1/86-3/31/87)				6/30/82-3/31/83	6/30/83-3/31/84	6/30/84-3/31/85	6/30/85-3/31/86	6/30/86-3/31/87
0-1MM	1-10MM	10-50MM	50-100MM	ALL	**ASSET SIZE**	ALL	ALL	ALL	ALL	ALL
342	**232**	**82**	**17**	**673**	**NUMBER OF STATEMENTS**	**522**	**514**	**535**	**592**	**673**
%	%	%	%	%	**ASSETS**	%	%	%	%	%
9.0	10.8	9.7	8.4	9.7	Cash & Equivalents	8.8	9.9	10.7	8.9	9.7
4.4	4.8	4.4	7.4	4.6	Trade Receivables - (net)	4.9	4.9	5.1	5.0	4.6
36.2	30.2	22.3	26.9	32.2	Inventory	33.4	32.8	32.9	33.7	32.2
1.7	2.7	2.3	1.7	2.1	All Other Current	1.9	2.0	2.8	2.5	2.1
51.4	48.5	38.6	44.4	48.6	Total Current	48.9	49.6	51.4	50.1	48.6
36.1	38.2	49.1	46.4	38.7	Fixed Assets (net)	39.2	39.0	36.3	37.5	38.7
2.7	1.2	.9	1.8	2.0	Intangibles (net)	1.5	1.5	1.8	1.8	2.0
9.8	12.1	11.3	7.4	10.7	All Other Non-Current	10.5	9.9	10.4	10.7	10.7
100.0	100.0	100.0	100.0	100.0	Total	100.0	100.0	100.0	100.0	100.0
					LIABILITIES					
6.7	5.0	3.1	3.1	5.6	Notes Payable-Short Term	4.5	4.9	4.8	5.3	5.6
4.7	5.1	4.7	2.6	4.8	Cur. Mat.-L/T/D	4.2	4.6	4.4	4.9	4.8
18.3	22.0	19.4	21.7	19.8	Trade Payables	20.4	21.1	22.0	21.1	19.8
.9	1.0	1.0	.5	1.0	Income Taxes Payable	–	–	1.2	.8	1.0
9.7	7.7	8.9	11.1	8.9	All Other Current	9.5	9.4	9.3	8.6	8.9
40.3	40.8	37.2	39.0	40.1	Total Current	38.7	40.0	41.6	40.9	40.1
31.0	23.9	26.8	26.1	27.9	Long Term Debt	25.3	24.5	23.5	26.5	27.9
.2	1.0	2.2	2.9	.8	Deferred Taxes	–	–	.5	.7	.8
1.5	2.1	1.5	4.3	1.8	All Other Non-Current	2.5	2.0	2.2	1.6	1.8
27.0	32.2	32.2	27.8	29.5	Net Worth	33.6	33.5	32.2	30.4	29.5
100.0	100.0	100.0	100.0	100.0	Total Liabilities & Net Worth	100.0	100.0	100.0	100.0	100.0
					INCOME DATA					
100.0	100.0	100.0	100.0	100.0	Net Sales	100.0	100.0	100.0	100.0	100.0
23.7	21.9	22.7	18.0	22.8	Gross Profit	21.4	22.2	22.1	22.1	22.8
21.7	20.8	20.8	16.5	21.2	Operating Expenses	19.8	20.4	20.5	20.9	21.2
2.0	1.0	1.9	1.5	1.6	Operating Profit	1.7	1.8	1.6	1.2	1.6
.5	.0	.1	– .5	.2	All Other Expenses (net)	.3	.2	.3	.2	.2
1.5	1.1	1.8	2.0	1.4	Profit Before Taxes	1.3	1.6	1.3	1.0	1.4
					RATIOS					
2.3	1.6	1.3	1.4	1.8		1.9	1.8	1.9	1.8	1.8
1.4	1.2	1.0	1.1	1.2	Current	1.3	1.3	1.3	1.2	1.2
.9	.9	.8	1.0	.9		.9	.9	.9	.9	.9
.7	.6	.6	.6	.6		.6	.7	.8	.6	.6
(331) .3	(230) .4	(81) .4	.4	(659) .3	Quick	(514) .3	(505) .3	(517) .3	(578) .3	(659) .3
.1	.2	.2	.2	.2		.2	.2	.2	.1	.2
0 INF	1 562.9	1 388.6	2 238.6	0 972.3		0 999.8	0 949.5	0 999.8	0 844.6	0 972.3
1 387.6	2 242.5	2 205.1	3 117.6	1 278.5	Sales/Receivables	1 328.5	1 291.4	1 332.4	1 307.2	1 278.5
3 131.4	3 112.2	3 106.6	7 54.6	3 117.5		3 113.9	3 118.0	3 107.9	3 119.0	3 117.5
18 19.9	16 23.0	14 25.2	14 25.5	16 22.3		16 22.9	17 21.7	16 23.1	16 22.4	16 22.3
25 14.7	21 17.4	20 18.4	19 19.5	22 16.3	Cost of Sales/Inventory	23 16.1	24 15.5	22 16.5	22 16.5	22 16.3
33 10.9	32 11.5	25 14.5	33 10.9	32 11.4		33 11.0	33 11.2	31 11.8	31 11.7	32 11.4
5 66.8	10 36.1	13 28.3	15 23.8	8 46.5		7 48.8	9 39.6	8 43.3	8 47.6	8 46.5
11 34.4	16 22.9	17 21.2	17 20.9	14 26.2	Cost of Sales/Payables	14 26.9	15 24.7	14 26.3	14 26.6	14 26.2
18 19.9	23 16.2	24 15.5	21 17.1	21 17.5		21 17.4	22 16.3	22 16.8	21 17.1	21 17.5
22.6	27.2	49.5	43.6	26.2		24.7	25.4	23.4	27.1	26.2
50.3	76.9	521.9	131.1	65.4	Sales/Working Capital	63.2	66.5	69.9	68.8	65.4
–147.9	–117.7	–66.6	±INF	–104.7		–103.1	–166.1	–119.8	–100.9	–104.7
6.0	4.8	5.6	10.6	5.6		5.2	5.9	5.8	5.4	5.6
(305) 2.5	(209) 2.4	(73) 3.0	3.2	(604) 2.5	EBIT/Interest	(452) 2.7	(442) 2.9	(471) 2.6	(518) 2.6	(604) 2.5
.9	1.2	2.0	1.7	1.2		1.3	1.5	1.3	1.2	1.2
4.8	4.4	5.4	4.3	4.6		5.0	5.8	5.6	4.0	4.6
(126) 1.9	(149) 2.1	(66) 2.4	(14) 3.0	(355) 2.1	Net Profit + Depr., Dep., Amort./Cur. Mat. L/T/D	(280) 2.4	(301) 2.4	(301) 2.6	(320) 2.2	(355) 2.1
.6	1.2	1.3	1.5	1.1		1.3	1.3	1.3	1.1	1.1
.5	.7	1.0	1.3	.6		.6	.7	.6	.6	.6
1.5	1.2	1.6	1.7	1.4	Fixed/Worth	1.3	1.2	1.2	1.4	1.4
8.2	2.4	2.7	3.5	3.7		2.5	2.6	2.8	3.3	3.7
1.0	1.2	1.4	1.6	1.2		1.1	1.1	1.0	1.2	1.2
2.9	2.3	2.3	3.2	2.5	Debt/Worth	2.1	2.0	2.2	2.4	2.5
16.4	3.8	3.8	4.2	6.8		4.9	5.5	5.4	6.3	6.8
63.0	34.1	38.2	41.1	45.0		38.1	37.2	38.6	36.1	45.0
(270) 29.3	(219) 18.5	(80) 26.6	(16) 31.7	(585) 24.0	% Profit Before Taxes/Tangible Net Worth	(474) 21.9	(457) 22.0	(476) 20.9	(517) 18.9	(585) 24.0
8.2	5.3	13.1	17.6	7.7		8.4	9.1	8.6	5.4	7.7
16.1	11.6	11.9	12.5	13.8		13.5	13.2	12.6	11.2	13.8
7.9	5.0	8.1	7.9	6.4	% Profit Before Taxes/Total Assets	6.9	7.6	6.5	5.9	6.4
– .2	1.3	4.0	3.5	1.3		1.8	2.2	1.9	.6	1.3
50.0	28.7	16.9	21.2	34.2		33.1	31.3	36.8	37.5	34.2
21.7	18.3	10.2	11.0	17.4	Sales/Net Fixed Assets	17.0	16.5	20.2	18.4	17.4
8.7	9.8	7.2	7.5	8.7		10.0	9.4	10.6	9.5	8.7
9.3	7.9	6.9	6.4	8.3		8.6	8.1	8.8	8.8	8.3
6.3	6.2	5.6	5.4	6.1	Sales/Total Assets	6.2	6.2	6.2	6.4	6.1
4.0	4.3	3.7	4.0	4.1		4.4	4.3	4.6	4.4	4.1
.7	.8	1.0	.4	.8		.6	.7	.7	.7	.8
(308) 1.2	(217) 1.2	(75) 1.4	.9	(617) 1.2	% Depr., Dep., Amort./Sales	(476) 1.0	(480) 1.1	(497) 1.0	(554) 1.1	(617) 1.2
2.1	1.6	1.9	1.3	1.8		1.4	1.5	1.5	1.6	1.8
1.1	.8	.3		.9		.8	.8	.8	.7	.9
(133) 2.1	(83) 1.2	(12) .9		(228) 1.7	% Officers' Comp/Sales	(192) 1.5	(160) 1.5	(174) 1.4	(192) 1.4	(228) 1.7
3.8	2.1	1.5		3.0		2.8	2.7	2.8	2.9	3.0
969766M	4860561M	8924746M	6734971M	21490044M	Net Sales ($)	21117789M	21896761M	18380619M	21348831M	21490044M
141135M	798397M	1778089M	1257206M	3974827M	Total Assets ($)	3586840M	3873056M	3221910M	3577750M	3974827M

©Robert Morris Associates 1987

M = $thousand   MM = $million
See Pages 1 through 13 for Explanation of Ratios and Data

SOURCE: *RMA Annual Statement Studies*, 1987. (Philadelphia: © Robert Morris Associates, 1987), p. 276.

Interpretation of
Statement Studies Figures

RMA cautions that the Studies be regarded only as a general guideline and not as an absolute industry norm. This is due to limited samples within categories, the categorization of companies by their primary Standard Industrial Classification (SIC) number only, and different methods of operations by companies within the same industry. For these reasons, RMA recommends that the figures be used only as general guidelines in addition to other methods of financial analysis.

---

or by asking the first few questions so as to indicate that the caller has some knowledge of the topic. These approaches will make the other party more likely to stay on the phone even if he or she is very busy and need not talk to the caller at all.

Once one is reasonably sure that the other party is willing to talk, it is appropriate to briefly set the scene for the discussion by giving

EXHIBIT 7-4

Sample Page from *Standard & Poor's Analyst's Handbook*

RETAIL STORES-FOOD CHAINS

Per Share Data—Adjusted to stock price index level. Average of stock price indexes, 1941-1943=10

	Sales	Oper. Profit	Profit Margin %	Depr.	Income Taxes	Earnings Per Share	Earnings % of Sales	Dividends Per Share	Dividends % of Earn.	Price 1941-1943-10 High	Price 1941-1943-10 Low	Price/Earn. Ratio High	Price/Earn. Ratio Low	Div. Yields % High	Div. Yields % Low	Book Value Per Share	Book Value % Return	Working Capital	Capital Expend-itures
1956	239.09	8.95	3.74	2.30	3.38	3.12	1.30	1.33	42.63	38.58	35.22	12.37	11.29	3.78	3.45	21.21	14.71	13.13	6.15
1957	255.70	9.96	3.90	2.51	3.90	3.62	1.42	1.40	38.67	44.25	34.47	12.22	9.52	4.06	3.16	23.36	15.50	14.10	6.64
1958	277.44	9.78	3.53	2.32	3.99	3.57	1.29	1.37	38.38	67.19	43.91	18.82	12.30	3.12	2.04	25.07	14.24	14.59	5.29
1959	286.32	10.17	3.55	2.52	3.97	3.63	1.27	1.56	42.98	68.46	54.91	18.86	15.13	2.84	2.28	27.41	13.24	15.43	4.59
1960	293.76	10.60	3.61	2.75	4.14	3.78	1.29	1.85	48.94	59.53	51.33	15.75	13.58	3.60	3.11	29.32	12.89	15.65	4.47
1961	302.82	10.73	3.54	2.97	4.06	3.78	1.25	1.97	52.12	90.33	57.83	23.90	15.30	3.41	2.18	31.33	12.07	16.67	4.67
1962	311.17	11.13	3.58	3.16	4.15	3.83	1.23	2.27	59.27	83.80	50.85	21.88	13.28	4.46	2.71	32.92	11.63	17.00	4.55
1963	318.81	10.87	3.41	3.23	3.85	3.79	1.19	2.25	59.37	71.05	58.35	18.75	15.40	3.86	3.17	34.27	11.06	18.13	3.93
1964	331.89	11.45	3.45	3.41	3.79	4.13	1.24	2.36	57.14	76.60	61.00	18.55	14.77	3.87	3.08	36.27	11.39	19.11	4.62
1965	339.20	11.29	3.33	3.50	3.56	4.16	1.23	2.45	58.89	81.32	65.67	19.55	15.79	3.73	3.01	37.45	11.11	18.72	5.23
1966	367.21	12.03	3.28	3.77	3.76	4.39	1.20	2.53	57.63	69.11	49.54	15.74	11.28	5.11	3.66	39.55	11.10	18.22	6.16
1967	377.07	11.61	3.08	3.98	3.46	4.13	1.10	2.61	63.20	57.90	49.00	14.02	11.86	5.33	4.51	41.08	10.05	19.25	5.48
1968	399.19	12.72	3.19	4.96	4.15	4.29	1.07	2.49	58.04	70.40	52.58	16.41	12.26	4.74	3.54	43.07	9.96	19.99	5.77
1969	439.97	13.97	3.18	4.37	4.68	4.70	1.07	2.54	54.04	67.01	56.28	14.26	11.97	4.51	3.79	46.14	10.19	18.29	7.94
1970	464.40	14.82	3.19	4.48	4.87	5.09	1.10	2.56	50.29	67.38	51.59	13.24	10.14	4.96	3.80	48.04	10.60	21.45	10.81
1971	482.38	13.35	2.77	4.77	3.76	4.44	0.92	2.66	59.91	79.36	58.99	17.87	13.29	4.51	3.35	50.10	8.86	22.37	10.12
1972	526.29	10.01	1.90	5.12	1.71	2.80	0.53	2.11	75.36	68.92	54.34	24.61	19.41	3.88	3.06	50.43	5.55	23.31	10.84
1973	563.16	13.94	2.48	5.46	3.26	4.37	0.78	1.83	41.88	63.35	43.59	14.50	9.97	4.20	2.89	52.38	8.34	25.65	11.12
1974	588.26	15.19	2.58	5.62	3.38	1.61	0.27	2.15	133.54	60.35	40.01	37.48	24.85	5.37	3.56	47.95	3.36	20.92	12.74
1975	637.67	16.16	2.53	6.05	4.46	5.71	0.90	2.08	36.43	60.39	43.90	10.58	7.69	4.74	3.44	50.61	11.28	23.25	10.67
1976	619.07	15.68	2.53	5.68	4.31	5.41	0.87	2.23	41.22	62.87	51.93	11.62	9.60	4.29	3.55	48.11	11.25	24.10	9.77
1977	667.55	18.40	2.76	6.95	4.31	5.49	0.82	2.49	45.36	62.31	51.93	11.35	9.46	4.79	4.00	50.19	10.94	23.44	14.18
1978	690.69	23.19	3.36	7.88	5.93	6.45	0.93	2.68	41.55	62.27	49.32	9.65	7.65	5.43	4.30	50.72	12.72	21.68	15.04
1979	R714.74	23.01	3.22	8.00	5.24	7.47	1.05	3.03	40.56	63.45	54.31	8.49	7.27	5.58	4.78	51.94	14.38	20.47	18.58
1980	808.53	23.47	2.90	9.27	4.95	6.71	0.83	3.24	48.29	58.50	46.13	8.72	6.87	7.02	5.54	54.61	12.29	20.73	22.08
1981	871.91	25.85	2.96	10.30	5.30	5.08	0.58	3.55	69.88	63.36	49.70	12.47	9.78	7.14	5.60	56.65	8.97	21.08	20.26
1982	904.98	30.11	3.33	10.95	6.50	9.98	1.10	3.94	39.48	89.54	52.01	8.97	5.21	7.58	4.40	60.85	16.40	23.73	22.13
1983	872.31	30.40	3.49	11.08	7.03	9.47	1.09	4.20	44.35	104.58	81.43	11.04	8.60	5.16	4.02	63.60	14.89	21.75	21.05
1984	937.78	33.08	3.53	12.20	8.08	10.70	1.14	4.32	40.37	107.28	83.48	10.03	7.80	5.17	4.03	69.56	15.38	21.15	37.46
1985	982.07	36.66	3.73	14.03	7.87	11.58	1.18	4.41	38.08	·141.30	105.07	12.20	9.07	4.20	3.12	79.24	14.61	19.55	28.36
1986	951.16	37.21	3.91	14.23	7.60	9.79	1.03	4.50	45.97	188.25	133.60	19.23	13.65	3.37	2.39	79.73	12.28	10.07	37.68

Stock Price Indexes for this group extend back to 1926.
*Albertson's (11-21-84)
*Amer. Stores (Acme Markets) (12-31-25)
*Great Atlantic & Pacific (12-17-58) (7-30-47 to 11-21-56)
*Kroger Co. (12-31-55) (Formerly Kroger Grocery-Bakery)
*Lucky Stores (1-14-76)

*Southland Corp (9-25-85)
*Supermarket General (10-8-86)
*Winn-Dixie Stores (11-28-56)
Allied Supermarkets (11-28-56 to 6-16-65) (Formerly ACF Wrigley)

First National Stores (12-31-25 to 5-30-73)
Food Fair Stores (11-28-56 to 10-11-78)
Grand Union (2-15-57 to 12-10-75)
Jewel Cos. (2-13-57 to 11-21-84)
National Tea (3-11-59 to 4-29-70) (12-31-25 to 12-10-58)
Safeway Stores (9-17-30 to 11-26-86)

SOURCE: *Standard & Poor's Analyst's Handbook,* 1987 (New York: Standard & Poor's Corporation, Inc., 1987), p.123.

the person some background on the reason for the call. Properly made telephone contacts can yield a surprising amount of useful information.

Indexes to Economic and Industry Data

There are several books and indexes available to assist in finding additional sources of economic and industry data. Some indexes were already mentioned, such as the *American Statistics Index* and *The Wall Street Journal/Barron's Index*. Other indexes, such as the *Business Periodical Index,* the *Public Affairs Information Service* (PAIS), which tends to have more economic information, and *Predicasts,* generally are available in public libraries.

Predicasts provides several business reference publications. Two of this company's publications, *Predicasts Basebook* and *Predicasts Forecasts,* provide summary information on economic indicators and refer the reader to the original source. The *Basebook* provides historical data on U.S. business and economic activities, while *Forecasts* cumulates both short- and long-range projections for products, markets, industries, and the economy. *Predicasts Forecasts* is published quarterly, with an annual cumulative volume. *Forecasts* is particularly valuable as a source of long-term inflation forecasts.

In addition to these indexes, several directories can provide additional sources of economic and industry information. Michael R. Lavin's book *Business Information: How to Find It, How to Use It* is particularly useful. Other helpful directories include *Where to Find Business Information* by David M. Brownstone and Gorton Carruth; the *Encyclopedia of Business Information Sources,* published by Gale Research Company in Detroit, Michigan; and the *Information USA Workbook,* which provides tips on finding information on a wide range of topics, from market studies to online data bases, as well as demographics and statistics.

Online data bases are revolutionizing the process of gathering and retrieving economic and other types of data. *Dow-Jones News Retrieval, Compuserve, The Source,* and *Dialog* are but a few of the online services now available.

Summary

This chapter has briefly described some of the sources of economic and industry data that business valuation analysts find particularly useful. Since the variety of potential sources is virtually boundless, the final section listed several of the most useful indexing services for locating sources relevant to a particular topic or industry. Locations of the sources' publishers and other information appear in the bibliography following the chapter.

In order to get maximum benefit from economic and industry research, the analyst must focus on the implications of the data for the value of the subject company. This focus must be maintained while conducting the research, using it in the process of arriving at an opinion as to value, and writing it up as an integral part of the ultimate appraisal report.

Bibliography: Economic and Industry Data Sources

American Statistics Index. Washington, D.C.: Congressional Information Services, annual with monthly supplements.
   American Statistics Index is a master index to the publications of more than 500 U.S. government agencies that issue statistics. The index began publication in 1972, but a retrospective edition covering 1960–1973 is available. Each edition is in two volumes, *Index* and *Abstracts.* Copies of the source documents on microfiche can be purchased from CIS. This source is also available online.

Board of Governors of the Federal Reserve System. *Federal Reserve Bulletin.* Washington, D.C., monthly.
   Current U.S. banking and monetary statistics. Includes such basic business statistics as employment, prices, national income, and construction. Includes the FRB index of industrial production.

Brownstone, David M., and Gorton Carruth. *Where to Find Business Information: A Worldwide Guide for Everyone Who Needs the Answers to Business Questions,* 2nd ed. New York: John Wiley & Sons, 1982.
   This volume lists over 5,000 sources of information, primarily magazines, looseleaf services, and online sources.

Business Index. Belmont, Calif.: Information Access Company, monthly.
   This service is provided on microfilm, with an updated film available monthly. Each current film includes three years' worth of articles arranged by subject. *Business Index* does cover-to-cover indexing of over 460 business periodicals and selected indexing of business information from over 1,100 general and legal periodicals. *The Wall Street Journal* (eastern and western editions) and *Barron's* are cover to cover. *The New York Times* financial section and selected relevant articles from the rest of the paper are also included. The result is the most comprehensive index of business periodical information available in one source.

Business Periodicals Index. New York: H. W. Wilson Company, monthly with annual cumulation.
   Covers a wide range of business topics, including industries, published in various journals, with indexing arranged alphabetically by subject and author. Available online and on disk.

Corporate and Industry Research Reports. Eastchester, N.Y.: JA Micro-publishing, quarterly.
   The 1986 edition of CIRR includes 23,000 research reports by 62 investment firms issued during 1985. The service consists of a set of microfiche and quarterly index.

Daniells, Lorna M. *Business Information Sources,* rev. ed. Berkeley: University of California Press, 1985.
   Annotates sources arranged by subject, such as industry statistics. Indexed by title, author, and subject.

Dun's Business Rankings. Parsippany, N.J.: Dun's Marketing Services, annual.

This source ranks 7,500 top U.S. public and private companies within 152 industries by annual sales volume and number of employees.

Executive Compensation Service. New York: American Management Association, annual.

Series of eight reports dealing with salaries for different levels of job categories. Includes top management, middle management, professional and scientific, first-line supervison, technicians, office personnel, and sales personnel. Offers job descriptions, further broken down into categories like durable goods industries, with some by industry segments. Offers median pay, base pay, bonuses, and average salary range.

Frank, Nathalie D., and John V. Ganley. *Data Sources for Business and Market Analysis,* 3rd ed. Metuchen, N.J.: Scarecrow Press, 1983.

Although it focuses on marketing information, this source is valuable because of its emphasis on sources of federal and local statistics and on nonpublished or nontraditional sources of data on companies or industries, products, and trends. One section is entirely devoted to the information resources of trade and professional associations. Another discusses grants, institutes, publications, and research available through university programs.

Grant, Mary McNierney, and Riva Berleant-Schiller. *Directory of Business and Financial Services,* 8th ed. Washington, D.C.: Special Libraries Association, 1984.

A fine companion to the Daniells book, this source deals with services that provide regularly or irregularly updated information on some category of business activity.

Growth Resources, Inc. *Growth Resources Officer Compensation Report.* Peabody, Mass.: Panel Publishers, annual.

A comprehensive study of validated annual compensation data for officers at over 1,400 companies with annual gross revenue of under $60 million.

Handbook of Basic Economic Statistics. Washington, D.C.: Economics Statistics Bureau of Washington, D.C., annual with monthly supplements.

Current and historical statistics on commerce, industry, labor, and agriculture, with more than 1,800 statistical series.

Harfax Guide to Industry Special Issues. Cambridge, Mass.: Harfax, 1984.

A brief abstract of 6,900 articles in 1,800 U.S., Canadian, and selected foreign journals, extensively indexed, makes it possible to search by industry, subject, or SIC code, geographically, and by type of information (statistics, directory, and so forth). This is one of many publications based on the Harfax Industry Data Sources data base.

Ibbotson Associates. *Stocks, Bonds, Bills, and Inflation 19— Yearbook: Market Results for 1926–19—.* Chicago: Ibbotson Associates, annual.

Key Business Ratios. New York: Dun & Bradstreet, Inc., annual.

Balance sheet and profit and loss ratios based on a computerized financial statements file. The 14 key ratios are broken down into median figures, with upper and lower quartiles. Covers over 800 lines of business, broken down into three size ranges by net worth for each SIC.

Lavin, Michael R. *Business Information: How to Find It, How to Use It.* Phoenix, Ariz.: Oryx Press, 1987.

Lesko, Matthew. *Information USA.* New York: Penquin Books, 1985.

Levine, Sumner N., ed. *The Dow Jones-Irwin Business and Investment Almanac.* Homewood, Ill.: Dow Jones-Irwin, annual.

The 10th edition of this standard reference tool includes several enhancements over previous editions. A statistics section brings together the major business and economic indicators.

Mattera, Philip. *Inside U.S. Business.* Homewood, Ill.: Dow Jones-Irwin, 1987.

National Trade and Professional Associations of the United States. Washington, D.C.: Columbia Books, annual.

Excellent source book for trade and industry sources of industry information. Restricted to trade and professional associations and labor unions with national memberships.

Nelson's Directory of Wall Street Research, 11th ed. Rye, N.Y.: W. R. Nelson & Company, annual.

The "Research Sources" section gives names, addresses, telephone numbers, and specialties of research personnel at over 600 firms.

O'Hara, Frederick M., and Robert Sicignano. *Handbook of United States Economic Indicators.* Westport, Conn.: Greenwood Press, 1985.

This guide covers some 200 indicators produced by 55 government and private organizations. Each entry provides a brief description of the indicator, together with a list of the major publications in which data are provided on a regular basis.

Paine Webber Handbook of Stock and Bond Analysis, ed. Kiril Sokoloff. New York: McGraw-Hill, 1979.

Discusses industry groups and offers keys for analyzing each industry.

Predicasts F & S Index. Cleveland, Ohio: Predicasts, Inc., weekly, monthly supplements, quarterly and annual cumulations.

Gleans company, product, and industry information from more than 750 periodicals, newspapers, and reports. The first section of each index includes a one-line description of articles on industries and products. The second section is arranged alphabetically by company name.

Predicasts Forecasts. Cleveland, Ohio: Predicasts, Inc., quarterly with annual cumulation.

Arranges products and industries under a modified SIC code. This source is an index to statistics, annual growth, and forecasts appearing in magazine and newspaper articles. The format is similar to that of other Predicasts products. Like its counterparts, it is available online as well as in book form.

Public Affairs Information Service Bulletin (PAIS). New York: Public Affairs Information Service, biweekly with quarterly and annual cumulations.

A selected subject list of the latest books, pamphlets, government publications, reports of public and private agencies and periodical articles relating to economic and social conditions, public administration, and international relations.

RMA Annual Statement Studies. Philadelphia: Robert Morris Associcates, annual.

Robert Morris Associates' member banks submit the raw data; thus, the contents are not strictly consistent from year to year. Although the financial data submitted reflect companies' overall operations, the data are categorized only by the companies' primary SICs. Comparative historical data are also included.

Standard & Poor's Analyst's Handbook. New York: Standard & Poor's Corporation, Inc., annual.

A statistical workbook that enables anyone concerned with company or industry performance to conveniently compare the most vital per share data and financial statistics for the S&P 400 Industrial Stocks and the

90 industries comprising the index. Also includes 15 transportation, financial, and utility groups. Contains industry charts. Available with monthly updating.

Standard & Poor's Industry Surveys. New York: Standard & Poor's Corporation, Inc., quarterly and annual.

Provides continuous economic and business information on all major U.S. industries and numerous related industries. Financial data on more than 1,000 companies are included in the 22 surveys now published. Publishes annual *Basic Survey* and periodic *Current Surveys* for each industry grouping. Also includes a monthly *Trends and Projections* Economics Letter and a monthly *Earnings Supplement.* Over 1,500 pages annually of accurate, timely information on important industry trends and developments. *Trends and Projections* reviews the state of the ecomomy by highlighting major topics and evaluating leading indicators. Makes specific projections for gross national product and several of its components. A variety of charts show trends in interest rates, employment, housing starts, industrial production, and retail sales.

Standard & Poor's Outlook. New York: Standard & Poor's Corporation, Inc., monthly.

In newsletter format, this publication analyzes and projects business and market trends while suggesting changes and additions to portfolios. Special features include an annual and mid-year forecast. Each issue features a particular industry with lists of favored stocks in that industry and "In the Limelight," which briefly discusses a specific company.

Standard & Poor's Statistical Service. New York: Standard & Poor's Corporation, Inc.

S&P's Statistical Service is a collection of important business statistics, including the Security Price Index Record, Business and Financial Statistics, and cumulative monthly Current Statistics providing new information. The Security Price Index Record, published every two years, provides information to help in determining the performance history of particular stock groups during recessions, recovery periods, or periods of increasing or declining interest rates. The Security Price Index Record provides performance/activity indicators, such as price/earnings ratios, earnings, and dividends on a quarterly and, in some cases, weekly basis.

Statistical Reference Index. Washington, D.C.: Congressional Information Service, monthly with annual cumulation.

Since 1980, *Statistical Reference Index* has indexed and abstracted statistical reports from agencies other than the federal government. Nonprofit organizations, trade and professional associations, state government agencies, university research centers, and commercial publishers are just some of the sources of statistical information included. Since January 1983, CIS has also published the *Index to International Statistics,* which includes the statistical publications of about 50 international, intergovernmental agencies such as the United Nations, OECD, and OAS.

Troy, Leo. *Almanac of Business and Industrial Financial Ratios.* Englewood Cliffs, N.J.: Prentice-Hall, annual.

The information is derived from corporate tax returns in the IRS files. Figures in the 1988 edition are based on 1984–85 returns.

Tyran, Michael R. *The Handbook of Business and Financial Ratios.* Englewood Cliffs, N.J.: Prentice-Hall, 1986.

Uhlan, Miriam, ed. *Guide to Special Issues and Indexes of Periodicals,* 3rd ed. Washington, D.C.: Special Libraries Association, 1985.
Includes 1,362 U.S. and Canadian periodicals that publish directories, buyers' guides, convention issues, statistical outlooks, and other features on a regular basis.

U.S. Bureau of Economic Analysis, Department of Commerce. *Business Conditions Digest.* Washington, D.C.: U.S. Government Printing Office, monthly.
Includes charts and statistical tables for leading economic time series. Sections include cyclical indicators: composite indicators and their components; cyclical indicators by economic process; diffusion indexes and rates of change; national income and product; prices, wages, and productivity; labor force, employment, and unemployment; government activities; U.S. international transactions and international comparisons. The U.S. Department of Commerce provides the Economic Bulletin Board online for current information, and current and historical data from *Business Conditions Digest* are available on diskette.

U.S. Bureau of Economic Analysis, Department of Commerce. *Business Statistics.* Washington, D.C.: U.S. Government Printing Office, biennial.
This publication constitutes an amazing collection of economic and industrial statistics. It covers 1,900 separate data series used by the BEA in calculating the gross national product. It is intended for publication on a biennial basis as a supplement to the monthly *Survey of Current Business.*

U.S. Bureau of Economic Analysis, Department of Commerce. *Survey of Current Business.* Washington, D.C.: U.S. Government Printing Office, monthly.
This periodical gives information on trends in industry, the business situation, outlook, and other points pertinent to the business world. It is the primary source of information on the National Income and Product Accounts. Although the Accounts are tabulated quarterly, they are revised each month and presented here. The *Survey of Current Business* contains the most extensive breakdown of current NIPA values found in any ongoing publication. Each segment of the model is shown in considerable detail, because many components are themselves critical economic indicators. Another regular feature is the monthly "Business Situation," which offers an overview of economic conditions. The balance of each issue consists of narrative and statistical articles on special topics. Many are quite technical, explaining the methodology of NIPA revisions or similar topics, but most are understandable and worthwhile for the serious reader.

U.S. Bureau of Industrial Economics, Department of Commerce. *U.S. Industrial Outlook.* Washington, D.C.: U.S. Government Printing Office, annual.
Information on recent trends and outlook for about five years on over 350 individual industries. Narrative with statistics contains discussions of changes in supply and demand, developments in domestic and overseas markets, price changes, employment trends, and capital investment. Published in January of each year. The *U.S. Industrial Outlook* is helpful not only for its succinct narratives and summary statistics but for its highly regarded forecasts. Together with the *Economic Report of the President,* it stands as one of the government's key sources of economic projections.

U.S. Bureau of Labor Statistics, Department of Labor. *Monthly Labor Review.* Washington, D.C.: U.S. Government Printing Office, monthly.

A compilation of economic and social statistics. Most are given as monthly figures for the current year and one prior year. Features articles on the labor force, wages, prices, productivity, economic growth, and occupational injuries and illnesses. Regular features include a review of developments in industrial relations, book reviews, and current labor statistics.

U.S. Bureau of the Census, Department of Commerce. *State and Metropolitan Area Data Book, 1986.* Washington, D.C.: U.S. Government Printing Office, 1986.

U.S. Bureau of the Census, Department of Commerce. *Statistical Abstract of the United States.* Washington, D.C.: U.S. Government Printing Office, annual.

The *Statistical Abstract* is as well known and frequently consulted as the *World Almanac and Book of Facts.* In it the user can find data on population, vital statistics, health, law enforcement, education, politics, and other areas of general interest. Although it contains much more than economic statistics, fully two thirds of the material can be characterized as economic or industrial data. Most of the information is provided by government agencies, but nongovernment sources are also utilized. In addition, the book contains an excellent bibliography of statistical publications arranged by subject, a list of state statistical abstracts, and a fairly detailed subject index to tables. While not always the best choice for obtaining general ecomonic statistics, with 1,600 tables it is a viable and convenient source.

U.S. Council of Economic Advisers. *Economic Indicators.* Washington, D.C.: U.S. Government Printing Office, monthly.

Includes statistical charts and tables for basic U.S. economic indicators. Statistics are reprinted for at least six years and monthly or quarterly for the past year. Covers total output, income, and spending; GNP in 1972 dollars; personal consumption expenditures; corporate profits; production and business activity; and money, credit, and security markets.

U.S. Council of Economic Advisers. *Economic Report of the President.* Washington, D.C.: U.S. Government Printing Office, annual.

This document is essentially a report from the Executive Branch to the Congress on the state of the economy. About two thirds of the publication is a narrative analysis of economic issues and conditions. An important feature of the narrative section is a five-year outlook for the United States, including specific projections for the GNP and other key indicators.

U.S. Internal Revenue Service. *Corporation Source Book: Statistics of Income.* Washington, D.C.: U.S. Government Printing Office.

Balance sheet, income statement, tax and investment credit items by major and minor industries, broken down by size of total assets. Tables provide more detailed industry data than those appearing in the annual *Statistics of Income: Corporation Income Tax Returns.* Comes out four to five years late.

Woy, James, ed. *Encyclopedia of Business Information Sources,* 6th ed. Detroit: Gale Research, 1986.

The introduction calls this "a bibliographic guide to approximately 22,000 citations covering more than 1,100 primary subjects of interest to business personnel." A good starting point for any search, this guide compiles sources under specific subject headings.

Chapter 8

Data on Required Rates of Return

It is apparent that the determination of a rate at which to capitalize the prospective earnings of a business is a hit-and-miss procedure. Its inaccuracies are generally conceded by the financial writers; but its wild crudeness has seldom been fully exposed even by the experts.[1]

Although written 50 years ago, this statement definitely retains a ring of truth today. We have all seen appraisal reports whose author takes countless pages to justify a figure or figures for normalized or expected earnings and then seems to just pull a capitalization or discount rate right out of the air.

IRS Revenue Ruling 59-60 succinctly notes:

A determination of the proper capitalization rate presents one of the most difficult problems in valuation [italics supplied].[2]

The above statement is so true! Using well-supported capitalization or discount rates is every bit as important as using well-documented earnings figures. This chapter deals with required rates of return in the market for equities, figures that are essential in determining appropriate discount rates. As discussed in Chapters 2 through 4, even if the valuation does not rely directly on the discounted future earnings or cash flow method, capitalization rates selected for valuation methods used should produce results compatible with those of a discounted future returns approach using reasonable values for the future benefits and a market discount rate.

General Rate-of-Return Guidelines from Past Literature

Following are three examples of broad guidelines offered for selection of rates at which to capitalize or to discount earnings. These examples span over half a century and demonstrate the consistency of the idea that higher risk demands higher returns. They also demonstrate the consistency as to the approximate ranges into which capitalization or discount rates might fall relative to broad, qualitative descriptions of the degree of risk.

1925: Ralph E. Badger

Ralph E. Badger, one of the earliest and most often quoted writers to opine on required rates of return by risk class, offers the following:[3]

Class I—low risk	12–14.99%
Class II—medium risk	15–19.99%
Class III—high risk	20–24.99%
Class IV—very high risk	25% and over

[1] James C. Bonbright, *Valuation of Property*, vol. 1 (Charlottesville, Va.: The Miche Company, 1965 [reprint of 1937 ed.]), p. 262.
[2] Revenue Ruling 59-60 (1959-1, C.B. 237).
[3] Ralph E. Badger, *Valuation of Industrial Securities* (New York: Prentice-Hall, 1925), p. 123.

The above represent capitalization rates applicable to current or normalized after-tax earnings, as opposed to discount rates, which would be applicable to a stream of projected future earnings.

1953: Arthur Stone Dewing

In the fifth and last edition of the classic *Financial Policy of Corporations,* Dewing suggests seven classifications, with rates ranging from 10 to 100 percent. These classifications are shown in Exhibit 8–1.

As with the suggested rates proffered by Badger, Dewing's suggested rates also represent capitalization rates to convert a single year's after-tax earnings figure into an indication of value, as opposed to discount rates to determine the present value of a projected earnings stream.

EXHIBIT 8-1

Dewing's "Summary Statement of Capitalization of Earnings"

It is possible to throw industrial businesses into diverse categories in accordance with which we can form some estimates of the value of a business by capitalizing its earnings. These categories could be described in the following manner:

1. Old established businesses, with large capital assets and excellent goodwill—10%, a value ten times the net earnings. Very few industrial enterprises would come within this category.
2. Businesses, well established, but requiring considerable managerial care. To this category would belong the great number of old, successful industrial businesses—large and small—12-1/2%, a value eight times the net earnings.
3. Businesses, well established, but involving possible loss in consequence of shifts of general economic conditions. They are strong, well established businesses, but they produce a type of commodity which makes them vulnerable to depressions. They require considerable managerial ability, but little special knowledge on the part of the executives—15%, a value approximately seven times the net earnings.
4. Businesses requiring average executive ability—and at the same time comparatively small capital investment. These businesses are highly competitive, but established goodwill is of distinct importance. This class includes the rank and file of medium-sized, highly competitive industrial enterprises—20%, a value approximately five times the net earnings.
5. Small industrial businesses, highly competitive, and requiring a relatively small capital outlay. They are businesses which anyone, even with little capital, may enter—25%, a

value approximately four times the net earnings.
6. Industrial businesses, large and small, which depend on the special, often unusual skill of one, or of a small group of managers. They involve only a small amount of capital; they are highly competitive and the mortality is high among those who enter the competitive struggle—50%, a value of approximately twice the net earnings.
7. Personal service businesses. They require no capital, or at the most a desk, some envelopes and a few sheets of paper. The manager must have a special skill coupled with an intensive and thorough knowledge of his subjects. The earnings of the enterprise are the objective reflection of his skill; and he is not likely to be able to create "an organization" which can successfully "carry on" after he is gone. He can sell the business, including the reputation and the "plan of business," but he cannot sell himself, the only truly valuable part of the enterprise—100%, a value equal, approximately, to the earnings of a single year.

This summary of categories is not a classification in the sense of clearly defined and marked classes. There are innumerable intermediate stages. These seven categories are of the nature of nodal points in the organization of industry, according to the relation of earnings and value. There may be businesses so highly stabilized, so immune to the shocks of industrial depression and incompetent management, that they are worth more than ten times their annual earnings; there may be businesses so peculiar and individual that they are, in the hands of another, not worth even the earnings of a single year.

SOURCE: Arthur Stone Dewing, *The Financial Policy of Corporations,* 5th ed. (New York: The Ronald Press Company, 1953), pp. 390-91.

1982: James H. Schilt

James H. Schilt, a long-time financial analyst and editor of the *Business Valuation Review,* adopted the notion of broad ranges of required rates of return by qualitatively defined risk class and classified the required-return guidelines within the modern capital market theory framework of required premiums *over* the prevailing risk-free rate of return. He describes his objective as follows:

> As discount or capitalization rates are fairly arbitrarily determined, I have attempted to set forth guidelines for using specific risk premiums. Beginning with the risk-free rate, a premium would be added according to the risk category, and the sum would be the risk-compensated discount rate.[4]

Schilt's risk premium guidelines are shown in Exhibit 8–2.

Note that, as opposed to Badger's and Dewing's systems, Schilt's rates represent discount rates to be applied to calculate the present value of a projected stream of pretax earnings.

"Equity Risk Premium" Based on Historical Studies

As noted in Chapter 2, the capital asset pricing model suggests that the required rate of return for an equity investment consists of the "risk-free" rate of return available in the market at the valuation date plus a premium for risk. Some practitioners start with the short-term Treasury bill rate for the risk-free rate, while others use long-term Treasury bonds. In any case, a suitable proxy for a risk-free rate is directly observable in the market at any given time. The data problem, then, in implementing the capital asset pricing model for valuations is to develop a suitable proxy for the equity risk premium.

Ibbotson Associates Studies

By far the most widely used data on equity risk premiums are currently published by Ibbotson Associates. The Ibbotson analyses make extensive use of the rate-of-return data bases compiled by the Center for Research in Security Prices at the University of Chicago Graduate School of Business. Summary tables of the Ibbotson statistics as of the end of 1987 (from the *1988 Yearbook*) are shown in Exhibit 8–3.

All Ibbotson Associates data are based on *total return,* that is, any dividends or interest paid plus or minus any change in the security's market price. The series of greatest interest for valuation are common stocks, small stocks, long-term government bonds, U.S. Treasury bills, equity risk premiums, small-stock premiums, and horizon premiums.

---

[4] James H. Schilt, "A Rational Approach to Capitalization Rates for Discounting the Future Income Stream of a Closely Held Company," *The Financial Planner,* January 1982, p. 56.

EXHIBIT 8-2

Schilt's Risk Premiums for Discounting
Projected Income Streams

Category	Description	Risk Premium
1	Established businesses with a strong trade position, are well financed, have depth in management, whose past earnings have been stable and whose future is highly predictable.	6-10%
2	Established businesses in a more competitive industry that are well financed, have depth in management, have stable past earnings and whose future in fairly predictable.	11-15%
3	Businesses in a highly competitive industry that require little capital to enter, no management depth, element of risk is high, although past record may be good.	16-20%
4	Small businesses that depend upon the special skill of one or two people. Larger established businesses that are highly cyclical in nature. In both cases, future earnings may be expected to deviate widely from projections.	21-25%
5	Small "one man" businesses of a personal services nature, where the transferability of the income stream is in question.	26-30%

NOTE: "The risk premium chosen is added to the risk-free rate . . . . The resulting figure is the risk-adjusted capitalization rate for use in discounting the projected income stream. Because of the wide variation in the effective tax rates among companies, these figures are designed to be used with pre-tax income."

SOURCE: James H. Schilt, "A Rational Approach to Capitalization Rates for Discounting the Future Income Stream of a Closely Held Company," *The Financial Planner,* January 1982, p. 58; table also reproduced in Nicholas L. Feakins, "Relevance of Financial Analysis to Standard Appraisal Methodology," *Business Valuation Review,* September 1987, p. 110.

The following sections briefly describe these items along with a brief explanation of the difference between the "arithmetic" and "geometric" means for these series.

Common Stocks.   The series used for common stocks is the Standard and Poor's (S&P) Composite Index. This series often is used to represent the "market" returns for common stocks within the framework of the capital asset pricing model.

Small Stocks.   The small-stock series from 1926 to 1981 was made up of the 20 percent of the stocks on the New York Stock Exchange with the smallest capitalization as measured by price times number of shares outstanding. The series from 1982 to 1986 is the total return achieved by the Dimensional Fund Advisors (DFA) small-company fund. The fund is a market-value-weighted index of the ninth and tenth deciles of the NYSE, plus the stocks on the AMEX and OTC with the same capitalization ceiling as that of the NYSE ninth decile and the same capitalization floor as that of the NYSE tenth decile.

Long-Term Government Bonds.   The long-term U.S. government bond series represents the total return on bonds with approximately 20 years to maturity, reasonably current coupons, and no special features such as tax benefits or unique redemption privileges.

EXHIBIT 8-3

Ibbotson Associates' Summary Rate-of-Return Statistics

Basic Series: 1926 - 1987
Summary Statistics of
Annual Returns

Series	Geometric Mean	Arithmetic Mean	Standard Deviation	Distribution
Common Stocks	9.9%	12.0%	21.1%	
Small Company Stocks	12.1	17.7	35.9	
Long-Term Corporate Bonds	4.9	5.2	8.5	
Long-Term Government Bonds	4.3	4.6	8.5	
Intermediate-Term Government Bonds	4.8	4.9	5.5	
U.S. Treasury Bills	3.5	3.5	3.4	
Inflation Rates	3.0	3.2	4.8	

−90%   0%   90%

Risk Premium Series   **Summary Statistics**   **(1926 - 1987)**
                          Of Annual Returns

Series	Geometric Mean	Arithmetic Mean	Standard Deviation
Equity Risk Premia (stocks−bills)	6.2%	8.3%	21.1%
Small Stock Premia (small stocks−stocks)	2.0	3.7	19.0
Default Premia (LT corps−LT govts)	0.6	0.7	3.0
Horizon Premia (LT govts−bills)	0.8	1.1	8.0
Long-horizon risk premia: Common stocks total returns minus long-term government bond yield (income) returns	4.7	6.8	20.5
Intermediate-horizon equity risk premia: Common stock total returns minus intermediate-term government bond yield (income) returns	5.2	7.3	20.6

SOURCE: Ibbotson, Roger G. and Rex A. Sinquefeld, *Stocks, Bonds, Bills, and Inflation* (SBBI), 1982, updated in *SBBI 1988 Yearbook,* Ibbotson Associates, Chicago, pp. 25, 76, and 81.

U.S. Treasury Bills. Returns on Treasury bills are based on bills with approximately 30 days to maturity.

Equity Risk Premiums. The equity risk premium for each time period is the return on common stocks (represented by the S&P Composite Index) less the return on Treasury bills.

Long-Horizon Equity Risk Premiums. The long-horizon equity risk premium for each time period is the return on common stocks (represented by the S&P Composite Index) less 20-year Treasury bond yield returns. (This is a new series introduced in the 1988 *Yearbook*.)

Intermediate-Horizon Equity Risk Premium. The intermediate-horizon equity risk premium for each time period is the return on common stocks (represented by the S&P Composite Index) less the five-year Treasury bond yield returns. (This also is a new series introduced in the 1988 *Yearbook*.)

Small-Stock Premiums. The small-stock premium for any period is the difference between the common stock returns (as measured by the S&P Composite Index) and the returns on small stocks (as defined above).

Horizon Premiums. The horizon premium (sometimes called the *maturity premium*) for any period is the difference between the return on long-term government bonds (as defined above) and the return on U.S. Treasury bills.

"Arithmetic" versus "Geometric" Means. Notice that Exhibit 8–3 shows two columns of averages for each series, the first labeled "Geometric Mean" and the second "Arithmetic Mean." The latter is the kind of average with which we are most familiar, computed simply by adding the values of all observations and dividing the result by the number of observations. The geometric mean, which is useful for computing such things as annually compounded rates of return, is computed by multiplying all the observations together and taking the nth root of the result, n being the number of observations. (When the observations are rates of return, one must add 1.0 to each observation and then subtract 1.0 from the final result in order to make the arithmetic work properly.) Exhibit 8–4 is a more complete description and example of the difference between the arithmetic and geometric means. Exhibit 8–5 shows Ibbotson Associates' rationale for considering the arithmetic mean the appropriate average on which to focus when using their data for estimating the cost of capital or the discount rate.

EXHIBIT 8-4

Computation of Arithmetic and Geometric
Mean Rates of Return

ARITHMETIC MEAN

As is known, the arithmetic mean (designated $\overline{X}$) is the sum of each value in a distribution divided by the total number of values.

$$\overline{X} = \Sigma X/n.$$

A problem occurs if there are large changes in the annual returns over time. Consider the example in which a nondividend paying stock goes from $50 to $100 during Year 1 and back to $50 during Year 2. The annual returns would be:
— Year 1: 100%
— Year 2: −50%
Obviously, during the two years there was *no* return on the investment. Yet the arithmetic mean return would be:

$$[(+100) + (-50)]/2 = 50/2 = 25\%.$$

In this case, although there was *no* change in wealth and, therefore, no return, the arithmetic mean return is computed at 25 percent.

GEOMETRIC MEAN

The geometric mean (designated G) is the nth root of the product arrived at by multiplying the values in the distribution by each other. Specifically, it is:

$$G = \Pi X^{1/n}$$

where Π stands for *product.* When calculating the geometric mean returns, it is customary to use holding-period returns, which are the yield plus 1.0 (e.g., a positive 10 percent return is designated 1.10; a negative 15 percent return is designated 0.85). This is done because a negative yield causes the geometric mean calculation to be meaningless. As an example, consider the extreme example used in the previous discussion of the arithmetic mean:

	Yield (percent)	Holding-Period Return
Year 1:	100	2.00
Year 2:	−50	0.50

$$G = (2.00 \times 0.50)^{1/2} = (1.00)^{1/2} = 1.00 - 1.00 = 0\%.$$

To get the yield, 1.00 is subtracted from the geometric holding-period return. As can be seen, this answer is consistent with the ending wealth position of the investor. He ended where he began and had a 0 percent return during the period.

SOURCE: *Investment Analysis and Portfolio Management* 2nd edition by Frank K. Reilly copyright © 1985 Holt, Rinehart and Winston, reprinted by permission of the publisher.

EXHIBIT 8-5

Ibbotson Associates' Discussion of Arithmetic versus Geometric Mean for Estimating Cost of Capital or Discount Rate

Arithmetic versus Geometric Mean

Q. In your initial example, you stated that you use the arithmetic mean historical risk premium as the forecast of the future risk premium. Why do you use the arithmetic mean, instead of the geometric mean (compound annual return)?

A. The arithmetic mean is the rate of return which, when compounded over multiple periods, gives the mean of the probability distribution of ending wealth values. (A simple mathematical example shows that this is true.) This makes the arithmetic mean return appropriate for calculation of a discount rate, since expected cash flows (i.e., the means of distributions of future values) are discounted to arrive at a present value. It is likewise appropriate for the cost of capital or market required rate of return.

Definitionally, the discount rate that equates expected (mean) future values with the present value of an investment is that investment's cost of capital (see James C. Van Horne, *Financial Management and Policy*, 4th edition, Prentice-Hall, Inc., 1977, p. 203). The logic of using the discount rate as the cost of capital can be reinforced by noting that investors will discount their expected (mean) ending wealth values from an investment back to the present using the arithmetic mean, for the reason given above. They will therefore require such an expected (mean) return prospectively (that is, in the present looking toward the future) in order to commit their capital to the investment. Thus once again, the discount rate is the market required rate of return or cost of capital.

Q. Can you give the mathematical example you referred to?

A. Assume that a dollar invested has two possible outcomes each year: it rises 30 percent or falls 10 percent. These outcomes occur with equal probability, that is, each with a probability of 0.5. After one year, the possible outcomes are:

Ending wealth value	Probability
$1.30	0.50
0.90	0.50

Now, let's extend the example one more year. The investment could start at $1.30 and rise 30 percent or fall 10 percent, i.e. rise to $1.69 or fall to $1.17 each with a probability of 0.25. Or, the investment could start at $0.90 and rise 30 percent or fall 10 percent, i.e. rise to $1.17 or fall to $0.81, again each with a probability of 0.25. This can be extended indefinitely, but we will spare the reader and stop at the second year. After two years, the possible outcomes are:

Ending wealth value	Probability	Value x Probability
$1.69	0.25	0.4225
1.17	0.50	0.5850
0.81	0.25	0.2025
	Summation	$1.2100

Note that an extra column has been added, value times probability, along with the sum of the figures in the extra column. This summation represents the statistical expectancy of the wealth an investor in this security would have after two years.

The return required in order for an investment to grow from $1.00 to (an expected) $1.21 in two years can now be calculated.

This is given by $(1.21/1.00)^{(1/2)} - 1$, and is 0.10 or 10 percent. Remarkably, 10 percent is also the arithmetic mean of the two returns, +30 and -10 percent. The geometric mean of the two returns is $(1.3 \times 0.9)^{(1/2)} - 1 = .082 = 8.2$ percent. Clearly, the arithmetic mean is the rate of return that equates the expected future value of an investment with its present value. This property makes it the correct return to use as the discount rate or cost of capital.

SOURCE: Ibbotson, Roger G. and Rex A. Sinquefeld, *Stocks, Bonds, Bills, and Inflation* (SBBI), 1982, updated in *SSBI 1988 Yearbook*, Ibbotson Associates, Chicago, pp. 139-141.

Selection of the Historical Base Period

The objective in studying historical realized rates of return is to find guidance as to rates of return that investors may expect in the future. Recognizing this, it seems useful to attempt to identify those historical time periods that might be most representative of results that one might expect in the future. The idea is to try to identify periods that are long enough to even out the high degree of volatility characteristic of equity returns but sufficiently recent that the historical forces generating the returns do not differ dramatically from the forces in place as of the valuation date. It would also seem desirable to try to select a period that starts and ends in roughly the same phase of the stock market cycle, since taking a period from trough to peak or vice versa obviously would introduce a potential bias. Toward this latter end it is helpful to consult a stock market chart, an example of which is shown in Exhibit 8–6.

Willamette Management Associates has selected several historical periods that investors might have reason to believe will provide some guidance as to future expectations. For each such period, they have summarized the geometric and arithmetic equity risk premium, small-stock premium, and horizon premium generated by the computer program and data base, SBBI/PC, from Ibbotson Associates, Inc. The comparative equity risk premium, small-stock premium, and horizon premium for five historical time periods are shown in Exhibit 8–7.

Applications of Historical Risk Premium Data to Estimation of Discount Rate

Use of equity risk premium data to develop a discount rate requires selecting the two basic components of the required rate of return: the risk-free rate and the equity risk premium. The following sections address selection of the rates for each component.

Risk-Free Rate.   The purest application of the capital asset pricing model would dictate use of the Treasury-bill rate for the risk-free rate. The T-bill rate, however, is much more volatile than longer-term rates, suggesting that the latter may be a more valid basis for building a current discount rate for equity investments, at least during periods of wide interest rate swings. Consequently, some practitioners use long-term government bond rates as a proxy for the risk-free rate. An alternative is to use the long-term government bond rates less the horizon premium as a proxy for the risk-free rate. This procedure escapes the extreme volatility that can characterize short-term rates while potentially eliminating an element of risk-related premium built into returns on long-term bonds.

With the introduction of the long-horizon and intermediate-horizon risk premium series in the 1988 *SBBI Yearbook,* the analyst can bypass use of the horizon premium by starting with the current 20-year or 5-year Treasury-bond rate and adding the appropriate equity risk premium.

Risk Premium.   The strictest application of the capital asset pricing model would require multiplying the beta of the subject stock by the equity risk premium for the market from which the beta was derived to get the applicable equity risk premium for the stock. As discussed in Part I, however, betas for closely held companies are difficult to estimate. Furthermore, most closely held companies are the same size as or smaller than the companies used to develop the small-stock risk premium. Therefore, it often is practical to add the small-stock risk premium to the equity risk premium based on the S&P 500 to develop an applicable risk premium, and then make further adjustments specific to the subject, if applicable, thus avoiding the necessity of estimating a beta for the subject company.

Sources of Betas

Some of the most popular sources of betas as of this writing are the *Value Line Investment Survey, Media General Financial Weekly, Merrill Lynch Quantitative Analysis,* and *Wilshire Associates.* Each of these

EXHIBIT 8-6

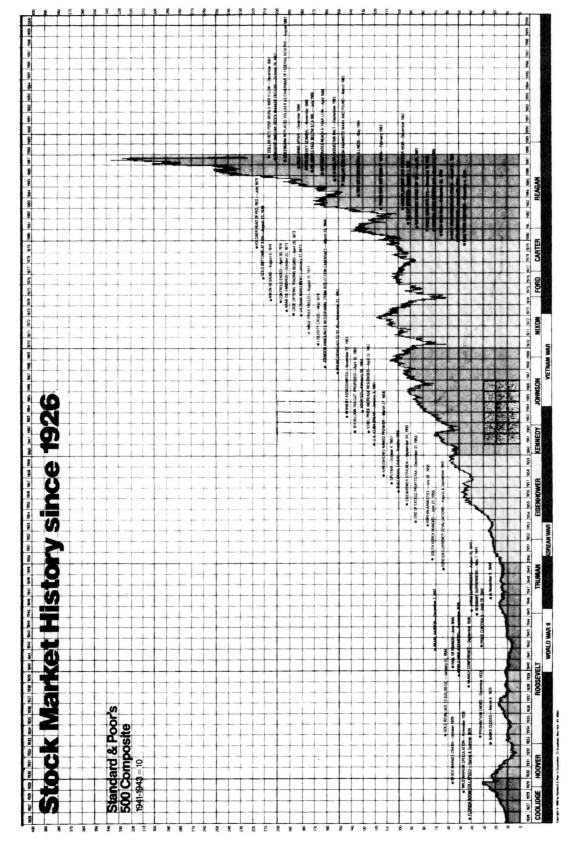

Stock Market History since 1926

Standard & Poor's
500 Composite
1941–1943 = 10

SOURCE: *Standard & Poor's Outlook*, January 6, 1988, copyright © 1988, Standard & Poor's Corporation, New York.

EXHIBIT 8-7

**Equity Risk Premiums, Small-Stock Premiums,
Horizon Premiums (Annualized) for Selected Historical Periods**

Variable	No. of Periods (Years)	Geometric Mean	Arithmetic Mean	Standard Deviation
Period: January 1926 to December 1986				
Equity Risk Premium	61	.063291	.086127	.217059
Small-Stock Premium	61	.039479	.060345	.222046
Maturity Premium	61	.008585	.011976	.084764
Period: January 1936 to December 1986				
Equity Risk Premium	51	.068306	.085635	.190037
Small-Stock Premium	51	.053224	.068921	.191405
Maturity Premium	51	.004429	.008073	.088103
Period: January 1946 to December 1986				
Equity Risk Premium	41	.064919	.079978	.179229
Small-Stock Premium	41	.030488	.042966	.169172
Maturity Premium	41	(.004712)	(.000507)	.095272
Period: January 1956 to December 1986				
Equity Risk Premium	31	.037209	.051633	.172319
Small-Stock Premium	31	.058405	.072369	.180014
Maturity Premium	31	(.006839)	(.001490)	.108049
Period: January 1966 to December 1986				
Equity Risk Premium	21	.016618	.031808	.174703
Small-Stock Premium	21	.062348	.080509	.206415
Maturity Premium	21	(.005711)	.001433	.126049

SOURCE: Calculations generated by the Computer program and database, SBBI/PC, from Ibbotson Associates, Inc., Chicago, Illinois.

services computes the betas slightly differently. *Value Line* computes betas for about 1,600 individual stocks, *Media General Financial Weekly* for about 500, *Merrill Lynch Quantitative Analysis* for about 800, and *Wilshire* for about 10,000. In addition, *Merrill Lynch* and *Media General* provide average betas for various economic and industry groups.

Implied Expected Returns in Current Market

As discussed in Part I, an alternative to building a discount rate by adding a historical risk premium to a current risk-free rate is to attempt to directly discern the total rates of return that participants in the market currently expect. In other words, the analyst can examine published projections to see directly the prospective rates of return that the market is expecting. Several services provide such data. Two of the most popular ones are *Value Line Investment Survey* and *Merrill Lynch Quantitative Analysis,* mentioned in the previous section.

Based on projected stock price and dividends, *Value Line* gives a low and a high projected total annual return for each stock (see item G in Exhibit 8–8). Based on assumptions regarding earnings growth and dividend payout ratios, the *Merrill Lynch Quantitative Analysis* gives a figure for "Implied Return" for each stock (see Exhibit 8–9).

As discussed in Part I, the quality of the implied returns such services publish depends directly on the quality of the projections from which they are derived.

Rates of Return Allowed to Regulated Companies

Public utility commissioners in all 50 states allow regulated utilities to charge rates to their customers that provide what supposedly is a fair rate of return on investment. These allowed rates of return generally are based on the respective commissions' perceptions of the cost of debt capital and the cost of equity capital based on studies by their staffs. Utility commissions' allowed rate of return orders usually also specify an allowed overall rate of return on invested capital based on their conclusions as to the appropriate capital structure. Megamillions of dollars are involved in these rate decisions, based on hard-fought negotiations and hearings which sometimes culminate in lawsuits and final decisions rendered in court.

Regulated companies usually are regulated because they have a captive market and are in a monopoly position to supply a needed service; thus, their cost of capital should be considerably lower than that for an average company. Therefore, allowed rates of return for regulated companies can be viewed as a reasonable benchmark for a minimum boundary of cost of capital.

Each year, *Public Utilities Fortnightly* publishes the results of research compiled on natural gas utility and electric utility rate orders issued during the previous year by state public utility commissions throughout the United States. The published research results include the rate of return on common equity authorized by each public utility commission order, along with various other information related to the order. The published research is organized by state and by individual utility within each state. The research published on the natural gas utility rate orders cover the 12-month period ending August 31, while the electric utility rate order published research covers the 12-month period ending April 30.

Research based on *Public Utilities Fortnightly* data indicates that during the 12 months ended August 1987, the authorized rates of return on common equity for natural gas utilities, as ordered by the state public utilities commissions, ranged from 10.29 to 15.55 percent after excluding outlying authorized rates of return that were affected by special circumstances. The average authorized rate of return on common equity for natural gas utilities throughout the nation was 13.15 percent during this 12-month period. Research indicates that

EXHIBIT 8-8

Sample Value Line Report

Ratings & Reports   A   B   BB   C   D

PHILIP MORRIS NYSE-MO	RECENT PRICE **85**	P/E RATIO **8.4**	(Trailing: 9.6 / Median: 9.5)	RELATIVE P/E RATIO **0.73**	DIV'D YLD **5.1%**	343

High → 17.8 29.6 34.2 30.7 29.6 31.6 32.4 38.4 38.6 48.5 55.1 67.8 72.4 83.3 95.1
Low → 11.7 16.9 24.4 17.0 20.4 24.9 25.8 27.9 31.1 29.1 42.0 44.1 54.0 62.1 79.0

Target Price Range 200 150 125 100 80 60

10.0 x Cash Flow p sh

2-for-1 split

Options Trade On ASE

Insider Decisions 1984
	F	M	A	M	J	J	A	S	O	N	D	J	F	M	A
to Buy	3	3	1	0	3	2	1	3	1	0	1	3	4	2	
to Sell	1	3	1	2	2	4	3	3	6	1	0	3	3	5	

Institutional Decisions
	1Q'84	2Q'84	3Q'84	4Q'84	1Q'85
to Buy	152	158	142	128	147
to Sell	146	130	141	172	183
Hldg's(000)	73666	75144	74487	74356	74952

Percent 9.0 / shares 6.0 / traded 3.0

1988 1989 1990
July 5, 1985 · Value Line
TIMELINESS **2** Above Average (Relative Price Perform-ance Next 12 Mos)
SAFETY **1** Highest (Scale 1 Highest to 5 Lowest)
BETA .90 (1.00 = Market)

1988-90 PROJECTIONS
	Price	Gain	Ann'l Total Return
High	190	(+125%)	26%
Low	155	(+80%)	20%

© Value Line, Inc.   88-90E

1970	1971	1972	1973	1974	1975	1976	1977	1978	1979	1980	1981	1982	1983	1984	1985	1986	1987			88-90E
15.62	17.70	19.57	23.50	26.29	30.68	36.09	43.41	53.37	66.67	78.73	86.81	93.06	103.82	113.79	123.30	133.50		Sales per sh (A)		178.00
.99	1.18	1.40	1.63	1.88	2.22	2.80	3.47	4.22	5.28	6.17	7.18	8.46	9.85	11.61	13.40	15.60		"Cash Flow" per sh		20.50
.84	1.01	1.17	1.36	1.58	1.84	2.24	2.80	3.39	4.08	4.63	5.28	6.23	7.17 (G)	8.43	10.10	12.00		Earnings per sh (B)		16.00
.26	.30	.32	.34	.38	.44	.58	.78	1.03	1.25	1.60	2.00	2.40	2.90	3.40	4.00	4.60		Div'ds Decl'd per sh (C)		6.50
.39	.57	1.10	1.61	1.88	2.06	1.85	2.34	4.56	5.07	6.06	8.15	7.31	4.53	2.46	2.70	2.75		Cap'l Spending per sh		4.00
4.47	5.36	6.28	7.33	8.43	10.32	12.00	14.08	17.00	19.84	22.87	26.35	29.09	32.27	33.72	38.30	44.75		Book Value per sh (D)		68.65
96.64	104.68	108.89	110.76	114.53	118.71	118.97	119.84	124.27	124.54	124.75	125.40	125.90	124.98	121.40	120.00	118.00		Common Shs Outst'g (E)		118.00
11.3	15.4	21.0	22.1	15.5	13.7	12.7	10.0	9.8	8.4	8.6	9.3	8.4	8.8	7.5				Avg Ann'l P/E Ratio		11.0
.81	.98	1.44	2.18	2.17	1.83	1.63	1.36	1.34	1.22	1.14	1.13	.93	.74	.69				Relative P/E Ratio		.90
2.8%	2.0%	1.3%	1.1%	1.5%	1.8%	2.0%	2.7%	3.1%	3.7%	4.0%	4.1%	4.6%	4.6%	4.7%				Avg Ann'l Div'd Yield		3.7%

Bold figures are Value Line estimates

CAPITAL STRUCTURE as of 12/31/84
Total Debt $2588.6 mill. Due in Yrs $1161.9 mill.
LT Debt $2059.5 mill. LT Interest $210.0 mill.

(LT interest earned: 8.0x; total interest coverage: 7.0x)   (33% of Cap'l)

Pension Liability None in '84 vs. None in '83

Pfd Stock None

Common Stock 121,395,290 shs. (67% of Cap'l)

4293.8	5202.0	6632.5	8302.9	9822.3	10886	11716	12976	13814	14800	15750		Sales ($mill) (A)		21000
15.2%	16.4%	16.3%	15.9%	14.9%	15.2%	16.5%	17.0%	18.3%	19.0%	19.5%		Operating Margin		19.5%
67.7	81.6	116.2	149.6	192.9	240.4	283.7	327.0	375.5	390	415		Depreciation ($mill)		525
265.7	334.9	408.6	507.9	576.8	659.7	781.8	903.5	1034.1	1220	1425		Net Profit ($mill) (F)		1890
43.7%	46.5%	45.2%	43.9%	40.5%	38.9%	40.0%	43.0%	45.2%	45.0%	45.0%		Income Tax Rate		44.0%
6.2%	6.4%	6.2%	6.1%	5.9%	6.1%	6.7%	7.0%	7.5%	8.2%	9.0%		Net Profit Margin		9.0%
1202.3	1415.8	1585.1	1833.2	1849.2	2053.0	2236.5	1116.5	1288.6	1500	1900		Working Cap'l ($mill)		4200
1247.8	1426.6	2147.0	2447.8	2598.1	3499.0	3749.3	2514.7	2059.5	1800	1600		Long-Term Debt ($mill)		1800
1430.0	1690.1	2114.7	2471.0	2853.0	3304.6	3662.9	4033.7	4092.9	4600	5275		Net Worth ($mill)		8100
11.7%	12.3%	11.1%	11.8%	12.0%	11.2%	12.3%	15.8%	18.6%	20.5%	22.0%		% Earned Total Cap'l		20.0%
18.6%	19.8%	19.3%	20.6%	20.2%	20.0%	21.3%	22.4%	25.3%	26.5%	27.0%		% Earned Net Worth		23.5%
13.8%	14.3%	13.4%	14.3%	13.2%	12.4%	13.1%	13.3%	15.1%	16.0%	16.5%		% Retained to Comm Eq		14.0%
26%	28%	31%	31%	35%	38%	39%	40%	40%	40%	38%		% All Div'ds to Net Prof		41%

CURRENT POSITION ($MILL)
	1982	1983	12/31/84
Cash Assets	53.9	29.8	93.7
Receivables	691.1	781.8	854.3
Inventory(LIFO)	3068.5	2599.2	2653.5
Other	36.8	42.0	38.6
Current Assets	3850.3	3452.8	3640.1
Accts Payable	423.7	437.3	471.9
Debt Due	– –	560.2	529.1
Other	1190.1	1338.8	1350.5
Current Liab.	1613.8	2336.3	2351.5

ANNUAL RATES of change (per sh)
	Past 10 Yrs	Past 5 Yrs	Est '82-'84 to '88-'90
Sales	16.0%	13.5%	9.5%
"Cash Flow"	20.0%	18.0%	13.0%
Earnings	19.0%	17.5%	15.0%
Dividends	24.0%	23.5%	14.5%
Book Value	15.5%	13.5%	13.5%

QUARTERLY SALES ($ mill.) (A)
Cal-endar	Mar. 31	June 30	Sep. 30	Dec. 31	Full Year
1982	2795	3065	3135	2721	11716
1983 (F)	3021	3400	3464	3091	12976
1984	3249	3609	3666	3290	13814
1985	3315	3900	3950	3635	14800
1986	3675	4100	4150	3825	15750

EARNINGS PER SHARE (B) Full
Cal-endar	Mar. 31	June 30	Sep. 30	Dec. 31	Full Year
1982	1.34	1.51	1.99	1.39	6.23
1983	1.47	1.75	2.27	1.68	7.17
1984	1.67	2.10	2.62	2.04	8.43
1985	2.12	2.50	3.05	2.43	10.10
1986	2.50	3.00	3.60	2.90	12.00

QUARTERLY DIVIDENDS PAID (C) Full
Cal-endar	Mar. 31	June 30	Sep. 30	Dec. 31	Full Year
1981	.40	.50	.50	.50	1.90
1982	.50	.60	.60	.60	2.30
1983	.60	.725	.725	.725	2.78
1984	.725	.85	.85	.85	3.28
1985	.85	1.00	1.00		

BUSINESS: Philip Morris Inc. is the nation's largest cigarette producer (estimated 35% of domestic consumption) and exporter. Major brands: *Marlboro, Benson & Hedges, Parliament, Merit, Virginia Slims, Players.* Acquired Miller, second largest beer manufacturer in U.S., in 1970. Sells *High Life, Lite* and *Lowenbrau.* Acquired Seven-Up, third leading soft drink co. in '78. Owns Mission Viejo, West Coast real estate developer. '84 depreciation rate: 6.7%. Estimated plant age: 5 yrs. Insiders own about 1.5% of common shares. Has 60,000 employees, 30,300 common stockholders. Chairman & C.E.O.: H. Maxwell. President: & C.O.O: J.A. Murphy. Inc: Virginia. Address: 120 Park Avenue, New York, NY 10017.

We look for Philip Morris to generate a huge amount of excess cash over the next three to five years. The company's core domestic tobacco business throws off an awesome level of profits—$1.7 billion in 1984 and an estimated $2.0 billion this year. Since capital requirements for this operation are relatively modest (and declining), much of these funds are available for other investment purposes. Indeed, our cash flow analysis suggests that through the end of this decade, PM's "free" cash flow will average about $1 billion annually and could be much more if the company decides to scuttle the Miller and/or Seven Up divisions, neither of which have lived up to expectations.

How will management utilize these monies? Completion of an announced share buyback program, coupled with a steady paring of the debt load and regular, double-digit dividend increases through the 1988-90 period, seem all but assured; such moves, however, would "sop up" only a portion of the excess cash flow. Further share repurchases could be undertaken, but we think the acquisition of a major consumer products outfit remains an intriguing possibility. Though

we won't factor the benefits from acquisitions into our estimates and projections until any deals are finalized, success in this regard could greatly enhance PM's earnings growth prospects—and stock price appreciation potential—to the 1988-90 period. As it is, based on current operations alone, we look for PM's share profits to grow at about a 15% rate, compounded annually, over the next three to five years.

These timely shares have been under pressure of late, as Wall Street struggled to determine the possible effect of pending product liability litigation against cigarette manufacturers, a very complicated and difficult to assess situation. Though PM does not expect any cases in which it is directly involved to go to trial this year and although to date the tobacco industry has *never* lost a

(Continued on page 389))

Restated Sales (and Operating* Margins) by Business Line
	1982	1983	1984	1985
Philip Morris Usa	4330.1(25.5%)	5520.0(24.2%)	6134.0(28.5%)	6600(31.0%)
Philip Morris Int	3564.0(12.5%)	3647.0(10.0%)	3741.0(11.3%)	4100(11.5%)
Miller Brewing	2929.0(5.4%)	2922.0(7.8%)	2928.0(4.0%)	3000(3.3%)
Seven Up	531.0(d0.1%)	650.0(d1.6%)	734.0(0.7%)	800(1.0%)
Philip Morris Intl	232.0(3.3%)	237.0(5.7%)	277.0(10.6%)	300(10.3%)
Mission Viejo	130.0(4.6%)	- (- -)	- (- -)	-(-)
Company Total	11716.1(14.7%)	12976.0(14.9%)	13814.0(16.8%)	14800(18.0%)

*After depreciation, before interest exp. & equity income.

(A) Includes Seven-Up from 6/78. (B) Based on avg. shs. outst'g. Next earnings report due late July. Est'd current cost eqs./sh. '84, $5.93. (C) Next div'd meeting about Aug. 29. Goes ex about Sept. 10. Approx. div'd payment dates: Jan. 10, Apr. 10, July 10, Oct. 10. ■ Div'd reinvestment plan available. (D) Incl. intangibles. In '84: $547 mill., $4.50/sh. (E) In mill., adj. for stock splits & div'ds. (F) Mission Viejo rept'd on equity basis from 1983. (G) Excl. nonrecur. writeoff of $1.19/sh. in 4th qtr. of '84.

Company's Financial Strength A+
Stock's Price Stability 90
Price Growth Persistence 60
Earnings Predictability 100

EXHIBIT 8-8

Sample Value Line Report
(Continued)

A **Recent price**—nine days prior to delivery date.

AA **Here is the core of Value Line's advice—the rank for Timeliness; the rank for Safety; Beta—the stock's sensitivity to fluctuations of the market as a whole.**

B **P/E ratio**—the most recent price divided by the latest six months' earnings per share plus earnings estimated for the next six months.

BB **P/E Median**—a rounded average of four middle values of the range of average annual price-earnings ratios over the past 10 years.

C **Relative P/E Ratio**—the stock's current P/E divided by the median P/E for all stocks under Value Line review.

D **Dividend Yield**—cash dividends *estimated to be declared in the next 12 months* divided by the recent price.

E **The 3-5 year target price range,** estimated. The range is placed in proper position on the price chart, and is shown numerically in the "1988-90 Projections" box in the lower right-hand corner of the price chart.

F **The date of delivery** to the subscribers. The survey is mailed on a schedule that aims for delivery to every subscriber on Friday afternoon.

G **Annual Total Return**—the estimated future average annual growth plus current dividend yield—plus possible annualized change in the trend of the price-earnings ratio.

H The stock's **highest and lowest price** of the year.

I The **Value Line**—reported earnings plus depreciation ("cash flow") multiplied by a number selected to correlate the stock's 3- to 5-year projected target price with "cash flow" projected out to 1988-90.

J **Monthly price ranges** of the stock—plotted on a ratio (logarithmic) grid to show percentage changes in true proportion. For example, a ratio chart equalizes the move of a $10 stock that rises to $11 with a $100 stock that rises to $110. Both have advanced 10% and over the same space on a ratio grid.

K **Relative price strength**—describes the stock's past price performance relative to the Value Line Composite Average of 1700 stocks. The Timeliness Rank usually predicts the future direction of this line.

L **The number of shares traded monthly** as a percentage of the total outstanding.

M **Statistical milestones** that reveal significant long-term trends. The statistics are presented in two ways: 1) The upper series records results on a per-share basis; 2) the lower records results on a

company basis. On pages 30 to 33, you will find conclusions that might be drawn from an inspection of these milestones. Note that the statistics for the year 1985 are estimated, as are the figures for the average of the years 1988-90. The estimates would be revised, if necessary, should future evidence require. The weekly *Summary & Index* would promptly call attention to such revisions.

N A condensed summary of the **business.**

O A 400-word **report on recent developments and prospects**—issued once every three months on a preset schedule.

P Most large corporations engage in several lines of business. Hence sales and profit margins are shown by **lines of business.**

Q Value Line indexes of **financial strength, price stability, price growth persistence,** and **earnings predictability.**

R **Footnotes** explain a number of things, such as the way earnings are reported, whether "fully diluted," on a "primary" basis, or on an "average shares outstanding" basis.

S **Quarterly dividends paid** are actual payments. The total of dividends paid in four quarters may not equal the figure shown in the annual series on dividends declared. (Sometimes a dividend declared at the end of the year will be paid in the first quarter of the following year.)

T **Quarterly earnings** are shown on a **per share** basis (estimates in bold type). Quarterly sales on a gross basis.

U **Annual rates of change** (on a per share basis). Actual past, estimated future.

V **Current position**—current assets, current liabilities, and other components of working capital.

W The **capital structure** as of recent date showing the percentage of capital in long-term debt (33%), and in common stock (67%); the number of times that total interest charges were earned (7.0 in 1984).

X A record of **the decisions taken by the biggest institutions** (over $70 million in equity holdings)—including banks, insurance companies, mutual funds, investment advisers, internally managed endowments, and pension funds—to buy or sell during the past five quarters and how many shares were involved, and the total number of shares they hold.

Y The **record of insider decisions**—decisions by officers and directors to buy or sell as reported to the SEC a month or more after execution.

Z **Options patch**—indicates listed options are available on the stock, and on what exchange they are most actively traded.

EXHIBIT 8-9

Merrill Lynch Quantitative Analysis User Guide to Company Profiles

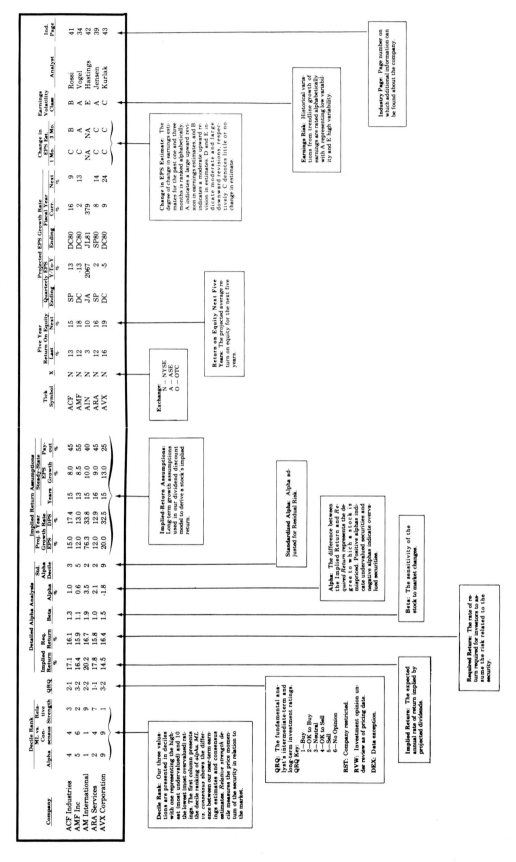

SOURCE: *Quantitative Analysis* (New York: Merrill Lynch, Pierce, Fenner & Smith, Inc., February 1988) pp. 42-43.

the average authorized rate of return on common equity for electric utilities throughout the nation was 13.36 percent during the 12 months ended April 1987, while the authorized rates of return on common equity ranged from 10.08 percent to 16.65 percent.

Summary

The determination of appropriate discount and/or capitalization rates is every bit as important to the valuation process as are accurate estimates of earning power. Nevertheless, many reports that claim to provide a supportable conclusion of value actually accord scant attention to this essential element of the valuation process. It is perhaps in the area of determining proper capitalization and discount rates that valuation analysts draw most heavily on their knowledge of financial theory and the data resources at their disposal to apply that theory to the unique circumstances of the subject company in the economic environment existing at a particular valuation date. This chapter has presented some of the most prominent sources of guidance for the valuation analyst's quest for supportable capitalization and discount rates.

Bibliography: Data on Required Rates of Return

Books

Badger, Ralph E. *Valuation of Industrial Securities.* New York: Prentice-Hall, 1925.

Dewing, Arthur Stone. *The Financial Policy of Corporations.* 5th ed. New York: Ronald Press, 1953.

Reilly, Frank K. *Investment Analysis and Portfolio Management.* 2nd ed. Hinsdale, Ill.: Dryden Press, 1985.

Williams, John Burr. *The Theory of Investment Value.* Cambridge, Mass.: Harvard University Press, 1938. (Reprinted in Amsterdam by North Holland Publishing Company, 1956.)

Periodicals

Corporate Earnings Estimator. Chicago: Zacks Investment Research, biweekly.

Earnings Forecaster. New York: Standard & Poor's Corporation, weekly.

Institutional Brokers Estimate System (I/B/E/S). New York: Lynch, Jones & Ryan, online daily; paper output weekly.

Media General Financial Weekly. Richmond, Va.: Media General Financial Services, weekly.

Public Utilities Fortnightly. Arlington, Va.: Public Utilities Reports, Inc., biweekly.

Quantitative Analysis. Washington, D.C.: Merrill Lynch, Pierce, Fenner & Smith, Inc., bimonthly.

Stocks, Bonds, Bills and Inflation 19— Yearbook: Market Results from 1926–19—. Chicago: Ibbotson Associates, annual.

Value Line Investment Survey. New York: Arnold Bernhard & Company, weekly.

Arbitrage Pricing Theory Data Sources:

Ibbotson Associates, Inc. *The Cost of Capital Quarterly-Utility Edition* (Chicago: Ibbotson Associates, Inc., beginning 1988).

Ibbotson Associates, Inc. *The Cost of Capital Quarterly-Industrial Edition* (Chicago: Ibbotson Associates, Inc., forthcoming).

See also The Alcar Group, Inc. *APT!*™ (Alcar's *Financial Policy Information Service*) (Skokie, Ill.: The Alcar Group, Inc., beginning 1988).

Chapter 9

Comparative Transaction Data

Throughout this book we have discussed using data from publicly traded companies as one source of guidance in the valuation of closely held businesses. This chapter presents step-by-step directions for locating and compiling such information. The final section outlines means of gathering data on mergers and acquisitions of both publicly traded and closely held companies, as well as information on control premiums paid in the acquisition of publicly traded companies.

Compiling a List of Publicly Traded Comparatives

The purpose of gathering data on comparative publicly traded companies is to derive some benchmarks by which to value the subject privately held company. For example, public companies in the industry selling at price/earnings ratios higher than the overall market average indicate that the public market is optimistic about the industry's future, and this optimism should also be reflected in the private companies' P/E ratios. Similarly, the public market can provide benchmarks concerning the relation of stock prices to such variables as book values, adjusted underlying net asset values, dividends, and gross revenues. Any or all of these parameters can be relevant to a specific valuation situation, as discussed throughout this book.

The process of compiling a comprehensive list of comparative publicly traded companies is not simple. No single source provides an exhaustive list. It is much easier to find good comparatives in some industries than in others. A complete search requires creativity, ingenuity, and experience. This chapter presents the most comprehensive general sources available. If not satisfied with the list developed through these sources, the analyst can consult trade association membership lists and regional investment publications or ask the management of the subject company and of the companies discovered through the conventional search for additional prospects.

Of all the criteria by which different companies may be judged as comparable for valuation purposes, the one that typically receives the most attention is the industry in which the subject company operates. In fact, Revenue Ruling 59-60 specifically states that of the factors that "are fundamental and require careful analysis in each case" for gift and estate tax valuations, one is "the market price of stocks of corporations engaged in the same or a similar line of business having their stocks actively traded on a free and open market, either on an exchange or over-the-counter."[1]

Therefore, the starting point in compiling a list of comparative companies is to form a list of the companies that operate in the subject company's industry group. The most widely accepted categorization of industry groups is the U.S. government's *Standard Industrial Classification Manual,* which publishes and defines Standard Industrial

---

[1]Revenue Ruling 59-60 (1959-1 C.B. 327), Section 4.

Classification (SIC) codes. (The SIC code is the statistical classification standard underlying all establishment-based federal economic statistics classified by industry.) The latest edition of the manual was published in 1987 and revised to take into account technological changes; institutional changes such as deregulation in the banking, communications, and transportation industries; and the tremendous expansion in the service sector.

The search for comparative public companies should be as exhaustive as the scope of the particular valuation case permits. Frequently, the most obvious public companies in an industry are the largest ones and, for this and related reasons, may be less comparable to most closely held companies than some of the smaller, more obscure public companies. Another purpose of conducting a comprehensive search for comparative companies is to demonstrate that the appraiser took into account all companies that might be considered reasonably comparable and selected for analysis the most comparative companies available. The analyst must establish and adhere to an objective set of selection criteria so that the final list will not tend to bias the valuation result either upward or downward.

Developing a List of "Suspects"

Three sources the analyst can use to develop a list of *suspects* (companies in the subject company's SIC group that might be useful as comparatives) are the *Directory of Companies Required to File Annual Reports with the Securities and Exchange Commission;* Standard & Poor's *Register of Corporations, Directors and Executives;* Standard & Poor's *Corporation Records* and *Moody's Manuals.*

SEC *Directory.* The latest SEC *Directory* as of this writing lists 13,425 companies. The coverage is defined as follows:

> The Directory contains listings of companies required to file annual reports under the Securities Exchange Act of 1934 as of September 30, 1987. The Directory includes companies with securities listed on national securities exchanges, companies with securities traded over the counter which are registered under Section 12(g) of the Securities Exchange Act, and certain companies required to file pursuant to Section 15(d) of the Securities Exchange Act as a result of having securities registered under the Securities Act of 1934.[2]

Although this is a good list, it omits thousands of smaller companies that trade over the counter. Only companies with $1 million or more in assets and 500 or more stockholders are subject to SEC filing requirements under Section 12(g) of the Securities Exchange Act. Furthermore, the SEC *Directory* excludes investment companies registered under the Investment Company Act of 1940, an important

---

[2]Securities and Exchange Commission, *Directory of Companies Required to File Annual Reports with the Securities and Exchange Commission* (Washington, D.C.: U.S. Government Printing Office, September 1987), p. 1.

group to use as comparables for family-owned investment holding companies. Data for investment companies can be found in Wiesenberger Investment Companies Service's *Investment Companies,* an annual publication with monthly supplements.

Another limitation of the SEC *Directory* is that it is usually a year or more out of date. As this book is being written in 1988, the latest issue is a listing as of September 30, 1987. Disclosure, Inc. publishes a more up-to-date list titled *SEC Filing Companies,* but it is arranged alphabetically only. It shows the SIC codes, but it would be necessary to comb through the whole list to pick out the companies in any particular SIC group.

Standard & Poor's *Register.* The S&P *Register* is perhaps the most comprehensive directory of companies by SIC group, but it does not distinguish which companies are public and which are private. However, if a company is public and has been quoted in the *National Daily Quotation Service* (referred to among stockbrokers as the *pink sheets*) within the preceding six months, it will be listed in the *National Monthly Stock Summary.* Therefore, the S&P *Register* and the *National Monthly Stock Summary* can be used together to develop a list of publicly quoted companies in a particular SIC group.

The *National Monthly Stock Summary* provides the price quotations at the end of the month in most cases. In compiling the list of companies, the analyst usually will want to use the monthly issue of the *National Monthly Stock Summary* that coincides with the valuation date.

Standard & Poor's *Corporation Records.* In cases in which budget or time constraints do not permit an exhaustive search for comparative companies, a shortcut is to use the *Classified Index of Industrial Companies* published annually as part of the Standard & Poor's *Corporation Records* instead of the S&P *Register.* The index, classified by SIC code, includes every public company that appears in the S&P *Corporation Records.* The limitation is that the *Corporation Records* excludes some smaller public companies included in the S&P *Register.*

Moody's Manuals. Another source that is useful in finding comparative publicly traded companies is *Moody's Manuals. Moody's Manuals* are separated into *Bank & Finance, Industrials, OTC Industrials, OTC Unlisted, Public Utilities,* and *Transportation.* Several of these manuals, particularly *Industrials* and *OTC Industrials,* list the companies included by general industry group.

Computer Data Bases. The online data base is an alternative to printed annual reports and 10-Ks. Predicasts, Inc. has been offering summary data from approximately 3,000 corporate reports through DIALOG Information Services, Inc. and BRS Information Technologies. Summary data from 10-Ks are accessible electronically for every company that files them. A service known as *Disclosure II* is available through several online vendors, such as DIALOG.

EDGAR (Electronic Data Gathering Analysis and Retrieval) is the Security and Exchange Commission's electronic filing, processing, and dissemination system. EDGAR permits corporations to make required filings electronically; however, currently only certain companies' filings are available through the system. The SEC expects to have the system fully operational in the near future.

Having used these sources, the analyst will have compiled a list of companies in a particular SIC code or several closely related codes that have a public trading market. Analysts in my firm call this the *suspect list*. The next step is to learn more about the companies so that those obviously not comparable can be eliminated at an early stage, narrowing the group to what we call a *prospect list*.

Before moving on to the next step, we should note that the suspect list does not necessarily include all public stocks that are potential comparatives. A stock price quotation is included in the *National Monthly Stock Summary* only if the stock is listed on an exchange or if a stockbrokerage firm pays a fee to have it quoted in the publication. There are many public stocks traded—mostly of smaller companies—for which no broker purchases the quotation services of the National Quotation Service. There is, however, no more comprehensive single price quotation source. Also, the S&P *Register* does not necessarily pick up every relevant company within an SIC group. Other potentially comparative companies may be added to the list from the analyst's personal knowledge, information from trade associations, trade publications, regional publications (e.g., the *Western Investor*), magazines and newsletters, and information obtained from stockbrokerage firms or the subject company's management.

Developing a List of "Prospects"

Another section of the S&P *Register* gives each company's address and a brief summary of the company's products or services. From these short descriptions, the analyst can eliminate some of the companies from consideration as possible comparatives.

Either of two fairly comprehensive services can provide more detailed company descriptions—Standard & Poor's *Corporation Records* or *Moody's Manuals*. Each of these services consists of several volumes. Although they are fairly comprehensive, they do not include every public company. The analyst can find some additional descriptions in regional publications such as *Western Investor, Walker's Manual of Western Corporations,* and similar publications covering other parts of the United States and Canada. From these more detailed descriptions, it usually will be possible to eliminate several more companies from consideration.

At this point, the analyst must start establishing the criteria by which to develop the final list of comparatives. The longer the list of potential comparatives, the more stringent the criteria should be while still resulting in a reasonably sized final list. Ideally, each comparative company will conduct 100 percent of its business in the same industry as the subject company. Rarely will it be possible to develop such a list, because companies' activities tend to become increasingly diversified over the years. It is best not to draw the criteria for comparability too tightly at this stage, since any questionable company can be eliminated from the list at a later stage.

At this point, on the basis of some preliminary screening using a few standard published sources, the analyst has narrowed down a suspect list to a *prospect list,* that is, a group of companies believed to be sufficiently comparable to the subject company to provide some guidance in the valuation. The suspect list may still contain some companies about which no information is available in the manuals consulted. The analyst will have to decide whether to carry these companies to the next step depending on time, budget, and the likelihood that a satisfactory group of comparatives will result from the remaining prospect list.

Narrowing the List to the Comparative Companies

The next step is to gather information on each of the *prospects* by contacting the companies themselves—by either mail or telephone— to request their financial reports or by obtaining their SEC filings. Even though they are publicly traded, the companies are not obligated to mail their financial reports to nonstockholders. Most of them will be glad to do so, however, whether just to help, to make their companies better known, or perhaps to gain new stockholders. In fact, I have serendipitously come across many good investments among smaller public companies in the process of doing research for the valuation of a closely held business.

A few companies, for whatever reasons, will refuse, or at least not bother, to send out the requested information. If they are not required to file annual reports with the SEC, this tactic may be a dead end unless it is possible to locate a stockholder or broker who has the reports. However, if they are one of the 13,425 corporations (as of September 30, 1987) required to file annual and quarterly reports with the SEC—forms 10-K and 10-Q, respectively (see Exhibit 9–2 on pages 228–231)—copies of the reports can be ordered from either Bechtel Information Services or Disclosure, Inc.

In deciding what information to request, the analyst should keep in mind that the data received from the companies serve two purposes. The first is to learn enough about the company to decide whether to use it as a comparative. The second is to obtain financial data for the companies selected as comparatives.

If the analyst has decided to rely on five years' data for the subject company, then it is desirable to get five years' data for each of the comparative companies. Most companies summarize five years' data in their annual reports. However, such summaries do not contain footnote data, which may be necessary in order to make certain adjustments. They also frequently omit items such as interest expense, depreciation, and so on. In addition, for companies that must meet SEC filing requirements, it is advisable to obtain 10-K forms for at least the latest year, because they are required to include a more detailed description of their businesses and properties in this report than they are in their annual reports to stockholders. In some cases, proxy statements or 8-K forms may have useful additional information, such as officer compensation and details of actual or proposed transactions.

A list of the various forms required to be filed with the SEC, and a synopsis of the content of each, is included as Exhibit 9–2. Different forms may contain information of particular relevance to various valuation situations. All the SEC filings may be ordered through either Bechtel Information Services or Disclosure, Inc.

After receiving and reviewing all the information, the analyst must decide which companies to include as comparatives for the case at hand. These decisions cannot be made lightly and must be based on objective criteria. If a company is eliminated, there should be good reason for it to be considered less comparable than the companies included. At all times, the analyst must be very careful to avoid any bias in the process of selecting comparatives—bias that could lead to some unjustified positive or negative impact on the valuation.

The Issue of Comparability

"It has been said that exact comparable company data is like a perfect vacuum, or a perfect spouse. It exists in theory but rarely, if ever, in the real world."[3]

The principal proponent of the use of comparative companies in the valuation of closely held companies is the IRS. Revenue Ruling 59-60 addresses the need to consider several relevant factors when deciding which companies are comparative:

> In selecting the corporations for comparative purposes, care should be taken to use only comparable companies. Although the only restrictive requirement as to comparable corporations specified in the statute is that their lines of business be the same or similar, yet it is obvious that consideration must be given to other relevant factors in order that the most valid comparison possible will be obtained. For illustration, a corporation having one or more issues of preferred stock, bonds, or debentures in addition to its common stock should not be considered to be directly comparable to one having only common stock outstanding. In like manner, a company with a declining business and decreasing markets is not comparable to one with a record of current progress and market expansion.[4]

In analyzing whether or not a particular public company should be considered comparable or which of those public companies considered

---

[3]Walter L. Zweifler, "Exact Comparable Company Data: Fact or Fiction?" *Fairshare* 4, no. 2 (February 1984), p. 3.
[4]Revenue Ruling 59-60 (1959-1 C.B. 237), Section 4(h).

comparable are most comparable and therefore deserve more weight in the valuation, the analyst must consider several important factors.

The comparability of publicly traded comparatives used in a valuation frequently has become a central issue in litigated valuations, partly because of the difficulty of choosing truly comparative companies. In *Tallichet* v. *Commissioner,* the Tax Court emphasized that there are "guideposts in determining comparability."[5] According to the court, the following factors are among those to consider in determining comparability:

1. Capital structure.
2. Credit status.
3. Depth of management.
4. Personnel experience.
5. Nature of competition.
6. Maturity of the business.

In *Estate of Victor P. Clarke,* the Tax Court re-emphasized that it is "imperative that the characteristics of the subject company and the purportedly comparable company relevant to the question of value be isolated and examined so that a significant comparison can be made."[6] In that case, the court cited the following as relevant factors:

1. Products.
2. Markets.
3. Management.
4. Earnings.
5. Dividend-paying capacity.
6. Book value.
7. Position of company in industry.

Although these lists are fairly comprehensive depending on the nature of the industry, the analyst may need to consider additional factors, such as number and size of retail outlets, sales volume, product mix, territory of operations, and customer mix. Clearly, even this additional list is not exhaustive, and I cannot overemphasize the necessity of tailoring the list of factors to be considered to fit each valuation. Much of this information can be gathered in a thorough review of each public company's 10-K form, but it may also be necessary to consult additional sources such as industry and trade publications (discussed in Chapter 7, "Economic and Industry Data") or to call the company for additional information.

It is also useful to analyze the financial statements for both the subject company and the comparative companies to uncover similarities and differences to consider in the valuation. Bearing in mind the company being valued and the nature of the industry, I generally compare the performance of the subject company to the comparative com-

---

[5]*Tallichet* v. *Commissioner,* 33 T.C.M. 1133 (1974).
[6]*Estate of Victor P. Clarke,* 35 T.C.M. 1482 (1976).

panies' by analyzing financial ratios that measure liquidity, leverage, activity, and profitability as well as historical trends in revenues, expenses, and profitability. This type of analysis is illustrated in Chapter 14, "A Sample Report," and the background necessary for this type of analysis is provided in Chapter 11, "Analyzing and Adjusting Financial Statements." In particular, if this analysis indicates that the comparative companies' capital structures significantly differ from that of the subject (one of the examples cited by the IRS in Revenue Ruling 59-60 regarding factors relevant to comparability), this difference can be factored out by using debt-free valuation approaches, which are discussed in Chapter 4, "Approaches Using Current or Historical Data."

In many valuation situations, the subject company is so unique that it is difficult to find a set of good comparatives. In these cases, the analyst may find a group of companies that can shed some light on the valuation question but may consider one or a few more directly comparable to the subject company than the rest. In such cases, the analyst may tabulate data for the whole group but elect to accord more weight to the data for those considered most comparable.

Sometimes, though, the subject company seems so unique that even an exhaustive search produces no companies for use as comparatives. The appraiser should keep in mind that there are over 30,000 small public companies out there that have sold stock through public offerings at one time or another and are still operating. Also, if the valuation is for federal gift or estate taxes, Revenue Ruling 59-60 states that the companies may be in the same "or similar" industries. This phrase gives the analyst latitude to exercise reasonable judgment in selecting companies from related industries if unable to find comparative companies in the subject company's industry group.

However, the analyst who finds it difficult to find suitable comparatives for the valuation at hand should also remember that in several cases courts have decided that the comparability between the subject company and the public company was insufficient. In *Righter* v. *U.S.*, for example, the court decided that companies that manufactured toys or toys and games were not sufficiently comparable to a company that produced two types of games partly because their products appealed to and were used by different age groups.[7] In *Estate of Joseph E. Salsbury* the Tax Court rejected several companies one of the experts had chosen as comparable because they "did not even have divisions engaged in the animal and poultry health industry" (which was the subject company's business). As a result, the court concluded that the selection of these companies "fails to satisfy the 'same or similar line of business' requirement of the regulations."[8] These two cases represent only the tip of the iceberg in terms of the rejection of comparable companies by various courts. Additional cases are listed in Exhibit 9–1.

---

[7]*Righter* v. *U.S.*, 439 F.2d 1244 (1971).
[8]*Estate of Joseph E. Salsbury*, 34 T.C.M. 1441 (1975).

A problem also arises if an appraiser establishes criteria that are too restrictive. By unnecessarily limiting the number of comparative companies considered, an appraiser may miss relevant market evidence that would have led to a different valuation conclusion. Several court cases have noted that experts were too selective, excluding companies that would have provided useful valuation guidance. A few of these court cases are also listed in Exhibit 9–1. In *Estate of Victor P. Clarke,* the Tax Court addressed this problem particularly forcefully by stating that the definition of a comparable corporation cannot be "unduly restrictive, as it strips the inquiry into the valuation of closely held stock of the flexibility needed to make an informed judgment."[9] The U.S. Court of Claims stated its opinion on this issue quite succinctly in *Central Trust Company* v. *U.S.* In employing the comparative appraisal method, "every effort should be made to select as broad a base of comparative companies as is reasonably possible, as well as to give full consideration to every possible factor in order to make the comparison more meaningful."[10] In *Estate of Mark S. Gallo,* this point was again emphasized when the Tax Court commended one of the experts for making "careful and reasoned comparisons with each comparable instead of arbitrarily relying upon the outer limit of a range."[11] Clearly, the message of these cases is that the appraiser must choose comparatives logically and be able to justify their selection. If there simply are no companies sufficiently comparable, the appraiser should, if at all possible, use other valuation methods that may be more reliable given the lack of comparative companies. This position was strongly emphasized in *Tallichet* v. *Commissioner:* "Moreover, in determining the fair market value of stock where no bid and asked prices and no relevant sales exist, a comparison with the values of securities of corporations engaged in the same or similar lines of business which are publicly traded is *only one factor to consider* [Emphasis supplied]."[12]

The Comparative Search—A Sample Exercise

For purposes of illustration, I have selected as our subject company a fairly large chain of consumer electronic "superstores" in the mid-Atlantic region. (This is also the subject company in Chapter 14, "A Sample Report.") I must emphasize at the outset that the depth of the comparative search will depend greatly on the appraiser's time and budget. It also will depend on how "easy" the particular search is (e.g., for some companies a rather cursory search will turn up a good list of comparatives). However, if good comparatives are not found initially, the appraiser will be forced to dig deeper.

---

[9]*Estate of Victor P. Clarke,* p. 1501.
[10]*Central Trust Company* v. *U.S.,* 305 F. 2d 393 (Ct.Cl., 1962).
[11]*Estate of Mark S. Gallo,* 50 T.C.M. 470 (1985).
[12]*Tallichet,* p. 1135.

EXHIBIT 9-1   **A Partial List of Court Cases**
Pertinent to the Issue of Comparability

Court rejected comparables:

Bader v. U.S., 172 F.Supp. 833 (D.C. Ill., 1959)

Blass v. U.S., 344 F.Supp. 669 (1972)

Central Trust Company v. U.S., 305 F.2d 393 (Ct. Cl., 1962)

Righter v. U.S., 439 F.2d 1244 (1971)

Estate of Joseph E. Salsbury, 34 T.C.M. 1441 (1975)

Tallichet v. Commissioner, 33 T.C.M. 1133 (1974)

Estate of Lida R. Tompkins, 20 T.C.M. 1763 (1961)

Worthen v. U.S., 192 F.Supp. 727 (D.C. Mass., 1961)

Court accepted comparables:

Cochran v. Commissioner, 1948 P-H TC Memo paragraph 48,094 (1948)

Estate of Mark S. Gallo, 50 T.C.M. 470 (1985)

Court found criteria for comparables chosen too restrictive:

Bowen v. Commissioner, 7 T.C.M. 325 (1948)

Estate of Victor P. Clarke, 35 T.C.M. 1482 (1976)

Estate of Ethyl L. Goodrich, 37 T.C.M. 1062 (1978)

Identifying an SIC Number

The first step in the search is to determine the appropriate SIC number. A review of the current edition of the *Standard Industrial Classification Manual* indicates that SIC 573, Radio, Television, Consumer Electronics, and Music Stores, is appropriate for a large retail chain of consumer electronic superstores. Within the major SIC category 573, SIC 5731, Radio, Television and Consumer Electronics Stores, is the most appropriate code for this search. One temporary problem that has arisen since the revision of the *Standard Industrial Classification Manual,* is that Standard & Poor's has not yet changed its SIC lists to comply with the new system and, therefore, the SIC codes in Standard & Poor's *Register* and the *Corporation Record* differ slightly from those in the *SIC Manual.* According to Standard & Poor's, these sources will have SIC lists comparable to those in the *SIC Manual* beginning in 1988.

Developing a List of Possible (Suspect) Companies

The second step is to determine how many suspects are available in the various sources. Skimming through the *Directory of Companies Required to File Annual Reports with the Securities and Exchange Commission,* we find the broad heading Wholesale & Retail Trade. Underneath is the heading we seek: SIC 5730, Retail Trade–Radio, TV & Music Stores, which lists only four companies. Looking in the S&P *Register,* we find approximately 78 companies in SIC 5732, Radio and Television Stores. A review of the directory in the S&P *Corporation Records* reveals 28 public companies under SIC 5732.

Given these lists, the analyst must decide how exhaustive the comparative search is to be. An all-encompassing search would require the analyst to cross-check all 78 companies in the S&P *Register* with the *National Monthly Stock Summary* to determine which are publicly traded. For 78 companies this process would not be onerous, but for some industries such a list might exceed 200—a much more formidable task. Moreover, there may be more companies on the SEC list that do not appear on the SIC list in Standard & Poor's. For comprehensiveness, the public companies in the SEC classification should be combined with those in the Standard & Poor's version of the SIC classification.

Budget or time constraints, particularly the latter, may send the appraiser directly to the SIC directory in S&P *Corporation Records*. If there is not enough lead time to call or write for annual reports or 10-K forms for prospective comparatives, the analyst may have to rely solely on data published by Standard & Poor's or Moody's or other secondary sources. In that case, there is no sense in searching exhaustively for the smallest comparatives for which no information will be available when they are found. Therefore, if Standard & Poor's or Moody's will be the source of the information, it might as well be the source of the list as well.

For our search for the sample report, our suspect list will contain the 28 companies in the *Corporation Records* and 5 other companies listed in a recent article in *Fortune* on the retail consumer electronics industry. All five companies in the *Fortune* article had initial public offerings in the past year or two and did not appear in Standard & Poor's *Corporation Records*.

Making the First Cut

The next step is to look up the companies in the *Corporation Records* to determine the principal lines of business. A company may be listed in an SIC group even though only a very small percentage of its business pertains to that industry; such a company can be quickly eliminated. The results of this initial screening, along with the description and size of each company, should be written down and kept in the case file. Other companies may be eliminated if they are in the process of being reorganized or liquidated or if they are subject to a merger or tender offer. (Companies that actually have been bought out may be useful as merger and acquisition comparatives. We will discuss sources of information about such transactions later in this chapter.)

From this initial screening, our original suspect list of 33 companies has been trimmed to a prospect list of 13. As noted earlier, the reasons for rejecting the others should be written down and kept in the case file for future reference. It is important to be able to track every suspect comparative company from its initial selection to either its ultimate use in the comparative company table or the reason for its rejection.

The Final Selection

The next step is to call for the annual and interim reports and SEC 10-K forms for the remaining 13 companies. After compiling the list of companies that survived the first pass, the analyst must establish some objective selection criteria. The relevant criteria for our chain of stores are the following:

1. Retailers of consumer electronics with at least 75 percent of revenues derived from consumer electronic sales.
2. Revenues between $12 million and $1.2 billion (plus or minus one order of magnitude based on the subject company's revenues).
3. Active public market for its stock.
4. Not currently involved in negotiations to be acquired or actually in the process of being acquired.
5. Not in financial distress.

After reviewing these documents, the analyst can apply these stricter selection criteria. The appraiser must continue to outline in detail why some companies were rejected and others retained.

Our search has finally resulted in 11 comparative publicly traded companies. Although I believe that it was an especially good comparative search, it does not ensure that the data derived will be conclusive, which can cause frustration for the appraiser.

The sample report in Chapter 14 presents the details of the comparative search. Of course, as discussed earlier, the objective of compiling the public company data is to derive some parameters that can be applied to the valuation of the subject company. Particularly important are the ratios of the public company's prices to whatever variables the analyst has decided are relevant in the subject company's case, such as earnings, revenues, book value, and dividends. The sample report in Chapter 14 contains two tables showing the data for the comparative companies, with an accompanying discussion of how the data were used valuing the subject company. Note that it is important to compile the prices for the comparative companies on the date of the subject company valuation or as close to it as possible.

Mergers, Acquisitions, and Other Transaction Data

The previous sections of this chapter dealt with data on day-to-day trading prices of stocks. However, one can also derive indications of value from data on the prices at which entire companies or operating units of companies have been sold or the prices at which significant interests in companies changed hands. Such data are harder to find than daily stock trading data, since there are far fewer such transactions and there is no centrally organized mechanism for collecting and making such price information available.

Merger and acquisition data are used primarily in valuing controlling interests, although they may be used in some minority interest valuations as well. In these situations, however, the analyst generally must take a minority discount, a topic that Chapter 15 addresses. An ancillary topic, control premiums, becomes relevant if comparative publicly traded companies are used to value a controlling interest. In this situation, the value determined may need to be adjusted to reflect the additional value of control. The "control premium," which is discussed later in this chapter, is useful in making this adjustment.

Sources of Merger and Acquisition (M&A) Data

The analyst can turn to a number of sources for data on mergers, acquisitions, and other significant transactions. Some of the most useful sources are the W. T. Grimm & Company *Mergerstat Review*, *Predicasts F & S Index of Corporate Change*, *The Merger Yearbook*, *The National Review of Corporate Acquisitions*, *Merger & Acquisition Sourcebook*, *Acquisition/Divestiture Weekly Report*, and *Mergers & Acquisitions. Mergers & Acquisitions* also has an online data base offered through ADP Data Services. Leads on mergers and acquisitions of comparative companies can also be obtained from company management, trade associations, and trade publications, as well as from brokers and other people familiar with the particular industry.

The W. T. Grimm *Mergerstat Review* is published annually in book form. In addition to a transaction roster covering transactions announced during the year and either completed or still pending at year's end, *Mergerstat Review* includes extensive analysis of the transaction data. In particular, it contains useful analyses of control premiums.

Predicasts F & S Index of Corporate Change is published quarterly and compiled annually. It lists acquisitions alphabetically and by SIC code. It also gives a one-line description of the transaction and a reference to a periodical or other publication that discusses the transaction in more detail.

Merger & Acquisition Sourcebook is published annually by Quality Services Company, which also publishes the *Acquisition/Divestiture Weekly Report*. For this reason, we generally use these two sources together, relying on the *Merger & Acquisition Sourcebook* for information on transactions for the years it covers and the *Acquisition/ Divestiture Weekly Report* for information on transactions announced or completed after the last *Sourcebook* was published. These sources are organized by SIC code and provide fairly comprehensive information on each transaction and the companies involved.

The Merger Yearbook is published annually by Cambridge Corporation. This publication summarizes selected information on merger activity for the year by general SIC code. Besides small minority investments of 1 percent or more, it includes the purchase or sale of product lines and companies with sales as low as $1 million per year. Cambridge Corporation also publishes biweekly supplements in a newsletter entitled *Mergers and Corporate Policy*.

The National Review of Corporate Acquisitions is published weekly by Tweed Publishing Company. While this source provides timely and interesting insights on current merger activity, it organizes brief summaries of transactions in very broad industry groups and does not include SIC codes.

Mergers & Acquisitions is published quarterly. Each issue contains articles about mergers and acquisitions and also a "Mergers & Acquisitions Roster." The amount of information shown for each merger varies quite a bit.

The M&A Database is an online data base of mergers and acquisitions offered through ADP Data Services and maintained by *Mergers & Acquisitions*. As of this writing, the data base has data on over 27,000 transactions valued at $1 million or more from 1979 to the present. This particular data base is indicative of the wealth of information that is being computerized for easy access.

The Merger and Acquisition Search

In searching for comparative mergers and acquisitions, the analyst should begin by focusing on the relevant SIC codes as was done for finding comparative publicly traded companies. Because there are fewer mergers and acquisitions and because the information may be less complete, it may be necessary to widen the scope of the search, that is, use less restrictive criteria in choosing comparative merger and acquisition transactions. Nevertheless, the analyst must continue to set objective standards and maintain scrupulous records of the reasons for choosing and rejecting comparatives.

The sources listed above are fairly comprehensive—and, in fact, there is considerable overlap among them—but they still do not provide all the data the investigator might want. Moreover, if there is no public company or unit of a public company involved in either side of the transaction, the parties are not obliged to disclose the transaction data to the public, and the information is available only if the parties are willing to disclose it.

If a public company is involved in the transactions, however, there is likely to be some kind of report to the SEC. Special proxy statements or Forms 8-K often are particularly useful. The special proxy statement is filed when it is sent to the stockholders of the public company that has a merger offer calling for a stockholders' meeting to vote on the proposal. The Form 8-K generally is filed when there has been an offer to buy out a public company, when a public company has acquired a private company, or when there has been any other change in the company's control. Exhibit 9–2 lists the various forms filed with the SEC and briefly summarizes the content of each. Copies of all filings with the SEC can be ordered, either as paper copies or on microfiche, from either Bechtel Information Services or Disclosure, Inc.

It is also useful to get the acquired company's proxy statement, 10-K forms or annual reports, and 10-Q forms (quarterly reports) if the acquired company must file with the SEC. Using the financial information in these documents, the appraiser can analyze the comparability of the various companies in more depth by calculating various financial ratios, assessing the companies' historical growth trends, and applying multiples of the sale prices to various underlying financial data.

EXHIBIT 9-2

A Guide to SEC Corporate Filings

Disclosure Statute

The purpose of the Federal securities laws is to provide disclosure of material financial and other information on companies seeking to raise capital through the public offering of their securities, as well as companies whose securities are already publicly held. This enables investors to evaluate the securities of these companies on an informed and realistic basis.

The Securities Act of 1933 is a *disclosure* statute. It generally requires that, before securities may be offered to the public, a registration statement must be filed with the Commission disclosing prescribed categories of information. Before the sale of securities can begin, the registration statement must become "effective," and investors must be furnished a prospectus containing the most significant information in the registration statement.

The Securities Act of 1934 deals in large part with securities already outstanding and requires the registration of securities listed on a national securities exchange, as well as Over-The-Counter securities in which there is a substantial public interest. Issuers of registered securities must file annual and other periodic reports designed to provide a public file of current material information. The Exchange Act also requires disclosure of material information to holders of registered securities in solicitations of proxies for the election of directors or approval of corporate action at a shareholders meeting, or in attempts to acquire control of a company through a tender offer or other planned stock acquisitions. It provides that insiders of companies whose equity securities are registered must report their holdings and transactions in all equity securities of their companies.

Prospectus

When the sale of securities as proposed in an "offering" registration statement is approved by the SEC, any changes required by the SEC are incorporated into the prospectus. This document must be made available to investors before the sale of the security is initiated. It also contains the actual offering price, which may have been changed after the registration statement was approved.

Annual Report to Shareholders

The Annual Report is the principal document used by most major companies to communicate directly with shareholders. Since it is not a required, official SEC filing, companies have considerable discretion in determining what types of information this report will contain and how it is to be presented.

In addition to financial information, the Annual Report to Shareholders often provides non-financial details of the business which are not reported elsewhere. These may include marketing plans and forecasts of future programs and plans.

Form 8 (Amendment)

Form 8 is used to amend or supplement any 1934 Act report previously submitted. 1933 Act registration statements are amended by filing an amended registration statement (pre-effective amendment) or by the prospectus itself, as previously noted.

Listing Application

Like the ARS, a listing application is not an official SEC filing. It is filed by the company with the NYSE, AMEX or other stock exchange to document proposed new listings. Usually a Form 8-A registration is filed with the SEC at about the same time.

10-K

This report provides a comprehensive overview of the registrant. The report must be filed within 90 days after close of company's fiscal year and contains the following items of disclosure:

ITEMS REPORTED
PART I

1. **Business.** Identifies principal products and services of the company, principal markets and methods of distribution and, if "material," competitive factors, backlog and expectation of fulfillment, availability of raw materials, importance of patents, licenses, and franchises, estimated cost of research, number of employees, and effects of compliance with ecological laws.

    If there is more than one line of business, a statement is included for each of the last three years. The statement includes total sales and net income for each line which during either of the last two fiscal years accounted for 10 percent or more of total sales or pretax income.

2. **Properties.** Location and character of principal plants, mines, and other important properties and if held in fee or leased.

3. **Legal Proceedings.** Brief description of material legal proceedings pending.

4. **Submission of Matters to a Vote of Security Holders.** Information relating to the convening of a meeting of shareholders, whether annual or special, and the matters voted upon.

PART II

5. **Market for the Registrant's Common Stock and Related Security Holder Matters.** Includes principal market in which voting securities are traded with high and low sales prices (in the absence thereof, the range of bid and asked quotations for each quarterly period during the past two years) and the dividends paid during the past two years. In addition to the frequency and amount of dividends paid, this item contains a discussion concerning future dividends.

EXHIBIT 9-2

A Guide to SEC Corporate Filings
(Continued)

6. **Selected Financial Data.** These are five-year selected data including net sales and operating revenue; income or loss from continuing operations, both total and per common share; total assets; long-term obligations including redeemable preferred stock; cash dividend declared per common share. This data also includes additional items that could enhance understanding of trends in financial condition and results of operations. Further, the effects of inflation and changing prices should be reflected in the five-year summary.

7. **Management's Discussion and Analysis of Financial Condition and Results of Operations.** Under broad guidelines, this includes: liquidity, capital resources and results of operations; trends that are favorable or unfavorable as well as significant events or uncertainties; causes of any material changes in the financial statements as a whole; limited data concerning subsidiaries; discussion of effects of inflation and changing prices.

8. **Financial Statements and Supplementary Data.** Two-year audited balance sheets as well as three-year audited statements of income and changes in financial condition.

9. **Disagreements on Accounting and Financial Disclosure.**

PART III

10. **Directors and Executive Officers of the Registrant.** Name, office, term of office and specific background data on each.

11. **Remuneration of Directors and Officers.** List of each director and three highest paid officers with aggregate annual remuneration exceeding $40,000. Also includes total paid all officers and directors.

12. **Security Ownership of Beneficial Owners and Management.** Identification of owners of 5 percent or more of registrant's stock in addition to listing the amount and percent of each class of stock held by officers and directors.

13. **Certain Relationships and Related Transactions.**

PART IV

14. **Exhibits, Financial Statement Schedules and Reports on Form 8-K.** Complete, audited annual financial information and a list of exhibits filed. Also, any unscheduled material events or corporate changes filed in an 8-K during the year.

FORM 10-K SCHEDULES

I. Investments other than investments in affiliates
II. Receivables from related parties and underwriters, promoters and employees other than affiliates
III. Condensed financial information
IV. Indebtedness of affiliates (not current)
V. Property, plant and equipment
VI. Accumulated depreciation, depletion, and amortization of property, plant and equipment
VII. Guarantees of securities of other issuers
VIII. Valuation and qualifying accounts
IX. Short-term borrowings
X. Supplementary income statement information
XI. Supplementary profit and loss information
XII. Income from dividends (equity in net profit and loss of affiliates)

10-Q

This is the quarterly financial report filed by most companies, which, although unaudited, provides a continuing view of a company's financial position during the year. The 10-Q report must be filed 45 days after close of fiscal quarter.

ITEMS REPORTED
PART I
Financial Statements

1. Financial Statements
2. Management Discussion
3. Statement of Source and Application of Funds
4. A narrative analysis of material changes in the amount of revenue and expense items in relation to previous quarters, including the effect of any changes in accounting principles

PART II

1. **Legal Proceedings.** Brief description of material legal proceedings pending; when civil rights or ecological statutes are involved, proceedings must be disclosed.
2. **Changes in Securities.** Material changes in the rights of holders of any class of registered security.
3. **Defaults upon Senior Securities.** Material defaults in the payment if principal, interest, sinking fund or purchase fund installment, dividend, or other material default not cured within 30 days.
4. **Submission of Matters to a Vote of Security Holders.** Information relating to the convening of a meeting of shareholders, whether annual or special, and the matters voted upon, with particular emphasis on the election of directors.
5. **Other Materially Important Events.** Information on any other item of interest to shareholders not already provided for in this form.
6. **Exhibits and Reports on Form 8-K.** Any unscheduled material events or corporate changes filed on an 8-K during the prior quarter.

EXHIBIT 9-2

A Guide to SEC Corporate Filings
(Continued)

8-K

This is a report of unscheduled material events or corporate changes deemed of importance to the shareholders or to the SEC. Corporate changes must be filed 15 days after the event, except for Other Materially Important Events which has no mandatory filing time.

1. Changes in Control of Registrant
2. Acquisition or Disposition of Assets
3. Bankruptcy or Receivership
4. Changes in Registrant's Certifying Accountant
5. Other Materially Important Events
6. Resignations of Registrant's Directors
7. Financial Statements and Exhibits

10-C

Over-The-Counter companies use this form to report changes in name or amount of NASDAQ-listed securities. It is similar in purpose to the 8-K and must be filed 10 days after change.

Proxy Statement

A proxy statement provides official notification to designated classes of shareholders of matters to be brought to a vote at a shareholders meeting. Proxy votes may be solicited for changing the company officers, or many other matters. Disclosures normally made via a proxy statement may in some cases be made using Form 10-K (Part III).

Registration Statements

Registration statements are of two principal types: (1) "offering" registrations filed under the 1933 Securities Act, and (2) "trading" registrations filed under the 1934 Securities Exchange Act.

"Offering" registrations are used to register securities before they may be offered to investors. Part I of the registration, a preliminary prospectus or "red herring," is promotional in tone; it carries all the sales features that will be contained in the final prospectus. Part II of the registration contains detailed information about marketing agreements, expenses of issuance and distribution, relationship of the company with experts named in the registration, sales to special parties, recent sales of unregistered securities, subsidiaries of registrant, franchises and concessions, indemnification of directors and officers, treatment of proceeds from stock being registered, and financial statements and exhibits.

"Offering" registration statements vary in purpose and content according to the type of organization issuing stock:

S-1   Companies reporting under the 1934 Act for less than 3 years. Permits no incorporation by reference and requires complete disclosure in the prospectus.

S-2   Companies reporting under the 1934 Act for 3 years or more but not meeting the minimum voting stock requirement. Reference of 1934 Act reports permits incorporation and presentation of financial information in the prospectus or in an annual report to shareholders delivered with the prospectus.

S-3   Companies reporting under the 1934 Act for 3 or more years and having at least $150 million of voting stock held by non-affiliates, or as an alternative test, $100 million of voting stock coupled with an annual trading volume of 3 million shares. Allows minimal disclosure in the prospectus and maximum incorporation by reference of 1934 Act reports.

S-4   Registration used in certain business combinations or reorganization. Replaces S-14, S-15, 7/85.

N-1A Filed by open-end management investment companies other than separate accounts of insurance companies.

N-2   Filed by closed-end management investment companies.

N-5   Registration of small business investment companies.

N-SAR Annual statement of management investment companies.

S-6   Filed by unit investment trusts registered under the Investment Act of 1940 on Form N-8B-2.

S-8   Registration used to register securities to be offered to employees under stock option and various other employee benefit plans.

S-11 Filed by real estate companies, primarily limited partnerships and investment trusts.

S-18 Short form initial registration up to $7.5 million.

SE   Non-electronically filed exhibits made by registrants filing with the EDGAR PILOT PROJECT.

F-1   Registration of securities by foreign private issuers eligible to use form 20-F, for which no other form is prescribed.

F-2   Registration of securities of foreign private issuers meeting certain 1934 Act filing requirements.

EXHIBIT 9-2

**Quick Reference
Chart to Contents
of SEC Filings**

A Guide to SEC Corporate Filings
(Continued)

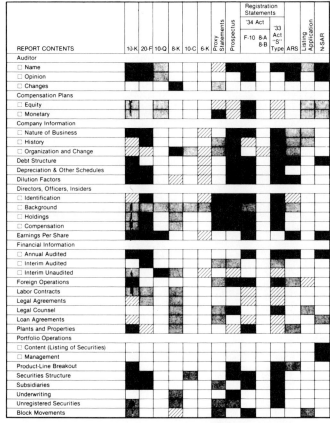

Legend

■ *always included*

▨ *frequently included*

▓ *special circumstances*

SOURCE: Disclosure, Inc., *A Guide to SEC Corporate Filings*. (Copies of the *Guide* may be acquired by contacting Disclosure, Inc. directly at 800/638-8241.)

Gathering Data on Control Premiums

It should be obvious that someone buying a business or an interest in one would pay extra for the right to have the final say in company decisions; the "extra" to be paid is called the *control premium*. (The value of control is discussed more fully in Chapter 2.) One means of quantifying control premiums is to compare the price at which the stock of the acquired company traded in the public market at some point in time prior to the announcement of the offer with the transaction price. The difference, figured as a percentage of the minority interest (publicly traded) price, is the control premium. There is considerable controversy over how far back in time one must go to get a minority interest value untainted by leaks or rumors of an upcoming buyout and yet close enough in time to be relevant despite changing market conditions. Although no one has found a definitive answer, the consensus seems to be that one must look one or two months prior to the announcement date for an unbiased price.

Currently there are several sources that provide data on control premiums. W. T. Grimm's *Mergerstat Review* provides control premium data annually and categorizes the information in several ways—by broad industry classification, price of stock prior to the transaction, seller's P/E, and distribution of premiums paid, among others. Also, Houlihan, Lokey, Howard, & Zukin, Inc. began a published control premium study in 1986. The publication presents control premiums on a quarterly basis as well as an annual summary. Two particularly useful features of this publication are that (1) it organizes the companies by SIC code and calculates mean and median premiums for each SIC category represented and (2) it gives brief descriptions of each company acquired that can help determine its comparability to the subject company.

Control premiums can also be calculated for those companies found in the merger and acquisition search that were publicly traded prior to the transaction. For more extensive research on control premiums, online services, such as the M&A Database discussed earlier, can be very useful.

After gathering all the pertinent control premium data available, the appraiser must analyze the data to arrive at a reasonable control premium, if one exists, to apply in adjusting an indicated value appropriate for a minority interest (e.g., a value derived from comparative publicly traded companies) to a control value.

Summary

A strong ability to locate and evaluate comparative transaction data is at once one of the most important and most challenging of the many skills needed by the professional business valuer. All too many business appraisals miss the mark or fail to be convincing because of inadequate attention to this essential element of the valuation process. This chapter has provided a "road map" for that all-important treasure hunt for the best available comparative transaction data. There is no complete and infallible set of sources that will ensure that no comparative transaction is overlooked, and the analyst often must call on experience and ingenuity to ferret out that special, obscure, and incredibly comparable transaction. However, by following the road map in this chapter, the analyst should be able to capture a very large proportion of comparative transaction data that are available.

Bibliography

General Information Sources

Acquisition/Divestiture Weekly Report. Quality Services Company, 5290 Overpass Road, Santa Barbara, CA 93111.
Reports weekly activity on acquisitions, mergers, offers, rumors to buy or sell, and terminations. Includes financial data on buyer and seller, plus purchase details. Weekly update on companies in negotiations.

Announcements of Mergers and Acquisitions. Conference Board, Inc., 845 Third Avenue, New York, NY 10022.
List of completed mergers and acquisitions reported in the month indicated. Covers independent corporate and noncorporate units, subsidiaries, affiliates, divisions, and stock acquisitions that bring the acquiring company's ownership to at least 50 percent of the voting stock of the acquired unit. Covers firms engaged in manufacturing, mining, wholesale and retail trade, services, agriculture, forestry and fisheries, and contract construction. Shows total assets (where available), business, and location. Monthly.

Directory of Companies Required to File Reports with the Securities and Exchange Commission. Securities and Exchange Commission. Washington, D.C.: U.S. Government Printing Office, annual.
Listing of companies required to file with the SEC under the Securities Exchange Act of 1934. Arranged alphabetically and by industry group.

Directory of Corporate Affiliations: Who Owns Whom. National Register Publishing Company, 5201 Old Orchard Road, Skokie, IL 60077.
Lists over 5,000 U.S. parent companies, their divisions, subsidiaries, and affiliates arranged alphabetically, with geographic and SIC indexes. Cross-indexed for indentification by either corporate or subsidiary's name.

HLHZ Control Premium Study. Houlihan, Lokey, Howard & Zukin, Inc., 1930 Century Park West, Los Angeles, CA 90067.
Tracks premiums paid to acquire controlling interests in public companies. It can be used to assess the overall takeover climate, ascertain the value of a controlling interest in private as well as public companies, and determine the fairness or adequacy of a takeover offer. Quarterly.

Merger and Acquisition Sourcebook. Quality Services Company, 5290 Overpass Road, Santa Barbara, CA 93111.
Covers purchase details on 3,000 major transactions, 92,000 merger and acquisition facts, the previous year's deals that fell through, prices paid by type of industry, merger terminology, premium paid for stocks on month before acquisition announcement, troubles in leveraged buyouts, takeover law revisions, tax benefits in ESOP acquisitions, industry surveys on acquisitions. Lists 125 takeover targets, premerger questions, and companies selling below book value. Annual.

The Merger Yearbook. Cambridge Corporation Publishers, Post Office Box 670, Ipswich, MA 01938-9989.
Summarizes selected information on merger activity for the year by general SIC code. Besides small minority investments of 1 percent or more, it includes the purchase or sale of product lines and companies with sales as low as $1 million per year. Cambridge Corporation also publishes

biweekly supplements in a newsletter entitled *Mergers and Corporate Policy*. Annual.

Mergers & Acquisitions. Information for Industry (Member of the Hay Group), 229 South 18th Street, Philadelphia, PA 19103.

Covers the merger/acquisition/divestiture field with articles on techniques and merger methodology; case studies of recent noteworthy deals; detailed records and evaluation of business deals for each quarter accompanied by tables analyzing merger activities in the past quarter; interviews with key people in the field; news of current legislation and regulations affecting the industry.

Mergerstat Review. W. T. Grimm & Company, 135 South LaSalle Street, Chicago, IL 60603.

Contains statistics on merger announcements, total dollar value paid, medium of payment, foreign buyers, divestitures, tender offers, and so forth. Provides historical statistics in each category. Each edition also contains analyses of the current year's transactions under a variety of categories. Annual.

Moody's Bank & Financial Manual. Moody's Investors Service, 99 Church Street, New York, NY 10007.

Covers insurance, finance, real estate, and investment companies. Includes five- to seven-year presentation of income accounts, balance sheets, financial and operating ratios, a detailed description of the company's business, including a complete list of subsidiaries, and a capital structure section with details on capital stock and long-term debt and bond and preferred stock ratings. Semiweekly, with annual cumulation.

Moody's Industrial Manual. Moody's Investors Service, 99 Church Street, New York, NY 10007.

Covers companies listed on the New York and American stock exchanges and those listed on regional American exchanges. Includes five to seven years of financial information on income accounts, balance sheets, financial and operating ratios, a detailed description of the company's business, including a complete list of subsidiaries and a capital structure section with details on capital stock and long-term debt. Semiweekly, with annual cumulation.

Moody's OTC Industrial Manual. Moody's Investors Service, 99 Church Street, New York, NY 10007.

Covers over-the-counter industrial corporations, with history, background, mergers and acquisitions, subsidiaries, business and products, principal plants and properties, names and titles of officers and directors. Includes financial statements and a description of capitalization with financial and operating ratios. Weekly, with annual cumulation.

Moody's Public Utility Manual. Moody's Investors Service, 99 Church Street, New York, NY 10007.

Includes electric and gas utilities, gas transmission companies, and telephone and water companies. Covers financial statements and operating and financial ratios, with history, background, mergers and acquisitions, subsidiaries, business, construction programs, principal plants and properties, and data relating to rates, franchises, and contracts. Semiweekly, with annual cumulation.

Moody's Transportation Manual. Moody's Investors Service, 99 Church Street, New York, NY 10007.

Covers railroads, airlines, shipping, bus, and truck lines. Also covers oil pipelines, bridge companies, and auto and truck leasing and rental companies. Includes maps of many of the larger railroad systems, plus route maps of some large airlines. Presents statistics showing financial and operating results, with historical data, location and mileage, and management and security descriptions. Semiweekly, with annual cumulation.

National Daily Quotation Service. National Quotation Bureau, Inc., Plaza Three, Harborside Financial Center, Jersey City, NJ 07302.

Provides daily stock price quotations (referred to by brokers as the *pink sheets*). The National Quotation Bureau provides the service of compiling, for a fee, any history of past price quotations that it has published. Daily.

National Monthly Stock Summary. National Quotation Bureau, Inc., Plaza Three, Harborside Financial Center, Jersey City, NJ 07302.

Summarizes market quotations that have appeared in *National Daily Quotation Service* or have been supplied by dealers on special lists. Lists many over-the-counter and inactively traded listed stocks. Monthly, with semiannual cumulations.

National Review of Corporate Acquisitions. Tweed Publishing Company, 49 Main Street, Tiburon, CA 94920.

While this source provides timely and interesting thoughts on current merger activity, it organizes brief summaries of transactions in very broad industry groups and does not include SIC codes. Weekly.

Official Summary of Security Transactions and Holdings. U.S. Securities and Exchange Commission. Washington, D.C. In tabular form, this monthly includes information on issuer, security, reporting person, nature of ownership, relationship of reporting person to issuer, date of transaction, quantity bought or sold, and price. Monthly.

Predicasts F&S Index of Corporate Change. Predicasts, Inc., 200 University Circle Research Center, 1101 Cedar Avenue, Cleveland, OH 44106.

Provides abstracts of articles on U.S. business information, including mergers, investments, legislation, and new products. Weekly report, with monthly and quarterly cumulatives.

Standard & Poor's Corporation Records. Standard & Poor's Corporation, Inc., 25 Broadway, New York, NY 10004.

Provides company descriptions and supplementary news items, plus an index. Comparable to Moody's manuals. Covers companies having both listed and unlisted securities. Company information includes history, list of subsidiaries, principal plants and properties, business and products, officers and directors, comparative income statements, balance sheet statistics, selected financial ratios, and description of outstanding securities. Daily News Section provides updates. Annual, with bimonthly supplements.

Standard & Poor's CUSIP Directories. Standard & Poor's Corporation, Inc., 25 Broadway, New York, NY 10004.

CUSIP service includes *CUSIP Master Directory, CUSIP Corporate Directory, CUSIP Directory of User Numbers,* and *Digest of Changes in CUSIP.* Master Directory lists CUSIP numbers alphabetically.

Standard & Poor's Register of Corporations, Directors, and Executives. Standard & Poor's Corporation, Inc., 25 Broadway, New York, NY 10004.

Vol. 1: Corporations; alphabetically lists over 45,000 companies, gives brief summary description with addresses, telephone numbers, corporate officers and directors. Vol. 2: Individual listings, directors and executives section; lists alphabetically the individuals serving as officers, directors, trustees, partners, and so on. Vol. 3: Indexes; gives SIC classification, geographic index, and new additions. Annual.

Standard Industrial Classification Manual. U.S. Office of Management and Budget. Washington, D.C.: U.S. Government Printing Office, 1987.
Useful for defining SIC codes.

Walker's Manual of Western Corporations. Walker's Manual, Inc., Long Beach, CA 92643.
Describes publicly owned financial institutions and corporations headquartered in the 13 western states and western Canada. Annual, with monthly supplements.

Western Investor. Willamette Publishing Company, Suite 1115, 400 Southwest Sixth Avenue, Portland, OR 97204.
Formerly *Northwest Stock Guide.* Oriented toward Pacific Northwest, western areas, Hawaii, and Alaska and how national trends affect those regions. Articles on industries, publicly traded corporations, individuals, regional stocks, and other investment opportunities. Each issue contains statistical tables on more than 525 public companies, including 6 years' earnings. Regular departments include: Western Investor Economic Indicators (indicators pertaining to the 13 western states); Index; Publisher's Comments; Index by Industry Group (companies listed in Investment Data Section); Technical Analysis (three selected companies each month); Broker Quotes (stocks of interest to regional brokers); New Listings (companies new to Investment Data Section); Investment Data Section (vital statistics on over 525 companies); Index to Advertisers; News Notes (people, mergers, acquisitions); Profiles (profiles on people behind companies in Investment Data Section); Research Reports (roundup of recent research reports). Quarterly. Willamette also publishes biweekly *Western Investor Newsletter.*

Wiesenberger Investment Companies Service. Warren, Gorham & Lamont, Inc., 210 South Street, Boston, MA 02111-9902.
Compendium of information about open- and closed-end mutual funds and investment companies, with a complete explanation of their functions and their various uses for the investor. Has data on the background, management policy, and salient features of all leading companies, management results, income and dividend records, price ranges, and comparative operating details. Annual, with quarterly supplements.

Online Sources

CompuServe. CompuServe Information Services, 5000 Arlington Centre Boulevard, Columbus, OH 43220.
Format: IBM PC/XT; Apple II, II+, III. 110/1200 baud modem.
Profile: Provides ticker retrieval, descriptive data on over 3,000 companies, historical information, and latest quotes. Includes access to SEC filings and Value Line data base via Disclosure 2.

CompuStat II. Standard & Poor's Corporation, 7400 South Alton Court, Englewood, CO 80112.
Format: Magnetic tapes, diskettes, and cartridges.
Distribution: Through authorized vendors. Weekly updates available.
Profile: Data base of financial statistics on over 6,500 companies. Information covers up to 20 years of annual and 10 years of quarterly income statement and balance sheet, market, and supplementary statistics.

M&A Data Base. ADP Network Services, Inc., 175 Jackson Plaza, Ann Arbor, MI 48106.
> Format: IBM PC or other PC.
> Distribution: Via Datapath.
> Profile: Online access to merger and acquisition data from *Mergers & Acquisitions.*

Mergers & Acquisitions. Securities Data Company, Inc., 62 William Street, New York, NY 10005.
> Format: Any computer with modem.
> Distribution: Via Telenet. All baud rates. 24 hours/7 days/week. Updated daily.
> Profile: 15,000 transactions, 1/81 to present. Information on tender offers and self-tenders, mergers, divestitures, repurchases, minority interests, target's financial position, managers, and fees, and specifics of each transaction. Compatible with *Lotus 1-2-3* and other spreadsheet packages.

SEC Documents Sources

Bechtel Information Services. 1570 Shady Grove Road, Gaithersburg, MD 20877, (301)258-4900.

Disclosure, Inc. 5161 River Road, Building 60, Bethesda, MD 20817, (800) 638-8241.

Federal Document Retrieval. 514 C Street, Washington, D.C. 20002, (202) 628-2229.

Washington Service Bureau. 655 15th Street N.W., Washington, D.C. 20005, (202) 833-9200.

Chapter 10

Data on Discounts for Lack of Marketability

> *Perhaps the most difficult aspect in the valuation of closely held stocks is the quantification of the size of the discount to apply to the gross value ascertained for the stock due to the absence of a public market for the stock.*[1]

All other things being equal, an interest in a business is worth more if it is readily marketable or, conversely, worth less if it is not. It is well known that investors prefer liquidity to lack of liquidity. Interests in closely held businesses are illiquid relative to most other investments. This problem may be further compounded by restrictions on transfer of interests found in buy-sell agreements in many companies. The problem that the appraiser of closely held businesses must solve, of course, is to quantify the effect of marketability, or lack of it, in terms of its impact on the value of the business interest being considered. In many valuations of closely held businesses or business interests, the discount for lack of marketability turns out to be the largest single issue to resolve—and an important issue in almost all such valuations.

This chapter covers three categories of empirical data to assist the appraiser in quantifying the discount for lack of marketability:

1. Discounts on sales of restricted shares of publicly traded companies.
2. Discounts on sales of closely held company shares compared to prices of subsequent initial public offerings of the same companies' shares.
3. Costs of floating a public offering.

As the above list indicates, the base from which to take the discount in each case is the actual or estimated price at which the shares could be sold if registered and freely tradable in a public trading market. As discussed conceptually in Chapter 2, the data presented in this chapter relate to the quantification of the discount for lack of marketability only, separately and distinctly from any discount for minority interest.

After presenting these data, this chapter discusses certain court decisions in which the discount for lack of marketability was a major issue.

Marketability Discounts Evidenced by Prices of Restricted Stocks

One body of empirical evidence specifically isolates the value of the factor of marketability from all other factors: the body of data on transactions in letter stocks. A *letter stock* is identical in all respects to the freely traded stock of a public company except that it is re-

---

[1]Milton Gelman, "An Economist-Financial Analyst's Approach to Valuing Stock of a Closely Held Company," *Journal of Taxation*, June 1972, p. 354.

stricted from trading on the open market for a certain period. The duration of the restrictions vary from one situation to another. Since marketability is the only difference between the letter stock and its freely tradable counterpart, the appraiser should try to find differences in the price at which letter stock transactions take place compared with open market transactions in the same stock on the same date. This difference will provide some evidence of the price spread between a readily marketable security and one that is identical but subject to certain restrictions on its marketability.

Publicly traded corporations frequently issue letter stock in making acquisitions or raising capital, because the time and cost of registering the new stock with the SEC would make registration at the time of the transaction impractical. Also, founders or other insiders may own portions of a publicly traded company's stock that has never been registered for public trading. Even though such stock cannot be sold to the public on the open market, it may be sold in private transactions under certain circumstances. Such transactions usually must be reported to the SEC and thus become a matter of public record. Therefore, there is available a body of data on the prices of private transactions in restricted securities or letter stocks that can be used for comparison with prices of the same but unrestricted securities eligible for trading on the open market.

Since the data represent hundreds of actual arm's-length transactions, anyone who might consider negotiating a deal involving these securities (such as receiving letter stock in connection with selling out to a public company) would be well advised to become familiar with the information. Furthermore, courts frequently reference the data on letter stock discounts in determining the amount of discount for lack of marketability appropriate in valuing interests in closely held companies.

SEC *Accounting Release No. 113* specifically points out that the discount for lack of marketability frequently is substantial:

> Restricted securities are often purchased at a discount, frequently substantial, from the market price of outstanding unrestricted securities of the same class. This reflects the fact that securities which cannot be readily sold in the public market place are less valuable than securities which can be sold, and also the fact that by the direct sale of restricted securities, sellers avoid the expense, time and public disclosure which registration entails.[2]

It is exceedingly important to keep in mind that restrictions on the transfer of letter stock eventually lapse, usually within 24 months. At that point the holder can sell the shares into the existing market, subject to whatever volume and other restrictions may be imposed by SEC Rule 144. Consequently, all other things equal, shares of closely held stock, which may never have the benefit of a public mar-

---

[2]Securities and Exchange Commission, *Accounting Series Release No. 113: Statement Regarding Restricted Securities* (Chicago: Commerce Clearing House, Federal Securities Law Reports, 1977), pp. 62, 285.

ket, would be expected to require a higher discount for lack of marketability than that applicable to restricted stock of a public company. The market does, indeed, impose a higher discount on closely held stock than on restricted stock of a public company, as we shall see in a later section.

SEC Institutional Investor Study

In a major SEC study of institutional investor actions, one of the topics was the amount of discount at which transactions in restricted stock (letter stock) took place compared to the prices of identical but unrestricted stock on the open market.[3] The most pertinent summary tables from that study are reproduced in Exhibits 10–1 and 10–2.

Exhibit 10–1 shows the amounts of discount from open market price on letter stock transactions broken down by the market in which the unrestricted stock trades. The four categories are the New York Stock Exchange, American Stock Exchange, over-the-counter (OTC) reporting companies, and over-the-counter nonreporting companies. A *reporting company* is a publicly traded company that must file Forms 10-K, 10-Q, and other information with the SEC. A *nonreporting company* is a company whose stock is publicly traded OTC but is not subject to the same reporting requirements. A company whose stock is traded OTC can avoid becoming an SEC reporting company either by maintaining its total assets under $1 million or by keeping its number of stockholders under 500.

Because many closely held companies are small compared to typical well-known public companies, the smaller nonreporting public companies often may have more characteristics comparable to the closely held subject company's. However, since they need not report to the SEC, the analyst may encounter difficulty in obtaining annual and interim reports for them.

Exhibit 10–1 shows that, compared to their free-trading counterparts, the discounts on the letter stocks were the least for NYSE-listed stocks, and increased, in order, for AMEX-listed stocks, OTC reporting companies, and OTC nonreporting companies. For OTC nonreporting companies, the largest number of observations fell in the 30 to 40 percent discount range. Slightly over 56 percent of the OTC nonreporting companies had discounts greater than 30 percent on the sale of their restricted stock compared with the market price of their free-trading stock. A little over 30 percent of the OTC reporting companies were discounted over 30 percent, and over 52 percent had discounts over 20 percent.

Using midpoints of the discount range groups from Exhibit 10–1— and even including the ones that sold at premiums for one reason or another—the overall mean average discount was 25.8 percent and the

---

[3]"Discounts Involved in Purchases of Common Stock," in U.S. 92nd Congress, 1st Session, House, *Institutional Investor Study Report of the Securities and Exchange Commission* (Washington, D.C.: U.S. Government Printing Office, March 10, 1971, 5:2444-2456, Document No. 92-64, Part 5).

Table XIV-45 of SEC *Institutional Investor Study*: Discount by Trading Market

Trading Mkt.	-15.0% to 0.0% No. of Trans-actions	Value of Purchases (Dollars)	0.1% to 10.0% No. of Trans-actions	Value of Purchases (Dollars)	10.1% to 20.0% No. of Trans-actions	Value of Purchases (Dollars)	Discount 20.1% to 30.0% No. of Trans-actions	Value of Purchases (Dollars)	30.1% to 40.0% No. of Trans-actions	Value of Purchases (Dollars)	40.1% to 50.0% No. of Trans-actions	Value of Purchases (Dollars)	50.1% to 80.0% No. of Trans-actions	Value of Purchases (Dollars)	Total No. of Trans-actions	Value of Purchases (Dollars)
Unknown	1	$1,500,000	2	$2,496,583	1	$205,000	---	---	2	$3,332,000	---	---	1	$1,259,996	7	$8,793,578
NY Stk. Exch.	7	3,760,663	13	15,111,798	13	24,503,988	10	$17,954,085	3	11,102,501	1	$1,400,000	4	5,005,068	51	78,838,103
Amer. Stk. Exch.	2	7,263,060	4	15,850,000	11	14,548,750	20	46,200,677	7	21,074,298	1	44,250	4	4,802,404	49	109,783,439
Over-the-Counter (Reporting Co.)	11	13,828,767	39	13,613,676	35	38,585,259	30	35,479,946	30	38,689,328	13	9,284,047	21	8,996,406	179	178,477,419
Over-the-Counter (Non-Reporting Co.)	5	8,329,369	9	5,265,925	18	25,122,024	17	11,229,155	25	29,423,584	20	11,377,431	18	13,505,545	112	104,253,033
Total	26	$34,681,849	67	$52,337,982	78	$102,965,021	77	$110,863,863	67	$123,621,711	35	$22,105,728	48	$33,569,418	398	$490,145,572

Table XIV-47 of SEC *Institutional Investor Study*: Discount by Sales of Issuer

Sales of Issuer (000's)	50.1% or More No. of Trans-actions	Size of Trans-actions (Dollars)	40.1% to 50.0% No. of Trans-actions	Size of Trans-actions (Dollars)	30.1% to 40.0% No. of Trans-actions	Size of Trans-actions (Dollars)	Discount 20.1% to 30.0% No. of Trans-actions	Size of Trans-actions (Dollars)	10.1% to 20.0% No. of Trans-actions	Size of Trans-actions (Dollars)	0.1% to 10.0% No. of Trans-actions	Size of Trans-actions (Dollars)	Total No. of Trans-actions	Size of Trans-actions (Dollars)
Less than $100	11	$2,894,999	7	$2,554,000	17	$19,642,364	16	$12,197,394	6	$12,267,292	9	$12,566,000	66	$62,122,049
$100 - $999	7	474,040	2	1,221,000	---	---	1	500,000	1	1,018,500	2	3,877,500	13	7,091,040
$1,000 - $4,999	8	4,606,505	13	8,170,747	12	10,675,150	15	9,865,961	10	9,351,738	3	2,295,200	61	44,964,291
$5,000 - $19,999	6	1,620,015	4	1,147,305	13	25,986,008	25	27,238,210	24	21,441,347	47	12,750,481	119	90,183,366
$20,000 - $99,999	3	605,699	3	4,372,676	6	11,499,250	8	11,817,954	18	22,231,737	17	36,481,954	55	87,009,260
$100,000 or More	2	1,805,068	---	---	2	2,049,998	3	7,903,586	10	24,959,483	7	10,832,925	24	47,551,060
Total	37	$12,006,316	29	$17,465,728	50	$69,852,770	68	$69,523,095	69	$91,270,097	85	$78,804,060	338	$338,921,066

SOURCE: "Discounts Involved in Purchases of Common Stock (1966-1969)." *Institutional Investor Study Report of the Securities and Exchange Commission.* H.R. Doc. No. 64, Part 5, 92d Cong., 1st Sess. (1971). pp. 2444-2456.

median is about the same. The study also noted that "average discounts rose over the period January 1, 1966 through June 30, 1969" and that average discounts were "27.9 percent in the first half of 1969."[4] For nonreporting OTC companies, which are more likely to resemble most closely held companies, the average discount was 32.6 percent and the median discount again was about the same.

Since the time of the SEC study, the efficiency of the OTC market has improved considerably, aided by the development of inexpensive and virtually instantaneous electronic communications and the advent of the NASDAQ system. Since the market in which restricted OTC shares will eventually trade once the restrictions expire or are removed is now somewhat more efficient, one would expect the differential in discount for restricted listed versus OTC stocks to be less pronounced, and this generally has been the case.

Exhibit 10–2 shows the discounts from open market prices on letter stock transactions broken down into six groups by the subject companies' annual sales volume. There was a strong tendency for the companies with the largest sales volumes to receive the smallest discounts and the companies with the smallest sales volumes the largest discounts. Well over half the companies with sales under $5 million (the three smallest of the six size categories used) had discounts of over 30 percent. However, this may not be a size effect but just further evidence of the influence of the trading market, since most of the largest companies were listed on the NYSE, by far the most liquid market at that time.

One of the outgrowths of the SEC *Institutional Investor Study* was *SEC Accounting Series Releases, No. 113,* dated October 13, 1969, and *No. 118,* dated December 23, 1970, which require investment companies registered under the Investment Company Act of 1940 to disclose their policies for the cost and valuation of their restricted securities. The result was that an ongoing body of data became available on the relationship between restricted stock prices and their freely tradable counterparts, which can provide empirical benchmarks for quantifying marketability discounts.

Gelman Study

In 1972, Milton Gelman published the results of his study of prices paid for restricted securities by four closed-end investment companies specializing in restricted securities investments.[5] From 89 transactions between 1968 and 1970, Gelman found that both the arithmetic average and median discounts were 33 percent and that almost 60 percent of the purchases were at discounts of 30 percent and higher. The distribution of discounts found in the Gelman study is shown in Table 10–1.

---

[4]Ibid., p. 2452.
[5]Gelman, "An Economist-Financial Analyst's Approach," pp. 353–54.

TABLE 10-1

Size of Discount	No. of Common Stocks	% of Total
Less than 15.0%	5	6
15.0 - 19.9	9	10
20.0 - 24.9	13	15
25.0 - 29.9	9	10
30.0 - 34.9	12	13
35.0 - 39.9	9	10
40.0 and Over	32	36
Total	89	100

SOURCE: MIlton Gelman, "An Economist-Financial Analyst's Approach To Valuing Stock Of A Closely-Held Company, "*Journal of Taxation* (June 1972), p. 354.

Trout Study

In a study of letter stocks purchased by mutual funds from 1968 to 1972, Robert Trout attempted to construct a financial model that would provide an estimate of the discount appropriate for a private company's stock.[6] His multiple regression model involved 60 purchases and found an average discount of 33.45 percent for restricted stock from freely traded stock. As the SEC study showed, he also found that companies with stock listed on national exchanges had lower discounts on their restricted stock transactions than did companies with stock traded over the counter.

Moroney Study

In an article published in the March 1973 issue of *Taxes*, Robert E. Moroney presented the results of a study of the prices paid for restricted securities by 10 registered investment companies.[7] The study reflected 146 purchases. The average discount for the 146 transactions was 35.6 percent, and the median discount was 33.0 percent. Exhibit 10–3 shows the results of the study.

Moroney points out:

> It goes without saying that each cash purchase of a block of restricted equity securities fully satisfied the requirement that the purchase price be one, "at which the property would change hands between a willing buyer and a willing seller, neither being under any compulsion to buy or to sell and both having reasonable knowledge of relevant facts." Reg. Sec. 20.2031-1(b)[8]

Moroney contrasts the evidence of the actual cash deals with the lower average discounts for lack of marketability adjudicated in most prior court decisions on gift and estate tax cases. He points out, however, that the empirical evidence on the prices of restricted stocks was not available as a benchmark for quantifying marketability discounts

---

[6]Robert R. Trout, "Estimation of the Discount Associated with the Transfer of Restricted Securities," *Taxes,* June 1977, pp. 381–85.

[7]Robert E. Moroney, "Most Courts Overvalue Closely Held Stocks," *Taxes,* March 1973, pp. 144–54.

[8]Ibid., p. 151.

EXHIBIT 10-3

Original Purchase Discounts for Restricted Stocks
(Discounts from the Quoted Market Value of the
Same Corporation's "Free" Stock of the Same Class)

Investment Company	Original Purchase Discount	Number of Blocks
Bayrock Growth Fund, Inc., New York City (formerly Fla. Growth Fund)	4 blocks bought at discounts of 12%, 23%, 26%, 66%, respectively	4
Diebold Venture Capital Corp., New York City	6 blocks bought at discounts of 16%, 20%, 20%, 23%, 23%, 50%, respectively	6
Enterprise Fund, Inc., Los Angeles	10 blocks bought at discounts of 31%, 36%, 38%, 40%, 49%, 51%, 55%, 63%, 74%, 87%, respectively	10
Harbor Fund, Inc., Los Angeles	1 block bought at a discount of 14%	1
Inventure Capital Corp., Boston	At acquisition dates all blocks were valued at cost	---
Mates Investment Fund, Inc., New York City	1 block bought at a discount of 62%	1
New America Fund, Inc., Los Angeles (formerly Fund of Letters, Inc.)	32 blocks bought at discounts of 3%, 3%, 14%, 14%, 16%, 21%, 25%, 26%, 27%, 33%, 33%, 33%, 35%, 36%, 36%, 37%, 37%, 39%, 40%, 40%, 43%, 44%, 46%, 47%, 49%, 51%, 53%, 53%, 56%, 57%, 57%, 58%, respectively	32
Price Capital Corp., New York City	7 blocks bought at discounts of 15%, 29%, 29%, 32%, 40%, 44%, 52%, respectively	7
SMC Investment Corp., Los Angeles	12 blocks bought at 30% premium, discounts 4%, 25%, 26%, 32%, 33%, 34%, 38%, 46%, 48%, 50%, 78%, respectively	12
Value Line Development Capital Corp., New York City	35 blocks bought at discounts of 10%, 15%, 15%, 15%, 15%, 15%, 20%, 23%, 28%, 28%, 28%, 30%, 30%, 30%, 30%, 30%, 32.5%, 35%, 40%, 40%, 40%, 40%, 40%, 40%, 45%, 50%, 50%, 50%, 50%, 53%, 55%, 55%, 65%, 70%, 90%, respectively	35
Value Line Special Situations Fund, Inc., New York City	38 blocks bought at discounts of 10%, 13%, 15%, 15%, 17%, 17%, 20%, 20%, 20%, 23%, 25%, 25%, 25%, 25%, 26.5%, 27%, 27%, 30%, 30%, 30%, 30%, 30%, 30%, 30%, 30%, 33%, 37.5%, 40%, 40%, 40%, 40%, 45%, 55%, 55%, 56%, 56%, 60%, 81%, respectively	38

SOURCE: Robert E. Moroney. "Most Courts Overvalue Closely Held Stocks." TAXES--The Tax Magazine (March 1973). pp. 154-155. Published and copyrighted (c)1973 by Commerce Clearing House. Inc.. in Chicago. Excerpted here with their permission.

at the times of the prior cases and suggests that higher discounts for lack of marketability be allowed in the future now that the relevant data are available. As Moroney puts it:

Obviously the courts in the past have overvalued minority interests in closely held companies for federal tax purposes. But most (probably all) of those decisions were handed down without benefit of the facts of life recently made available for all to see.

Some appraisers have for years had a strong gut feeling that they should use far greater discounts for nonmarketability than the courts had allowed. From now on those appraisers need not stop at 35 percent merely because it's perhaps the largest discount clearly approved in a court decision. Appraisers can now cite a number of known arm's-length transactions in which the discount ranged up to 90 percent.[9]

Maher Study

Another well-documented study on marketability discounts for closely held business interests was done by J. Michael Maher and published in the September 1976 issue of *Taxes*.[10] Maher's approach was similar to Moroney's in that it compared prices paid for restricted stocks with the market prices of their unrestricted counterparts. He found that mutual funds were not purchasing restricted securities during 1974 and 1975, which were very depressed years for the stock market. Therefore, the data actually used covered the five-year period from 1969 through 1973. The study showed that "the mean discount for lack of marketability for the years 1969–73 amounted to 35.43 percent."[11] He further eliminated the top and bottom 10 percent of purchases in an effort to remove especially high- and low-risk situations. The result was almost identical with the "outliers" removed, with a mean discount of 34.73 percent.

Maher concludes:

> The result I have reached is that most appraisers underestimate the proper discount for lack of marketability. The results seem to indicate that this discount should be about 35 percent. Perhaps this makes sense because by committing funds to restricted common stock, the willing buyer (a) would be denied the opportunity to take advantage of other investments, and (b) would continue to have his investment at the risk of the business until the shares could be offered to the public or another buyer is found.
>
> The 35 percent discount would not contain elements of a discount for a minority interest because it is measured against the current fair market value of securities actively traded (other minority interests). Consequently, appraisers should also consider a discount for a minority interest in those closely held corporations where a discount is applicable.[12]

Standard Research Consultants Study

In 1983, Standard Research Consultants (SRC) analyzed recent private placements of common stock to test the current applicability of the SEC study.[13] SRC studied 28 private placements of restricted common stock from October 1978 through June 1982. Discounts ranged from 7 percent to 91 percent, with a median of 45 percent.

---

[9]Ibid., p. 154.
[10]J. Michael Maher, "Discounts for Lack of Marketability for Closely-Held Business Interests," *Taxes*, September 1976, pp. 562–71.
[11]Ibid., p. 571.
[12]Ibid., p. 571.
[13]"Revenue Ruling 77-287 Revisited," *SRC Quarterly Reports*, Spring 1983, pp. 1–3.

Willamette Management Associates Study

Willamette Management Associates, Inc. analyzed private placements of restricted stocks for the period of January 1, 1981, through May 31, 1984. The early part of this unpublished study overlapped the last part of the SRC study, but very few transactions took place during the period of overlap. Most of the transactions in the Willamette study occurred in 1983.

Willamette identified 33 transactions during that period that could reasonably be classified as arm's length and for which the price of the restricted shares could be compared directly with the price of trades in identical but unrestricted shares of the same company at the same time. The median discount for the 33 restricted stock transactions compared to the prices of their freely tradable counterparts was 31.2 percent.

The slightly lower average percentage discounts for private placements during this time may be attributable to the somewhat depressed pricing in the public stock market, which in turn reflected the recessionary economic conditions prevalent during most of the period of the study. I believe this study basically supports the long-term average discount of 35 percent for transactions in restricted stock compared with the prices of their freely tradable counterparts.

Summary of Studies on Restricted Stock Transactions

The seven independent studies of restricted stock transactions reported above cover several hundred transactions spanning the late 1960s through 1984. Considering the number of independent researchers and the very long time span encompassing a wide variety of market conditions, the results are remarkably consistent, as summarized in Table 10–2.

In many of the cases of restricted stock transactions tabulated in Table 10–2, the purchaser of the stock had the right to register the stock for sale in the existing public market. Sometimes investors get a commitment from the issuer to register the securities at a certain future date, sometimes investors have "demand" rights, where they can force the issuer to register the securities at a time of their choosing. Sometimes they get "piggyback" rights where there is no obligation other than to include the securities on any future registration that the issuer undertakes. And sometimes the purchaser has to rely on Rule 144, where they can sell after two years if other parts of the rule are followed. In any case, they generally expect to be able to resell the stock in the public market in the foreseeable future.

Revenue Ruling 77-287

In 1977, the Internal Revenue Service specifically recognized the relevance of the data discussed in the foregoing sections in Revenue Ruling 77-287. The purpose of the ruling is "to provide information and

TABLE 10-2

Summary of Restricted Stock Studies

Study	Years Covered in Study	Average Discount %
SEC, Overall Average [a]	1966-1969	25.8
SEC, Nonreporting OTC Companies [a]	1966-1969	32.6
Gelman [b]	1968-1970	33.0
Trout [c]	1968-1972	33.5 [i]
Moroney [d]	[h]	35.6
Maher [e]	1969-1973	35.4
Standard Research Consultants [f]	1978-1982	45.0 [i]
Willamette Management Associates, Inc. [g]	1981-1984	31.2 [i]

[a] From "Discounts Involved in Purchases of Common Stock (1966-1969)," *Institutional Investor Study Report of the Securities and Exchange Commission*, H.R. Doc. No. 64, Part 5, 92d Cong., 1st Sess. 1971, pp. 2444-2456.

[b] From Milton Gelman, "An Economist-Financial Analyst's Approach to Valuing Stock of a Closely Held Company," *Journal of Taxation*, June 1972, pp. 353-354.

[c] From Robert R. Trout, "Estimation of the Discount Associated with the Transfer of Restricted Securities," *Taxes*, June 1977, pp. 381-385.

[d] From Robert E. Moroney, "Most Courts Overvalue Closely Held Stocks," *Taxes*, March 1973, pp. 144-154.

[e] From J. Michael Maher, "Discounts for Lack of Marketability for Closely-Held Business Interests," *Taxes*, September 1976, pp. 562-571.

[f] From "Revenue Ruling 77-287 Revisited," *SRC Quarterly Reports*, Spring 1983, pp. 1-3.

[g] From Willamette Management Associates study (unpublished).

[h] Although the years covered in this study are likely to be 1969-1972, no specific years were given in the published account.

[i] Median discounts

guidance to taxpayers, Internal Revenue Service personnel, and others concerned with the valuation, for Federal tax purposes, of securities that cannot be immediately resold because they are restricted from resale pursuant to Federal security laws."[14]

The ruling specifically references the SEC *Institutional Investor Study* and the values of restricted securities purchased by investment companies as part of the "relevant facts and circumstances that bear upon the worth of restricted stock." The complete text of Revenue Ruling 77-287 is shown as Exhibit 19–4 in Chapter 19, "Estate Planning and Tax Valuations."

Studies of Private Transactions Prior to Public Offerings

Before the 1980s, virtually all the empirical research directed at quantifying the value of ready marketability, or the discount for lack of it, focused on comparisons between the prices of freely tradable shares of stock and restricted but otherwise identical shares of stock.

---

[14]Revenue Ruling 77-287 (1977-2 C.B. 319), Section 1.

Observers agreed that discounts for lack of marketability for shares of closely held companies were greater than those for restricted shares of publicly held companies, since the closely held shares had no established market in which they could eventually sell following the removal of certain trading restrictions. However, data for quantifying how much greater this discount should be had not yet been developed and analyzed.

During the 1980s, an investment banking firm and a business valuation firm independently undertook development of data with which to address this question. The research proceeded along basically parallel lines, although each firm was unaware of the other's efforts until their respective research was far along and each had enough data to reach some conclusions.

Both firms utilized data from *registration statements,* forms that companies must file with the SEC when they sell securities to the public. Each of the series of studies reported in the following sections used data from these forms to analyze prices of the private transactions relative to the public offering prices and market prices following the initial public offerings.

Robert W. Baird & Company Studies

Two studies were conducted under the direction of John D. Emory, vice president of appraisal services at Robert W. Baird & Company, a large, regional investment banking firm headquartered in Milwaukee, Wisconsin.[15] The first study encompassed stocks of companies that had successful public offerings between January 1, 1980, and June 30, 1981. The second study encompassed stocks of companies that went public from January 1, 1985, through June 30, 1986.

The basic methodology for the two studies was identical. The population of companies in each study consisted entirely of initial public offerings during the respective period in which Baird & Company either participated in or received prospectuses for a total of 97 companies in the 1980–1981 study and 130 companies in the 1985–1986 study. The prospectuses of these 227 offerings were analyzed to determine the relationship between the price at which the stock was initially offered to the public and the price at which the latest private transaction took place up to five months prior to the initial public offering. Emory gives the following explanatory statements regarding the studies:

> In all cases, the transactions were to have been at fair market value and ultimately would have had to be able to withstand judicial review, particularly in light of the subsequent public offering. The transactions took one of two forms—either the granting of options to purchase common stock, or the direct sale of common stock.

---

[15]John D. Emory, "The Value of Marketability as Illustrated in Initial Public Offerings of Common Stock—January 1980 through June 1981," *Business Valuation News,* September 1985, pp. 21–24; also in *ASA Valuation,* June 1986, pp. 62–66; and "The Value of Marketability as Illustrated in Initial Public Offerings of Common Stock—January 1985 through June 1986," *Business Valuation Review,* December 1986, pp. 12–14.

In order to provide a reasonable comparison between the fair market value of stock prior to an initial public offering and the subsequent offering price, we felt it necessary both for the company to have been financially sound prior to the offering, and for the transaction to have occurred within a period of five months prior to the offering date.[16]

Following the above guidelines, and after eliminating development-stage companies (companies with a history of operating losses) and companies with no transactions within five months prior to the initial public offering, 13 companies remained in the 1980–1981 study and 21 companies in the 1985–1986 study. Comparative private transaction and public offering prices for the 34 companies' shares are shown in Exhibit 10–4.

The private transactions in the 1980–1981 period took place at a 60 percent average and 66 percent median discount from the price at which the stock subsequently came to market. The discount for the 1985–1986 period was 43 percent for both the average and the median. The range of discounts in the 1980–1981 period was 4 to 87 percent; the range in the 1985–1986 period was 3 to 83 percent.

Emory concludes with the following observations:

Since a public offer often takes four or five months from conception to completion, the above transactions mentioned in the prospectuses in our study would almost certainly have reflected the likelihood of marketability within the next half year. This is not unlike the marketability situation for the blocks of securities being purchased with registration rights by registered investment companies in the 1960s and early 1970s. In both of these situations the companies were promising in nature, and their securities had good potential for becoming readily marketable. . . .

The final question to be answered is that if these kinds of discounts are appropriate for promising situations where marketability is probable, but not a certainty, how much greater should discounts be for the typical company's stock that has no marketability, little if any chance of ever becoming marketable, and is in a neutral to unpromising situation? The inability to get out of a once promising investment that has turned sour is something to be avoided. . . .

It is apparent that the lack of marketability is one of the more important aspects to value, and the marketplace itself emphasizes this point.[17]

Willamette Management Associates Studies

Over the last several years, Willamette Management Associates, Inc. has conducted a series of five studies on the prices of private stock transactions relative to those of subsequent public offerings of stock of the same companies. The five studies covered the following time periods for a total of 10 years:

---

[16]Emory, "The Value of Marketability," p. 13.
[17]Ibid., pp. 13–14. Further elaboration is to be found in "Letters to the Editor," *Business Valuation Review,* June 1987, pp. 93–94, and September 1987, pp. 143–45.

EXHIBIT 10-4

Fair Market Value TransactionsThat Occurred Within Five Months
Prior to an Inital Public Offering as Disclosed in the Prospectus

Company	Principal Business	Last Transaction Date	Price[1]	Public Offering Date	Price	%Discount From Public Offer Price[2]	Type of Transaction
		January 1, 1980 to June 30, 1981					
Alpha Microsystems	Microcomputer systems	2/81	$6.00	6/18/81	$15.00	60	Sale
Anthem Electronics, Inc.	Semiconductor distributor	1/80	6.00	3/04/80	13.50	56	Option
Apple Computer, Inc.	Personal computer systems	8/80	5.44	12/12/80	22.00	75	Sale
Computer Magnetics Corp.	Transformer mfg.	1/81	3.90	4/14/81	8.00	51	Sale
Diagnostic/Retrieval Systems, Inc.	Military computer systems	9/80	1.28	1/22/81	10.00	87	Option
Emulex Corp.	Disk/tape controllers	1/81	1.73	3/26/81	12.00	86	Option
Intergraph Corp.	Computer graphic systems	1/81	4.17	4/07/81	18.00	77	Sale
Inter-Tel	Key phone systems	12/80	12.00	2/05/81	12.50	4	Option
Kimbark Oil & Gas Company	Oil & gas exploration & production	3/81	10.44	6/04/81	13.00	20	Option
Monolithic Memories	Computer circuits; bipolar	3/80	4.80	8/06/80	21.00	77	Sale
Management Science America, Inc.	Computer software packages	2/81	7.75	4/08/81	16.00	52	Taxes
Network Systems Corp.	Ultra high-speed computer networks	9/80	5.00	2/25/81	14.62	66	Option
SEI Corp.	Services to bank trust departments	1/81	4.01	3/25/81	17.00	76	Option
Average						60	
Median						66	
		January 1, 1985 to June 30, 1986					
Bridge Communications Inc.	Local area network systems	2/85	$2.00	4/18/85	$12.00	83	Option
Sbarro Inc.	Italian restaurants	3/85	8.00	5/08/85	10.37	23	Sale
Carver Corp.	Audio system components	1/85	7.44	5/09/85	11.00	32	Option
Central Sprinkler Corp.	Sprinkler heads	12/84	10.80	5/17/85	12.75	15	Sale
VM Software Inc.	Software products	1/85	5.75	5/29/85	16.00	64	Option
Reebok International Ltd.	Athletic footwear	1/06/85	5.56	7/26/85	17.00	67	Sale
Hose Club, Inc.	Membership warehouses	9/10/85	6.30	10/29/85	9.00	30	Option
Sandy Corp.	Media-based programs	10/85	6.00	11/19/85	13.00	54	Sale
Mercury General Corp.	Small auto insurance	10/08/85	10.00	11/20/85	19.00	47	Option
Seacraft, Inc.	Family residential units	8/15/85	2.00	12/13/85	8.00	75	Option
Century Communications Corp.	Cable systems	12/05/85	12.00	2/11/86	12.50	4	Option
General Computer Corp.	Integrated computer systems	12/08/85	7.80	3/04/86	13.00	40	Option
Poly-Tech Inc.	Trash bags	12/85	7.50	3/11/86	11.00	32	Sale
Capital Wire & Cable Corp.	Wire and cable	3/86	5.00	4/29/86	13.00	62	Option
Sterling Inc.	Fine jewelry retailer	3/86	10.40	5/14/86	15.50	33	Option
Sigma Designs Inc.	IBM Enhancement products	3/25/86	2.79[4]	5/15/86	5.75	51	Option[3]
Modular Technology Inc.	Nonresidential structures	4/86	7.00	5/29/86	7.25	3	Option
Hana Biologics Inc.	Cell biology	1/86	6.25	6/05/86	10.00	38	Perf. Units
Marietta Corp.	Guest amenity programs	3/86	6.60	6/11/86	11.50	43	Option
Cytogen Corp.	Biochemical systems	3/01/86	7.00	6/18/86	13.00	46	Option
Health Management Assoc. Inc.	Health care services	2/26/86	4.50	6/20/86	10.00	55	Option
Average						43	
Median						43	

[1] In all cases, the fair market value was determined by the Board of Directors on or near the date of the last transaction prior to the offering.
[2] 1 minus (last transaction price divided by offering price).
[3] Net Realized Value x Fair Market Value less Price Paid.
[4] Computed from [3].

SOURCE:John D. Emory, "The Value of Marketability As Illustrated in Initial Public Offerings of Common Stock--January 1980 through June 1981," *Business Valuation News* (September 1985), p. 24; and John D. Emory, "The Value of Marketability As Illustrated in Initial Public Offerings of Common Stock--January 1985 through June 1986," *Business Valuation Review* (December 1986), p. 15.

1. 1975–1978.
2. 1979.
3. 1980–1982.
4. 1984.
5. 1985.

The Willamette studies differed from the Baird studies in several respects. One important difference was that the source documents for the Willamette studies were complete SEC registration statements, primarily on Form S-1 and Form S-18, whereas the source documents for the Baird studies were prospectuses. Although the prospectus constitutes a portion of the registration statement, it is required to disclose only transactions with affiliated parties. Form S-1 and Form S-18 registration statements requires disclosure of *all* private transactions in the stock within the three years prior to the public offering, in a section of the registration statement separate from the prospectus portion. The Willamette studies attempted to include only transactions that were on an arm's-length basis. The data analyzed included sales of stock in private placements and repurchases of treasury stock by the companies. All stock option transactions and sales of stock to corporate insiders were eliminated unless there was reason to believe that they were bona fide transactions for full value. In some cases, the companies were contacted by telephone to either validate the arm's-length nature of the transaction or eliminate the transaction from the study. Therefore, although there was considerable overlap in the three years of public offerings studied by Baird and the 10 years of offerings studied by Willamette, the actual transactions included in the two sets of studies differed almost totally.

The Willamette study considered all public offerings in the files of the *IPO Reporter.* According to the *IPO Reporter,* they included all public offerings during the respective periods. Eliminated from each of the studies were financial institutions, natural resource companies, offerings priced at $1 or less per share, and offerings that included units or warrants, since such offerings might be thought to have unique characteristics. The private transactions analyzed took place from 1 to 36 months prior to the initial public offering. If a company had more than one transaction that met the study's criteria, all such transactions were included.

Each private transaction price was compared with the subsequent public offering price. In addition, for each transaction for which meaningful earnings data were available in the registration statement as of both the private transaction and public offering dates, the price/earnings ratio of each private transaction was compared with the subsequent public offering price/earnings ratio. Because some of the companies had no meaningful earnings as of the private transaction date and/or the public offering date, the population of transactions compared on a P/E ratio basis was a subset of the population of transactions compared on a price basis.

Also, because the private transactions occurred over a period of up to three years prior to the public offering, Willamette made certain adjustments to reflect differences in market conditions for stocks of the respective industries between the time of each private transaction and the time of each subsequent public offering. Prices were adjusted by an industry stock price index. P/E ratios were adjusted for differences in the industry average P/E ratio between the time of the private transaction and that of the public offering.

For the price comparison, the formula used to derive the discount for the private transaction price from the public offering price was as follows:

Formula 10–1

$$\frac{P_0 - P_p\left(\dfrac{I_0}{I_p}\right)}{P_0}$$

where:

P_0 = Price per share of the public offering
P_p = Price per share of the private transaction
I_0 = Industry price index at time of offering
I_p = Industry price index at time of private transaction

As an example, consider the public offering at $10 per share of Paola's Pizza Parlours, an upscale gourmet pizza chain, whose largest stockholder and chairman of the board was Louis Paola, a prominent business valuation analyst who knew a good thing when he saw it. About a year before the $10 per share offering, Paola had arranged for the company to buy back the stock held by a major outside investor for $4 per share. The restaurant industry stock price index stood at 77 at the time of the public offering and at 70 at the time of the private transaction. Substituting in the above formula, the percentage discount of the private transaction price from the public offering price, adjusted for the change in the industry price index, was as follows:

Formula 10–2

$$\frac{\$10 - \$4\left(\dfrac{77}{70}\right)}{\$10} = \frac{\$10 - \$4.40}{\$10} = 56\%$$

$10 = Price per share of the public offering
$4 = Price per share of the private transaction
77 = Industry price index at time of offering
70 = Industry price index at time of private transaction

For the price/earnings ratio comparison, the formula used to derive the discount for the private transaction price from the public offering price was as follows:

Formula 10–3:

$$\frac{P/E_0 - P/E_p \left(\frac{IP/E_0}{IP/E_p}\right)}{P/E_0}$$

where:

P/E_0 = Price/earnings ratio of the public offering
P/E_p = Price/earnings ratio of the private transaction
IP/E_0 = Industry average price/earnings ratio at the time of the public offering
IP/E_p = Industry average price/earnings ratio at the time of the private transaction

Continuing with the same example, assume that Paola's earnings for the year prior to the offering were $1 per share. Thus, the offering was at a P/E ratio of 10 ($10/$1 = 10) and Paola's earnings for the year prior to the private transaction were $.80 per share and the private transaction was at a P/E ratio of 5 ($4/$.80 = 5). At the time of the public offering the restaurant industry average P/E ratio was 12, and at the time of the private transaction it was 10. Substituting the information in the above formula, the percentage discount of the private transaction P/E ratio from the public offering P/E ratio, adjusted for the change in the industry average P/E ratio, was as follows:

Formula 10–4:

$$\frac{10 - 5\left(\frac{12}{10}\right)}{10} = \frac{10 - 6}{10} = 40\%$$

10 = Price/earnings ratio of the public offering
 5 = Price/earnings ratio of the private transaction
12 = Industry average price/earnings ratio at the time of the public offering
10 = Industry average price/earnings ratio at the time of the private transaction

The results of the five Willamette studies described above are summarized in Exhibit 10–5. As the table shows, the average discounts varied from period to period but in all cases were higher than the average discounts shown in the studies for restricted stocks of companies that already had an established public trading market—which is the result one would expect.

While both sets of discount data deserve attention, I believe that the data based on P/E ratios present a more accurate estimate of the amount of discount attributable to lack of marketability, since it eliminates the effects of both changes in the subject company's earnings and changes in market P/E ratios.

EXHIBIT 10-5

**Average Discounts for Private Transaction Prices
Compared with Public Offering Prices**

Summary of discounts for private transaction prices
compared to public offering prices
adjusted for changes in industry stock price indexes

Time Period	No. of Companies Analyzed	No. of Transactions Analyzed	Median Discount %
1975-1978	28	59	64.3
1979	11	30	68.1
1980-1982	98	185	68.2
1984	53	94	80.0
1985	39	75	60.0

Summary of discounts for private transaction p/e ratios
compared to public offering p/e ratios
adjusted for changes in industry p/e ratios

Time Period	No. of Companies Analyzed	No. of Transactions Analyzed	Median Discount %
1975-1978	20	34	49.6
1979	9	17	62.9
1980-1982	58	113	55.5
1984	20	33	74.4
1985	18	25	41.7

SOURCE: Willamette Management Associates, Inc.

In one of the studies, Willamette checked trading prices six months after the initial public offering to see whether the IPO prices were upwardly or downwardly biased compared to a more seasoned market price. While after six months some prices went up and some down, the *average* change from the IPO price was insignificant.

Summary of Conclusions from Private Transaction Studies

The evidence from the Baird and Willamette studies taken together seems quite compelling. The studies covered hundreds of transactions over a span of 11 years. Average differentials between private transaction prices and public market prices varied under different market conditions, ranging from about 42 to 74 percent. This is very strong support for the hypothesis that the fair market values of minority interests in privately held companies are greatly discounted from their publicly traded counterparts.

Cost of Flotation of Public Stock Offerings

The previous sections presented empirical evidence on the quantification of discounts for lack of marketability for minority stock interests. However, controlling interests also lack the virtually immediate liquidity of a publicly traded stock. As discussed in Chapter 26, "Going Public," some companies' primary motivation for going public is to gain liquidity, and this is a significant factor in the motivation behind most public offerings. Consequently, the concept of a discount for lack of marketability applies to controlling as well as minority interests.

Since a controlling stockholder has the right to cause the company to register its stock for a public offering, the *cost of flotation* (cost of selling stock to the public, called *floating an issue* in securities trade jargon) often is used as a benchmark for quantifying the discount for lack of marketability for controlling interests. The most comprehensive and still most often quoted study on the cost of flotation is one published by the SEC in December 1974, which covered 1,599 public offerings. The average direct expenses of the offering, broken down by size of offering, are shown in Exhibit 10–6.

Costs of public flotation today are considerably greater than those in 1972. For example, for an offering under $7.5 million (the maximum allowed at the time of this writing under an S–18 registration), you rarely see direct compensation to the underwriters of less than 12–13 percent, compared to the 6.7 percent shown in Exhibit 10–6 for issues of $5.0 million–$9.99 million. Futhermore, other direct expenses currently tend to run higher than those shown in Exhibit 10–6.

In addition to the underwriting commissions and direct expenses shown in Exhibit 10–6, underwriters frequently receive warrants, especially in connection with smaller initial public offerings. Although this is not an immediate cash expense, it is a very real cost if the company is successful, amounting to a few percentage points of dilution. There are also other indirect costs, such as a large commitment of top management's time to negotiate and carry out a successful offering. If the marketability discount is a critical issue in the valuation, it might be appropriate to obtain more current data on the cost of flotation.

There is always considerable risk as to whether a public offering can actually be completed at any given price, or even at all, until it is an established fact. The market is more receptive to stocks of companies in different industries at different times, and some companies will not be accepted by the public markets at all.

One frequent mistake is to use costs of flotation to quantify the discount for lack of marketability for minority interests. It is inappropriate to do so, because minority interest holders do not have the right to register their stock for a public offering.

An alternative to liquidating a company's stock through a public offering is to attempt to sell it in a single transaction through an investment banker, merger and acquisition specialist, or business broker. Commission costs for such transactions for large companies

EXHIBIT 10-6

Cost of Flotation

Size of Issue (Millions)	No.	Compensation (Percent of Gross Proceeds)	Other Expense (Percent of Gross Proceeds)
Under .5	43	13.24	10.35
.5-.99	227	12.48	8.26
1.0-1.99	271	10.60	5.87
2.0-4.99	450	8.19	3.71
5.0-9.99	287	6.70	2.03
10.0-19.99	170	5.52	1.11
20.0-49.99	109	4.41	.62
50.0-99.99	30	3.94	.31
100.0-499.99	12	3.03	.16
Over-500.00	0	---	---
Total / Averages	1,599	8.41	4.02

SOURCE: *Cost of Flotation of Registered Issues 1971-72.* Washington, D.C.: Securities and Exchange Commission, 1974, p.9.

under the well-known *Lehman formula* are 5 percent on the first $1 million, 4 percent on the second million, 3 percent on the third million, 2 percent on the fourth million, and 1 percent on the balance. Business brokers, which typically sell smaller businesses, usually charge 10 to 12 percent. In addition to commissions, of course, are all the expenses of management time and costs of preparing the offering materials. Typically it takes six months to a year to effect those transactions that eventually are successful. A significant proportion of the businesses thus offered for sale are never sold, and a large number of those sold are finally transacted at a figure well below the initial offering price. Furthermore, in many cases, unlike in public stock offerings, all or part of the consideration received is something other than cash, requiring careful analysis of the consideration to determine a cash-equivalent value.

Court Decisions on Discounts for Lack of Marketability

Four years after Moroney's 1973 article, referenced earlier, Moroney wrote that courts have started to recognize higher discounts for lack of marketability:

> The thousands and thousands of minority holders in closely held corporations throughout the United States have good reason to rejoice because the courts in recent years have upheld illiquidity discounts in the 50 percent area. (*Edwin A. Gallun*, CCH Dec. 32,830(M), 33 T.C.M. 1316 (1974) allowed 55 percent. *Est. of Maurice Gustave Heckscher*, CCH Dec.

33,023,63 T.C. 485 (1975) allowed 48 percent. Although *Est. of Ernest E. Kirkpatrick*, CCH Dec. 33,524(M), 34 T.C.M. 1490 (1975) found per share values without mentioning discount, expert witnesses for both sides used 50 percent—the first time a government witness recommended 50 percent. A historic event, indeed!)

Nevertheless, perhaps we appraisers ought to think of 75 percent or thereabouts as the norm, subject to adjustment up or down according to the facts of each case. We shall certainly gain strong support from many minority stockholders who have tried to sell at that level without getting so much as a nibble.[18]

Solberg Study of Court Decisions on Restricted Shares

Thomas A. Solberg conducted a study of 15 cases in which the courts valued restricted securities.[19] He discussed Revenue Ruling 77-287 and federal securities law, especially Rules 144 and 237. Of the 15 cases, the range of discounts from market value was 10 to 90 percent, with a median of 38.9 and a mean of 37.4 percent. He concluded:

> The valuation of restricted securities is not a numbers game, and each case must stand on its own facts as presented to the court. Legal precedent, in terms of discounts granted in cases previously decided, is not as important as the nature, quality, and quantity of the evidence and the skill with which that evidence is marshalled and presented. The cases indicate that the courts, if provided with the factual basis to do so, are willing to grant significant discounts for restricted securities to properly reflect the economic realities of the marketplace.[20]

The results of the Solberg study are shown in Exhibit 10–7.

Recent Court Decision on Restricted Shares

At his death, Saul Gilford was the largest stockholder in a company that traded OTC; he owned 23 percent of the stock, all restricted shares. The IRS contended that the stock should be valued at a substantial premium over the market price at the time of death based on the price of a merger six months later. Expert for taxpayer, Allyn Joyce, testified that the stock should be discounted 35 percent from the public trading price, 33 percent to reflect the lack of marketability of the restricted shares, and an additional 2 percent to reflect blockage. The IRS presented no expert testimony. The court rejected reflecting the subsequent merger, ruled that the stock should be discounted 33 percent to reflect lack of marketability, and rejected the additional 2 percent for blockage.[21]

---

[18]Robert E. Moroney, "Why 25 Percent Discount for Nonmarketability in One Valuation, 100 Percent in Another?" *Taxes*, May 1977, p. 320.

[19]Thomas A. Solberg, "Valuing Restricted Securities: What Factors Do the Courts and the Service Look for" *Journal of Taxation*, September 1979, pp. 150–54.

[20]Ibid., p. 153.

[21]*Estate of Saul R. Gilford*, 88 T.C. 38 (1987).

EXHIBIT 10-7

Cases in Which the Court Valued Restricted Securities

	Case Name and Citation	Discounts Considered	Market Price	IRS Value	Taxpayer's Value	Court's Value	Discount From Market
1.	*Goldwasser*, 47 BTA 445 (1942) aff'd 142 F.2d 556 (CA-2, 1944) *cert. den.*	Restricted Securities	$ 82.25	$ 75.88	$ 54.87	$ 68.00	17.3%
2.	*Conroy*, TCM 1958-6	Restricted Securities	$ 5.00	NA	$1.00-$2.00	$ 3.50	30%
3.	*Victorson*, TCM 1962-231	Restricted Securities	$ .85	$ .85	NA[1]	$ .50	40%
4.	*Simmons*, TCM 1964-237 (involved two securities)	Restricted Securities and Blockage	$ 3.50 $ 1.00	$ 2.75 $ 1.00	NA[1] NA[1]	$ 2.75 $ .75	21.4% 25%
5.	*Specialty Paper and Board Co., Inc.*, TCM 1965-208	Restricted Securities and Blockage	$ 5.12	$ 4.50	NA[1]	$ 2.85	44.4%
6.	*LeVant*, 45 TC 185 (1965) *rev'd* 376 F.2d 434 (CA-7, 1967)	Restricted Securities	$ 39.06	$ 39.06	$ 31.50	$ 31.50	19.4%
7.	*Husted*, 47 TC 644 (1967)	Restricted Securities and Blockage	$ 11.25	$ 11.25	$4.20-$5.25	$ 7.00	37.7%
8.	*Jacobowitz*, TCM 1968-261	Restricted Securities	$ 10.00[2]	$ 10.00	$ 1.00[3]	$ 4.50	55%
9.	*Alves*, DC Mo., 4/11/69	Restricted Securities and Voting Trust Certificates	$103.00[4]	$103.00	$ 77.25	$ 77.25	25%
10.	*Bolles*, 69 TC 342 (1977) (involved three securities)	Restricted Securities and Blockage	$ 22.62 $ 14.30 $ 12.60	$ 15.00 $ 6.50 $ 12.00 $ 12.00[6]	NA[5] NA[5] NA[5] $ -0-	$ 12.44 $ 1.43 $ 9.83 $ -0-	45% 90% 22%
11.	*Roth*, TCM 1977-426	Restricted Securities and Blockage	$ 2.68	$ 2.00	$ .75[7]	$ 1.07	60%
12.	*Stroupe*, TCM 1978-55 (involved two dates)	Restricted Securities	$ 36.00 $ 34.00	$ 34.00 $ 32.00	$ 6.00 $ 6.00	$ 21.00 $ 19.20	40% 43.5%
13.	*Estate of Doelle*, DC Mich., 5/19/78.	Restricted Securities and Voting Trust	NA[8]	$ 3.12	$ .083	$ .085[9] $ .09[9]	NA[10]
14.	*Wheeler*, TCM 1978-208	Restricted Securities, Blockage Denied	$ 5.87	NA	$ 2.15	$ 5.29	10%
15.	*Kessler*, TCM 1978-491	Restricted Securities	$ 7.09	$ 4.96	$ .50	$ 3.67	48.2%

[1] Taxpayer argued that the stock had no ascertainable value due to Securities Act restrictions.
[2] Public offering took place 2½ months after the valuation date. Offering price to public was $10.
[3] Taxpayer reported value initially at $5.50, but later changed his value to $1.00. Taxpayer's expert testified stock was worth $1.10.
[4] Market price for shares was $101 bid, $105 asked. Plaintiff made gift of voting trust certificates representing shares and valued them at 75% of mean share value.
[5] Taxpayer sought greater discounts than court allowed on debentures.

The court probably adopted the taxpayer's value on the warrants and common stock, but this is not clear from opinion.
[6] Taxpayer had a guaranty of questionable enforceability that the three securities would have a total value of $45.50. IRS valued the guaranty agreement at $12.00. The Court disregarded the guaranty.
[7] Reduced from $1.00 claimed on original tax return.
[8] No evidence introduced as to market price.
[9] Stock in voting trust was valued at $.085 and stock not in voting trust at $.09.
[10] Cannot be computed without a market value figure.

SOURCE: Thomas A. Solberg, "Valuing Restricted Securities: What Factors do the Courts Look For?" *Journal of Taxation* (September 1979), pp. 150-54. (c)1979 *The Journal of Taxation*. Reprinted with permission of author and publisher.

There have been a substantial number of other court cases on restricted stock in recent years, but I think the Gilford case is the most on target.

Moore Study of Court Decisions on Closely Held Interests

Philip W. Moore, president of J. & W. Seligman Valuations Corporation, published a study analyzing 14 decisions of the U.S. Tax Court involving discounts for lack of marketability for interests in closely held businesses from 1969 through 1982.[22] Such an analysis is quite difficult, because the wording of some opinions leaves the reader somewhat uncertain as to exactly what weight was accorded to lack of marketability in the discounts finally arrived at. As Moore explains,

> The discounts vary quite considerably, depending on many factors. However, it is oftentimes not easy to isolate the weight of the so-called "lack-of-marketability" factor, and difficult to compare even equal discounts when taken from the varied basis, i.e., net asset value, book value or appraised value.[23]

Moore concludes, however, that "the tendency seems to have been for discounts for lack of marketability to have risen slowly in size over the years."[24] He groups the 14 cases into three time periods, as shown in Table 10–3.

Recent Court Decisions on Closely Held Interests

Several U.S. Tax Court cases since the Moore study have addressed the issue of discount for lack of marketability. The following four cases are described in more detail in Chapter 22, "Other Federal Gift and Estate Tax Cases," because they involve several interesting valuation issues; I will comment briefly here on only the discount for lack of marketability. I selected these cases for inclusion here because they are particularly relevant among the many recent cases in which discount for lack of marketability has been an issue.

***Virginia Z. Harwood* v. *Commissioner.*[25]**   In this case, the court ruled for a combined discount from net asset value of 50 percent to reflect combined minority interest and lack of marketability, the latter influenced by a restrictive agreement. The court recognized that lack of marketability was the basis for a further discount beyond the dis-

---

[22]Philip W. Moore, "Valuation Revisited," *Trusts & Estates*, February 1987, pp. 40–52.
[23]Ibid.
[24]Ibid.
[25]*Virgina Z. Harwood* v. *Commissioner*, 82 T.C. 239 (1984).

TABLE 10-3

| | Discounts for Lack of Marketability | | |
Years	Number of Cases	Range	Average
		%	%
1969-1976	4	15 to 25	18.75
1978-1979	5	10 to 35	24.00
1980-1982	5	10 to 50	28.00

SOURCE: Philip W. Moore, "Valuation Revisited." *Trusts & Estates* (February 1987), p.48.

count for minority interest, even though in the final decision the discount was given as a lump amount.

One witness said that the marketability discount could be between 20 and 50 percent and chose 35 percent. The court said, "He failed to adequately substantiate the discount he chose to apply." This leads me to believe that the combined discount would have been higher had the 35 percent marketability discount been adequately substantiated.

Estate of Mark Gallo* v. *Commissioner.[26]   At trial, the estate presented three expert witnesses. The primary valuation expert for the estate testified that the per share value was $237. This value was derived by using a price/earnings multiple based on comparative publicly traded companies' price/earnings ratios and then discounting by 36 percent to reflect the stock's lack of marketability.

The Tax Court held for a value of $237 per share, holding, among other findings, that a company's size and market dominance do not necessarily mean that a lack of marketability discount should be lower than normal.

Roy O. Martin, Jr. and Barbara M. Martin* v. *Commissioner.[27] This complicated case involved a series of gifts of minority interests of common stock in a closely held personal holding company. The holding company owned minority interests in each of seven closely held companies. The court determined that the one company that clearly was an operating company should be valued on a capitalization of earnings basis, that two companies that clearly were nonoperating companies should be valued on an asset value basis, and that four companies should be valued with one third of the weight given to capitalized earnings and two thirds to asset values. To the values thus derived, the court applied a 70 percent discount "to reflect the marketability/minority considerations." Finally, the court allowed a 5 percent second-stage discount at the holding company level.

---

[26]*Estate of Mark Gallo* v. *Commissioner,* 50 T.C.M. 470 (1985).
[27]*Roy O. Martin, Jr. and Barbara M. Martin* v. *Commissioner,* 50 T.C.M. 768 (1985).

Estate of Martha B. Watts.[28]   In this case, the court allowed a discount for lack of marketability of 35 percent from the estimated price at which minority interests would have traded in a public market had such a market existed for them.

Conclusion

This chapter presented a substantial amount of evidence to assist in determining appropriate discounts for lack of marketability for both minority and controlling interests in closely held businesses. In the final analysis, however, as with many other valuation issues, the determination must be made in light of a careful examination of the facts and circumstances of each case. The specific data that the analyst collects and relies on for each situation must relate as closely as possible in time and other characteristics to the particular valuation for which they are being used.

Shares of closely held companies, most of which will never be freely tradable, suffer much more from lack of marketability than do restricted shares of publicly traded companies. In general, they also have less prospect of being marketable than do shares of companies that are considering or already in the process of attempting to go public.

Courts have tended to recognize higher discounts for lack of marketability in recent years than earlier. However, the levels of discounts for lack of marketability allowed in most court decisions still seem to be well below those at which the empirical evidence indicates that arm's-length transactions tend to take place in the real-world market between willing buyers and willing sellers. Each court decision must rely on the facts and circumstances of the individual case and the evidence that experts and others submit to the court for its consideration. Hopefully the data presented in this chapter, along with continuing related research, will help to correct the disparity between marketability discounts usually recognized in prior court decisions and marketability discounts typically evidenced in actual market transactions.

---

[28]*Estate of Martha B. Watts,* 87–2 U.S.T.C., paragraph 13726 (11th Cir. 1987); 51 T.C.M. 60 (1985).

Part III

Analyzing Financial Statements

Chapter 11

Analyzing and Adjusting Financial Statements

Computation of Book Value per Share
An Example of the Effect of Alternative Accounting Methods
Adjusting the Balance Sheet to Current Values
Summary

> *. . . within the framework of generally accepted accounting principles
> (GAAP) there is some latitude permitted in the preparation of financial
> statements.*[1]

The financial analyst knows not only that the above statement is true
but that it may be the understatement of the century. Rarely do any
two firms follow exactly the same set of accounting practices in keeping their books and preparing their financial statements, even within
the broad confines of generally accepted accounting principles. Furthermore, the typical closely held company does not go to the expense
of having financial statements audited, and many deviate from GAAP.
Therefore, the analyst must evaluate each item and adjust for differences in accounting practices in order to compare two or more companies or measure a company against some industry or other
standard.

Where there is latitude for choice among accounting practices,
some private companies may account more conservatively to avoid unnecessary taxes, while some public companies may account more aggressively to please stockholders. This difference between public and
private companies tends to be more pronounced for very small private
companies and less so for medium-size and large ones. Also, at least a
few public companies attempt to "manage" their earnings in order to
ameliorate earnings volatility, electing more conservative accounting
decisions in good years and more aggressive accounting decisions in
bad ones.

As we will note at various points in this chapter and elsewhere in
the book, certain adjustments to financial statements may be appropriate when valuing controlling interests, because a controlling interest, unlike a minority interest, may have the right to change things.
Furthermore, all discussions of financial statement analysis in this
book are subject to the caveat that generally accepted accounting principles are constantly being reviewed and changed. Accounting principles were prescribed by the Accounting Principles Board (APB) until
1974, when the Financial Accounting Standards Board (FASB) assumed that function. The FASB is broader than the APB in that it
includes representation from financial analysts and corporate issuers
of financial statements as well as from the accounting profession. The

---

[1] George D. McCarthy and Robert E. Healy, *Valuing a Company: Practices and Procedures* (New York:
John Wiley & Sons, 1971), p. 16.

first FASB statement was issued toward the end of 1974, and as of this writing there already have been 97 such statements, many with sweeping implications for the use and interpretation of financial statements. In addition to the accounting requirements prescribed by the FASB, publicly traded companies are subject to certain disclosure requirements of the SEC.

The material in Part III is intended primarily as a framework for the nonspecialist rather than as a comprehensive treatise on financial statement analysis; complete books on the subject are referenced in Appendix D, at the back of this book. Anyone who appraises a business must have the resources with which to keep abreast of the current status of accounting principles as they affect the business being valued.

Since earning power is the most important element in the majority of business valuations, the purpose of analyzing income statements is to better understand and interpret the earning power that they represent. Adjustments to the earning power as shown in the income statements generally fall into any or all of three categories:

1. Adjustments to the way the company has elected to account for its activities.
2. Adjustments to reflect the likelihood that certain things in the future may differ from those in the past, since some aspects of past operations, such as nonrecurring events or discontinued operations, may not be representative of future earning power.
3. Adjustments for certain discretionary items, such as generous management bonuses.

Asset values also play a greater or lesser role in different valuation situations; thus, it may be appropriate to adjust certain balance sheet accounts for analytical purposes. Since the income statement and balance sheet are interdependent, some variables adjusted for income statement analysis will imply adjustments to the balance sheet. In other cases there may be appropriate balance sheet adjustments, especially to nonoperating assets, that will not affect the company's ongoing earning power, or adjustments to the income statement that will not affect the balance sheet.

This chapter discusses the most common categories of adjustments to the income statement and balance sheet in the business valuation. It begins with adjustments for different means of measuring asset and liability items. Then it examines a number of items arising from the treatment of revenue and expense items. Finally, it looks at a number of miscellaneous items. The reader may refer to Appendix D for more complete discussions of the various items, including comprehensive books on financial statement analysis.[2]

---

[2] See, for example, Leopold A. Bernstein, *Financial Statement Analysis,* 3rd ed. (Homewood, Ill.: Richard D. Irwin, 1983).

Adequacy of Allowance and Reserve Accounts

The analyst may encounter an endless variety of reserve or allowance accounts from time to time and should question and analyze each on its own merits. Some so-called reserve accounts should not be considered reserve accounts at all but merely portions of equity that management has chosen to earmark for some future expenditure or contingency. It is common to find that a company is either under- or overreserved for certain items. If underreserved, the effect is an overstatement of earnings due to inadequate reserve charges to expenses, with an accompanying overstatement of net asset value. If overreserved, the opposite occurs.

Allowance for Doubtful Accounts

Accounts Receivable. Most companies carry accounts receivable and deduct some allowance for potentially uncollectible accounts. The typical policy is to charge some percentage of credit sales to bad debt expense at the time the sales are made. Often a charge at the end of each month, reflecting that month's credit sales, is made with a credit to the allowance for doubtful accounts, which shows up as a deduction from accounts receivable on the balance sheet. Then, as individual accounts are written off, they are credited against accounts receivable and debited against the allowance for doubtful accounts, with no direct effect on either earnings or net asset value at the time of the write-off.

Since the expense charge actually represents an estimate of future write-offs, the analyst must make some judgment as to that estimate's accuracy, at least if the effect might be material. One way is to compare the historical percentage of bad debt losses from past credit sales with the percentage of current credit sales being charged to bad debt expense to see if too little or too much is currently being charged. Another approach is to compare the aged accounts receivable schedule with the current allowance for doubtful accounts to judge whether the allowance is reasonable relative to the amount of overdue accounts. Some companies tend to carry receivables on their books indefinitely, with little or no doubtful account allowance, resulting in overstatement of earnings and net asset value. Other companies follow a very aggressive write-off policy, removing from their books many accounts that eventually are collected; this tends to understate earnings and net asset value.

Notes Receivable. While examining accounts receivable, the analyst should check to see whether any notes or other receivables are questionable and make any appropriate adjustments. Notes receivable may be taken to improve the company's chance of collecting a delinquent trade receivable, but their collectibility may be in question. Notes receivable from stockholders may really be more in the nature of long-term loans, or even undeclared dividends, even though they may be carried on the balance sheet in the current asset section. A review of prior balance sheets to see how long some "current" items have been carried often can provide some insight into the probability of collection during the company's normal operating cycle.

Pension Liabilities

The FASB *Statement of Financial Accounting Standards No. 87,* issued in December 1985, dramatically revised the procedures for pension plan accounting, including the treatment of unfunded pension liabilities. Although explanation of the revision is beyond the scope of this book, the analyst should become familiar with the revised accounting procedures and be aware that they must be in place for all companies with audited financial statements no later than fiscal years beginning after December 15, 1988. For companies still not using GAAP accounting in 1989 and beyond, this could be a major item of financial statement adjustment.

Inventory Accounting Methods

FIFO, LIFO, and Other Methods

The *FIFO,* or *first-in, first-out,* inventory accounting method, assumes, for accounting purposes, that the first unit of an inventory item purchased is the first unit sold. The *LIFO,* or *last-in, first-out,* method assumes that the last unit of an inventory item purchased is the first unit sold. The difference between FIFO and LIFO accounting shows up in the ending inventory on the balance sheet, affecting both the cost of goods sold and earnings. To the extent that prices go up, LIFO produces lower figures for earnings and inventory than does FIFO. Since LIFO accounting is acceptable for federal income tax purposes, many companies have adopted LIFO over FIFO inventory accounting in response to inflation. However, it should be noted that if an inventory has been accounted for using LIFO, and if that inventory *declines* over the course of the year—that is, withdrawals from inventory exceed purchases—an accounting phenomenon known as *LIFO liquidation* occurs. This reduces inventories to a point at which cost layers from prior years are matched to current inflated prices. If prices from the "old" inventory are much lower than current prices, a distortion of income occurs. Audited and reviewed financial statements should disclose whether LIFO liquidation has occurred and the extent of its effects. If a decline in inventory that is being accounted for using LIFO occurs, and the financial statements lack proper disclosures, the analyst should conduct further examination and inquiry in order to eliminate the distorting effects of LIFO liquidation.

If one is comparing two or more companies for valuation purposes, all of the companies' earnings and asset values should have been derived based on the same inventory method if the difference is substantial enough to affect the valuation. If they do not all use the same method, the analyst must adjust the earnings and asset values to the same basis using information in the financial statements.

As a simple example, imagine a company that started its accounting period with 30 widgets, purchased for $10 each. Later in the period, it purchased 60 more widgets at $15 each, and before its next fiscal year-end it sold 50 widgets, ending the period with 40 widgets in inventory. The cost of goods sold would be computed under the FIFO and LIFO methods as shown in Table 11–1. In other words, LIFO accounting perpetrates the fiction that the original units in the inventory are the ones that are still there. In the above case, if sales were $1,000, the gross margin would be $400 under FIFO accounting and $250 under LIFO accounting.

For most companies that report on FIFO, the information the analyst needs in order to adjust earnings and inventory to the LIFO basis is not readily available. If a company reporting on LIFO has audited statements, however, the footnotes will provide a figure for the LIFO inventory reserve that the analyst can use to adjust earnings and inventory values from LIFO to FIFO. If the statements are not audited, the company's accountant should be able to provide the analyst with the necessary information for adjusting to a FIFO basis. Therefore, because of the availability of this information, if one or more companies' inventory accounting needs to be adjusted for comparative purposes, the analyst usually must adjust the LIFO-reporting companies to a FIFO basis rather than vice versa.

The appraiser should keep in mind that if earnings are adjusted from LIFO to FIFO, the adjustment should be net of the income tax effect (either additional taxes or benefit) associated with it. Choosing the correct income tax rate to use in making the adjustment may be more complicated than just using the effective or marginal tax rate. The analyst should carefully scrutinize the income tax characteristics of the company whose income is being adjusted to determine the most likely consequences of the additional income or losses, as adjusted, on income taxes.

Besides adjusting the income statement from a LIFO to a FIFO basis, it may be necessary to adjust the balance sheet, generally in three areas. First, the inventory level should be adjusted to the FIFO

TABLE 11-1

	FIFO		LIFO	
Beginning inventory	30 Units @ $10 =	$ 300	30 Units @ $10 =	$ 300
Purchases	60 Units @ $15 =	$ 900	60 Units @ $15 =	$ 900
Goods available for sale		$1,200		$1,200
Ending inventory	40 Units @ $15 =	$ 600	30 Units @ $10 =	$ 300
			10 Units @ $15 =	$ 150
				$ 450
Cost of goods sold		$ 600		$ 750

TABLE 11-2

Continuing with the example above,
Assume:

	Tax rate	30%
	LIFO reserve	$150
Adjust ending inventory to FIFO:		
	LIFO inventory	$450
	Add LIFO reserve	150
	Adjusted ending inventory	$600
Compute accrued income tax liability, and		
Add to an income tax liability account:		
	LIFO reserve	$150
	Multiply by tax rate	0.30
	Addition to accrued income tax liability	$ 45
Add net effect to retained earnings:		
	LIFO reserve	$150
	Less related accrued income tax	45
	Addition to retained earings	$105

basis. Second, an income tax liability account should be adjusted to account for the additional income taxes that would have resulted from the adjustment to inventory. Third, retained earnings should be adjusted by the net difference between the inventory and income tax liability adjustments.

Continuing with the our widget company example, assume that the company is using LIFO accounting and the appropriate tax rate for the adjustment is 30 percent. The company has a LIFO reserve of $150; therefore, to adjust the inventory to FIFO, the analyst adds $150 to the ending inventory level of $450 to reach an adjusted inventory level of $600. Then the analyst adds $45 ($150 × 30% tax rate) to an income tax liability account and $105 ($150 − $45) to retained earnings. Table 11–2 illustrates the calculations.

In some lines of business, specific inventory items are clearly identifiable from the time of purchase through the time of sale and are accounted for and costed on this basis. Some companies also account for inventory on some type of average cost basis.[3] In particular, in some industries it is possible to adjust inventory from LIFO only to average cost, not to FIFO. The adjustment is calculated in the same way as the adjustment to FIFO.

Write-Down and Write-Off Policies

Regardless of whether the company uses FIFO, LIFO, specific identification, or average cost inventory accounting, most companies adhere to the *lower-of-cost-or-market* principle, which says that the carrying value should be reduced if the market value is less than cost. *Market value* for this purpose is defined as "current replacement cost except

---

[3] For a discussion of the average cost method, see Bernstein, *Financial Statement Analysis*, pp. 144–45.

that market shall not be higher than net realizable value nor should it be less than net realizable value reduced by the normal profit margin."[4] Implementation of the lower-of-cost-or-market principle varies tremendously—one company may have stockrooms full of obsolete inventory and another an aggressive program of automatic write-downs and write-offs of inventory based on the number of months it has been in stock. If the company goes to one extreme or the other in its implementation of this principle, the analyst may need to adjust earnings and asset values.

Depreciation Methods and Schedules

The five most common methods of computing depreciation charges— all acceptable to the IRS for income tax purposes—are the straight-line, declining-balance, sum-of-the-years'-digits, accelerated cost recovery system (ACRS), and modified accelerated cost recovery system (MACRS) introduced by the Tax Reform Act of 1986. Regardless of which method is used, the number of years' useful life over which the asset will be depreciated is a crucial decision.

The *straight-line method* simply charges depreciation on the asset in even increments over the asset's useful life. The declining-balance, sum-of-the-years'-digits, ACRS, and MACRS methods are called *accelerated methods* because, unlike the straight-line method, they charge a higher proportion of the total depreciation in the early years of the asset's useful life than in later years.

Declining-Balance Method

The *declining-balance method* uses some multiple, such as two times or one and one-half times the straight-line depreciation rate. For example, if an asset had a useful life of 10 years, straight-line depreciation would be at the rate of 10 percent per year. Double-declining-balance depreciation would be at twice that rate, or 20 percent, but with the percentage always applied to the remaining book value. In other words, in the first year a $100,000 piece of equipment with a 10-year life would be depreciated at 20 percent of $100,000, or $20,000, leaving a depreciated balance of $80,000. In the second year, the asset would be depreciated at 20 percent of $80,000, or $16,000, leaving a depreciated balance of $64,000.

Sum-of-the-Years'-Digits Method

In the *sum-of-the-years'-digits method,* the depreciation charge is a fraction whose denominator is the sum of the years' digits of the asset's useful life and the numerator is the number of years of remaining

---

[4] Ibid., p. 149.

useful life. Thus, for a 10-year useful life, the denominator is 55 (1 + 2 + 3 + 4 + 5 + 6 + 7 + 8 + 9 + 10 = 55), and the numerator the first year is 10. Therefore, the first year's depreciation charge is 10/55 of the asset's value, in the second year 9/55, and so on.

For some assets, the company assumes a residual or salvage value at the end of the depreciable life. In these cases, the difference between the cost and salvage value is the depreciable amount. Salvage value may not be deducted from cost in the declining-balance method, however, because that method never results in the asset being depreciated to zero.

ACRS and MACRS[5]

The fourth widely used depreciation method is *ACRS,* (accelerated cost recovery system), which was enacted as part of the Economic Recovery Tax Act of 1981. It is used mainly for federal tax purposes. The Tax Reform Act of 1986 revised the use of ACRS for property placed in service after 1986, thus creating the MACRS (modified accelerated cost recovery system). One can consult a periodic tax guide for a presentation of the original and revised provisions of ACRS.

Still another depreciation method sometimes used is *units of production* (also referred to as *units of utilization*). For example, if a $100,000 asset is expected to provide 10,000 hours of useful service, it might be depreciated on the basis of $10 for each hour it is used.

Exhibit 11–1 illustrates the depreciation computations under the straight-line, declining-balance, sum-of-the-years' digits, and ACRS methods assuming an asset with a cost of $50,000, no salvage value, and an estimated useful life of five years.

Analytical Implications

The analyst should make some judgment of the appropriateness of the depreciation schedule both as it stands alone and in relation to other companies, if such comparisons are to be made. For example, a company may use an eight-year useful life for equipment that it manufactures and leases to customers, but most other companies in the industry may use a six-year useful life for the same type of equipment, assuming that the machinery will be technologically obsolete in six years. In valuing the company using an eight-year depreciation schedule, the analyst should apply a downward adjustment to both the earnings base and the equipment's net remaining book value to reflect the apparently inadequate depreciation charges. There can be a fairly wide range of normal practices within any industry, and the analyst must be prepared to do considerable research to reach an informed judgment of the reasonable depreciation life for some types of assets.

---

[5] The MACRS example is quite complex and beyond the scope of this book. The reader may wish to refer to the *U.S. Master Tax Guide,* 71st ed. (Chicago: Commerce Clearing House, 1987), for a comprehensive discussion of MACRS.

EXHIBIT 11-1

Alternate Depreciation Methods

Data used for the following examples:
Piece of equipment, purchased at beginning of Year 1
Cost of equipment $50,000
Estimated useful life   5 years

Straight-line method

Year	Computation	Year's Depreciation Charge	Balance Accumulated Depreciation	Book Value Year-End
1	1/5 (20%) x $50,000	$10,000	$10,000	$40,000
2	20% x 50,000	10,000	20,000	30,000
3	20% x 50,000	10,000	30,000	20,000
4	20% x 50,000	10,000	40,000	10,000
5	20% x 50,000	10,000	50,000	—

200%-Declining-balance method

1	40% x $50,000[a]	$20,000	$20,000	$30,000
2	40% x 30,000	12,000	32,000	18,000
3	40% x 18,000	7,200	39,200	10,800
4	40% x 10,800	5,400[b]	44,600	5,400
5	40% x 6,480	5,400	50,000	—

[a] Based on double the straight-line rate of 20%, multiplied by the remaining book value.
[b] Generally, when the asset has been depreciated to the point that the straight-line method yields a higher depreciation charge than the declining balance method, the company will convert the asset to straight-line depreciation for the remaining useful life of the asset. Thus, in this example, the asset's book value divided by its remaining useful life provides a depreciation charge of $5,400 per year ($10,800 ÷ 2); under the declining-balance method, the depreciation charge would be only $4,320 ($10,800 x 40%).

Sum-of-the-years'-digits method

1	5/15 x $50,000[c]	$16,667	$16,667	$33,333
2	4/15 x 50,000	13,333	30,000	20,000
3	3/15 x 50,000	10,000	40,000	10,000
4	2/15 x 50,000	6,667	46,667	3,333
5	1/15 x 50,000	3,333	50,000	—

[c] Numerator is the remaining estimated useful life. Denominator is the sum of the years (5 + 4 + 3 + 2 + 1 = 15).

The accelerated cost recovery system (ACRS)

1	15% x $50,000[d]	$ 7,500	$ 7,500	$42,500
2	22% x 50,000	11,000	18,500	31,500
3	21% x 50,000	10,500	29,000	21,000
4	21% x 50,000	10,500	39,500	10,500
5	21% x 50,000	10,500	50,000	—

[d] Statutory percentages for ACRS five-year property placed in service before 1986.

The above are examples of the more popular depreciation methods now in use. Salvage value has not been considered in the examples. An introductory accounting text can be consulted for a thorough presentation of potential depreciation methods. ACRS was enacted as part of the Economic Recovery Tax Act of 1981 and is used for federal tax purposes for assets placed in service between January 1, 1981, and December 31, 1986. For assets placed in service after December 31, 1986, MACRS is used for tax purposes under the Tax Reform Act of 1986. One of the periodic tax guides can be consulted for a thorough presentation of the provisions of the ACRS and MACRS.

Let's say we are valuing a closely held company by a multiple of earnings approach and that about 10 times earnings seems appropriate based on current market multiples of earnings at which publicly traded companies in the industry are selling. Suppose, however, that the publicly held companies are reporting straight-line depreciation for financial statement purposes while our company is reporting on an accelerated depreciation basis. The analyst would want to adjust the closely held company's earnings to a straight-line basis (remembering to also adjust the related income taxes) before applying the publicly traded-company multiple so that the earnings to be capitalized will be stated on a comparable basis. Usually a reasonable approximation suffices for this kind of adjustment.

Depletion

Depletion is the process of charging the cost of a natural resource to expense over the time during which it is extracted. It applies to such natural resources as metals and hydrocarbons in the ground and to timber stands. The basic concept of depletion accounting is simple: If a natural resource costs $1 million and 5 percent of it is removed in a year, the depletion expense charge is $5\% \times \$1,000,000 = \$50,000$. A like amount is credited to the allowance for depletion account on the balance sheet, reducing the net carrying value of the natural resource asset. The IRS also accepts this method of calculating depletion and refers to it as *cost depletion.*

A nonrelated method, *percentage depletion,* also appears in the Tax Code and is defined so as to allow an excess tax deduction in prescribed circumstances. Percentage depletion, as defined by the IRS, has no conceptual basis and is allowed only for calculating a depletion deduction for tax purposes. The problems of applying depletion are basically ones of measurement. How much of the natural resource is there? What is included in "cost" of a natural resource undergoing continuous development? If depletion is involved, the analyst should ask how it is measured and how thoroughly the company's depletion accounting practices conform to (or depart from) industry norms. Although depletion is relatively easy to define, it is very difficult to measure. Reasonable estimates can be subject to wide variations.

Treatment of Intangibles

It may be necessary to adjust the balance sheet and income statement for the diverse accounting treatments (or lack thereof) for intangible assets.

Leasehold Interests

If a company owns a leasehold at something other than fair market rent, the balance sheet may be adjusted to show an asset or liability representing the present value of the difference between the leasehold rent and the current fair market rent. The formula for this calculation is as follows:

Formula 11–1

$$PV = \sum_{i=1}^{n} \frac{A}{(1 + r)^i}$$

where:

PV = Present value
A = Amount of difference per period between leasehold rent and fair market rent
n = Number of periods remaining on the lease
r = Capitalization (discount) rate per period at which to capitalize the leasehold interest
i = ith period

For example, suppose a company has 25 months remaining on its lease at $5,000 per month and a new lease on comparable space today would cost $6,500 per month. (Alternatively, the company could sublet the space at $6,500 per month for the 25 months remaining on the lease.) The company's cost of capital is 12 percent per annum. The present value of the company's leasehold interest is computed as follows:

Formula 11–2

$$PV = \sum_{i=1}^{25} \frac{\$6,500 - \$5,000}{\left(1 + \frac{.12}{12}\right)^i}$$
$$= \sum_{i=1}^{25} \frac{\$1,500}{(1 + .01)^i}$$

An upward adjustment of $33,035 could be made to the asset side of the balance sheet to recognize the value of the leasehold interest.

Other Intangible Assets

Following are some other examples of intangible assets:

1. Patents.
2. Trademarks.
3. Copyrights.
4. Goodwill.
5. Customer lists.
6. Employment contracts.
7. Covenants not to compete.
8. "Intangible drilling costs" or similar natural resource development costs.
9. Natural resource exploration rights.
10. Franchises.
11. Licenses.

Accounting principles state that intangibles are to be carried on the books at cost and amortized over their useful economic lives. However,

The costs of developing, maintaining, or restoring intangibles which are unidentifiable, have indeterminate lives, or are inherent in a continuing enterprise should be expensed as incurred. By contrast, such intangible assets which are purchased must be carried at cost and amortized over their useful lives and cannot be written down or written off at date of acquisition.[6]

Thus, a company may have spent a great amount of money internally developing valuable intangible assets without showing their value on the balance sheet, while another company may show comparable intangible assets on the balance sheet and be charging amortization expenses as deductions from earnings because it purchased the intangibles instead of developing them internally. If a company's intangible assets have true economic value, that value is likely to be reflected in earnings. For that reason, the more heavily a company depends on its intangible as opposed to tangible assets to generate earnings, the more reliance the appraiser should put on earnings rather than asset valuation approaches. In comparing companies with very different accounting practices, the simplest way for an analyst to adjust for intangible items on the financial statements is to eliminate intangible assets from the balance sheets and amortization charges from the income statements.

Capitalization versus Expensing of Various Costs

Many cost items fall into a "gray" area, in which the decision which to expense or to capitalize the expenditure is subjective. One such decision is the dividing line between maintenance expenditures, which are expenses, and capital improvements, which are capitalized. For example, many seasonal operations, such as resorts and food processing plants, maintain skeletal crews year-round. Their compensation generally is expensed, even though they may do improvements that probably would be capitalized if outside contractors were hired for the same job. Companies that want to show a good bottom line will capitalize items that fall into this gray area, and companies that want to minimize income taxes will elect to expense rather than capitalize whenever possible. In analyzing the quality of the company's earnings and balance sheets, the appraiser should watch for opportunities to choose between capitalization and expensing and should ask management about the company's practice of accounting for these items.

Timing of Recognition of Revenues and Expenses

Certain types of companies have considerable latitude in their choice of accounting practices in the timing of recognition of some of their revenues and expenses.

---

[6] Ibid., p. 176.

Contract Work

Contract work can be accounted for either on a completed-contract or percentage-of-completion basis. The latter is conceptually preferable, but it can be implemented only under strict guidelines established by the AICPA.[7] Furthermore, the method is only as good as the estimates of the percentages completed. If the company being valued is in the contracting business, its accounting practices deserve careful scrutiny. This can be one of the most difficult areas for the outside analyst to evaluate critically. If it is a major issue in the valuation, it may necessitate considerable inquiry into the company's records as well as investigation of industry experience in comparable situations.

Installment Sales

When is a sale a sale? For years many companies booked huge profits by selling land on high-face-value contracts with 5 or 10 percent down and the balance over extended periods at low interest. The down payments were not high enough to deter many buyers from defaulting, and even good contracts were worth nowhere near their face value because of the low interest rate. In 1982, the FASB released *Statement of Financial Accounting Standards No. 66*[8] to help prevent such abuses, but there is still some latitude for differences in treatment from one company to another. If installment sales are a significant part of the company's business, the analyst should look into their accounting treatment.

Sales Involving Actual or Contingent Liabilities

Generally, sales involving actual future liabilities are those in which certain services are due to the customer in conjunction with the transaction. Such sales would include service contracts and subscriptions or products with future servicing warranted for some period. The unearned portion of the revenues is usually carried on the balance sheet as a liability item, commonly labeled deferred income, and then transferred to income as it is earned. When to recognize such income as revenues may require considerable judgment. Thus, the analyst should scrutinize the accounting treatment in companies that make sales involving future liabilities.

Sales involving contingent liabilities most commonly are those in which the customer has certain rights to return the product for a refund. If contingent liabilities exist, the analyst should assess the adequacy of their accounting treatment because they will affect the reported earnings and assets.

---

[7] *AICPA Statement of Position 81-1.*
[8] *FASB Statement of Financial Accounting Standards No. 66,* "Accounting for Sales of Real Estate."

Prior-Period Adjustments

For a variety of reasons a company may find that its revenues or expenses, or both, were under- or overstated in certain prior accounting periods. The most common reasons are errors in accounting and under- or overpayment of income taxes. The company usually records such an adjustment in the accounting year in which it is discovered by charging or crediting the adjustment to the opening balance of retained earnings. Thus, the adjustment does not affect net income during the current period. In assessing the company's earnings history, the analyst should spread the effect of the adjustment back over the prior periods to which it applies. Sometimes the information needed for accurately allocating the adjustment to the appropriate prior periods is available; in other cases, it is not. Even if a rough estimate of the appropriate prior-period allocation is the best one can make, usually it is better, for analytical purposes, to spread the adjustment on the basis of such an estimate rather than leave it in the period in which it was reported.

Accounting for Leases

According to the *Statement of Financial Accounting Standards No. 13* as amended and interpreted, leases that are of a financial nature (those that transfer essentially all of the benefits and risks incident to ownership of the property) must be capitalized as assets on the lessee's balance sheet. All other leases are accounted for as operating leases; that is, the lease payments are simply expensed as they are incurred. Since there is sometimes room for argument about which method of accounting is appropriate, and because unaudited closely held companies are less prone than audited public companies to strictly adhere to GAAP, the analyst should examine leases to judge whether to make any adjustments to the company's accounting treatment for analytical purposes.

Accounting for Certain Tax Aspects

Investment Tax Credits

The Tax Reform Act of 1986 repealed the regular investment tax credit for most property placed in service after 1985. Therefore, in assessing a company's earning power base, the analyst should determine how much of each year's earnings resulted from investment tax credits and whether similar credits will be generated in the future under the new tax law.

Tax Loss Carryforwards

An item that frequently causes controversy in a business valuation is the value of a tax loss carryforward. The amounts are shown in footnotes to the balance sheet rather than in the body, because their value is contingent upon generating future profits against which to use them. The ability to generate such profits usually is questionable, since if the company had an unbroken profit history there would be no loss carryforwards.

As far as the income statement is concerned, tax loss carryforwards properly are classed as extraordinary credits in the periods in which they are used. They should be adjusted out of the earnings base in those periods for analytical purposes. It may be reasonable to spread back the tax loss carryforward credits that actually were used to offset the losses in the periods in which the tax loss carryforwards were generated.

Treatment of Interests in Affiliates

If a company owns 50 to 100 percent of another company's stock, it generally prepares consolidated statements. However, in some situations the parent company properly accounts for the subsidiary by the equity method, defined below. If a company owns 20 to 50 percent of another company's stock, it may account for it by either the equity method or the cost method, depending on whether the parent exerts "significant influence"[9] over the company in which it holds the ownership interest. If a company owns less than 20 percent of another company's stock, it almost always accounts for it by the cost method, although accounting principles leave the door open for using the equity method if a significant degree of control can be demonstrated.

Consolidated statements treat the parent and subsidiaries as if they were all one company, with minority interests in subsidiaries, if any, shown as deductions on the financial statements. When accounting is done by the equity method, the parent's share of the subsidiary's earnings or losses (net of intercorporate eliminations, if any) is shown on its income statement and the carrying value of the interest in the subsidiary is adjusted accordingly on its balance sheet. When accounting is done by the cost method, the parent shows only dividends received on its income statement and continues to carry the investment on its balance sheet at cost except if it has a permanent impairment in its value, in which case accounting principles state that the investment should be written down. Frequently an analyst would consider an adjustment appropriate on the basis of the evaluation, even though the accountant would not necessarily recognize permanent impairment.

---

[9] *APB Opinion No. 18*, 1971.

The greatest distortions in the reporting of a parent company's overall results, of course, arise under the cost method, which does not reflect earnings or losses of the subsidiary interest in the parent's financial statement. If a subsidiary's earnings and losses are significant, the analyst may wish to make appropriate adjustments. On the other hand, presenting consolidated statements or accounting using the equity method implies that a dollar of the subsidiary's earnings is worth a dollar to the parent, which is not necessarily true. There may be restrictions on distributions of the subsidiary's earnings due to loan agreements, regulatory authorities, or other reasons. Also, the analyst should ensure that the parent has allowed for any income taxes incident to potential transfer of funds from subsidiary to parent.

Extraordinary or Nonrecurring Items

In analyzing a company's historical earnings as a guide to estimating the company's earnings base, the analyst should make every reasonable effort to distinguish between past earnings that represent ongoing earning power and those that do not. The analyst should adjust the income statements to eliminate the effects of past items that would tend to distort the company's current and future earning power. Implementation of this analysis and adjustments requires much judgment.

Ordinary versus Extraordinary Items

Accounting Principles Board Opinion No. 30, issued in 1973, is very restrictive as to what may be reported as an "extraordinary" gain or loss. *APB Opinion No. 30* states that an item must be *both* unusual in nature and infrequent in occurrence to be categorized as extraordinary. It defines these two requirements as follows:

> *Unusual nature*—the underlying event or transaction should possess a high degree of abnormality and be of a type clearly unrelated to, or only incidentally related to, the ordinary and typical activities of the entity, taking into account the environment in which the entity operates.
> *Infrequency of occurrence*—the underlying event or transaction should be of a type that would not reasonably be expected to recur in the foreseeable future, taking into account the environment in which the entity operates.[10]

If an item meets these definitions, it almost certainly cannot be considered representative of ongoing earning power. That does not

---

[10] *APB Opinion No. 30,* 1973.

necessarily mean it should be totally ignored, however, since an extraordinary item could indicate a risk that the company may face again in the future.

Other Nonrecurring Items

Since the use of the "extraordinary" designation is so restrictive, obviously many items do not meet the strict definition for accounting purposes but nevertheless should be regarded as nonrecurring for analytical purposes. Some examples of such items would be:

1. Gains or losses on the sale of assets, especially when the company clearly lacks a continuing supply of assets available for sale.
2. Gains or losses on disposition of a segment of the business.
3. Insurance proceeds from life insurance on a key person or from some type of property and casualty claim.
4. Proceeds from the settlement of lawsuits.
5. Effects of a strike or of an extended period in which critical raw materials are unavailable.
6. Effects of abnormal price fluctuations, such as the astronomical but short-lived inflation in sugar prices that occurred in 1974.

It is possible, of course, for most of these unusual events to recur, resulting in a greater or smaller effect on the company's financial results. The analyst must carefully consider the likelihood of their recurrence and decide whether and how to adjust the financial statements to produce a best estimate of the company's continuing earning power.

Discontinued Operations

Apart from any one-time gain or loss associated with the disposal or discontinuation of an operating segment, the analyst must also determine how to treat the operating earnings or losses that were generated by that segment before its discontinuation. If the amounts can be distinguished from the results of the ongoing operations, the analyst may decide to adjust the earnings of the ongoing operations by removing the effect of the discontinued operations. The analyst must also consider the effect on the company's overall resources, however, because lost earnings from one source may be replaced by redeploying the resources in other efforts.

Operating versus Nonoperating Items

Depending on the method of valuation, it may be useful to distinguish between operating and nonoperating earnings even if the latter are recurring. The nonoperating item most commonly found on financial statements is income from investments. I suggest elsewhere in this book that it may be appropriate to value certain portions of a company, such as investments, with a market value approach and operating portions primarily on a capitalization of earnings approach. If the analyst values nonoperating assets separately, he or she must be sure to exclude any income generated or expenses incurred by the nonoperating assets from the earnings base capitalized in valuing the company's operations.

Management Compensation and Perquisites

In closely held companies, compensation and perquisites to owners and managers may be based on the owners' personal desires and the company's ability to pay rather than on the value of the services these individuals perform. How much to adjust the earnings base to reflect discrepancies between compensation paid and value of services performed depends on the valuation's purpose.

Owners of successful closely held businesses tend to take out what normally would be considered profits in the form of compensation and discretionary expenses. This practice may be an effort to avoid the double taxation that arises from paying a corporate income tax and then paying a personal income tax on what the closely held business pays to the owner in the form of dividends. It is not uncommon to find an owner/manager of a successful company drawing $250,000 in annual compensation even though his or her services to the company could be replaced for $100,000 per year. The extreme cases go much further.

If the above owner/manager wants to sell the business and retire, the difference between the compensation and the cost to replace the owner's services will become available as a part of pretax profits, and the company's earning power should be adjusted accordingly in establishing the business's selling price. On the other hand, if the principal owner wants to establish an ESOP but plans to continue working and maintain a similar compensation program for the next 10 years, the analyst should not adjust the earnings base for an ESOP valuation, since the level of compensation can be expected to continue.

It is also common for management to be undercompensated because the company lacks the ability to pay. Usually the analyst should assume that the underpayment will be corrected when adequate resources are available and should make an appropriate upward adjustment to the management compensation expense in estimating the company's earnings base.

In general, adjustments for compensation, if appropriate, will be made when valuing controlling interests, because it will be within the power of the controlling interest's owner to change such compensation. Adjustments for compensation may *not* be appropriate when valuing minority interests, because the minority stockholder may receive no benefit from such compensation and lacks the power to change it.

Transactions Involving Company Insiders

The analyst should carefully scrutinize and evaluate any transaction involving owners or management. One of the most common situations is one in which the business leases premises from a person associated with the company. In such cases, the analyst usually should evaluate whether the lease amounts are equivalent to what the company would pay on an arm's-length basis. If not, the appropriate adjustment will depend on the situation, especially the length of time over which the present lease arrangement can be expected to continue, and the ability of the stockholder whose stock is being valued to change the arrangement.

Another common occurrence in closely held businesses is loans to or from stockholders or officers. Here the analyst should examine the borrowers' ability and intent to repay. If there is little or no likelihood of collecting a receivable from an insider, it should be removed from the balance sheet for analytical purposes. If interest is being accrued and is unlikely to be collected, it should be adjusted out of the earnings used to evaluate the earning power. It is also common to find a demand note payable in the current liability section of the balance sheet, even though there is no intent to pay the note any time soon or even ever. Interest may or may not be paid on it. For analytical purposes, it may be more appropriate to treat such an item as if it were long-term debt or even subordinated capital of a nature more like equity than debt.

Contingent Assets and Liabilities

One of the most difficult categories of items to treat analytically for valuation purposes is contingencies. The very fact that an item is a contingency defies precise quantification. Nevertheless, the valuation analyst must try to discover contingent assets and liabilities, whether or not they are on the financial statements in some form, and deal with them within the scope of the available information.

The most common categories of contingent assets and liabilities are those that arise from existing or potential litigation. If the outcomes were known, there would be no need for litigation. These situations are so varied that it is virtually impossible to generalize about how to treat them for valuation purposes. The analyst should at least be alert to opportunities to investigate and evaluate contingencies.

Adjustments to Asset Valuations

Marketable Securities

It is generally agreed that marketable securities should be adjusted to fair market value for most asset valuation purposes. However, there is not necessarily total agreement that such an adjustment should be accompanied by a partially offsetting adjustment for the related income tax effects implied by the unrealized gain or loss to which the adjustment gives rise. Making the offsetting tax adjustment seems logical. As the chapters on gift and estate tax cases discuss in detail, the courts' treatment of the matter has been inconsistent.

Other Assets

The appropriateness of adjusting various other categories of balance sheet assets for business valuation purposes is very controversial and depends partly on the situation. Revenue Ruling 59-60 states that for gift and estate tax purposes, values of assets of an investment nature (as opposed to operating assets) should be adjusted. The theory apparently is that such assets could be liquidated without impairing the company's operations. Sometimes, however, that will not be true, such as if the assets must be maintained as loan collateral or are necessary for maintaining certain financial ratios that lenders or regulatory agencies require. Other portions of this book discuss the appropriateness of adjusting different categories of asset values under various circumstances.

Computation of Earnings per Share

Weighted-Average Basis

Earnings per share should be computed on a weighted-average basis, that is, the number of shares weighted by the length of time they have been outstanding. Let's say that a company had 100,000 shares outstanding at the beginning of the year and issued 30,000 more shares on May 1. The 100,000 shares would be outstanding for four months and the 130,000 shares for eight months, or two thirds of the year. The weighted-average number of shares outstanding for the year would be computed as follows:

Formula 11–3

$\frac{1}{3} \times 100{,}000$	$= 33{,}333$
$\frac{2}{3} \times 130{,}000$	$= \underline{86{,}667}$
Weighted average shares outstanding	$= 120{,}000$

If the earnings were \$300,000, the proper computation of earnings per share would be \$300,000/\$120,000 = \$2.50 per share.

Primary versus Fully Diluted Earnings

In general, primary earnings per share are computed by dividing the earnings available to common equity by the weighted average number of common shares outstanding, plus "dilutive common stock equivalents." The definition and computations can be very technical, and the reader who needs this detail should turn to a technical, accounting-oriented manual, such as Bernstein's.[11]

For analytical purposes, it seems that the earnings per share are best stated on a fully diluted basis, that is, showing the maximum potential dilution that could have resulted had all possible conversions and exercises of options and warrants been exercised. Naturally, the effect of any interest or dividends paid on the convertible issues would have to be added back to the earnings base. Any conversions that would be antidilutive in their effect should not be included.

Computation of Book Value per Share

Book value per share is based on the number of shares outstanding at the end of the accounting period rather than the weighted average used in computing earnings per share. Also, book value normally is computed without considering possible dilutive effects of conversions, although the analyst may wish to make such a computation for analytical purposes. Thus, the computation of book value per share usually is a simple matter of dividing the total common equity by the number of shares outstanding. (Treasury stock—that is stock once issued and subsequently reacquired—is *not* included in the number of shares outstanding.) On most balance sheets, the common equity consists of the common stock account, any paid-in capital in excess of par or stated value, any unrealized currency translation gains or losses, and the accumulated retained earnings or deficit. Of course, if there were any contingent payments on senior securities not shown on the balance sheet, such as preferred dividends in arrears, such amounts would have to be deducted from common equity in computing book value per share. Several investment services, including S&P *Corporation Records* (referenced elsewhere in this book), exclude intangibles in their computed book values per share.

An Example of the Effect of Alternative Accounting Methods

Exhibit 11–2 illustrates the impact on reported earnings of using different methods of accounting for a particular set of operations.

---

[11] Bernstein, *Financial Statement Analysis,* pp. 368–72.

EXHIBIT 11-2

Example of the Effect of the Variety of Accounting Principles on Reported Income

Rival Manufacturing Company
Consolidated Statement of Income
For Year Ended 19xx

	Method A	Method B
Net sales	$ 365,800,000	$ 365,800,000
Cost of goods sold (1) (2) (3) (4) (5)	(276,976,200)	(274,350,000)
	88,823,800	91,450,000
Selling, general, and administrative expenses (5) (6)	(51,926,000)	(42,700,000)
	36,897,800	48,750,000
Other Income (expenses):		
Interest expenses	(3,085,000)	(3,095,000)
Net income--subsidiaries	1,538,000	1,460,000
Amortization of goodwill (7)	(390,000)	(170,000)
Miscellaneous expenses	(269,000)	(229,000)
Income before taxes	34,691,800	46,716,000
Taxes:		
Income taxes--deferred	(556,000)	(850,000)
Income taxes--current	(13,906,500)	(18,639,500)
Net income	$ 20,229,300	$ 27,226,500
Earnings per share	$6.98	$9.39

Explanations:
  (1) Inventories
        A uses last-in, first-out
        B uses first-in, first-out
        Difference--$1,780,000
  (2) Administrative costs:
        A includes some administrative costs as period costs
        B includes some adminis trative costs as inventory costs
        Difference--$88,000
  (3) Depreciation.:
        A uses sum-of-the-years'-digits method
        B uses straight-line mehtod
        Difference--$384,200
  (4) Useful lives of assets:
        A uses conservative assumption--8 years (average)
        B uses liberal assumption--14 years (average)
        Difference--$346,000
  (5) Pension costs:
        A uses realistic assumptions regarding rates of return on assets and future inflation
        B uses less realistic assumptions regarding rates of return on assets and future inflation
        Difference--$78,000
  (6) Executive compensations:
        A compensates executives with cash bonuses
        B compensates executives with stock options
        Difference--$840,000
  (7) Goodwill from acquisition:
        A amortizes over 10 years
        B amortizes over 40 years
        Difference--$220,000

SOURCE: Leopold A. Bernstein, *Financial Statement Analysis: Theory, Application and Interpretation,* 4th ed. (Homewood, Ill.: Richard D. Irwin, Inc., 1989), p. 379.

Adjusting the Balance Sheet to Current Values

If it is appropriate to rely heavily on an asset approach in the valuation, the analyst may prepare a pro forma balance sheet with some or all of the line items adjusted to current values. Depending on the valuation criteria to be used, the adjustments may affect only non-operating assets or may affect all assets.

Summary

Adjustments to the financial statements require both an understanding of accounting and analytical judgment. This chapter has presented the categories of financial statement adjustments that are required most frequently in the course of the business valuation process. The chapter has presented both the accounting mechanics and also some discussion of the judgmental factors that the analyst should consider in analyzing the financial statements for appropriate adjustments for valuation purposes. The analyst should be guided by common sense, experience, and an understanding of the company in determining what adjustments should be made to present the statements in the manner most appropriate for valuation purposes.

Chapter 12

Comparative Ratio Analysis

Use and Interpretation of Ratio Analysis

When properly used, analysis of financial statement ratios can be a useful tool in a business valuation. In particular, it can help identify and quantify some of the company's strengths and weaknesses both on an absolute basis and relative to other companies or industry norms.

The implications gleaned from financial statement analysis may be considered in arriving at the value of the business or business interest in several ways. The most common method of incorporating the results of ratio analysis of financial statements into the final valuation is to make appropriate adjustments to the capitalization rate used when valuing earnings. To the extent that the ratios indicate sustainable growth, the business should be worth a higher multiple of current earnings than it would if they did note indicate growth. Ratio analysis can also be helpful in determining appropriate multiples of book value and other variables. The higher the degree of risk factors the ratios reveal, the lower should be the business's worth relative to earnings, book value, and other fundamental financial variables.

One use of ratio analysis is to compare a company's own figures over time, a method sometimes called *trend analysis*. In this way, one can identify aspects of the business that demonstrate any trends of improvement or deterioration. It can also indicate levels of the different variables that have been normal within the period studied, as well as ranges that reveal high and low points for each variable over time.

Another way to use ratio analysis is to compare the subject company with other companies, either specific companies or industry averages. Patterns of strength in the subject company relative to comparative companies would tend to support a price/earnings or price/asset multiple in the high end of the industry range. Conversely, poor performance ratios relative to similar companies would suggest lower multiples for the subject company's earnings and asset values.

In comparing ratios from one period to another or from company to company, one should inquire into the extent to which comparative ratios are based on comparable accounting policies. The previous chapter noted that different choices among accounting methods can result in wide variations in reported figures. If one is making a comparative analysis of a company's financial statements over time, one should make an appropriate allowance for any changes in accounting policies that occured during the period. When comparing a company with others in its industry, one should allow for any differences in accounting policies between the subject company and industry norms.

Another consideration is whether to calculate the ratios before or after any adjustments in the balance sheet or income statement for things such as nonrecurring items, inventory adjustments, or pro forma adjustments. In many cases, these adjustments can significantly affect the magnitude of the company's ratios.

Two factors should guide the analyst in making this decision. First, if the ratios are to be compared to those of similar publicly traded companies, the analyst should make the same adjustments to the statements of both the subject company and the comparative companies. Second, if the computed ratios are to be compared to industry norms, the analyst should make only those adjustments that are likely to put the subject company on a basis comparable to other companies in the industry. In most cases, however, ratios calculated on adjusted statements will reveal a more accurate picture of the company's financial health.

The relative significance of the various ratios will differ in each valuation. Certain ratios have greater significance for value in particular industries. A ratio may be especially significant in some situations because it departs markedly from industry norms. The analyst must apply judgment to each individual case in selecting and evaluating the significance of figures as they apply to the particular situation.

If the analyst does the ratio computations prior to making the field trip to interview company personnel, the ratio analysis usually will generate some questions about any departures from industry norms. Of course, if the ratio work follows the field trip, the analyst can cover such questions in later telephone interviews.

This chapter discusses ratios that help evaluate the company's financial position. First it looks at those that measure short-term liquidity, followed by the commonly used longer-term balance sheet leverage ratios. Then the chapter discusses a variety of operating ratios. Each ratio is illustrated with an example from our hypothetical manufacturer, Ace Widget Company. A summary of Ace Widget Company ratios appears at the end of the chapter.

Common-Size Statements

Usually, the first step in ratio analysis of financial statements is to prepare what are sometimes called *common-size statements*. On these statements, each line item is expressed as a percentage of the total. On the balance sheet, each line item is shown as a percentage of total assets. On the income statement, each item is expressed as a percentage of sales.

Exhibit 12–1 shows five years of balance sheets and Exhibit 12–2 five years of income statements for Ace Widget Company presented on a common-size basis. Chapter 14 also presents a set of common-size statements as part of the sample case.

Short-Term Liquidity Measures

Generally, *liquidity ratios* demonstrate the company's ability to meet its current obligations. Liquidity ratios can help resolve one of the common controversies in business valuations: whether the company has any assets in excess of those required for its operating needs or, conversely, whether its assets fall short of its needs.

EXHIBIT 12-1

Ace Widget Company
Balance Sheets

	As of December 31					As of December 31				
	1987 $	1986 $	1985 $	1984 $	1983 $	1987 %	1986 %	1985 %	1984 %	1983 %
ASSETS										
Current Assets:										
Cash & Equivalents	225,000	187,500	187,500	150,000	150,000	7.8	7.2	8.0	7.0	7.4
Trade Notes & Accounts Rec.	600,000	600,000	562,500	525,000	525,000	20.7	23.2	23.9	24.6	25.9
Inventory	562,500	525,000	525,000	487,500	487,500	19.4	20.3	22.3	22.9	24.1
Prepaid Expenses	37,500	37,500	37,500	37,500	37,500	1.3	1.4	1.6	1.8	1.9
Total Current Assets	1,425,000	1,350,000	1,312,5000	1,200,000	1,200,000	49.2	52.1	55.8	56.3	59.3
Fixed Assets:										
Land	300,000	300,000	300,000	225,000	225,000	10.4	11.6	12.8	10.5	11.1
Plant & Equipment	1,500,000	1,275,000	1,087,500	1,087,500	965,000	51.8	49.2	46.3	51.0	47.7
Total Fixed Assets, Cost	1,800,000	1,575,000	1,387,500	1,312,500	1,190,000	62.1	60.8	59.0	61.5	58.8
Accumulated Depreciation	(600,000)	(525,000)	(450,000)	(412,500)	(375,000)	(20.7)	(20.3)	(19.1)	(19.3)	(18.5)
Total Fixed Assets, Net	1,200,000	1,050,000	937,500	900,000	815,000	41.4	40.5	39.9	42.2	40.2
Total Other Assets	273,000	190,500	100,500	33,000	10,000	9.4	7.4	4.3	1.5	0.5
TOTAL ASSETS	2,898,000	2,590,500	2,350,500	2,133,000	2,025,000	100.0	100.0	100.0	100.0	100.0
LIABILITIES & EQUITY										
Liabilities:										
Current Liabilities:										
Notes Payable	75,000	75,000	75,000	75,000	75,000	2.6	2.9	3.2	3.5	3.7
Trade Accounts Payable	262,500	225,000	225,000	225,000	225,000	9.1	8.7	9.6	10.5	11.1
Curr. Portion L-T Debt	112,500	75,000	75,000	75,000	75,000	3.9	2.9	3.2	3.5	3.7
Accrued Expenses	225,000	150,000	150,000	150,000	150,000	7.8	5.8	6.4	7.0	7.4
Contingent Liab., Oper. Lease	270,000	225,000	187,500	157,500	120,000	9.3	8.7	8.0	7.4	5.9
Interest Payable	30,000	37,500	37,500	30,000	30,000	1.0	1.4	1.6	1.4	1.5
Total Current Liabilities	975,000	787,500	750,000	712,500	675,000	33.6	30.4	31.9	33.4	33.3
Long-Term Debt	525,000	637,500	600,000	562,500	600,000	18.1	24.6	25.5	26.4	29.6
Total Liabilities	1,500,000	1,425,000	1,350,000	1,275,000	1,275,000	51.8	55.0	57.4	59.8	63.0
Equity:										
Common Stock	150,000	150,000	150,000	150,000	150,000	5.2	5.8	6.4	7.0	7.4
10% Preferred Stock	150,000	150,000	150,000	150,000	150,000	5.2	5.8	6.4	7.0	7.4
Retained Earnings	1,098,000	865,500	700,500	558,000	450,000	37.9	33.4	29.8	26.2	22.2
Total Shareholders' Equity	1,398,000	1,165,500	1,000,500	858,000	750,000	48.2	45.0	42.6	40.2	37.0
TOTAL LIABILITIES & EQUITY	2,898,000	2,590,500	2,350,500	2,133,000	2,025,000	100.0	100.0	100.0	100.0	100.0
Common Shares Outstanding	150,000	150,000	150,000	150,000	150,000					
Per-Share Book Value	$8.32	$6.77	$5.67	$4.72	$4.00					

SOURCE: Company's audited financial statements.

Current Ratio

The most commonly used short-term liquidity ratio is the *current ratio,* which is defined as current assets divided by current liabilities. Its greatest significance is as an indicator of the firm's ability to pay its short-term liabilities on time. The old rule of thumb that a satisfactory current ratio is 2.0:1, is not widely followed because of vastly different conditions typical in various industries, such as accounts receivable collection periods and inventory turnover periods. As with

EXHIBIT 12-2

Ace Widget Company
Income Statements

	Years Ended December 31					Years Ended December 31				
	1987 $	1986 $	1985 $	1984 $	1983 $	1987 %	1986 %	1985 %	1984 %	1983 %
Total Sales	5,250,000	4,650,000	4,500,000	4,125,000	3,750,000	100.0	100.0	100.0	100.0	100.0
Cost of Goods Gold	3,750,000	3,375,000	3,300,000	3,075,000	2,812,500	71.4	72.6	73.3	74.5	75.0
Gross Margin	1,500,000	1,275,000	1,200,000	1,050,000	937,500	28.6	27.4	26.7	25.5	25.0
Operating Expenses										
General & Administrative	600,000	550,000	525,000	500,000	480,000	11.4	11.8	11.7	12.1	12.8
Depreciation and Amortization	100,000	75,000	50,000	40,000	35,000	1.9	1.6	1.1	1.0	0.9
Other Operating Expenses	350,000	312,500	325,000	285,000	235,000	6.7	6.7	7.2	6.9	6.3
Total Operating Expenses	1,050,000	937,500	900,000	825,000	750,000	20.0	20.2	20.0	20.0	20.0
Operating Income	450,000	337,500	300,000	225,000	187,500	8.6	7.3	6.7	5.5	5.0
Interest Expense	(30,000)	(37,500)	(37,500)	(30,000)	(30,000)	(0.6)	(0.8)	(0.8)	(0.7)	(0.8)
Pretax Income, Continuing Operations	420,000	300,000	262,500	195,000	157,500	8.0	6.5	5.8	4.7	4.2
Provision for Income Taxes	172,500	120,000	105,000	72,000	52,500	3.3	2.6	2.3	1.7	1.4
Net Income from Continuing Operations	247,500	180,000	157,500	123,000	105,000	4.7	3.9	3.5	3.0	2.8
Preferred Dividends	15,000	15,000	15,000	15,000	15,000	0.3	0.3	0.3	0.4	0.4
Net Income Allocated to Common Stock	232,500	165,000	142,500	108,000	90,000	4.4	3.5	3.2	2.6	2.4
Average Shares Outstanding	150,000	150,000	150,000	150,000	150,000					
Per-Share Net Income from Continuing Operations	$1.65	$1.20	$1.05	$0.82	$0.70					

SOURCE: Company's audited financial statements.

most ratios, the adequacy of the current ratio for a given company can be better gauged by comparison with industry norms than by comparison with any absolute standard.

Using figures from Exhibit 12–1, the current ratio for Ace Widget Company for 1987 is calculated as follows:

Formula 12–1

$$\frac{\text{Current assets}}{\text{Current liabilities}} = \frac{\$1,425,000}{\$975,000} = 1.46{:}1$$

Quick (Acid-Test) Ratio

The next most commonly used ratio is the *quick ratio,* which some analysts refer to as the *acid-test ratio.* It is defined as the sum of cash and cash equivalents plus receivables (usually all current assets listed above inventory) divided by current liabilities. For most companies, the only other significant current asset is inventory—usually the slowest of the current assets to be converted to cash. The old rule of thumb is that a satisfactory quick ratio is 1.0:1; but, as with the current ratio, comparison with industry norms is more meaningful in most cases than comparison with an absolute standard.

Using figures from Exhibit 12–1, the quick or acid-test ratio for 1987 is calculated as follows:

Formula 12–2

$$\frac{\begin{array}{c} \text{Cash} \\ + \text{ Cash equivalents} \\ + \text{ Receivables} \end{array}}{\text{Current liabilities}} = \frac{\$225{,}000 + \$600{,}000}{\$975{,}000} = .85{:}1$$

It is important to realize that both the current ratio and the quick ratio measure liquidity at a point in time and may not reflect a company's use of short-term credit to finance its short-term liquidity needs.

Activity Ratios

Activity ratios generally measure how efficiently a company uses its assets.

Accounts Receivable Turnover

The *accounts receivable turnover* can be expressed either as the number of times per year the accounts turn over on average or as the average number of days required for collecting accounts. A slow accounts receivable turnover (long average collection period) not only puts a strain on a company's short-term liquidity; it can indicate excessive bad debt losses. On the other hand, a fast accounts receivable turnover (short average collection period) can indicate an overly stringent credit policy that may be limiting sales.

The accounts receivable turnover typically is computed by dividing net credit sales by average accounts receivable. If cash sales (as opposed to credit sales) are insignificant, or if the available figures do not distinguish between cash and credit sales, total sales may be used in the computation. Because of limitations on available data, average accounts receivable may have to be computed by averaging the receivables at the beginning and at the end of the period. The procedure of averaging receivables figures at the end of each quarter or each month gives a more accurate picture, especially if the business is subject to seasonal variations. In any case, if the ratio is for comparative purposes, the amount of data available for the comparative companies may limit the extent of fine-tuning that is possible in computing this ratio.

Using data from Exhibits 12–1 and 12–2, the accounts receivable turnover for Ace Widget Company for 1987 is computed as follows:

Formula 12–3

$$\frac{1987\ Sales}{(Accounts\ receivable\ end\ 1987\ +\ Accounts\ receivable\ end\ 1986)/2}$$

$$= \frac{\$5,250,000}{(\$600,000\ +\ \$600,000)/2} = 8.75\ times$$

The accounts receivable turnover is divided into 365 days to express this variable in terms of average collection period. For Ace Widget Company, we divide 365 days by the turnover of 8.75 times a year for an average collection period of 41.7 days. Incidentally, some analysts use 360 days instead of 365 days—one of many inconsistencies in valuation practice.

The sales-to-receivables ratio reported in Robert Morris Associates' (RMA) *Annual Statement Studies*[1] is net sales for the year divided by accounts and trade notes receivable as of the end of the year. Therefore, if the analyst wishes to compare the subject company with RMA statistics, the ratio for the subject company should be computed in the same manner as the RMA ratio. For Ace Widget Company, this simplifies the computation to the following:

Formula 12–4

$$\frac{1987\ Sales}{Accounts\ receivable\ end\ 1987} = \frac{\$5,250,00}{\$600,000} = 8.75\ times$$

Note that the ratio according to RMA would differ from the initial ratio calculation if the average accounts receivable did not equal those of the year-end, which was the case with Ace Widget in 1987. This level of accounts receivable turnover is equivalent to (365/8.75) = 41.7 average days collection period.

Inventory Turnover

The *inventory turnover ratio* typically is computed by dividing the cost of goods sold by the average inventory. As is true of accounts receivable turnover, a slow inventory turnover (long average holding period) not only puts a strain on the company's liquidity but can indicate obsolete or otherwise undesirable inventory. On the other hand, a fast inventory turnover may indicate that sales are being lost due to insufficient inventory on hand.

Also, as with accounts receivable turnover, the ratio is more meaningful if it can be computed using quarterly or monthly inventory data, especially for companies with seasonal aspects in their operation; however, data limitations more often than not make these computations impractical.

---

[1]*RMA Annual Statement Studies*, 1987 (Philadelphia: Robert Morris Associates, Inc.). Published annually. See Exhibit 7–3 for Interpretation of Statement Studies Figures.

Using data from Exhibits 12–1 and 12–2, the inventory turnover for Ace Widget Company for 1987 is computed as follows:

Formula 12–5

$$\frac{1987 \text{ Cost of goods sold}}{(\text{Inventory end } 1987 + \text{Inventory end } 1986)/2}$$

$$= \frac{\$3,750,000}{(\$562,500 + \$525,000)/2} = 6.9 \text{ times}$$

Like accounts receivable turnover, inventory turnover can be expressed as the average number of days in inventory. For Ace Widget Company, average days in inventory is calculated by dividing 365 days by an inventory turnover of 6.9 times per year for an average of 52.9 days needed for selling inventory.

RMA Annual Statement Studies[2] reports inventory turnover in the same manner as accounts receivable turnover—dividing cost of sales by ending inventory. For making comparisons with RMA data, this ratio should be computed by RMA's formula. For Ace Widget, this ratio is computed as follows:

Formula 12–6

$$\frac{1987 \text{ Cost of goods sold}}{\text{Inventory end } 1987} = \frac{\$3,750,000}{\$562,500} = 6.7 \text{ times}$$

From an inventory turnover of 6.7 times per year, we calculate an average of 54.5 days in inventory (365/6.7 = 54.5).

Sales to Net Working Capital

Net working capital is defined as current assets minus current liabilities. If a company's current ratio, accounts receivable collection period, and inventory turnover remain constant as its sales go up, the working capital must rise, because the company will have to carry more receivables and inventory to support the increased sales level. A simple way to compute the sales-to-net-working-capital ratio is to divide sales for the fiscal year just ended by net working capital at the fiscal year-end. This ratio can be useful in comparing the company's own history and with those of other companies in the industry.

Using the figures from Exhibits 12–1 and 12–2, the sales-to-net-working-capital ratio for Ace Widget Company is calculated as follows:

Formula 12–7

$$\frac{\text{Sales}}{\text{Current assets} - \text{Current liabilities}}$$

$$= \frac{\$5,250,000}{\$1,425,000 - \$975,000} = 11.7{:}1$$

---

[2]Ibid. See Exhibit 7–3 for Interpretation of Statement Studies Figures.

A more sophisticated way to compute the ratio would be to use average net working capital rather than ending net working capital as the denominator. Again using the figures from Exhibits 12–1 and 12–2, sales to average net working capital is calculated as follows:

Formula 12–8

$$\frac{1987 \text{ Sales}}{(\text{Working capital end 1987} + \text{Working capital end 1986})/2}$$

$$= \frac{\$5,250,000}{[(\$1,425,000 - 975,000) + (\$1,350,000 - \$787,500)]/2} = 10.4$$

A high ratio of sales to net working capital results from a favorable turnover of accounts receivable and inventory and indicates efficient use of current assets. However, a high sales-to-net-working-capital ratio also can indicate risk arising from possibly inadequate short-term liquidity. The economy and most industries are subject to some degree of cyclicality in economic activity and liquidity that do not necessarily run exactly in tandem. In order to assess the company's ability to meet peak needs, the analyst should consider the highest reasonable level of sales that might be anticipated, couple it with the largest accounts receivable and longest inventory turnover periods that might occur, and assess the adequacy of the working capital under that scenario.

Sales to Fixed Assets and Total Assets

Sales-to-fixed-assets and *sales-to-total-assets ratios,* sometimes called *asset utilization ratios,* measure how efficiently a company's assets are generating sales. They are calculated by dividing sales by either ending asset levels or by an average of the asset levels over the last two years. The results indicate the number of dollars of sales being generated by a dollar of assets. When observed over time, these ratios can indicate changing levels of asset productivity and reveal possible non-operating assets relative to comparative companies.

Using the figures in Exhibits 12–1 and 12–2, the simplest way to calculate these ratios is as follows:

Formula 12–9

$$\frac{\text{Sales}}{\text{Fixed assets}} = \frac{\$5,250,000}{\$1,200,000} = 4.4:1$$

$$\frac{\text{Sales}}{\text{Total assets}} = \frac{\$5,250,000}{\$2,898,000} = 1.8:1$$

A more sophisticated approach would be to use the average asset levels over the last two years. In this instance, monthly or quarterly figures are less important, since one would not expect to see seasonality in total or fixed asset levels in the same manner as current assets. Using the figures in Exhibits 12–1 and 12–2, the calculation of these ratios using this method is as follows:

Formula 12–10

$$\frac{1987\ Sales}{(Fixed\ assets\ end\ 1987\ +\ Fixed\ assets\ end\ 1986)/2}$$

$$=\frac{\$5,250,000}{(\$1,200,000\ +\ \$1,050,000)/2}=4.7{:}1$$

$$\frac{1987\ Sales}{(Total\ assets\ end\ 1987\ +\ Total\ assets\ end\ 1986)/2}$$

$$=\frac{\$5,250,000}{(\$2,898,000\ +\ \$2,590,500)/2}=1.9{:}1$$

These ratios are subject to misinterpretation. The age and, thus, depreciated book value of the assets used in these calculations should be considered, particularly when comparing them to those of other, similar companies.

Risk Analysis

At this point it is appropriate to briefly investigate risk analysis, since it is closely related to the leverage ratios and coverage ratios discussed in the following sections. The purpose of risk analysis is to ascertain the uncertainty of the income flows to the company's various capital suppliers. Generally, there are two classes of capital suppliers—those that provide debt capital and receive a fixed return and those that provide equity capital and receive a variable return but can participate in the firm's growth through increased future returns. As discussed in Part I and in the chapters on valuing debt securities and preferred stocks, the higher the risk to any category of capital suppliers to the firm, the higher the cost of that class of capital.

As discussed in Chapter 2, the capital asset pricing model suggests using the factor called *beta* to measure risk. However, because of a lack of regularly quoted market prices for their stocks, betas for most closely held companies cannot be measured directly. Studies have demonstrated that there is significant correlation between betas and risk measures that can be computed from companies' financial statements.[3] Furthermore, as also discussed in Part I, one can make a good case for the fact that the nonsystematic portions of risk (those not reflected in beta) are more important for closely held companies than for publicly traded companies. Therefore, the risk analysis portion of financial statement analysis is a very important part of the valuation process.

---

[3]For a summary of several such studies, see Donald J. Thompson II, "Sources of Systematic Risk in Common Stocks," *Journal of Business* 49, no. 2 (April 1976), pp. 173–88.

It is possible to examine the uncertainty of income to the various suppliers of capital by investigating the uncertainty of income to the company. The greater the uncertainty of income to the company, the greater the uncertainty of income to the investor in the company. There are two general classes of risk of the company: business risk and financial risk.

Business Risk

Business risk is the uncertainty of income due largely to two factors: (1) fluctuation in sales and (2) the level of the firm's fixed operating costs, which is a function of how the firm operates. There are basically two ways to measure a company's business risk.

The first—and simpler—way is to measure the coefficient of variation of earnings, which is equal to the standard deviation of operating earnings divided by the mean of operating earnings:

Formula 12–11

$$\text{Business risk} = \frac{\text{Standard deviation of operating earnings}}{\text{Mean of operating earnings}}$$

For example, using the figures from Exhibit 12–2, the standard deviation of operating earnings is \$55,729 and the mean of operating earnings is \$162,600. Substituting into the above equation produces a measure of business risk:

Formula 12–12

$$\text{Business risk} = \frac{\$55,729}{\$162,600} = 0.34$$

For many companies, sales volatility is the most important determinant of the fluctuation of operating earnings measured by the standard deviation. Although companies have some control over this variable, sales volatility is, to a considerable extent, a function of the economy's overall health and consumers' willingness to spend their disposable income.

The second method used to measure business risk is the calculation of the degree of operating leverage. *Operating leverage* reflects both the variability of sales and the level of the company's fixed operating costs. These fixed operating costs are a function of the manner in which the company produces its product. The operating earnings of companies with high variable operating costs fluctuate at about the same rate as sales do, whereas those of companies whose production processes entail high fixed-operating-costs fluctuate more widely than sales. This fluctuation in operating earnings introduces risk to the company's investors, since the income to debtholders as well as equityholders is derived from the firm's operating earnings.

Operating leverage is measured by the percentage change in operating earnings relative to the percentage change in sales during any given period:

Formula 12–13

Degree of operating leverage

$$= \frac{\text{Percentage change in operating earnings}}{\text{Percentage change in sales}}$$

For example, using the figures from Exhibit 12–2, the degree of operating leverage for Ace Widget Company for 1987 is:

Formula 12–14

Degree of operating leverage

$$= \frac{(\$247{,}500 - \$180{,}000)/\$180{,}000}{(\$5{,}250{,}000 - \$4{,}650{,}000)/\$4{,}650{,}000} = 2.91$$

This result indicates that 1.0 percent change in sales results, on average, in a 2.9 percent change in operating earnings.

Financial Risk

The second type of risk to investigate is financial risk. Whereas business risk, as measured by operating leverage, reflects the incidence of fixed operating costs and their effect on the income flows to capital suppliers, *financial risk* reflects the incidence of fixed financial costs, or interest, and their effect on the fluctuation of income flows to investors. A company's financial risk occurs in addition to business risk. If there were only business risk, the fluctuation of earnings available to stockholders would be the same as that of operating earnings. However, when fixed financial costs—that is, the interest associated with the use of financial leverage—are introduced, the fluctuation of earnings available to shareholders is greater than that of operating earnings. When the company uses debt to finance some of its activities, the payments to the holders of this debt come before any payments to shareholders. During good times, there is plenty left over for the shareholders and the fluctuation in earnings available to them is reduced. In bad times, however, much of the company's operating earnings is used to pay the interest on the debt and little is left over for the shareholders, increasing the fluctuation in their earnings.

Financial risk is measured in two ways: (1) through calculating the degree of financial leverage and (2) through calculating various leverage ratios. The degree of financial leverage is similar to the degree of operating leverage in that both measure relative volatility. Financial leverage measures the fluctuation of earnings available to the common shareholders relative to the fluctuation of operating earnings:

Formula 12–15

Degree of financial leverage

$$= \frac{\text{Percentage change in income to common stockholders}}{\text{Percentage change in operating income}}$$

For example, using figures from Exhibit 12–2, the degree of financial leverage for Ace Widget for 1987 is:

Formula 12–16

Degree of financial leverage

$$= \frac{(\$232,500 - \$165,000)/\$165,000}{(\$247,500 - \$180,000)/\$180,000} = 1.09$$

This result indicates that a 1 percent change in operating income is accompanied by approximately a 1.1 percent change in income available to common shareholders.

The higher the degree of financial leverage, the more risk exists for the company's equity investors because there is a greater possibility that they will receive lower cash flows both today and in the future.

The balance sheet leverage ratios discussed in the next section are also used to measure financial leverage. They are used in conjunction with the degree of financial leverage to indicate the company's overall financial riskiness.

Balance Sheet Leverage Ratios

The general purpose of capital structure or *balance sheet leverage ratios* is to aid in making some quantifiable assessments of the long-term solvency of the business and its ability to deal with financial problems and opportunities as they arise. As with most ratios, such analysis generally is most meaningful when compared with other companies in the same industry. Comparisons within the same company over time also can be useful.

There are numerous variations of balance-sheet leverage ratios, but the following are the ones most frequently used.

Total Debt to Total Assets

Of the various balance sheet ratios designed to measure the long-term adequacy of the company's capital structure, the *total-debt-to-total-assets ratio* probably is the most popular. It is defined as total debt divided by total assets and measures the total amount of the company's funding provided by all categories of creditors as a percentage of the company's total assets.

Using figures from Exhibit 12–1, the total-debt-to-total-assets ratio for Ace Widget Company at the end of 1987 is calculated as follows:

Formula 12–17

$$\frac{\text{Total liabilities}}{\text{Total assets}} = \frac{\$1,500,000}{\$2,898,000} = 0.52$$

Equity to Total Assets

The *equity-to-total-assets ratio,* or simply *equity ratio,* is computed by dividing the company's total equity by its total assets. It is equal to 1 minus the total-debt-to-total-assets ratio. Since these two ratios are merely alternative ways of stating the same thing, most analysts would include one or the other, but not both, in the presentation.

Using figures from Exhibit 12–1, the equity-to-total-assets ratio for Ace Widget at the end of 1987 is calculated as follows:

Formula 12–18

$$\frac{\text{Total equity}}{\text{Total assets}} = \frac{\$1,398,000}{\$2,898,00} = 0.48$$

Long-Term Debt to Total Capital

Unfortunately, there is considerable ambiguity in the terminology of financial statement analysis, especially in ratio definitions. By *debt ratio,* some analysts mean "debt divided by total assets," the ratio just discussed, but others mean "long-term debt divided by total capital." Therefore, to avoid misinterpretation, it seems best to avoid the term *debt ratio* entirely and use the more specific term *long-term-debt-to-total-capital ratio.* There is a reasonably strong consensus that *total capital* should be defined as total assets minus current liabilities.

Using figures from Exhibit 12–1, the long-term-debt-to-total-capital ratio for Ace Widget Company is computed as follows:

Formula 12–19

$$\frac{\text{Long-term debt}}{\text{Total assets} - \text{Current liabilities}} = \frac{\$525,000}{\$2,898,000 - \$975,00} = 0.27$$

The analyst should check to ensure that any ratios used for comparisons actually are computed by the same definitions, or the comparisons may be misleading. For example, some analysts include deferred taxes in the denominator as part of long-term capital, and others do not.

Equity to Total Capital

The *equity-to-total-capital-ratio* is simply 1 minus the long-term-debt-to-total-capital ratio, so there usually is no need to compute both.

Using figures from Exhibit 12–1, the equity-to-total-capital-ratio for Ace Widget at the end of 1987 is figured as follows:

Formula 12–20

$$\frac{\text{Total equity}}{\text{Total assets} - \text{Current liabilities}}$$

$$= \frac{\$1,398,000}{\$2,898,000 - \$975,000} = 0.73$$

Fixed Assets to Equity

One can get another view of the company's leverage by looking at the proportion of the fixed assets that are financed by equity as opposed to long-term debt. A larger value for the *fixed-assets-to-equity ratio* indicates that much of the company's productive capacity is being financed by borrowed funds rather than owners' funds.

Using the figures from Exhibit 12–1, the fixed-assets-to-equity ratio for Ace Widget Company in 1987 is calculated as follows:

Formula 12–21

$$\frac{\text{Net fixed assets}}{\text{Total equity}} = \frac{\$1,200,000}{\$1,398,00} = .86$$

Debt to Equity

Sometimes the firm's debt is expressed as a ratio to equity rather than to total assets. Again, some analysts prefer to focus on total debt and others just on long-term debt. The *RMA Annual Statement Studies* use total debt and only tangible equity.[4] In other words, the RMA *debt-to-equity ratio* is computed as follows:

Formula 12–22

$$\frac{\text{Total liabilities}}{\text{Total equity } - \text{ Intangible assets}}$$

This ratio is also sometimes expressed in reverse, that is, equity to total debt or equity to long-term debt.

Income Statement Coverage Ratios

In general, *income statement coverage ratios* are designed to measure the margin by which certain of the company's obligations are being met.

Times Interest Earned

The most popular income statement coverage ratio is times interest earned (referred to as the *interest coverage ratio*). It is designed to measure the firm's ability to meet interest payments. The *times-interest-earned ratio* is defined as earnings before interest and taxes (EBIT) divided by interest expense.

Using figures from Exhibit 12–2, the times-interest-earned ratio for Ace Widget Company for 1987 is:

---

[4]*RMA Annual Statement Studies,* 1987. See Exhibit 7–3 for Interpretation of Statement Studies Figures.

Formula 12–23

$$\frac{\text{Earnings before interest and taxes}}{\text{Interest expense}} = \frac{\$450,000}{\$30,000} = 15.0 \text{ times}$$

Note that the Ace Widget Company statements are presented in the conventional manner, showing interest expense as a separate deduction after operating income. Since some closely held companies do not present the statements in this way, the EBIT figure may have to be computed rather than taken directly from a line item on the income statement.

Another way to look at interest coverage is to calculate the ratio based on earnings before depreciation, interest, and taxes (EBDIT) rather than EBIT. EBDIT is basically pretax, preinterest cash flow that is available to pay the interest expense.

Using figures from Exhibit 12–2, the EBDIT interest coverage ratio for Ace Widget Company for 1987 is computed as follows:

Formula 12–24

$$\frac{\text{Earnings before depreciation, interest, and taxes}}{\text{Interest expense}}$$

$$= \frac{\$450,000 + \$100,000}{\$30,000} = 18.3 \text{ times}$$

Coverage of Fixed Charges

The *coverage of fixed charges* is a more inclusive ratio than the times-interest-earned ratio in that it includes coverage of items in addition to interest. It is defined as the sum of earnings before interest and taxes and fixed charges divided by fixed charges. This definition leaves open an almost unlimited spectrum of possibilities for determining which items of fixed charges to include. The most common items are lease payments and required installments of principal payments toward debt retirement.

In the Ace Widget Company example, the information shown in Exhibits 12–1 and 12–2 is inadequate for computing this ratio. Typically, the analyst must request some schedules or ask questions beyond the normal statement presentations in order to acquire the information necessary for computing this ratio. Audited financial statements normally contain such information in the footnotes.

Let's assume that the current portion of long-term debt shown in the current liability section of the balance sheet in Exhibit 12–1 is an annual required reduction of debt principal and that the operating expenses shown in Exhibit 12–1 include $180,000-per-year lease payments on the premises the company occupies. The coverage of fixed charges for Ace Widget, then, can be computed as:

Formula 12–25

$$\frac{\text{Earnings before interest and taxes} + \text{Lease payments}}{\text{Interest} + \text{Current portion of long-term debt} + \text{Lease payments}}$$

or

$$\frac{\$450,000 \ + \ \$180,000}{\$30,000 \ + \ \$112,500 \ + \ \$180,000} = 2.0 \text{ times}$$

Coverage of Preferred Dividends

If a company has a preferred stock issue outstanding, it may be useful to compute how adequate the earnings are for covering the preferred dividends. The simple way to calculate *preferred dividend coverage* is to divide the net income after taxes by the preferred dividend requirement, which can provide a useful ratio. However, most analysts concur that a more meaningful coverage ratio includes coverage of the interest payments on debt obligations as well as the preferred dividends. Since preferred stock dividends must be paid with after-tax dollars, the computation also must consider the tax requirements.

The balance sheet in Exhibit 12–1 shows 50,000 shares of 10 percent preferred stock outstanding with a par value of $1. Therefore, there is a preferred dividend requirement of $.10 per share. The choice of tax rate to use in the computation is arbitrary, because the rate will go up as the earnings (and thus the coverage) rise. In the Ace Widget example, the taxes are $172,500 on $420,000 of pretax income, or a 41.1 percent average rate. Using that rate and the EBIT from Exhibit 12–2, the preferred dividend coverage can be computed as follows:

Formula 12–26

$$\frac{\text{Earnings before interest and taxes}}{\text{Interest} + \text{Preferred dividends} \left(\dfrac{1}{1 - \text{Tax rate}} \right)}$$

$$= \frac{\$450,000}{\$30,000 \ + \ \$15,000 \left(\dfrac{1}{1 - .41} \right)} = 8.1 \text{ times}$$

Depending on the purpose of the analysis, some fixed charges in addition to interest (such as lease payments) also may be reflected in the calculations. If the company is considering issuing preferred stock, a computation of the preferred dividend coverage will help determine whether the firm can realistically be expected to meet anticipated dividend payments.

Income Statement Profitability Ratios

The four most commonly used measures of operating performance, are *gross profit to sales, operating profit to sales, pretax income to sales,* and *net profit to sales*. Since all are percentages of sales, they may be read directly from the common-size income statements shown in Exhibit 12–2.

Return-on-Investment Ratios

Analysts will argue until doomsday whether return on equity, return on investment, or return on assets is the most meaningful measure of investment return. Proponents of return on equity say that the return on stockholder investment is what counts, and most adhere to this argument. Return on investment recognizes both the shareholders and the debtholders and can be quite important if the company is contemplating a change in the capital structure. However, proponents of return on assets say that management should be measured by the return on total assets utilized, without regard for the company's capital structure, which can have a considerable bearing on return on equity if return on assets is held constant. Each measure is useful for its own purpose.

Return on Equity

Return on equity usually means return on common equity capital. If a company has preferred stock outstanding, the analyst might consider computing return on total equity and return on common equity, since both can be useful measures. If comparing one or more ratios of return on equity for other companies with preferred stock outstanding, the analyst should ensure that the ratios are being computed on the same basis for the subject company as for the comparative companies.

Unless otherwise specified, return on equity means *after* taxes. Once in a while, someone—perhaps a broker trying to sell a business— quotes return on equity computed on a pretax basis. This definition can be very misleading, since *income taxes are a very real cost,* and the investor's return is what remains after corporate taxes. In fact, if the computation is being made for a Subchapter S corporation, a partnership, or a sole proprietorship, many analysts recommend that the taxes the company would pay if it were a regular corporation be deducted from the net income before making the calculations. Sometimes there are legitimate reasons for comparing companies' returns on equity on a pretax basis, but when doing so it should be clearly specified—and recognized by the parties using the data—that it is a departure from the conventional meaning and computation of return on equity. Perhaps the best way to specify this is to use the expression *pretax return on equity* when that is what in fact is being shown.

One other issue to be resolved in the return-on-equity analysis is whether the selected equity base is the one at the beginning of the period, the end of the period, or the average for the period. There is consensus among analysts that the average equity provides the basis for the most meaningful analysis. However, an emerging group believe that beginning equity is the most important measure, since that is the equity *base* on which the earnings are generated. Still, the most commonly used method is to divide the earnings for the year by the average of the beginning and ending equity. If adequate information is available, return on equity can be further fine-tuned by averaging quarterly or monthly equity figures.

Since return on equity is a percentage, the result should be the same whether the computations are made on a total-company basis or on a per share basis, at least if there is no dilution. If a weighted average number of shares has been used in the per-share earnings computation, the calculation will work out if the average equity base is weighted in the same manner.

Using the data from Exhibits 12–1 and 12–2, the return on equity for Ace Widget Company for 1987 is calculated as follows:

Formula 12–27

$$\frac{\text{Net income}}{\text{Average common stockholders' equity}}$$

$$= \frac{\$232,500}{(\$1,398,000 + \$1,165,500)/2} = 18.1\%$$

Using beginning equity yields the following:

Formula 12–28

$$\frac{\text{Net income for 1987}}{\text{Stockholders' equity for 1986}} = \frac{\$232,500}{\$1,165,500} = 20.0\%$$

On a per share basis with 150,000 shares outstanding for Ace Widget, the computation is as follows:

Formula 12–29

$$\frac{\text{Earnings per share}}{\text{Average book value per share}} = \frac{\$1.65}{(\$8.32 + \$6.77)/2} = 21.9\%$$

Return on Investment

The computations for *return on investment,* sometimes called *return on total capital,* are similar to those for return on equity. One key difference is that interest should be added back to net income to reflect the return to *both* equity *and* debt. Whether interest should be adjusted for taxes depends on the information to be conveyed in the ratio presentation. One may adjust interest for taxes by multiplying interest by 1 minus the tax rate, yielding a product that is the equivalent of computing the ratio on a debt-free basis, as if all of the investment were in the form of equity. If, on the other hand, there is no adjustment for taxes, the ratio will reflect the return under the company's existing capital structure. Again the issue of average investment versus beginning investment must be recognized. In addition, the debt portion of the investment figure in the denominator could be long-term debt plus interest-bearing short-term debt, since the interest expense in the numerator is *total* interest expense.

Looking at it all four ways and using figures from Exhibits 12–1 and 12–2, the computation of return on investment for Ace Widget Company for 1987 is as follows:

Formula 12–30

$$\frac{\text{Net income} + \text{Interest} \,(1 - \text{Tax rate})}{\left[\left(\begin{array}{c}\text{Beginning stockholders' equity}\\ + \text{Long-term debt}\end{array}\right) + \left(\begin{array}{c}\text{Ending stockholders' equity}\\ + \text{Long-term debt}\end{array}\right)\right]/2}$$

$$\frac{\$232,500 + \$30,000\,(1 - .41)}{[(\$1,165,000 + \$637,500) + (\$1,398,000 + \$525,000)]/2} = 13.4\%$$

or

$$\frac{\text{Net income} + \text{Interest}}{\left[\left(\begin{array}{c}\text{Beginning stockholders' equity}\\ + \text{Long-term debt}\end{array}\right) + \left(\begin{array}{c}\text{Ending stockholders' equity}\\ + \text{Long-term debt}\end{array}\right)\right]/2}$$

$$\frac{\$232,500 + \$30,000}{[(\$1,165,000 + \$637,500) + (\$1,398,000 + \$525,000)/2} = 14.1\%$$

Based on beginning investment, return on investment becomes:

Formula 12–31

$$\frac{\text{Net income} + \text{Interest}\,(1 - \text{Tax rate})}{\text{Beginning stockholders' equity} + \text{Long-term debt}}$$

$$= \frac{\$232,500 + \$30,000\,(1 - .41)}{\$1,165,000 + \$637,500} = 13.9\%$$

or

$$\frac{\text{Net income} + \text{Interest}}{\text{Beginning stockholders' equity} + \text{Long-term debt}}$$

$$= \frac{\$232,500 + \$30,000}{\$1,165,000 + \$637,500} = 14.6\%$$

It is important to note that conceptually the amount of interest expense that should be added back is only the interest expense that relates to the company's long-term debt, since that is the figure in the denominator. However, in practice, while one may be able to get this information for the subject company, the data for the comparative companies will rarely be available. Another alternative is to use total interest expense in the numerator and total interest-bearing debt in the denominator. The problem with this, however, is that often the fiscal year-end amount of short-term interest-bearing debt does not relate to the amount of interest expense that was paid over the year on the average amount of short-term interest-bearing debt utilized. One would have to find out what the average amount of short-term interest-bearing debt was over the course of the year.

Due to these complexities, for practical purposes it is acceptable to use the ratio as we have defined it. However, the analyst is well advised to research both the subject and comparative companies' use of short-term debt to determine whether to adjust this ratio to include all interest-bearing debt.

Return on Total Assets

The computations for *return on total assets* are similar to those for return on investment, with the same issues of tax adjustments and beginning or average assets. A realistic analysis of return on total assets should not be influenced by how the company chooses to use debt in its capital structure.

Again using figures from Exhibits 12–1 and 12–2, the computation of return on assets for Ace Widget Company for 1987 is as follows:

Formula 12–32

$$\frac{\text{Net income} + \text{Interest} (1 - \text{Tax rate})}{(\text{Beginning total assets} + \text{Ending total assets})/2}$$

$$= \frac{\$232,500 + \$30,000 (1 - .41)}{(\$2,590,500 + \$2,898,000)/2} = 9.1\%$$

or

$$\frac{\text{Net income} + \text{Interest}}{(\text{Beginning total assets} + \text{Ending total assets})/2}$$

$$= \frac{\$232,500 + \$30,000}{(\$2,590,000 + \$2,898,000)/2} = 9.6\%$$

Based on beginning assets, the ratio becomes:

Formula 12–33

$$\frac{\text{Net income} + \text{Interest} (1 - \text{Tax rate})}{\text{Beginning total assets}}$$

$$= \frac{\$232,500 + \$30,000 (1 - .41)}{\$2,590,500} = 9.7\%$$

or

$$\frac{\text{Net income} + \text{Interest}}{\text{Beginning total assets}} = \frac{\$232,500 + \$30,000}{\$2,590,500} = 10.1\%$$

One must be careful when comparing these ratios to published ratios to determine whether the base is an average or whether beginning or ending figures are being used. The return-on-investment ratios shown in Exhibit 12–5 are calculated using beginning equity, total capital, and total assets.

Asset Utilization Ratios

Asset utilization ratios indicate how efficiently the firm is employing its assets in its operations. These are almost always based on average asset levels, unless a study used for industry comparative ratio analysis calculates them using year-ending asset figures. This series of ratios relates sales to each of several assets or asset groups. Ratios sometimes computed include sales to cash, to accounts receivable, to inventories, to working capital, to fixed assets, to other assets, and to total assets (discussed under "Activity Ratios").

Sample Summary of Ratio Analyses

Exhibits 12–3 and 12–4 provide samples of summaries of the ratio analyses discussed in the foregoing sections as applied to Ace Widget Company. They show a number of statistics for Ace Widget in comparison with industry averages compiled by *RMA Annual Statement Studies*. Exhibit 12–5 shows ratios for Ace Widget over a five-year period. Minor discrepancies between the figures shown in Exhibits 12–3 and 12–4 and those in the text occur because the former are computed on ending statement figures only rather than on averages of beginning and ending statement figures.

Interpretation of
Statement Studies Figures

RMA cautions that the Studies be regarded only as a general guideline and not as an absolute industry norm. This is due to limited samples within categories, the categorization of companies by their primary Standard Industrial Classification (SIC) number only, and different methods of operations by companies within the same industry. For these reasons, RMA recommends that the figures be used only as general guidelines in addition to other methods of financial analysis.

EXHIBIT 12-3

Ace Widget Company
and Robert Morris Associates (RMA)
SIC No. 3544, Widget Makers
Common-Size Financial Statements

	1987	
	Ace	RMA
Number of observations	1	481
Average asset size ($000s)	2,898	2,452
Average sales volume ($000s)	5,250	4,122
	%	%

Common-size balance sheets
ASSETS
Current assets:

Cash and equivalents	7.8	8.4
Accounts & notes receivable (trade)	20.7	26.5
Inventory	19.4	17.5
All other current assets	1.3	2.2
Total current assets	49.2	54.6
Net fixed assets	41.4	38.3
Net intangible assets	—	0.7
Net other assets	9.4	6.5
TOTAL ASSETS	100.0	100.0

Liabilities & equity
Liabilities:
Current liabilities

Notes payable	2.6	9.1
Current maturities of long term debt	3.9	6.2
Accounts & notes payable (trade)	9.1	10.5
Income taxes payable	—	1.1
All other current liabilities	18.1	9.5
Total current liabilities	33.6	36.4
Total long-term debt	18.1	19.8
Total other noncurrent debt	—	2.8
Total liabilities	51.8	59.0
Total equity	48.2	40.9
TOTAL LIABILITIES & EQUITY	100.0	100.0

Common-size income statements

Net sales	100.0	100.0
Cost of goods sold	71.4	69.7
Gross profit	28.6	30.3
Operating expenses	20.0	24.6
Operating income	8.6	5.8
Other income (expense), net	(0.3)	(1.8)
Pretax profit	8.3	4.0

SOURCE: Company's audited financial statements and Robert Morris Associates' *Annual Statement Studies*, copyright (c)1987.

EXHIBIT 12-4

Ace Widget Company
and Robert Morris Associates (RMA)
SIC No. 3544, Widget Makers
Comparative Ratio Analysis

		1987	
		Ace	**RMA**
Number of observations		1	481
Average asset size ($000s)		2,898	2,452
Average sales volume ($000s)		5,250	4,122
Liquidity ratios			
	HI		2.3
Current ratio	MD	1.5	1.6
	LO		1.1
	HI		1.5
Quick ratio	MD	0.8	1.0
	LO		0.7
Working capital ($000s)	MN	450.0	446.3
Activity ratios			
	HI		9.6
Sales/receivables	MD	8.8	7.5
	LO		5.7
	HI		16.5
Cost of sales/inventory	MD	6.7	8.7
	LO		5.0
	HI		28.5
Cost of sales/payables	MD	14.3	15.8
	LO		8.5
	HI		5.8
Sales/working capital	MD	11.7	10.0
	LO		34.3
	HI		8.2
Sales/net fixed assets	MD	4.4	5.1
	LO		3.3
	HI		2.3
Sales/total assets	MD	1.8	1.8
	LO		1.4
Debt ratios			
Earnings before interest	HI		5.6
and taxes/interest expense	MD	14.5	2.7
	LO		1.2
Cash flow/current	HI		4.0
maturities of long term debt	MD	4.6	2.3
	LO		1.3
	HI		0.5
Fixed assets/net worth	MD	0.9	0.9
	LO		1.7
	HI		0.8
Debt/net worth	MD	1.1	1.4
	LO		3.0
Equity/total capital (%)	MN	72.7	67.4
Profit ratios			
Pretax profit/	HI		34.7
tangible net worth (%)	MD	29.0	17.9
	LO		4.9
Pretax profit/	HI		12.4
total assets (%)	MD	14.0	6.9
	LO		1.4
Pretax profit/sales (%)	MN	7.7	4.0

SOURCE: Company's audited financial statements and Robert Morris Associates' *Annual Statement Studies*, copyright (c)1987.

EXHIBIT 12-5

Ace Widget Company
Financial and Operating Ratios

	1987	1986	1985	1984	1983
Liquidity ratios					
Current ratio	1.46	1.71	1.75	1.68	1.78
Quick ratio	0.85	1.00	1.00	0.95	1.00
Working capital ($000s)	450.00	562.50	562.50	487.50	525.00
Activity ratios					
Sales/receivables	8.75	8.00	8.28	7.86	NA
Days in receivables	42	46	44	46	NA
Cost of sales/inventory	6.90	6.43	6.52	6.31	NA
Days in inventory	53	57	56	58	NA
Working capital turnover	10.37	8.27	8.57	8.15	NA
Fixed asset turnover	4.67	4.68	4.90	4.81	NA
Asset turnover	1.91	1.88	2.01	1.98	NA
Coverage/leverage ratios					
Times interest earned:					
EBIT	15.00	9.00	8.00	7.50	6.25
EBDIT	18.33	11.00	9.33	8.83	7.42
Fixed charge coverage	2.0	1.8	1.6	1.4	1.3
Preferred dividend coverage	8.1	5.4	4.8	4.2	3.6
Total debt/total assets (%)	51.8	55.0	57.4	59.8	63.0
Fixed assets/equity (%)	85.8	90.1	93.7	104.9	108.7
Equity/total capital (%)	72.7	64.6	62.5	60.4	55.6
Profitability ratios (%)					
Net income/equity	21.2	18.0	18.4	16.4	NA
Net income/investment	13.9	11.7	11.6	9.4	NA
Net income/assets	9.6	7.7	7.4	6.1	NA

EBIT   =   Earnings before interest and taxes.
EBDIT =   Earnings before depreciation , interest, and taxes.
NA   =   Not available.

SOURCE: Exhibits 12-1, 12-2, and Willamette Management Associates, Inc., calculations.

Part IV

Presenting a Written Report

Chapter 13

Writing an Appraisal Report

The objectives of the written appraisal report are:

1. To communicate the analysis and conclusions in a clear and convincing manner.
2. To document the details of the appraisal for reference purposes.

A well-written report leads the reader along a logical path through the relevant facts and analysis to the same conclusion as the writer.

The form, scope, and content of a written business appraisal report can vary considerably depending on the size and complexity of the business being valued and especially the use or uses to which the report will be put. The two major factors influencing the scope, content, and style of the written report are:

1. Legal requirements.
2. Needs of the audience.

For example, if a report is for tax purposes, it must address the factors enumerated in Revenue Ruling 59-60. If it is for an ESOP, it must contain the additional content required in Department of Labor Regulations. If it is for a lawsuit, it should address issues raised in relevant case law precedents.

The audiences could include prospective parties at interest and their beneficiaries, representatives of any regulatory authorities involved, a judge and possibly a jury if there is existing or potential litigation, and all other relevant parties, such as attorneys, CPAs, and trustees.

If the report's audience will be people unfamiliar with the company, a good description of the firm is important. If the report is for internal use by company officers and directors, a description of the company may be unnecessary or may allude only to certain salient points that directly affect the valuation. If the audience is financially sophisticated, one may presume that they have some knowledge of finance. If the report is for a lay audience, such as a jury, the concepts must be spelled out in language that a layperson will understand.

In the early planning of the valuation case, the appraiser should think through the various legal requirements and parties to be satisfied and plan the general form of the written report and the steps leading to it. If changes are made in the assignment during the course of the project, any implications for changes in the written report should be noted by a memo to the file, with a copy to the client, if appropriate.

In preparing a written report, it is a good idea to follow the American Society of Appraisers (ASA) *Principles of Appraisal Practice*, which lists the items the society requires its designees to include in any complete, formal appraisal report, whether the property being appraised is real estate, antiques, a business enterprise, or whatever. The relevant section of the *ASA Principles of Appraisal Practice* is presented in Exhibit 13–1.

EXHIBIT 13-1

Report Requirements Section of
ASA Principles of Appraisal Practice

8   APPRAISAL REPORTS

In preceding sections it was stated that good appraisal practice, as defined by the Society, requires the inclusion of certain specific explanations, descriptions, and statements in an appraisal report. These are summarized herewith. (These requirements do not apply to reports prepared by a staff appraiser for the exclusive and non-public use of his employer; but do apply to reports prepared by a public appraiser, i.e., one who offers his services for a fee to the general public.)

8.1   Description of the Property Which Is the Subject of an Appraisal Report

It is required that the property with which an appraisal report is concerned, whether tangible, intangible, real, or personal, be fully described therein, the elements of such description being: (a) identification, (b) legal rights and restrictions encompassed in the ownership, where these are not obvious, (c) value characteristics, and (d) physical condition, where applicable. (See Sec. 6.8)

8.2   Statement of the Objectives of the Appraisal Work

It is required that an appraisal report include a statement of the objectives for which the work was performed: to determine a value, to estimate a cost, to forecast an earning power, to ascertain certain facts, to reach conclusions and make recommendations for action in specified matters, etc. (See Sec. 2.1)

It is required that the meaning attached by the appraiser to any specific kind of value or estimated cost which is the objective of the appraisal undertaking be described and explained in the appraisal report. (See Sec. 6.1)

It is required that an appraisal report include a statement as to the date which the value estimate, cost estimate or forecast of income applies.

When appropriate, an analysis of the highest and best use of the property should be included in the investigation and study.

8.3   Statement of the Contingent and Limiting Conditions to Which the Appraisal Findings Are Subject

It is required that statements, information, and/ or data, which were obtained by the appraiser from members of other professions, or official or other presumably reliable sources, and the validity of which affects the appraisal findings, be summarized or stated in full in the appraisal report and the sources given, so that verification desired by any user of the report may be accomplished. (See Sec. 6.4)

If an appraisal is a hypothetical one, it is required that it be labeled as hypothetical, that the reason a hypothetical appraisal was made be stated, and that the assumed hypothetical conditions be set forth. (See Sec. 6.5)

If an appraisal is a fractional appraisal, it is required that it be labeled as fractional and that the limitations on the use of the reported figure be stated. (See Sec. 6.3)

If a preliminary appraisal report is issued, namely, one in which the figures are subject to refinement or change, it is required that the report be labeled as preliminary and that the limitations on its use be stated (See Sec. 7.6)

8.4   Description and Explanation in the Appraisal Report of the Appraisal Method Used

It is required that the method selected by the appraiser as applicable to the subject appraisal undertaking be described and explained in the appraisal report. (See Sec. 6.2)

8.5   Statement of the Appraiser's Disinterestedness

It is required that the appraiser include a statement in his appraisal report that he has no present or contemplated future interest in the subject property or any other interest which might tend to prevent his making a fair and unbiased appraisal or, if he does have such an interest, to set forth fully the nature and extent of that interest. (See Sec. 7.3)

8.6   Signatures to Appraisal Reports and the Inclusion of Dissenting Opinions

It is required that the party who makes the appraisal or who has the appraisal made under his supervision sign the appraisal report. (See Sec. 7.4)

It is required that all collaborating appraisers, issuing a joint appraisal report, who agree with the findings, sign the report; and that any collaborating appraiser who disagrees with any or all of the findings of the others, prepare, sign, and include in the appraisal report his dissenting opinion. (See Sec. 7.4)

Reprinted with permission, Principles of Appraisal Practice and Code of Ethics, Reprint Series #24, April 1988, American Society of Appraisers.

This chapter is intended to help not only writers of business appraisal reports but their readers. If the users or reviewers have a good idea of what the report's content *should* be, they will be in a much better position to evaluate whether the report meets normally accepted professional standards.

General Principles of Good Report Writing

The basic principles for writing a good business valuation report are similar to those for writing a good term paper or thesis. The reader must be able to understand:

1. The purpose and scope of the assignment.
2. The steps taken to carry it out.
3. The conclusion reached.
4. The logical flow of data and rationale that led to and supported the conclusion.

The report should be well organized, as comprehensive as the purpose calls for, well documented, and presented in a correct, consistent, and easily readable style. The entire content should be relevant to the report's purpose, avoiding extraneous material.

The report writer should be conscious of the intended audience and write in such a manner that they will understand it and find it convincing. The report should be free of obscure jargon. If required to use terminology or references unfamiliar to the intended audience, the appraiser should explain such items sufficiently that their relevance to the report and the points being made will be understood. Each aspect of the conclusion(s) should be so clearly supported that no link in the chain of data and rationale leading to the conclusion need be left to the reader's imagination.

The report must be *coherent*. This means that the topics should flow smoothly from one to another, linked by logical transitions when necessary. Topics should be completed under topic headings, and subjects irrelevant to them should not be included under those headings. The reader should never be led to focus on one topic only to find that the writer has suddenly and without warning decided to talk about something else.

The report should be *replicable*. One of the most common shortcomings of all too many business valuation reports is inadequate documentation. Research people who employ the "scientific method" use the term *replicability* as one of the hallmarks of an acceptable research report. It means that the documentation should describe all the steps taken so thoroughly that the reader will be able to duplicate the exercise and reach the same conclusion. Whenever information or opinion is attributable to anyone besides the report's author, the source should be cited such that the reader can find and consult it personally. In those instances in which it is necessary to omit source citations because of confidentiality, the reasons for omitting them should be explained. Such documentation becomes particularly important if the work must ever be defended in court.

The report should be *internally consistent*. If one has promised in the introduction that certain factors will be considered, such as the list of factors in Revenue Ruling 59-60, one should be sure that each of those factors is indeed addressed in the report. If one has stated somewhere that a particular approach should be accorded the greatest weight, one should ensure that what one actually did is consistent with that statement.

One of my favorite adjectives to ascribe to a good report is *incisive*, for which my dictionary offers the following definitions:

1. Having a cutting edge or piercing point—facilitating cutting or piercing, as sharp . . .
2. Marked by sharpness and penetration—especially in keen, clear, unmistakable resolution of matter at issue or in pointed decisive effectiveness of presentation . . .
3. Clear genius which states in a flash the exact point at issue . . .
4. Keen penetration and sharp presentation that is decisive or effective—rapier quality of highly tempered steel . . .
5. Unmistakably clear outlining, analysis, and presentation that defies disbelief or question.[1]

Report Organization and Content

This section discusses a generalized report format that is useful for most appraisal purposes, including, for example, gift and estate taxes, ESOPs, dissenting-stockholder suits, and a variety of other uses. Naturally, the scope and organization must be tailored to the requirements of the particular assignment. Different formats or variations that may be appropriate for certain specialized purposes are discussed briefly in a subsequent section. Chapter 14 presents a sample report generally organized along the lines discussed in this chapter.

Exhibit 13–2 is a memo that our case editor wrote to our analysts on how to organize and write certain sections of an appraisal report. We found it edifying as well as amusing.

General Organization

Following a brief introductory section that defines the assignment, summarizes the conclusion, and sets the stage for the detailed report, an organizational pattern that moves from the general to the specific seems to serve many purposes quite well. It provides a logical flow of data and analysis within which all the necessary considerations can be incorporated, leading to the appraisal conclusion.

Most situations lend themselves well to organization into seven major sections, often but not necessarily in the following order:

1. Introduction.
2. Economic Data.
3. Industry Data.

---

[1]*Webster's Third New International Dictionary*, p. 1142.

EXHIBIT 13-2

Tips on Organizing and Writing Appraisal Reports

A few words about organization

Imagine going on a field trip and having company management blindfold you, then walk you around and take off the blindfold at various points in the facilities. "Here," the factory director would say, "is where we package the widgets, 95,000 of them a day." Then later, off with the blindfold, and the director says, "This is the grommetizing process--43,000 per day here." And somewhere, "This is our raw materials bin--14 tons of widget stuff per week." And you had no opportunity to ask about the relationship between the 43,000 being grommetized and the 95,000 being packaged or how many widgets 14 tons of widget stuff actually make. It would hardly be surprising if at the end you had no real sense of how the factory worked or of the total widget process.

I imagine, though, (never having been on a field trip myself) that the factory director actually takes you through in an orderly manner. He probably begins by making sure you understand what a widget is and what it does. Then he shows you the widget stuff, then walks you through the production process (including grommetizing), and then shows how the widgets are packaged. And along the way, the factory director explains how many widgets 14 tons of widget stuff will make, and why they package 95,000 but grommetize only 43,000, and furthermore, as he passes through various rooms in the factory, he might point out the relation of this portion of the process to one you saw a half hour ago. At the end, you come back to the office well enough informed (except for a few details maybe) to write a report section describing the process. Organization makes all the difference.

When you write an industry, economy, or company description section, you are in the role of that factory director and the reader is on the field trip. Once again, organization makes all the difference. There are various ways of organizing information, and any or all of them are applicable in different circumstances. Chronological organization sets things in order from past to future (or future to past). Journalistic organization sets things in their order of importance, from most important to least important. Logical order arranges things from the general to the specific or from the specific to the general (not as useful for our purposes).

If you're describing a process, the chronological organization is probably most appropriate. You can begin by explaining what the thing is and then go back to the beginning and explain how it came to be. Or you can start at the beginning and explain the history of the thing and end with its outlook. If you're describing a group of characteristics (as in the Financial Statement Analysis section, for instance), the journalistic approach is good. It would also be useful for discussing competitors or qualitative factors, and many other applications. The logical organization is

often used to introduce the reader to a new concept. In our valuation sections, we describe the general approaches used before going into the details of each. In our industry and economy sections, we almost always start with an overview or a general description of the industry before going into specific characteristics. As you can see, these organizational forms can be mixed and modified--indeed, they must be to be appropriate to their topics--and two good sections on the same topic might be organized somewhat differently. It is important, though, that your reader feel that he's been led around the factory and not brought blindfolded into various rooms with no sense of their relation to each other.

These organizational techniques apply at all levels: section, subsection, paragraph, and, often, sentence. The Industry or Economy section often leads off with a paragraph telling how the section relates to the company being valued. The section may then continue with an Overview or a General Description of the Industry. This subsection is an application of the logical organization and tells the reader general information about the industry, so that he'll be better able to understand the specific information to follow. From this point, you're on your own for a while, because every economy, industry, and company section is different. Some involve a process (historical, or a movement from raw materials to finished goods); some involve a group of related characteristics that are best listed in order of decreasing importance (for example federal, state, and local regulations or various contributors to total revenues); and some topics involve categories and subcategories (such as international, national, regional, and local markets). Finally, often, the sections end with an Outlook or Long-term Outlook, which is another application of the chronological organization.

The same observations apply to the information within the subsections. The reader should have a sense of a reasonable order of the paragraphs. And each paragraph should be organized as well. A topic sentence, usually coming first, tells the reader what to expect to learn from this paragraph, and how the information in the paragraph relates to the rest of the paragraph, to the subsection, to the section, and/or to the company as a whole. A paragraph without a topic sentence runs the risk of being just a handful of facts. Finally, within each sentence, as applicable, these structures can give form to lists of dates, percentages, competitors, and so on.

The irony is that people hardly ever notice good organization; they are more likely to notice if it is poor. Like the blindfolded person touring the factory, they come out more annoyed at what they didn't see than comprehending what they did. On the other hand, a well-conducted factory tour leaves one thinking about (and remembering) the factory, not its presentation.

EXHIBIT 13-2   Tips on Organizing and Writing Appraisal Reports (Continued)

Suggested steps in writing

1. *Read and collect relevant materials.*

Take note of facts that should go into the report. There are several ways of taking notes, and you should work out a system that works for you. Some people photocopy and underline. Some handwrite notes on paper or 3x5 cards. One important thing to remember in this step is to be sure that you get a sense of the subject, not just data, because it's that sense that you want to communicate; the data are just tools.

2. *Create an outline* (it can be rough).

Determine the best means of organizing the section and list the major categories of information that are important.

3. *Distribute the facts to their relevant sections* (also known as "writing").

If you are working on a word processor, you can type in your headings (which came from your outline) first, then type in the information under each heading as it comes to you. As the subsections and paragraphs develop, you flesh them out with your observations about the data, what ties them together, and what distinguishes among them. You can work

with a fact under one subsection until you realize that it fits better in another and move it. And so forth.

If you don't do word processing, another method is to write the facts on 3x5 cards and arrange them according to your outline. Then, as you write, you fold the information into your description of the topic.

4. *Edit.*

Wait a day or two, or even a week, if possible, and read the section with a fresh eye. Does it flow smoothly? Does it raise unanswered questions? Did some fact wander away from home and lodge with neighbors where it doesn't belong? Do the subjects and verbs of the sentences agree (Or do they quarrel? Or have they already separated? Every writer is a grammatical marriage counselor).

Pretend that you're the client (or whoever the expected reader may be) and think about the section as it relates to his business or his concerns.

Remember that writing is writing, whether it's an essay about *The Scarlet Letter* that you had to write to escape from English Comp 51 or a survey of the nuclear power industry. The same principles apply, and the whole purpose is communication.

SOURCE: Written by Jan Bear, case editor, Willamette Management Associates, Inc.

4. Description of the Company.
5. Search for Comparative Transaction Data.
6. Financial Statement Analysis.
7. Valuation Approaches and Conclusion.

Some reports have a separate section containing a general discussion of valuation principles. If included, such a section often follows the introduction. If both national and regional economic data are important to the company, each may have its own major section. The financial statement analysis may be included as a subsection under the company description. Comparative transaction data may be addressed within the section on valuation approaches. In any case, the above constitute the major elements of most valuation reports.

Most reports also contain certain prefatory material and/or appendixes. The most common of these are:

1. Statement of the appraisers' independence.
2. Appraisers' qualifications.
3. Assumptions and limiting conditions.

Some appraisers tend to put most or all of their tabular data in the body of the report where it is discussed, while others prefer to put tabular data in appendixes. Supporting documents that must be included usually are in appendixes. Also, if the research has resulted in extensive supporting detail, that might be placed in an appendix.

Introduction

The introduction usually is brief and may cover any or all of half a dozen key points in summary form:

1. Description of the assignment.
2. Summary description of the company.
3. Capitalization and ownership.
4. Definition of the applicable standard of value.
5. Sources of information.
6. Valuation approach or approaches and conclusion.

Description of the Assignment.   I usually like to make the description of the appraisal assignment the very first paragraph in the report. As discussed in detail in Chapter 1, this description includes the following elements:

1. Who was retained by whom to do the appraisal.
2. Applicable standard of value.
3. Definition of the property being appraised.
4. Effective date of the appraisal.
5. Purpose or purposes of the appraisal.

Summary Description of the Company.   For the reader's convenience, it is often helpful to include in the introduction a brief statement of what the company does, where it is located, some idea of its size, and possibly one or more salient or unique aspects of the company.

Capitalization and Ownership. This paragraph can give the reader a quick view of the class or classes of stock or partnership interests and the distribution of ownership.

Definition of the Applicable Standard of Value.   This paragraph defines the applicable standard of value, already stated in the description of the assignment. If the applicable standard of value is derived from a statute or regulation, the exact source of the governing standard of value should be referenced. If the statutory or regulatory source includes a definition or explanation of the standard of value, that definition or explanation should be included. Often it is helpful to list or briefly discuss some of the factors included or implied in the applicable standard of value, such as the eight major factors listed in Revenue Ruling 59-60 if the valuation is for gift or estate taxes, an ESOP, or some other tax-related matter. If the definition of the standard of value derives from case law (such as with state statutes governing dissolutions or dissenting-stockholder actions), a statement to that effect is appropriate, perhaps along with a summary statement of interpretation of the case law from a financial analysis point of view.

Sources of Information.   A convenient place to present a generalized list of the sources of information used is after the description of the assignment. The degree of detail that is appropriate depends on the case. In essence, this section of the report is a summary of the sources used as discussed in Chapters 5 through 10.

This section should list the financial statements and supporting schedules that were examined, including the years studied for each statement or category. The statements should be described as having been audited, reviewed, or compiled. Other company financial information used should be listed. If one or a few asset appraisal reports were examined, they might be listed separately; if many such reports were examined, they might be described in summary as a group. The same thing applies to leases or contracts. Other significant company data consulted should be cited.

Facilities visited should be listed. If only a few interviews were conducted, the names and positions of the interviewees might be given; if many interviews were conducted, the categories and scope of the interviews might be summarized.

Major sources of economic data, such as periodicals, may be specified and other sources referred to generally. The same applies to industry data. The extent and nature of relevant economic and industry data vary greatly from one case to another. The point is to summarize the sources that were called upon for the case at hand.

Sources used to compile comparative company data should be listed. If specific sources were used in determining such factors as marketability, minority interest discounts, or both, it would be appropriate to reference them in the information sources section.

In most cases it is not necessary to include exact citations in this section, since these will appear in later sections when necessary. The purpose of the information source section is to summarize for the reader the sources that were consulted in the course of preparing the report. Optimally, at this early stage of the written report the reader will think that the background information collected and considered was adequate and appropriate for the analysis and conclusion.

Valuation Approach or Approaches and Conclusion.   This section should briefly indicate the broad criterion or criteria used in reaching the valuation conclusion, such as capitalization of earnings, net asset value or adjusted asset values, or whatever. This should be followed by a brief statement of the conclusion.

Economic Data

The key word in choosing what to include in the economic section is *relevance*. What the reader wants to know about are those aspects of economic conditions that may have a bearing on the subject company's prospects. If a company's business is tied to the economy of a particular region, it might be appropriate to divide the economic section into two parts: the national economy and the relevent regional economy. It is helpful to point out how the economic data being discussed affect the subject company.

Remember: If the report is a retrospective valuation (a valuation as of an earlier date), the economic section must follow the same rules as other sections—that is, the writer must be standing in time on the valuation date, using only economic data and forecasts available then even if subsequent events have produced different results. A discussion of what economic data to include and where to find them is the subject of Chapter 7.

Industry Data

Subject to the industry data available and the need to acquaint the reader with the industry, the industry section should give the reader a primer on the nature of the industry involved and current conditions therein. This section should discuss the markets and uses for the industry's products or services and the factors that affect the potential growth and volatility of demand. Any special supply factors should be pointed out.

The writer should discuss the structure of the industry—how big the industry is, how many competitors there are, and how they compete. Is the industry characterized by commodity-like price competition or by product differentiation?

Although this section applies to the industry rather than to the subject company, it may be a good idea to briefly mention how the company fits into the industry, perhaps noting such things as its size relative to competitors, any specialized segments of the market it serves, and its competitive strengths and weaknesses. Such observations can give the reader some grasp of the subject company's niche within its industry group.

Some companies clearly are engaged in two or more different industries. In such cases, it usually is necessary to include a separate industry section in the report for each industry in which the company is significantly involved. Gathering industry data is discussed in Chapter 7.

Description of the Company

The company section should be both descriptive and analytical; that is, it should present the facts the reader needs to know to understand the company and analyze those facts and make qualitative judgments on the positive and negative aspects of the company that bear on its value.

The description and analysis of the company can be organized into any number of subsections and in any of several logical sequences. If the financial statement analysis is to be a separate section of the report (as I generally prefer), the main topics to be covered in the company description section usually are background, operations, markets, competition, suppliers, facilities, employees, and management. In some cases, it is appropriate to include further discussion of the capitalization of the company and distribution of stock ownership. If there is or has been a market for the stock, or past transactions in the stock, that topic could be discussed in this section. It often is helpful to conclude the section with a summary of positive and negative factors.

Background. The reader will gain some perspective on the company by learning when it started and being given a brief chronology of major changes or events in its history. Such changes would be changes in name, in form of organization (e.g., from partnership to corporation), in location, and in major line or lines of business, mergers with or acquisitions of other companies, start-ups of new operations, and changes in ownership control. Any significant or unusual events during or affecting the period under analysis should be mentioned, such as a major fire or strike that may have disrupted operations.

The section should conclude with a summary statement about the company's present position. Some companies' operations can be described in a single sentence, such as "The company presently operates as a corporation manufacturing pine boxes in a single plant in Waukesha, Wisconsin." Other companies may require elaborate organization charts. They may have one or more subsidiaries or subunits, some of which are wholly or partially owned. Subsidiaries are separately incorporated. There may be other forms of suborganization, such as unincorporated divisions, general or limited partnerships, or joint ventures. All may be in different business lines or segments. Not all the subsidiaries may have the same fiscal year as the parent company. The parent company may reflect different affiliates by consolidated statements or by the equity or cost methods of accounting. The reader should receive a clear and complete picture of the company's structure.

Exhibit 13–3 is a sample organization chart designed to help the reader understand a company with several affiliates. Note that for each affiliate the information indicates the form of organization, the ownership percentage, the fiscal year, and the accounting method by which the affiliate is reflected on the parent company's financial statements.

Operations. The operations section should list the company's operating locations, describe its products and services, markets, facilities, and employee structure, and give key information about supplies and suppliers, if applicable. It is at the appraiser's discretion, of course, whether to include all this information in a single section or separate it into several, such as marketing, facilities and production, personnel, and supply sources.

If the company has proprietary products, this section should explain how the products serve the perceived market and how they differ from competition. In a sense, this section explains the economic justification for the company's existence, at least conceptually. This could be a good place in the report to include some qualitative judgments

EXHIBIT 13-3

Northern Hospitality Company, Inc. and Affiliates
Organization Chart

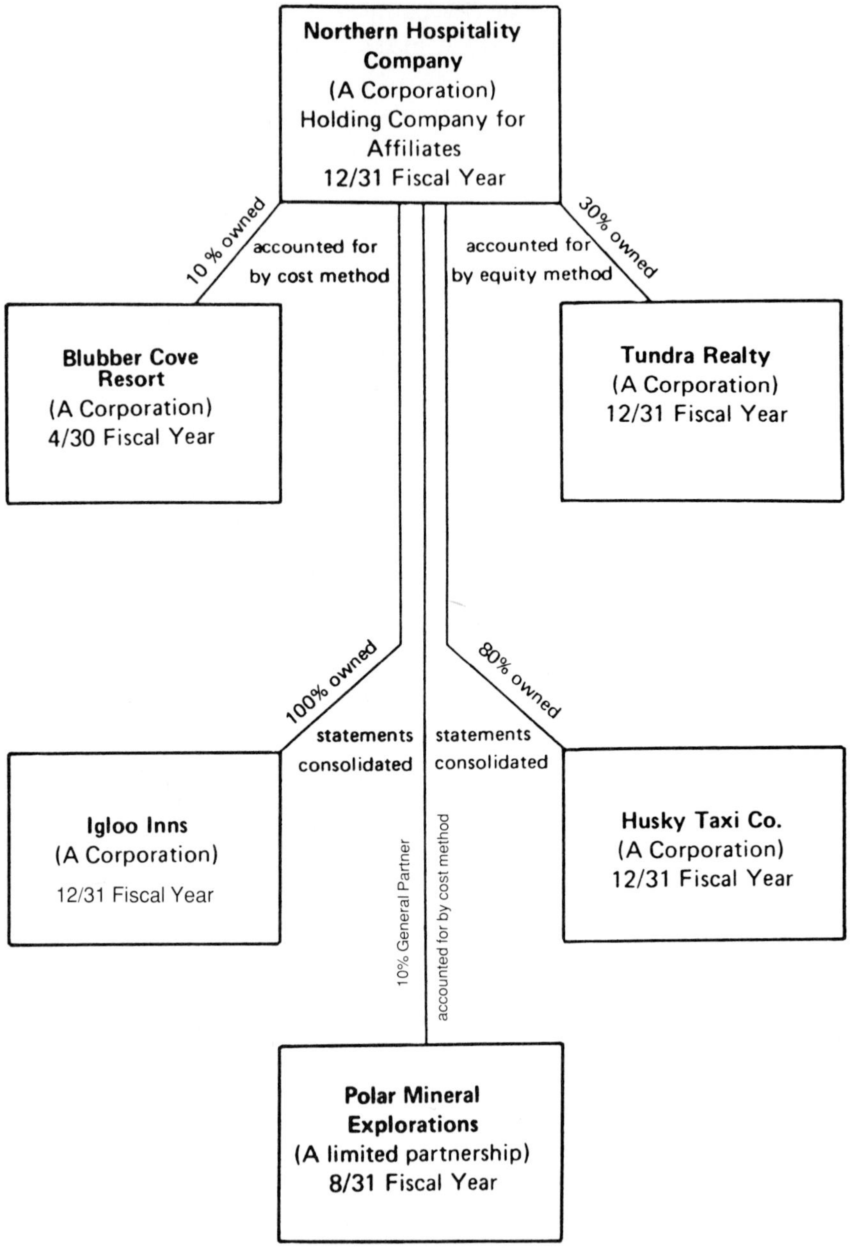

about how strongly the company's existence is justified. A discussion of the company's competition would be an appropriate part of this section. It is particularly important that the reader understand the primary basis on which the company competes. What is the relative importance of product uniqueness, product quality, service, advertising, and pricing?

The report should indicate which facilities are leased and which are owned. It should note the terms of current leases, including expiration dates, and the extent to which they appear to be above, below, or near current market rates. Square footage of each facility also should be noted. It is desirable to include some qualitative judgment on the facilities' apparent condition and efficiency. Any major problems on the horizon, such as a forced move or sharply increased costs because of a lease expiring or some major cash outlays for replacing or updating equipment, should be pointed out.

The report should indicate approximately how many employees there are and how many are seasonal and part-time versus full-time, if applicable. It is desirable to indicate whether the employees are unionized and, if so, which unions and when the current contracts expire. It also may be useful to include some qualitative comments about employee turnover or longevity and labor relations.

For some kinds of companies, continuity of sources of supply is a critical consideration. If so, the adequacy of supply sources should be addressed. If applicable, a list of key suppliers may be included at this point.

A review of Chapters 5 and 6 on gathering company data will bring to mind many other factors that might be included in the operations section for any given company.

Management.   The management section can be handled by briefly describing the position and background of each key person, along with some qualitative evaluation of the adequacy of present management, provisions for management succession, and, when appropriate, the experience of the board of directors. Most closely held companies suffer from some weakness in this respect, and the report should address this issue.

Capitalization and Distribution of Ownership.   If the capitalization and ownership were not covered in the introduction or were presented only summarily, it may be necessary to elaborate on this topic. Particularly, if there is more than one class of security, it usually is important to understand the features of each class. It may also be desirable to describe the various owners' relationships to the company and to one another.

Past Transactions in the Stock.   This section should describe any market in the stock or any transactions in it within a reasonable period prior to the valuation date. If there were no transactions, it should state that fact.

Transactions that did occur should be discussed in terms of whether or not they were on an arm's-length basis, if that information is available, so that the appraiser can analyze their appropriateness as evidence of fair market value.

Summary of Positive and Negative Factors.   In order to tie the description of the company into the valuation, it often helps to conclude the description with a summary of factors that the appraiser believes have either a positive or negative impact on the company's value.

Comparative Transaction Data

The comparative transaction data section typically includes a description of the criteria for comparability that were used in the search for comparative companies, a description of the search process itself, including the population of companies considered and the sources used, and a brief description of each company determined to be comparable enough for use in the valuation process.

As discussed in Chapter 9, "Comparative Transaction Data," these companies generally fall into either or both of two categories: publicly traded companies for which daily minority interest trading prices are available or companies that have merged or been acquired. A tabular presentation of the relevant data for the comparative companies may be presented in this section, in a later section, or in the appendix material.

Financial Statement Analysis

The financial statement analysis section usually examines the company's financial statements, explains the adjustments necessary for the valuation, and discusses comparative ratios as calculated from the financial data. This section, of course, contains the critical quantitative analysis of the company.

The analysis and adjustments to the financial statements typically cover the topics presented in Chapter 11, "Analyzing and Adjusting Financial Statements." It is important to remember, of course, that any types of adjustments to the subject company's financial statements, such as the elimination of nonrecurring items, should also be made to the statements of any comparative companies being used for valuation purposes, if appropriate.

The ratio analysis typically covers the topics and may more or less follow the format presented in Chapter 12, "Comparative Ratio Analysis." The comparisons may be made with the subject company over time (to identify trends), with general industry averages, and/or with the specific comparative companies identified in the previous section.

The appraiser should highlight and comment on the aspects of the financial statement analysis that have positive or negative implications for the company's value, either on an absolute basis or compared to other companies. In some cases, the financial statement analysis will reveal that some comparative companies are more similar than others to the subject company in certain respects. If such a pattern becomes apparent, it is desirable to point it out.

Valuation Approaches and Conclusion

The valuation section usually proceeds more or less along the following lines:

1. Discussion of valuation approaches.
2. Description of the procedure, data, and results for each approach used.

3. Relative weight to be accorded the various approaches.
4. Premiums and/or discounts, if applicable.
5. Summary and conclusion.

If the analyst considered one or more past transactions in the subject company's stock, an analysis based on these transactions may be one of the approaches used. Alternatively, such transaction(s) may be discussed separately—usually just before the conclusion—indicating whether the transaction data corroborate or modify the indications of value from other approaches or should not be accorded weight because the transactions were too old, not at arm's length, or whatever.

The important thing is to make everything clear, complete, and supportable. In addition to discussing the valuation approaches used, the analyst should explain the reasons for rejecting any other approaches that the reader might expect to find in the report.

It is important that valuation methodology be spelled out explicitly so that there will be no mystery in the reader's mind as to exactly what was done. Data sources should be specified in sufficient detail that the reader could go to the same sources and find the same data. This includes the data on which discount or capitalization rates utilized are based, as discussed in Chapter 8, "Data on Required Rates of Return." If multiples based on comparative company data are used, the reasoning behind the choice of mulitiple should be presented, even if the multiple is the average or median of comparative companies.

As noted earlier, *the work should be replicable. The reader should be able to find the data in the sources referenced, follow the procedures outlined, and reach the same conclusion.*

If the analysis is based on publicly traded stocks, the value indicated will be equivalent to a publicly traded, minority interest value. To this indicated value it may be appropriate to apply premiums or discounts for control, lack of marketability, or other qualitative factors. All such premiums or discounts should be adequately supported, in terms of both the rationale leading to them and the amount.

If the analysis is based on merger and acquisition data or another basis for arriving at the value of the entire company, and what is actually being valued is a minority interest, it may be necessary to apply discounts for *both* minority interest and lack of marketability. Again, the rationale behind and amount of any discounts must be supported.

The summary and conclusion section usually is quite brief. It often helps to summarize the indications of value from the various approaches in tabular form, summarize the relative weight accorded the respective approaches, and state the conclusion in terms of the standard of value that it represents.

Prefatory Material and Appendixes

Statement of Appraiser's Disinterest. A statement that the appraiser has no interest in the property or other conflict that could cause bias should be included in either the prefatory material or an appendix. If the appraiser does have any interest in the property or potential conflict of interest, this interest should be disclosed.

Assumptions and Limiting Conditions. The assumptions and limiting conditions also may appear in either the prefatory material or an appendix. Such topics usually cover the facts that the appraisers relied on data supplied without further verification, the appraiser is not obligated to provide testimony unless arrangements for doing so have been made, and the appraisal is valid only for the effective date and the purpose specified in the statement of the appraisal assignment.

Qualifications of Appraisers. This is usually an appendix, presenting the appraisers' relevant academic and professional credentials, experience, and other information indicating that they are qualified to appraise the type of property that is the subject of the report. Note that the American Society of Appraisers is a multidisciplinary appraisal organization, and it is a breach of its code of ethics to use the professional designation *ASA* in connection with an appraisal report without specifing the appraisal discipline in which the member is certified.

Other Appendixes. There can be any number of other appendixes, which usually provide supporting or explanatory data that did not fit conveniently into the body of the report.

Common Errors and Shortcomings in Presentation in Business Appraisal Reports

This section briefly touches on some of the errors and/or shortcomings I have encountered most frequently among the thousands of appraisal reports I have reviewed over the last 20 years. I hope this section will help appraisers to avoid these errors and help users of appraisals to identify and evaluate them when they occur.

Failure to Conform to Applicable Standard of Value

Amazingly, one of the most common errors is failure to identify and conform to the applicable standard of value. In some cases, this is merely an omission from the written report. In other cases, it has become apparent, from either reading the report or questioning the analyst, that the analyst has gone off heedlessly to do an "appraisal" without ever determining the applicable standard of value.

In some cases, the applicable standard of value is identified but apparently not understood because the analysis and conclusion do not conform to the standard of value identified. The standard of value may be misconstrued, or the report may simply fail to address some of the factors implied in the standard of value or mandated for consideration as a matter of law or regulation.

Internal Inconsistencies

I sometimes review reports that read as if they were written by two or more people who did not read the others' sections. I have read many reports saying that certain approaches should be used or accorded the most weight, only to read on and find that something contrary was actually done in the valuation methodology leading to the conclusion.

Extensive and Irrelevant Boilerplate

To a professional appraiser, a fat report filled with irrelevant boiler-plate is more an annoyance than an out-and-out error. I have seen clients, however, who were impressed with the sheer length of a report without really evaluating the quality of the content. I suggest that reports be read carefully to determine whether all the content is relevant to the appraisal as well as internally consistent. Large sections of unedited boilerplate should alert the user to evaluate the quality of the content very carefully to determine the comprehensiveness and craftsmanship with which the critical parts of the report fulfill their mission.

Undefined Jargon

The use of abstruse or ambiguous terms without definition is one of the greatest hindrances to a reader's ability to understand what the author is trying to say and exactly what was done in the appraisal process. *Abstruse* language is language that simply is not clear. When language is abstruse, the reader legitimately wonders whether the author really has any clear-cut concept to convey. *Ambiguous* language is language that has two or more possible meanings; however, the real meaning may become clear once the context is understood. Unfortunately, many commonly used terms in finance are ambiguous. A good example is *cash flow*, which has many definitions but can be very precise once the author has specified which definition applies.

The problem can be handled by defining each term the reader could possibly find abstruse or ambiguous the first time it is used in the text or by providing a list of definitions in the prefatory material or an appendix. The report reader should be alert to language that may be abstruse or ambiguous and not automatically assume definitions when the author in fact may have no clear idea in mind or may mean something quite specific but different from the reader's interpretation.

Inadequate Comparative Data

Inadequate gathering or presentation of comparative transaction data tends to be one of the most common shortcomings in the preparation and writing of business appraisal reports. Good comparative transaction data and clear exposition of it are critical if the analyst bases the valuation methodology in whole or in part on market valuation parameters (capitalization rates and multiples of fundamental variables such as revenues, earnings, cash flow, and book value) derived from such data.

In some cases, the analyst simply does not seek out and evaluate comparative transaction data (publicly traded companies and/or merger and acquisition data) thoroughly, as discussed in Chapter 9, "Comparative Transaction Data." The appraiser may say that the search yielded no comparative companies beyond those presented in the report (or none at all), but the "search" itself may have been sorely lacking. Sometimes the problem is lack of careful analysis of the comparative companies to evaluate their degree of comparability. As noted in the prior section on organization and content of the report, the search process, including the definition of the population of companies considered, should be clearly explained. The reader should critically evaluate the adequacy of the process as explained in the report.

The other common problem with comparative company data is lack of clear exposition. For example, companies have varying fiscal years. Often, when earnings or other data are presented, it is not clear exactly what time period each piece of data represents, so the reader cannot evaluate whether or not the comparative and subject company data are for the same time period. Reports often are silent on the question of whether or not comparative company data have been adjusted (or even whether the writer checked to see whether they need adjustment) to be comparable with the subject company data. To compound the problem, the comparative company data sources may not be shown explicitly, so that the user or reviewer of the report does not know where to go to verify data or find answers to the unanswered questions.

Inadequacies such as these necessarily leave the appraisal product suspect, since the reader has no way of knowing precisely what was done and thus no way of evaluating it.

Leaps of Faith

By a *leap of faith* I mean the presentation of a fact or conclusion with no accompanying documentation as to source or supporting analysis or data. This is especially critical, of course, if the unsupported fact or conclusion is part of an integral link in the valuation process, such as a capitalization rate, so that the valuation conclusion depends on it.

The variety of leaps of faith to which readers of business valuation reports may be subjected is almost boundless. The writer should be careful not to leave such gaps. The reader should evaluate whether all critical assertions are supported and consider the evaluation in determining the extent to which he or she is willing or able to rely on the report.

Emphasis of Items Not in Proportion to Their Relative Importance

Another common problem in the writing of appraisal reports is the emphasis given various aspects of the analysis presented in relation to their importance in reaching the conclusion. Probably the most common example of this error is the emphasis often accorded to developing the earnings base and the capitalization rates in a capitalization of earnings approach. The two variables are more or less equally critical to a valid conclusion using that approach. Yet many reports devote 20 pages to painstakingly developing the earnings base to be capitalized and then cavalierly capitalize that earnings base at a capitalization rate supported only by one or two flimsy sentences.

In one report I reviewed, the appraiser took great pains and several well-crafted pages to justify the discount rate (in a discounted future earnings approach) to the nearest one-tenth of 1 percent. He then took one sentence to apply a 90 percent discount for lack of marketability to the result of the painstaking exercise!

The report writer should be conscious of what really matters in the final opinion of value when writing the report and not give short shrift to factors that substantially impact on the conclusion. The reader should evaluate the report in light of whether the factors that really matter in reaching the final conclusion are indeed given their due consideration.

Reports for Special Purposes

Appraisal reports written for certain purposes may have requirements that are greater than, smaller than, or different from the generalized format just outlined.

Employee Stock Ownership Plans

For an ESOP stock appraisal, it is appropriate to include the report content and use a format along the lines discussed in this chapter and shown in the sample report in Chapter 14. However, certain additional factors peculiar to ESOPs must be addressed, as discussed in Chapter 23, "Employee Stock Ownership Plans." Also, Department of Labor regulations require written reports valuing ESOP stock to contain certain specialized information such as that shown in Exhibit 23–2.

Buy-Sell Agreements

It is desirable to have a written valuation report on a buy-sell agreement, as discussed in Chapter 20. The report can range from a single-page memorandum to a full formal report, as discussed in the previous section.

Normally, written appraisal reports done for the purpose of entering into buy-sell agreements are somewhat abbreviated compared to the full-length format just described, since they need satisfy only the parties to the agreement and their beneficiaries rather than any regulatory authorities or legal requirements. Frequently, however, valuation reports prepared for buy-sell agreements also serve other purposes, such as to establish values for gift and estate taxes. In such cases, the more detail included in the report, the better.

Due Diligence Reports for Public Stock Offerings

When a company contemplates an offering of stock to the public, the SEC requires that certain due diligence work be undertaken to ensure that the underwriters and all parties marketing the stock understand the selling company, including its financial condition and limitations. This work may be done by the underwriter or by an independent third party.

The report is made available to representatives of the underwriting firm and the selling group. The written report usually is quite comprehensive and is supplemented by one or more meetings between the person or persons preparing the report and the representatives of the underwriter and selling group to discuss the proposed offering and answer questions.

The due diligence report contains most or all of the elements of a report prepared for tax purposes but puts much more emphasis on the company's future prospects. It usually contains earnings and cash flow projections and analyses of the factors that tend to support or prevent the attainment of the projections. Subjective evaluative judgments, possibly obtained from persons outside the company, such as customers, distributors, suppliers, competitors, and bankers, should be included and, in some cases, may be one of the longest sections in the report. The written report may identify the comments attributable to such sources by name or, in some cases of confidentiality, by category of source.

Fairness Opinion Letters

It is becoming increasingly common for boards of directors to retain an independent financial adviser to assist them in carrying out their fiduciary duty when a major decision that affects noncontrolling as well as controlling stockholders is pending. In some cases, the financial adviser will work with and report to a special committee of the board, often composed of independent outside directors not directly affiliated with management and/or controlling stockholders. Sometimes the financial adviser is retained by the ESOP or some other trustee representing a particular group of stockholders to protect that group's interests. The role of the financial adviser can vary widely, but usually involves assistance in pricing and/or structuring a proposed transaction or reviewing and rendering an opinion on the fairness of a proposed transaction. The financial adviser usually has one or more meetings with the board, committee, or trustee to discuss the opinion and typically provides them with a somewhat detailed memorandum explaining the opinion, although without much of the background data of full written reports discussed earlier.

Ultimately, if the financial adviser is satisfied and a transaction is imminent, the adviser will issue a fairly brief letter to the effect that it is the adviser's opinion that the transaction is fair to the stockholders in question from a financial point of view. This letter usually is published in the proxy or other materials that are distributed to stockholders prior to a vote on the proposed transaction. An example of such a letter, commonly known as a *fairness opinion* (this one in connection with a public company going private), is shown in Exhibit 13–4.

Normally the financial adviser reviews events between the time of issuing the fairness opinion and the time of the stockholder vote and issues a supplemental letter to the board, committee, or fiduciary as to whether or not any material events that would cause the financial adviser to change the opinion have occurred.

In the past, this type of financial advisory role and the issuance of fairness opinions has been largely the province of investment bankers. However, many think that there is a potential conflict of interest between an investment banker's financial interest in the successful consummation of the proposed transaction, or other possible relationships with the company, and the issuance of an opinion as to its fairness to a group of stockholders. As a consequence of this perception—and possibly of some differential in the level of fees typically charged—the role of financial adviser and the issuance of fairness opinions in this context are shifting somewhat toward independent business valuation firms.

Summary

This chapter discussed both the content and organization of a good written appraisal report, as well as some of the shortcomings most commonly encountered in business appraisal reports. Certain minimum legal and professional standards must be met in writing appraisal reports for some purposes. Beyond those somewhat limited minimum requirements, though, there can be great flexibility in the quantity, quality, and format of material presented.

Well-researched and documented written appraisal reports, presented in a complete, logical, and readable manner, can be instrumental in expediting sound transactions and in reducing the risks of subsequent litigation pursuant to the subject transactions. Conversely, poorly written appraisal reports may delay or prevent transactions

EXHIBIT 13-4

Fairness Opinion

October 5, 1987

Board of Directors
Reser's Fine Foods, Inc.
15570 S.W. Jenkins Road
Beaverton, Oregon 97006-6009

Gentlemen:

Willamette Management Associates, Inc., (Willamette) was retained by Reser's Fine Foods, Inc., (Reser's) to express an opinion as to the fairness from a financial point of view to Reser's common stock shareholders of a price of $12.50 per share to be paid to the stockholders pursuant to a proposed transaction, whereby all the outstanding stock of Reser's not held by RAI Acquisition, Inc., will be acquired.

Willamette's principal business is the valuation of businesses and business interests, including both privately held and publicly traded companies, for all purposes, including mergers and acquisitions, divestitures, public offerings, gift and estate taxes, Employee Stock Ownership Plans, corporate and partnership recapitalizations, dissolutions, and other objectives.

In arriving at our opinion, we have considered the nature of the business and history of the enterprise, the economic outlook in general, the outlook for the meat and specialty food processing industry in particular, the company's earnings and cash flow for the last five years, the outlook for future earnings, the book value of the stock, the company's financial condition, its dividend-paying capacity, past transactions in the company's stock, and prices at which other public companies in related lines of business are selling both on a minority and on a control basis.

Specific documents relied upon in arriving at our opinion included audited financial statements for the periods ending April 30, 1982, through April 30, 1986; preliminary audited financial statements for the period ending April 30, 1987; three-month interim financial statements for the period ending July 31, 1987; Securities and Exchange Commission Forms 10-K filed by the company for the fiscal years ending April 30, 1980, April 30, 1985, and April 30, 1986; company Articles of Incorporation and Bylaws; 1986/1987 Washington County property tax assessments; company stock transfer records from April 1985 through September 1987; common stock trading prices from September 1984 through May 1987; proxy statements for annual shareholder meetings from 1983 through 1986; various other current company documents, including but not limited to current marketing literature, accounts receivable aging schedule and fixed asset schedule. We also analyzed financial statements and other material regarding comparative public companies, acquisition data for the meat and specialty food processing industry, required rates of return on common stocks in general, material discussing the economic outlook and the meat and specialty foods processing industry outlook, and such other material as we deemed appropriate. In addition, we toured Reser's facilities, interviewed company management, and met with Reser's board of directors.

In rendering this opinion, we have relied, without independent verification, on the accuracy, completeness, and fairness of all financial and other information that was publicly available or furnished to us by Reser's.

Based on our analysis of the factors deemed relevant, it is our opinion that the proposed cash offer for all the outstanding common stock of Reser's not held by RAI Acquisition, Inc., at a price of $12.50 per share is fair from a financial point of view to the shareholders of Reser's.

Yours very truly,

WILLAMETTE MANAGEMENT ASSOCIATES, INC.

EXHIBIT 13-5

Checklist for Evaluating an Appraisal Report

Is the assignment clearly stated?
[ ] Clear definition of interest being appraised
[ ] Purpose of appraisal
[ ] Valuation date
[ ] Standard of value clearly stated, including reference to statute if a statutory standard is applicable

[ ] Are sources of information absolutely clear throughout the report so that the reader can locate the source and check all data used by the appraiser if he so desires?

Is the company adequately described?
[ ] Background
[ ] Physical facilities
[ ] Products and/or services
[ ] Management
[ ] Capitalization and ownership

[ ] Are all terms used in the report defined so that they are unambiguous (e.g., if "cash flow" is used, is it defined so that the reader can take the same raw data, make the computation, and arrive at exactly the same number?)

Are the criteria and procedures for selection of comparative companies clearly stated?
[ ] Population from which comparatives drawn
[ ] Criteria for selection from among population considered
[ ] Sources and procedures used clearly spelled out

[ ] Are the steps taken to carry out the assignment clearly described so that the reader can perform all the steps and calculations with the data and methods presented and arrive at the same answer?

Is the rationale clearly and convincingly presented?
[ ] Rationale for selection of comparative data
[ ] Rationale for choosing methodologies (or rejecting certain methodologies in some cases)
[ ] Rationale for selection of discount rates, capitalization rates, and multipliers
[ ] Rationale for weighting approaches in arriving at conclusion

Is the report internally consistent?
[ ] Did data for comparative and subject companies cover the same time periods?

[ ] Were data for comparative and subject companies presented or adjusted on consistent basis?
[ ] Did the research and analysis fully conform to criteria set forth in the report? (Did the report actually do what it said that it would or should do?)

[ ] Is there reference to whether or not there have been past transactions in the stock, and, if so, whether they are indicative of value for the purpose of this valuation?

Does the appraiser's statement of qualifications present relevant qualifications for the particular assignment?
[ ] Education
[ ] Technical training
[ ] Professional designations
[ ] Professional organization memberships and activities
[ ] Type and years of experience
[ ] Expert witness experience

Reviewer's judgments
[ ] Is the analysis and conclusion consistent with the stated purpose of the appraisal and standard of value, including any statutory, regulatory, or other legal requirements?
[ ] Is the conclusion consistent with the economic and industry analysis presented?
[ ] Did the appraiser identify and utilize the best available comparative companies?
[ ] Are the proper financial statement adjustments made for both the subject and the comparative companies?
[ ] Is the conclusion consistent with the implications of the financial statement analysis?
[ ] Is the use of each discount rate, capitalization rate, and multiple adequately and convincingly supported?
[ ] Have all relevant factors been addressed?
[ ] Are factors accorded treatment and weight commensurate with their significance for the valuation purpose and circumstances at hand?
[ ] Are the approaches used apropos to the valuation purpose and the company circumstances?
[ ] Do the data steps and rationale lead logically and convincingly to the conclusion presented?
[ ] Is the conclusion reasonable in light of all the facts and circumstances?

and invite litigation even if the transaction itself was basically sound. I hope this chapter will help report writers to prepare sound reports that will be readable by and acceptable to the parties who must be satisfied, whether buyers, sellers, beneficiaries, fiduciaries, regulators, or others related to the subject appraisal in some way. I hope it will also assist users of reports by providing some objective guidelines with which to evaluate the reports they read. Exhibit 13–5 is a handy checklist to help both the writer and the user evaluate some of the factors essential to a good valuation report.

Chapter 14

A Sample Report

Appraisal Report
JMK Inc.

Prepared by

Jacie R. Daschel
Valuation Analyst

Mary B. McCarter, CFA, ASA
Valuation Analyst

Kathryn F. Aschwald, CFA
Valuation Analyst

JMK Inc. is a case contrived to illustrate the application of many of the principles and procedures presented in the first 13 chapters of this book.

This hypothetical company is not intended to be patterned after any real-world company. The reader should not be concerned whether or not any of the assumptions bear resemblance to the reader's perception of reality in the consumer electronics industry. The point of the case simply is to demonstrate one possible way of organizing a written valuation report, and to illustrate by example the application of a variety of procedures commonly used in valuation reports.

This report has been prepared for the confidential use of the Estate of Robert Johnson. It was made by and/or under the direct supervision of the undersigned using standard valuation techniques and practices.

Neither Willamette Management Associates, Inc., nor the individuals involved in this appraisal, have any present or contemplated future interest in the subject property or any other interest that might tend to prevent making a fair and unbiased appraisal.

The American Society of Appraisers has a mandatory recertification program for all of its senior members. All senior members employed by Willamette Management are in compliance with that program's requirements.

Jacie R. Daschel
Valuation Analyst

Mary B. McCarter, CFA, ASA
Valuation Analyst

Kathryn F. Aschwald, CFA
Valuation Analyst

TABLE OF CONTENTS

Introduction

      Description of the Assignment
      Summary Description of the Company
      Capitalization and Ownership
      Definition of Fair Market Value
      Sources of Information
      Valuation Approaches and Conclusion

U.S. Economic Outlook

      Overview
      Consumer Spending and Retail Sales
      Outlook

Economic Outlook for the Metropolitan Areas of Baltimore, Maryland;
      Washington, D.C.; and Norfolk, Virginia

Consumer Electronics Industry

      Overview
      The Superstore Concept
      Products
      Dependence on Imports
      Outlook

Fundamental Position of the Company

      Background
      Operations
      Employees and Management
      Marketing
      Suppliers
      Competition
      Facilities
      Expansion Plans
      Summary of Positive and Negative Factors
      Prior Transactions in the Stock

The Search for Comparatives

      Selection of Comparative Companies
      Description of Comparative Companies

Financial Statement Analysis

      Adjustments to Income Statements
      Trend Analysis
      Analysis of Comparative Publicly Traded Companies

Appraisal of Fair Market Value

      Valuation Approaches
      Approaches Considered but Not Used
      Capitalization of Earnings
      Price/Revenues Approach
      Price/Book Value Approach
      Valuation Summary
      Discount for Lack of Marketability
      Prior Transaction
      Conclusion

INTRODUCTION

Description of the Assignment

Willamette Management Associates, Inc., was retained by the Estate of Robert Johnson to appraise the fair market value of 3,000 shares of the common stock of JMK Inc. (JMK) as of July 21, 1987, the date of death, for estate tax purposes. The 3,000 shares of common stock represent a 15 percent interest in JMK's total common shares outstanding.

Summary Description of the Company

JMK, a Maryland corporation headquartered in Baltimore, is a retailer of consumer electronics. The company operates 29 retail stores in the metropolitan areas of Baltimore; Washington, D.C.; and Norfolk, Virginia.

Capitalization and Ownership

JMK is capitalized with one class of common stock with a par value of $100 per share. As of July 21, 1987, there were 50,000 shares authorized, 21,000 shares issued, and 20,000 shares outstanding (1,000 shares held in treasury). The ownership of these shares was as follows:

	No. of Shares Owned	%
Sam Adams	2,900	14.5
Robert Johnson	3,000	15.0
Kathleen Kelly	4,700	23.5
James Miller	4,700	23.5
William Smith	4,700	23.5
	20,000	100.0

Definition of Fair Market Value

Fair market value is considered to represent a value at which a willing seller and willing buyer, both informed of the relevant facts about the business, could reasonably conduct a transaction, neither person acting under compulsion to do so. Among other factors, this appraisal considers all elements of appraisal listed in Internal Revenue Service Ruling 59-60, which generally outlines the valuation of closely held stocks and includes the following:

1. The nature of the business and history of the enterprise.
2. The economic outlook in general and condition and outlook of the specific industry in particular.
3. The book value of the stock and the financial condition of the business.
4. The company's earning capacity.
5. The company's dividend-paying capacity.
6. Whether or not the enterprise has goodwill or other intangible value.
7. Sales of stock and size of the block to be valued.
8. The market prices of stocks of corporations engaged in the same or similar lines of business whose stocks are actively traded in a free and open market, either on an exchange or over the counter.

Sources of Information

In September 1987, Kathryn Aschwald, Jacie Daschel, and Mary McCarter visited the company's headquarters in Baltimore, Maryland, and interviewed

James Miller, executive vice president; Kathleen Kelly, vice president–operations; and William Smith, vice president–finance, and toured several of the stores in Baltimore and Washington, D.C., plus the newest store in Norfolk. The sources of information used in this appraisal included the following:

1. Financial statements reviewed by One, Two, Three & Company, P.C., for the fiscal years ended April 30, 1983, through 1987.
2. Corporate income tax returns over the same period.
3. Internally prepared budget for fiscal 1988.
4. Equipment list and depreciation schedule as of April 30, 1987.
5. Inventory list as of April 30, 1987.
6. Stockholders' list for fiscal 1983 through 1987.
7. Schedule of total owners' compensation.
8. Copies of store leases.
9. Recent minutes of board of directors' meetings.
10. Articles of incorporation and bylaws.
11. Industry information gathered from the *1987 Electronic Market Data Book* by the Electronic Industries Association, the *U.S. Industrial Outlook 1987, Fortune, Value Line Investment Survey, Consumer Electronics, The Economist, Television Digest,* Donald Trott, consumer electronics industry analyst for Dean Witter Reynolds, and public companies' annual reports.
12. Information on the U.S. economy from *The Wall Street Journal, Fortune, Business Week,* Standard & Poor's (S&P) *Trends & Projections,* the Federal Reserve Bank of Cleveland's *Economic Trends, The Federal Reserve Bulletin,* and First Interstate Bank's *Forecast 1987–1988.*
13. In researching the economies of Baltimore, Washington, D.C., and Norfolk, we reviewed the following:
    a. Baltimore Regional Planning Council's *Economic Review* (December 1985 and June 1987).
    b. Washington Metropolitan Council of Governments *Economic Trends in Metropolitan Washington, 1980–1986, Commercial Construction Indicators Fourth Quarter 1986 and Annual Report.*
    c. Salomon Brothers Inc., *Washington, D.C. Real Estate Market.*
    d. *Sales and Marketing Management* magazine, "1984 Survey of Buying Power."
    e. *The Washington Post,* August 19, 1985.
    f. *Tidewater Virginian, Statistical Digest 1987.*
    g. Information from Hampton Roads Chamber of Commerce.
14. Information on comparative publicly traded companies from S&P *Corporation Records,* individual companies' annual reports, SEC Forms 10-K and 10-Q, Institutional Brokers Estimate System (I/B/E/S), and various brokerage reports on these companies.

Valuation Approaches and Conclusion

Using data from publicly traded companies, we arrived at indicated values based on the following five approaches: capitalization of latest 12 months' earnings, capitalization of five years' average earnings, capitalization of projected 1988 earnings, price/latest 12 months' revenues, and price/book value. After appropriate weighting of these approaches, we arrived at an indicated publicly traded equivalent value of JMK's common stock. We then discounted this value to reflect the lack of marketability of JMK's common stock, developing a per share indicated fair market value of $1,430. We then analyzed a prior arm's-length transaction in JMK's common stock and found that the value we determined was consistent with the price paid in that transaction.

After a complete analysis of all relevant factors surrounding JMK, it is our opinion that the fair market value of a minority interest in JMK's common stock for estate tax purposes, as of July 21, 1987, was $1,430 per share. The Estate of Robert Johnson holds 3,000 shares of JMK common stock. Therefore, as of July 21, 1987, the aggregate minority interest fair market value of the common stock held in the estate was $4,290,000 (3,000 × $1,430).

U.S. ECONOMIC OUTLOOK

In the appraisal of any company, the general economic factors prevailing at the date of the appraisal must be considered in order to gain insight into the economic climate in which investors are dealing. Although individual factors may or may not have a direct impact on a particular industry, the overall economy (and the outlook for it) strongly influences how investors perceive the investment opportunities in all industries. In our analysis of JMK, we have considered the general economic climate that prevailed in July 1987, as well as the outlook for the future. In particular, we have focused on the outlook for consumer spending and retail sales, since this aspect of the economy is most directly related to the consumer electronics industry and JMK.

Overview

The latest U.S. Commerce Department report suggests that the economy is expanding at a balanced pace, even though growth slowed to 2.6 percent in the second quarter of 1987, adjusted for inflation. Economic growth is measured by real gross national product (GNP), which is the inflation-adjusted value of the nation's output of goods and services. Although the rise in real GNP is below the revised 4.4 percent increase for the first quarter of 1987, it is considerably higher than the 1.9 percent that most private forecasters expected. As in the first quarter, improvement in international trade contributed to growth, but the latest period also saw strength in domestic demand, with increases in consumer spending, business fixed investment, and government purchases. The quarterly figures bring the growth rate for the first half to 3.5 percent.

Although forecasters generally expect that the economy will continue to expand steadily in 1987, weakness in consumer spending, housing, business investment, and government spending is expected to temper the influence of significant export growth. In addition, while the outlook for capital spending and business investment appears to be improving, according to McGraw Hill and Conference Board capital spending surveys, capital spending is expected to be somewhat restrained in 1987 due to tax reform.

The real strength in the 1987 economy is expected to lie in expanding exports and reducing the trade deficit. However, even though the latest free-fall of the dollar in foreign exchange markets is finally improving the trade deficit, it has also forced the Fed to tighten credit conditions and has stirred up fears of renewed inflation. As a result, banks raised their prime rate to 8.25 percent in mid-May, the third increase in two months.

A jump in energy prices fueled a 0.4 percent rise in the consumer price index in June 1987, the Labor Department said, underscoring a troubling aspect of the inflation outlook. The June increase amounted to a 4.3 percent annual compound rate and included a 1.5 percent rise in energy costs. For the first six months of the year, the CPI rose at a 5.4 percent annual rate, largely because of the surge in energy prices. For comparison, in 1986, consumer prices increased only 1.1 percent overall, and only 3.8 percent excluding the big decline in energy prices.

Consumer Spending and Retail Sales

Consumer spending rose at a 2.1 percent annual rate during the second quarter of 1987, with the gain coming primarily in services and durables (which would include consumer electronics). According to the U.S. Department of Commerce, consumer spending fell 0.1 percent during the first quarter. However, S&P *Industry Surveys* indicates that if auto sales were excluded, consumer spending increased at a more respectable real annual rate of 2.2 percent during the first quarter.

Much of the general slowdown in the growth of consumer spending in 1987 is related to spending on consumer durables. While spending on consumer durables increased 8 percent (before adjusting for inflation) in 1986, outpacing growth in total consumer spending, spending on consumer durables (before adjusting for inflation) is expected to increase only 3.5 percent in 1987 and 3.4 percent in 1988, according to S&P *Outlook*. This compares with an expected 6.2 percent increase in total consumer spending for 1987 and 6.5 percent increase in 1988 (before adjusting for inflation).

Retail sales slipped 0.6 percent in May, to $124 billion, seasonally adjusted, according to *Business Week*. The malaise in retailing is general; soft goods have gone up only slightly since winter, and hard goods have been declining even in dollar terms. Autos are no longer the only segment pulling down the retail sales numbers. Excluding automobiles, sales of hard goods totaled $19.9 billion in May. That marks the third consecutive monthly decline and brings sales down below the level reached in December 1986.

The decline in consumer spending has had one positive effect: The anemic savings rate, which fell to 1.2 percent of disposable income in December 1986, has rebounded to a somewhat healthier 3.5 percent in the first quarter of 1987. In 1986, the savings rate fell to 3.8 percent, compared to an average savings rate of 5.2 percent in the first four years of the recovery and a postwar average of 6.8 percent. The consensus forecast for the savings rate in 1987 is slightly below 1986's 3.8 percent. "The fundamentals simply do not support optimism," says Data Resources Inc., a consulting firm. "With inflation on the rise, real disposable income should grow only 1 percent in 1987. Our spending projection assumes that the saving rate drops to 3.2 percent. Because tax reform raises the after-tax cost of consumer installment debt, households may begin to rein in debt, in which case the savings rate would drop less sharply but consumer spending would be even weaker."

According to the Federal Reserve Bank of Cleveland's *Economic Trends*, many forecasts for 1987 say that consumer spending will slow to about half the growth rate for 1986. *Fortune* predicts that consumer spending will be back on a modest upswing before long, primarily because personal income will be rising faster than in recent years—3.0 percent in 1987. According to S&P, "While the economy continues to show signs of picking up, consumer spending is no longer the leading sector. Though buoyed by some recent employment gains, consumers are not likely to increase spending faster than the overall economy. At the same time, consumers may bring their built-up credit financing under control, partly by taking advantage of new home equity loans. Confidence remains high, although it is not rising rapidly."

Overall, it appears that growth in consumer spending will continue to be somewhat slow in 1987. In fact, S&P expects consumer spending to increase only 2 percent after adjusting for inflation in 1987, compared to 4.1 percent real growth in 1986. This slowdown could significantly crimp the economic expansion as a whole, since consumer spending accounts for about two thirds of overall business activity.

Outlook

Although the second-quarter increase of 2.6 percent in the nation's real GNP was better than expected and may lead economic forecasters to revise their estimates upward somewhat, current forecasts for 1987 indicate that real GNP is expected to increase by 2.4 percent to 3.2 percent for all of 1987. S&P forecasts 3.5 percent growth in real GNP during the third quarter, followed by 3.0 percent in the fourth quarter. For the year, S&P expects real GNP to increase 2.8 percent. The *Blue Chip Economic Indicators,* a Sedona, Arizona, newsletter that polls 51 leading forecasters each month, indicates that the July 1987 consensus is for real GNP to increase by 2.5 percent in 1987, followed by 2.8 percent in 1988. *Fortune* forecasts only a 2.4 percent increase in real GNP in 1987, followed by a 2.6 percent increase in 1988. According to the *Federal Reserve Bulletin,* the central tendency of the forecasts of the Federal Reserve Committee members and other Reserve Bank presidents is for growth in real GNP of about 2.5 percent to 3.0 percent for 1987. *The Wall Street Journal* reports that the Reagan administration is predicting 3.2 percent growth in real GNP 1987. Overall, the national economic outlook is for slow growth with some weakness in consumer spending relative to the past few years.

ECONOMIC OUTLOOK FOR THE METROPOLITAN AREAS OF BALTIMORE, MARYLAND; WASHINGTON, D.C.; AND NORFOLK, VIRGINIA

The economic outlook for the metropolitan areas of Baltimore, Maryland; Washington, D.C.; and Norfolk, Virginia, is particularly relevant in an appraisal of JMK, since the company's consumer electronics stores are located there. Due to the nature of the company's business, JMK will be more directly influenced by changes in the economic outlook for these specific areas than by the U.S. economy as a whole. Therefore, we considered the economic outlook for the metropolitan areas of Baltimore, Maryland; Washington, D.C.; and Norfolk, Virginia, as of July 1987.

Norfolk (Hampton Roads), Virginia[1]

The Norfolk, Virginia, metropolitan area is commonly called "Hampton Roads." Hampton Roads includes the areas of five cities: Norfolk, Suffolk, Portsmouth, Virginia Beach, and Chesapeake, and covers nearly 2,000 square miles in the southeastern corner of Virginia.

---

[1]Due to space limitations in this book, we have included a summary of the economic outlook for only Norfolk, Virginia, as a condensed sample of a regional economic section.

The dominant factor of the area is the location of the world's largest natural harbor within its bounds. The harbor is home to the world's largest naval base, as well as the U.S. Atlantic fleet. Twenty-five percent of all U.S. naval personnel call the area home. Furthermore, Norfolk Naval Shipyard is the largest ship repair facility in the world, employing 27,000 workers. The harbor provides a base for a strong regional economy that has shown growth far above that of the national economy as a whole. The economy is further enhanced because of its large percentage of government and military personnel, which traditionally remains stable even in times of economic downturn.

Population. The Virginia Department of Planning and Budget predicts strong population growth for Hampton Roads.

From 1980 to 1990, the area's overall population is expected to grow 19.4 percent, from 796,000 to 951,000, with an additional 12.6 percent growth from 1990 to 2000. Thus, the area's total population is expected to exceed 1 million persons in 2000.

Employment. The strength of the area's economy is best demonstrated by its employment growth. According to the National Planning Association, a Washington, D.C.–based research group, the overall employment growth rate was 3.9 percent for 1986, with construction leading the way at 10.7 percent. Historically, the area's overall employment growth rate has exceeded that of the United States as a whole. For the period 1960 to 1984, the area's rate of growth was 3.4 percent annually, compared to 2.3 percent for the United States as a whole.

The area's economy has proven much more stable than other areas for several reasons. Manufacturing provides only 14 percent of the jobs for the region, compared to nearly 20 percent for the United States as a whole. With a smaller percentage involved in manufacturing, fewer people are affected by the sometimes volatile nature of the industry. The area has a higher percentage of government civilians in the work force—25 percent compared to 17 percent for the U.S. as a whole. Government employment tends to be much more stable than that of the economy as a whole.

The unemployment rate reflects the economy's health. The region's unemployment rate has trailed the national average for many years. For 1986 it was 4.6 percent, and it has never exceeded 7 percent in the last 13 years.

Income. The Bureau of Economic Analysis, U.S. Department of Commerce, predicted that the area's total personal income will increase annually by 2.8 percent from 1983 to 1990, with a 1.9 percent increase from 1990 to 2000. However, the region's per capita income lags slightly behind both the U.S. and Virginia per capita incomes. In 1984 the region's per capita income was $12,177, compared to $12,772 for the United States and $13,291 for Virginia. This relationship reflects the historical trend as well.

A measure of retail activity, taxable sales including both goods and services shows very strong growth. The Department of Taxation, Commonwealth of Virginia, reported an 80.0 percent increase in taxable sales from 1980 to 1986, for a 13.4 percent annual increase. This rate cannot be expected to continue, but it does point to a very strong economy.

Outlook. Hampton Roads is a strong economic environment that appears to have a very good future. However, growth has its costs. Because of the strong population growth, the current transportation network is already strained, with future growth expected to put additional burden on the system. An aggressive construction program is currently under way, but it may be unable to keep up with the expected growth. In addition, local taxes have increased significantly in the last year or two, which will affect consumers' disposable income. If the area can manage its growth problems, Hampton Roads will continue to grow and prosper at a rate exceeding that of the nation as a whole.

CONSUMER ELECTRONICS INDUSTRY

An understanding of the outlook for the consumer electronics industry, as well as its nature, is very important for an appraisal of JMK, since it is necessary to evaluate a company in the context of the industry and markets in which it participates. Therefore, we considered the outlook for the consumer electronics industry as of July 1987 in our valuation of JMK. In particular, we focused on video products (primarily VCRs), audio products, and televisions, since these constitute the bulk of JMK's sales.

Overview

The retail consumer electronics industry recently was characterized by *Consumer Electronics* as an industry in flux. Its evolution is part of an overall trend toward consolidation in retailing. Change in the industry's manufacturing sector has paved the way for the shift. Prior to the 1980s, the industry was dominated by domestic manufacturers with local channels of distribution who sold to small "mom-and-pop" dealers. Japanese manufacturers, who now account for approximately 40 percent of American consumer electronics, undermined the traditional methods of distribution and made possible the concepts of the national retailer and the superstore chains.

The videocassette recorder (VCR) and other new products, along with a relatively strong economy, caused explosive growth in the industry from 1980 to 1986. Between 1980 and 1985, retail sales grew at an annual rate of 15 percent to 20 percent. In 1986, the Electronic Industries Association reported growth of 13.6 percent. In response to this growth, national retailers have expanded. Funded by cash raised in public offerings, most of the national retailers have almost doubled their number of stores in the past few years. For example, Newmark & Lewis, located in the Northeast, grew from 25 to 44 outlets in two years.

Now the industry is in a state of adjustment. National retailers' wild expansion set off price wars, which have trimmed margins and threatened the profitability of many existing stores. In addition, whereas the prices of many consumer electronic products traditionally have decreased over time due to advancing technology, the devaluation of the dollar has slowed the fall in prices for imported products, which has affected sales somewhat. Moreover, flat sales, along with bloated inventories resulting from a record volume of imports in 1986, have added to the retailers' problems. The result has been a record number of consolidations, mergers, and bankruptcies among the top 300 consumer electronics dealers. The shakedown of the industry is expected to continue, as retail consumer electronic sales are expected to increase only approximately 5 percent in 1987 and 1988. In the meantime, national retailers will have to concentrate on tighter management of their superstores in order to remain competitive.

The Superstore Concept

Superstores generally range in size from 10,000 to 30,000 square feet of retail space depending on the size of the market. They are referred to as *destination stores,* generating their own traffic instead of relying on traffic created by other stores in the area. The superstore's biggest advantage is that it can offer consumers lower prices than the smaller, independent store, since it receives volume purchase discounts from manufacturers and, due to its size, has achieved economies of scale in its operations. The superstore also is able to offer a wide selection of national brand-name merchandise. Most of the superstores pride themselves on customer service, maintaining a highly trained sales force and offering many additional services to consumers, such as extended warranties, financing of purchases, and liberal exchange policies.

In order to be profitable, a superstore must capture at least 10 percent of its overall market. According to *Fortune,* a store of 20,000 square feet must generate annual sales of approximately $10 million, yielding a gross margin of 25 percent to 30 percent of sales and a net profit margin of less than 4 percent. To support such a high sales volume, the superstore uses extensive advertising, which generally accounts for 5 percent to 8 percent of sales revenue. The superstore usually offers such product lines as televisions, video equipment, stereo components, car stereos, and personal electronics, including personal computers. Some superstores also sell appliances.

Products

The VCR, which hit the mass market only five years ago, is estimated to be in 40 percent of all households. Industry experts estimate that approximately two thirds of all U.S. households will have a VCR by 1990, offering room for considerable growth. The Electronic Industries Association reports that VCR sales in 1986 totaled over 13.5 million units, a 14.8 percent increase in unit sales over 1985. Currently, slackening demand for VCRs remains a problem, causing *Fortune* to predict that VCR sales will remain flat in the current year. The sale of camcorders is an area of potential growth within the video sector, with only 3 percent penetration and growing sales. According to *Television Digest,* camcorder sales to dealers are up 48 percent for the first 27 weeks in 1987 compared to the comparable 1986 period.

Unit sales of televisions, as reported by the Electronic Industries Association, reached 22.9 million units in 1986, an 11 percent increase, after declining in 1985. Since approximately 98 percent of all homes have at least one television set, sales come mainly from consumers buying replacement sets, with replacements accounting for approximately 40 percent of total TV sales. The trend in television is toward larger screens, higher-resolution pictures, and the addition of MTS stereo, which enables a TV set to receive stereo broadcasts. VCR sales could boost TV sales as consumers replace or upgrade equipment.

In the audio sector, technological innovations have come in the form of compact disk (CD) players and digital audiotape. Despite declining prices for CD players, sales have been slow. *U.S. Industrial Outlook* reported a glut of CD players at the end of 1986 as a result of the sluggish sales and inventory buildups. However, there is considerable room for growth in CD player sales, since the household penetration of these products is only 7 percent. Because of the new products being introduced, the audio sector should be much stronger than the video sector, in contrast to the past, when the video sector dominated because of the VCR.

Dependence on Imports

Due to the high level of imports in consumer electronics, the United States is increasingly depending on foreign suppliers for consumer electronic products. Domestic shipments (sales by domestic manufacturers to the U.S. market) of consumer electronics, measured in constant dollars, decreased approximately 2.7 percent in 1986, according to the *U.S. Industrial Outlook.* In contrast, imports reached a record level of $15.7 billion, an increase of 9.7 percent over the 1985 level, as reported by the Electronic Industries Association. Japan was the largest foreign supplier, producing approximately 65 percent of total consumer electronic imports in 1986. Following Japan were Korea and Taiwan, with each contributing less than 10 percent of the total. VCRs accounted for the largest dollar amount of consumer electronic imports.

Although the value of the dollar has fallen against the yen for the past two years, the Japanese reportedly have absorbed the loss by continuing to lower their prices in order to capture market share. Now that the Japanese have captured a substantial portion of the U.S. market, the drop in prices seems to have slowed recently. According to *U.S. Industrial Outlook,* Japan supplied 97 percent of all VCRs sold in the United States in 1986 and a major portion of the color television sets. As the dollar continues to drop against the yen, the Japanese are moving some of their production facilities to the United States. Meanwhile, some U.S. suppliers are moving their operations offshore to capitalize on cheaper labor.

Slower import growth is predicted in 1987 as the dollar continues to weaken and retailers sell the large inventories they accumulated in 1986. For the long term, *U.S. Industrial Outlook* is expecting imports to continue to increase at an annual rate of 2.3 percent, and domestic shipments to decrease at 1.6 percent annually.

Outlook

Overall, growth prospects for the industry appear modest. Although retail sales reached $40 billion in 1986 for a 13.6 percent increase, the Electronic Industries Association predicts increases of only 4.6 percent in 1987 and 5.7 percent in 1988. Sales of consumer electronics are closely tied to personal disposable income, which *U.S. Industrial Outlook* estimates will grow 2.4 percent in 1987, following a 1.4 percent increase in 1986, measured in 1982 dollars. Consumers, having become accustomed to declining prices for consumer electronic products, are expected to reduce their spending if prices stabilize. A slow economy, large inventory accumulations, and increased competition from overexpanded retailers also should work to keep revenue growth down.

Analyst Donald Trott of Dean Witter Reynolds explains that growth in the industry is heavily influenced by two factors: overall consumer spending and "product cycle influence." He goes on to explain that the products that have had the most significant effect on expanding growth in the industry over the past few years were the VCR, the microwave oven, and, to a lesser degree, telephone devices such as the answering machine. Now, Trott says, these products are approaching a more mature phase of their product cycles and, because of tremendous price cutting, revenue growth has not kept pace with unit growth.

Overall, the shakedown and consolidation in the industry is expected to continue. The industry is still highly fragmented, with a lot of room for consolidation, as sales slow and competition intensifies. Many national retailers have expanded to the point of invading one another's markets. Many analysts think that most markets can support only two national retailers. Therefore, the shakedown will not only affect smaller companies but will compress the national retailers into a few tightly run organizations. Consequently, the emphasis of consumer electronic retailers is going to have to shift from merchandising to mastering the operational aspects of the retailing business.

Clearly, these changes will also have an impact on JMK and force the company to remain competitive in all aspects of its operations. In addition, slower growth may compel the company to expand in markets where it faces less competition and reduce its activity in the more competitive areas. This will be discussed more in depth in the next section.

FUNDAMENTAL POSITION OF THE COMPANY

Background

JMK Inc. was formed in 1970 by three high school friends, Robert Johnson, James Miller, and Kathleen Kelly. They opened their first store that year—a 5,000-square-foot store located in a strip shopping center and specializing in stereo (both car and in-home) products. Over the next eight years, they opened eight new stores in the Baltimore area and expanded the product line to include television and video products. These stores ranged in size from 4,000 to 7,000 square feet.

Due to these stores' success in the late 1970s, the founders decided to aggressively expand the operation. In 1978, Mark Williams was brought on board to direct the company's expansion. Over the next five years, JMK added 10 stores in the Washington, D.C., market that were slightly larger—at 8,000 to 10,000 square feet—and expanded the product line to include other portable and personal electronics. Mr. Williams left the firm in 1983 but not before developing plans for the company to enter the Hampton Roads market, which includes Norfolk, Suffolk, Portsmouth, Virginia Beach, and Chesapeake, Virginia. From 1983 through the first part of 1987, JMK opened 10 stores in the Hampton Roads area and moved from some of its older locations in Baltimore to larger, more updated facilities. The company's most recent store additions have been in the superstore format, which have approximately 20,000 square feet of selling space and carry a broad line of audio/video and other electronic products.

Operations

JMK Inc. currently operates 29 retail stores located in freestanding and strip-center locations. The company has about 300,000 square feet of selling space in all of its stores combined. Six of the stores are in a superstore format with approximately 20,000 square feet of selling space. Future expansion will emphasize the superstore concept. The remaining stores have from 5,000 to 10,000 square feet of selling space.

JMK's product mix is as follows:

Video Products (Primary VCRs)	40%
Audio Products	30
Televisions	15
Car Stereos	7
Portable and Personal Electronics	6
Tapes and Related Products	2
	100%

The company carries about 4,000 different items in inventory, purchased from about 100 vendors.

JMK has centralized operations, including purchasing, distribution, and advertising. It has an in-house advertising department and, like most of its competitors, spends heavily on advertising and promotion.

JMK's strategy, like that of others in the industry, is to be the leading consumer electronics retailer in its geographic area. The company offers a low-price guarantee, extensive selection, and good service after a sale.

Employees and Management

At fiscal year-end 1987, JMK employed approximately 550 employees, of whom 380 were hourly or salaried and 170 worked on a commission basis against a draw. Substantially all of the employees are employed full-time, and there are no collective bargaining agreements covering any of the employees.

Store personnel. Each store is staffed with a full-time manager, an assistant manager, sales personnel, stock personnel, and office personnel. The store managers are responsible for training the sales force, who are also instructed by manufacturers' representatives and attend outside sales training seminars. All store personnel receive continuous training by company management on products, product innovations, and selling techniques.

Executive management. *Robert Johnson* (40), prior to his death, was president of JMK. He was with the company since its formation in 1970 and was responsible for overall corporate strategy and expansion.

James Miller (40), executive vice president (also with the firm since its inception), worked very closely with Mr. Johnson on corporate planning and is also responsible for the company's marketing strategy, although a marketing manager handles day-to-day marketing decisions.

Kathleen Kelly (40), vice president–operations, is also one of the original company founders. She is responsible for the direct supervision of all store managers and for analyzing and improving store performance.

William Smith (38), vice president–finance, joined the company in 1980 after seven years in public accounting with Price Waterhouse. Mr. Smith is a CPA and a graduate of Ohio State University with a degree in finance. He is responsible for all of the company's accounting and financial functions.

It is anticipated that Mr. Miller will assume Mr. Johnson's responsibilities and take over as president of the company. Jane Hill, presently the marketing manager, will become vice president of marketing and assume Mr. Miller's marketing responsibilities. Ms. Hill has a master's degree in marketing from Cornell and started full-time with the company in 1985 as its marketing manager. She previously worked part-time for the company as a salesperson.

Total executive compensation is expected to be comparable to what it was in prior years.

Marketing

The company promotes its stores through an extensive advertising program. Advertising expense has accounted for 5 percent to 7 percent of total revenues over the past five years. Most of the company's advertisements appear on television and radio and in newspapers. Advertisements emphasize JMK's name and low prices, broad product selection, and customer service. Newspaper ads focus on specific products and prices, generally in connection with particular sales events and promotions. Most of JMK's advertisements are designed by its in-house staff, enabling the company to make timely changes in advertising copy. The company clusters its stores in its three marketing areas to maximize the efficiency of advertising and publicity as well as distribution.

Suppliers

The merchandise carried at the company stores consists almost entirely of nationally recognized, well-advertised, brand-name products purchased directly from about 100 different manufacturers. The company has no long-term merchandise purchase contracts, and during fiscal year 1987, no single supplier accounted for more than 10 percent of company purchases.

JMK, like many others in the industry, belongs to the National Association of Television Merchants (NATM), a purchasing group that, due to its size, can take advantage of volume discounts from manufacturers. NATM consists of a group of appliance and electronics retail sales companies, some of which are competitors of JMK. JMK makes approximately 25 percent of its purchases through this group, although it is not obligated to make any purchases and does not believe its ability to buy merchandise on favorable terms would be adversely affected if it were not a member of NATM. The company believes that adequate sources of supply will continue to exist for the merchandise sold in its stores.

Competition

The consumer electronics industry is highly competitive, with price and customer service being the primary competitive factors. The company's principal competitors include other specialty consumer electronic retailers, department stores, discount chain stores, and catalog showrooms.

The company believes it has established a leading market position in the Baltimore and Hampton Roads areas but commands only a number two or three market position in Washington, D.C. JMK's primary competitors, especially in Washington, D.C., are Circuit City Stores, Inc. (Circuit City) and Luskins, Inc. (Luskins). Circuit City is much larger than JMK. Washington, D.C. is one of the top retail markets in the country, and Circuit City is considered to have the largest market share. Luskins is comparable in size to JMK and competes with the company in all of its marketing areas. However, JMK believes it has the largest market share in Baltimore and Hampton Roads. Circuit City has announced plans to enter the Baltimore market, and although JMK has good locations for its stores, Circuit City has greater financial resources. Also, many of JMK's Baltimore stores are older and need remodeling and upgrading.

Facilities

JMK's headquarters are in Baltimore, Maryland. The headquarters facility, consisting of 8,000 square feet of office space and a 60,000-square-foot warehouse, was built approximately five years ago. Due to the company's rapid expansion in recent years, the warehouse facility is less than adequate for servicing JMK's 29 stores. JMK is looking for a warehouse to lease or purchase in the Norfolk area to service stores in that market.

Information on the company's leases for its retail stores is contained in Appendix 14A. The unexpired lease terms range from 6 months to 17 years, including options to renew. The average unexpired lease term of leased stores is approximately seven years. To date the company has had no difficulty in securing leases for suitable locations for retail stores. The company believes that as current leases expire, it will be able to either renew leases or obtain leases for comparable or better locations in the same general areas. Management believes that terms of leases are comparable to those of other companies in the industry.

Expansion Plans

The company has grown rapidly over the past five years, opening two stores per year. Given the outlook for lower growth in the consumer electronics market in the next few years, company management has indicated that it will be discontinuing its aggressive growth policy. JMK does plan to open one new store per year, preferably in a superstore format, but it will carefully analyze the market and location for each addition. It plans to continue expanding in the Hampton Roads area, where competition is less intense. It will focus in the near term on finding additional warehouse space in Norfolk and on upgrading some of its older stores in Baltimore and Washington, D.C. JMK plans to be able to finance the upgrading of stores and potential addition of one store per year through cash flows generated from operations and through additional debt, if necessary.

Summary of Positive and Negative Factors

Positive factors

1. The company has a leading market position in the Baltimore and Hampton Roads markets.
2. The company has secured key locations in the Baltimore and Hampton Roads market areas with fairly long-term leases.
3. The company has a strong, though fairly thin management team that is able to motivate its employees.
4. The company has a strong reputation for competitive prices and excellent service.

Negative factors

1. The industry is extremely price competitive, and JMK's major competitor, Circuit City, is much larger and has greater financial resources. Circuit City has secured the number-one market position in Washington, D.C. Luskins is another substantial competitor.
2. Circuit City has announced plans to enter the Baltimore market, which should increase price competition and reduce margins in the Baltimore stores.
3. The company currently has inadequate warehouse space and is therefore operating less efficiently than it should.
4. Many of the company's older stores, especially in Baltimore, need remodeling and enlargement. These improvements will involve finding new locations for some.

Prior Transactions in the Stock

On February 29, 1984, JMK repurchased 1,000 shares of common stock from a former employee, Mark Williams. The company paid $1,000 per share for the stock. The price was based on a previously agreed upon formula. This was not an arm's-length transaction, and this price does not necessarily represent the fair market value of the 1,000 shares at that time. Because this transaction occurred more than three years ago, and because it was not an arm's-length transaction, we did not use this transaction information in our appraisal of JMK's common stock for estate tax purposes as of July 21, 1987.

On September 30, 1986, Robert Johnson sold 1,700 shares of JMK's common stock to William Smith, another stockholder, for $1,300 per share. Mr. Smith paid Mr. Johnson a down payment of $250,000, with the balance paid over 10 years at an interest rate of prime plus 1 percent. Mr. Johnson sold the stock to diversify his assets. This was an arm's-length transaction that represented evidence of the stock's fair market value at that time. Since this transaction was at arm's length and took place less than one year ago, we considered it in our determination of the common stock's fair market value as of July 21, 1987.

THE SEARCH FOR COMPARATIVES

It often has been stated that all values are best tested and determined in the marketplace. However, when valuing the shares of a privately held company, no such marketplace exists. In valuing a minority interest, often the best alternative is to seek guidance from the prices investors are willing to pay for securities of similar, publicly traded companies with comparable financial and operating characteristics. With this information, it is then possible to come to the fair market value of shares that have no active market. Since we are not valuing a controlling interest, it is not necessary to analyze comparative merger and acquisition transactions.

The "willing buyer/willing seller" concept underlying this fair market value approach comes from the assumption that the buyer is seeking an equity participation in a particular industry and that "value" to the buyer is a function of the strength and quality of earnings, assets, dividend yield, and/or some other relevant variables.

To gain valuation guidance from this approach, we must identify a group of publicly traded comparative companies.

Selection of Comparative Companies

A first step in the search for comparative publicly traded companies is determining the appropriate Standard Industrial Code (SIC) number. JMK most closely resembles those companies appearing in SIC 5731, Radio, Television, and Consumer Electronics Stores. (Because S&P had not yet adjusted its SIC directories to the revised SIC codes as of this writing, this code number is SIC 5732, Radio and TV stores, in S&P *Corporation Records*.)

A search using the directory by SIC code in S&P's *Corporation Records* revealed 28 publicly traded companies in SIC 5732 (see Appendix 14B). Using S&P's *Corporation Records*, we examined a description of each of these companies in order to determine which of them were involved in businesses comparable to JMK's. We found eight companies to be comparable to JMK. After analyzing annual reports and SEC Forms 10-K for all of these companies, we eliminated Crazy Eddie, Inc., because it was in the process of being acquired, and Stereo Village, because it was in Chapter 11. We were left with six comparative companies. We also reviewed the descriptions of five more companies listed in a recent *Fortune* article about the retail consumer electronics industry and found all five to be comparable. All five companies had initial public offerings in the past year or two and did not appear in Standard & Poor's *Corporation Records*. Our final determination was based on the following selection criteria:

1. Retailer of consumer electronics with at least 75 percent of revenues derived from consumer electronics sales.
2. Revenues between $12 million and $1.2 billion.
3. Active public market for its stock.
4. Not currently involved in negotiations to be acquired or actually in the process of being acquired, because this typically affects the normal minority interest trading price of the stock.
5. Not in financial distress.

Based on these criteria, we determined that 11 companies were involved in businesses similar to JMK's. A brief description of each of these companies follows. Financial and market data on these companies are presented in subsequent sections of this report.

Description of Comparative Companies

Audio/Video Affiliates, Inc.   Audio/Video sells home entertainment and consumer electronic equipment at discount prices through 111 retail stores in 18 midwestern and southeastern states. For the year ended January 31, 1987, video products accounted for 62 percent of total sales; audio products, 23 percent; microwave ovens, 6 percent; and other appliances, 8 percent.

Best Buy Co., Inc.   Best Buy sells nationally recognized brand-name consumer video, audio, and photographic equipment and major home appliances through 27 superstores located in western Illinois, Iowa, Minnesota, Missouri, South Dakota, and Wisconsin. The company also operates videocassette rental stores adjacent to 19 of its 27 superstores.

Circuit City Stores, Inc.   Circuit City is one of the nation's leading specialty retailers of brand-name audio/video products and major appliances. It operates 87 stores in 11 southeastern states and California, and 53 of its retail outlets are superstores. The company plans to enter the Baltimore and Memphis markets and add six to ten superstores in the San Francisco Bay area in the coming year. During fiscal 1987, TVs accounted for 25 percent of Circuit City's total sales; VCRs, 27 percent; audio products, 21 percent; appliances, 18 percent; and other electronics, 9 percent.

The Federated Group, Inc.   Federated operates a chain of 65 home entertainment and consumer electronics superstores in California, Arizona, Texas, and Kansas.

Fretter, Inc.   Fretter is a large specialty retailer of brand-name home entertainment products, consumer electronics, and appliances. Fretter operates 47 stores in Michigan, Illinois, Ohio, Indiana, and Massachusetts. Video products, accounting for approximately 46 percent of total sales in fiscal 1987, represented the company's largest-volume product. Appliances accounted for approximately 25 percent of total sales and microwave ovens, audio, and personal electronics for the remaining 29 percent.

The Good Guys. Good Guys is a leading specialty retailer of competitively priced, brand-name consumer electronics products in the San Francisco Bay area, where it presently operates 12 stores. It plans to open new stores in northern California over the next two years, expanding its market area to a 200-mile radius from San Francisco.

Highland Superstores. Highland is one of the largest-volume retailers of consumer electronics and major home appliances. As of January 31, 1987, Highland operated 53 stores in major urban areas of Michigan, Ohio, Indiana, Illinois, Texas, and Louisiana. The company plans to add stores in the Milwaukee and Minneapolis/St. Paul areas and in New England.

Luskins, Inc. Luskins operates 53 specialty retail stores that sell nationally recognized brand-name home entertainment, consumer electronic, and major appliance products. The company's stores are located in Maryland, Washington, D.C., Virginia, Ohio, Kentucky, Connecticut, Indiana, and Michigan. Luskins' stores generally are located on major commercial thoroughfares. The company's total fiscal 1987 sales breakdown was as follows: TVs, 22 percent; video products, 21 percent; major appliances, 12 percent; audio and audio systems, 16 percent; and portable and personal electronics, 9 percent.

Newmark & Lewis, Inc. Newmark & Lewis is a specialty retailer of home entertainment and consumer electronic products and major appliances operating 42 stores in the New York metropolitan area and Connecticut. Newmark & Lewis' stores generally are located in freestanding buildings as opposed to shopping mall locations. The company plans to open six to eight new stores in fiscal 1988. During fiscal 1987, electronic products accounted for approximately 60 percent of sales. Appliances and air conditioners accounted for the remaining 40 percent.

Sound Advice, Inc. Sound Advice is a specialty retailer of brand-name entertainment and consumer electronic products. The company operates 12 stores in Florida. During fiscal 1986, audio products accounted for 47 percent of total sales; car stereos, 15 percent; televisions and VCRs, 34 percent; and miscellaneous items, 4 percent.

Tipton Centers, Inc. Tipton Centers is a large volume specialty retailer of brand-name consumer electronic products and major appliances. The company operates 24 stores in Missouri, Tennessee, Indiana, Iowa, Kentucky, and Illinois, 10 of which are in the St. Louis metropolitan area. During fiscal 1987, video products accounted for approximately 28 percent of total sales; televisions, 27 percent; major appliances, 20 percent; microwave ovens, 6 percent; audio products, 7 percent; air conditioners, 5 percent; service contracts and other items, 7 percent.

FINANCIAL STATEMENT ANALYSIS

Adjustments to Income Statements

Often adjustments must be made to a company's income statements to get a more accurate picture of long-term normal earning capacity and to depict a consistent set of operating data for analysis. Typical adjustments include those for extraordinary and/or nonrecurring items that may understate or overstate the reported results of normal operations.

Before presenting an analysis of JMK's performance over time, it is necessary to adjust the company's income statements for the fiscal years ending April 30, 1983, and April 30, 1987. During these two fiscal years, JMK's income statements included nonrecurring items.

During fiscal 1983, there was a fire in JMK's Baltimore headquarters warehouse. Portions of the fire loss were uninsured. As a result, JMK recorded a nonrecurring expense of $112,000 during fiscal 1983.

In fiscal 1987, JMK recorded nonrecurring income of $160,000. The company had been involved in litigation against a small competitor for trade-name infringement. The litigation was settled in February 1987 and, as a result, JMK recorded nonrecurring litigation settlement income of $160,000, net of legal fees, during fiscal 1987. There were no material costs associated with this litigation in prior years.

The following table shows the calculation of JMK's net income before nonrecurring items for fiscal 1983 and 1987.

	Fiscal Year Ended April 30	
	1987 **$000**	**1983** **$000**
Net Income as Reported	3,598	1,215
Nonrecurring Item	(160)	112
Tax Provision @ 46% Effective Tax Rate	74	(52)
Net Income before Nonrecurring Items	3,512	1,275

Trend Analysis

An essential step in the valuation of any company is an analysis of its performance over time. Past sales and earnings growth can indicate future growth and can put the company's current performance in a historical context. Other things being equal, a company with rapidly rising sales and earnings is worth more than one with little or no growth. The following sections examine the trend of JMK's income statements, balance sheets, and pertinent financial ratios over time.

Balance sheets. Exhibit 14–1 presents JMK's balance sheets as of April 30, 1983, through April 30, 1987. Total assets increased every year over the period and as of April 30, 1987, totaled $64.9 million, which translates into an average annual compound growth rate of 14 percent.

Total assets consisted mostly of current assets (64 to 67 percent of total assets) and amounted to $41.9 million at April 30, 1987. Inventory consistently has accounted for 41 percent to 45 percent of total assets and was $28.9 million at April 30, 1987. Inventories are stated at the lower of cost or market, with cost being determined by the first-in, first-out (FIFO) method. Accounts receivable typically have amounted to 6 percent of total assets. The remainder of current assets is primarily cash and marketable securities.

EXHIBIT 14-1

JMK, INC.
BALANCE SHEETS

| | As of April 30 | | | | | As of April 30 | | | | |
	1987 $000	1986 $000	1985 $000	1984 $000	1983 $000	1987 %	1986 %	1985 %	1984 %	1983 %
ASSETS										
Cash & Equivalents	7,009	7,451	8,166	6,225	5,072	10.8	13.6	16.6	14.3	13.4
Accounts & Notes Receivable	3,699	2,301	3,394	2,699	2,082	5.7	4.2	6.9	6.2	5.5
Inventory	28,878	23,338	20,316	18,806	16,694	44.5	42.6	41.3	43.2	44.1
Other Assets	2,336	1,698	1,181	1,175	946	3.6	3.1	2.4	2.7	2.5
Total Current Assets	41,922	34,788	33,057	28,905	24,794	64.6	63.5	67.2	66.4	65.5
Total Fixed Assets, Cost	27,145	24,120	20,123	17,891	16,089	41.8	44.0	40.9	41.1	42.5
Accumulated Depreciation	(4,886)	(4,672)	(4,333)	(3,656)	(3,408)	(7.5)	(8.5)	(8.8)	(8.4)	(9.0)
Total Net Fixed Assets	22,259	19,448	15,790	14,235	12,681	34.3	35.5	32.1	32.7	33.5
Other Assets	714	548	344	392	379	1.1	1.0	0.7	0.9	1.0
Total Assets	64,895	54,784	49,191	43,532	37,854	100.0	100.0	100.0	100.0	100.0
LIABILITIES & EQUITY:										
Liabilities:										
Current Liabilities:										
Accounts Payable, Trade	13,563	9,971	8,461	7,226	5,943	20.9	18.2	17.2	16.6	15.7
Current Maturity, L-T Debt	389	274	295	261	114	0.6	0.5	0.6	0.6	0.3
Accrued Liabilities	5,386	4,657	4,526	3,439	2,347	8.3	8.5	9.2	7.9	6.2
Total Current Liabilities	19,338	14,902	13,282	10,926	8,404	29.8	27.2	27.0	25.1	22.2
Long-Term Debt	7,369	5,424	4,919	4,397	2,163	11.4	9.9	10.0	10.1	5.7
Deferred Income Taxes	999	868	737	561	372	1.5	1.6	1.5	1.3	1.0
Total Liabilities	27,706	21,194	18,938	15,884	10,939	42.7	38.7	38.5	36.5	28.9
Stockholders' Equity:										
Common Stock	2,000	2,000	2,000	2,000	2,100	3.1	3.7	4.1	4.6	5.6
Retained Earnings	36,189	32,591	29,253	26,648	24,815	55.8	59.5	59.5	61.2	65.5
Treasury Stock	(1,000)	(1,000)	(1,000)	(1,000)	—	(1.5)	(1.8)	(2.0)	(2.3)	—
Total Stockholders' Equity	37,189	33,591	30,253	27,648	26,915	57.3	61.3	61.5	63.5	71.1
TOTAL LIABILITIES & STOCKHOLDERS' EQUITY	64,895	54,785	49,191	43,532	37,854	100.0	100.0	100.0	100.0	100.0
No. Shares Outstanding	20,000	20,000	20,000	20,000	21,000					
Book Value per Share	$1,859.45	$1,679.55	$1,512.65	$1,382.40	$1,305.48					

SOURCE: Reviewed financial statements, 1983-1987, and Willamette Management Associates, Inc. calculations.

Gross fixed assets totaled $27.1 million at April 30, 1987, and were only 18 percent depreciated, resulting in net fixed assets of $22.3 million. Net fixed assets typically have accounted for 32 to 36 percent of total assets. Property, buildings, and equipment are stated at cost. Depreciation is computed on the straight-line and declining-balance methods based on the assets' useful lives. The relatively low level of accumulated depreciation reflects JMK's addition of new superstores during the last five years. Other assets, typically accounting for about 1 percent of total assets, represent primarily officers' life insurance.

On the liability side of the balance sheet, current liabilities have increased slightly every year, from 22.2 percent of total assets in 1983 to 29.8 percent in 1987. Current liabilities consist mostly of accounts payable ($13.6 million at April 30, 1987) and accrued liabilities ($5.4 million at April 30, 1987). Total current liabilities have increased over the period, due primarily to increases in accounts payable.

JMK's long-term debt also has increased every year, from $2.2 million (5.7 percent of total assets) as of April 30, 1983, to $7.4 million (11.4 percent) as of April 30, 1987. The long-term debt has been used to finance remodeling of older stores and, more recently, construction of new stores.

Deferred income taxes amounted to $1.0 million, or 1.5 percent of total assets, as of April 30, 1987. Deferred taxes arise primarily from timing differences between depreciation expense reported for income tax and financial statement purposes.

Stockholders' equity stood at $37.2 million as of April 30, 1987, or $1,859.45 per share based on 20,000 shares outstanding. Over the 1983–1987 period, stockholders' equity has grown at an average annual compound rate of 8.4 percent. Overall, JMK was capitalized with 43 percent debt and 57 percent equity as of April 30, 1987.

Income statements. Exhibit 14–2 shows JMK's income statements over the 1983–1987 period. Total sales grew from $42.3 million in 1983 to $120.8 million in 1987, for a compound annual growth rate of 30.0 percent.

Gross profit margins have remained stable over the period at 28.5 to 30.5 percent. However, JMK's gross profit margin fell to 29.0 percent in 1987 from 30.5 percent in 1986 (the company's highest margin over the period). JMK's 1986 margin was somewhat higher due to some special discount prices obtained on a large purchase during the year. However, margins also declined in 1987 due to increased price competition, especially in the Washington, D.C., market.

Operating expenses also have been stable, at about 23 percent of sales, and were 23.4 percent in fiscal 1987. Payroll typically has made up the largest portion of operating expenses, accounting for 10.5 percent of sales in fiscal 1987. The next largest expense item is advertising, which accounted for 7.0 percent of sales in 1987. Advertising expense is the only operating expense item that has increased noticeably over the period. According to company management, it has been necessary to increase advertising due to increased competition in JMK's market areas.

JMK's operating margins increased every year from 5.4 percent in 1983 to 6.5 percent in 1986. However, in 1987 a higher cost of sales and higher advertising expenses relative to sales resulted in a fall in the company's operating margin to 5.6 percent, the second lowest over the period. Management expects the increased advertising expenses to continue.

Other income and expenses consist primarily of interest income on cash and equivalents and interest expense on long-term debt. Interest income has

EXHIBIT 14-2

JMK, INC
INCOME STATEMENTS

	Fiscal Years Ended April 30					Fiscal Years Ended April 30				
	1987 $000	1986 $000	1985 $000	1984 $000	1983 $000	1987 %	1986 %	1985 %	1984 %	1983 %
Total Sales	120,780	95,885	75,979	57,343	42,288	100.0	100.0	100.0	100.0	100.0
Cost of Goods Sold	85,754	66,640	53,793	40,484	30,236	71.0	69.5	70.8	70.6	71.5
Gross Margin	35,026	29,245	22,186	16,859	12,052	29.0	30.5	29.2	29.4	28.5
Sell., General & Administrative Expense:										
General & Administrative	6,160	5,178	4,179	3,269	2,580	5.1	5.4	5.5	5.7	6.1
Advertising	8,455	6,233	4,787	3,383	2,241	7.0	6.5	6.3	5.9	5.3
Payroll	12,682	10,659	8,054	6,365	4,609	10.5	11.2	10.6	11.1	10.9
Depreciation & Amortization	1,002	853	380	401	338	0.8	0.9	0.5	0.7	0.8
Total Operating Expenses	28,299	23,003	17,400	13,418	9,768	23.4	24.0	22.9	23.4	23.1
Operating Income	6,727	6,242	4,786	3,441	2,284	5.6	6.5	6.3	6.0	5.4
Other Income (Expenses):										
Interest Income	430	575	686	489	566	0.4	0.6	0.9	0.9	1.3
Interest Expense	(681)	(641)	(691)	(480)	(475)	(0.6)	(0.7)	(0.9)	(0.8)	(1.1)
Misc. Income (Expense)	142	(30)	25	(66)	(133)	0.1	—	—	(0.1)	(0.3)
Total Other Income (Expense)	(109)	(96)	20	(58)	(42)	(0.1)	(0.1)	—	(0.1)	(0.1)
Inc. (Loss) before Provision for Inc. Taxes	6,618	6,146	4,806	3,383	2,242	5.5	6.4	6.3	5.9	5.3
Provision for Taxes	3,020	2,809	2,201	1,549	1,027	2.5	2.9	2.9	2.7	2.4
Net Income	3,598	3,337	2,605	1,833	1,215	3.0	3.5	3.4	3.2	2.9
Net Income before Nonrecurring Items	$3,512[a]	$3,337	$2,605	$1,833	$1,275[b]	2.9	3.5	3.4	3.2	3.0
Weighted Average Shares Outstanding	20,000	20,000	20,000	20,833	21,000					
Earnings per Share before Nonrecurring Items	$175.60	$166.85	$130.25	$87.99	$60.71					

a. Before nonrecurring litigation settlement income of $86,000, net of tax effect.
b. Before nonrecurring fire loss expense of $60,000, net of tax effect.
SOURCE: Reviewed financial statements, 1983-1987, and Willamette Management Associates, Inc., calculations

declined as a percent of sales since 1983 due to a combination of declining interest rates and the fact that cash and marketable securities are a lower percentage of total assets. Interest expense as a percentage of total sales also has declined since 1983, despite increasing debt levels, due primarily to lower interest rates and rapidly increasing sales. Interest expense was $681,000, or 0.6 percent of sales, in fiscal 1987. JMK recorded net miscellaneous expenses in 1983, 1984, and 1986 and net miscellaneous income in 1985 and 1987. Included in this category is officers' life insurance premiums. For fiscal 1983, miscellaneous expenses of $133,000 included the nonrecurring fire loss charge of $112,000 noted earlier. During fiscal 1987, JMK recorded miscellaneous income of $142,000, or 0.1 percent of sales. This figure includes $160,000 of nonrecurring litigation settlement income, also discussed earlier.

JMK's net profit margins before nonrecurring items rose from 3.0 percent in 1983 to 3.5 percent in 1986 and fell to 2.9 percent in 1987 due to increased cost of sales and advertising expenses.

Overall, JMK's revenues have increased rapidly over the period, but the year-to-year increase has begun to slow. Sales increased 36 percent in 1984, 33 percent in 1985, and 26 percent in 1986 and 1987. The company's profitability peaked in fiscal 1986 and has since fallen to its lowest level over the period as increased competition and oversupply have led to price discounting.

Ratios.   Exhibit 14–3 illustrates some pertinent financial ratios for JMK from 1983 to 1987. Appendix 14C defines how these ratios were calculated. Ratios probably give an even better indication of changes in a firm's profitability or financial condition over time than either the income statements or

EXHIBIT 14-3

JMK, INC.
FINANCIAL AND OPERATING RATIOS

	1987	1986	1985	1984	1983
LIQUIDITY					
Current Ratio	2.2	2.3	2.5	2.6	3.0
Quick Ratio	0.6	0.7	0.9	0.8	0.9
Working Capital ($000s)	22,584	19,886	19,775	17,979	16,390
ACTIVITY					
Days in Receivables (Average)	9	11	15	15	NA
COGS/Inventory (Average)	3.3	3.1	2.8	2.3	NA
Sales/Working Cap. (Average)	5.7	4.8	4.0	3.3	NA
Sales/Net Fixed Assets (Average)	5.8	5.4	5.1	4.3	NA
Sales/Total Assets (Average)	2.0	1.8	1.6	1.4	NA
COVERAGE/LEVERAGE					
Interest Expense Coverage	10.4	10.6	8.0	8.0	6.0
Cash Flow/Current Maturity of LTD	11.6	15.3	10.1	8.6	14.1
Total Debt/Equity	0.75	0.63	0.63	0.57	0.41
LTD/LTD + Equity	0.17	0.14	0.14	0.14	.07
Fixed Assets/Equity	0.6	0.6	0.5	0.5	0.5
PROFITABILITY					
% Net Income/Sales	2.9	3.5	3.4	3.2	3.0
% Net Income/Equity (Average)	9.9	10.5	9.0	6.7	NA
% Net Income/Assets (Average)	7.8	6.4	5.6	4.5	NA
ANNUAL AVERAGE COMPOUND GROWTH					
% Growth in Sales	30.0	—	—	—	—
% Growth in Earnings	28.8	—	—	—	—

NOTE: All ratios using pretax and after-tax income in 1983 and 1987 have been adjusted to exclude nonrecurring items.

COGS = Cost of goods sold.
LTD = Long-term debt.
NA = Not available.
SOURCE: Reviewed financial statements, 1983-1987, and Willamette Management Associates, Inc. calculations.

balance sheets. The ratios utilizing pretax and after-tax income in 1983 and 1987 have been adjusted to exclude the nonrecurring items noted earlier.

The current ratio (current assets/current liabilities) provides a rough indication of a company's ability to service its current obligations. JMK's ratio generally declined over the period, from 3.0 to 2.2. The quick ratio (cash plus accounts receivable/current liabilities) measures the degree to which a company's current liabilities are covered by its most liquid assets. JMK's quick ratio also declined over the period, from 0.9 to 0.6.

Working capital measures the margin of protection of current creditors and reflects a company's ability to finance current operations. The dollar amount of working capital for JMK increased from $16.4 million in 1983 to $22.6 million as of April 30, 1987.

Activity ratios indicate how efficiently a company is utilizing its assets. All of JMK's activity ratios have improved over the period. JMK's average collection period (days in receivables) improved from 15 days in 1984 to 9 days in 1987. Inventory turnover (cost of sales/inventory) rose from 2.3 in 1984 to 3.3 in 1987. Working capital turnover indicates how efficiently a company employs its working capital. A low ratio may indicate an inefficient use of working capital, and a very high ratio often signifies "overtrading"—a vulnerable position for creditors. JMK's working capital turnover increased from 3.3 in 1984 to 5.7 in 1987 and would appear to be reasonable, although its reasonableness can be determined more adequately when compared to the ratios of the comparative companies. The company's fixed asset turnover and total asset turnover also have increased over the period, from 4.3 and 1.4, respectively, in 1984 to 5.8 and 2.0, respectively, in 1987. These activity ratios were not available in 1983 because they are based on average asset levels, and 1982 figures were unavailable.

A company's coverage ratios and leverage ratios indicate how heavily leveraged the company is. Highly leveraged firms are more vulnerable to business downturns than those with lower debt/net worth positions. However, while JMK became more leveraged over the period, it is important to compare its degree of leverage to the comparative companies' to see if it is in line with that of the industry. JMK's total debt/equity ratio rose from 0.41 in 1983 to 0.75 as of April 30, 1987, indicating that the company became more leveraged. JMK's long-term debt to total capital (long-term debt plus equity) has also increased, from 0.07 in 1983 to 0.17 in 1987. Fixed assets/equity remained fairly stable at 50 percent to 60 percent over the period. Despite increased leverage, JMK's coverage ratios generally have risen from 1983 to 1986 due to increased profitability and lower interest expense. However, both coverage ratios fell off slightly in 1987. The interest expense coverage ratio (earnings before interest and taxes/interest) measures the amount by which earnings could decline without impairing the firm's ability to meet its fixed interest payments. This ratio rose from 6.0 in 1983 to 10.4 in 1987. The cash flow/current maturities of long-term debt measures the amount by which cash flow (net income plus depreciation and amortization) could decline without impairing the firm's ability to meet its fixed principal payments. This ratio increased from a low of 8.6 in 1984 to a high of 15.3 in 1986 but fell off to 11.6 in 1987.

Profitability ratios typically assist in evaluating management performance. As noted earlier, JMK's net-income-to-sales ratio rose steadily from 1983 to 1986 and then declined to 2.9 percent (as adjusted) in 1987. The company's return on equity followed the same pattern. JMK's return on equity rose from 6.7 percent in 1984 to 10.5 percent in 1986 before falling to 9.9 percent in 1987. However, return on assets rose steadily, from 4.5 percent in 1984 to 7.8 percent in 1987.

Overall, JMK's ratios over time give mixed signals. The company's liquidity has declined from 1983 to 1987, but its activity ratios, and therefore asset utilization efficiency, have improved steadily. JMK's leverage has increased steadily but not dramatically, while coverage ratios generally have improved. The company's profitability generally peaked in 1986 and has since fallen off slightly.

Analysis of Comparative Publicly Traded Companies

While trend analysis is particularly helpful in identifying any trends of improvement or deterioration or deviations from the norm, it gives no indication of how JMK's balance sheet and operating performance compare with those of other firms in the industry. A comparison of JMK to publicly traded companies chosen as comparatives is particularly useful. Not only are the companies in this sample comparable to JMK in their size and lines of business, but this exercise can assist in choosing capitalization rates applicable to the value of JMK, which is the ultimate objective of this report.

Adjustments to comparative company income statements. In order to present JMK and the comparative publicly traded companies on a comparable basis, we analyzed the comparative companies financial statements to determine if any extraordinary and nonrecurring items were present. As a result, we made specific adjustments for nonrecurring and/or extraordinary items to two of the comparative companies' last fiscal year-end earnings.

Comparative Company	Nonrecurring and/or Extraordinary Item	Amount, Net of Tax Effect
Federated	Cumulative Effect of Charge	$864,000
Newmark & Lewis	Gain on Sale of Securities	332,828

None of the remaining nine comparative companies had nonrecurring or extraordinary items in their last fiscal year-end income statements.

Exhibit 14–4 and Exhibit 14–5 illustrate the last fiscal year-end balance sheet and income statement composition and various ratios of JMK and the comparative publicly traded companies.

Balance sheet composition. Exhibit 14-4 shows common-size balance sheets and income statements for JMK and the companies chosen as comparatives. Overall, JMK's total current assets as a percentage of total assets are less than the comparative companies'. All of the comparative companies use either a FIFO or average cost (which approximates FIFO) basis of inventory accounting. As noted earlier, JMK uses the FIFO inventory accounting method. Therefore, no adjustments for differences in inventory accounting methods are necessary. The average percentage of current assets for JMK was 64.6 percent, while the comparative companies' current assets represented 74.0 percent of total assets. JMK compares most closely to Fretter and Audio/Video with respect to percentage of current assets. Fretter and Audio/Video's current assets were 62.0 percent and 67.0 percent of total assets respectively, at their last fiscal year-ends.

At 34.3 percent of total assets, JMK's percentage of net fixed assets was larger than the 23.0 percent average for the comparative companies. In this category, JMK corresponds most closely to Highland and, again, Fretter and Audio/Video, whose net fixed assets accounted for 31.5 percent, 37.9 percent, and 32.3 percent of total assets, respectively.

JMK's other assets accounted for 1.1 percent of total assets, while for the comparative companies other assets (including goodwill) accounted for an average of 3.0 percent of total assets.

EXHIBIT 14-4

JMK INC.
AND COMPARATIVE PUBLICLY TRADED COMPANIES
COMPOSITION OF BALANCE SHEETS AND INCOME STATEMENTS

	Audio Video 1/87 %	Best Buy 3/87 %	Circuit City 2/87 %	Federated 3/87 %	Fretter 1/87 %	Good Guys 9/86 %	Highland 1/87 %	Luskins 1/87 %	Newmark & Lewis 1/87 %	Sound Advice 6/86 %	Tipton Centers 3/87 %	Average %	JMK 4/87 %
BALANCE SHEET ASSETS													
Cash & Equivalents	8.9	2.9	9.3	0.9	7.8	22.2	17.8	19.6	8.4	2.4	2.0	9.3	10.8
Accounts Receivable	1.8	7.8	3.4	6.7	2.2	6.0	3.6	4.3	4.7	42.8	10.0	8.5	5.7
Inventory	53.8	71.2	39.9	51.0	48.9	32.0	45.6	52.2	60.8	42.0	73.1	51.9	44.5
Other Current Assets	2.4	3.3	1.4	5.0	3.1	25.4	1.1	1.9	1.7	1.8	1.8	4.4	3.6
Total Current Assets	67.0	85.2	54.1	63.5	62.0	85.5	68.2	78.1	75.6	88.2	86.9	74.0	64.6
Net Fixed Assets	32.3	14.8	40.7	29.2	37.9	13.3	31.5	16.5	15.0	10.3	11.3	23.0	34.3
Goodwill	0.7	—	—	1.2	—	—	—	3.7	8.5	—	1.6	1.4	—
Other Assets	—	0.1	5.2	6.1	0.1	1.1	0.4	1.7	1.0	1.5	0.2	1.6	1.1
TOTAL ASSETS	100.0	100.0	100.0	100.0	100.0	100.0	100.0	100.0	100.0	100.0	100.0	100.0	100.0
LIABILITIES & EQUITY													
Liabilities:													
Current Liabilities:													
Accounts & Notes Payable	20.7	19.2	17.7	20.0	26.1	36.4	12.0	28.4	33.5	25.7	26.7	24.2	20.9
Accrued Expenses	—	4.1	9.2	3.0	1.3	6.4	7.7	4.1	13.8	1.6	3.1	4.9	8.3
Current Maturities LTD	0.2	0.5	0.3	0.5	—	—	0.4	0.1	—	15.9	2.3	1.8	0.6
Other Current Liabilities	3.9	5.7	—	—	6.4	2.7	5.2	6.2	4.1	0.7	1.3	3.3	—
Total Current Liabilities	24.8	29.5	27.1	23.5	33.8	45.5	25.3	38.8	51.4	43.9	33.4	34.3	29.8
Long-Term Debt	4.2	6.8	28.0	38.7	10.3[b]	—	26.3	21.3	3.8	1.1	—	12.8	11.4
Deferred Revenues	0.7	—	3.2	—	—	2.2	1.8	1.4	1.7	—	0.1	1.1	—
Other Liabilities	1.1	—	0.4	6.8	0.3	—	0.1	0.1	—	1.0	0.9	1.0	1.5
Total Liabilities	30.7	36.3	58.7	69.0	44.4	47.7	53.5	61.6	56.9	46.1	34.4	49.0	42.7
Stockholders' Equity	69.3	63.7	41.3	31.0	55.6	52.3	46.5	38.4	43.1	53.9	65.6	51.0	57.3
TOTAL LIABILITIES & EQUITY	100.0	100.0	100.0	100.0	100.0	100.0	100.0	100.0	100.0	100.0	100.0	100.0	100.0
INCOME STATEMENTS													
Net Sales	100.0	100.0	100.0	100.0	100.0	100.0	100.0	100.0	100.0	100.0	100.0	100.0	100.0
Cost of Sales	69.3	74.9	71.3	75.2	74.3	71.2	68.3	72.6	72.5	68.2	72.0	71.8	71.0
Gross Profit	30.7	25.1	28.7	24.8	25.7	28.8	31.7	27.4	27.5	31.8	28.0	28.2	29.0
Operating Expenses	24.5	18.8	21.1	26.5	22.9	25.9	25.8	26.5	22.6	24.0	22.9	23.8	23.4
Operating Profit	6.2	6.4	7.6	(1.7)	2.7	2.8	5.9	0.9	4.9	7.8	5.0	4.4	5.6
Other Income (Exp) Net	(0.3)	0.1	(0.5)	(1.1)	(0.2)	0.1	(0.4)	0.4	0.1	(0.4)	—	(0.2)	(0.2)
Pretax Income	6.0	6.5	7.1	(2.3)[a]	2.5	2.9	5.5	1.3	5.0[c]	7.4	5.1	4.2	5.4[d]
Income Taxes	2.7	3.3	3.6	(1.3)	1.0	1.4	2.4	0.6	2.5	3.4	2.4	2.0	2.5
NET INCOME	3.3	3.2	3.5	(1.4)[a]	1.5	1.6	3.1	0.7	2.5[c]	4.0	2.7	2.0	2.9

LTD = Long-term debt; LFYE = Last fiscal year end.
a. Before nonrecurring income from cumulative effect of change in accounting principle.
b. Included in other current liabilities.
c. Before nonrecurring gain on sale of securities, net of tax.
d. Before nonrecurring litigation settlement income.
SOURCE: Individual companies annual reports and Forms 10-K and Willamette Management Associates, Inc. calculations.
NOTE: Medians are not presented because they do not sum to 100%.

EXHIBIT 14-5

JMK, INC.
AND COMPARATIVE PUBLICLY TRADED COMPANIES
FINANCIAL AND OPERATING RATIOS

	Audio/ Video 1/87	Best Buy 3/87	Circuit City 2/87	Federated 2/87	Fretter 1/87	Good Guys 9/86	Highland 1/87	Luskins 1/87	Newmark & Lewis 1/87	Sound Advice 6/86	Tipton Centers 3/87	Average	Median	JMK 4/87
LIQUIDITY														
Current Ratio	2.7	2.9	2.0	2.7	1.8	1.9	2.7	2.0	1.5	2.0	2.6	2.3	2.0	2.2
Quick Ratio	0.4	0.4	0.5	0.3	0.3	0.6	0.8	0.6	0.3	1.0	0.4	0.5	0.4	0.6
Working Capital ($000)	48,156	48,750	97,320	77,596	30,758	13,310	105,172	18,603	13,857	5,297	14,505	43,029	30,758	22,584
ACTIVITY														
Days in Receivables (Avg.)	7	8	4	10	1	7	6	4	3	6	9	6	6	9
COGS/Inventory (Avg.)	3.2	4.2	5.5	3.7	4.7	7.5	3.8	4.1	5.7	4.2	3.6	4.6	4.2	3.3
Sales/Working Cap. (Avg.)	4.4	7.8	13.4	6.3	12.3	11.0	7.7	8.8	17.3	6.1	7.7	9.3	7.8	5.7
Sales/Net Fixed Assets (Avg.)	7.7	29.6	8.8	8.0	13.7	24.9	10.9	21.6	30.1	27.1	36.8	19.9	21.6	5.8
Sales/Total Assets (Avg.)	2.1	4.0	3.3	2.3	3.2	3.8	3.0	3.2	4.1	3.1	3.8	3.3	3.2	2.0
COVERAGE/LEVERAGE														
Int. Expense Coverage	23.9	NA	14.8	Df	5.0	NM	11.1	3.8	17.6[c]	23.8	27.0	15.9	16.2	10.4[d]
Cash Flow/Curr. Mat. LTD	31.6	29.3	28.6	0.3[a]	18.2	NM	34.8	44.5	NM	0.9	5.3	21.5	28.6	11.6[d]
Fixed Assets/Equity	0.5	0.2	1.0	0.9	0.4	0.3	0.7	0.2	0.3	0.2	0.2	0.4	0.3	0.6
LTD/LTD + Equity	0.06	0.10	0.40	0.56	0.16	—	0.36	0.18	0.08	0.02	—	0.17	0.10	0.17
Total Debt/Equity	0.44	0.57	1.42	2.22	0.80	0.91	1.15	0.62	1.32	0.65	0.52	1.0	0.85	0.75
PROFITABILITY														
% Net Income/Sales	3.3	3.2	3.5	(1.4)[a]	1.5	1.6	3.1	0.7	2.5[c]	4.0	2.7	2.2	2.7	2.9[d]
% Net Income/Equity (Avg.)	10.0	22.1	27.1	(9.5)[a]	9.7	12.1	19.4	2.1	24.5[c]	25.6	18.9	14.7	18.9	9.9[d]
% Net Income/Assets (Avg.)	6.9	13.0	11.7	(3.2)[a]	4.7	5.9	9.3	2.1	10.3[c]	12.2	10.1	7.5	9.3	7.8[d]
ANNUAL AVERAGE COMPOUND GROWTH														
% Growth in Sales	32.3	103.3	42.4	48.2	32.6	30.2	39.0	27.4	35.1	31.7	36.8	41.7	35.1	30.0
% Growth in Earnings	27.5	201.0	59.1	—[b]	13.9	24.4	45.3	1.1	93.2[c]	45.3	87.9	59.9	45.3	28.8[d]
OTHER														
Sales per Store ($000)	2,159	9,979	11,617	6,717	5,799	7,456	12,386	2,642	5,344	2,129	3,484	6,337	5,799	4,165
Sales per Sq. Ft. Sell. Space ($)	965	1,053	1,489	NA	NA	1,427	909	NA	800	NA	456	1,014	965	403

COGS = Cost of goods sold.
LTD = Long-term debt.
NA = Not available
Df = Deficit
NM = Not meaningful.

[a] Before nonrecurring income from cumulative effect of change in accounting principle.
[b] Company had a deficit; therefore, growth calculation was not meaningful.
[c] Before nonrecurring gain on sale of securities.
[d] Before nonrecurring litigation settlement income.

Overall, JMK holds fewer of its assets in the form of current assets than the majority of the comparative companies, while more of its assets are in the form of fixed assets. The comparative companies whose asset structures are most similar to JMK's are Highland, Fretter, and Audio/Video.

On the liability side, JMK has a slightly smaller percentage of current liabilities than the comparatives (29.8 percent versus 34.3 percent for the comparatives). JMK also operates with a slightly smaller percentage of long-term debt than the comparative companies (11.4 percent vs. 12.8 percent).

Overall, JMK's capitalization of 42.7 percent debt and 57.3 percent equity corresponds closely with the average comparative company capitalization of 49.0 percent debt and 51.0 percent equity.

Income statement composition. As Exhibit 14–4 shows, JMK's gross margin was very similar to the comparative companies'. The average gross margin for the comparative companies was 28.2 percent, while JMK's was 29.0 percent.

JMK's operating margin of 5.6 percent was above the 4.4 percent average exhibited by the comparative companies, due mainly to JMK's slightly higher gross margin.

JMK's other expenses (excluding nonrecurring income) were 0.2 percent of total revenues, the same as the average for the comparative companies.

The combination of slightly lower cost of sales (71.0 percent versus 71.8 percent) and operating expenses (23.4 percent versus 23.8 percent) resulted in JMK exhibiting a higher net profit margin than the average of the comparative companies. JMK's net income (excluding nonrecurring income) as a percentage of total revenues was 2.9 percent, while the average for the comparative companies was 2.0 percent.

Ratios. Exhibit 14–5 shows various operating and financial ratios for JMK and the comparative publicly traded companies. All ratios utilizing pretax and after-tax income have been adjusted to exclude nonrecurring items.

JMK's liquidity, as measured by the current and quick ratios, was close to the median of the comparative companies. As Exhibit 14-5 shows, all of JMK's activity ratios are below the comparative company medians, indicating that the company uses its assets less efficiently than the comparatives. However, as noted in the "Trend Analysis" section, JMK's activity ratios have improved steadily since 1984. Working capital turnover is on the low side but is similar to that of three of the comparative companies.

JMK's coverage ratios, as measured by interest expense coverage and cash flow coverage of currently maturing long-term debt, are significantly below the median of the comparative companies. However, at 10.4 and 11.6, respectively, JMK's interest expense coverage and cash flow coverage of currently maturing long-term debt are more than adequate.

JMK has slightly more of its total capital in the form of long-term debt than the comparative companies, as is evidenced by JMK's long-term-debt-to-total-capital ratio of .17 versus .10 for the comparative company median. However, JMK's total debt-to-equity ratio of .75 is less than the comparative company median of .85.

The profitability ratios indicate that JMK's less efficient use of assets and slightly lower use of leverage have resulted in return-on-equity and return-on-asset ratios that are below the comparative company medians. JMK's return on equity was 9.9 percent versus a median of 18.9 percent for the comparative companies and its return on assets 7.8 percent versus a median of 9.3 percent. JMK's net profit margin of 2.9 percent was slightly above the comparative company median of 2.7 percent.

JMK's sales and earnings growth at 30.0 percent and 28.8 percent, respectively, were also below the comparative company medians of 35.1 percent and 45.3 percent, respectively.

In the consumer electronics industry, the sales per store and sales per square foot of selling space are analyzed to determine potential profitability on a per-store basis. JMK's sales per store, at $4.165 million, was below the median of $5.799 million but higher than Audio/Video, Luskins, Sound Advice and Tipton Centers'. Also, many of these stores sell appliances, which greatly increases sales per store. JMK's sales per square foot of selling space was $403, well below the median of $965 but this information was unavailable for four companies, three of which had below-average sales per store. Tipton Centers, with $456 of sales per square foot of selling space, was the most comparable to JMK.

The preceding ratio analysis indicates that JMK's liquidity is about average when compared to the comparative companies, its coverage is below average but adequate, and its overall capitalization is about average. However, JMK's less efficient use of assets has resulted in below-average return on equity, return on assets, and growth.

APPRAISAL OF FAIR MARKET VALUE

Valuation Approaches

Several approaches for valuing closely held companies are available. The conventional approaches typically include some form of earning power appraisal, asset appraisal, or a combination of the two. After a review of several approaches, it is our opinion that the most appropriate approaches to consider for appraising JMK's fair market value are capitalization of earnings, price/revenues and price/book value. These three approaches rely on data from publicly traded comparative companies. We also looked at the value indicated by a prior arm's-length transaction in JMK's stock.

Comparative valuation analysis is a technique that provides an indicated publicly traded equivalent value based on direct comparison of the subject company stock to stocks of publicly traded companies involved in the same or similar lines of business. As provided in the comparative search section of this report, we have identified a group of publicly traded companies that we consider suitable for comparison with JMK. The public market stock price data and underlying fundamental data will be used in these approaches.

A *value measure* (multiple or divisor) relates a stock's price to various underlying fundamental data, such as earnings, revenues, and book value. Each measure provides an easily identifiable basis for ascertaining the public market's perception of a stock's value or, stated in investment jargon, the market's capitalization or discounting of a company's underlying fundamentals. Value measures generally take into account the trends in growth, performance, and stability of these underlying fundamental data. In this manner, the business and financial risk associated with an industry or group of companies can be viewed in relation to return expectations. For example, as discussed in the industry section, the growth prospects for this industry are much lower than what was realized over the past five years. In fact, expectations for the industry fell in the first six months of 1987 as price competition reduced margins and profitability. As would be expected, these lower expectations were followed by a significant drop in value measures in the first six months of 1987.

The value measures also reflect the outlook for the economy as a whole. In addition, the value measures for each comparative company reflects the economic outlook of the geographic region in which it operates. Several of the comparative companies operate in the same geographical region as JMK. In analyzing the historical and projected growth in earnings for both the comparative companies and JMK, we have considered the regional economic outlooks of the comparative companies as compared to JMK.

In analyzing the consumer electronics industry and the comparative companies, we chose the standard underlying fundamental data of earnings, revenues, and book value as the variables to relate to their market prices as of July 21, 1987. We developed a series of value measures for each comparative company. Exhibit 14–6 reflects financial data for JMK and the comparative companies and the market value measures compiled for our group of comparative companies. We have reviewed and analyzed the financial statements of the comparative companies. In doing so, we discovered certain nonrecurring and/or extraordinary items. The data in Exhibit 14–6 exclude these items, and any adjustments are footnoted. The range, mean, and median for the comparatives for each value measure as of July 21, 1987, are summarized below.

Value Measures	Mean	Median	Range
Price/Current Earnings	15.7	12.1	10.7 -21.0
Price/5-Year Average Earnings	14.7	15.5	7.3 -19.3
Price/Current Revenues	0.39	0.30	0.15- 0.74
Price/Book Value	2.03	1.71	1.07- 5.13

In our opinion, the median is more representative than the mean because it is not skewed by one or two relatively high or low numbers.

Approaches Considered but Not Used

Capitalization of dividends. We did not use a capitalization of dividends approach because not only has JMK never paid a dividend but only one of the eleven comparative companies paid a dividend, and that was very small (Circuit City pays a $.06 annual dividend for a dividend yield of only .2 percent). JMK's management indicated to us that it does not intend to pay a dividend in the near future, as it is going to retain earnings to fund the remodeling of older stores and opening of new ones.

Capitalization of cash flow. We did not use a capitalization of cash flow approach because the comparative publicly traded retail consumer electronic stores have a relatively small amount of depreciation and therefore there was little difference between earnings and cash flow for JMK and the comparative companies. Also, JMK and the comparative companies for the most part utilized similar depreciation methods and had similar levels of fixed assets. Therefore, a capitalization of cash flow approach, while not inappropriate, was not necessary in this case.

Debt-free approach. In some cases, it is appropriate to use a debt-free approach in the valuation. In the debt-free approach, market valuation parameters are developed on a debt-free basis, that is, assuming the company has no financial leverage. Using debt-free approaches helps eliminate distortions in value that might occur if the subject company has a capital structure that differs significantly from the comparative companies'. Market value ratios are computed with the market value of invested capital in the numerator

EXHIBIT 14-6

JMK INC.
AND COMPARATIVE PUBLICLY TRADED COMPANIES--FINANCIAL AND MARKET DATA

	Mkt.	Lat. 12 Mos. Revenues $000s	FYE	Lat. 12 Mos. RPS $	Lat. 12 Mos. EPS $	End	Earnings per Share 1987 $	1986 $	1985 $	1984 $	1983 $	5-Yr. Avg. EPS $	1983-1987 EPS Cmpd Grth Rate %
Audio / Video Affiliates, Inc. [a]	NYSE	232,115	Jan	14.78	0.43	Apr	0.48	0.58	0.54	0.48	0.30	0.48	12.5
Best Buy Co., Inc. [b]	OTC	239,496	Mar	30.18	0.98	Mar	0.98	0.66	0.29	0.07	0.05	0.41	110.4
Circuit City Stores, Inc.	NYSE	1,010,692	Feb	48.59	1.72	May	1.58	0.99	0.97	0.62	0.31	0.89	50.3
Federated Group, Inc.	OTC	431,266	Feb	40.05	(0.71)	May	(0.57)	0.98	0.92[g]	0.77	0.13	0.45	NM
Fretter, Inc. [c]	NASD	269,752	Jan	17.53	0.03	Apr	0.27	0.54	0.31	0.27	0.18	0.31	10.7
The Good Guys [d]	NASD	89,473	Sep	23.94	0.40	Mar	0.35	0.64	0.21	0.24	0.17	0.37	19.8
Highland Superstores	OTC	667,317	Jan	36.55	0.99	Apr	1.11	1.36	0.97[h]	0.54[i]	0.30[i]	0.86	38.7
Luskins, Inc.	NASD	138,487	Jan	29.62	0.07	Apr	0.20	0.92	0.94	0.74	0.20[j]	0.60	0.0
Newmark & Lewis, Inc. [d]	ASE	224,589	Jan	36.20	0.75[f]	Apr	0.86[f]	0.67	0.51	0.25	0.08	0.47	81.1
Sound Advice, Inc. [d]	NASD	32,939	Jun	11.37	0.45	Mar	0.41	0.27	0.11	0.09[j]	(0.10)[k]	0.27[j]	NM
Tipton Centers, Inc.	NASD	83,633	Mar	27.99	0.75	Mar	0.75	0.31	0.67	0.35	0.07[k]	0.53	80.9
JMK Inc. [e]	-	120,780	Apr	6,039.00	175.60	Apr	175.60	166.35	130.25	87.99	60.71	124.28	30.4

	Bid/Close Price 7/21/87 $	P/E Ratio Latest 12 Mos.	5-Yr. Average	Price/ Lat. 12 Mos. RPS Ratio	Latest 12 Mos. ROS %	Latest Interim Book Value[m] per Share $	Price/ Book Value Ratio	Latest 12 Mos. ROE %	5-Yr. Average ROE %	Ind. Annual Dividend $	Dividend Yield %
Audio / Video Affiliates, Inc. [a]	7.750	18.0	16.3	0.52	2.9	5.08	1.52	8.5	9.4	None	-
Best Buy Co., Inc. [b]	16.250	16.6	NM	0.54	3.2	6.75	2.41	14.5	6.0	None	-
Circuit City Stores, Inc.	36.125	21.0	NM	0.74	3.5	7.04	5.13	24.4	12.7	0.06	0.2
Federated Group, Inc.	6.000	Df	13.3	0.15	(1.8)	5.51	1.09	(12.9)	8.1	None	-
Fretter, Inc. [c]	4.875	NM	15.5	0.28	0.2	3.80	1.28	0.8	8.3	None	-
The Good Guys [d]	4.750	11.9	12.9	0.20	1.7	4.46	1.07	9.0	8.3	None	-
Highland Superstores	11.000	11.1	12.9	0.30	2.7	6.42	1.71	15.4	13.3	None	-
Luskins, Inc.	4.375	NM	7.3	0.15	0.2	3.40	1.29	2.1	17.6	None	-
Newmark & Lewis, Inc. [d]	8.000	10.7	16.9	0.22	2.1	3.21	2.49	23.4	14.8	None	-
Sound Advice, Inc. [d]	5.125	11.4	19.3	0.45	4.0	2.46	2.08	18.3	10.8	None	-
Tipton Centers, Inc.	9.250	12.3	17.5	0.33	2.7	5.41	1.71	13.9	9.8	None	-
Mean		15.7	14.7	0.39	1.8		2.03	8.5	9.5		
Median		12.1	15.5	0.30	2.7		1.71	13.9	9.8		
Low		10.7	7.3	0.15	1.8		1.07	(12.9)	6.0		
High		21.0	19.3	0.79	4.0		5.13	24.4	17.6		
JMK Inc. [e]	-	-	-	-	2.9	1,859.45	-	9.4	6.7	None	

FYE = Fiscal year-end.
EPS = Earnings per share.
RPS = Revenues per share.
P/E = Price / earnings.
Df = Deficit.
NM = Not meaningful.
ROS = Return on sales.
ROE = Return on equity.

[a] Company changed fiscal year-end in 1985 from October to January; unaudited statements were used for 1985.
[b] All per-share data adjusted for January 1987 3-for-2 stock split; 1983 data are for the seven months ended March 31, 1983.
[c] Company changed its fiscal year-end from April 30 to January 31 in 1986.
[d] Data are for fiscal years ending 1982-1986.

[e] All earnings-per-share figures adjusted to exclude nonrecurring items in 1983 and 1987.
[f] Before nonrecurring gain on sale of securities of $0.06 per share, net of tax.
[g] Before net gain on sale of leasehold interest of $2,502,000, or $0.25 per share.
[h] Earnings per share after charges, in lieu of income tax for Subchapter S corporation.

[i] Before extraordinary income of $0.03 per share, net of tax.
[j] Before extraordinary gain of $0.05 per share, net of tax.
[k] Before extraordinary income of $0.05 per share, net of tax.
[l] Includes latest 12 months as fifth year.
[m] Book value of common equity less intangible assets.

SOURCE: Standard & Poor's Corporation Records; company annual reports; SEC Forms 10-K and 10-Q; The Wall Street Journal, July 22, 1987; CompuServe; and Willamette Management Associates, Inc. calculations.

and the pro forma values of relevant variables (earnings, cash flow, book value), as though the company had no interest-bearing debt, in the denominator. In this particular case, since JMK's capital structure is very similar to the average of the comparative companies, it was not necessary to use a debt-free approach.

Capitalization of Earnings

In using a capitalization of earnings approach, two variables must be determined—an appropriate earnings base to capitalize and a capitalization rate to apply to those earnings. In the case of JMK, we chose to capitalize the company's fiscal 1987 earnings (which were the latest 12 months' earnings available as of July 21, 1987), five-year average earnings, and 1988 projected earnings. While in high-growth industries such as this a weighted average earnings approach often is appropriate, the current industry outlook indicates that this level of growth probably will not continue. In addition, many of the comparative companies had a significant drop in earnings in the latest 12-month period, but, according to industry earnings estimates, these earnings levels are expected to bounce back. Thus, in our opinion a five-year weighted average earnings base is less representative of a sustainable level of earnings for either JMK or the comparative companies because it would place the greatest weight on the most recent earnings. In addition, we take into account JMK's most recent earnings in the capitalization of latest 12 months' earnings approach.

In choosing capitalization rates for these earnings bases, we looked at the P/E ratios of the comparative publicly traded companies.

Latest 12 months' earnings. JMK's fiscal 1987 earnings per share (EPS) before nonrecurring income were $175.60. In choosing an appropriate P/E ratio for JMK's earnings, it is important to compare JMK's earnings pattern and growth to the comparative companies'. JMK's earnings increased steadily over the period, although growth slowed considerably in 1987. Three of the comparative companies (Federated, Fretter, and Luskins) had significant earnings drops in 1987 and the latest 12-month period and, due to the substantial differences in their earnings patterns from JMK's, should not be considered in this approach. Two of the companies (Best Buy and Circuit City) continued to have substantial growth in earnings and their historical earnings, growth has been substantially above JMK's (110 percent and 50 percent versus 30 percent); thus, they were also excluded from consideration in this aproach. The remaining six comparative companies have experienced either a slowdown in earnings growth or a slight earnings decline in the latest 12-month period and therefore were most suitable for comparison with JMK. These companies and their P/E ratios and growth rates are shown below.

	Latest 12 Months P/E Ratio	1983-1987 Average Annual Compound Earnings Growth
Audio/Video	18.0	12.5
Good Guys	11.9	19.8
Highland	11.1	38.7
Newmark & Lewis	10.7	81.1
Sound Advice	11.4	NM
Tipton	12.3	80.9
Median	11.7	38.7
JMK Inc.	—	30.4

JMK's historical growth was below the average of these six companies, but there was very little correlation in this case between earnings growth and P/E ratios. Therefore, we chose a multiple of 11.5, close to the median for this group as appropriate for JMK. With the exception of Audio/Video, these P/E ratios fell in a very narrow range from 10.7 to 12.3, thus providing a good indication of value and supporting the choice of a P/E ratio of 11.5 for JMK. Applying a P/E ratio of 11.5 produced the following indicated value:

$$\frac{\text{Latest 12 Mos.}}{\text{EPS}} \times \frac{\text{P/E Ratio}}{11.5} = \frac{\text{Indicated Value Per Share}}{\$2,019.40}$$
$$\$175.60$$

Five-year average earnings. JMK's five-year average earnings per share before nonrecurring items were $124.28. Again, in choosing an appropriate P/E ratio for these earnings, it is important to focus on the comparative companies with the most similar earnings pattern and growth. We again looked at the P/E ratios of the same six companies for reasons discussed earlier; these are shown in the following table:

	P/E Ratio
Audio/Video	16.3
Good Guys	12.9
Highland	12.9
Newmark & Lewis	16.9
Sound Advice	19.3
Tipton	17.5
Mean	16.6

These ratios also fell in a fairly tight range, from 12.9 to 19.3, thus providing a good indication of value. We chose a multiple of 16.5, which was close to this median of 16.6 as appropriate for JMK, producing the following indicated value:

$$\frac{\text{Five-Year Average EPS}}{\$124.28} \times \frac{\text{P/E Ratio}}{16.5} = \frac{\text{Indicated Value per Share}}{\$2,050.62}$$

Projected 1988 earnings. JMK prepares no formal projections or forecasts. However, management has indicated to us that it expects to realize bottom-line net income of $3.9 million in fiscal 1988, or $195.00 per share, which represents an 11.0 percent increase over 1987's earnings before nonrecurring items of $175.60 per share.

Exhibit 14–7 presents 1988 earnings estimates for all of the comparative companies and the indicated P/E ratios based on them. The P/E ratios ranged from 8.8 to 18.2, with a mean of 11.9 and a median of 10.5. In our opinion, the median is more representative than the mean, which is skewed upward by Federated's and Fretter's multiples of 18.2 and 16.3, respectively. Both these companies are coming off losses in the current year, and their 1988 forecasted earnings are not yet expected to be back to a normal level.

Long-term earnings growth forecasts were available for only 8 of the 11 comparative companies, but they do indicate that forecasted growth is, in

EXHIBIT 14-7

JMK INC.
Comparative Publicly Traded Companies
1988 Earnings Estimates

	Bid/Close Price 7/21/87 $	1988 Median Earnings Estimates $	No. of Estimates	Price/Earnings Ratio	Median Long-Term Growth Projection %
Audio /Video Affiliates	7.750	0.55	11	14.1	15.0
Best Buy Co.	16.250	1.32	8	12.3	25.0
Circuit City Stores	36.125	2.24	14	16.1	25.0
Federated Group, Inc.	6.000	0.33	9	18.2	15.0
Fretter, Inc.	4.875	0.30	3	16.3	6.2
The Good Guys	4.750	0.53[a]	4	9.0	11.0
Highland Superstores	11.000	1.05	9	10.5	18.0
Luskins, Inc.	4.375	0.50	1	8.8	NA
Newmark & Lewis, Inc.	8.000	0.90	4	8.9	12.0
Sound Advice, Inc.	5.125	0.70	1	7.3	NA
Tipton Centers, Inc.	9.250	1.00	1	9.3	NA
			Mean	11.9	
			Median	10.5	

NA = Not available
[a] Average of fiscal 1987 and 1988 earnings because company has a September 30 fiscal year-end.
SOURCE: Institutional Brokers Estimate System, Exhibit 14-6, and Willamette Management Associates, Inc. calculations.

most cases, anticipated to be less than half of historical growth. Since this is also expected for JMK, and because the earnings growth JMK's management expects is in line with what is expected for the comparative companies, we chose the median ratio of 10.5 as appropriate for JMK, producing the following indicated value:

$$\frac{1988 \text{ EPS}}{\$195.00} \times \frac{\text{P/E Ratio}}{10.5} = \frac{\text{Indicated Value per Share}}{\$2,047.50}$$

Price/Revenues Approach

A capitalization of revenues approach often is considered an appropriate approach to valuation. In a way, it can be considered a derivative of a capitalization of earnings approach, since generally there is an implicit assumption that a certain level of sales should be able to generate a particular level of earnings in a given type of business.

Like the earnings approach, the price/revenues approach requires determining two variables—the revenues base and an appropriate price/revenues (P/R) multiple. In the case of JMK, we chose to use only the latest 12 months' revenues because current revenues represent a sustainable base for JMK and the comparative companies. Revenues for all companies have grown considerably, and growth is expected to continue at a moderate pace in the future. In choosing an appropriate P/R multiple for JMK's revenues, we analyzed the correlation between net profit margin for the latest 12 months and the P/R ratios for the comparative companies. We found a fairly good correlation after excluding the outliers, as can be seen in Table 14–8. However, there is a sizable gap between the P/R multiple for a company with a 2.7 percent profit margin and one with a 2.9 percent margin. Tipton, with a 2.7 percent profit margin, traded at a P/R multiple of 0.33, while Audio/Video, with a 2.9 percent margin, traded at a P/R multiple of 0.52. This is a considerable gap in multiples for a small increase in profitability.

	P/R Ratio	Latest 12 Months' Net Profit Margin
		%
Luskins	0.15	0.2
Good Guys	0.20	1.7
Newmark & Lewis	0.22	2.1
Highland	0.30	2.7
Tipton	0.33	2.7
Audio/Video	0.52	2.9
Best Buy	0.54	3.2
Circuit City	0.74	3.5

We chose a P/R multiple of 0.40 for JMK, which is above the median of 0.30. We found 0.40 to be appropriate considering the facts that JMK has an above-median (2.7 percent) net profit margin of 2.9 percent and Audio/Video's multiple appears to be on the high side relative to the company's current profit margin. Applying this multiple to JMK's latest 12 months' revenues per share (RPS) of $6,039.00 results in an indicated value as follows:

$$\frac{\text{Latest 12 Months' RPS}}{\$6,039.00} \times \frac{\text{P/R Ratio}}{0.40} = \frac{\text{Indicated Value per Share}}{\$2,415.60}$$

Price/Book Value Approach

Several empirical studies have shown that how much an investor will pay for a given amount of equity in a company depends heavily on how great a return on its equity capital that company has made or is expected to make. Therefore, a relationship between return-on-equity (ROE) and the price/book value (P/BV) multiple for the comparative publicly traded companies should exist. In general, the greater a company's ROE, the higher its P/BV multiple tends to be. In developing a P/BV multiple to apply to JMK's latest fiscal year-end book value per share of $1,859.45, we looked at the publicly traded comparative companies shown in Exhibit 14–6 for guidance. For our 11 comparative companies, P/BV multiples ranged from a low of 1.07 to a high of 5.13, with a median of 1.71. Analysis of the comparative companies' ROEs for both the latest 12 months and five-year average indicates that while there is some correlation, the relationship is less clear than one would expect.

However, comparison of JMK's latest 12-month ROE and 5-year average ROE of 9.3 percent and 6.6 percent, respectively, with the medians for the comparative companies of 13.9 percent and 9.8 percent respectively, indicates that the P/BV multiple applicable to JMK should be somewhat below the median of 1.71. We found that JMK's ROE was most comparable to the ROE for Fretter, at 9.0 percent (latest 12 months) and 8.3 percent (5-year average), and for Audio/Video Affiliates, 8.5 percent and 9.4 percent, respectively. Fretter had a P/BV multiple of 1.07, while Audio/Video's P/BV multiple was 1.52. The average of the two is 1.30, which represents a roughly 24 percent discount from the median multiple for the entire group. We consider such a discount reasonable considering that JMK's latest 12 months' ROE and five-year average ROE are approximately 33 percent below the respective medians for the comparative companies. Applying a multiple of 1.30 to JMK's book value per share (BVPS) of $1,859.45 gives us an indicated value of $2,417.29 per share:

$$\frac{\text{BVPS}}{\$1,859.45} \times \frac{\text{P/BV Ratio}}{1.30} = \frac{\substack{\text{Indicated} \\ \text{Value} \\ \text{per Share}}}{\$2,417.29}$$

Valuation Summary

Based on the three different approaches (earnings, revenues and book value) we have arrived at the following indications of value for JMK stock on a publicly traded equivalent basis:

Approach	Per-Share Indicated Value
Capitalization of Earnings:	
Latest 12 Months	$2,019.40
Five-Year Average	2,050.62
Projected 1988	2,047.50
Price/Revenues	2,415.60
Price/Book Value	2,417.29

In concluding the relative weights to be accorded the various approaches, one must consider the mandates of Revenue Ruling 59-60, generally accepted appraisal practices, and the appraiser's experience. Revenue Ruling 59-60 discusses weighting to be accorded various approaches as follows:

> Earnings may be the most important criterion of value in some cases, whereas asset value will receive primary consideration in others. In general, the appraiser will accord primary consideration to earnings when valuing stocks of companies which sell products or services to the public; conversely, in the investment or holding type of company, the appraiser may accord the greatest weight to the assets underlying the security to be valued.[2]

Clearly, JMK is an operating company and not an investment or holding company, so the values indicated by capitalization of earnings and price/revenues should be accorded primary consideration. This weighting is also consistent with generally accepted practices in business appraisals in other contexts.

We therefore accorded 75 percent of the weight to the earnings and revenues approaches and 25 percent to the price/book value approach (the only asset approach). We accorded less weight to the revenues approach than the earnings approach because of the wide spread in the P/R multiples for companies with profitability comparable to JMK's. Within the earnings approach, it is our opinion that the most weight should be given to the latest 12 months' earnings, slightly less to average earnings, and the least to projected earnings. Current earnings should be given the most weight due to the very tight range of the multiples of the most comparable companies; projected earnings should get the least weight because not only does JMK not prepare formal projections, but there was only limited information on the forecasts for the comparative companies. In our opinion taking into account the above weight-

---

[2]Revenue Ruling 59-60, 1959-1, C.B. 237.

ing, the publicly traded equivalent value of JMK's common stock as of July 21, 1987, was $2,200.00 per share. The fact that the publicly traded equivalent value is higher than JMK's book value indicates that the company has some intangible value that may be attributable to goodwill, although we did not attempt to analyze the source of the intangible value.

Discount for Lack of Marketability

A major difference between JMK's shares and those of its publicly traded counterparts is their lack of marketability. All other things being equal, an investment is worth more if it is marketable than if it is not, since investors prefer liquidity over lack of liquidity. Interests in closely held businesses are illiquid relative to most other investments.

The market places a far greater value differential on the liquidity factor alone in its pricing of common stocks than in its pricing of any other class of investment assets, for sound reasons. For common stocks as a group, investors expect to realize the majority of their return in the form of capital gains at the time of the stock's sale and only a small part of their total return in the form of dividends while they hold the stock. This situation is taken to the extreme, of course, in the case of common stock that has not paid dividends in the past, such as JMK's. Thus, the ability to sell the stock is crucial to the realization of the investor's expected return for buying and holding it.

A stock that pays no dividends, has no market, and cannot be legally offered to the general public but might possibly be salable under certain limited circumstances and at a totally undeterminable price must be discounted heavily from an otherwise comparable stock that is both legally salable to the general public and has an established market.

Another reason that liquidity takes on a high degree of importance for common stocks is that the stocks' prices tend to be much more volatile than prices of real estate or other securities such as preferred stocks or bonds. Consequently, the investor's choice as to the timing of the sale of the stock is much more important in determining the amount of return to be earned on the investment than is the case with other security investments. Numerous studies concerning the size of marketability discounts have been published.[3]

Applying a discount for lack of marketability of 35 percent to our previously determined publicly traded equivalent value of $2,200 per share results in an indicated fair market value of $1,430 per share ($2,200 × .65).

Prior Transaction

On September 30, 1986, Robert Johnson sold 1,700 shares of JMK common stock to William Smith. The price of $1,300 per share was based on arm's-length negotiations between the two parties. As noted in the fundamental position of the company section of this report, Mr. Smith paid Mr. Johnson a down payment of $250,000, with the balance to be paid over 10 years at an interest rate of prime plus 1 percent. Because this interest rate represents a

---

[3]These studies normally would be presented in an appraisal report. However, due to the limited amount of space available in presenting this sample case, we have not presented them here. See Chapter 10, "Data on Discounts for Lack of Marketability," for a detailed discussion. The studies discussed in Chapter 10 indicate an average discount for lack of marketability of at least 35 percent.

market rate of interest, the $1,300-per-share price is equal to its cash equiv-
alent value.

Comparing JMK's indicated fair market value as of July 21, 1987, of
$1,430 per share to the $1,300-per-share September 30, 1986, transaction
price indicates that the per share minority interest value of JMK's common
stock increased 10 percent from September 30, 1986, to $1,430 per share as
of July 21, 1987. In our opinion, this represents a reasonable increase in
value. JMK's earnings per share increased 5 percent from April 30, 1986, to
April 30, 1987. The company's book value increased 11 percent over the same
period, and revenues increased 26 percent.

Conclusion

Based on an analysis of all relevant factors surrounding JMK, it is our opinion that the fair market value of JMK's common stock on a minority interest
basis as of July 21, 1987, was $1,430 per share.

The Estate of Robert Johnson holds 3,000 shares of JMK common stock.
Therefore, as of July 21, 1987, the aggregate minority interest fair market
value of the common stock held in the estate was $4,290,000 (3,000 × $1,430).

APPENDIX 14-A

Retail Store Lease and Size Information

Store Number	Leased/Owned	Gross Square Footage	Lease Expires[a]
1	Leased	5,000	1990
2	Leased	4,000	1991
3	Leased	6,000	1988
4	Leased	5,500	1989
5	Leased	6,500	1992
6	Leased	4,500	1991
7	Leased	4,000	1989
8	Leased	7,000	1990
9	Leased	6,000	1994
10	Leased	8,500	1993
11	Leased	8,000	1996
12	Owned	9,500	---
13	Leased	8,000	1995
14	Leased	10,000	1997
15	Leased	8,500	1998
16	Leased	9,000	1996
17	Leased	8,500	1998
18	Leased	10,000	2002
19	Leased	8,500	2000
20	Leased	9,500	1996
21	Leased	8,000	1997
22	Leased	10,000	1995
23	Leased	9,500	2001
24	Owned	20,000	---
25	Leased	20,000	1999
26	Leased	22,000	2000
27	Owned	21,000	---
28	Leased	22,000	2004
29	Owned	21,000	---
		300,000	

[a] Includes renewal options
SOURCE: Company management

APPENDIX 14-B

Standard & Poor Corporation Records
Directory of Companies by SIC Code
March 1987

5732 Radio and Television Stores

BALTIMORE GAS & ELECTRIC CO., Baltimore, Md.
BEN WA INTERNATIONAL, Los Angeles, Cal.
BEST BUY CO., Bloomington, Minn.
CHYRON CORP., Melville, N. Y.
CIRCUIT CITY STORES INC., Richmond, Va.
COMPUTERCRAFT, INC., Houston, Texas
CRAZY EDDIE INC., Brooklyn, N. Y.
CYCLOPS CORP., Pittsburgh, Pa.
FEDERATED GROUP, INC., City of Commerce, Cal.
FIRST FAMILY GROUP, INC., Akron, Ohio
FRETTER INC., Livonia, Mich.
GENDIS INC., Winnipeg, Can.
GOOD GUYS INC., San Francisco, Cal.
HAMMER TECHNOLOGIES, INC., Larkspur, Cal.

HARVEY GROUP INC. (THE), Great Neck, N. Y.
HIGHLAND SUPERSTORES, INC., Taylor, Mich.
LADBROKE GROUP PLC, London, England
NEWMARK & LEWIS INC., Hicksville, N. Y.
PRESENT CO., INC. (THE), Rochester, N. Y.
SCHAAK ELECTRONICS, INC., St. Paul, Minn.
SOUND ADVICE INC., Ft. Lauderdale, Fla.
STEREO VILLAGE, INC., Decatur, Ga.
TANDY CORP., Fort Worth, Texas
U. S. ELECTRONICS GROUP, INC., Aurora, Colo.
U. S. VIDEO VENDING CORP., Winooski, Vt.
VIDEO CONNECTION OF AMERICA, INC., Malibu, Cal.
VISION COMMUNICATIONS CORP., Ridgefield, N. J.
WALL TO WALL SOUND & VIDEO, INC.,
          Cinnaminson, N. J.

APPENDIX 14-C

Willamette Management Associates, Inc.
Definition of Financial and Operating Ratios

Current ratio

Year-end current assets divided by year-end current liabilities.

Quick ratio

(Year-end cash, accounts receivable, and all assets shown between cash and accounts receivable) divided by year-end total current liabilities.

Working capital ($000s)

(Year-end current assets less year-end current liabilities) divided by 1,000.

Days in receivables

365 divided by (year's sales divided by average of year-beginning and year-end accounts receivable).

Cost of sales/inventory

Year's cost of sales divided by the average of the year-beginning inventory and year-end inventory.

Sales/working capital

Year's sales divided by the year's average working capital ((year-beginning total current assets plus year-end total current assets less year-beginning total current liabilities less year-ending total current liabilities) divided by 2).

Sales/net fixed assets

Year's sales divided by average of year-beginning and year-end net fixed assets.

Sales/total assets

Year's sales divided by average of year-beginning and year-end total assets.

Interest expense coverage

(Year's pretax income from continuing operations plus year's interest expense) divided by year's interest expense.

Cash flow/current maturities of long-term debt

(Year's net income from continuing operations plus year's depreciation/amortization expense) divided by the average of year-beginning current maturities of long-term debt and year-end current maturities of long-term debt.

Total debt/total equity

Year-end total debt divided by year-end common equity.

Long-term debt/long-term debt plus equity

Year-end long-term debt divided by (year-end equity plus year-end long-term debt).

Fixed assets/equity

Year-end net fixed assets divided by year-end net worth.

Net income/sales

Year's net income divided by year's sales.

Net income/equity

Year's net income divided by the average of year-beginning common equity and year-end common equity.

Net income/assets

Year's net income divided by the average of year-beginning total assets and year-end total assets.

APPENDIX 14-D

Qualifications of Appraisers

This appraisal report was prepared by Willamette Management Associates, Inc., a firm specializing in financial research and analysis, especially the valuation of businesses and business interest. Willamette Management conducts valuation studies of both publicly held and privately held ongoing business enterprises for a variety of purposes, including public stock offerings, tender offers, mergers and acquisitions, federal gift and estate tax cases, employee stock ownership trusts, divorces, and other cases involving litigation.

In addition, Willamette Management publishes the quarterly *Western Investor* and semimonthly *Western Investor Newsletter*, which include statistics and analysis of publicly held companies operating in the western United States. Willamette Management also maintains an extensive investment research library with files and reference manuals on publicly held companies throughout the nation.

Mary McCarter is a valuation analyst with Willamette Management Associates, Inc. Ms. McCarter is also a Chartered Financial Analyst (C.F.A.) and a Senior Member, Business Valuation, of the American Society of Appraisers (A.S.A.). She holds a Masters of Business Administration from the University of Portland and a Bachelor of Arts degree from Kenyon College, with a major in mathematics.

Kathryn F. Aschwald is a valuation analyst for Willamette Management Associates, Inc. Ms. Aschwald, also a Chartered Financial Analyst (C.F.A.), has a Bachelor of Science degree in business administration from Portland State University, with a major in finance and emphasis in economics.

Jacie Daschel, a valuation analyst for Willamette Management Associates, Inc., has a Bachelor of Arts degree in business administration from Portland State University, with a major in finance and emphasis in economics.

APPENDIX 14-E

Assumptions and Limiting Conditions

This appraisal is subject to the following assumptions and limiting conditions:

1. Information, estimates, and opinions contained in this report are obtained from sources considered reliable; however, no liability for such sources is assumed by the appraiser.

2. Client company and its representatives warranted to appraiser that the information supplied to appraiser was complete and accurate to the best of client's knowledge. Information supplied by management has been accepted without further verification as correctly reflecting the company's past results and current condition in accordance with generally accepted accounting principles, unless otherwise noted.

3. Possession of this report, or a copy thereof, does not carry with it the right of publication of all or part of it, nor may it be used for any purpose by anyone but the client without the previous written consent of the appraiser or the client and, in any event, only with proper attribution.

4. Appraiser is not required to give testimony in court, or be in attendance during any hearings or depositions, with reference to the company being appraised, unless previous arrangements have been made.

5. The various estimates of value presented in this report apply to this appraisal only and may not be used out of the context presented herein. This appraisal is valid only for the appraisal date or dates specified herein and only for the appraisal purpose or purposes specified herein.

Part V

Valuing Partial Interests

Chapter 15

Valuing Minority Interests

The Minority Stockholder's Situation
Problems in Liquidating Minority Shares of Closely Held Companies
    Restrictive Agreements
    Lack of Right to Partition
    Lack of Right to Participate in a Sale
State Statutes Affecting Minority Stockholder Rights
    Requirements for Supermajority Votes
    Rights to Dissolution or Sale of Stock
    Dissenting-Stockholder Appraisal Rights
Effect of Distribution of Ownership
Voting versus Nonvoting Shares
How the Applicable Standard of Value Affects Minority Interests
    Fair Market Value
    Investment Value
    Intrinsic Value
    Fair Value
Broad Approach #1: Proportion of the Enterprise Value Less Discount(s),
    If Applicable
    Determining the Enterprise Value
    Computing the Minority Pro Rata Interest
    Determining Applicable Discount(s) from Enterprise Value
Broad Approach #2: Direct Comparison with Sales of Other
    Minority Interests
    Sources of Comparative Minority Interest Data
    Courts Accept Direct Comparison Approach
Broad Approach #3: The "Bottom-Up" Approach
Errors to Avoid
    The Public Offering Myth
    Irrelevant Financial Statement Adjustments
    Comparing a "Mom-and-Pop" Operation with a Giant Public Corporation
Summary

Minority stock interests in a "closed" corporation are usually worth much less than the proportionate share of the assets to which they attach.[1]

The above statement, from a 1935 stock valuation case that is still widely quoted 53 years later, captures the essence of the minority stockholder's situation. Yet this revelation comes as a shock to many people, who may have always assumed that a partial interest is worth a pro rata portion of the value of the total enterprise.

The Minority Stockholder's Situation

Chapter 2 discussed the important and valuable elements of control, rights that do *not* attach to minority stock. H. Calvin Coolidge, a former bank trust officer with extensive experience in dealing with and selling (or attempting to sell) minority interests in closely held companies, presents a cogent précis of the minority stockholder's position:

> The holder of a minority interest can at best elect only a minority of the directors and for corporations chartered in states which do not permit cumulative voting, he may not be able to elect even one director. Lacking control of the board of directors, he cannot compel payment of dividends which must be declared equally and which would give him his pro rata share of earnings. Lacking control of the board of directors, he cannot compel his election as an officer or his employment by the corporation, which the holders of the controlling interest can do, often with resultant handsome compensation. In short, the holder of a minority interest has no voice in corporate affairs and is at the mercy of the holders of the controlling interest who have no reason to pay anything but a token dividend, if any, and no reason to buy out the minority holder except at a nominal price.
>
> A willing buyer contemplating purchase from a willing seller of a minority interest, being under no compulsion to buy (which would exclude a buyer already owning some shares whose new purchase would cover control), would suffer the same disadvantages of lack of control. The buyer is asked to make an investment with no assurance as to certainty of current yield or as to when, or the amount at which, he may be able to liquidate his investment. Regardless, therefore, of the value of 100% of the corporation, the buyer will not purchase a minority interest except at a discount from its proportionate share of the value of 100% of the corporation.[2]

The lack of concurrence between the value of stock and the corporation's underlying assets was clearly established by the U.S. Supreme Court back in 1925:

---

[1]*Cravens* v. *Welch,* 10 Fed. Supp. 94 (1935).

[2]H. Calvin Coolidge, "Discount for Minority Interest: Rev. Rul. 79-7's Denial of Discount Is Erroneous," *Illinois Bar Journal* 68 (July 1980), p. 744.

> The capital stock of a corporation, its net assets, and its shares of stock are entirely different things. . . . The value of one bears no fixed or necessary relation to the value of the other.[3]

An oft-cited U.S. Tax Court case quoted the above, adding:

> This is particularly true as to minority interests in a closed corporation. . . .[4]

That minority shareholders often find themselves disadvantaged compared to controlling shareholders is attested to by the fact that the oft-quoted, lengthy, and scholarly two-volume treatise *O'Neal's Oppression of Minority Shareholders* is doing well in its second edition, published in 1985. In the preface to that edition, the authors comment on the growing amount of minority shareholder litigation:

> Most American lawyers do not realize the tremendous amount of litigation in this country arising out of shareholder disputes. Since the publication of the first edition of this treatise, the volume of litigation grounded on minority shareholder oppression—actual, fancied, or fabricated—has grown enormously, and the flood of litigation shows no sign of abating. The increase in litigation has been pronounced in both federal and state courts, with an especially large number of suits challenging the validity of "cash-out" mergers. Also worthy of note is that in the last four or five years there has been a substantial increase in the number of suits minority shareholders have brought for involuntary dissolution of their corporation or to force majority shareholders to purchase their shares.[5]

This chapter first comments on certain unique problems in liquidating shareholder interests. It then looks at how the degree of control (or lack of it) and the applicable standard of value affect minority interest values. The chapter suggests three broad approaches to the valuation of minority interests:

1. Determine the value of the total enterprise on a control basis, and deduct any discounts appropriate for minority interest and/or lack of marketability.
2. Value the interest by direct comparison with other minority interest transactions. (Since most available data on minority interest transactions deal with publicly traded stocks, this approach usually requires the further step of deducting a discount for lack of marketability but no further deduction for minority interest.)
3. Value the interest with a "bottom-up" approach based on the dis-

---

[3]*Ray Consol. Copper Co.* v. *United States,* 45 S. Ct. 526 (1925).
[4]*Drayton Cochran et al.,* 7 T.C.M. 325 (1948).
[5]F. Hodge O'Neal and Robert B. Thompson, *O'Neal's Oppression of Minority Shareholders,* 2nd ed., vol. 1 (Wilmette, Ill.: Callaghan & Company, 1985), p. iii. The term *cash-out merger* is sometimes used to mean a *squeeze-out* or *freeze-out merger,* in which minority shareholders receive cash for their shares. They cannot block the merger or demand consideration other than cash. If they are not satisfied with the amount of cash offered, their remedy is to demand an appraisal of the stock under dissenters' appraisal rights statutes. See, for example, *Roland International Corp.* v. *Najjar,* 407 A.2d 1032, 1033 (Del. S. Ca. 1979).

counted future returns the shareholder may expect to realize through dividends and/or liquidation of the interest at some future date.

Problems in Liquidating Minority Shares of Closely Held Companies

A corollary to the disadvantages associated with lack of control is lack of marketability. Although the minority interest status and degree of liquidity (marketability) of the investment are two different concepts, as discussed in Chapter 2, they are interrelated. The disadvantages associated with the minority status make it very difficult to find buyers for minority shares of nonpublic companies, which further reduces the value of such shares. In fact, unless there is some provision for sale of the shares through either the articles of incorporation or a contract, the minority shareholder may be unable to find anyone willing to buy the shares at any price. Data on discounts for lack of marketability (separate from and beyond any discounts for minority interest) are presented in Chapter 10.

Restrictive Agreements

Many minority shares are subject to restrictions on transfer. The typical restriction gives the company and/or each of the company's stockholders a right of first refusal, thus putting any potential sale of the shares on hold for two or three months or even longer. As a practical matter, few potential buyers would make a firm offer to buy and leave their offers open for that length of time. Thus, such restrictive agreements further reduce the marketability and, hence, the value of the shares. Some restrictions on sale are far more onerous than a simple right of first refusal, thus limiting the shares' marketability even further.

Lack of Right to Partition

Discounts for minority interests in direct investment in real estate, when taken at all, usually are only about 15 to 20 percent below a pro rata proportion of the value of the total parcel. Sometimes people more familiar with direct investments in real estate than with investments in businesses accord similarly low minority interest discounts to investments in business interests.

As discussed earlier, the controlling owner of a business enterprise has an extremely wide diversity of options available, some of which may benefit control owners without benefiting minority owners. Of particular importance in protecting the interests of minority owners of real estate is the legal right to *partition,* the right to demand that the property be divided up and the minority owner given title to his or her share (or to demand sale of the property if partitioning is impractical). With a few exceptions (noted subsequently in the Rights to Dissolution or Sale of Stock section), no such rights are available to minority stockholders. Whether such rights may be available to minority interests in a business partnership depends on the articles of partnership (partnership agreement) and applicable state law.

Lack of Right to Participate in a Sale

Many minority stockholders assume that if a controlling interest is sold, they have the right to receive the same price for their shares as the controlling stockholders. Generally speaking, however, unless there are special state laws or protective provisions in the articles of incorporation, this is not true. There have been many situations in which controlling stockholders sold out and minority stockholders subsequently accepted offers for their shares at a fraction of the price per share the controlling stockholders received.

O'Neal and Thompson make the following statement regarding the traditional doctrine on sale of control:

> The traditional view is that a shareholder, irrespective of whether he is also a director, officer, or both, may sell his shares, just as other kinds of personal property, for whatever price he can obtain, even if his shares constitute a controlling block and the price per share is enhanced by that fact. Further, he is under no obligation to obtain for other shareholders an opportunity to sell their shares on the same favorable terms he is receiving or even to inform them of that price or of the terms of the sale.[6]

There has been much bitter litigation over this point, and the authors footnote many court case citations. The flavor of the decisions is capured in their paraphrasing of the findings in two cases:

> Majority shareholder has no duty to see that minority shareholders are allowed to join in a sale of stock at the same price per share and on the same terms offered for shares constituting the controlling interest [*Claget* v. *Hutchinson,* 583 F.2d 1259 (CA4, 1978)].
>
> . . . .
>
> Majority shareholders did not breach their fiduciary duty by selling control at a premium, by inviting some (but not all) minority shareholders to sell also and share in the premium, or by failing to disclose these facts to the other minority shareholders [*Ritchie* v. *McGrath,* 1 Kan App.2d 481, 571 P2d 17 (1977)].[7]

---

[6] O'Neal and Thompson, *O'Neal's Oppression,* p. 4.
[7] Ibid., p. 10.

State Statutes Affecting Minority Stockholder Rights

Statutes affecting minority stockholders' rights vary greatly from state to state. These statutes, and the case law developed pursuant to each, can have an extremely important bearing on the values of certain minority interests in many situations.

Requirements for Supermajority Votes

In some states, a simple majority can approve major actions such as a merger or sale of the company. Other states require a two-thirds or even greater majority to approve such actions, which means that a minority of just over one third has the power to block them thus giving large minority interests a form of "blocking power."

Both the types of actions that require a supermajority vote and the size of the supermajority required for each action vary considerably from state to state, and many states are undergoing processes of review and change. The tendency is toward requiring only a simple majority (anything above 50 percent) rather than a supermajority to authorize most or all corporate actions.

Rights to Dissolution or Sale of Stock

An increasing number of states are enacting statutes enabling minority shares aggregating some specified percentage of the total outstanding to petition the courts to force dissolution of the corporation under certain circumstances. Such statutes generally provide that controlling stockholders can prevent dissolution in such cases by paying the petitioners for dissolution the fair value of their shares. By far the largest amount of litigation regarding the value of shares under such statutes has been pursuant to California Corporation Code Section 2000.

Dissenting-Stockholder Appraisal Rights

Most states have statutes allowing minority stockholders to dissent if a company merges, sells nearly all of its assets, or undergoes some other fundamental change. In most cases, the dissenters' remedy is to have their shares appraised and be paid that value in cash. In most states, the standard of value for dissenting-stockholder actions is "fair value," as discussed in Chapter 2 and later in this chapter. A few state statutes still specify "fair market value," but recently several have changed their dissenting-stockholder statutory standard of value to "fair value."

Most states require that if a minority stockholder wishes to dissent to a corporate action, the decision to dissent must be registered in writing at or within a few days following the stockholder meeting at which the action is approved by the majority of stockholders. This registration of the dissent often is referred to as *perfecting dissenters' appraisal rights.* The courts are virtually unanimous in prohibiting dissenters' appraisal rights unless they have been perfected within the amount of time specified in the statute.

Effect of Distribution of Ownership

If one person owns 49 percent of a company's stock and another owns 51 percent, the 49 percent holder has little or no control of any kind. However, if two stockholders own 49 percent each and a third owns 2 percent, the 49 percent stockholders may be on a par with each other depending on who owns the other 2 percent. The 2 percent stockholder may be able to command a premium over the normal minority interest value for that particular block of stock because of its swing vote power.

If each of three stockholders or partners owns a one-third interest, no one has complete control. However, no one is in a relatively inferior position, unless two of the three have close ties with each other that the third does not share. Each of equal individual interests normally are worth less than a pro rata portion of the total enterprise's worth; thus, the sum of the values of the individual interests usually is less than what the total enterprise could be sold for to a single buyer. However, the percentage discount from pro rata value for each such equal interest normally would be smaller than that for a minority interest with no control whatever.

Each situation must be analyzed individually with respect to the degree of control, or lack of it, and the implications for the minority interest's value.

Voting versus Nonvoting Shares

The difference in value, if any, between voting and nonvoting minority shares depends largely on the size of the block and the distribution of ownership. In general, the greater the extent to which the issue of control is involved, the greater the impact of voting rights on the stock's value. As noted earlier, when swing votes are involved, the value impact can be considerable.

There have been several empirical studies on the price differentials between voting and nonvoting publicly traded stocks. The market data indicate that for small minority interests, the market generally accords very little or no value to voting rights. Where differentials in favor of voting stock exist, they generally have been under 5 percent, and no study has indicated a differential of over 10 percent. Again, the distribution of the stock can have a bearing. If one stockholder has total control anyway and there is no cumulative voting, the question of whether the minority shares are voting or nonvoting is academic unless a split-up of the control block is foreseeable.

Restrictive agreements also can have a bearing. Some voting stocks are subject to an agreement that causes them to be converted to nonvoting stock in the event of transfer. Such a provision can render voting rights virtually impotent for valuation purposes.

How the Applicable Standard of Value Affects Minority Interests

As discussed in Chapter 1, the applicable standard of value for the vast majority of valuation situations falls into one of four categories: (1) fair market value, (2) investment value, (3) intrinsic value, or (4) fair value. The applicable standard of value is determined primarily by the purpose and circumstances of the valuation. In some situations, the applicable standard of value is mandated by law. In others, the choice of standard of value lies within the discretion of the parties involved.

Fair Market Value

Recall from Chapter 1 that the *fair market value* standard implies a price at which an arm's-length transaction would be expected to take place between normally motivated investors under open market conditions, without considering any special benefits for any particular buyer or seller. Considering the unattractiveness of minority interests in closely held companies to investors at large, the discount from a proportionate share of enterprise value under the fair market value standard normally is quite large.

Investment Value

In Chapter 1, we defined the *investment value* standard as the value to a particular investor considering that investor's cost of capital, perception of risk, and other unique characteristics. Because of the particular attributes of ownership that may have unique appeal to any specific investor, the investment value of a minority interest in a certain enterprise may be equal to, greater than, or less than fair market value and also equal to, greater than, or less than a pro rata portion of the total enterprise value.

Intrinsic Value

Intrinsic value (sometimes called *fundamental value*), as defined in Chapter 1, is the value inherent in the characteristics of the investment itself. It is rarely used as a standard of value in and of itself. More commonly, the term is referred to, and some of the notions it implies used, in the context of one of the other three standards of value.

Fair Value

As noted in Chapter 1, the *fair value* standard suffers from lack of consistent definition from one context to another. It most often crops up as the statutory standard of value applicable to appraisals under dissenting-stockholders' rights or rights to dissolution. Such valuations by their nature are valuations of minority interests. The need to interpret the meaning of this standard of value from a study of the legal precedents in minority stockholder actions in each of the 50 states and Canada poses a continuing challenge to the appraisal profession. Certain precedents—including, for example, those pursuant to California Corporations Code Section 2000—have suggested that fair value be interpreted to mean fair market value without a minority interest discount (a proportionate share of enterprise value). However, I cannot emphasize enough that research of the specifically applicable legal precedents is very important in each context to which the fair value standard is determined to apply.

Even when a proportionate share of enterprise value is an indicated interpretation of "fair value," precedents as to which factors to consider, and the relative weights to accord each vary considerably. Generally, but not always, unless liquidation is in prospect, emphasis will be on factors that bear on the enterprises's going-concern value rather than on its liquidation value. This concept is discussed in more detail in Chapter 25, "Divorces, Dissolutions, Dissenting Stockholders' Suits, and Damages."

Broad Approach #1: Proportion of the Enterprise Value Less Discount(s), If Applicable

The first broad approach to the valuation of a minority interest involves a three-step process:

1. Determine the value of the total enterprise.
2. Compute the minority owner's pro rata interest in the total.
3. Determine the amount of discounts, if any, applicable to the pro rata value of the total enterprise to properly reflect the value of the minority interest. This step must also include determination of whether or not a further discount for lack of marketability is applicable, and if so, how much.

Determining the Enterprise Value

The Business Valuation Committee of the American Society of Appraisers has defined a *business enterprise* as "a commercial, industrial, or service organization pursuing an economic activity." This definition itself suggests that an enterprise be viewed as any integral, operating unit rather than as a collection of individual assets and liabilities.

This is consistent with quotes presented earlier in the chapter from the U.S. Supreme Court and other sources, indicating that there is little, if any, direct relationship between the value of stock in the enterprise and the value of assets the enterprise owns. One of the quotes cited earlier notes that this is particularly true for minority interests in close corporations.

All of the basic valuation methods discussed in earlier chapters could bear on the value of the entire enterprise or on the value of minority interests. However, my own experience, as well as my study of the literature and of court decisions on valuation issues, reveals a thread of distinction, in terms of the relative weight accorded to various factors, between determining the enterprise value for a controlling interest and determining the enterprise value as a starting point for valuing a minority interest. This distinction is that in determining an enterprise value as a starting point for valuing minority shares, greater emphasis is on operating factors, such as earnings and dividends or dividend-paying capacity, than on values of assets.

An example of this focus is illustrated in the following quote from an oft-cited estate tax case:

> A prospective buyer would give some consideration to the book value of $145 a share. He would realize, however, that the company was a going concern, and that, even if it be assumed that the book value could be realized upon the liquidation of the corporation, there was no indication that it was to be liquidated. Moreover, he would also realize that "minority stock interests in a 'closed' corporation are usually worth much less than the proportionate share of the assets to which they attach." *Cravens* v. *Welch,* 10 Fed. Supp. 94. In our opinion, the factor which he would consider as the most important would be what the stock would earn.[8]

In the above case, the court determined a value of $45 per share, a little less than one third of the $145 per share book value.

The following excerpt is typical of statements of the same position from the literature:

> Control evaluations differ markedly from noncontrol evaluations, because the way in which control buyers analyze businesses is different from the way in which passive investors analyze stocks. Control buyers generally concentrate on only a few situations and tend to analyze asset values. Situations are evaluated from a long-term perspective, because the control buyer is contemplating a large economic reevaluation in a single move. Alternatively, passive or noncontrol investors generally emphasize earnings.[9]

Another distinction between determining the enterprise value for a controlling interest and determining the enterprise value as a starting point for valuing a minority interest is in the assumptions inherent in adjustments to financial statements or in projections. The

---

[8]*Hooper* v. *C.I.R.,* 41 U.S.B.T.A. 114 (1949).

[9]Arthur N. Haut and William P. Lyons, "Issues in the Valuation of Control and Noncontrol Shares in Connection with the Acquisition of Stock by Employee Stock Ownership Plans," *Journal of Pension Planning & Compliance,* Winter 1986, p. 319.

control buyer normally will assume changes that the buyer would make, while the minority interest valuation will not assume any changes that the existing control owners do not contemplate.

Computing the Minority Pro Rata Interest

In cases in which there is only a single class of stock and no warrants or contingent interests outstanding, the proportionate value per share is given by the straightforward exercise of dividing the enterprise value by the number of shares outstanding. If there are different classes of interests, the total enterprise value must be allocated among the classes and the dilution resulting from any contingent interests must be reflected.

Determining Applicable Discount(s) from Enterprise Value

Discounts and premiums have no meaning unless the basis for the discount or premium and the base from which it is calculated are clearly identified. Failure to do so has resulted in much confusion over use of the terms *minority interest discount* and *control premium.*

Such confusion exists particularly because some writers and appraisers fail to distinguish between a minority interest discount and a discount for lack of marketability. As discussed in Chapter 2, these are two separate concepts, but there is some interrelationship between them.

The concept of *minority interest* deals with the relationship between the interest being valued and the total enterprise. The primary factor bearing on the value of the minority interest in relation to the value of the total entity is how much control the minority interest has over that entity. The concept of *marketability* deals with the liquidity of the interest, that is, how quickly and certainly it can be converted to cash at the owner's discretion.

Since a minority interest discount reflects lack of control, the base from which it is subtracted is its proportionate share in the total entity value, including all rights of control. Since a discount for lack of marketability reflects lack of liquidity, the base from which it is subtracted is the value of an interest that is comparable but enjoys ready liquidity.

This important distinction is reflected in the definitions of terms adopted by the Business Valuation Committee of the American Society of Appraisers. The term *minority discount* is defined as "the reduction, from the pro rata share of the value of the entire business, to reflect the absence of the power of control." The term *marketability discount* is defined as "an amount or percentage deducted from an equity interest to reflect the lack of marketability."

Besides the conceptual preference for distinguishing between the discount for minority interest and the discount for lack of marketability, far more empirical evidence is available for quantifying each of the two discounts taken one at a time than for quantifying them taken together. (Data on discounts for lack of marketability were explored quite thoroughly in Chapter 10.) In terms of the definition of minority interest discount cited above, extensive empirical evidence for guidance in quantifying that discount is available in the public market.

Control Premium Studies. Extensive studies have been undertaken and published on *control premiums,* defined by the Business Valuation Committee as "the additional value inherent in the control interest, as contrasted to a minority interest, that reflects its power of control." Using this definition, the minority interest discount is the reverse of the control premium. As law professors Fellows and Painter have pointed out, "A minority discount . . . is a corollary of a majority premium and depends on the latter for its validity."[10]

The thousands of daily transactions on stock exchanges are, of course, minority interest transactions. Each year, a controlling interest in a few hundred of these public companies is purchased, in almost all cases at a price representing a premium over the market price at which the stock previously had traded as a minority interest. Several services follow these acquisitions and publish data on the control premiums. Table 15–1 shows the average percentage discount from the buyout price at which stocks were selling immediately prior to the announcements of acquisitions for the years 1980 to 1987. It is based on statistics published by W. T. Grimm & Company in their annual *Mergerstat Review.* It should be noted that the data in Table 15–1 are based on market prices only one workweek (five business days) prior to the merger announcement. Studies have shown that stocks have some tendency to rise in anticipation of such events, starting considerably more than five days prior to the public announcement. To that

TABLE 15-1

W.T. Grimm Control Premiums

Year of Buyout	No. of Transactions	Average Premium Paid over Market[a] %	Median Premium Paid %	Implied Minority Interest Discount[b] %
1980	169	49.9	44.6	33.3
1981	166	48.0	41.9	32.4
1982	176	47.4	43.5	32.2
1983	168	37.7	34.0	27.4
1984	199	37.9	34.4	27.5
1985	331	37.1	27.7	27.1
1986	333	38.2	29.9	27.6
1987	237	38.3	30.8	27.7

[a] The premium paid over market is a percentage based on the buyout price over the market price of the seller's stock five bsuiness days prior to the announcement date.
[b] Formula: 1 - (1 ÷ (1 + Average Premium Paid)), for example 1 - (1 ÷ 1.499) = 1 - .667 = .333

SOURCE: *Mergerstat Review 1987.* (Chicago: W.T. Grimm & Co., 1988). Discount calculated by Willamette Management Associates, Inc..

---

[10]Mary Louise Fellows and William H. Painter, "Valuing Close Corporations for Federal Wealth Transfer Taxes: A Statutory Solution to the Disappearing Wealth Syndrome," *Stanford Law Review* 30 (May 1978), p. 909.

extent, the above figures may understate the control premium and implied minority interest discounts. The *Mergerstat Review* breaks down the data by broad industry group to permit analysis of control premiums for any relevant time period by that category.

Published by Houlihan, Lokey, Howard & Zukin, Inc., the quarterly *Control Premium Study,* with data starting in 1986, analyzes the prices of the target company's stock prior to the transaction date and attempts to select a price that is unaffected by preannouncement speculation about the proposed transaction. For all of calendar year 1986, the publisher analyzed 134 transactions. It found that the average control premium for the 134 transactions was 41.5 percent, which implies a minority interest discount of about 29 percent $(1 - [1/(1 + .415)] = .29)$.[11] For calendar year 1987, it analyzed 84 transactions. It found that the average control premium was 48.3 percent, which implies a minority discount of about 32.6 percent. The HLHZ data are also broken down by SIC code.

I again emphasize that the public market control premium studies are useful for guidance in quantifying the minority interest discount, resulting in an estimate of what the stock might sell for if a public market existed. From this "publicly traded equivalent value," it is still necessary to deduct an additional discount for lack of marketability if the subject minority interest is closely held.

Trust and Estate Sales.   H. Calvin Coolidge, a bank trust officer responsible for administering trusts and estates that owned all or portions of closely held businesses, did two studies in which he compiled data on actual sales prices of closely held businesses. As an introduction, he offers the following generalities:

> A number of years of experience has demonstrated that it is extremely difficult to find any market for minority interests . . . , despite efforts to do so. . . . On the relatively rare occasions when an offer is made to buy a minority interest, it is almost always for an amount far less than the fiduciary and the beneficiary expect to get.[12]

In his first study, Coolidge compiled data on 30 actual sales of minority interests. He found that the average transaction price was 36 percent below book value and concluded with the following observations:

> Only 20 percent of the sales were made at discounts less than 20 percent. A little more than half the sales (53⅓ percent) were made at discounts that ranged from 22 percent to 48 percent, and 23⅓ percent of the sales were made at discounts of from 54.4 percent to 78 percent.
>
> It would be dangerous to draw too many generalizations from the survey, but those sales where the discounts were below 20 percent involved, with one exception, purchases from close relatives where friendly rela-

---

[11]*HLHZ Control Premium Study.* Houlihan, Lokey, Howard & Zukin, Inc. (Los Angeles, Calif., 1987).
[12]H. Calvin Coolidge, "Fixing Value of Minority Interest in a Business; Actual Sales Suggest Discount as High as 70 Percent," *Estate Planning,* Spring 1975, p. 141.

tions existed. The exception was the sale by a holder of swing shares who used his leverage well, but still took a 4.3 percent discount. At the other end of the spectrum was the settlement of a three year bitter dispute between two families; the majority family raised its token offer only after threat of a lawsuit, but the price the minority interest took nonetheless represented a 78 percent discount.[13]

Note that the discounts in the foregoing surveys were from book value, not from the value of the enterprise as a whole. Book value, of course, recognizes no appreciation in assets above depreciated net asset value, although, in a very few cases in the above survey, the discounts were computed from an adjusted book value, reflecting appreciation in real estate values. I would expect that the total enterprise value would be above the book value in most cases. If that was true in the survey, then the discounts from the owners' proportionate shares of the total enterprise values were even greater than the discounts as shown in the survey, which were from book value.

An update published in 1983 indicated a trend toward even higher discounts when disposing of minority interests in closely held corporations. That study found a much higher concentration of discounts from book value at the high end of the range, and the average discount for the two studies combined was approximately 40 percent. The updated study concludes as follows:

> Each of the sales used in the survey involved a combination of factors that made it somewhat unique. To use any of the data, or any classification of the data, as definitive proof of the discount to be applied in a prospective valuation would be dangerous. This should not, however, obscure the true significance of the data, which is that in the actual marketplace, the typical discount is not of token size, but of substantial magnitude.[14]

Broad Approach #2: Direct Comparison with Sales of Other Minority Interests

Perhaps the simplest and most straightforward approach to valuing minority interests is by direct comparison with other sales of minority interests. In this approach, the appraiser need not go through the steps of estimating a value for the total enterprise and figuring out how much discount to apply for the minority interest status. The appraiser can value the subject minority interest using parameters similar to those used for valuing a total company. Such parameters would include, for example, capitalization of earnings, capitalization of cash flow, capitalization of dividends, discounted future returns, a ratio of price to book value or adjusted net asset value, and so on. Guidance

---

[13]Ibid., p. 141.
[14]H. Calvin Coolidge, "Survey Shows Trend Toward Larger Minority Discounts," *Estate Planning,* September 1983, p. 282.

for quantifying the market value parameters would come from the comparative minority interest transaction data.

As discussed in the previous section, it should be remembered that when valuing minority interests, more weight usually should be put on earnings-related approaches and less on asset-related approaches than when valuing a controlling interest. Also, when valuing minority interests, actual dividends rather than dividend-paying capacity are relevant, since the minority stockholder can't force the payment of dividends, regardless of how much dividend-paying capacity the company has.

Sources of Comparative Minority Interest Data

One source of comparative data could be prior arm's-length transactions involving minority interests in the same company, with data updated to reflect any changes in fundamental factors. Such transactions must be analyzed extremely carefully, however, to ensure that they are truly at arm's length and also that they represent the standard of value applicable to the current valuation, such as fair market value.

There is no generally available source of data on any broad group of minority interest transactions in closely held companies, but there is, of course, a readily available data base on daily transactions in minority interests in thousands of publicly traded companies. The nature and sources of these data are discussed at considerable length in Chapter 8, "Data on Required Rates of Return," and Chapter 9, "Comparative Transaction Data." If earnings (or some other measure of earning power, such as cash flow) projections are available or can be developed for the subject company, it may be possible to use a discounted future returns approach using data discussed in Chapter 8. In most cases, a comparative company analysis can be done using data discussed in Chapter 9.

It must be remembered that the result of a direct comparison of minority interest transactions using public stock market data results in a value as if publicly traded. To apply this approach to a minority interest in a private company usually requires one more step, a discount for lack of marketability, using data sources presented in Chapter 10.

Courts Accept Direct Comparison Approach

The approach of direct comparison with publicly traded minority interests was used successfully, for example, in both the Gallo and the Watts estate tax cases. In the Gallo case, neither the IRS nor the taxpayer's experts attempted to determine an enterprise value. Both valued the subject minority stock by comparing it with stocks of comparative publicly traded companies and then subtracting a discount for lack of marketability.[15] In the Watts case, experts for the taxpayer

---

[15]*Estate of Mark S. Gallo*, 50 T.C.M. 470 (1985).

similarly valued the subject minority interest, in this case a general partnership interest, by comparison with stocks of comparative publicly traded companies and then subtracted a discount for lack of marketability. The expert for the IRS presented a similar approach but also introduced an enterprise value approach. The direct comparison with publicly traded stocks carried the day.[16]

Broad Approach #3: The "Bottom-Up" Approach

The two broad approaches just discussed could be thought of as "top-down" approaches in that one starts with something (such as enterprise value or comparative minority interests) and subtracts whatever discounts, if any, are applicable. The "bottom-up" approach, in contrast, starts with nothing and builds up whatever elements of value to ownership of the minority interest exist.

This approach is the preference of Joel Adelstein, partner in charge of closely held company valuations for the Toronto office of Coopers & Lybrand. In a presentation at the 1985 ASA Advanced Business Valuation Seminar, Adelstein explained:

> Starting with zero and trying to find some value is my preference—why try to value the total enterprise at all? For many minority interests, ownership is just a long-shot speculation on something happening to get something out of the stock. The interest may have value someday, but it's sometime between now and never.[17]

In most cases, the values the minority interest holder may realize fall into two categories: (1) distributions, usually in the form of dividends, and (2) proceeds to be realized upon the sale of the interest. The mechanics of this approach are the same as those discussed in Chapter 3, "The Discounted Future Returns Approach to Valuation," with expected cash contributions as the returns to be discounted. The steps in this approach are as follows:

1. Project the flow of expected distributions (timing and amounts).
2. Project an amount realizable on sale of the interest (timing and amount).
3. Discount the results of steps 1 and 2 to present value at an appropriate discount rate, reflecting the degree of uncertainty of realizing the expected returns at the times and in the amounts projected.

As an alternative to projecting an amount realizable on sale, the analyst could, of course, project the flow of expected distributions into perpetuity and not assume any residual sale value.

---

[16]*Estate of Martha B. Watts*, 51 T.C.M. 60 (1985), appealed and affirmed, U.S. Court of Appeals, Eleventh Circuit, August 4, 1987.

[17]Joel Adelstein, "Real World Challenges in Valuing Minority Shareholdings in Private Corporations (Fourth Annual ASA Advanced Business Valuation Seminar, New Orleans, November 7–8, 1985).

In doing this exercise, the analyst may want to project a "best-case" and "worst-case" scenario and perhaps one or more scenarios in between. The analyst might base the value on the "most-likely" scenario or assign probabilities to each scenario and compute the "expected value" (weighted average) of the possible values indicated by the various scenarios.

The lack of marketability of the closely held minority interest can be reflected in either of two ways. First, the discount rate can be increased to reflect the disadvantages of illiquidity as well as the other risks inherent in the investment. Second, the discount for lack of marketability can be handled as a separate step.

Errors to Avoid

The following points should help the reader avoid certain common errors in the valuation of minority interests and to identify such errors when they appear in others' minority interest valuation analyses.

The Public Offering Myth

Incredibly, I frequently have seen authors and analysts use the estimated cost of public offering as a method for quantifying the discount for lack of marketability for a minority interest in a closely held company. The rationale for such an approach is that if the difference in value compared to a publicly traded minority interest is lack of marketability, the discount should be no more than the cost of overcoming that deficiency. The fallacy in that approach is the basic fact that a minority stockholder does not have the legal right to register the company's stock for a public offering. Since registration for a public offering is not an alternative available to a minority stockholder, the cost of doing so is not pertinent.

Irrelevant Financial Statement Adjustments

In Chapter 11, "Analyzing and Adjusting Financial Statements," we suggested that in analyzing the company's earning capacity the appraiser might want to remove from expenses any items that would be considered excess compensation to the business's owners if the business were being appraised for a possible sale. Under these circumstances, we were assuming that it was within the controlling owner's discretion to remove such expenses with no significant impairment to revenues. The minority stockholder, however, has no such power; thus, these adjustments may be irrelevant in estimating an earnings base for the valuation of minority interests, unless there is reason to believe that the changes actually will be made.

The same general concept applies to adjustments to the balance sheet to reflect the values of excess assets. Unless the controlling person or group is expected to take action to liquidate such assets, their value to the minority stockholders is dubious.

Comparing a "Mom-and-Pop" Operation with a Giant Public Corporation

Every once in awhile, we find some misdirected character such as Alan Analyst applying P/E ratios and other valuation parameters from large publicly traded companies to mom-and-pop operations such as Richard's Donuts (gross sales, $60,000; pretax profit before compensation to Dick, $10,000). There are so many differences between such small businesses and large publicly traded corporations that such a comparison usually is meaningless. For exactly this reason, I wrote *Valuing Small Businesses and Professional Practices*,[18] an entire book devoted to valuing businesses worth less than $1 million. Often, however, due to a lack of smaller comparative publicly traded companies, the analyst is forced to use large publicly traded companies. It is still possible to gain value guidance from these companies as long as the analyst recognizes the differences between the small subject company and the large publicly traded comparatives and takes them into account when selecting the appropriate multiples.

As a rule of thumb, I try to keep comparative companies within an order of magnitude of the subject company in terms of size. For example, if the subject company has $20 million in revenues, I usually try to find comparative companies with revenues between $2 million and $200 million.

Summary

Because of lack of control, minority interests usually are worth somewhat less than a proportionate share of the value of the total enterprise, if there are no contractual or legal provisions to the contrary. Furthermore, minority interests in closely held companies suffer more from lack of marketability than do controlling interests, thus further reducing minority interest value.

Many of the same indicators of market value (price/earnings ratios, capitalization of dividends, discounted future returns, price/book value ratios, and so on) used in valuing controlling interests can also be used to value minority interests. However, in valuing minority interests, the focus of value normally is on the business as a going concern rather than in either total or partial liquidation, and relatively more emphasis goes to operating variables, such as earnings and dividends, and less to asset values than when valuing a controlling interest. Also the assumptions underlying the minority interest valuation usually

---

[18]Shannon P. Pratt, *Valuing Small Businesses and Professional Practices* (Homewood, Ill.: Dow Jones-Irwin, 1986).

reflect business as usual rather than any changes that an outside party buyer might introduce.

One approach to valuing minority interests is to determine the value of the total enterprise, compute the minority's pro rata interest, and subtract whatever discounts are applicable for the minority interest status and lack of marketability. However, in many cases, if comparative minority interest transaction data are available, such as from publicly traded stocks, it is not necessary to address the question of the value of the entire enterprise. The minority interest can be valued by direct comparison with values of comparative minority interests, subtracting a discount for lack of marketability, if appropriate. Another approach to valuing a minority interest is to project dividends and an expected selling price at some future date and discount those projected returns to a present value at a discount rate reflecting the risks involved. In this approach, the matter of lack of marketability can be reflected either in the discount rate applied to the future returns or by a separate discount.

If existing or potential litigation is involved, it is important to understand relevant statutory standards of value and their interpretation by the courts. The range of court case outcomes in disputes regarding valuations of minority interests is extremely wide, even under comparable statutory law. Therefore, in litigated situations, a thorough analysis of the facts and circumstances of the particular interest is essential, along with strong supporting data and careful reasoning that lead to an objective conclusion that is consistent with applicable statutes and legal precedent.

Chapter 16

Valuing Debt Securities

Although debt securities play an important role in the analysis and appraisal of closely held companies, their valuation can in no way be thoroughly discussed in a single chapter. Therefore, this chapter confines discussion to general areas of reference that the analyst may want to consider when valuing debt securities. References to more extensive discussions of the areas of interest to the reader, including complete books on fixed-income analysis and valuation, are included in the bibliography at the end of this chapter.[1]

This chapter first discusses common situations that require the valuation of debt securities; then it moves to the general approach to valuing them. The chapter discusses the discount for lack of marketability, if any, and then examines the impact on value of special characteristics that many debt securities have.

Common Situations Requiring Valuation of Debt Securities

The most frequently encountered reasons for needing to value debt securities are the following:

1. Purchase or sale for cash.
2. Exchange of equity for debt, or vice versa.
3. Gift and estate taxes.
4. Allocating total enterprise value among classes of securities in a leveraged buyout, recapitalization, or bankruptcy reorganization.
5. Adjusting a balance sheet for debt securities owned or owed.

Purchase or Sale for Cash

From time to time, a company may have occasion to purchase or sell debt securities for cash. If they are existing securities, it is necessary to determine their cash-equivalent value. If they are to be newly issued securities, it is necessary to structure the provisions so that the value will be equal to the price paid or received.

Exchange of Equity for Debt

If debt securities are to be exchanged for some consideration other than cash, such as stock or other property, it usually is most expedient to determine the cash-equivalent values of both the debt securities and the stock or other consideration to be exchanged.

Most typically, a company or some or all of its stock is to be sold and a debt security received as all or part of the consideration. The seller needs to know the cash-equivalent value of the consideration

---

[1]See, for example, Frank J. Fabozzi and Irving M. Pollack, *The Handbook of Fixed Income Securities*, 2nd ed. (Homewood, Ill: Dow Jones-Irwin, 1987).

being received for the company or stock being given up. It is not un-common for notes or other debt securities issued in connection with the acquisition of a company to have a cash-equivalent value of 20 percent or more below the securities' face value.[2]

Gift and Estate Taxes

Debt securities may be gifted or be an asset in an estate. As in all gift and estate tax situations, the standard of value is fair market value. Quite often, debt securities presented as a gift or included in an estate have a fair market value considerably below the face value.

Allocation of Total Enterprise Value among Classes of Securities

A leveraged buyout, by its nature, results in the creation of new classes of securities, almost always including at least one class of debt. There-fore, in dealing with a valuation for a leveraged buyout, it usually is necessary not only to value the entire enterprise but to allocate the total value among the various classes of participants.

Recapitalizations involving debt securities may be undertaken for a variety of reasons. An increasingly popular purpose in the late 1980s has been leveraged recapitalizations—issuing debt for the purpose of redeeming a substantial portion of outstanding equity to create a more optimal capital structure.

Bankruptcy recapitalizations, by their nature, involve debt secur-ities, sometimes both before and after the recapitalization. Creative structuring of debt and other securities to meet the varying objectives of the parties at interest can be an essential tool in achieving a suc-cessful bankruptcy reorganization.

Adjusting a Balance Sheet for Debt Securities Owned or Owed

For various reasons, the balance sheet may be analyzed to adjust each line item to its fair market value. In many cases, debt may need to be adjusted to market on both the asset and liabilities sides of the balance sheet. An example of the latter would be the use of "debt-free" ap-proaches to value the common stock, as discussed in Chapter 4.

The amount of analysis undertaken for the valuation of debt se-curities will vary with the assignment and the accuracy required. For example, generally more analysis will be undertaken in the valuation of a debt security when that security is to be gifted (and thus subject to gift tax consequences) than when the assignment is to value the

---

[2]While this may be true in a business of any size, it is particularly prevalent in the sale of small businesses. For an extended discussion of this, see Chapter 17, "Tradeoff between Cash and Terms," in Shannon P. Pratt, *Valuing Small Businesses and Professional Practices* (Homewood, Ill.: Dow Jones-Irwin, 1986).

common stock of a closely held company by a debt-free valuation approach. Even if the analyst does not contemplate going through all the steps in the analysis of debt securities, it is important to understand them in order to have a general idea of the potential impact of an adjustment in the value of a debt security to market value.

Method of Valuation

Valuation theory states that the fair market value of a future stream of cash flows is equal to the present value of the future cash flows, discounted back to the current time at an appropriate interest rate. The higher the risk or uncertainty associated with the cash flows, the higher the appropriate interest rate will be. This is precisely how the value of a debt security is determined. The value of this type of security can be determined by the following present value formula:

Formula 16–1: Present Value of Nonconvertible Debt Securities

$$\text{Present value} = \sum_{i=1}^{n} \frac{C_i}{(1 + r)^i}$$

where:

C_i = Cash flow in the ith period in the future
i = Period when cash flows are generated
r = Interest rate at which cash flows are to be discounted back to the present
n = Maturity of the debt, in periods

There are extensive public trading markets for many debt securities, including corporate bonds and notes, U.S. government and agency bonds and notes, some municipal government bonds and notes, and various short-term money market instruments. If the debt security being valued can be bought and sold in one of the public trading markets, its observed market price at any given time will reflect the present value of the future cash flows as determined by the market. The rate of interest that, when applied to the expected future cash flows of a debt security, produces a present value of the cash flows equal to the debt security's observed market price is called the *yield to maturity* of that security.

If the debt security cannot be purchased or sold in a public market (a closely held debt security), its value must be determined by using the above formula. The information needed for determining the value of a closely held debt security from the above formula is the following: (1) the amount of future cash flows generated by the debt security; (2) the timing of the future cash flows generated by the security; and (3) the appropriate rate of interest or yield to maturity to apply to the future cash flows to determine the present value. The timing and amounts of the contractually obligated cash flows can be determined from the debt instruments themselves. The third item, an appropriate interest rate or yield to maturity to apply to the future cash flows, requires both quantitative analysis and the appraiser's judgment.

Amount and Timing of Future Cash Flows

The amount of future cash flows generally is set by the contract establishing the debt security. Interest payments are specified at a certain amount, and, as determined by the contract, the principal will be repaid at some specific future time. Certain characteristics of some debt securities may alter the amount and timing of the future cash flows. Some of these characteristics include call provisions and sinking fund provisions, the debt's income taxation status, and whether the debt is a "zero coupon" debt issue or has conversion privileges. The nature of each of these characteristics is discussed later in the chapter.

Determination of Yield to Maturity

The critical step in the final determination of the value of a debt security is to choose an appropriate interest rate or yield to maturity to apply to the future cash flows. Many quantitative and qualitative factors help to determine this figure at any point in time.

The yield to maturity for a debt security may differ from the security's coupon rate of interest (the rate expressed as a percentage of face value) at any point in time. If the market-determined yield to maturity for a debt security is equal to the security's coupon interest rate, the security's fair market value is equal to its face or par value. If the coupon interest rate is greater than the yield to maturity, as indicated by the market yields of comparable bonds, the debt security's market value is greater than its face or par value. Conversely, if the coupon interest rate for a debt security is less than the yield to maturity as indicated by the market, the security's market value is less than its face or par value. The coupon rate of interest determines the amount of the cash flows that can be expected from holding a debt security, but the yield to maturity required by the market establishes the market value of the cash flows generated by the debt security at any particular point in time.

Comparative Analysis. In order to determine the yield to maturity to apply to a closely held debt security, it is necessary to examine several characteristics related to the security's issuer. By comparing the various characteristics of the closely held debt issuer with comparable characteristics of issuers of publicly traded debt securities that already have a market-determined yield to maturity, the analyst can gain insight into the proper yield to maturity to apply to the closely held debt security.

The first step in the comparative analysis is the quantitative analysis of the debt security issuer's operating performance and financial position. This analysis is very similar to that described in Chapter 12,

"Comparative Ratio Analysis," and generally includes analysis of the debt issuer's balance sheet leverage ratios, income statement coverage ratios, short-term liquidity ratios, profitability ratios, and return on investment. The relative importance of the various ratios may vary with the type of debt security being valued. For example, the short-term liquidity ratios are far more important in the valuation of short-term debt securities than in the valuation of long-term debt securities, since short-term liquidity ratios demonstrate the debt issuer's ability to meet its current obligations, one of which is the short-term debt.

The closely held debt issuer's operating performance and financial condition can be compared to those of a broad population of issuers of publicly traded debt securities. For example, Exhibit 16–1 shows key financial ratios calculated by Standard & Poor's Corporation for industrial long-term debt issuers for which it provides debt ratings. The exhibit also shows median three-year financial ratios for the debt issuers, by rating classification, for both 1983 to 1985 and 1984 to 1986. Exhibit 16–2 shows the definition of credit ratings issued by Standard & Poor's Corporation. By calculating these same ratios for the issuer of the closely held debt security over the same time period, the analyst can determine into which rating classification the closely held debt might fall if it were rated by Standard & Poor's.

After having gained an idea of the general rating classification into which the closely held debt security might fall, the analyst can select specific publicly traded debt securities similar in debt rating and nature to the subject security. Several rating agencies, including Moody's Investors Service[3] and Standard & Poor's Corporation,[4] provide listings of publicly traded debt securities, along with credit ratings for nearly all of the securities. Exhibit 16–3 shows the yields to maturity for various bond indexes, segregated by rating, compiled by Standard & Poor's Corporation for 1977 through 1987. As would be expected, the lower-rated indexes have higher yields to maturity than the higher-rated indexes at any point in time.

The list of prospective comparative publicly traded debt securities compiled from one of these two debt listings should then be narrowed to those with characteristics or provisions similar to the privately held debt security. Thus winnowing the selection will help eliminate securities whose yields to maturity differ because of varying contract provisions. If unable to eliminate any publicly traded debt securities whose provisions differ from those of the closely held debt security from the comparative list, the analyst should carefully consider the differences in the securities' provisions and the associated risk characteristics when determining the appropriate yield to maturity to apply to the closely held debt security.

Standard & Poor's attaches one of approximately 200 industry codes or subcodes to nearly all the corporate bonds included in its listing. The analyst may want to consider including only publicly traded debt securities within the same general industry as that of the

---

[3]*Moody's Bond Record* (New York: Moody's Investors Service, 1987).
[4]*Standard & Poor's Bond Guide* (New York: Standard & Poor's Corporation, 1988).

EXHIBIT 16-1

Standard &Poor's Corporation
Key Financial Ratios and Definitions
by Rating Classification for Long-Term Debt Issuers

Industrial long-term debt

Three-year (1984–1986) medians	AAA	AA	A	BBB	BB	B	CCC
Pretax interest coverage (x)	12.63	9.06	5.24	3.19	2.49	1.83	0.22
Pretax interest coverage including rents (x)	7.39	4.62	3.02	2.32	1.83	1.54	0.52
Funds from operations/long-term debt (%)	226.67	124.00	67.51	46.05	28.94	19.43	12.26
Funds from operations/total debt (%)	135.22	90.32	54.63	40.45	24.64	16.43	10.19
Pretax return on permanent capital employed (%)	24.80	21.38	18.16	13.30	12.75	11.40	1.40
Operating income/sales (%)	20.63	14.85	12.21	10.91	11.44	10.55	7.09
Long-term debt/capitalization (%)	11.31	17.67	26.85	31.61	43.10	53.15	64.71
Total debt/capitalization including short-term debt (%)	18.59	24.11	31.52	34.81	45.77	55.67	67.10
Total debt/capitalization including short-term debt (including 8 times rents) (%)	30.39	35.40	46.14	48.18	58.24	65.78	71.07
Total liabilities/tangible shareholders' equity and minority interest (%)	78.89	107.26	118.28	146.11	188.22	224.97	379.66
Three-year (1983–1985) medians	AAA	AA	A	BBB	BB	B	CCC
Pretax interest coverage (x)	10.46	8.21	5.53	3.05	2.47	1.87	0.09
Pretax interest coverage including rents (x)	7.48	4.43	2.93	2.30	2.04	1.51	0.75
Funds from operations/long-term debt (%)	309.03	118.44	75.40	45.74	27.02	18.95	15.07
Funds from operations/total debt (%)	151.40	84.31	60.73	39.44	23.28	16.88	8.12
Pretax return on permanent capital employed (%)	25.60	22.05	18.03	12.10	13.80	12.01	2.70
Operating income/sales (%)	18.67	15.20	11.73	10.18	10.90	8.83	10.50
Long-term debt/capitalization (%)	8.85	18.88	24.46	31.54	42.52	52.04	69.28
Total debt/capitalization including short-term debt (%)	17.85	24.87	29.11	34.02	45.85	55.69	71.99
Total debt/capitalization including short-term debt (including 8 times rents) (%)	27.44	38.69	43.00	47.02	58.30	63.45	74.19
Total liabilities/tangible shareholders' equity and minority interest (%)	74.44	103.28	109.16	130.54	186.50	238.51	413.17

Glossary

Balances for pretax returns and coverages Net income from continuing operations before (1) special items, (2) minority interests, (3) gains on re-acquisition of debt, plus income taxes plus interest expense.

Gross interest. Gross interest accrued before (1) capitalized interest, (2) interest income.

Interest expense. Interest accrued net of capitalized interest.

Gross rents. Gross operating rents paid before sublease income.

Long-term debt. As reported, including capitalized lease obligations on the balance sheet.

Total debt. Long-term debt, current maturities, commercial paper, and other short-term borrowings.

Equity. Shareholders' equity, plus minority interest, plus deferred investment tax credits.

Operating income. Sales minus cost of goods manufactured (before depreciation), selling, general and administrative, and research and development costs.

Eight times rents. Gross rents paid multiplied by capitalization factor of eight.

Tangible net worth. Equity less goodwill, patents, "deferred" assets, "other assets."

Formulas for key ratios

$$\text{Pretax interest coverage} = \frac{\text{Balances for pretax returns and coverages}}{\text{Gross interest}}$$

$$\text{Pretax interest coverage including rents} = \frac{\text{Balances for pretax returns and coverages} + \text{gross rents}}{\text{Gross interest} + \text{gross rents}}$$

$$\text{Funds from operations as \% of long-term debt} = \frac{\text{Working capital from operations}}{\text{Long-term debt}}$$

$$\text{Funds from operations as a \% of total debt} = \frac{\text{Working capital from operations}}{\text{Total debt}}$$

$$\text{Pretax return on permanent capital} = \frac{\text{Balances for pretax returns and coverages}}{\substack{\text{Sum of (1) the average of the beginning of year and end of year current maturities, long-term debt, noncurrent deferred} \\ \text{taxes, minority interest, and stockholders' equity, and (2) average short-term borrowings during year per footnotes to} \\ \text{financial statements}}}$$

$$\text{Operating income as a \% of sales} = \frac{\text{Operating income}}{\text{Sales}}$$

$$\text{Long-term debt as a \% of capitalization} = \frac{\text{Long-term debt}}{\text{Long-term debt} + \text{equity}}$$

$$\text{Total debt as a \% of capitlization} + \text{short-term debt} = \frac{\text{Total debt}}{\text{Total debt} + \text{equity}}$$

$$\text{Total debt} + 8 \text{ times rents as a \% of capitalization} + \text{short-term debt} + 8 \text{ times rents} = \frac{\text{Total debt} + 8 \text{ times gross rentals paid}}{\text{Total debt} + \text{equity} + 8 \text{ times gross rentals paid}}$$

$$\text{Total liabilities as of \% of tangible net worth} = \frac{\text{Total liabilities}}{\text{Tangible net worth}}$$

SOURCE: *Standard & Poor's Credit Week* (New York: Standard & Poor's Corporation, September, 1987).

closely held debt security issuer, if enough publicly traded debt securities within that industry are available to provide meaningful insight into yields to maturity within that industry. Standard & Poor's description of the impact of industry analysis on its debt rating methodology is shown in Exhibit 16–4.

EXHIBIT 16-2

Standard & Poor's Corporation
Corporate and Municipal Rating Definitions

DEBT

A Standard & Poor's corporate or municipal debt rating is a current assessment of the creditworthiness of an obligor with respect to a specific obligation. This assessment may take into consideration obligors such as guarantors, insurers, or lessees.

The debt rating is not a recommendation to purchase, sell or hold a security, inasmuch as it does not comment as to market price or suitability for a particular investor.

The ratings are based on current information furnished by the issuer or obtained by Standard & Poor's from other sources it considers reliable. Standard & Poor's does not perform any audit in connection with any rating and may, on occasion, rely on unaudited financial information. The ratings may be changed, suspended or withdrawn as a result of changes in, or unavailability of, such information, or for other circumstances.

The ratings are based, in varying degrees, on the following considerations:
I. Likelihood of default-capacity and willingness of the obligor as to the timely payment of interest and repayment of principal in accordance with the terms of the obligation;
II. Nature of and provisions of the obligation;
III. Protection afforded by, and relative position of, the obligation in the event of bankruptcy, reorganization or other arrangement under the laws of bankruptcy and other laws affecting creditors' rights.

AAA Debt rated AAA has the highest rating assigned by Standard & Poor's. Capacity to pay interest and repay principal is extremely strong.

AA Debt rated AA has a very strong capacity to pay interest and repay principal and differs from the higher rated issues only in small degree.

A Debt rated A has a strong capacity to pay interest and repay principal although it is somewhat more susceptible to the adverse effects of changes in circumstances and economic conditions than debt in higher rated categories.

BBB Debt rated BBB is regarded as having an adequate capacity to pay interest and repay principal. Whereas it normally exhibits adequate protection parameters, adverse economic conditions or changing circumstances are more likely to lead to a weakened capacity to pay interest and repay principal for debt in this category than in higher rated categories.

BB, B, CCC, CC, C Debt rated BB, B, CCC, CC and C is regarded, on balance, as predominantly speculative with respect to capacity to pay interest and repay principal in accordance with the terms of the obligation. BB indicates the lowest degree of speculation and C the highest degree of speculation. While such debt will likely have some quality and protective characteristics, these are outweighed by large uncertainties or major risk exposures to adverse conditions.

CI The rating CI is reserved for income bonds on which no interest is being paid.

D Debt rated D is in default, and payment of interest and/or repayment of principal is in arrears.

Plus (+) or Minus (−): The ratings from "AA" to "CCC" may be modified by the addition of a plus or minus sign to show relative standing within the major rating categories.

Provisional Ratings: The letter "p" indicates that the rating is provisional. A provisional rating assumes the successful completion of the project being financed by the debt being rated and indicates that payment of debt service requirements is largely or entirely dependent upon the successful and timely completion of the project. This rating, however, while addresssing credit quality subsequent to completion of the project, makes no comment on the likelihood of, or the risk of default upon failure of such completion. The investor should exercise his own judgment with respect to such likelihood and risk.

L The letter "L" indicates that the rating pertains to the principal amount of those bonds where the underlying deposit collateral is fully insured by the Federal Savings & Loan Insurance Corp. or the Federal Deposit Insurance Corp.
* Continuance of the rating is contingent upon S&P's receipt of an executed copy of the escrow agreement or closing documentation confirming investments and cash flows.

NR indicates that no rating has been requested, that there is insufficient information on which to base a rating, or that S&P does not rate a particular type of obligation as a matter of policy.

Debt Obligations of issuers outside the United States and its territories are rated on the same basis as domestic corporate and municipal issues. The ratings measure the creditworthiness of the obligor but do not take into account currency exchange and related uncertainties.

Bond Investment Quality Standards: Under present commercial bank regulation issued by the Comptroller of the Currency, bonds rated in the top four categories (AAA, AA, A, BBB, commonly known as "Investment Grade" ratings) are generally regarded as eligible for bank investment. In addition, the Legal Investment Laws of various states may impose certain rating or other standards for obligations eligible for investment by savings banks, trust companies, insurance companies and fiduciaries generally.

SOURCE: *Standard & Poor's Bond Guide* (New York: Standard & Poor's Corporation, January 1988).

EXHIBIT 16-3

Standard & Poor's Corporation
Yield to Maturity for Bond Indexes
1977-1987

STANDARD & POOR'S CORPORATE & GOVERNMENT BOND YIELD INDEX—BY RATINGS

Weekly Averages 1987	†PUBLIC UTILITY			INDUSTRIAL				†COMPOSITE			U.S.GOVERNMENT			MUNI-CIPALS
	AA	A	BBB	AAA	AA	A	BBB	AA	A	BBB	LONG TERM	INTER-MEDIATE	SHORT TERM	
December 30	----	----	----	----	----	----	----	----	----	----	----	----	----	----
December 23	9.88	10.13	10.68	9.59	9.98	10.79	11.24	9.93	10.46	10.96	9.05	8.60	7.57	8.03
December 16	10.20	10.47	10.89	9.88	10.25	10.98	11.49	10.23	10.73	11.19	9.29	8.73	7.56	8.13
December 9	10.11	10.33	10.89	9.85	10.23	10.98	11.49	10.17	10.66	11.19	9.40	8.76	7.54	8.14
December 2	10.10	10.36	10.83	9.83	10.22	10.96	11.41	10.16	10.66	11.12	9.33	8.71	7.45	8.07
Monthly Averages 1987–1986														
December	10.07	10.32	10.82	9.79	10.17	10.93	11.41	10.12	10.63	11.12	9.27	8.70	7.53	8.09
November	9.91	10.32	10.75	9.71	10.07	10.69	11.22	9.97	10.51	10.99	9.16	8.65	7.45	8.09
October	10.54	10.82	11.38	10.41	10.70	11.14	11.70	10.62	10.98	11.55	9.80	9.30	8.23	8.84
September	10.34	10.68	11.14	10.26	10.62	10.88	11.35	10.48	10.77	11.25	9.78	9.16	8.14	8.36
August	9.72	10.07	10.57	9.67	9.95	10.24	10.64	9.83	10.16	10.61	9.14	8.47	7.51	7.90
July	9.57	9.89	10.40	9.31	9.71	9.91	10.44	9.64	9.90	10.42	8.86	8.24	7.28	7.83
June	9.62	9.94	10.39	9.31	9.77	9.86	10.36	9.70	9.89	10.38	8.76	8.29	7.46	7.89
May	9.69	9.98	10.45	9.29	9.93	9.84	10.43	9.81	9.91	10.44	8.92	8.52	7.68	8.10
April	9.18	9.45	9.94	8.80	9.43	9.33	9.94	9.31	9.39	9.95	8.36	7.80	6.97	7.62
March	8.64	8.92	9.22	8.41	8.92	8.89	9.63	8.78	8.91	9.42	7.65	7.05	6.44	6.71
February	8.70	8.98	9.21	8.49	8.94	8.89	9.79	8.82	8.94	9.50	7.77	7.12	6.50	6.67
January	8.63	8.96	9.22	8.47	9.09	9.18	9.72	8.86	9.07	9.47	7.64	6.97	6.32	6.63
December	8.78	9.09	9.44	8.53	9.22	9.38	9.87	9.01	9.23	9.65	7.68	7.03	6.37	6.93
Annual Ranges														
1987 High	10.96	11.27	11.78	10.74	11.09	11.48	12.06	11.03	11.37	11.92	10.30	9.89	8.90	9.31
Low	8.59	8.89	9.13	8.37	8.89	8.83	9.52	8.76	8.88	9.36	7.57	6.90	6.26	6.53
1986 High	10.24	10.69	11.06	9.80	10.41	10.58	11.26	10.32	10.58	11.15	9.51	9.15	8.44	8.21
Low	8.76	9.05	9.36	8.50	9.18	8.99	9.81	8.98	9.19	9.61	7.23	6.98	6.73	6.73
1985 High	12.54	12.87	13.24	12.00	12.43	12.50	13.19	12.48	12.62	13.14	11.84	11.89	10.82	9.93
Low	10.01	10.49	10.93	9.50	10.13	10.20	11.13	10.07	10.34	11.03	9.24	8.86	8.11	8.41
1984 High	14.45	14.78	15.60	13.66	14.13	14.42	15.12	14.23	14.54	15.32	13.89	13.79	13.22	11.14
Low	11.94	12.31	12.80	11.40	11.73	12.06	12.78	11.84	12.18	12.79	11.25	11.30	10.19	9.48
1983 High	13.05	13.14	13.74	12.38	12.62	12.94	13.67	12.83	13.04	13.63	11.99	12.03	11.26	10.01
Low	10.85	11.10	11.49	10.51	10.72	11.07	11.68	10.78	11.08	11.58	10.18	9.83	9.21	8.72
1982 High	16.13	16.39	17.14	14.76	15.13	15.57	17.03	15.63	15.91	17.08	14.32	14.56	14.57	13.34
Low	11.39	11.78	12.68	10.55	10.96	11.75	13.28	11.18	11.80	13.17	10.18	9.91	9.57	9.16
1981 High	16.63	17.01	18.19	15.67	15.89	16.23	16.82	16.26	16.62	17.51	15.08	15.56	16.13	13.20
Low	13.05	13.19	14.35	12.03	12.27	12.77	13.20	12.66	12.98	13.77	11.52	12.10	12.37	9.47
1980 High	13.99	14.23	15.27	13.10	13.29	13.61	14.24	13.64	13.90	14.61	12.68	13.62	14.66	10.46
Low	10.07	10.55	11.93	9.87	10.05	10.67	11.50	10.23	10.61	11.75	9.55	9.10	8.49	6.96
1979 High	11.24	11.52	12.26	10.64	11.01	11.16	12.32	11.10	11.33	12.25	10.59	11.25	12.07	7.29
Low	9.41	9.57	10.03	8.87	9.05	9.33	10.00	9.23	9.47	10.02	8.74	8.67	8.77	5.98
1978 High	9.57	9.75	10.11	9.14	9.29	9.38	10.16	9.41	9.57	10.09	8.95	9.46	10.26	6.48
Low	8.68	8.83	8.99	8.33	8.45	8.59	9.04	8.61	8.71	9.07	8.04	7.50	6.68	5.49
1977 High	8.67	8.84	9.03	8.32	8.46	8.59	9.26	8.58	8.72	9.07	8.02	7.49	6.95	5.81
Low	8.27	8.39	8.51	7.83	7.97	8.16	8.64	8.12	8.27	8.64	7.26	5.90	5.39	5.33

†"AAA" Public Utility & Composite bond yields discontinued January, 1984

SOURCE: *Standard & Poor's Bond Guide* (New York: Standard & Poor's Corporation, January, 1988).

EXHIBIT 16-4

Standard & Poor's Rating Methodology

Each rating analysis begins with an assessment of the company's environment. To determine the degree of operating risk that faces a participant in a given business, S&P analyzes the dynamics of that business. This analysis focuses on the strength of the industry prospects, as well as the competitive factors that affect that industry.

The many factors that are assessed include: Is the industry in a growth, stable, or declining phase? Does the business display cycles independent of the economy as, for example, agriculture? Or, if it moves with the economy in general, is it more or less volatile? Does it lead or lag economic trends or does it have contracyclical tendencies?

What is its vulnerability to technological change, labor unrest, or regulatory interference? Are assets typically concentrated in receivables and inventory, or is there a need for fixed plant of a specialized nature? The list goes on. The implications of increasing competition are obviously crucial. S&P's knowledge of the investment plans of the major players in an industry offers a unique vantage point from which to assess competitive prospects.

While any particular profile category can be *the* overriding consideration, it must be noted that the industry risk assessment will go a long way toward setting the upper limit on the rating to which any participant in the industry can aspire. Specifically, it would be very difficult to imagine S&P assigning 'AA' and 'AAA' bond ratings or 'A-1+' commercial paper ratings to companies with heavy participation in industries considered to be of above-average risk regardless of how conservative a financial posture is maintained.

Examples of some of the industries S&P would so characterize are integrated steel makers, tire and rubber companies, homebuilders, and most of the mining sector.

Conversely, some industries are regarded favorably by S&P. They are distinguished by such traits as steady demand growth, an ability to maintain margins without impairing future prospects, flexibility in the timing of capital outlays, and moderate capital intensity. Industries possessing one or more of these attributes include manufacturers of branded consumer products, drug firms, and publishing and broadcasting. Again, high marks in this category do not translate into high ratings for all industry participants, but it certainly doesn't hurt to have the cushion of strong industry fundamentals to fall back on.

Often a changed industry outlook will lead to rating changes for firms competing in that industry. Whether a specific company's rating is raised or lowered as a result of a changed industry outlook depends on that company's ability to achieve the attributes for success and avoid the pitfalls in that business. A change in an industry's outlook certainly prompts S&P to closely examine its ratings in that area, but all participants may not be affected equally by the revised outlook. For example, decline of the aluminum industry fundamentals led to a review and subsequent downgrading of every industry participant with rated debt in the spring of 1985. However, Alumax Inc.--by virtue of its more protected niche in fabricated aluminum for construction--was reduced less than the others.

SOURCE: *Standard & Poor's Debt Ratings Criteria:* Industrial Overview (New York: Standard & Poor's Corporation, 1986) pp. 21-22.

After gathering an appropriate set of publicly traded equivalent securities, the analyst should examine several quantitative and qualitative factors of the privately held debt security issuer and compare them to those of the publicly traded debt security issuers. This analysis is similar to that for valuing common stock in a closely held business.

The analyst should quantitatively analyze and compare the operating performance and financial position of the debt security issuer to those of the comparative publicly traded debt security issuers. This analysis is similar to that described above in comparing the operating performance and financial condition of the closely held debt security issuer to the broad population of its publicly traded counterparts. This comparison will offer the analyst insight into the appropriate yield to maturity for the closely held debt security relative to those of the comparative publicly traded debt securities.

If the valuation is to be done in considerable depth, the appraiser may wish to analyze relevant economic and industry data, as well as the company's fundamental position, in some detail, as discussed elsewhere in the book.

After completing the quantitative and qualitative analysis discussed above, the analyst must develop an opinion of the risk associated with the cash flows from the closely held debt security in relation to the risk associated with the cash flows of the publicly traded debt securities. Based on the closely held security's risk and the publicly traded debt securities' yields to maturity, the analyst determines the appropriate yield to maturity to apply to the closely held debt security cash flows.

Valuation Conclusion.   Having determined the appropriate yield to maturity to apply to the future cash flows associated with a closely held debt security, the analyst may value the debt security simply by computing the present value of its cash flows, using Formula 16–1.

Marketability Aspects of Closely Held Debt Securities

Chapter 10, "Data on Discounts for Lack of Marketability," presents a great deal of evidence in support of a discount for lack of marketability for the common stock of closely held businesses. On the surface, it appears that such a discount might also be appropriate for closely held debt securities. However, such a discount often is not required or, if required, would be much less than such a discount for a common stock. Unlike investment returns on common stock, which are generated primarily by appreciation in the price of the common stock and contingent on the ability to sell the stock to realize the price appreciation, investment returns on most debt securities are generated predominantly by cash flows in the form of interest payments over the securities' lives. These cash flows are anticipated to be received by the debt security holder regardless of the security's marketability, and the repayment of principal is a contractual obligation for a given amount at a fixed point in time. Therefore, if the marketability of a debt security is to be considered at all, the discount associated with the security's lack of marketability should be much less than that associated with closely held common stock. If the analyst thinks that marketability is a valid consideration in the valuation of a particular closely held debt security, the adjustment can be handled by either increasing the appropriate yield to maturity to apply to the debt security cash flows to compensate for the additional risk associated with lack of marketability or taking a discount from the value determined by applying a yield to maturity unadjusted for marketability considerations.

Special Characteristics of Various Debt Securities

In determining the value of a debt security, it is extremely important to analyze the security's various characteristics or provisions that will impact on its value. In addition, if comparative publicly traded debt securities are used in the valuation, any differences between the provisions of the security being valued and those of the comparatives should be considered. The following discussion focuses on some of the most common provisions of various debt securities that should be analyzed in the valuation process.

Call Provisions

A feature associated with some debt securities is a *call* provision. This allows the debtor to repay the debt prior to its maturity. Usually, the debt may not be called for some period early in its life, often the first five years. Furthermore, the debtor usually must pay a premium in addition to the amount of debt outstanding to the debtholder when the debt is called. A call provision benefits the debtor, since it allows the debtor to repay the debt early in a period of declining interest rates. A debt security with a call provision usually will require a higher yield to maturity than an identical security without such a provision. This is due to the fact that if the debt security is called, the investor usually will be unable to find a comparable alternative investment vehicle with a yield to maturity as high as that of the original debt issue that was called. If the stated interest rate on the debt is above market rates, making exercise of the call provision likely, the analyst usually will focus on the yield-to-call date rather than on the yield to maturity.

Sinking Fund Provisions

A debt security may also have a *sinking fund* provision. This provision requires the debt issuer to call or retire a contractually determined portion of the entire debt issue periodically over time prior to the issue's maturity date. When a portion of a debt issue is retired under sinking fund provisions, the actual debt security to be retired is usually determined by lottery and the holder of the security typically is paid the security's face or par value. Although sinking fund provisions increase the uncertainty of the timing of future cash flows associated with a particular debt security, they are also thought to reduce the risk associated with the security. The sinking fund provisions ensure that a portion of the debt is retired periodically, thus reducing the amount of debt that will have to be paid off at maturity and lowering the risk of default on the debt.

Collateral Provisions

A debt security that has no pledge of specific property or assets as collateral for the debt is called a *debenture*. Although a debenture clearly will require a higher yield to maturity than an identical security secured by a specific asset, the relative risk associated with it will be reduced by indenture provisions designed to protect the debtholder. Such indenture provisions might include restrictions on the amount of additional debentures the debtor can issue before paying off the original debentures; restrictions on the payment of cash dividends to equity owners of the debt issuer while the debentures are outstanding; and provisions that require the issuer to meet minimum liquidity (such as working capital) requirements while the debentures are outstanding. Despite the protection such provisions provide, however, debentures generally are considered more risky than similar secured debt.

Income Tax Status

Interest earned on debt is subject to federal and state income taxation, with several exceptions. Interest earned on U.S. Treasury obligations and on many U.S. government agency obligations generally is exempt from income tax at the state level. Interest earned on most municipal obligations is exempt from federal income taxation and may also be exempt from state income taxation if the obligation originated in the state assessing the income tax. In addition, the purchaser must reside in the same state. As a result of this preferential tax status, debt securities not subject to some form of income taxation will require a lower yield to maturity than an identical security subject to income taxation. Conversely, a debt security subject to income taxation will require a higher yield to maturity than an identical security exempt from income taxation to compensate for the income tax liability associated with the interest on the debt security.

Zero Coupon Debt

An interesting form of debt security, known as a *zero coupon* debt security, allows the issuer to avoid paying cash to the debtholder for interest prior to the debt's maturity. The only cash payment from the debt issuer comes at maturity, when the debt's face value is repaid to the security holder. However, when the debt is originally issued, the debtor will receive proceeds substantially discounted from the debt's face amount. The difference between the amount of the proceeds the debtor receives at issue and the amount of debt the debtor repays at the maturity date is the investor's compensation in lieu of interest. The yield to maturity is simply the compound rate of return that equates the present value with the face value.

Convertible Debt

Corporations periodically issue bonds with conversion privileges, known as convertible bonds. These conversion privileges give the holder the right to convert the bond into a given number of shares of the issuing corporation's common stock at some future point. The bondholder has no obligation to convert the bond to stock if the conversion is not to the holder's advantage. The terms of the conversion privilege are usually set such that at the time the convertible debt is issued, there is no economic benefit in immediately converting the debt to stock. For example, if a $1,000-par-value convertible bond is issued for $1,000 and is convertible into 20 shares of the issuer's common stock that pays no dividend, there will be no economic benefit in converting the debt to stock as long as the common stock is selling for less than $50 per share.

A convertible bond is unique in that its value depends, to a certain extent, on the value of the common stock into which it can be converted. The convertible bond has a minimum value equal to its value as straight debt with no conversion privilege. However, as the value of the common stock into which the bond is convertible rises, the bond's value also will begin to depend on the common stock's value. Finally, as the common stock price continues to rise, there will be a point at which the incremental increase in the bond's value is nearly equal to the increase in the aggregate value of the number of common shares into which the bond can be converted. Once this relationship begins, the bond value has entered what is known as the *equity-equivalent region*. Continuing with the above example, if the bond value is indeed in the equity-equivalent region, as the value of a single share of common stock increased $1, the bond's value will increase $20 ($1 increase × 20 common shares per bond).

The valuation of closely held convertible debt securities presents a problem not associated with publicly traded convertible debt securities. Closely held debt securities are usually convertible into closely held stock with no readily determinable market price. Although it is theoretically correct to value closely held convertible debt by direct comparison with publicly traded convertible debt with comparable conversion privileges and other provisions, it is extremely difficult to find publicly traded convertible debt that meets these criteria. As a consequence, it is difficult to determine the value of the closely held convertible debt by comparison with publicly traded convertible debt other than when determining the minimum value of the convertible debt as a straight, nonconvertible issue.

One reasonable alternative approach to this dilemma is to segregate the convertible debt security into two parts: a straight, nonconvertible debt security and a derivative security in the form of an option or warrant to purchase the common stock at a given price. The nonconvertible debt portion of the security would then be valued in the manner for valuing nonconvertible debt securities described above. The option portion of the security would be valued in a manner described in Chapter 18, "Valuing Stock Options." Then these two values would be added together to determine the value of the convertible debt security.

Summary

Debt security valuations are required for a wide range of purposes. Some of the most frequent reasons include the possible purchase or sale of a debt security, an exchange of equity securities for debt securities, gift and estate taxes on debt securities, allocation of the enterprise value of a business entity among debt and other classes of securities, and the adjustment of the balance sheet for debt securities owned or owed.

The debt security valuation process includes an analysis of the debt security contract provisions to determine the amount and timing of cash flows associated with the security's ownership. Various contract provisions or characteristics that affect the amount, timing, and riskiness of cash flows include call provisions, sinking fund provisions, collateral provisions, income tax status, and whether the debt is a zero coupon issue or has conversion privileges.

The risk or uncertainty associated with the cash flows is further assessed through the use of comparative quantitative and qualitative analysis. This involves comparing the closely held debt security with a broad population of debt securities in order to determine the general ratings classification into which the security would fall if it were publicly traded. Then the closely held debt security is compared with specific comparative publicly traded debt securities similar in debt rating and nature in order to determine an appropriate yield to maturity to apply to the subject security. The present value of the debt security cash flows is determined by discounting the future cash flows at the appropriate yield to maturity. The analyst should consider the marketability of the debt security and determine whether a discount for lack of marketability or an increase in the debt security's yield to maturity is appropriate. However, such discounts, if any, are minor compared to discounts for lack of marketability for common stocks.

Finally, if a convertible debt security is being valued, the valuation process is further complicated by the security's "optionlike" features. In this case, further analysis similar to that described in Chapter 18 on the valuation of options may be used for assistance in the valuation process.

Bibliography: Valuing Debt Securities

CFA Readings in Fixed Income Securities Analysis. Charlottesville, Va.: The Institute of Chartered Financial Analysts, 1985.

Cohen, Jerome B.; Edward D. Zinbarg; and Arthur Zeikel. *Investment Analysis and Portfolio Management,* 4th ed. Homewood, Ill.: Richard D. Irwin, 1982.

Cottle, Sidney; Roger F. Murray; and Frank E. Block. *Graham and Dodd's Security Analysis,* 5th ed. New York: McGraw-Hill, 1988.

Fabozzi, Frank J., and Irving M. Pollack, eds. *The Handbook of Fixed Income Securities,* 2nd ed. Homewood, Ill.: Dow Jones-Irwin, 1987.

Graham, Benjamin; David L. Dodd; and Sidney Cottle. *Security Analysis: Principles and Techniques,* 4th ed. New York: McGraw-Hill, 1962.

Knecht, Luke D., and Michael L. McCowin. *Valuing Convertible Securities.* Chicago: Harris Trust & Savings Bank, 1986.

Levine, Sumner N., ed. *The Financial Analyst's Handbook,* 2nd ed. Homewood, Ill.: Dow Jones-Irwin, 1988.

Moody's Bond Record. New York: Moody's Investors Service, 1987.

Reilly, Frank M. *Investment Analysis and Portfolio Management*, 2nd ed. Hinsdale, Ill.: Dryden Press, 1985.

Sokoloff, Kiril, ed. *The Paine Webber Handbook of Stock and Bond Analysis.* New York: McGraw-Hill, 1979.

Standard & Poor's Bond Guide. New York: Standard & Poor's Corporation.

Standard & Poor's Credit Week. New York: Standard & Poor's Corporation.

Standard & Poor's Debt Ratings Criteria: Industrial Overview. New York: Standard & Poor's Corporation.

Chapter 17

Valuing Preferred Stock

Preferred stock commonly is found in closely held corporations. Despite this fact, very little has been written on the subject of the valuation of closely held preferred stock. This chapter presents a comprehensive discussion of the considerations in valuing closely held preferred stock.

Because preferred stock is similar in many respects to debt securities, this chapter takes the same format as Chapter 16, "Valuing Debt Securities." Like Chapter 16, this chapter first discusses common situations that require the valuation of preferred stock and then examines the method of valuation, marketability considerations, Revenue Ruling 83-120, and special characteristics typically found in closely held preferred stock.

Common Situations Requiring Valuation of Preferred Stock

There are many reasons for valuing preferred stock; these reasons are very similar to those for valuing debt securities discussed in Chapter 16. The most frequently encountered reasons are:

1. Purchase or sale for cash.
2. Exchange of common equity or debt for preferred stock, or vice versa.
3. Gift and estate taxes.
4. Allocating total enterprise value among classes of securities in a leveraged buyout, recapitalization, or bankruptcy reorganization.
5. Adjusting a balance sheet for preferred securities owned or outstanding.

Purchase or Sale for Cash

As is the case with debt securities, a company may have occasion to purchase or sell preferred stock for cash. If the preferred stock is existing stock, it is necessary to determine the cash-equivalent value. If it is to be newly issued, it will be necessary to structure the provisions so that the value will be equal to the price paid or received.

Exchange of Common Equity or Debt for Preferred Stock

If preferred stock is to be exchanged for some consideration other than cash, such as common stock, debt securities, or other property, it usually is most expedient to determine the cash-equivalent values of both the preferred stock and the other consideration.

The most typical situation encountered is one in which a company, or some or all of its stock, is to be sold and a preferred stock received as all or part of the consideration. In this case, it is important that the seller know the cash-equivalent value of the consideration being received for the company or stock being sold.

Gift and Estate Taxes

Preferred stock may be gifted or may be an asset in an estate. In either situation, a determination of the preferred stock's fair market value is needed for tax purposes. It is not at all uncommon to find that the fair market value of a preferred stock is considerably less than its par value.

Allocating Total Enterprise Value among Classes of Securities

As noted in Chapter 16, a leveraged buyout, by its very nature, results in the creation of new classes of securities, almost always including at least one class of debt. In addition, preferred stock may be issued in a leveraged buyout. Therefore, it is usually necessary not only to value the total enterprise but also to allocate the total value among the various classes of securities.

The issuance of preferred stocks in leveraged buyouts is becoming increasingly popular in situations involving ESOPs. Typically, the preferred stock is issued to the ESOP with other shareholders taking common stock. Issuing the preferred stock to the ESOP gives the ESOP a claim that is senior to the common shareholders' and at the same time allows a form of equity participation, thereby reducing the risk to the employees in a leveraged situation. One of the attractions of preferred stocks for ESOPs is the fact that, under the current tax law, dividends paid on preferred ESOP stock can be a tax-deductible expense to the corporation in most circumstances. (See Chapter 23 on Employee Stock Ownership Plans.)

Recapitalizations very often involve preferred stock, thereby requiring a valuation of the security. In recapitalizations involving preferred stock, a new class of preferred is issued, which the current owners of the business typically retain, while the common stock is passed along to other shareholders.

As noted in Chapter 16, bankruptcy reorganizations, by their nature, involve debt securities. Preferred stock often is issued along with the debt securities. As Chapter 16 notes, creative structuring of debt and preferred stock can be an essential tool in achieving a successful bankruptcy reorganization.

Adjusting a Balance Sheet for Preferred Stock Owned or Outstanding

The most common situation requiring a balance-sheet adjustment for preferred stock outstanding occurs when the appraiser is using debt-free approaches to valuing common stock. In this situation, the market value of any preferred stock must be determined as well as the market value of any debt outstanding. As discussed in Chapter 4, when the market value of debt and preferred stock is deducted from the value of the company's total capital, what remains is the value of the company's equity.

Also, the company may own some preferred stock that may need valuing if the analyst is adjusting the various line items on the balance sheet to fair market value.

Method of Valuation

Simply stated, the value of a preferred stock lacking any common equity kicker, such as convertibility or other special features, is equal to the present value of its future income stream discounted at its required rate of return, or yield. The higher the risk inherent in the investment, the higher the required yield.

Assessing Dividend and Liquidation Payment Risk

The single most important factor in the value of most preferred stock is the stock's dividend rate. Another factor would be redemption in the case of a preferred stock that has a prospect of being redeemed. In most instances, the primary source of value to the preferred stockholder is the right to future levels of income through the receipt of dividends. Therefore, in determining the appropriate required yield for the subject company preferred, the risk that the dividends on the preferred stock will not be paid is critical.

The most prevalent measure for assessing the likelihood of receiving future preferred dividends is the company's fixed-charge coverage ratio, defined as the sum of pretax income plus interest expense divided by the sum of interest expense plus preferred dividends adjusted for taxes.[1] The higher this ratio, the greater the subject company's capacity to pay its preferred dividends (or, conversely, the lower the risk that the company will miss dividend payments) and, therefore, the lower the required yield. Rating agencies use the fixed-charge coverage ratio as part of the analysis conducted to determine the appropriate rating to assign a particular preferred stock issue. Moreover, the Internal Revenue Service Revenue Ruling 83-120 (to be discussed later) specifically requires analysis of the fixed-charge coverage ratio for preferred stock valuations involving federal gift, estate, or income taxes.

Other ratios than the fixed-charge coverage ratio are used to assess the subject company's dividend payment risk. One example is the re-

---

[1]The fixed-charge coverage ratio has many definitions. However, Standard & Poor's uses this definition of fixed-charge coverage in its preferred stock rating process. See *Standard & Poor's Debt Ratings Criteria: Industrial Overview* (New York: Standard & Poor's Corporation, 1986).

turn on total capital, defined as the sum of pretax income plus interest expense divided by the sum of long-term debt and shareholders' preferred and common equity. Several variations of this ratio also can be used, such as pretax cash flow return on total capital or pretax earnings before interest and depreciation charges return on total capital. A higher ratio indicates superior profitability and, thus, a greater ability to meet preferred dividend obligations.

Another often-calculated ratio is the liquidation coverage ratio, defined as the sum of the market value of total assets less the market value of total liabilities divided by the aggregate liquidation value of the preferred stock. This ratio helps the analyst identify the risk that the preferred shareholder will not receive the full liquidation payment in the event of the corporation's liquidation. Analysis of this ratio also is specifically required in Revenue Ruling 83-120. A higher ratio implies greater protection of the shareholder's investment in the event of liquidation of company assets.

The problem with the above ratios is that they address the subject company's dividend payment risk only as of a certain point in time. Because many companies exhibit cyclical earnings fluctuations, recent operating results may not accurately reflect a company's long-term dividend payment risk. A company subject to large swings in profits is more likely to suspend preferred dividends in down years, even though its average earnings may far exceed the annual preferred stock dividend requirements. Depending on the situation, the analyst may want to compute the above ratios using historical average financial statement figures.

The subject company's capitalization ratio is another measure of long-term dividend payment risk. The capitalization ratio is defined as the sum of long-term debt and the aggregate liquidation value of preferred stock divided by the sum of long-term debt and total equity. This ratio measures the company's leverage and indicates how vulnerable the company will be in cyclical downturns. The higher the capitalization ratio, the greater the company's vulnerability to cyclical downturns; therefore, the risk of losing out on preferred dividend payments over the long term is higher.

The methods of calculating these ratios are shown in Exhibit 17–1. If the analyst is valuing a preferred stock that has not yet been issued, a situation that often occurs in recapitalizations, the subject company ratios must be calculated on a pro forma basis, assuming that the subject preferred issue is outstanding.

Comparison with Publicly Traded Preferred Stocks

None of the ratios discussed above imply, in and of themselves, the appropriate required yield to apply to the subject preferred stock's income stream. In order to determine the appropriate required yield, and thus the value of the preferred stock, the ratios determined for the subject company must be compared to similarly calculated ratios

EXHIBIT 17-1

Preferred Stock Dividend and Liquidation Payment Risk Ratios

Fixed charge coverage $\quad = \quad$ $$\frac{\text{EBIT}}{\text{I} + (\text{Preferred dividends}) \div (1 - t)}$$

Liquidation coverage $\quad = \quad$ $$\frac{(\text{Market value of assets - Market value of liabilities})^a}{\text{Aggregate liquidation value of preferred stock}}$$

Capitalization ratio $\quad = \quad$ $$\frac{(\text{Total debt + Liquidation value of all preferred stock})}{(\text{Total debt + Total equity})}$$

Pretax return on
total capital $\quad = \quad$ $$\frac{(\text{Pretax income + Interest expense})}{(\text{Long-term debt + Total equity})}$$

---

[a] From a practical standpoint, total book value of equity is often used.

NOTE: All net income and cash flow figures are before preferred stock dividends, discontinued operations, nonrecurring items, and extraordinary items.

EBIT $\quad=\quad$ Earnings before interest expense and taxes
I $\quad=\quad$ Interest expense
T $\quad=\quad$ Taxes
t $\quad=\quad$ Effective tax rate

for a group of publicly traded preferred stocks having the *same rights and privileges as the subject company*. Once these ratios are calculated, the comparable publicly traded preferred stocks must be grouped by rating category.

Quantitative Comparison. Both Moody's and Standard & Poor's rate publicly traded preferred stock issues. Exhibit 17–2 shows Standard & Poor's ratings and its explanation of the nature of the risk of the preferred stocks contained in each category. Exhibit 17–3 shows the yields of nonconvertible publicly traded preferred stocks as they existed in mid-1987. As can be seen from Exhibit 17–3, there were 256 nonconvertible fixed-dividend-rate preferred stocks issued by 131 different companies listed in the June 1987 Standard & Poor's *Stock Guide*.

It is extremely important that the comparative publicly traded preferred stocks used to determine appropriate yields for the subject stock be as similar as possible to the subject stock in rights, privileges, and all relevant characteristics. Differences in these factors can have a dramatic impact on the required yield. In addition, I suggest that when selecting publicly traded preferred stocks to use as comparatives, preferred stocks issued by utilities, banks, insurance companies, and other financial institutions be excluded (unless the preferred stock to be valued is issued by a utility, bank, or insurance company). The criteria the rating agencies use differ somewhat for these types of issues due to their unique financial statement presentation and the

EXHIBIT 17-2

Standard & Poor's
Preferred Stock Ratings

"AAA"   This is the highest rating that may be assigned by Standard & Poor's to a preferred stock issue and indicates an extremely strong capacity to pay the preferred stock obligations.

"AA"   A preferred stock issue rated "AA" also qualifies as a high-quality, fixed income security. The capacity to pay preferred stock obligations is very strong, although not as overwhelming as for issues rates "AAA."

"A"   An issue rates "A" is backed by a sound capacity to pay the preferred stock obligations, although it is somewhat more susceptible to the adverse effects of changes in circumstances and economic conditions.

"BBB"   An issue rated "BBB" is regarded as backed by an adequate capacity to pay the preferred stock obligations. Whereas it normally exhibits adequate protection parameters, adverse economic conditions or changing circumstances are more likely to lead to a weakened capacity to make payments for a preferred stock in this category than for issues in the "A" category.

"BB," "B," "CCC"   Preferred stock rated "BB," "B," and "CCC" are regarded, on balance, as predominantly speculative with respect to the issuer's capacity to pay preferred stock obligations. "BB" indicates the lowest degree of speculation and "CCC" the highest degree of speculation. While such issues will likely have some quality and protective characteristics, these are outweighed by large uncertainties or major risk exposures to adverse conditions.

"CC"   The rating "CC" is reserved for a preferred stock issue in arrears on dividends or sinking fund payments but that is currently paying.

"C"   A preferred stock rated "C" is a non-paying issue.

"D"   A preferred stock rated "D" is a non-paying issue with the issuer in default on debt instruments.

NR   indicates that no rating has been requested, that there is insufficient information on which to base a rating, or that S&P does not rate a particular type of obligation as a matter of policy.

Plus (+) or **Minus (-)**   To provide more detailed indications of preferred stock quality, the ratings from "AA" to "BB" may be modified by the addition of a plus or minus sign to show relative standing within the major rating categories.

SOURCE: Standard & Poor's *Stock Guide.* (New York: Standard & Poor's Corporation, 1987).

EXHIBIT 17-3

Preferred Stock--Dividend Yield Summary

	Companies	Issues	Range Low %	Range High %	Mean %	Median %
AA	8	22	7.2	9.5	8.3	8.2
AA—	5	7	7.8	9.2	8.4	8.5
A+	4	6	7.7	9.8	8.8	9.1
A	14	23	7.4	11.0	8.9	8.9
A—	13	19	6.2	10.4	9.0	9.3
BBB+	14	30	8.8	13.6	10.0	9.7
BBB	14	33	8.2	12.4	9.9	9.7
BBB—	10	18	7.3	12.3	9.5	9.7
BB+	12	31	8.1	13.7	11.0	10.8
BB	5	6	7.9	11.7	9.9	9.9
BB—	2	2	10.2	11.8	11.0	11.0
B	4	12	9.5	14.0	12.0	12.8
B+	2	3	11.4	16.0	13.1	11.8
CCC	3	3	0.0	13.4	11.9[a]	11.9[a]
NR	16	20	0.0	30.7	12.3[a]	9.7[a]
C[b]	5	20				

[a]   Excludes non-dividend paying issues.
[b]   Non-dividend paying by definition.
SOURCE: All nonconvertible, fixed-rate preferred shares listed in the June 1987 *Standard & Poor's Stock Guide.*

fact that they are regulated. Because preferred stock ratings affect the investor's perception of risk, they also impact the required yield.

Once the ratios are calculated for both the subject company and the publicly traded comparatives and the publicly traded issues categorized by rating, the yields of each issue must be calculated and averaged for each rating category. The ratios for each issue also need to be averaged in each rating category. Exhibit 17–4 shows an example of the end result of this process. As can be seen there, generally the more favorable the ratios, the higher the rating and the lower the yield. In addition, once financial institutions and utilities are excluded, the number of comparative preferred stocks drops significantly. In most circumstances, it is not necessary to compute dividend yields and ratios for each rating category. This is because once the dividend and liquidation payment risk ratios for the subject company have been calculated, it often becomes clear to the analyst into which rating category the subject preferred generally would fit.

Once all the necessary comparative data are available, the next step is to determine the rating category into which the subject preferred stock would fall given the subject company's dividend and liquidation payment risk. The appropriate yield is selected for the subject company based on the yields in the appropriate rating category.

Qualitative Factors. At this point, the analyst must consider any unique qualitative factors that might cause the required yield to be higher or lower than that determined based on the quantitative ratio analysis. These include many of the nonquantitative factors generally considered in valuing common stock that would increase or decrease the issuing company's risk. However, when assessing risk, the preferred shareholder will be most concerned with qualitative factors that may change the company's ability to meet its preferred stock obliga-

EXHIBIT 17-4

Nonconvertible, Non-Sinking Fund, Fixed-Rate, Cumulative Preferred Stocks
Excluding Financial Institutions and Utilities

S&P Rating	No. Issues	Yield Range Low %	Yield Range High %	Yield %	Average Fixed Charge Coverage	Average Liquidation Coverage	Average Tot. Debt/ Tot. Equity	Average Rtn. on Tot. Cap. %
AAA	0	—	—	—	—	—	—	—
AA	3	8.1	8.5	8.2	13.6	76.5	0.9	21.6
A	5	7.9	9.8	9.0	4.0	54.9	2.2	17.4
BBB	4	9.0	12.1	10.2	0.8	18.3	3.2	6.6
BB	1	—	—	9.2	2.0	3.8	1.5	19.7
B	2	10.8	12.6	11.7	0.2	60.6	1.9	1.7
CCC	0	—	—	—	—	—	—	—

NOTE: For companies that have several nonconvertible, non-sinking fund, fixed-rate, cumulative preferred stocks outstanding, the most senior preferred stock was used.

SOURCES: *Standard & Poor's Stock Guide,* December 1987; *Standard & Poor's Corporation Records;* prices obtained from *The Wall Street Journal,* December 10, 1987 and CompuServe; and Willamette Management Associates, Inc. calculations.

tions. As suggested in an article in *Taxes* magazine, these qualitative factors might include the following:

1. The competitive environment in the industry.
2. Depth and competence of management.
3. Proposed federal regulation of the business.
4. Rights of lenders and other stockholders to influence dividend policy.
5. Trends in and diversification of supply sources.
6. Trends in and diversification of revenue sources.[2]

Standard & Poor's performs an extensive analysis of a company's qualitative factors in determining a security's appropriate rating. In addition, the outlook for the industry and economy also play an important role in assessing the subject company's preferred stock income stream risk.

Capitalizing the Income Stream

Once the appropriate required yield is determined, the next step is to capitalize the preferred stock's future income stream by its required yield. Mechanically, this is a simple present value calculation. For a noncallable, nonsinking-fund preferred stock with no maturity and lacking a conversion feature, the formula for determining the value is as follows:

Formula 17–1: Present Value of Noncallable, Nonsinking-Fund Preferred Stock with No Maturity, and Lacking a Conversion Feature

$$\text{Present value} = \frac{\text{Dividend}}{\text{Required yield}}$$

If the issue is nonconvertible and callable or subject to a sinking fund, its value is calculated as follows:

Formula 17–2: Present Value of a Nonconvertible Preferred Stock That Either Is Callable or Has a Sinking Fund

$$\text{Present value} = \sum_{i=1}^{n} \frac{C_i}{(1 + r)^i}$$

where:

C_i = Cash flow (including redemption price and dividends) in the ith period in the future
i = Period when cash flows are generated
r = Required yield at which cash flows are to be discounted back to the present
n = Number of periods until redemption

---

[2]Gerald R. Martin and E. Halsey Sandford, "Applying Fair Market Value Appraisal Techniques to Closely Held Preferred Stock," *Taxes*, February 1978, pp. 108–15.

It is important to note that even if a preferred stock is callable at the company's option, it usually is appropriate to value the issue as if it were noncallable if the stated dividend rate is below the rate currently required by the market for comparable issues. For example, if a $100-par-value preferred stock, callable at $100 per share and with a stated dividend of 6 percent, requires a yield of 10 percent under current market conditions, the call feature has little or no effect as a practical matter. If the required yield is above the stated yield, the company will not exercise its option to call the issue, which renders the call feature irrelevant for the preferred stockholder.

Marketability Aspects of Closely Held Preferred Stock

Chapter 10, "Data on Discounts for Lack of Marketability," presented a great deal of evidence in support of a discount for lack of marketability on common stock of closely held businesses. On the surface, it appears that such a discount might also be appropriate for closely held preferred stocks. However, such a discount often is not required for preferred stocks or, if required, would be much less than such a discount for common stocks. Unlike investment returns on closely held common stock, which are predominantly generated by appreciation in the common stock's price and contingent upon the ability to sell the stock to realize the price appreciation, investment returns on most preferred stocks, as on debt securities, are predominantly generated by cash flows in the form of dividend payments over the life of the security. These cash flows are anticipated to be received by the holder of the preferred stock regardless of how marketable the preferred stock happens to be. Therefore, if the marketability aspects of a preferred stock are to be considered at all, the discount associated with the lack of marketability should be much less than that associated with closely held common stock.

If the analyst thinks that marketability is a valid consideration in the valuation of a particular closely held preferred stock, the adjustment can be handled by either increasing the appropriate yield to apply to the preferred stock's dividends or by taking a discount from the value determined by applying a yield unadjusted for marketability considerations.

Revenue Ruling 83-120

At this writing, the only regulatory guidelines established for the valuation of closely held preferred stock are those issued by the Internal Revenue Service in Revenue Ruling 83-120 (see Exhibit 17–5). Although applicable to any valuation of preferred stock in a closely held corporation, the ruling was specifically designed to prevent the relative overvaluation of preferred stock and concurrent undervaluation

EXHIBIT 17-5

Revenue Ruling 83-120

Section 1. Purpose

The purpose of this Revenue Ruling is to amplify Rev. Rul. 59-60, 1959-1 C.B. 237, by specifying additional factors to be considered in valuing common and preferred stock of a closely held corporation for gift tax and other purposes in a recapitalization of closely held businesses. This type of valuation problem frequently arises with respect to estate planning transactions wherein an individual receives preferred stock with a stated par value equal to all or a large portion of the fair market value of the individual's former stock interest in a corporation. The individual also receives common stock which is then transferred, usually as a gift, to a relative.

Sec. 2. Background

.01 One of the frequent objectives of the type of transaction mentioned above is the transfer of the potential appreciation of an individual's stock interest in a corporation to relatives at a nominal or small gift tax cost. Achievement of this objective requires preferred stock having a fair market value equal to a large part of the fair market value of the individual's former stock interest and common stock having a nominal or small fair market value. The approach and factors described in this Revenue Ruling are directed toward ascertaining the true fair market value of the common and preferred stock and will usually result in the determination of a substantial fair market value for the common stock and a fair market value for the preferred stock which is substantially less than its par value.

.02 The type of transaction referred to above can arise in many different contexts. Some examples are:

(a) *A* owns 100% of the common stock (the only outstanding stock) of *Z* Corporation which has a fair market value of 10,500x. In a recapitalization described in section 368 (a) (1)(E), *A* receives preferred stock with a par value of 10,000x and new common stock, which *A* then transfers to *A*'s son *B*.

(b) *A* owns some of the common stock of *Z* Corporation (or the stock of several corporations) the fair market value of which stock is 10,500x. *A* transfers this stock to a new corporation *X* in exchange for preferred stock of *X* corporation with a par value of 10,000x and common stock of corporation, which *A* then transfers to *A*'s son *B*.

(c) *A* owns 80 shares and his son *B* owns 20 shares of the common stock (the only stock outstanding) of *Z* Corporation. In a recapitalization described in section 368(a)(1)(E), *A* exchanges his 80 shares of common stock for 80 shares of new preferred stock of *Z* Corporation with a par value of 10,000x. *A*'s common stock had a fair market value of 10,000x.

Sec. 3. General Approach to Valuation

Under section 25.2512-2(f)(2) of the Gift Tax Regulations, the fair market value of stock in a closely held corporation depends upon numerous factors, including the corporation's net worth, its prospective earning power, and its capacity to pay dividends. In addition, other relevant factors must be taken into account. *See* Rev. Rul. 59-60. The weight to be accorded any evidentiary factor depends on the circumstances of each case. *See* section 25.2512-2(f) of the Gift Tax Regulations.

Sec. 4. Approach to Valuation–Preferred Stock

.01 In general the most important factors to be considered in determining the value of preferred stock are its yield, dividend coverage and protection of its liquidation preference.

.02 Whether the yield of the preferred stock supports a valuation of the stock at par value depends in part on the adequacy of the dividend rate. The adequacy of the dividend rate should be determined by comparing its dividend rate with the dividend rate of high-grade publicly traded preferred stock. A lower yield than that of high-grade preferred stock indicates a preferred stock value of less than par. If the rate of interest charged by independent creditors to the corporation on loans is higher than the rate such independent creditors charge their most credit worthy borrowers, then the yield on the preferred stock should be correspondingly higher than the yield on high quality preferred stock. A yield which is not correspondingly higher reduces the value of the preferred stock. In addition, whether the preferred stock has a fixed dividend rate and is nonparticipating influences the value of the preferred stock. A publicly traded preferred stock for a company having a similar business and similar assets with similar liquidation preferences, voting rights and other similar terms would be the ideal comparable for determining yield required in arms length transactions for closely held stock. Such ideal comparables will frequently not exist. In such circumstances, the most comparable publicly-traded issues should be selected for comparison and appropriate adjustments made for differing factors.

.03 The actual dividend rate on a preferred stock can be assumed to be its stated rate if the issuing corporation will be able to pay its stated dividends in a timely manner and will, in fact, pay such dividends. The risk that the corporation may be unable to timely pay the stated dividends on the preferred stock can be measured by the coverage of such stated dividends by the corporation's earnings. Coverage of the dividend is measured by the ratio of the sum of pre-tax and pre-interest earnings to the sum of the total interest to be paid and the pre-tax

EXHIBIT 17-5

Revenue Ruling 83-120
(Continued)

earnings needed to pay the after-tax dividends. *Standard & Poor's Ratings Guide, 58* (1979). Inadequate coverage exists where a decline in corporate profits would be likely to jeopardize the corporation's ability to pay dividends on the preferred stock. The ratio for the preferred stock in question should be compared with the ratios for high quality preferred stock to determine whether the preferred stock has adequate coverage. Prior earnings history is important in this determination. Inadequate coverage indicates that the value of preferred stock is lower than its par value. Moreover, the absence of a provision that preferred dividends are cumulative raises substantial questions concerning whether the stated dividend rate will, in fact, be paid. Accordingly, preferred stock with noncumulative dividend features will normally have a value substantially lower than a cumulative preferred stock with the same yield, liquidation preference and dividend coverage.

.04 Whether the issuing corporation will be able to pay the full liquidation preference at liquidation must be taken into account in determining fair market value. This risk can be measured by the protection afforded by the corporation's net assets. Such protection can be measured by the ratio of the excess of the current market value of the corporation's assets over its liabilities to the aggregate liquidation preference. The protection ratio should be compared with the ratios for high quality preferred stock to determine adequacy of coverage. Inadequate asset protection exists where any unforeseen business reverses would be likely to jeopardize the corporation's ability to pay the full liquidation preference to the holders of the preferred stock.

.05 Another factor to be considered in valuing the preferred stock is whether it has voting rights and, if so, whether the preferred stock has voting control. See, however, Section 5.02 below.

.06 Peculiar covenants or provisions of the preferred stock of a type not ordinarily found in publicly traded preferred stock should be carefully evaluated to determine the effects of such covenants on the value of the preferred stock. In general, if covenants would inhibit the marketability of the stock or the power of the holder to enforce dividend or liquidation rights, such provisions will reduce the value of the preferred stock by comparison to the value of preferred stock not containing such covenants or provisions.

.07 Whether the preferred stock contains a redemption privilege is another factor to be considered in determining the value of the preferred stock. The value of a redemption privilege triggered by death of the preferred shareholder will not exceed the present value of the redemption premium payable at the preferred shareholder's death (i.e., the present value of the excess of the redemption price over the fair market value of the preferred stock upon its issuance). The value of the redemption privilege should be reduced to reflect any risk that the corporation may not possess sufficient assets to redeem its preferred stock at the stated redemption price. See .03 above.

Sec. 5. Approach to Valuation–Common Stock

.01 If the preferred stock has a fixed rate of dividend and is nonparticipating, the common stock has the exclusive right to the benefits of future appreciation of the value of the corporation. This right is valuable and usually warrants a determination that the common stock has substantial value. The actual value of this right depends upon the corporation's past growth experience, the economic condition of the industry in which the corporation operates, and general economic conditions. The factor to be used in capitalizing the corporation's prospective earnings must be determined after an analysis of numerous factors concerning the corporation and the economy as a whole. *See* Rev. Rul. 59-60, at page 243. In addition, after-tax earnings of the corporation at the time the preferred stock is issued in excess of the stated dividends on the preferred stock will increase the value of the common stock. Furthermore, a corporate policy of reinvesting earnings will also increase the value of the common stock.

.02 A factor to be considered in determining the value of the common stock is whether the preferred stock also has voting rights. Voting rights of the preferred stock, especially if the preferred stock has voting control, could under certain circumstances increase the value of the preferred stock and reduce the value of the common stock. This factor may be reduced in significance where the rights of common stockholders as a class are protected under state law from actions by another class of shareholders, *see Singer v. Magnavox Co.*, 380 A.2d 969 (Del. 1977), particularly where the common shareholders, as a class, are given the power to disapprove a proposal to allow preferred stock to be converted into common stock. See ABA-ALI Model Bus. Corp. Act, Section 60 (1969).

Sec. 6. Effect on Other Revenue Rulings

Rev. Rul. 59-60, as modified by Rev. Rul. 65-193, 1965-2 C.B. 370 and as amplified by Rev. Rul. 77-287, 1977-2 C.B. 319, and Rev. Rul. 80-213, 1980-2 C.B. 101, is further amplified.

of common stock in "estate-freezing recapitalizations" in closely held corporations.

In the section entitled "Approach to Valuation—Preferred Stock," Revenue Ruling 83-120 invokes the standard tools of security analysis for the valuation of the closely held preferred stock based on the issuing company's ability to pay its dividend yield and its liquidation preference. Revenue Ruling 83–120 specifically addresses the following factors affecting the value of preferred stock:

1. Stated dividend rate and the risk associated with payment of it.
2. Cumulative versus noncumulative dividends.
3. Ability to pay the preferred stock's liquidation preference at liquidation.
4. Voting rights.
5. Redemption privileges.

Specifically, the ruling calls on the valuation analyst to compute "coverage ratios" for the subject company's preferred stock dividend and liquidation value and to compare these ratios to those found for comparable publicly traded preferred stocks. The ruling indicates that if the ratios for the subject stock are substandard, the value of the subject preferred should be discounted from its par value on the basis of these criteria. Although the ruling is very specific with respect to these two factors, it leaves a wide area of uncertainty as to the value of features such as voting control and redemption rights, two extremely valuable features often found in closely held preferred stocks that will be discussed in the next section.

Special Characteristics of Closely Held Preferred Stocks

The difficulties encountered in valuing closely held preferred stock result primarily from determining the required yield rate given the stock's myriad characteristics. Because of the flexibility in characteristics such as dividend yield, voting rights, liquidation preference, redemption, and conversion rights, the ability to determine the value of preferred stock of a closely held business depends on the appraiser's experience and subjective judgment. The following discussion focuses on some of the most common special characteristics found in closely held preferred stock.

Dividend Rate

The dividend rate in and of itself is not special, but the type of dividend can be unique.

Fixed Dividend Rate. The most common form of dividend is one that is fixed at an amount usually stated as a percentage of the preferred stock's par value. For example, a $100-par-value, 10 percent preferred stock would pay an annual dividend of $10 per share. The value attributable to the stated dividend rate of the preferred stock depends on the issuing company's current and expected ability to pay the stated dividend rate and the current market yields of preferred stocks with similar dividend payment risk.

Adjustable Dividend Rate. A somewhat less common form of dividend is an adjustable-rate dividend. This form of dividend typically is adjustable within a stated range and is pegged to the general level of interest rates. However, the adjustable rate can be pegged to just about anything. I have seen situations in which the dividend rate was adjustable based on a given time period—for example, 10 percent from 1987 to 1990, 11 percent from 1990 to 1993, and so forth. I have also seen situations in which the dividend rate was adjusted based on the corporation's profits (in effect, a specialized form of participating preferred stock). In this case, the dividend might have equaled some percentage of the average of the corporation's last three fiscal years' earnings or some other measure of profits.

In order to determine the appropriate yield, or discount rate, to apply to the subject company's adjustable-rate preferred stock, publicly traded adjustable-rate preferred stocks can be used as a benchmark. However, the appraiser must be careful to note the differences between the basis for the adjustability of the subject company's preferred stock dividend and that of the publicly traded comparatives' preferred stock dividends. The adjustability differences in the subject preferred stock compared to its publicly traded adjustable counterparts will require either an increase or a decrease in the adjustable dividend yield evidenced in the market. Just as the case with a "straight" or fixed-dividend preferred stock, the subject company's ability to pay the adjustable dividend and its liquidation preference must also be analyzed, making appropriate adjustments to the publicly traded adjustable dividend yields as necessary.

In general, all other things being equal, adjustable-rate preferred stocks require a lower dividend yield, thereby increasing the preferred stock's value. As shown in Exhibit 17–6, in December 1987 market

EXHIBIT 17-6

Adjustable- and Fixed-Rate Preferred Stock Yields

S&P Rating	Average Yield As of 12/9/87				Yield Differential in Basis Points
	Adjustable %	No. Obs.	Fixed Rate %	No. Obs.	
AA	7.7	1	8.2	3	50
A	8.5	1	9.0	5	50
BBB	9.3	3	10.2	4	90
BB & B	10.1	4	10.9	3	80

SOURCE: Exhibit 17-4; all adjustable-rate preferred stocks, excluding financial institutions and utilities, listed in *Baird's Handbook,* December 1987; *Standard & Poor's Stock Guide,* December 1987; CompuServe; and Willamette Management Associates, Inc. calculations.

evidence indicated that adjustable-rate preferred stocks generally require yields in the range of 50 to 90 basis points[3] below the yields required on similar fixed-rate preferred stocks. However, at any given time, the reduction in required yield will depend on the level of interest rates prevailing in the market at the valuation date and the stated range of the adjustable dividend rate of the subject company's closely held preferred stock. For example, if market interest rates are at historically high levels at the valuation date, the likelihood of their going much higher is smaller. In this situation, the potential for a higher dividend rate in the future is diminished, thereby reducing the necessary adjustment to the yield. If the adjustable-rate range (or *collar*) on the closely held preferred stock is very small, there is less potential for an increase in the dividend, thereby reducing the required yield adjustment relative to an issue with a wider adjustable-dividend-rate range.

Cumulative versus Noncumulative Dividends

The term *cumulative,* when applied to preferred stock dividends, means that if the dividends are not paid for one or more periods, the corporation has a contractual obligation to make up the lapsed payments before declaring and paying any dividends on the common stock or on other junior issues. Furthermore, most cumulative issues also give preferred stockholders voting rights and/or the right to elect one or more members to the board of directors following the nonpayment of one or more dividends.

Cumulative dividends imply that the risk of nonpayment of dividends becomes secondary, because the cumulative feature requires that the shareholder not suffer a loss in income in the long run unless the company is never able to pay. In addition, when dividends are cumulative, liquidation coverage tends to become more important than dividend coverage, because in the event of liquidation cumulative dividends in arrears must be paid in addition to the stated liquidation preference before making any assets available for distribution to common shareholders.

Noncumulative preferred stocks are rare in the public market, and those few that do exist typically have special characteristics, making them unlikely to be useful as comparative securities. In general, all other things being equal, the value of a noncumulative preferred stock would be significantly less than an otherwise comparable cumulative preferred stock, because dividends not paid on a noncumulative issue are lost permanently. Revenue Ruling 83-120 addresses the cumulative-versus-noncumulative feature as follows:

> The absence of a provision that preferred dividends are cumulative raises substantial questions concerning whether the stated dividend rate will, in fact, be paid. Accordingly, preferred stock with noncumulative dividend features will normally have a value substantially lower than a cumulative

---

[3]100 basis points = 1 percentage point.

preferred stock with the same yield, liquidation preference and dividend coverage.

According to Graham, Dodd, and Cottle:

> One of the chief objections to the noncumulative provision is that it permits the directors to withhold dividends even in good years, when they are amply earned, the money thus saved inuring to the benefit of the common stockholders. Experience shows that noncumulative dividends are seldom paid unless they are necessitated by the desire to declare dividends on the common; and if the common dividend is later discontinued, the preferred dividend is almost invariably suspended soon afterward.[4]

However, the appraiser must also look at the subject company's history of dividend payments on noncumulative preferred stock and evidence of the company's intention to pay or not to pay preferred stock dividends. If the company has a solid history of paying dividends on its noncumulative preferred stock and a stated intention to do so in the future, and the company has the financial capability to pay dividends in the future, the diminution in value resulting from the noncumulative feature will be minimal. In addition, if the holder of a noncumulative preferred stock has full voting control of the corporation, the noncumulative feature becomes moot, since the shareholder controls the votes to pay or withhold dividends. With all these factors to consider, the impact of the noncumulative feature on value requires a considerable amount of experienced subjective judgment.

Liquidation Preference

Another important characteristic of a preferred stock is its liquidation preference and the subject company's ability to pay it in full at liquidation. In almost all cases, preferred stock carries a contractual right to preference (advantage) in the distribution of the issuing corporation's assets upon liquidation. The preferred stock's liquidation preference usually is stated as a certain dollar amount per share, such as $100 per share. Revenue Ruling 83-120 requires that the issuing corporation's ability to pay the full liquidation preference at liquidation be taken into account in determining the preferred stock's fair market value. According to the ruling, this risk can be measured by the protection afforded by the corporation's net assets. The ruling sets out the method of measuring this protection as follows:

Formula 17–3: Liquidation Coverage

$$\frac{\text{Market value of assets} - \text{Market value of liabilities}}{\text{Aggregate liquidation preference of preferred stock}}$$

This ratio should be high enough that any unforeseen business downturns would not jeopardize the issuing corporation's ability to pay

---

[4]Benjamin Graham, David L. Dodd, and Sidney Cottle, *Security Analysis—Principles and Technique* (New York: McGraw Hill, 1962), p. 391.

the liquidation preference. This ratio should be compared with ratios of publicly traded preferred stocks. All other things being equal, if the subject company's preferred stock liquidation coverage ratio is higher than the publicly traded preferred stock ratios, a lower yield (or, conversely, a higher value) will be required on the subject company preferred stock due to the lower risk of nonpayment of the liquidation preference upon liquidation. However, it should be noted that since most investors look at investments in preferred stock on a going-concern basis, the liquidation coverage ratio generally is a less important factor in the valuation than the dividend coverage ratio.

It should be noted that it is extremely difficult, if not impossible, to obtain adequate data about the comparative publicly traded preferred stocks to compute the market value of assets called for in the above liquidation coverage ratio. Therefore, as a practical matter, analysts will often use the book value of the issuing corporation's assets and liabilities in calculating the liquidation coverage ratios.

Redeemable versus Nonredeemable

Most privately held preferred stock is nonredeemable; that is, the issue has an infinite life. However, in many instances a preferred stock has a contractual redemption provision. The type of redemption provision can vary significantly. The most common forms of redemption provision found in privately held companies are as follows:

1. The entire issue is redeemable at the option of the issuing corporation at a specified price (typically par value) over a designated time period. These types of issues are commonly referred to as *callable*.
2. The entire issue is redeemable at the option of the issuing corporation at a specified price contingent upon a certain event, such as the death of a major shareholder, a change in ownership control, or issuance of other securities.
3. Future redemption by the issuing company is mandatory and based on a specific redemption schedule. These types of issues have sinking fund provisions similar to the vehicle by which bonds are retired at intervals up to their maturity dates and are referred to as *sinking fund preferreds*.

The impact on value of the redemption privilege varies depending on the specific redemption provisions. Therefore, it is extremely important that the analyst be aware of all the contractual provisions and contingencies of the redemption.

In general, the most important factors of the redemption provisions that affect value are:

1. Call (or redemption) price.
2. Length of time the issuing company is *not* permitted to call the preferred.

3. Likelihood that the contingent event triggering redemption will occur.
4. Redemption schedule.
5. Whether or not a sinking fund or some other means of financing the redemption is established.
6. Issuing company's financial ability to cash out the preferred shares without some sort of redemption financing fund.

For a preferred issue that is redeemable at the issuing corporation's option at a specified price, the most important provisions affecting value are the call price and the length of time the issuing company is not permitted to call the preferred stock (the call protection period). All other things being equal, the shorter the call protection period, the lower the preferred stock's value. This is because redemption of the entire issue of preferred stock eliminates the shareholder's right to a future stream of income and forces the shareholder to accept a price (equal to the call price) for the stock that may be substantially lower than the fair market value the preferred stock might have in the absence of the redemption feature. A lower redemption, or call, price also reduces value to the shareholder, both by increasing the probability that the preferred will be called (assuming that redemption is not contingent upon some future event) and by reducing the proceeds to shareholders upon redemption.

Fortunately, the public market for preferred stocks makes the task of determining the appropriate yield rate to apply to a callable preferred stock, such as that described above, relatively straightforward. To value this type of issue, the analyst uses the same procedure discussed in the section "Method of Valuation" with one important distinction: The publicly traded preferred stocks used as comparatives will be callable preferred stocks with similar call protection periods. As discussed in that section, the analyst chooses the appropriate yield based on a comparison of the dividend and liquidation payment risk of the subject preferred and the publicly traded callable preferred stock. An additional risk factor to consider in valuing callable preferred stock is the subject company's ability to fund redemptions.

When the preferred stock is redeemable contingent upon a future event, it is extremely difficult to ascertain the impact on value. This stems from the fact that the analyst is forced to make an educated guess as to the likelihood that the event triggering redemption will or will not occur. In addition, "contingent" redemption privileges are extremely rare, if not nonexistent, in the public market. Because the redemption of this type of issue is contingent upon some certain event, the importance of the likelihood of its occurring may outweigh the importance of the issuing corporation's financial ability to redeem the preferred shares should the contingent event occur when determining the appropriate yield to apply to the stock's future income stream.

I think the best way to approach the valuation of a "contingently" redeemable preferred stock is to determine the appropriate yield to apply to the future income stream absent the contingent redemption privilege and then adjust the yield based on an analysis of the likelihood of the contingent event occurring. Alternatively, the matter of the contingency can be handled as a separate adjustment. It should be noted that if the redemption is contingent upon the death of a major stockholder, the ability to use life insurance proceeds to redeem the preferred stock and the adequacy of those proceeds, or other evidence of the company's ability to pay, are important factors to consider in determining the appropriate yield adjustment.

Sinking fund preferred stocks differ from the types of redeemable preferred stocks discussed above in that it is known with certainty that the preferred stock will be redeemed at a specified price over a given time period. Both the redemption price and the redemption schedule are specified in the preferred stock contract. Sinking fund preferred stocks provide two advantages to their holders that are worth noting. First, the continuous reduction in the issue's size allows greater certainty that dividends will be paid. Second, the specified redemption guarantees a market, albeit limited, for the preferred stock.

The primary impact on the value of a sinking fund preferred stock results from the fact that redemption creates a finite stream of income to the investor plus a terminal value versus an infinite stream of income available to the nonsinking fund preferred stockholder. This can be illustrated with a simplified example. Assume that issue A is $100-par-value nonredeemable, fixed-rate, voting, cumulative preferred stock that requires a yield (based on market comparisons) of 10 percent. Issue A's fixed dividend rate is 7 percent, or $7 per share. The value of issue A before consideration of lack of marketability is calculated as follows:

Formula 17–4:

$$\text{Value} = \frac{\text{Dividend}}{\text{Required yield}} = \frac{\$7.00}{.10} = \$70 \text{ per share}$$

Now assume that issue B is identical to issue A in all respects except that it is a sinking fund preferred stock that is redeemable at par value beginning in year 5, with 10 percent of the entire issue redeemable each year. There are 100 shares of issue B outstanding. In order to determine the appropriate required yield for issue B, the procedure outlined in the "Method of Valuation" section is followed using publicly traded, redeemable, fixed-rate, voting, cumulative, sinking fund preferred stocks *with similar redemption schedules* as comparatives. It is important to note that the appropriate yield measure for sinking fund preferred stock is yield to maturity (YTM) as opposed to the stated yield implied by the dividend rate alone.

For simplicity, we will assume that the appropriate yield to maturity given an analysis of issue B's dividend and liquidation payment risk is 10 percent. The value of issue B before consideration of lack of marketability, if applicable, is calculated as shown in Exhibit 17–7. In these examples, the value of issue B (the sinking fund preferred) is greater than the value of issue A (nonsinking fund preferred) because issue B is redeemed at par value, which, because the required yield is

EXHIBIT 17-7

Value of Sinking Fund Preferred

Year End	Income Stream		Total $	Present Value Factor @ 10.0% YTM	$
	Dividends $	Redemption $			
1	700	0	700	.909	636.3
2	700	0	700	.826	578.2
3	700	0	700	.751	525.7
4	700	0	700	.683	478.1
5	700	1,000	1,700	.621	1,055.7
6	630	1,000	1,630	.564	919.3
7	560	1,000	1,560	.513	800.3
8	490	1,000	1,490	.467	695.8
9	420	1,000	1,420	.424	602.8
10	350	1,000	1,350	.386	521.1
11	280	1,000	1,280	.350	448.0
12	210	1,000	1,210	.319	386.0
13	140	1,000	1,140	.290	330.6
14	70	1,000	1,070	.263	281.4
					8,259.3
				Shares Outstanding	÷ 100
				Value per Share	82.59

YTM = Yield to maturity

higher than the stated yield, is higher than its value absent the sinking fund provision. Therefore, a portion of issue B's return is derived from capital gains from the time of purchase to the time of redemption. If the stated yield and required yield in both issue A and issue B were equal, their values would be equal to par in both instances.

Put Option

A common characteristic of closely held preferred stock is a *put* option on the preferred shareholder's behalf. This option allows the shareholder to require the issuing corporation to buy back the stock at some fixed price, usually par value. When a preferred stock can be put back to the company at par value, its value usually is, at a minimum, its par value assuming the company has the financial ability to honor the put. This is true because if the preferred stock's value is determined to be less than par value based on the stock's other characteristics, the holder always has the right to put the stock back to the company at par value.

Voting versus Nonvoting

In general, voting rights increase the value of preferred stock, for obvious reasons. My staff and I have conducted numerous studies of publicly traded preferred stocks in an attempt to isolate the reduction in yield (and thus increase in value) investors accord to voting preferred stock. Unfortunately, these studies have yet to produce any meaningful results. I have been unable to isolate any significant patterns of yield differentials due to voting versus nonvoting preferred stocks in the public market. Generally, this is because voting rights in publicly traded preferred stocks are incidental relative to the total outstanding voting power. Therefore, they have no significant impact on yield.

Lacking any concrete public market evidence, it is thus necessary for the analyst to subjectively adjust the required yield downward in valuing voting preferred stock. It has been my experience that industry practice dictates a discount in yield for voting stock ranging from 5 to 10 percent of the yield otherwise indicated.

In closely held companies, it is common for the preferred stock as a class to have voting control of the corporation. If the voting preferred stock being valued represents a controlling interest, the value increases considerably more (or the yield decreases even more). Perhaps the easiest way to approach the valuation of preferred stock in this situation is to value the stock absent the control feature and then add a premium for control.

Participating versus Nonparticipating

A participating preferred stock gives the preferred stockholder the right to share in additional earnings beyond the amount described in the preferred stock contract (beyond the stated dividend rate). On the other hand, a nonparticipating preferred stockholder can receive dividends only in the amount specified in the contract. A fully participating preferred stock allows the stockholder to share with the common stockholder in any earnings disbursements after the common stockholders have received a certain specified annual payment. The incremental amount to the preferred shareholders in such a case normally is equal to that paid to the common stockholders.

Another form of participating preferred stock, which is something less than fully participating, allows the preferred stockholder to share earnings disbursements with the common stockholder up to a certain dividend rate, and after this dividend has been paid in any one year, the right of the preferred stock to participate in the earnings ceases. The degree of participation allowed in any preferred stock can vary significantly from one issue to another, limited only by the creativity of financial advisers, legal counsel, and controlling stockholders' imaginations in designing the features of the issue. This is especially true of privately held participating preferred stock. Therefore, it is critical that the analyst review the preferred stock provisions to determine the level of participation.

The value of the participating feature in a preferred stock is derived from the stockholder's right to *potentially* higher dividends and depends on the likelihood that these potentially higher dividends will in fact be paid. Thus, the increment to value attributable to the participating feature is higher the greater the likelihood that dividends exceeding the stated dividend rate will be paid and the greater the participation (the higher the potential dividend).

When valuing a participating preferred stock, the analyst will need to analyze projected income statements, if available, and look at the common stock dividend payment history in order to determine a level of future dividends to capitalize that can reasonably be expected given the preferred stock's contractual participation features.

A variation of a participating stock is a hybrid cumulative preferred stock. For example, a company might issue a preferred stock that has a stated cumulative dividend and also participates in common stock dividends. Theoretically, one might logically approach a valuation of this type of preferred stock by valuing the fixed dividend and participating dividends separately and then adding these values together to get the preferred's total value. This approach requires that the required yield to be applied to the participating dividends be higher than the yield applied to the cumulative fixed dividends, because the risk of nonpayment of the participating dividends is much higher. Whether or not the preferred shareholder will receive additional dividends as a result of the participating feature depends on whether or not dividends are declared on the common. The analyst must look at the subject company's history of paying dividends on common stock and assess the likelihood that its payment history will continue in order to assess the additional risk inherent in the preferred shareholder's receipt of participating dividends. In addition, the analyst should not view the appropriate required yield on the participating dividend portion of the preferred stock in isolation from the fact that the stock does, in fact, carry a stated cumulative dividend right. This fact, combined with the participation, reduces the overall risk of the participating portion of the issue compared to an issue that has only participating dividend rights. Thus, determining the appropriate required yield for the participating dividend requires a great deal of subjectivity.

Given these factors, perhaps a more appropriate approach to the valuation of such a hybrid preferred stock is to value both the cumulative stated dividends and the participating dividends together, adjusting the required yield to compensate for the added risk of nonpayment of the participating dividends. This process somewhat lessens the subjectivity required in determining the appropriate required yield. Using this approach, the analyst can determine the appropriate required yield to apply to the issue assuming that it lacked the participation feature by using public market evidence. Then the required yield is adjusted to reflect the added dividend payment risk attributable to the participating feature. If the valuation is approached by separating the cumulative stated dividend and the participating dividend, the analyst will be forced to determine the required yield on the participating dividend portion with no empirical market evidence base from which to start.

Convertible versus Nonconvertible

Convertible preferred stock is similar to a convertible bond in that it is a combination of a preferred stock issue and an option on a common equity issue. The conversion feature gives the preferred stock a speculative quality in addition to its investment value as a fixed-income security, which is derived through future dividend payments. Because of the speculative quality that the equity conversion feature imparts to the preferred stock, the stock's value depends not only on its conversion rights and expected future income stream but on the value of the common stock as well.

Conversion rights typically take one of the following forms:

1. Convertible into a fixed number of shares of common stock, expressed as a conversion ratio.
2. Convertible into common stock on the basis of the preferred stock's par value and the common stock's fair market value at the time of conversion.
3. Convertible into common stock based on the preferred stock's fair market value and the common stock's fair market value at the time of conversion.

Preferred stocks with conversion rights described in item 1 above are the types of convertible preferred stocks found in the public market. Preferred stocks with conversion rights such as those described in items 2 and 3 are found almost exclusively in closely held companies. In most cases, convertible preferred stocks are convertible at the holder's option at any time, although some are convertible only after some specified date.

The valuation of closely held convertible preferred stock presents a problem not associated with publicly traded convertible preferred stock. Closely held preferred stock usually is convertible into closely held common stock with no readily determinable market price. Theoretically, the best way to approach the valuing of a convertible preferred stock would be to compare it with publicly traded convertible preferred stocks. However, just as in the case of closely held convertible debt securities, it is difficult, if not impossible, to find publicly traded convertible preferred stocks that have conversion privileges and other rights and privileges similar enough to the closely held preferred to generate a meaningful comparison. In addition, because a convertible preferred stock derives a portion of its value from the underlying fundamentals of the common stock into which it is convertible, it is desirable for comparative purposes to find publicly traded convertible preferred issues whose issuers are also comparable in terms of lines of business and other fundamentals. Comparability on a fundamental basis is not nearly as critical when valuing nonconvertible preferreds, because their value is driven primarily by the rights to future dividends rather than by the prospects for capital appreciation in the underlying common.

As with closely held debt securities, discussed in Chapter 16, a reasonable approach to valuing convertible preferred is to segregate it into two parts: a straight nonconvertible preferred stock and a derivative security in the form of an option to purchase the common stock at a given price. The nonconvertible debt portion of the security will then be valued in the manner for valuing nonconvertible preferred stock described in this chapter. The option portion of the security will be valued in a manner described in Chapter 18, "Valuing Stock Options." Then these two values are added together to determine the value of the convertible preferred stock.

Summary

The combination of rights and privileges found in closely held preferred stock are limited only by the imaginations of the issuer, the financial adviser, and legal counsel. It is the flexibility of the myriad characteristics of closely held preferred stock that makes the determination of value so difficult. Some guidance is found in Revenue Ruling 83-120, but the ruling fails to address the value implications of several of the most important features often found in closely held preferred stocks but not in publicly traded preferreds.

A judge's opinion in a 1981 estate tax case, in which the fair market value of closely held preferred stock was at issue, sums up the difficulties in valuing closely held preferred stock with many features not found in publicly traded preferred stocks:

> Since these consummate negotiators, who invariably achieve an agreeable bargain, are mythical persons endowed with characteristics prescribed in authoritative writings, the undertaking of determining what they would decide on given evidence not exactly like any recounted in precedents, might better be discharged with the benefit of interpretive insights and skills associated more often with the theater than with the court. Like the actor or actress who recreates the character from the guidelines the playwright has given, I must try first to understand the characters created in the authoritative statute regulations and precedents, and then, departing from the custom of the stage, occupy not one but two roles simultaneously—those of the willing buyer and the willing seller—coming finally to an agreement with myself—or more precisely between the two whom I am simultaneously impersonating—on the value of the stock at issue. A judge might be daunted by such an undertaking were it not for the reassuring thought that as surely as one who.
>
>   . . . never saw a moor,
> [And] never saw the sea;
> Yet [may] know . . . how the heather looks,
> And what a wave must be.[5]

---

[5]*Wallace v. United States,* 82-1 U.S.T.C. paragraph 13,442 (D. Mass. 1981). Verse from, "Time and Eternity," in *Poems by Emily Dickinson,* vol. IV, ed. George Monteiro (Scholars' Facsimiles & Reprints, 1967), p. XVII.

Chapter 18

Valuing Stock Options*

*This chapter draws heavily on "Valuing Stock Options, with Applications to Closely Held Companies," *Journal of Business Valuation*, 1987, originally presented at the First Joint Business Valuation Conference of the Canadian Institute of Chartered Business Valuators and the American Society of Appraisers (October 1986); and "Valuing Stock Options," presented at the American Society of Appraisers' 6th Annual Business Valuation Conference (October 1987). Both papers by Shannon P. Pratt and Philip M. Smith.

Introduction

This chapter explores methods available for valuing options to purchase common stock when there is no established market price for the option. It discusses the nature of these options and the factors relevant to their value, explains and discusses four models in current use for the valuation of stock options, and presents some new empirical evidence gauging the ability of three of the models to accurately estimate option prices.

Origins of Nonmarketable Options and Situations Requiring Valuation

The options this chapter addresses are those issued by the company on whose stock the option constitutes a call, which is the right to buy the stock, usually either as a part of incentive compensation for executives or in conjunction with raising capital for the company. The situations most commonly requiring valuation of such options are the following:

1. Divorce of an executive who holds an option.
2. Repurchase of an option by the issuing company.
3. Transfer of ownership of the option to a third party.
4. Damage suits in which the value of the option is at issue, such as a breach of contract suit between an existing or former executive and the issuing company.
5. Determination of compensation of executives for income tax.

Characteristics of Nonmarketable Stock Options

The term *option* as used in this chapter is a contract giving the holder the right, but not the obligation, to buy a stated number of shares of stock at a fixed price within a predetermined time period. The fixed stock price at which the option is exercisable is called the *exercise price* or sometimes, the *strike price*.

The options this chapter addresses have the following characteristics:

1. They are options to purchase stock of either a publicly traded or closely held company, but in either case there is no public trading market for the option itself.
2. In most cases, they have more than a year remaining until expiration.
3. At the time of exercise, the company will issue either treasury stock or authorized but previously unissued shares, resulting in cash or some consideration coming into the company and additional shares outstanding.

Instruments that have these characteristics but are publicly traded are called *warrants*. Instruments called *options* in the public stock market differ from those addressed here in that they are issued by third parties rather than the company itself (so that at exercise they are satisfied by already outstanding shares) and are issued for periods of months rather than years. Although the instruments we will discuss in this chapter are called *warrants* rather than *options* in the public stock market, we will use the term *options* here because these instruments arise most frequently in the familiar context of incentive stock options (ISOs) and because contracts conveying such instruments in connection with private placements of capital usually use the term *option* rather than *warrant*.

The price at which an option trades in the public market is referred to as the *premium* on the option. Publicly traded call options need not be exercised in order to realize the profits from an increase in the price of the underlying security, because they can be sold to another investor, who receives the rights associated with the contract. Executive or employee stock options do not have this advantage, since they are usually nonmarketable; however, the basic determinants of the value of traded options are also relevant to the value of any option-type contract.

Components of Stock Option Values

The value of a stock option can be broken down into two components: the intrinsic value and the time value.

Intrinsic Value of Stock Options

In stock option jargon, the *intrinsic value* of an option is the difference between the stock's value and the exercise price, or the price at which the option holder can purchase the stock. The intrinsic value can never be less than zero. For example, the Wilcox & Gibbs warrant that expires in April 1990 (one of the publicly traded warrants used to test the models presented later in this chapter) has an exercise price of $14.00 and the share price on December 15, 1986, was $16.37. In this case, then, the warrant's intrinsic value is $2.37. Note that this definition of intrinsic value of a stock option completely differs from the definition of intrinsic value as the term is commonly used in reference to the value of the stock itself (see Chapter 2).

The intrinsic value of a stock option may be either positive or zero, but it can never be negative since the contract involves no liability on the part of the option holder. If the value of the underlying stock is above the exercise price, the option is referred to as being *in the money,* and the option accordingly has positive intrinsic value. If the value of the underlying stock and the exercise price are equal, the option is referred to as being *at the money*. If the value of the underlying stock is less than the exercise price, the option is referred to as being *out of the money*. For options that are at the money or out of the money, the intrinsic value is zero; nevertheless, such options may still have time value, as discussed in the next section.

Time Value of Stock Options

In its simplest form, the *time value* of a stock option is the present value of the expected difference between the value of the stock at the option's expiration date and the option's exercise price (see Exhibit 18–1). If one knew the future value of the stock as of the option's expiration date, one could merely compute the present value to determine the option's value. It would be a matter of simply subtracting the stock's value as of the expiration date from the option's exercise price and discounting the difference back to a present value at an appropriate discount rate.

In fact, this approach sometimes is used to value an option. However, since it requires the appraiser to both estimate the stock value at the option's expiration date and select an appropriate discount rate, the approach can produce a wide range of estimated values for an option depending on the appraiser's determination of the two critical independent variables. Consequently, several models for valuing options based on observable data have been developed. I have chosen four models to discuss in this chapter based on the objective of valuing

EXHIBIT 18-1

Option Value vs. Stock Price

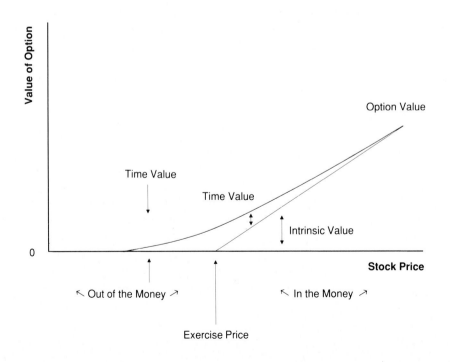

long-term options and the scarcity of models available for accomplishing this task. Three models appear to meet these criteria, but we will also briefly discuss the best-known one, the Black-Scholes option valuation model. First, however, we will consider factors that affect option values.

Factors Influencing Stock Option Values

A variety of factors might be expected to influence the value of a stock option: the time to the option's expiration, the leverage the option affords, the growth in the value of the underlying stock, the volatility of the value of the underlying stock, whether or not the company pays dividends on its stock, the level of interest rates in the economy at large, the dilutive effect of the option's exercise, and the liquidity of the underlying stock and the option itself. Obviously, some of these factors are interrelated, and other factors may affect the value of an option for any given company. All the valuation models described in this chapter incorporate certain of these factors, but none incorporates them all.

Time to Expiration

The longer the time to expiration, the greater the stock's opportunity to appreciate in value, thus enhancing the option's value. All four models incorporate the time to expiration.

Degree of Leverage the Option Affords

There are two ways to view the leverage involved in holding an option. First, if an investor who buys the underlying security must pay the full price, any change in price accrues to the investor. However, the option's purchase price is small relative to the price of the underlying stock. As the underlying share price increases, the option's price also increases, but from a much lower base; thus, the percentage change in value is much larger for the option than for the underlying security. This relationship between underlying share price and option price causes the option's time value to be higher when its price is low.

In addition, leverage is the relationship between the growth in the option's value and the growth in the value of its underlying stock. A stock option is attractive to an investor because it offers prospects of maximum appreciation in proportion to the amount invested. As an option's intrinsic value increases, leverage decreases; in other words, the greater the difference between the option's exercise price and the stock's underlying value, the less the option's value will increase in relation to the increase in value of the underlying stock. All the models incorporate the degree of leverage in one way or another.

Rate of Growth in Value of the Underlying Stock

If one knew the future compound rate of growth in the value of the underlying stock, one could simply apply the discounted present value calculations previously discussed to value the option. However, most evidence indicates that historical earnings growth rates are not good predictors of future earnings growth rates. Since it is impossible to quantify this important variable by merely observing empirical data, this factor is omitted from the applied versions of any of the models discussed in this chapter.[1]

Volatility of Value of the Underlying Stock

Generally, the wider the fluctuations in the value of the underlying stock over time, the greater the option's time value. Fluctuations add to the value because upside fluctuations theoretically enhance the option's value infinitely, while downside fluctuations cannot drive the option value below zero. (This characteristic is in contrast to a direct investment in the stock on margin. Whereas an investor in an option can lose only the price paid for the option—an amount much smaller than the price of the stock—an investor who buys a stock on margin can lose the entire investment and be required to pay back portions of the margin loan if the stock price declines precipitously.)

Empirical research has shown that volatility in the stock price tends to persist; that is, stocks whose prices have been relatively volatile in the past are likely to have relatively volatile prices in the future as well. Three of the models incorporate a measure of the historical volatility of the underlying stock price in determining the option's value.

Dividends

The payment of dividends on the underlying stock detracts from an option's value, because the option holder does not receive the dividends and the company pays out retained earnings that otherwise might be available for reinvestment and would contribute to the growth in value of the underlying stock. Three of the four models discussed incorporate dividend payments.

General Level of Interest Rates

Higher interest rate levels in the economy tend to produce higher option value. One reason is that as interest rates go up, required rates of return on all investments rise, including common stocks. Concurrently, stock values decline; thus, their expected total rates of return

---

[1]Kassouf, who developed one of the models discussed in the chapter, attempts to use a short-term historical growth variable, but this proves to be insignificant in his multiple regression formulas.

to the investor, including dividends and capital appreciation, will equate to rates of return available in the market on other investments of comparable risk. Therefore, to the extent that the values of the underlying common stocks reflect efficient capital markets, the higher the level of interest rates, the higher the expected rate of appreciation in the underlying stock's value. Moreover, as interest rates go up, so does the investor's carrying cost (or opportunity cost, as the case may be) for direct investment in the underlying stock, thus enhancing the attractiveness of the stock option's leverage feature. For example, if the interest rate is 10 percent, an investor in a stock priced at $10 is forgoing the opportunity to earn $1 interest on that $10 investment in the hope of earning a higher return by investing in the stock. If the investor paid $2 for an option on the stock rather than $10 for the stock itself, only $.20 of interest would be forgone.

Potential Dilution from Exercise of Options

The more options outstanding in relation to the existing number of shares of underlying stock outstanding, the greater the common stock dilution if all the options are exercised. Potential dilution, therefore, has a negative impact on the value of an option. Two of the models we discuss address this factor.

Degree of Liquidity of the Underlying Stock

Since investors have a strong desire for liquidity, the more readily marketable the underlying stock, the greater the option's value. Only one of the models discussed herein addresses this important factor.

Degree of Liquidity of the Option Itself

All four models discussed in this chapter arrive at values on the premise that the option itself has an active public trading market. If the option to be valued lacks ready marketability, any values indicated by these models should be discounted to reflect that factor. It is important to recognize that the discount for lack of marketability for an option is less than that for common stock due to the leverage effects discussed earlier. The topic of discounts for lack of marketability is discussed in Chapter 10.

Discussion of Option Valuation Models

Econometric versus Theoretical Models

The models currently in use for the valuation of stock options can be classified into two groups based on how they were developed: econometric models and theoretical models. This chapter describes and discusses two models in each group and presents results of empirical testing on the two econometric models and one of the theoretical models.

Econometric Models.   An *econometric model,* sometimes called an *empirical model,* is a statement of a functional relationship that uses regression analysis of historical relationships among economic variables to estimate statistically the expected value of an economic variable. Econometric stock option valuation models were developed by studying historical relationships observed in the market between factors thought to have a bearing on the values of options and the options' actual market prices. The historical relationships thus observed are used to predict the current market price of an option contract given current values of the independent variables incorporated in the model and the assumption that the relationship between those variables and the option's value remains somewhat stable through time. The Shelton and Kassouf models discussed in this chapter currently are the two best known and most widely used econometric option valuation models.

Theoretical Models.   *Theoretical models,* sometimes called *statistical* or *probability models,* can be distinguished from econometric models in several ways. The most important distinction is that econometric models deal with historical relationships and, therefore, do not produce a theoretical value, while theoretical models are forward looking and attempt to determine what the option *should* sell for in the market given the option terms and the underlying stock's salient characteristics. Theoretical stock option valuation models are premised on a number of assumptions, generally similar to those implicit in capital asset pricing theory models, regarding the nature and behavior of the markets for both the underlying stock and the option. One essential assumption is that the price of the underlying stock behaves in such a way that possible future prices can be accurately modeled by some probability distribution. Other assumptions are listed in the context of the discussion of the individual models. Given these assumptions and the data regarding the relevant independent variables, the models determine the theoretical value of the instrument, that is, the price at which the option should sell in the marketplace. The Black-Scholes and Noreen-Wolfson models discussed in this chapter serve to introduce the reader to the concepts behind these theoretical models.

Shelton Model

In a two-part article in the *Financial Analysts Journal* beginning in May–June 1967, John Shelton discussed an econometric model that enables the analyst to value warrants with almost any period of life remaining.[2] In the article, Shelton argues that there are minimum

---

[2] J. P. Shelton, "The Relation of the Price of a Warrant to the Price of Its Associated Stock," *Financial Analysts Journal,* May–June, July–August 1967.

and maximum values for a warrant. The minimum value must be the warrant's intrinsic value, which can never be less than zero because the warrant has no liability attached to it. If the warrant's price falls below its intrinsic value, investors will buy the warrant and exercise it, simultaneously driving the price of the warrant back to its intrinsic value and purchasing the stock at a price below its current market price. This argument needs no empirical support because it is strictly logical.

The Shelton model assumes that if the stock price is four times the exercise price or more, the warrant will seldom trade above its intrinsic value. Shelton supports this assumption by empirical observation. All of his 157 warrant price observations were very close to their intrinsic values when the stock price approached four times the warrant's exercise price. Therefore, Shelton assumes that the maximum value of a warrant is three fourths of the stock price. The time value and, particularly, the leverage advantages of the option are virtually completely exhausted at this point, and the warrant is selling only at its intrinsic value. The upper and lower limits of the range of plausible prices is illustrated graphically in Exhibit 18–2.

Within the range determined by the minimum and maximum value lines shown in Exhibit 18–2, Shelton determined through regression analysis that a good approximation of prices of long-term warrants is given by using the adjustment factor calculated using the following expression:

EXHIBIT 18-2

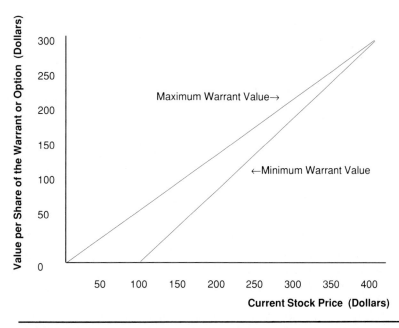

**Shelton Model
Maximum and Minimum Lines**

SOURCE: *The Stock Options Manual* by Gary Gastineau. (New York: McGraw-Hill, 1979) p. 218.
Reproduced with permission of publisher.

Formula 18–1

$$\sqrt[4]{\frac{M}{72}} \left(.47 - 4.25\frac{D}{P_s} + .17L \right)$$

where:

M = Number of months remaining to expiration
D = Annual dividend payment
P_s = Current price of the stock
L = 1 if the warrant is listed and 0 if it is traded over the counter

Once the value of this expression has been calculated, the resulting decimal fraction is multiplied by the difference between the minimum value (the intrinsic value) and the maximum value (three fourths of stock price), and the product is added to the minimum value.

An example may clarify the use of this model. The Wilcox & Gibbs warrant mentioned earlier has the following characteristics:

$$Dividend = \$.10 \text{ per share}$$
$$Expiration \ date = April \ 15, \ 1990$$
$$Stock \ price \ on \ December \ 15, \ 1986 = \$16.37/share$$
$$Exercise \ price = \$14.00$$
$$Actual \ warrant \ price \ on \ December \ 15, \ 1986 = \$5.00$$

Substituting into the relationship described above, we get:

M = Time to expiration = 40.6 months
D = Dividend = $.10
P_s = Stock price = $16.37
L = 0

This results in a value for the adjustment factor of .3833. The minimum value of the warrant is its intrinsic value, which is determined by subtracting the exercise price from the stock price:

$16.37 − $14.00 = $2.37

The maximum value as stated above is:

.75 × $16.37 = $12.28

The value of the warrant from the Shelton model is then determined as follows:

Minimum value + (Adjustment factor) × (Maximum value − Minimum value)
2.37 + (.3833) × (12.28 − 2.37) = $6.17

The result is intuitively pleasing, since the above expression includes many characteristics that we would expect to affect the warrant's value. The model produces higher estimated values for warrants with longer terms to expiration and warrants that are traded on an exchange but produces lower values if the stock has a high dividend yield, which the warrant holder forgoes.

One drawback to the Shelton formula is that it makes no adjustment for the historical fluctuations in the stock price. Shelton tested this volatility factor in his original empirical work but did not find that it affected the warrant's value when the other variables were included in the regression. The best features of the Shelton model are that it is simple to apply and it gives plausible results for currently traded warrants. Our testing of its results using real-world warrants is described on pages 460–63.

Kassouf Model

The Kassouf econometric model was developed by Sheen T. Kassouf and described in a doctoral dissertation written in 1965.[3] The model itself is very straightforward to use, provided that all the necessary information for the specific warrant is available. Following are the formulae of the model and the variable definitions.[4]

Formula 18–2

$$V_e = S \left[\sqrt[z]{\left(\frac{P_s}{S}\right)^z + 1} - 1 \right]$$

where:

$$z = k_1 + \frac{k_2}{t} + k_3 R + k_4 d + k_5 E_1 + k_6 E_2 + k_7 x + k_8 S + \epsilon$$

V = Expected price of warrant
S = Strike or exercise price
P_s = Price of underlying stock
$k_1 \dots k_8$ = Coefficients derived by multiple regression analysis
t = Number of months before expiration
R = Dividend yield on common stock
d = Number of outstanding warrants divided by number of outstanding shares (i.e., potential dilution ratio)
E_1 = Slope of least-squares line fitted to logarithms of monthly mean price of common stock for previous 11 months
E_2 = Standard deviation of natural logarithms of monthly mean price of common stock for previous 11 months
$x = \dfrac{P_s}{S}$
ϵ = Error term

Once again, an example may help clarify the use of the Kassouf model. However, it is important to note that complex mathematical

---

[3]Sheen T. Kassouf, *A Theory and an Econometric Model for Common Stock Purchase Warrants* (New York: Analytical Publishers, 1965).
[4]Gary Gastineau, *The Stock Options Manual* (New York: McGraw-Hill, 1979), p. 230.

calculations are required for updating the regression coefficients that are used in the following demonstration. The additional information relevant to the Wilcox & Gibbs warrant described earlier is as follows:

Formula 18–3

P_s = \$16.37
S = \$14.00
R = Dividend yield = .0183
t = 40.6 months; $1/t$ = .0247
E_2 = Volatility factor = .0834
x = Stock price $\div$ Exercise price = 1.169

Using the coefficients derived from a regression analysis run for the 12 months prior to December 15, 1987, yields the following value for z:

Formula 18–4

$$z = 1.1351 + 37.269(1/t) + 26.997(R) - 2.81(E_2) + .867(x) = 3.33$$

Then, substituting this calculated value of z into the formula for the value of a warrant as outlined above yields:

Formula 18–5

$$V_e = 14.00 \left[\sqrt[3.33]{\left(\frac{16.37}{14.00}\right)^{3.33} + 1} - 1 \right] = \$4.83$$

The Kassouf model considers more variables than the Shelton model, a point of superiority—it permits the user to include several different variables in the regression and to demonstrate their efficacy in predicting warrant values. Since it is an econometric model, the Kassouf model assumes that past relationships, from which regression coefficients are determined, will continue in the present—an assumption that, unfortunately, hardly ever proves true. Kassouf's formula does, however, provide a basis from which to update the coefficients using current data. Furthermore, regression analysis enables the user to eliminate variables that do not appear to affect warrant prices in the relevant period.

The Kassouf model does take into account stock price volatility. Although intuitively it would seem that volatility influences warrant pricing, Kassouf did not find that variable to be significant during the second of the two time periods he studied.

The major disadvantage of the Kassouf model is the cost of using it, because it must be updated regularly to ensure that the variables and coefficients used to determine z reflect recent market relationships.

Black-Scholes Model

In 1973, Fisher Black and Myron Scholes derived what is today the most widely used and best-known theoretical model for the valuation of marketable options.[5] The model is based on the assumption that it is possible to set up a perfectly hedged position consisting of owning the shares of stock and selling a call option on the stock. Any movement in the price of the underlying stock will be offset by an opposite movement in the option's value, resulting in no risk to the investor. This perfect hedge is riskless and, therefore, should yield the riskless rate of return. If it does not yield the riskless rate, the option is mispriced, the hedge is not perfect, and the option should be revalued until the hedge yields the riskless rate. Black and Scholes inferred that when the option is correctly priced, the perfect hedge results.

The assumptions underlying the Black-Scholes model are not intuitively pleasing; nevertheless, it is important to be aware of them in order to avoid misapplying the model. These assumptions are as follows:

1. The short-term interest rate is known and is constant through time.
2. The stock price follows a random walk in continuous time with a rate of variance in proportion to the square of the stock price.
3. The distribution of possible stock prices at the end of any finite interval is lognormal.
4. The variance of the rate of return on the stock is constant.
5. The stock pays no dividends and makes no other distributions.
6. The option can be exercised only at maturity.
7. There are no commissions or other transaction costs in buying or selling the stock or the option.
8. It is possible to borrow any fraction of the price of a security to buy it, or to hold it, at the short-term interest rate.
9. A seller who does not own a security (a short seller) will simply accept the price of the security from the buyer and agree to settle with the buyer on some future date by paying him or her an amount equal to the price of the security on that date. While this short sale is outstanding, the short seller will have the use of, or interest on, the proceeds of the sale.
10. The tax rate, if any, is identical for all transactions and all market participants.[6]

The model is as follows:

Formula 18–6

Call value $= S \times N(d_1) - Ee^{-rt} \times N(d_2)$

where:

S = Stock price
E = Exercise (strike) price

[5]Fisher Black and Myron Scholes, "The Pricing of Options and Corporate Liabilities," *Journal of Political Economy,* June 1973.
[6]Gastineau, *Stock Options Manual.*

$N(\ ) =$ Value of cumulative normal distribution at the point ($\ $)

$$d_1 = \frac{\ln(S/E) + (r + .5\sigma^2)t}{\sigma\sqrt{t}}$$

$d_2 = d_1 - \sigma\sqrt{t}$

$\ln =$ Natural logarithm

$r =$ Short-term riskless rate (continuously compounded)

$t =$ Time to expiration, in years

$e =$ Base of natural logarithms

$\sigma =$ Annual standard deviation of return (usually referred to as *volatility*)

The Black-Scholes model is elegant, but its usefulness is reduced by the many assumptions necessary for its derivation. The first problem is that the model was developed to value a "European call," that is, one that can be exercised only at expiration.[7] Such options are not currently available in the United States. Second, the model does not allow for the payment of dividends on the stock. Although one could adjust the interest rate used in the computation to allow for dividends, it should be remembered that dividends are paid discretely, whereas the interest rate in the model is a continuous rate. The frequent adjustment necessary for maintaining the perfect hedge would require transaction costs that would eliminate any advantages from determining the option's true or theoretical value. Another problem is that the model assumes a single riskless rate of interest, constant through time, yet fluctuations in the economy preclude rational acceptance of this assumption. Furthermore, investors are assumed to be able to both borrow and lend at this riskless rate, while in fact borrowing rates are almost always well above lending rates.

Even if all these problems could be overcome and the assumptions could somehow be accepted, a very practical problem would confront the appraiser who is applying this model to the valuation of a closely held interest: the measurement of the volatility factor in the formula. This volatility factor is a function of the past variability in the returns on the stock as measured by changes in the stock price. When valuing the options of publicly traded stock, one simply records historical prices and determines the standard deviation of the natural logarithm of the price relatives (the price in the current period divided by the price in the previous period). However, historical prices on the stocks of closely held companies are seldom available. The appraiser may have a series of five or six previous valuations to use, but that number is hardly sufficient to determine the true volatility. Some practitioners suggest finding a closely comparable publicly traded stock and using the price series of that stock as a proxy to estimate the volatility factor. If an analyst chooses to estimate volatility in this way, he or she should carefully analyze the comparative to determine whether its risk is sufficiently similar to the closely held company under consideration.

---

[7]Richard Roll subsequently developed a modification to the model to handle options that may be exercised at any time prior to expiration. See Richard Roll, "An Analytic Valuation Formula for Unprotected American Call Options on Stocks with Known Dividends," *Journal of Financial Economics*, November 1977.

Noreen-Wolfson Model

In 1981, Eric Noreen and Mark Wolfson adapted the Black-Scholes model for use in valuing executive stock options.[8] Noreen and Wolfson thought that the accounting treatment of executive stock options seriously undervalued the true worth of these instruments as recorded on the company's financial statements. The purpose of their work was to estimate the magnitude of the errors introduced by generally accepted accounting principles, which required recording the expense associated with executive stock options at essentially zero. They used a modified form of the Black-Scholes model to value executive stock options as though they had the characteristics of publicly traded warrants.

Noreen and Wolfson argued that publicly traded warrants are similar to executive stock options in many ways, the two most important of which are that both have lives measured in years instead of months and the exercise of either one results in the company's issuing additional shares. However, there are differences that should be noted as well. First, warrants are usually issued out of the money and executive stock options at the money. Second, executive stock options normally are not transferable and can be exercised only while the executive is employed by the firm. All other things held constant, these restrictions reduce the value of the executive stock option relative to a publicly traded warrant.

The assumptions associated with the Noreen-Wolfson variation of the Black-Scholes model are primarily the same as the Black-Scholes model itself. Two differences should be noted. First, the Noreen-Wolfson model allows for dividends and assumes they are paid continuously. Second, it considers the dilution that would take place upon exercise of the option.

The model takes the following form, using the same definitions of variables as those used in the Black-Scholes model except for the following differences:

Formula 18–7

$$P_w = \frac{N}{N + n} [Se^{-dt} \times N(d_1) - Ee^{-rt} \times N(d_2)]$$

where:

N = Number of common shares outstanding

n = Number of common shares to be issued if warrants are exercised

d = Continuous dividend yield

$$d_1 = \frac{\ln (S/E) + (r - d + .5\sigma^2)t}{\sigma \sqrt{t}}$$

$$d_2 = d_1 - \sigma \sqrt{t}$$

---

[8] Eric Noreen and Mark Wolfson, "Equilibrium Warrant Pricing Models and Accounting for Executive Stock Options," *Journal of Accounting Research*, Autumn 1981.

The complexity of this model prohibits the development of an example to demonstrate its use.

This variation of the Black-Scholes model has some of the same problems that its parent does. However, as said above, this model allows for dividends and incorporates the dilution that will occur on exercise. The problem of estimating the volatility factor will continue to limit its usefulness for appraisers of closely held companies.

Empirical Tests of Option Valuation Models

In the course of preparing for a case that involved valuing some executive stock options, we undertook empirical testing of the Shelton, Kassouf, and Noreen-Wolfson models. The Shelton model is simple to use and explain and, if it accurately predicts the value of publicly traded warrants, would be quite useful, particularly in litigation. Although the Kassouf model involves extensive empirical estimation, it has an advantage in that it can be reestimated at any time to provide timely estimates of warrant values. On the other hand, the Noreen-Wolfson adaptation of the Black-Scholes model has the problems highlighted above, but it too may be useful for an appraiser since it incorporates some features unique to nonmarketable stock options and could provide a corroboration of a value determined by another method.

Method Used

We determined the models' validity by comparing the prices they indicated with actual prices of warrants on the public market. A comparative warrant had to meet the following criteria:

1. Be in the money or less than 20 percent out of the money.
2. Have an expiration date at least three years in the future.
3. Be a call on common stock.
4. If callable, have a call date two years or more in the future.

We searched all the warrants listed in the *R.H.M. Survey of Warrants, Options, and Low-Price Stocks* and found 45 that initially fit the criteria. Both the Kassouf and Noreen-Wolfson models incorporate a volatility factor calculated from a weekly stock price series; some of these stock price series were incomplete, and this additional criterion further narrowed the number of comparative warrants to 25. The list of warrants and their salient characteristics is shown in Exhibit 18–3.

Exhibit 18–3 also summarizes the estimated values for the 25 comparative warrants, determined using each of the three models tested. It also shows pertinent characteristics of each warrant and the warrant's and stock's market prices on December 15, 1986. By dividing the estimated price determined by each model by the actual warrant price on December 15, 1986, we determined a "ratio statistic" indicat-

EXHIBIT 18-3

Comparative Results of Shelton, Kassouf, and Noreen-Wolfson Stock Option Valuation Models

Warrant	Div. $	Expire Date	Stock Price 12/15/86 $	Exercise Price $	Warrant Price 12/15/86 $	Shelton Estimated Price $	Shelton Ratio Stat.	Kassouf Estimated Price $	Kassouf Ratio Stat.	Noreen-Wolfson Estimated Price $	Noreen-Wolfson Ratio Stat.
NYSE/AMEX Stocks											
Asarco Inc. '91	0.00	8/15/91	14.00	16.09	6.37	4.63	0.73	5.13	0.81	4.89	0.77
Fed. Nat'l Mtge 'A'	0.16	2/25/92	38.00	44.25	11.50	11.79	1.03	10.00	0.87	11.78	1.02
Geoth. Resc. Int'l	0.00	11/15/91	11.62	13.50	3.87	3.90	1.01	3.51	0.91	3.80	0.98
Lilly (Eli)	1.80	3/31/91	75.75	75.98	20.62	19.28	0.94	19.13	0.93	16.68	0.81
Lomas & Nettleton	1.88	3/1/90	31.12	27.00	4.00	7.63	1.91	6.75	1.69	4.52	1.13
McDermott Int'l	1.80	4/1/90	20.87	25.00	3.12	1.39	0.45	1.95	0.63	3.42	1.10
M.D.C. Holdings	0.36	4/15/90	13.25	14.10	3.00	3.04	1.01	2.89	0.96	4.05	1.35
Mtge & Rlty Trust	1.87	1/15/92	22.87	20.50	3.37	4.11	1.22	4.72	1.40	3.29	0.98
Pub Serv Co of NH	0.00	10/15/91	8.12	5.00	4.37	4.44	1.02	3.73	0.85	3.42	0.78
Storage Equities	1.40	12/4/89	16.00	17.00	2.06	0.99	0.48	1.96	0.95	1.64	0.80
Turner Broad. Sys	0.00	12/15/91	14.00	22.50	5.00	4.72	0.94	5.91	1.18	5.68	1.14
Webb '90	0.20	2/1/90	23.00	23.00	6.00	6.35	1.06	5.96	0.99	6.78	1.13
Wickes Cos Inc	0.00	1/26/92	3.75	4.43	2.37	1.27	0.54	1.30	0.55	0.93	0.39
Wilcox & Gibbs	0.10	4/15/90	16.37	14.00	5.00	6.17	1.23	4.83	0.97	5.14	1.03
Class "A" OTC Stocks											
Biotechnology Dev	0.00	12/19/89	2.87	4.50	0.62	0.85	1.37	0.62	1.00	0.80	1.29
Cronus Ind.	0.00	2/1/90	16.62	17.63	5.25	4.98	0.95	5.19	0.99	5.14	0.98
DNA Plant Tech	0.00	1/17/90	13.50	10.50	3.37	5.85	1.74	5.06	1.50	4.72	1.40
First Exec Corp	0.00	11/15/90	16.75	17.50	6.12	5.31	0.87	6.31	1.03	5.78	0.94
Judicate Inc 'A'	0.00	2/27/90	3.31	2.00	1.12	1.78	1.59	0.83	0.74	1.13	1.01
Moto Photo	0.00	11/25/89	4.43	4.25	2.25	1.41	0.63	1.44	0.64	1.66	0.74
Pharmacontrol Corp	0.00	6/4/90	9.25	8.50	6.06	3.29	0.54	3.86	0.64	4.16	0.69
Tri Star Pictures	0.00	6/1/92	11.87	8.50	6.12	5.91	0.97	5.00	50.82	3.79	0.62
Class "B" OTC Stocks											
Care Plus 'A'	0.00	8/13/90	0.68	1.00	0.31	0.21	0.68	0.31	0.99	0.23	0.74
Great Western Sys 'A'	0.00	8/21/89	0.31	1.50	0.18	0.09	0.50	0.20	1.13	0.08	0.44
Scientific Meas Sys	0.00	4/5/90	0.93	1.00	0.37	0.28	0.76	0.36	0.96	0.20	0.54
Mean							0.965		0.965		0.912
Standard deviation							0.386		0.267		0.265
Median							0.945		0.955		0.940
Coefficient of variation							0.400		0.276		0.291

Div. = Most recent annual dividend

Ratio Stat. = Estimated price ÷ warrant price

Coefficient of variation = Standard deviation ÷ mean

ing the relative accuracy of each approach (1.0 would be perfectly accurate).

The ratio statistic, as mentioned above, is calculated by dividing the estimated price of the warrant by its actual market price. If the ratio is greater than 1.0, the warrant price has been overestimated. For example, Exhibit 18–3 shows the Shelton ratio statistic for Asarco Inc. to be 0.73, which indicates that the Shelton model has underestimated the warrant's market price by 27 percent. For each model, some values are considerably larger than 1.0 and some considerably smaller, but many of the ratio values are quite close to the perfect 1.0.

Shelton Model Results

We tested the Shelton model against actual warrant prices from the public market in two ways. Recall that there is a variable in the Shelton model, L, that is equal to 1 when the option is traded on the AMEX and zero when the option is traded over the counter.[9] Today, however, the OTC market provides excellent marketability, and the liquidity of warrants and stocks does not suffer (as it did in the 1960s when the Shelton model was developed) because these instruments are traded over the counter rather than on an exchange. Therefore, we tested Shelton's model using his "listed" variable and omitting it.

The results of our testing suggest that using the Shelton model without the AMEX variable (i.e., $L = 0$) produced predicted warrant values that were significantly closer to actual market values than when the AMEX variable was included. Therefore, all results reported in Exhibit 18–3 reflect values developed with $L = 0$, in other words, without considering in which segment of the public market the warrant trades.

Kassouf Model Results

In order to test the Kassouf model against the sample of publicly traded warrants, we first collected historical observations to establish the relevant regression variables, as shown in the earlier description of the Kassouf formula. We then used them to estimate the coefficients of the regression relationship described above and estimated the appropriate value of z for each warrant in the sample. This process requires the use of regression analysis as well as other, rather sophisticated quantitative techniques. Once these estimates are developed, the actual valuation of the warrants in the sample is simply a matter of solving Kassouf's equation for V_e.

Exhibit 18–3 shows the results of the estimates using the Kassouf model. For this sample in this time period, the Kassouf model performed the best of the three at estimating the warrants' actual market price. The average ratio statistic for the Kassouf sample, 0.965, indicates only 3.5 percent underestimation, the same as for the Shelton

---

[9]At the time of the study, the New York Stock Exchange did not allow options to be traded.

model but with a much smaller standard deviation. More important, the coefficient of variation for the Kassouf model is lower than for either the Shelton or Noreen-Wolfson models.

Noreen-Wolfson Model Results

Testing the Noreen-Wolfson adaptation of the Black-Scholes model involved using both the market data for the warrants in the sample and statistical tables for the normal distribution. As shown on Exhibit 18–3, the Noreen-Wolfson adaptation underestimates the market prices of the warrants by an average of about 9 percent. By comparison, both the Shelton and Kassouf models underestimate the same set of warrant values by an average of only 3 percent.

Summary

We concluded from these data that the Noreen-Wolfson adaptation does not provide as accurate an estimate of the market prices of warrants as either the Shelton or Kassouf model. The Kassouf model worked best, in both accurately estimating the values and maintaining low variability of the estimates relative to the actual market prices. The difficulty of using the Kassouf model—namely estimating the volatility of the stock price and reestimating the coefficients of the regression relationship—points to the Shelton model as an easy and relatively accurate model for estimating warrant values. In a sense, that is comforting to business appraisers, because most warrants or options they would encounter are on closely held stocks with little or no historical pricing data, which are necessary for calculating the volatility factor incorporated in both the Kassouf model and the Noreen-Wolfson adaptation.

On the whole, the evidence indicates that for stock options on closely held interests, the Shelton model generates plausible results given the general lack of data available on these interests. However, more sophisticated models, such as the Kassouf model and the Noreen-Wolfson adaptation, may be useful if the appraiser recognizes the necessity of extensive quantitative analysis and the assumptions implicit in the models.

Part VI

Valuations for Specific Purposes

Chapter 19

Estate Planning and Tax Valuations

"Say not that you know another entirely untill you have shared an inheritance with him."

Johann Kaspar Lavater
Swiss theologian, 1788

Introduction

The three most important objectives of estate planning for owners of closely held businesses are:

1. Provision for liquidity for themselves or their heirs, or both.
2. Minimization of federal gift and estate taxes and state inheritance taxes.
3. Provision for continuity of the business.

Liquidity during the owner's lifetime can be achieved by going public, selling the company, selling shares to an employee stock ownership plan (ESOP), or selling shares by other means. Liquidity at the owner's death can be provided by any of the same means or through a buy-sell agreement funded by life insurance. The need for liquidity relates to the business owner's desires not only to cash in on the company's successful growth but also to have funds available to pay the associated income or estate taxes that the above transactions typically trigger. This chapter discusses the valuation issues that arise in connection with estate and gift planning based on these three key objectives.

Other chapters in Part VI carry this topic further. Chapter 20 focuses on buy-sell agreements. Chapters 21 and 22 analyze a number of particularly instructive cases in which disputed tax valuations have been resolved in court. Additional estate-planning-related information is contained in Chapter 23 on ESOPs. Elsewhere in the book, Chapter 17 discusses the valuation of preferred stocks, which often have been utilized in estate freezing recapitalizations, while Chapter 15 covers the valuation of minority interests, which currently is receiving much attention from both estate planners and the IRS.

The first section of this chapter sets forth the nature of estate and gift taxes and the current rates, exemptions, special provisions, and penalties under the current Internal Revenue Code and Regulations. The next section discusses the guidelines for valuation for estate and gift tax purposes (which also can be applied to income tax matters) and includes the complete texts of the most relevant IRS Revenue Rulings. The last section deals with valuation issues arising from specific estate and gift tax planning techniques. No doubt new techniques will be developed in response to the constantly changing economic and tax environment.

The material in this book generally is limited to discussion of valuation issues. Because there have been major tax law changes almost every year during this decade, the reader should use caution when referring to information contained in articles listed in the bibliography to this chapter. They may have been written during a period with different tax laws. Anyone involved in appraisal work with tax planning or tax litigation implications should consult a competent attorney and CPA for guidance in legal and tax issues.

Current Tax Rates and Penalties

Estate and gift taxes are a unified system of excise taxes levied on the transfer of wealth during life and at death. In other words, for purposes of calculating an individual's final estate taxes, the amount of all taxable gifts that were made during life are added to the estate's gross value and all gift taxes that were paid during life are subtracted from the estate tax payable. The current rates on taxable amounts are set forth in Exhibit 19–1.

It should be noted that the law provides for several basic exemptions and exclusions from the amount of net assets that otherwise would be taxable for:

EXHIBIT 19-1

Unified Transfer Tax on Gifts and Estates 1985-1992

If the Amount Is:		Tentative Tax Is: [1]			
Over	But Not Over	Tax	+	%	Of Excess Over
$	$	$			$
0	10,000	0		18	0
10,000	20,000	1,800		20	10,000
20,000	40,000	3,800		22	20,000
40,000	60,000	8,200		24	40,000
60,000	80,000	13,000		26	60,000
80,000	100,000	18,200		28	80,000
100,000	150,000	23,800		30	100,000
150,000	250,000	38,800		32	150,000
250,000	500,000	70,800		34	250,000
500,000	750,000	155,800		37	500,000
750,000	1,000,000	248,300		39	750,000
1,000,000	1,250,000	345,800		41	1,000,000
1,250,000	1,500,000	448,300		43	1,250,000
1,500,000	2,000,000	555,800		45	1,500,000
2,000,000	2,500,000	780,800		49	2,000,000
2,500,000	3,000,000	1,025,800		53	2,500,000
3,000,000	-----	1,290,800		55	3,000,000

NOTE: There is a 5% additional tax levied on amounts between $10,000,000 and $21,040,000. This additional tax essentially recaptures the benefits received from the lower brackets and the unified credit for large estates.

[1] Tentative tax is applied to the sum of the taxable estate and all taxable gifts made by the deceased after 1976. The tentative tax shown above is calculated before the application of the unified credit and other credits and certain adjustments. (After 1986 this is $192,800 in tax-equal to $600,000 in assets.)

- The first $600,000 of the fair market value of estate and gifted assets.[1]
- Any amounts given to one's spouse, either by gift or by will.[2]
- Up to $10,000 gifted annually from any one donor to each of any number of donees.

Other special provisions affect:

- The value of farm or small-business special-use real estate (Internal Revenue Code [IRC] Section 2032A).
- The time over which estate tax payments can be made and the interest rate changed on such payments on the portion of the estate consisting of interests in a privately owned company engaged in an active trade or business (IRC Section 6166).
- The income tax treatment of redemptions of corporate stock owned by the estate whose proceeds are used to pay estate expenses and taxes (IRC Section 303).

An additional tax can be levied on certain generation-skipping transfers of assets.

There are also penalties for undervaluation of estate and gift assets (IRC Section 6660); these are given in Table 19–1. The Section 6660 penalties shown in Table 19–1 are triggered by asset undervaluation and computed as a percentage of the tax underpayment. The IRS may decide not to apply these penalties if the returned value was made in good faith and had a reasonable basis. A qualified appraisal prepared by a competent appraiser may constitute part of the establishment of a "reasonable basis."

Appraisers are subject to a civil penalty of $1,000 for aiding and abetting an understatement of tax liability (IRC Section 6701). Even more serious, the IRS may impose an administrative sanction barring the appraiser from submitting probative evidence in future IRS tax proceedings.

These penalties are similar to the overvaluation penalties imposed on taxpayers who overstate charitable gift values (IRC Section 6659) or depreciable investment asset values for income tax deductions. The

TABLE 19-1

Undervaluation Penalties

For estate and gift taxes over $1,000:

Value claimed on the tax return as a Percentage of the value finally determined	Additional Penalty
Between 66-2/3% and 50%	10%
Below 50%, but 40% or over	20%
Below 40%	30%

---

[1]There is a unified credit of $192,800 applicable against either the gift or estate tax. This credit is equal to the tax on the first $600,000 of taxable value.

[2]The transfers to the spouse must be "qualified," i.e., they must be in a form which would cause the property to be taxed in the spouse's estate if retained until death.

charitable contribution penalty is a flat 30 percent of the tax under-payment due to a valuation overstatement if the latter exceeds the finally determined value by 150 percent or more. Charitable gift valuation issues are discussed later in the chapter.

Guidelines for Federal Gift and Estate Tax Valuations

The basic guidelines for the valuation of closely held common stocks for federal gift and estate tax purposes are contained in Revenue Ruling 59-60, which Exhibit 19–2 shows in its entirety. Revenue Ruling 59-60 is modified slightly by Revenue Ruling 65-193, shown in Exhibit 19–3.

Revenue Ruling 68-609, discussed in Chapter 4, presents a "formula method" (sometimes referred to by practitioners as the "excess earnings method" or "Treasury method") for arriving at values for intangibles, but it states, "The 'formula' approach should not be used if there is a better evidence available from which the value of intangibles can be determined." In addition, Revenue Ruling 68-609 endorses the application of Revenue Ruling 59-60 for valuations for income tax and other tax purposes and for valuations of business interests of any type. Revenue Ruling 68-609 states:

> The general approach, methods, and factors, outlined in Revenue Ruling 59-60, as modified, are equally applicable to valuations of corporate stocks for income and other tax purposes as well as for estate and gift tax purposes. They apply also to problems involving the determination of the fair market value of business interests of any type, including partnerships and proprietorships, and of intangible assets for all tax purposes.

Revenue Ruling 77-287, presented as Exhibit 19–4, amplifies Revenue Ruling 59-60 by specifically recognizing criteria for determining an appropriate discount for lack of marketability. It also provides guidance for discounts to be applied to publicly traded securities restricted under federal securities laws (see Chapter 22). Revenue Ruling 81-253, shown in Exhibit 19–5, extends Revenue Ruling 59-60 by stating the IRS's position that in the absence of family discord, no minority discount will be available for blocks of shares transferred to family members when the family as a group owns a controlling interest in company's stock. Revenue Ruling 83-120, discussed in Chapter 17, contains guidelines for valuing preferred stock.

If the analyst follows the valuation procedures presented in this book with reasonable thoroughness, the requirements of these Rulings should be satisfied. Consequently, beyond including the relevant rulings as exhibits, this section will simply call attention to a few points in Revenue Ruling 59-60. The following chapters discuss a variety of key factors in the context of various positions taken and decisions reached in court cases. I should note at this point that, unlike the other cited rulings, 81-253 has been rejected by every court which considered it.

EXHIBIT 19-2

Revenue Ruling 59-60

In valuing the stock of closely-held corporations, or the stock of corporations where market quotations are not available, all other available financial data, as well as all relevant factors affecting the fair market value must be considered for estate tax and gift tax purposes. No general formula may be given that is applicable to the many different valuation situations arising in the valuation of such stock. However, the general approach, methods and factors which must be considered in valuing such securities are outlined.

Section 1. Purpose.

The purpose of this Revenue Ruling is to outline and review in general the approach, methods and factors to be considered in valuing shares of the capital stock of closely-held corporations for estate tax and gift tax purposes. The methods discussed herein will apply likewise to the valuation of corporate stocks on which market quotations are either unavailable or are of such scarcity that they do not reflect the fair market value.

Section 2. Background and Definitions.

.01 All valuations must be made in accordance with the applicable provisions of the Internal Revenue Code of 1954 and the Federal Estate Tax and Gift Tax Regulations. Sections 2031(a), 2032 and 2512(a) of the 1954 Code (sections 811 and 1005 of the 1939 Code) require that the property to be included in the gross estate, or made the subject of a gift, shall be taxed on the basis of the value of the property at the time of death of the decedent, the alternate date if so elected, or the date of gift.

.02 Section 20.2031-1(b) of the Estate Tax Regulations (section 81.10 of the Estate Tax Regulations 105) and section 25.2512-1 of the Gift Tax Regulations (section 86.19 of Gift Tax Regulations 108) define fair market value, in effect, as the price at which the property would change hands between a willing buyer and a willing seller when the former is not under any compulsion to buy and the latter is not under any compulsion to sell, both parties having reasonable knowledge of relevant facts. Court decisions frequently state in addition that the hypothetical buyer and seller are assumed to be able, as well as willing, to trade and to be well informed about the property and concerning the market for such property.

.03 Closely-held corporations are those corporations the shares of which are owned by a relatively limited number of stockholders. Often the entire stock issue is held by one family. The result of this situation is that little, if any, trading in the shares takes place. There is, therefore, no established market for the stock and such sales as occur at irregular intervals seldom reflect all of the elements of a representative transaction as defined by the term "fair market value."

Section 3. Approach to Valuation.

.01 A determination of fair market value, being a question of fact, will depend upon the circumstances in each case. No formula can be devised that will be generally applicable to the multitude of different valuation issues arising in estate and gift cases. Often, an appraiser will find wide differences of opinion as to the fair market value of a particular stock. In resolving such differences, he should maintain a reasonable attitude in recognition of the fact that valuation is not an exact science. A sound valuation will be based upon all the relevant facts, but the elements of common sense, informed judgment and reasonableness must enter into the process of weighing those facts and determining their aggregate significance.

.02 The fair market value of specific shares of stock will vary as general economic conditions change from "normal" to "boom" or "depression," that is, according to the degree of optimism or pessimism with which the investing public regards the future at the required date of appraisal. Uncertainty as to the stability or continuity of the future income from a property decreases its value by increasing the risk of loss or earnings and value in the future. The value of shares of stock of a company with very uncertain future prospects is highly speculative. The appraiser must exercise his judgment as to the degree of risk attaching to the business of the corporation which issued the stock, but that judgment must be related to all of the other factors affecting value.

.03 Valuation of securities is, in essence, a prophesy as to the future and must be based on facts available at the required date of appraisal. As a generalization, the prices of stocks which are traded in volume in a free and active market by informed persons best reflect the consensus of the investing public as to what the future holds for the corporations and industries represented. When a stock is closely-held, is traded infrequently, or is traded in an erratic market, some other measure of value must be used. In many instances, the next best measure may be found in the prices at which the stocks of companies engaged in the same or similar line of business are selling in a free and open market.

Section 4. Factors to Consider.

.01 It is advisable to emphasize that in the valuation of the stock of closely-held corporations or the stock of corporations where market quotations are either lacking or too scarce to be recognized, all available financial data, as well as all relevant factors affecting the fair market value, should be considered. The following factors, although not all-inclusive are fundamental and require careful analysis in each case:

(a) The nature of the business and the history of the enterprise from its inception.

(b) The economic outlook in general and the condition and outlook of the specific industry in particular.

(c) The book value of the stock and the financial condition of the business.

(d) The earning capacity of the company.

(e) The dividend-paying capacity.

(f) Whether or not the enterprise has goodwill or

EXHIBIT 19-2

Revenue Ruling 59-60
(Continued)

other intangible value.

(g) Sales of the stock and the size of the block of stock to be valued.

(h) The market price of stocks of corporations engaged in the same or a similar line of business having their stocks actively traded in a free and open market, either on an exchange or over-the-counter.

.02 The following is a brief discussion of each of the foregoing factors:

(a) The history of a corporate enterprise will show its past stability or instability, its growth or lack of growth, the diversity or lack of diversity of its operations, and other facts needed to form an opinion of the degree of risk involved in the business. For an enterprise which changed its form of organization but carried on the same or closely similar operations of its predecessor, the history of the former enterprise should be considered. The detail to be considered should increase with approach to the required date of appraisal, since recent events are of greatest help in predicting the future; but a study of gross and net income, and of dividends covering a long prior period, is highly desirable. The history to be studied should include, but need not be limited to, the nature of the business, its products or services, its operating and investment assets, capital structure, plant facilities, sales records and management, all of which should be considered as of the date of the appraisal, with due regard for recent significant changes. Events of the past that are unlikely to recur in the future should be discounted, since value has a close relation to future expectancy.

(b) A sound appraisal of a closely-held stock must consider current and prospective economic conditions as of the date of appraisal, both in the national economy and in the industry or industries with which the corporation is allied. It is important to know that the company is more or less successful than its competitors in the same industry, or that it is maintaining a stable position with respect to competitors. Equal or even greater significance may attach to the ability of the industry with which the company is allied to compete with other industries. Prospective competition which has not been a factor in prior years should be given careful attention. For example, high profits due to the novelty of its product and the lack of competition often lead to increasing competition. The public's appraisal of the future prospects of competitive industries or of competitors within an industry may be indicated by price trends in the markets for commodities and for securities. The loss of the manager of a so-called "one-man" business may have a depressing effect upon the value of the stock of such business, particularly if there is a lack of trained personnel capable of succeeding to the management of the enterprise. In valuing the stock of this type of business, therefore, the effect of the loss of the manager on the future expectancy of the business, and the absence of management-succession potentialities are pertinent factors to be taken into consideration. On the other hand, there may be fac-

tors which offset, in whole or in part, the loss of the manager's services. For instance, the nature of the business and of its assets may be such that they will not be impaired by the loss of the manager. Furthermore, the loss may be adequately covered by life insurance, or competent management might be employed on the basis of the consideration paid for the former manager's services. These, or other offsetting factors, if found to exist, should be carefully weighed against the loss of the manager's services in valuing the stock of the enterprise.

(c) Balance sheets should be obtained, preferably in the form of comparative annual statements for two or more years immediately preceding the date of appraisal, together with a balance sheet at the end of the month preceding that date, if corporate accounting will permit. Any balance sheet descriptions that are not self-explanatory, and balance sheet items comprehending diverse assets or liabilities, should be clarified in essential detail by supporting supplemental schedules. These statements usually will disclose to the appraiser (1) liquid position (ratio of current assets to current liabilities); (2) gross and net book value of principal classes of fixed assets; (3) working capital; (4) long-term indebtedness; (5) capital structure; and (6) net worth. Consideration also should be given to any assets not essential to the operation of the business, such as investments in securities, real estate, etc. In general, such non-operating assets will command a lower rate of return than do the operating assets, although in exceptional cases the reverse may be true. In computing the book value per share of stock, assets of the investment type should be revalued on the basis of their market price and the book value adjusted accordingly. Comparison of the company's balance sheets over several years may reveal, among other facts, such developments as the acquisition of additional production facilities or subsidiary companies, improvement in financial position, and details as to recapitalizations and other changes in the capital structure of the corporation. If the corporation has more than one class of stock outstanding, the charter or certificate of incorporation should be examined to ascertain the explicit rights and privileges of the various stock issues including: (1) voting powers, (2) preference as to dividends, and (3) preference as to assets in the event of liquidation.

(d) Detailed profit-and-loss statements should be obtained and considered for a representative period immediately prior to the required date of appraisal, preferably five or more years. Such statements should show (1) gross income by principal items; (2) principal deductions from gross income including major prior items of operating expenses, interest and other expense on each item of long-term debt, depreciation and depletion if such deductions are made, officers' salaries, in total if they appear to be reasonable or in detail if they seem to be excessive, contributions (whether or not deductible for tax purposes) that the nature of its business and its com-

EXHIBIT 19-2

Revenue Ruling 59-60
(Continued)

munity position require the corporation to make, and taxes by principal items, including income and excess profits taxes; (3) net income available for dividends; (4) rates and amounts of dividends paid on each class of stock; (5) remaining amount carried to surplus; and (6) adjustments to, and reconciliation with, surplus as stated on the balance sheet. With profit and loss statements of this character available, the appraiser should be able to separate recurrent from nonrecurrent items of income and expense, to distinguish between operating income and investment income, and to ascertain whether or not any line of business in which the company is engaged is operated consistently at a loss and might be abandoned with benefit to the company. The percentage of earnings retained for business expansion should be noted when dividend-paying capacity is considered. Potential future income is a major factor in many valuations of closely-held stocks, and all information concerning past income which will be helpful in predicting the future should be secured. Prior earnings records usually are the most reliable guide as to the future expectancy, but resort to arbitrary five-or-ten-year averages without regard to current trends or future prospects will not produce a realistic valuation. If, for instance, a record of progressively increasing or decreasing net income is found, then greater weight may be accorded the most recent years' profits in estimating earning power. It will be helpful, in judging risk and the extent to which a business is a marginal operator, to consider deductions from income and net income in terms of percentage of sales. Major categories of cost and expense to be so analyzed include the consumption of raw materials and supplied in the case of manufacturers, processors and fabricators; the cost of purchased merchandise in the case of merchants; utility services; insurance; taxes; depletion or depreciation; and interest.

(e) Primary consideration should be given to the dividend-paying capacity of the company rather than to dividends actually paid in the past. Recognition must be given to the necessity of retaining a reasonable portion of profits in a company to meet competition. Dividend-paying capacity is a factor that must be considered in an appraisal, but dividends actually paid in the past may not have any relation to dividend-paying capacity. Specifically, the dividends paid by a closely-held family company may be measured by the income needs of the stockholders or by their desire to avoid taxes on dividend receipts, instead of by the ability of the company to pay dividends. Where an actual or effective controlling interest in a corporation is to be valued, the dividend factor is not a material element, since the payment of such dividends is discretionary with the controlling stockholders. The individual or group in control can substitute salaries and bonuses for dividends, thus reducing net income and understating the dividend-paying capacity of the company. It follows, therefore, that dividends are less reliable criteria of fair market value than other applicable factors.

(f) In the final analysis, goodwill is based upon earning capacity. The presence of goodwill and its value, therefore, rests upon the excess of net earnings over and above a fair return on the net tangible assets. While the element of goodwill may be based primarily on earnings, such factors as the prestige and renown of the business, the ownership of a trade or brand name, and a record of successful operation over a prolonged period in a particular locality, also may furnish support for the inclusion of intangible value. In some instances it may not be possible to make a separate appraisal of the tangible and intangible assets of the business. The enterprise has a value as an entity. Whatever intangible value there is, which is supportable by the facts, may be measured by the amount by which the appraised value of the tangible assets exceeds the net book value of such assets.

(g) Sales of stock of a closely-held corporation should be carefully investigated to determine whether they represent transactions at arm's length. Forced or distress sales do not ordinarily reflect fair market value nor do isolated sales in small amounts necessarily control as the measure of value. This is especially true in the valuation of a controlling interest in a corporation. Since, in the case of closely-held stocks, no prevailing market prices are available, there is no basis for making an adjustment for blockage. It follows, therefore, that such stocks should be valued upon a consideration of all the evidence affecting the fair market value. The size of the block of stock itself is a relevant factor to be considered. Although it is true that a minority interest in an unlisted corporation's stock is more difficult to sell than a similar block of listed stock, it is equally true that control of a corporation, either actual or in effect, representing as it does an added element of value, may justify a higher value for a specific block of stock.

(h) Section 2031(b) of the Code states, in effect, that in valuing unlisted securities the value of stock or securities of corporations engaged in the same or a similar line of business which are listed on an exchange should be taken into consideration along with all other factors. An important consideration is that the corporations to be used for comparisons have capital stocks which are actively traded by the public. In accordance with section 2031(b) of the Code, stocks listed on an exchange are to be considered first. However, if sufficient comparable companies whose stocks are listed on an exchange cannot be found, other comparable companies which have stocks actively traded on the over-the-counter market also may be used. The essential factor is that whether the stocks are sold on an exchange or over-the-counter there is evidence of an active, free public market for the stock as of the valuation date. In selecting corporations for comparative purposes, care should be taken to use only comparable companies. Although the only restrictive requirement as to comparable corporations specified in the statute is that their lines of business be the same or similar, yet it is obvious that

EXHIBIT 19-2

Revenue Ruling 59-60
(Continued)

consideration must be given to other relevant factors in order that the most valid comparison possible will be obtained. For illustration, a corporation having one or more issues of preferred stock, bonds or debentures in addition to its common stock should not be considered to be directly comparable to one having only common stock outstanding. In like manner, a company with a declining business and decreasing markets is not comparable to one with a record of current progress and market expansion.

Section 5. Weight to be Accorded Various Factors.

The valuation of closely-held corporate stock entails the consideration of all relevant factors as stated in section 4. Depending upon the circumstances in each case, certain factors may carry more weight than others because of the nature of the company's business. To illustrate:

(a) Earnings may be the most important criterion of value in some cases whereas asset value will receive primary consideration in others. In general, the appraiser will accord primary consideration to earnings when valuing stocks of companies which sell products or services to the public; conversely, in the investment or holding type of company, the appraiser may accord the greatest weight to the assets underlying the security to be valued.

(b) The value of the stock of a closely-held investment or real estate holding company, whether or not family owned, is closely related to the value of the assets underlying the stock. For companies of this type the appraiser should determine the fair market values of the assets of the company. Operating expenses of such a company and the cost of liquidating it, if any, merit consideration when appraising the relative values of the stock and the underlying assets. The market values of the underlying assets give due weight to potential earnings and dividends of the particular items of property underlying the stock, capitalized at rates deemed proper by the investing public at the date of appraisal. A current appraisal by the investing public should be superior to the retrospective opinion of an individual. For these reasons, adjusted net worth should be accorded greater weight in valuing the stock of a closely-held investment or real estate holding company, whether or not family owned, than any of the other customary yardsticks of appraisal, such as earnings and dividend-paying capacity.

Section 6. Capitalization Rates.

In the application of certain fundamental valuation factors, such as earnings and dividends, it is necessary to capitalize the average or current results at some appropriate rate. A determination of the proper capitalization rate presents one of the most difficult problems in valuation. That there is no ready or simple solution will become apparent by a cursory check of the rates of return and dividend yields in terms of the selling prices of the corporate shares listed on the major exchanges of the country. Wide variations will be found even for companies in the same industry. Moreover, the ratio will fluctuate from year to year depending upon economic conditions. Thus, no standard tables of capitalization rates applicable to closely-held corporations can be formulated. Among the more important factors to be taken into consideration in deciding upon a capitalization rate in a particular case are: (1) the nature of the business; (2) the risk involved; and (3) the stability or irregularity of earnings.

Section 7. Average of Factors.

Because valuations cannot be made on the basis of a prescribed formula, there is no means whereby the various applicable factors in a particular case can be assigned mathematical weights in deriving the fair market value. For this reason, no useful purpose is served by taking an average of several factors (for example, book value, capitalized earnings and capitalized dividends) and basing the valuation on the result. Such a process excludes active consideration of other pertinent factors, and the end result cannot be supported by a realistic application of the significant facts in the case except by mere chance.

Section 8. Restrictive Agreements.

Frequently, in the valuation of closely-held stock for estate and gift tax purposes, it will be found that the stock is subject to an agreement restricting its sale or transfer. Where shares of stock were acquired by a decedent subject to an option reserved by the issuing corporation to repurchase at a certain price, the option price is usually accepted as the fair market value for estate tax purposes. See Rev. Rul. 54-76, C.B. 1954-1, 194. However, in such case the option price is not determinative of fair market value for gift tax purposes. Where the option, or buy and sell agreement, is the result of voluntary action by the stockholders and is binding during the life as well as at the death of the stockholders, such agreement may or may not, depending upon the circumstances of each case, fix the value for estate tax purposes. However, such agreement is a factor to be considered, with other relevant factors, in determining fair market value. Where the stockholder is free to dispose of his shares during life and the option is to become effective only upon his death, the fair market value is not limited to the option price. It is always necessary to consider the relationship of the parties, the relative number of shares held by the decedent, and other material facts, to determine whether the agreement represents a bonafide business arrangement or is a device to pass the decedent's shares to the natural objects of his bounty for less than an adequate and full consideration in money or money's worth. In this connection see Rev. Rul. 157 C.B. 1953-2,255, and Rev. Rul. 189, C.B. 1953-2,294.

Section 9. Effect on Other Documents.

Revenue Ruling 54-77, C.B. 1954-1,187, is hereby superseded.

SOURCE: 1959-1, C.B. 237.

EXHIBIT 19-3

Revenue Ruling 65-193

Revenue Ruling 59-60, C.B. 1959-1, 237, is hereby modified to delete the statements, contained therein at section 4.02(f), that "In some instances it may not be possible to make a separate appraisal of the tangible and intangible assets of the business. The enterprise has a value as an entity. Whatever intangible value there is, which is supportable by the facts, may be measured by the amount by which the appraised value of the tangible assets exceeds the net book value of such assets."

The instances where it is not possible to make a separate appraisal of the tangible and intangible assets of a business are rare and each case varies from the other. No rule can be devised which will be generally applicable to such cases.

Other than this modification, Revenue Ruling 59-60 continues in full force and effect.

SOURCE: 1965-2, C.B. 370.

Revenue Ruling 59-60, Section 3, "Approach to Valuation," makes the general point that the public marketplace best reflects the consensus of the investing public, and it concludes by suggesting as a measure of value "the prices at which the stocks of companies engaged in the same or similar line of business are selling in a free and open market." The section also recognizes that the value can change as a result of factors internal to the company and external economic factors. The section emphasizes the complexity of the factors affecting valuation and the degree of uncertainty involved.

Section 4, "Factors to Consider," lists the eight key factors and elaborates on each. In any appraisal involving taxes, the appraiser should review Section 4 to ensure that each of the eight points has been addressed at some point in the total valuation process.

Section 4.01(c) notes, "In computing the book value per share of stock, assets *of the investment type* should be revalued on the basis of their market price and the book value adjusted accordingly [Emphasis supplied]." It is important to recognize that this requirement to adjust asset values specifically applies to assets "of the investment type," not operating assets.

Section 4.02(d) notes that the profit and loss statements to be considered should be for a "representative period." The section states that the appraiser should separate recurrent from nonrecurrent items and operating income from investment income. It suggests putting more weight on recent years if there appears to be a trend in the earnings pattern.

Section 4.02(h) re-emphasizes that the prices of stocks of publicly traded companies in the same or similar lines of business should be considered and the greatest care possible taken in analyzing the companies to select the ones that are most comparable. Chapter 9 discusses the identification and selection of comparative publicly traded stocks.

Weight to Be Accorded Various Factors

Section 5, "Weight to Be Accorded Various Factors," essentially makes the point that earnings should be accorded the most weight in valuing

EXHIBIT 19-4

Revenue Ruling 77-287

Valuation of securities restricted from immediate resale. Guidelines are set forth for the valuation, for Federal tax purposes of securities that cannot be immediately resold because they are restricted from resale pursuant to Federal securities laws; Rev. Rul. 59-60 amplified. (1977-2, C.B. 319).

Section 1. Purpose.

The purpose of this Revenue Ruling is to amplify Rev. Rul. 59-60, 1959-1 C.B. 237, as modified by Rev. Rul. 65-193, 1965-2 C.B. 370, and to provide information and guidance to taxpayers, Internal Revenue Service personnel, and others concerned with the valuation, for Federal tax purposes, of securities that cannot be immediately resold because they are restricted from resale pursuant to Federal securities laws. This guidance is applicable only in cases where it is not inconsistent with valuation requirements of the Internal Revenue Code of 1954 or the regulations thereunder. Further, this ruling does not establish the time at which property shall be valued.

Section 2. Nature of the Problem.

It frequently becomes necessary to establish the fair market value of stock that has not been registered for public trading when the issuing company has stock of the same class that is actively traded in one or more securities markets. The problem is to determine the difference in fair market value between the registered shares that are actively traded and the unregistered shares. This problem is often encountered in estate and gift tax cases. However, it is sometimes encountered when unregistered shares are issued in exchange for assets or the stock of an acquired company.

Section 3. Background and Definitions.

.01 The Service outlined and reviewed in general the approach, methods, and factors to be considered in valuing shares of closely-held corporate stock for estate and gift tax purposes in Rev. Rul. 59-60, as modified by Rev. Rul. 65-193. The provisions of Rev. Rul. 59-60, as modified, were extended to the valuation of corporate securities for income and other tax purposes by Rev. Rul. 68-609, 1968-2 C.B. 327.

.02 There are several terms currently in use in the securities industry that denote restrictions imposed on the resale and transfer of certain securities. The term frequently used to describe these securities is "restricted securities," but they are sometimes referred to as "unregistered securities," "investment letter stock," "control stock," or "private placement stock." Frequently these terms are used interchangeably. They all indicate that these particular securities cannot lawfully be distributed to the general public until a registration statement relating to the corporation underlying the securities has been filed, and has also become effective under the rules promulgated and enforced by the United States Securities & Exchange Commission (SEC) pursuant to the Federal securities laws. The following represents a more refined definition of each of the following terms along with two other terms -- "exempted securities" and "exempted transactions."

(a) The term "restricted securities" is defined in Rule 144 adopted by the SEC as "securities acquired directly or indirectly from the issuer thereof, or from an affiliate of such issuer, in a transaction or chain of transactions not involving any public offering."

(b) The term "unregistered securities" refers to those securities with respect to which a registration statement, providing full disclosure by the issuing corporation, has not been filed with the SEC pursuant to the Securities Act of 1933. The registration statement is a condition precedent to a public distribution of securities in interstate commerce and is aimed at providing the prospective investor with a factual basis for sound judgment in making investment decisions.

(c) The terms "investment letter stock" and "letter stock" denote shares of stock that have been issued by a corporation without the benefit of filing a registration statement with the SEC. Such stock is subject to resale and transfer restrictions set forth in a letter agreement requested by the issuer and signed by the buyer of the stock when the stock is delivered. Such stock may be found in the hands of either individual investors or institutional investors.

(d) The term "control stock" indicates that the shares of stock have been held or are being held by an officer, director, or other person close to the management of the corporation. These persons are subject to certain requirements pursuant to SEC rules upon resale of shares they own in such corporations.

(e) The term "private placement stock" indicates that the stock has been placed with an institution or other investor who will presumably hold it for a long period and ultimately arrange to have the stock registered if it is to be offered to the general public. Such stock may or may not be subject to a letter agreement. Private placements of stock are exempted from the registration and prospectus provisions of the Securities Act. of 1933.

(f) The term "exempted securities" refers to those classes of securities that are expressly excluded from the registration provisions of the Securities Act of 1933 and the distribution provisions of the Securities Exchange Act of 1934.

(g) The term "exempted transactions" refers to certain sales or distributions of securities that do not involve a public offering and are excluded from the registration and prospectus provisions of the Securities Act of 1933 and distribution provisions of the Securities Exchange Act of 1934. The exempted status makes it unnecessary for issuers of securities to go through the registration process.

Section 4. Securities Industry Practice in Valuing Restricted Securities.

.01 Investment Company Valuation Practices. The Investment Company Act of 1940 requires open-end investment companies to publish the valuation of their portfolio securities daily. Some of these companies have portfolios containing restricted

EXHIBIT 19-4

Revenue Ruling 77-287
(Continued)

securities, but also have restricted securities of the same class traded on a securities exchange. In recent years the number of restricted securities in such portfolios has increased. The following methods have been used by investment companies in the valuation of such restricted securities:

(a) Current market price of the unrestricted stock less a constant percentage discount based on purchase discount;

(b) Current market price of unrestricted stock less a constant percentage discount different from purchase discount;

(c) Current market price of the unrestricted stock less a discount amortized over a fixed period;

(d) Current market price of the unrestricted stock; and

(e) Cost of the restricted stock until it is registered.

The SEC ruled in its Investment Company Act Release No. 5847, dated October 21, 1969, that there can be no automatic formula by which an investment company can value the restricted securities in its portfolios. Rather, the SEC has determined that it is the responsibility of the board of directors of the particular investment company to determine the "fair value" of each issue of restricted securities in good faith.

.02 Institutional Investors Study. Pursuant to Congressional direction, the SEC undertook an analysis of the purchases, sales, and holding of securities by financial institutions, in order to determine the effect of institutional activity upon the securities market. The study report was published in eight volumes in March 1971. The fifth volume provides an analysis of restricted securities and deals with such items as the characteristics of the restricted securities purchasers and issuers, the size of transactions (dollars and shares), the marketability discounts on different trading markets, and the resale provisions. This research project provides some guidance for measuring the discount in that it contains information, based on the actual experience of the marketplace, showing that, during the period surveyed (January 1, 1966, through June 30, 1969), the amount of discount allowed for restricted securities from the trading price of the unrestricted securities was generally related to the following four factors:

(a) **Earnings.** Earnings and sales consistently have a significant influence on the size of restricted securities discounts according to the study. Earnings played the major part in establishing the ultimate discounts at which these stocks were sold from the current market price. Apparently earnings patterns, rather than sales patterns, determine the degree of risk of an investment.

(b) **Sales.** The dollar amount of sales of issuers' securities also has a major influence on the amount of discount at which restricted securities sell from the current market price. The results of the study generally indicate that the companies with the lowest dollar amount of sales during the test period accounted for

most of the transactions involving the highest discount rates, while they accounted for only a small portion of all transactions involving the lowest discount rates.

(c) **Trading Market.** The market in which publicly-held securities are traded also reflects variances in the amount of discount that is applied to restricted securities purchases. According to the study, discount rates were greatest on restricted stocks with unrestricted counterparts traded over-the-counter, followed by those with unrestricted counterparts listed on the American Stock Exchange, while the discount rates for those stocks with unrestricted counterparts listed on the New York Stock Exchange were the smallest.

(d) **Resale Agreement Provisions.** Resale agreement provisions often affect the size of the discount. The discount from the market price provides the main incentive for a potential buyer to acquire restricted securities. In judging the opportunity cost of freezing funds, the purchase is analyzing two separate factors. The first factor is the risk that underlying value of the stock will change in a way that, absent the restrictive provisions, would have prompted a decision to sell. The second factor is the risk that the contemplated means of legally disposing of the stock may not materialize. From the seller's point of view, a discount is justified where the seller is relieved of the expenses of registration and public distribution, as well as of the risk that the market will adversely change before the offering is completed. The ultimate agreement between buyer and seller is a reflection of these and other considerations. Relative bargaining strengths of the parties to the agreement are major considerations that influence the resale terms and consequently the size of discounts in restricted securities transactions. Certain provisions are often found in agreements between buyers and sellers that affect the size of discounts at which restricted stocks are sold. Several such provisions follow, all of which, other than number (3), would tend to reduce the size of the discount:

(1) A provision giving the buyer an option to "piggyback," that is, to register restricted stock with the next registration statement, if any, filed by the issuer with the SEC;

(2) A provision giving the buyer an option to require registration at the seller's expense;

(3) A provision giving the buyer an option to require registration, but only at the buyer's own expense;

(4) A provision giving the buyer a right to receive continuous disclosure of information about the issuer from the seller;

(5) A provision giving the buyer a right to select one or more directors of the issuer;

(6) A provision giving the buyer an option to purchase additional shares of the issuer's stock; and

(7) A provision giving the buyer the right to have a greater voice in operations of the issuer, if the issuer does not meet previously agreed upon operating standards.

EXHIBIT 19-4

Revenue Ruling 77-287
(Continued)

Institutional buyers can and often do obtain many of these rights and options from the sellers of restricted securities, and naturally, the more rights the buyer can acquire, the lower the buyer's risk is going to be, thereby reducing the buyer's discount as well. Smaller buyers may not be able to negotiate the large discounts or the rights and options that volume buyers are able to negotiate.

.03 Summary. A variety of methods have been used by the securities industry to value restricted securities. The SEC rejects all automatic or mechanical solutions to the valuation of restricted securities, and prefers, in the case of the valuation of investment company portfolio stocks, to rely upon good faith valuations by the board of directors of each company. The study made by the SEC found that restricted securities generally are issued at a discount from the market value of freely tradable securities.

Section 5. Facts and Circumstances Material to Valuation of Restricted Securities.

.01 Frequently, a company has a class of stock that cannot be traded publicly. The reason such stock cannot be traded may arise from the securities statutes, as in the case of an "investment letter" restriction; it may arise from a corporate charter restriction, or perhaps from a trust agreement restriction. In such cases, certain documents and facts should be obtained for analysis.

.02 The following documents and facts, when used in conjunction with those discussed in Section 4 of Rev. Rul. 59-60, will be useful in the valuation of restricted securities:

(a) A copy of any declaration of trust, trust agreement, and any other agreements relating to the shares of restricted stock;

(b) A copy of any document showing any offers to buy or sell or indications of interest in buying or selling the restricted shares;

(c) The latest prospectus of the company;

(d) Annual reports of the company for 3 to 5 years preceding the valuation date;

(e) The trading prices and trading volume of the related class of traded securities 1 month preceding the valuation date, if they are traded on a stock exchange (if traded over-the-counter, prices may be obtained from the National Quotations Bureau, the National Association of Securities Dealers Automated Quotations (NASDAQ), or sometimes from broker-dealers making markets in the shares);

(f) The relationship of the parties to the agreements concerning the restricted stock, such as whether they are members of the immediate family or perhaps whether they are officers or directors of the company; and

(g) Whether the interest being valued represents a majority or minority ownership.

Section 6. Weighing Facts and Circumstances Material to Restricted Stock Valuation.

All relevant facts and circumstances that bear upon the worth of restricted stock, including those set forth above in the preceding Sections 4 and 5, and those set forth in Section 4 of Rev. Rul. 59-60, must be taken into account in arriving at the fair market value of such securities. Depending on the circumstances of each case, certain factors may carry more weight than others. To illustrate:

.01 Earnings, net assets, and net sales must be given primary consideration in arriving at an appropriate discount for restricted securities from the freely traded shares. These are the elements of value that are always used by investors in making investment decisions. In some cases, one element may be more important than in other cases. In the case of manufacturing, producing, or distributing companies, primary weight must be accorded earnings and net sales; but in the case of investment or holding companies, primary weight must be given to the net assets of the company underlying the stock. In the former type of companies, value is more closely linked to past, present, and future earnings while in the latter type of companies, value is more closely linked to the existing net assets of the company. See the discussion in Section 5 of Rev. Rul. 59-60.

.02 Resale provisions found in the restriction agreements must be scrutinized and weighed to determine the amount of discount to apply to the preliminary fair market value of the company. The two elements of time and expense bear upon this discount; the longer the buyer of the shares must wait to liquidate the shares, the greater the discount. Moreover, if the provisions make it necessary for the buyer to bear the expense of registration, the greater the discount. However, if the provisions of the restricted stock agreement make it possible for the buyer to "piggyback" shares at the next offering, the discount would be smaller.

.03 The relative negotiation strengths of the buyer and seller of restricted stock may have a profound effect on the amount of discount. For example, a tight money situation may cause the buyer to have the greater balance of negotiation strength in a transaction. However, in some cases the relative strengths may tend to cancel each other out.

.04 The market experience of freely tradable securities of the same class as the restricted securities is also significant in determining the amount of discount. Whether the shares are privately held or publicly traded affects the worth of the shares to the holders. Securities traded on a public market generally are worth more to investors than those that are not traded on a public market. Moreover, the type of public market in which the unrestricted securities are traded is to be given consideration.

Section 7. Effect on Other Documents.

(Rev. Rul. 59-60, as modified by Rev. Rul. 65-193, is amplified.)

SOURCE: 1977-2, C.B. 319

EXHIBIT 19-5

Revenue Ruling 81-253

Issue

Whether minority discounts should be allowed in valuing for federal gift tax purposes three simultaneous transfers of all of the stock in a closely held family corporation to the donor's three children.

Facts

The donor, *A*, owned all of the 90 outstanding shares of stock in corporation *X*, the sole asset of which is a parcel of real estate. On December 30, 1978, *A* made simultaneous gifts of one-third (30 shares) of the stock in *X* to each of *A*'s three children. On that date, the established fair market value of each share of *X* stock, if all the stock were sold together, was $100*x* per share.

At the time the gifts were made, there were no corporate bylaws or other instruments restricting the voting or disposition of corporate shares by any shareholder, and there were no negotiations underway for the disposition of the corporation's assets or the disposition of the shares in question before or subsequent to the date of the gifts. In addition there is no evidence of the kind of family discord or other factor that would indicate that the family would not act as a unit in controlling the corporation. The corporation still owns the parcel of real estate and *A*'s children still own the corporate shares.

Law and Analysis

Section 2501(a)(1) of the Internal Revenue Code provides that a tax is imposed for each calendar quarter on the transfer of property by gift during such calendar quarter. Section 2512(a) provides that the value of the property at the date of the gift shall be considered the amount of the gift.

Section 25.2512-1 of the Gift Tax Regulations defines the value of property as the price at which such property would change hands between a willing buyer and willing seller, neither being under compulsion to buy or sell, and both having reasonable knowledge of relevant facts. The regulations provide that the value of a particular kind of property is not the price that a forced sale of the property would produce, and that all relevant facts and elements of value as of the time of the gift shall be considered.

Section 25.2512-2(a) of the regulations provides that the value of stocks and bonds is the fair market value per share or bond on the date of the gift. Section 25.2512-2(f) provides that the degree of control of the business represented by the block of stock to be valued is among the factors to be considered in valuing stock where there are not sales prices or bona fide bid and asked prices. See also Rev. Rul. 59-60, sections 4.01(g), 4.02(g), 1959-1 C.B. 237.

The fair market value of a piece of property depends on the facts and circumstances. Section 3.01, Rev. Rul. 59-60, 1959-1 C.B. 237, *Messing v. Commissioner*, 48 T.C. 505, 512 (1967), *acq.* 1968-1

C.B. 2. Thus questions of valuation cannot be resolved by mechanical application of formulae and cases involving valuation can often be distinguished. Nonetheless, certain overriding legal principles to which each set of facts is applied govern valuation. *Powers v. Commissioner*, 312 U.S. 259 (1941); *Maytag v. Commissioner*, 187 F.2d 962 (10th Cir. 1951).

Judicial authority is inconsistent regarding the correct legal principle governing the availability of a minority discount in the instant case. Therefore, this ruling is intended to state the Service's position.

Several cases have held or implied that no minority discount is available when the transferred stock is part of a family controlling interest. *Driver v. United States*, No. 73C 260 (W.D. Wis., Sept. 13, 1976); *Blanchard v. United States*, 291 F. Supp. 248 (S.D. Iowa, 1968); *Richardson v. Commissioner*, No. 95770 (T.C.M. 1943), *aff'd*, 151 F.2d 102 (2d Cir. 1945), *cert. denied*, 326 U.S. 796 (1946); *Hamm v. Commissioner*, T.C.M. 1961-347, *aff'd*, 325 F.2d 934 (8th Cir. 1963), *cert. denied*, 377 U.S. 993 (1964). The Service will follow these decisions. Other cases have allowed a minority discount on similar facts. *Whittemore v. Fitzpatrick*, 127 F. Supp. 710 (D. Conn. 1954); *Obermer v. United States*, 238 F. Supp. 29, 34 (D. Hawaii, 1964), *Estate of Piper v. Commissioner*, 72 T.C. 1062 (1979); *Clark v. United States*, Civil Nos. 1308, 1309 (E.D.N.C., May 16, 1975); *Bartram v. Graham*, 157 F. Supp. 757 (D. Conn. 1957); *Estate of Lee v. Commissioner*, 69 T.C. 860 (1978), *nonacq.* 1980-2 C.B. 2; *Estate of Bright v. United States*, No. 78-2221 (5th Cir., Oct. 1, 1981). The Service will not follow these and similar cases.

It is the position of the Service that ordinarily no minority discount will be allowed with respect to transfers of shares of stock among family members where, at the time of the transfer, control (either majority voting control or de facto control) of the corporation exists in the family, *Dattel v. United States*, No. D.C. 73-107-S, (N.D. Miss., Oct. 29, 1975), *Cutbirth v. United States*, Civil No. CA-6-75-1 (N.D. Tex., June 16, 1976). However, when there is evidence of family discord or other factors indicating that the family would not act as a unit in controlling the corporation, a minority discount may be allowed. Although courts have recognized that where a shareholder is unrelated to other shareholders a minority discount may be available because of absence of control, *Estate of Schroeder v. Commissioner*, 13 T.C. 259 (1949), *acq.* 1949-2 C.B. 3, where a controlling interest in stock is owned by family members, there is a unity of ownership and interest, and the shares owned by family members should be valued as part of that controlling interest. This conclusion is based on an evaluation of the facts and circumstances that would affect the price received for the shares in a hypothetical sale. It is unlikely that under circumstances such as exist in the instant case, shares that are part of a controlling

EXHIBIT 19-5

Revenue Ruling 81-253
(Continued)

interest would be sold other than as a unit except to a family member in whose hands the shares would retain their control value because of the family relationship. Thus, where a controlling interest in stock is owned by a family, the value per share of stock owned by one family member is the same as stock owned by any other family member and is the same value that would exist if all the stock were held by one person.

Holding

No minority discount is allowable and the value of each share of stock for federal gift tax purposes is $100.

SOURCE: 1981-2 CB 187.

operating companies and asset values the most weight in valuing holding companies.

The section also notes that assets should be adjusted to market values for closely held investment or real estate holding companies in the same manner that investment-type assets should be adjusted to market values if they are a factor in an operating company. For family-held investment companies, comparisons of per share value to underlying asset value can then be made on the basis of the ratios of market value to net asset value for closed-end investment companies, since such companies report the values of their assets at market on a regular basis. For closely held real estate holding companies, deriving a per share value by reference to publicly traded real estate holding companies is not quite as easy, since most real estate companies do not report their assets' market values. However, in the last few years quite a few Real Estate Investment Trusts (REITs) have started reporting market values. There now are enough reporting such market values that a table of REITs with the ratios of market prices to adjusted asset values can be constructed to provide guidance in valuing closely held real estate holding company shares.

Capitalization Rates

Section 6, "Capitalization Rates," makes further reference to publicly traded shares and notes that appropriate capitalization rates vary considerably both among companies and over time due to economic conditions.

Average of Factors

Section 7, "Average of Factors," is the section referred to in Chapter 2 that discourages use of a mathematical weighting of various factors. The reason is that "such a process excludes active consideration of other pertinent factors." However, as noted in Chapter 2 and in the examples presented in Chapter 21, mathematical weighting frequently is used in practice, even by government representatives, and relied on in court decisions despite the wording of this section. My firm uses the mathematical weighting process in some cases, for the reasons discussed in Chapter 2, but takes care not to exclude active consideration of any other pertinent factors.

Restrictive Agreements

Section 8, "Restrictive Agreements," makes the point that in order to be binding for estate tax valuation purposes, a price fixed under a buy-sell agreement must be binding during the life as well as at the death of the stockholder and not "a device to pass the decedent's shares to the natural objects of his bounty for less than an adequate and full consideration in money or money's worth." See Chapter 20, "Buy-Sell Agreements," for additional discussion.

Summary of Guidelines

Although Revenue Ruling 59-60 was written almost 30 years ago, it still offers considerable insight into the basic criteria and processes for valuing closely held common stocks. With minor modifications and amplification, it has stood the test of time.

Nevertheless, the nature of the process necessarily leaves much room for subjectivity and disagreement. Interpretations by IRS agents and courts have been somewhat less than consistent. It is not a subject that lends itself to such sharp definition of criteria that gray areas can be eliminated. Chapters 21 and 22 demonstrate the issues, opposing positions, and outcomes for a group of cases representative of most of the major issues commonly involved in disagreements in federal tax valuation cases.

Valuation Issues in Estate and Gift Tax Planning Techniques

Placing Family Assets in Corporate or Partnership Form

It may be worthwhile to consider incorporating various family assets into a family-controlled holding company before transferring interests to heirs. Aside from the business purposes of such transfers, such as centralization of supervision, reduction of potential personal exposure to creditors, assurance of smoother management succession, and prevention of the assets' waste by inexperienced heirs, there may also be estate planning advantages. The assets could be almost anything, such as marketable securities, real estate, art, coins, or any kind of collectibles. Since publicly traded securities of companies holding such assets (such as closed-end investment companies and REITs) tend to sell at a discount from underlying net asset value, so should shares of family-controlled corporations. Interests in this type of closely held company also are valued at a further discount for lack of marketability.

Of course, in making the decision to incorporate a family holding company to execute a portion of the family estate plan in this manner, one must realize that the justification for the discounted values is real, not contrived; that is, the heir who receives a gift of minority shares of a family holding company representing an undivided interest in a portfolio of assets will not have control over those assets. Owning 15 percent of the assets and owning 15 percent of the stock of the company that owns them are two different things. The power to liquidate, transfer assets, declare dividends, and exercise all the other various elements of control will not go to the donee. There also may be income tax considerations, so such a move should not be undertaken without the aid of competent tax counsel. If the donor understands and is satisfied with the various implications, the creation of a family-owned holding company could be a tax-saving feature of the total estate plan.

An extension of this technique has been placement of family assets in S corporations, which allows pass-through of most types of income generated by the underlying assets without being subjected to income tax at the corporate level. This technique has become more important with the repeal of the *General Utilities* doctrine in the Tax Reform Act of 1986. Under the *General Utilities* doctrine, a corporation selling its assets to another corporation, as in an acquisition, generally was allowed to liquidate within one year of sale without having to recognize gain on the assets' sale at the corporate level.[3]

Family assets also have been placed in partnerships to facilitate the estate planning techniques described in the next two sections on minority interest transfers and recapitalizations. With the advent of some forms of public markets for limited partnership interests, such as master limited partnerships, and secondary markets, such as the National Partnership Exchange (NAPEX), reliable information has become available indicating that limited partnership interests also often tend to trade at prices below their underlying net asset values.[4]

Minimizing Taxes by a Series of Timely Minority-Interest Transfers

In general, estate planning techniques for minimizing transfer taxes revolve around timing transfers when the value of the stock is relatively low and structuring them such that they have the least possible value.

The more rapidly a company is growing in value, the more important it is to effect stock transfers to heirs early rather than later, after the value has increased. However, if the business is cyclical in nature, it may be possible to time transfers at a cyclical trough in the company's value.

For structure, the best technique usually is to plan transfers as a series of small minority interests. To begin, a married couple can give up to $20,000 ($10,000 per donor) in value to each of as many persons as they wish each year without paying federal gift tax. More important for transfers of substantial size, however, is that, at least under the law and court rulings at this writing, minority interests are subject to substantial discounts in value per share compared with the per share

---

[3]Mitchell M. Gans, "The Repeal of *General Utilities*: Estate Tax Implications," *Trusts & Estates*, July 1987, pp. 43–48.

[4]The National Partnership Exchange is a computerized, seven-day auction market for secondary market trading of units of public limited partnerships. Membership is available only to broker/dealers and registered representatives.

value of a controlling interest. Generally, the less significant the fractional interest as it relates to the company's control or potential control, the greater the discount that applies. Minority interests are further discussed in Chapter 15.

Discounts for lack of marketability are discussed in Chapter 10. Minority shares in closely held companies can be valued for tax purposes by estimating their potential market value as publicly traded stock and then discounting them for lack of marketability. In general, the smaller the minority interest, the greater the extent to which this approach can be applied. The net result may be that transfers of shares of closely held companies can be made at quite large discounts below net asset values. Illustrations of such discounts are included in the analyses of certain tax valuation cases in Chapters 21 and 22.

Note that in Revenue Ruling 81-253 (see Exhibit 19–5) the IRS takes the position that a minority interest valuation is not available for gifts of shares that are part of a family-owned controlling block of shares, absent any evidence of family discord. However, recent court decisions have not followed this valuation theory. Chapter 22 reviews some of these decisions.

Recapitalizations

The Revenue Act of 1987 created a new IRC Section 2036(c) that requires that for federal estate tax purposes all property transferred by a decedent after December 17, 1987, in which the decedent retained a disproportionately large share of the income or rights in an enterprise and transferred a disproportionately large share of the potential appreciation in the decedent's interest be brought back and included in the estate and valued at fair market value as of the date of death. This section will be triggered if the deceased owned directly or indirectly (calculated by including the cumulative ownership interests of all other family members or other controlled enterprises) 10 percent or more of the voting power or income stream or both of the enterprise and if the share of the rights or income was retained for a period which did not end before the decedent's death.

The Technical and Miscellaneous Revenue Act of 1988 (TAMRA 88) contained additional amendments to Section 2036(c) which further increased the potential scope of this Section. Also, under TAMRA 88 some very narrowly defined "safe harbor" types of transactions among family members are granted freedom from inclusion under the harsh tax effects of Section 2036(c).

The broad wording of IRC Section 2036(c) appears to encompass many of the estate-freezing recapitalization techniques discussed below. Because of the drastic estate tax consequences of any transfers of securities qualifying under Section 2036(c) issued in an estate-freezing recapitalization, it is unlikely that this technique will find much use after 1987.

However, the appraiser may face assignments to value securities issued in estate freezing recapitalizations prior to the passage of the Revenue Act of 1987. Therefore, a discussion of the objectives and mechanics of such recapitalizations is useful.

Prior to the passage of the 1987 changes in the law, recapitalizations were an effective tool in estate planning for freezing the value of the older generation's estate and having the future appreciation in the business's value accrue to the younger generation. In the past, such recapitalization accomplished several other desirable objectives, such as allowing active members of management to maintain continuity of voting control and providing income to selected owners who need it. Although it was most common to use the recapitalization technique for a corporation, it also was possible to use essentially the same technique to create a multiclass partnership.[5]

A corporate recapitalization involves dividing the company's equity into two or more classes of stock, with the provisions of each class designed to serve the objective of a particular owner or group of owners. In its simplest form, a recapitalized company would have the value of its common stock divided into one class of common and one class of preferred, but the possible variations for serving different circumstances and objectives are limitless.

Example of a Recapitalization.   Let's say that we have a growing company operated by a father and son, that the father owns all the stock, and that we have estimated the fair market value at $1 million. Assume also that the father desires that all the future growth in the company's value accrue to the benefit of the son rather than further building the value of the father's estate. The total value of the $1 million can be reallocated to a common stock and a fixed-dividend preferred—say, on the basis of $100,000 worth of common and $900,000, worth of preferred. If the father has not used his gift and estate tax unified credit, he can give the $100,000 of common stock to his son with no gift tax payment. If in five years the value of the total business grows to $2.5 million but the value of the preferred stays constant, the value of the business interest in the older generation's estate will have been frozen at $900,000 and the value of the younger generation's interest grown to $1.6 million.

Valuation Issues.   The recapitalization technique obviously can be a tremendously powerful tool for reducing potential estate tax consequences in a growing family company. This technique used to be perfectly acceptable to the IRS as long as two criteria were met.[6] First, the total value assigned to the company at the time of the recapitalization had to be acceptable under the guidelines of Revenue Rulings 59-60 and 83-120. Second, the allocation of total value had to be properly made among whatever classes of stock were used. The essence of the problem here usually was to avoid the possible pitfall of allocating too little to the common and too much to the preferred, since the common typically was transferred and the taxpayer did not want to be in

---

[5]Byrle M. Abbin, "Using the Multi-class Partnership to Freeze Asset Values for Estate Planning Purposes," *Journal of Taxation*, February 1980, pp. 66–69.

[6]Of course, a business purpose must be met. However, courts have found that estate planning for shareholders in a closely held company does constitute a valid business purpose. If one is in doubt about being able to satisfy the business purpose requirement, it may be advisable to seek a private letter ruling. For a good discussion of basic requirements of a recapitalization and tax treatment as well as other aspects of recapitalizations, see Robert L. Littenberg, "The Use of Recapitalizations in Estate Plans under the 1976 Tax Reform Act," University of Southern California Tax Institute, 1978, pp. 719–73.

the position of incurring a substantial gift tax if the IRS subsequently determined that the value of the transfer was considerably above the amount allocated in the recapitalization.

As Littenberg states:

> Accurate valuation of a corporation and the stocks and/or securities to be exchanged and issued in connection with a recapitalization is absolutely essential. Failure to achieve accurate valuation can result in either unexpected gift tax or income tax liabilities. . . .
>
> In most instances the most prudent course to pursue is to engage the services of a qualified expert to make the valuation and prepare a supporting written report which can be provided to the Service on audit.[7]

The income, voting, redemption, and liquidation rights can be assigned to the various classes of stock in almost any manner desired. Typically, those who want income, such as a retiring key owner or family member, will receive dividend-paying preferred stock, and those desiring growth of value will receive common. Stock with voting rights may be used for persons active in the company's affairs and nonvoting stock for inactive owners. Sometimes voting rights on a class of stock will be conditioned on some event, such as failure to pay dividends for a two-year period. A class of stock can even have voting rights that terminate with the death of a specified individual so that control of the corporation will not remain in the estate of the deceased.

All of the foregoing factors bear on the value of each class of security issued, as discussed in relevant sections of chapters throughout the book.

The appraiser must make a reasoned judgment of the factors affecting the relative value of the securities of each class in a recapitalization situation in light of all the facts unique to the specific case. Because of the considerable impact on value that can result from the securities' various features, it is becoming increasingly common for an appraiser to work intimately with the attorney, CPA, and client from the very outset of a proposed recapitalization program. Given the adverse tax impacts of estate-freezing recapitalizations as a result of the changes in the law, this kind of close coordination is more important than ever.

Common-on-Common Recapitalizations.   A different form of this estate-planning technique involves the recapitalization of a corporation or partnership into classes of securities that are the same in all respects except for voting control. Typically, this technique requires the creation of voting and nonvoting shares of common stock for a corporation. For partnerships, this requires general and limited partnership interests with carefully drawn liquidation and control rights.[8] This type of common-on-common recapitalization may avoid the new IRC Section 2036(c) provisions and may allow the gifting of minority, permanently noncontrolling interests with the valuation advantages described in the previous two sections. In addition, under current tax law S corporations can issue this type of otherwise identical voting

---

[7]Ibid., pp. 732–33.
[8]See *Estate of Daniel J. Harrison, Jr.*, T.C. Memo 1987-8 (1987).

and nonvoting common stock, which makes this technique especially applicable to family holding companies.

The valuation issues in the recapitalization of ownership interests into voting and nonvoting interests revolves around the differential due to voting control. The nonvoting stock in a closely held company would have all the noncontrol characteristics of minority interests, and would also be subject to further discount for lack of marketability. Based on a number of studies, a further discount because the stock is nonvoting would be relatively small if taken from the amount at which the stock is valued as a voting minority interest in a closely held company.

Buy-Sell Agreements or Sale of Options

Chapter 20 discusses buy-sell agreements in detail. For now, let us note that there are three factors that determine whether the buy-sell agreement is conclusively binding for estate tax purposes:

1. The agreement must restrict the transfer of the securities to the buy-sell price during the owner's life as well as at death.
2. There must be a valid business purpose for establishing the agreement.
3. The value established in the agreement must have been an adequate and fair price at the time the agreement was executed.

Thus a properly drawn buy-sell agreement with a fixed transfer price may, over time, have provided a way to freeze the value of family members' shares at a value perhaps less than fair market value as a subsequent date of death. Since December 17, 1987, this technique is unworkable from an estate tax standpoint due to the passage of Section 2036(c).

In a similar fashion, the sale of a fixed-price option in order to purchase a security would tend to freeze the security's estate tax value; thus, the option must satisfy the same rules that apply to buy-sell agreements.[9] The valuation of options is discussed in Chapter 18.

Loss of Key Person

Often the appraiser faces the valuation of closely held stock in the estate of the president, founder, or other key executive of a business. In this circumstance, it is reasonable to investigate the possibility that the value of the company—and, thus, of its securities—has been impaired due to the loss of the services of a "key person" in the business's management.

Whether such decline in value actually has occurred depends on the facts of the case. Following are the elements to be investigated in establishing any discount or diminution from the loss of a key person.

First, the appraiser determines the deceased executive's actual duties and areas of active involvement. A key person may contribute value to a firm in both day-to-day management duties and from strategic judgment responsibilities based on long-standing contacts and reputation within an industry.

---

[9]*Dorn, et al.* v. *U.S.*, 86-2 U.S.T.C. paragraph 13,701 (1986).

Second, the appraiser assesses the ability of existing successor management to move up the organizational ladder and take over the duties of the vacated position. Ideally, a strong and stable corporate organization will provide this capability. This assumes that a succession plan actually exists. All too often, however, private business owners create "spider web" organization structures with themselves at the center—that is, all management decisions are made by the key executive-owner. The extent of organizational damage may also be related to the suddenness of the key manager's death.

Third, the appraiser calculates the amount of compensation necessary for replacing the key executive or filling the positions vacated or created when successors move up.

Fourth, to this quantitative calculation the appraiser adds the damages arising from risks to the firm in bringing in replacement executives who may be unfamiliar with the company's operations. These risks can be compounded by the appraiser's assessment of the complexity or precariousness of the firm's competitive or financial position. This is especially true if the deceased was personal guarantor of the firm's debts, as often is the case with closely held business loans. Sometimes these risks can be quantified as estimates of sales losses or profit margin declines over estimated future periods.

There are at least two offsets to these potential losses. One is the compensation, net of any continuing obligations, that the company ceases to pay to the deceased executive. The other is any insurance on the key person's life that is payable to the firm and not earmarked for other purposes, such as repurchase of the deceased's stock in the company.

The estimates of key-person losses can be directly incorporated into the valuation methods appropriate for the particular case. This may be accomplished by adjusting normalized earnings or price-to-earnings multiples, or as reductions in estimated future cash flows to be discounted. Otherwise, the loss can be subtracted from the firm's indicated value as a separate item, much like the discount for lack of marketability.

Evidence for the amount of the loss from the key person's death from securities' values in the public market shows that the magnitude of the decline varies with the particular circumstances. Generally, public companies have larger and more flexible professional management teams and thus can better absorb the shock of the loss of any one key person. An instructive example of a catastrophic loss of key executives, however, was the tragic death of most of the top management of Arrow Electronics in a hotel fire in December 1980. Arrow's New York Stock Exchange listed common stock fell approximately 20 percent after the announcement of the news.

Other Estate Planning Techniques Requiring Valuations

Strictly speaking, the three techniques reviewed below do not require consideration of any valuation factors different than those mandated under Revenue Ruling 59-60. But an appraiser ought to be aware of these techniques, as he or she may be called upon to prepare a valuation of a closely held business that will be used in this fashion.

Sale of Remainder Interest. In this technique, the owner of a closely held business security sells to an heir a remainder interest in the security and retains a life interest in the current enjoyment of income and the security's voting rights. The *remainder interest* is valued by taking the security's appraised fair market value and discounting it to a present value under the IRS actuarial tables based on the seller's projected remaining life. At this writing, the present value interest factor of the tables is 10 percent. Thus, the present value of the remainder interest can be a small fraction of the security's current fair market value if the seller is relatively young. Upon the seller's death the life interest terminates, leaving the security, including any appreciation after the sale, to pass, untaxed, to the heir outside the seller's gross estate.

Valuation is crucial to this technique, because if the sale transaction is not for full and adequate consideration, the asset's entire value will be brought back into the seller's estate at fair market value as of the date of death .

It should be noted that if the new IRC Section 2036(c) under the Revenue Act of 1987 and TAMRA 88 is read literally, the sale of a remainder interest might be characterized as a transfer of a disproportionately large share of the potential appreciation in the seller's interest in the enterprise where the seller has retained a life interest in the income and voting rights. This would require that the fair market value of the remainder interest be included in the seller's estate at date-of-death value and thus defeat the objective of this technique.

Grantor-Retained Income Trusts (GRITs). This technique requires the owner of a closely held business security to transfer the security to a *grantor-retained income trust (GRIT)* that will remain outstanding for only a certain number of years. The owner receives the income from the trust, and the remainder interest passes to the trust's beneficiaries, typically the heirs. The transfer to the trust is subject to gift taxes only on the smaller discounted present value of the remainder interest based on the same IRS actuarial tables referred to above. If the owner does not die while the trust is in existence, the security passes to the heirs outside the owner's gross estate.

Once again, valuation is important in establishing the value to be discounted. TAMRA 88 provisions appear to allow a limited use of GRITS that remain in existence for a period not exceeding 10 years that comply with other restrictions in Section 2036(c).

Sale for a Private Annuity or a Self-Canceling Note. The business owner utilizes this technique to sell the entire business to an heir in exchange for a *private annuity*—a fixed periodic payment made to the seller for the rest of his or her life.

A *self-canceling note* is similar to an annuity but has the additional advantage that part of the periodic payment of principal and interest due from the heir can be forgiven (waived) by the seller under the annual $10,000 gift tax exclusion. One of the key issues in the structure of this technique is the correct valuation of the closely held business interest sold and the terms of the annuity or note received so as to avoid gift taxes on the initial sale and estate taxes at the seller's death.

The use of various types of debt or other time payments on transfers of interests in enterprises between family members, especially intergenerational transfers, is severely restricted to certain types of qualified debt under the provisions of Section 2036(c).

Other Valuation Issues

There are four other issues regarding valuation for estate and gift taxes of which an appraiser should be aware.

In Revenue Ruling 85-75, 1985-1 C.B. 376, the IRS has held that it will not necessarily be bound by values that it accepted for estate tax purposes as the correct cost basis for determining depreciation deductions or income taxes on capital gains from an asset's subsequent sale.

In a similar manner, in Private Letter Ruling 8447005 (July 26, 1984), the IRS states that it may revalue gifts made in previous years, even if the values were not fraudulent and the filings exceed the statute of limitations, for the purpose of increasing the tax bracket applicable to taxable transfers reported on a business owner's subsequent gift or estate tax return.

On the other hand, it may be possible to use one value for calculating the gross estate value of a block of closely held stock and a different value for calculating the value of a portion of the block of stock that will be exempted from estate taxes as a marital deduction (i.e., the portion of the estate transferred to a spouse).[10]

The final valuation issue is the lower value for closely held business stock that may result if real estate used in a family-owned trade or business is valued for estate tax purposes for actively involved family members under the provisions of Section 2032A, "Special-Use Valuation." A detailed discussion of this section is beyond the scope of this book. Here simply note that closely held company valuation methods based on net asset values may be lower if an appraisal of the underlying operating real property follows the guidelines of this section. This issue is particularly relevant for family-owned farming or other agricultural business securities.

Charitable Gift Valuation

Since charitable gifts are also deductible for federal income tax purposes, a business owner may use charitable gifts to reduce the size of the estate during life or may place closely held securities in trusts with charitable institutions as beneficiaries and receive favorable income and estate tax treatment. The elements of value set forth in Revenue Ruling 59-60 apply to this type of transaction.

In the case of non–publicly-traded securities, a qualified appraisal is required if the gift's value is over $10,000. A special appraisal sum-

---

[10]See *Estate of Chenoweth*, 88 T.C. No. 90 (1987).

mary form (IRS Form 8283) must be signed by the appraiser and submitted by the taxpayer with his or her annual income tax return to substantiate the charitable deduction. A copy of Form 8283 is shown in Exhibit 19–6.

A *qualified appraisal* is an appraisal document that [Temporary Reg. S1.170A-13T(c)(3)]:

1. Relates to an appraisal that is made no earlier than 60 days prior to the date of contribution of the appraised property.
2. Is prepared, signed, and dated by a qualified appraiser.

EXHIBIT 19-6

Form 8283
Noncash Charitable Contributions

Form **8283** (Rev. October 1986) Department of the Treasury Internal Revenue Service	**Noncash Charitable Contributions** ► Attach to your Federal income tax return if the total claimed value of all property contributed exceeds $500.	OMB No. 1545-0908 Expires 9-30-88 Attachment Sequence No. **55**
Name(s) as shown on your income tax return		Identification number

Section A   Include in Section A **only** items (or groups of similar items) which have a claimed value of **$5,000** or less per item or group and certain publicly traded securities (see instructions).

Part I   **Information on Donated Property**

1	(a) Name and address of the donee organization	(b) Description of donated property (attach a separate sheet if more space is needed)
A		
B		
C		
D		
E		

Note: Columns (d), (e), and (f) do not have to be completed for items with a value of $500 or less.

	(c) Date of the contribution	(d) Date acquired by donor (mo., yr.)	(e) How acquired by donor	(f) Donor's cost or adjusted basis	(g) Fair market value	(h) Method used to determine the fair market value
A						
B						
C						
D						
E						

Part II   **Other Information**—Complete questions 2 and 3 only if you gave less than the entire interest in property or if restrictions were attached to the contribution.

2   If less than the entire interest in the property is contributed during the year, complete the following:

(a) Enter letter from Part I which identifies the property _____. (Attach a separate statement if Part II applies to more than one property.)

(b) Total amount claimed as a deduction for the property listed in Part I for this tax year _____; for any prior tax year(s) _____.

(c) Name and address of each organization to which any such contribution was made in a prior year (complete only if different from the donee organization above).

Charitable organization (donee) name

Number and street

City or town, state, and ZIP code

(d) The place where any tangible property is located or kept. _____

(e) Name of any person, other than the donee organization, having actual possession of the property. _____

3   If conditions were attached to the contribution, answer the following questions:

	Yes	No
(a) Is there a restriction either temporarily or permanently on the donee's right to use or dispose of the donated property?		
(b) Did you give to anyone (other than the donee organization or another organization participating with the donee organization in cooperative fundraising) the right to the income from the donated property or to the possession of the property, including the right to vote donated securities, to acquire the property by purchase or otherwise, or to designate the person having such income, possession, or right to acquire?		
(c) Is there a restriction limiting the donated property for a particular use?		

For Paperwork Reduction Act Notice, see separate instructions.   Form **8283** (Rev. 10-86)

EXHIBIT 19-6

Form 8283
Noncash Charitable Contributions
(Continued)

Form 8283 (Rev. 10-86)   Page **2**

Name(s) as shown on your income tax return. (Do not enter name and identification number if shown on the other side.)	Identification number

Section B Appraisal Summary—Include in Section B only items (or groups of similar items) which have a claimed value of more than $5,000 per item or group. *(Report contributions of certain publicly traded securities only in Section A.)*

Part I Donee Acknowledgment *(To be completed by the charitable organization.)*

1 This charitable organization acknowledges that it is a qualified organization under section 170(c) and that it received the donated property as described in Part II on _____
(Date)
Furthermore, this organization affirms that in the event it sells, exchanges, or otherwise disposes of the property (or any portion thereof) within two years after the date of receipt, it will file an information return (**Form 8282,** Donee Information Return) with the IRS and furnish the donor a copy of that return. This acknowledgment does not represent concurrence in the claimed fair market value.

Charitable organization (donee) name	Employer identification number
Number and street	City or town, state, and ZIP code
Authorized signature	Title Date

Part II Information on Donated Property *(To be completed by the taxpayer and/or appraiser.)*

2 Check type of property:
   ☐ Art*   ☐ Real Estate   ☐ Gems/Jewelry
   ☐ Stamp Collections ☐ Coin Collections   ☐ Books   ☐ Other
*Art includes paintings, sculpture, watercolors, prints, drawings, ceramics, antique furniture, decorative arts, textiles, carpets, silver, rare manuscripts, historical memorabilia, and other similar objects.

3	(a) Description of donated property (attach a separate sheet if more space is needed)	(b) Date acquired by donor (mo., yr.)	(c) How acquired by donor	(d) Donor's cost or adjusted basis	(e) Appraised fair market value
A					
B					
C					
D					

4 If tangible property was donated, write a brief summary of the overall physical condition of the property at the time of the gift.
....
....
....

Part III Taxpayer (Donor) Statement *(To be completed for items listed in Section B, Part II, with appraised value of $500 or less per item.)*

I declare that item(s) (enter letter(s) identifying property) _____ listed in Part II above has (have) to the best of my knowledge and belief an appraised value of not more than $500 (per item).
Signature of taxpayer (donor) ▶   Date ▶

Part IV Certification of Appraiser *(To be completed by the appraiser of the above donated property.)*

I declare that I am not the donor, the donee, a party to the transaction in which the donor acquired the property, employed by or related to any of the foregoing persons, or a person whose relationship to any of the foregoing persons would cause a reasonable person to question my independence as an appraiser.

Also, I declare that I hold myself out to the public as an appraiser and that because of my qualifications as described in the appraisal, I am qualified to make appraisals of the type of property being valued. I certify the appraisal fees were not based upon a percentage of the appraised property value. Furthermore, I understand that a false or fraudulent overstatement of the property value as described in the qualified appraisal or this appraisal summary may subject me to the civil penalty under section 6701(a) (aiding and abetting the understatement of tax liability). I affirm that I have not been barred from presenting evidence or testimony by the Director of Practice.

Please
Sign
Here | Signature ▶   Title ▶   Date of appraisal ▶
Business address   Identification number

City or town, state, and ZIP code

3. Does not involve a prohibited type of appraisal fee, such as occurs when part or all of the fee arrangement is based on a percentage of the property's appraised value (except for certain fee arrangements with not-for-profit associations that regulate appraisers [Reg. S1.170A-13T(c)(6)]).

4. Includes the following information:
   a. A description of the property.
   b. In the case of tangible property, the property's physical condition.
   c. The date of contribution.
   d. The terms of any agreement the donor enters into that relates to the use, sale, or other disposition of the contributed property.
   e. The name, address, and tax identification number of the qualified appraiser and the appraiser's employer corporation or partnership.
   f. The qualifications of the qualified appraiser.
   g. A statement that the appraisal was prepared for income tax purposes.
   h. The date on which the property was valued.
   i. The property's appraised fair market value on the date of contribution.
   j. The method of valuation used.
   k. The specific basis for valuation, if any, such as certain comparable sales transactions.
   l. A description of the fee arrangement between the donor and the appraiser.

In order to be a qualified appraiser, a person must [Temporary Reg. S1.170A-13T(c)(5)]:

1. Hold himself or herself out to the public as an appraiser.
2. Be qualified to make appraisals of the type of property being valued.
3. Understand that he or she can be subject to penalties for a false or fraudulent overvaluation statement under Code Section 6701.

The person who claims a deduction, the donee, and an employee of any of these persons cannot qualify as an appraiser. In addition, the person who sold, exchanged, or gave the contributed property to the donor cannot be a qualified appraiser unless the property was donated within two months of the date of acquisition and the appraised value did not exceed the acquisition price. Also, any person whose relationship with any of the above persons would cause a reasonable person to question the appraiser's independence cannot be a qualified appraiser.

Summary

The entire area of estate and gift tax valuation can be a constantly shifting mine field of laws, regulations, and court decisions. Because of this, it is important that the appraiser be able to function as a knowledgeable contributor to the client's team of estate planning professionals.

With the top marginal federal estate tax rate at 55 percent, the tax implications of estate planning and gift and estate tax valuations can be huge. Inclusion of assets back into an estate that were originally gifted or transferred away via estate freezing transactions can also create tremendous problems. The tax implications are exacerbated by the penalties that may be imposed on taxpayers for undervaluation for gift and estate tax purposes and overvaluation for charitable contibution purposes. Appraisers are also subject to significant penalties.

It is essential that valuations involving federal tax implications be done in accordance with guidelines discussed in this chapter, as clarified and modified by ever-evolving case law. Chapters 21 and 22 discuss some of the most relevant case law for tax valuation purposes.

Bibliography

Articles

Abbin, Byrle M. "Is Bifurcation a Dirty Word?" 11 *Estates, Gifts and Trusts Journal*, 1986, p. 35 +.

Abbin, Byrle M., and David K. Carlson. "Significant Recent Developments Concerning Estate Planning (Part I)." *Tax Adviser*, June 1987, pp. 415–31.

Abbin, Byrle M., and David K. Carlson. "Significant Recent Developments Concerning Estate Planning (Part II)." *Tax Adviser*, July 1987, pp. 467–84.

Abbin, Byrle M., and James Zukin. "Have They Nuked the Freeze? Evaluating the Impact of Recent Decisions, Regulations and Rulings." Philip E. Heckerling Institute on Estate Planning, University of Miami Law Center, 1985, pp. 5.1–5.129.

Abernethy, Lynn Jr., and Frank S. McGaughey III. "Gift and Estate Tax Returns: Practical Problems and Procedures." 32nd Estate Planning Institute, University of Georgia, February 27–28, 1987, pp. 1–26.

Allen John T., Jr. "Washington Saves the Farm? The Peculiar Remedy of IRC Section 2032A." *Taxes*, April 1978, pp. 205–12.

Averill, Lawrence A., Jr. "Valuing Oil and Mineral Interests for Estate Planning Purposes." *Land & Water Law Review*, 1982, pp. 367–400.

Bakay, Gregory H., and Steven N. Kaplan. "Estate Planning Options Available for Owners of Closely-Held Businesses." *Taxation for Accountants*, May 1985, pp. 290–95.

Bettigole, Bruce J. "Use of Estate Freeze Severely Restricted by Revenue Act of '87." *Journal of Taxation*, March 1988, pp. 132–35.

Blake, John Freeman. " 'Control' and the Estate Tax Implications of Retained Voting Rights under Section 2036(b)." *Estate Planning*, January–February 1988, pp. 22–26.

Blake, John Freeman. "*Estate of Samuel I. Newhouse*: High Stakes Dispute over Valuation and Civil Fraud." *Estates, Gifts and Trusts Journal*, May–June 1984, pp. 76–83.

Blattmachr, Jonathan G., and Mitchell M. Gans. "Putting the Heat on Freezes." *Probate and Property*, May–June 1988, pp. 11–17.

Bock, C. Allen, and John H. McCord. "Estate Tax Valuation of Farmland under Section 2032A of the Internal Revenue Code: An Analysis of the Recently Proposed Treasury Regulations." *Southern Illinois University Law Journal*, August 1978, pp. 145–77.

Bortek, Robert D. "Estate Tax Relief for Business Owners' Estates after the Tax Reform Act of 1986." *Financial and Estate Planning*. Commerce Clearing House, May 1987, pp. 23,781–23,798.

Bringardner, Bruce W. "Planning to Qualify Nonfarm Business Real Estate for Special-Use Valuation." *Journal of Taxation*, March 1986, pp. 130–36.

Bromley, Robert G. "A Closer Statistical Look at Tax Court Compromise." *Taxes*, May 1979, pp. 325–30.

Butala, John H., Jr. "Estate Planning for Securities Burdened with Securities Law Restrictions." Philip E. Heckerling Institute on Estate Planning, University of Miami Law Center, 1981, pp. 9.1–9.35.

Carter, T. Heyward, Jr. "Application of Section 2032A to the Valuation of Timberland for Federal Estate Tax Purposes." *South Carolina Law Review*, 1978, pp. 577–625.

Childs, James W. "Valuation of Real Property Based on Farm or Other Business Use: How Well Do the Proposed Regulations Track with the Internal Revenue Code Provisions and Existing Case Law?" *South Dakota Law Review*, Summer 1980, pp. 528–60.

Committee on Federal Death Tax Problems of Estates and Trusts. "Internal Revenue Service Challenge to Valuation of Assets after Statute of Limitations Has Expired" *Real Property, Probate and Trust Journal*, 1985, p. 111+.

Coolidge, H. Calvin. "Valuation of Closely-Held Businesses: Emphasis on Full Disclosure of Facts." *Illinois Bar Journal*, November 1976, pp. 160–62.

Cooper, George. "A Voluntary Tax? New Perspectives of Sophisticated Estate Tax Avoidance." *Columbia Law Review*, March 1977, pp. 161–247.

Cordier, Henry K. "Charitable Donations: The 1986 Tax Law Impact." *ASA Valuation*, February 1988, pp. 80–86.

Crandall, Arthur L. "Valuing the Closely Held Business." *Financial and Estate Planning*. Commerce Clearing House, 1983, pp. 22401–22411.

Cummins, John R.; Turney P. Berry; and Martin S. Weinberg. "Using the Service's New Handbook for Estate Tax Examiners." *Journal of Taxation*, May 1988, pp. 276–82.

Cummins, John R.; Martin D. Weinberg; and D. M. Roth. "Current Attitudes towards Estate Tax Discounts for Restricted Securities and Underwriting Fees." *Estate Planning*, September 1983, pp. 276–81.

Dant, Thomas W., Jr. "Courts Increasing Amount of Discount for a Minority Interest in a Business." *Journal of Taxation*, August 1975, pp. 113–18.

Dougherty, J. Chrys. "Business Interests in an Estate." Institute on Federal Taxation, New York University, 1982, pp. 5.1–5.42.

Eastland, S. Stacy, and Robert M. Weylandt. "Partnerships Solve Problems." *Trusts & Estates*, September 1987, pp. 10–28.

Englebrecht, Ted D. "A Reply, Analysis, and Extension of a Closer Statistical Look at Tax Court Compromise." *Taxes*, September 1979, pp. 607–14.

Englebrecht, Ted D. "Valuation of Closely-Held Oil and Gas Corporations for

Estate and Gift Tax Purposes." *Oil and Gas Tax Quarterly*, December 1977, pp. 273–88.

Englebrecht, Ted D., and Dale L. Davison. "A Statistical Look at Tax Court Compromise in Estate Gift Tax Valuation of Closely Held Stock." *Taxes*, June 1977, pp. 395–400.

"Estate Planning: Protecting Business and Family Interests." *Small Business Report*, December 1987, pp. 48–53.

Fellows, Mary Louise, and William H. Painter. "Valuing Close Corporations for Federal Wealth Transfer Taxes: A Statutory Solution to the Disappearing Wealth Syndrome." *Stanford Law Review*, May 1978, pp. 895–933.

Fiore, Owen G. "Ownership Shifting to Realize Family Goals, Including Tax Savings." Institute on Federal Taxation, New York University, 1979, pp. 38.1–38.52.

Fiore, Owen G. "The Value Shifting Approach." *ALI-ABA Resource Materials: Estate Planning in Depth*, 1984, pp. 903–56.

Fiore, Owen G., and Paul L. Lion III. "Using Valuation Uncertainty in Estate Planning." University of Southern California Law Center Tax Institute, 1984, pp. 18.1–18.59.

Foster, Frances H. "Towards a Uniform Standard: The Effect of Close Corporation and Partnership Restrictive Agreements on Federal Estate Tax Valuation." *Yale Law Journal*, March 1981, pp. 863–88.

Gans, Mitchell M. "The Repeal of *General Utilities:* Estate Tax Implications." *Trusts & Estates*, July 1987, pp. 43–48.

Gardner, Merritt A. "Death and Taxes Aren't Certain, Either." *The Tax Times*. Prentice-Hall, March 1987, p. 29.

Gardner, Merritt A. "Do Life Estate Splits Make Sense?" *The Tax Times*. Prentice-Hall, July 1987, pp. 5, 9.

Gelman, Milton, "An Economist-Financial Analyst's Approach to Valuing Stock of a Closely-Held Company." *Journal of Taxation*, June 1972, pp. 353–54.

Gibbs, Larry W. "Basic Federal Estate and Gift Taxation." *St. Mary's Law Journal*, 1986, pp. 809–67.

Goggans, Travis P., and Bruce K. Benesh. "Pre-Mortem and Post-Mortem Valuation Techniques for Closely-Held Stock Relative to Estate Tax Reporting—An Application." *Taxes*, February 1984, pp. 99–108.

Goggans, Travis P., and Anne Keller. "Current Use Valuation: Opportunities and Restrictions for Estate Planning." *Trusts & Estates*, November 1980, pp. 41–47.

Gordon, Emanuel L. "What Is Fair Market Value?" *Tax Law Review*, 1952, pp. 35–62.

Hall, Thomas H. "Valuing Closely Held Stock: Control Premiums and Minority Discounts." *Emory Law Journal* 31 (1982), pp. 137–99.

Harline, N. La Var. "Valuation of Partnership Interests in Implementing a Partnership Capital Freeze for Farming Enterprises." *Journal of Agricultural Taxation and Law*, Summer 1984, pp. 504–44.

Haynsworth, Harry J. IV. "Valuation of Business Interests." *Mercer Law Review*, Winter 1982, 457–517.

Hill, J. Jeptha. "Estate Planning for the Closely-Held Corporation and Its Owner." *Alabama Lawyer*, January 1979, pp. 122–48.

Hocky, Joseph S. "When and How to Elect the Alternate Valuation Date in Light of Changes Made by the DRA." *Estate Planning*, May–June 1986, pp. 164–67.

Horsman, Steven E. "Minority Interest Discounts on Gifts among Family Members." *Trusts & Estates*, July 1987, pp. 54–55.

Keir, Loyal E., and Douglas W. Argue. "Choosing a Forum for Tax Litigation." *Practicing Lawyer*, October 1976, pp. 63–68.

Kelley, Donald H. "After the Disaster: Salvage for the Estate Lawyer." Philip E. Heckerling Institute on Estate Planning, University of Miami Law Center, 1985, pp. 14.1–14.43.

Kelly, James P. III. "IRS Expands Definition of Gift to Launch New Attack on Two Estate Freezing Techniques." *Estate Planning*, July–August 1988, pp. 230–36.

Kozaczek, Kim Marie. "The Restrictive Stock Transfer Agreement: Still a Valid Means of Establishing the Value of Stock for Estate Tax Purposes after *St. Louis County Bank?*" *Syracuse Law Review*, 1986, p. 181+.

Leung, T. S. Tony. "Valuing Preferred Stock in a Recapitalization: What Weight to Give Its Special Provisions." *Estate Planning*, September 1980, pp. 270–74.

Lindeberg, Frederic H. "Estate Planning Benefits for Small Farmer Increased by Provisions of Tax Reform Act." *Taxation for Accountants*, April 1977, pp. 238–43.

Llewellyn, Don W., et al. "Selling a Close Corporation: Should Stock or Assets Be Sold for Maximum Tax Benefits?" *Taxation for Accountants*, 1976, pp. 98–103.

Low, Tony. "All Things Considered . . ." *Financial Planning*, August 1987, pp. 114–19.

Maher, John Michael. "The Impact of Keyperson Insurance on the Valuation of Closely-Held Business Interests." *Trusts & Estates*, August 1979, pp. 39–40.

Martin, Gerald R., and E. Halsey Sandford. "Applying Fair Market Value Appraisal Techniques to Closely Held Preferred Stock." *Taxes*, February 1978, pp. 108–15.

Marvel, C. C. "Valuation for Taxation Purposes as Admissible to Show Value for Other Purposes." 39 *A.L.R.* 2d (1955, Supp. 1977, 1979), pp. 209–53.

McCoy, Jerry J., and Neill G. McBryde. "The Use of Subchapter S Corporations and Personal Holding Companies after 1986." Real Property, Probate and Trust Section, American Bar Association, 1986, pp. 129–204.

McGaffey, Jere D. "Estate Planning Consequences of Corporate Tax Reform." Philip E. Heckerling Institute on Estate Planning, University of Miami Law Center, 1987, pp. 3-1–3-20.

McGuire, John A. "Partnership Interests and Fair Market Value." *Journal of Partnership Taxation*, 1985, pp. 324–39.

Merritt, James E., and Tony M. Edwards. "DRA Changes Affecting Charitable Contributions, Estate and Gift Tax Valuations and Appraisers." *Tax Adviser*, March 1985, pp. 140–42, 144–48.

Moerschbaecher, Lynda S. "Substantiation of Charitable Contributions: New

Appraisal Regulations." *Estate, Gifts and Trusts Journal*, May–June 1985, pp. 84–93.

Moore, Philip W. "Valuation Revisited." *Trusts & Estates*, February 1987, pp. 40–52.

Moreland, Everett R. "The Control Value of Noncontrolling Shares." *The Review of Taxation of Individuals*, Autumn 1984, pp. 291–348.

Much, Paul J., and Chester A. Gougis. "IRS Stock Value View Questioned." *National Law Journal*, November 3, 1980.

Padwe, Gerald W. "Undoing the Estate Freeze for S Corporations." *Tax Adviser*, March 1987, pp. 160–61.

"Post-Death Events Affect Estate Asset Valuation." *Estate Planning*, November 1985, p. 355.

Pratt, Shannon P. "Estate Planning, ESOPs, Buy-Sell Agreements, and Life Insurance for Closely Held Businesses." *Journal of the American Society of CLU*, September 1986, pp. 74–79.

Rhine, David S. "The Estate and Trust Rules of the Tax Reform Act of 1986." *Tax Adviser*, May 1987, pp. 301–11.

Ridley, James I. "Establishing Proper Basis in a Nontaxable Estate Can Prevent Later Income Tax Problems." *Estate Planning*, May–June 1986, pp. 146–62.

Schlenger, Jacques T.; Marianne Schmitt Hellauer; and Robert L. Waldman. "Buy-Sell Agreement Established Value of Stock of Closely Held Business for Estate Tax Purposes." *Estate Planning*, January–February 1986, pp. 49–51.

Schlenger, Jacques T.; Stephen L. Owen; and John B. Watkins. "Freezing the Value of Closely-Held Business Interests." *Financial and Estate Planning.* Commerce Clearing House, 1984, pp. 22,125–22,143.

Schneider, Willys H., and Sarah G. Austrian. "Widespread Changes for Corporations in 1987 Act." *Journal of Taxation*, April 1988, pp. 196–202.

Smith, Gordon W. "Valuing Closely-Held Stock of Regulated Companies." *ASA Valuation*, March 1979, pp. 9–14.

Stann, John A. "Valuations and Control of the Corporate Enterprise." *Trusts & Estates*, May 1987, pp. 54–55.

Stechel, Ira. "Restrictive Buy-Sell Agreements Can Limit Estate Tax Value of a Business Interest." *Journal of Taxation*, June 1976, pp. 360–67.

Stukenberg, Michael W. "Election and Other Planning Choices Facing Executors Affect Income, Estate and Gift Taxes." *Estate Planning*, May–June 1987, pp. 154–58.

Tarlow, Edward D., and Richard P. Breed III. "Knowledge of the IRS's Approach Can Increase Taxpayers' Success on Questions of Valuation." *Estate Planning*, May 1983, pp. 136–42.

Tarlow, Edward D., and Richard P. Breed III. "Using Acquisitive, Divisive Reorganizations to Achieve Estate Planning Objectives." *Estate Planning*, May–June 1988, pp. 164–71.

Teitell, Conrad. "IRS on Stock Gifts and Redemption: They're OK Unless . . ." *Trusts & Estates*, November 1986, pp. 57–58.

Teitell, Conrad. "Post IRA '84 Regs. for Charitable Deductions." *Trusts & Estates*, March 1985, pp. 29–32.

Ullman, Samuel C. "The Personal Holding Company in the Estate Plan: A

New Look." Philip E. Heckerling Institute on Estate Planning, University of Miami Law Center, 1980, pp. 8.1–8.20.

"Valuation of Closely Held Stock for Federal Estate Tax Purposes under Section 2031(b) of Internal Revenue Code of 1954 [26 USCS Section 2031(b)], and Implementing Regulations." 22 *A.L.R.* Fed. 31 (1975, Supp. 1979).

"Valuation of Gift Property for Purposes of Gift Tax." 60 *A.L.R.* 2d 1034 (1958, Supp. 1976).

Waldron, Gary L. "Valuation of an Estate." *Journal of the American Society of CLU*, May 1986, pp. 82–84.

Wallace, John A. "Valuation Problems in Planning with Family Assets—A Comprehensive Analysis." Fiduciary Law Seminar, State Bar of Georgia, July 23–25, 1987, pp. 16.1–16.54.

Watts, David E. "The Fair Market Value of Actively Traded Securities." *Tax Lawyer*, Fall 1976, pp. 51–84.

Zampino, John P. "Use of Personal Holding Companies in Estate Planning." *Financial and Estate Planning*, Commerce Clearing House, July 1982, pp. 21,491–21,502.

Zankel, Jeffrey A. "Choosing the Best Method of Handling the Partnership Interest of a Deceased Partner." *Estate Planning*, July–August 1986, pp. 198–201.

Zaritsky, H. "Amortization of Intangibles: How the 1976 TRA and *Laird* Affect Sports Franchises." *Journal of Taxation*, May 1978, pp. 292–96.

Zweifler, Walter L. "Stock Appraisals under the Tax Reform Act of 1984." *Practical Lawyer*, April 15, 1985, pp. 45–60.

Books

Averill, Lawrence H., Jr. *Estate Valuation Handbook*. New York: John Wiley & Sons, 1983.

Bishop, John, A., and Idelle A. Howitt. *Federal Tax Valuation Digest*. Cumulative edition. Boston: Warren, Gorham & Lamont, annual.

Bittker, Boris I., and James S. Eustice. *Federal Income Taxation of Corporations and Shareholders*. 5th ed. New York: Warren, Gorham & Lamont, 1987.

Federal Estate and Gift Taxes Explained. Chicago: Commerce Clearing House, 1987.

Freeman, Douglas K. *Estate Tax Freeze: Tools and Techniques*. New York: Mathew Bender, 1985.

IRS Valuation Guide for Income, Estate and Gift Taxes. Standard Federal Tax Reports, Extra Edition No. 44. Chicago: Commerce Clearing House, 1985.

Mertens, Jacob, Jr. *Law of Federal Income Taxation*. Revised by James J. Doheny. Wilmette, Ill.: Callaghan & Company, 1987.

Rabkin, Jacob, and Mark H. Johnson. *Federal Income, Gift and Estate Taxation*. New York: Mathew Bender, 1987 (Originally published 1942).

Stephens, Richard B.; Guy B. Maxfield; Stephen A. Lind; and Dennis A. Calfee. *Federal Estate and Gift Taxation*. 5th ed. New York: Warren, Gorham & Lamont, 1983.

Westfall, David. *Estate Planning Law and Taxation*. New York: Warren, Gorham & Lamont, 1985.

Chapter 20

Buy-Sell Agreements

A buy-sell agreement can effectively prevent many potential problems regarding disposition of stock or a partnership interest of a departing or deceased stockholder or partner. The buy-sell agreement can accomplish the following objectives:

1. Provide a mechanism with which the departing owner or the estate can liquidate the ownership interest.
2. Set a price or provide a mechanism for determining a price for the ownership interest.
3. Under some circumstances, set a price that will determine a binding value for estate tax purposes.
4. Prevent the ownership interest from being sold or otherwise transferred to any party not acceptable to the other owners.
5. Provide a mechanism for pricing and liquidating the interest of a departing spouse in the event of a divorce.[1]

It should be noted that, with the passage of the Revenue Act of 1987 and TAMRA 88, only buy-sell agreements that provide for a transaction price at fair market value as of the time of the exercise of the agreement will not be subject to the harsh tax effects of Section 2036(c).

Types of Buy-Sell Agreements

Buy-sell agreements used in closely held corporations or partnerships to provide for liquidation of the interest of a withdrawing or deceased shareholder or partner fall into one of three categories:

1. *Repurchase agreements* (also called *entity purchase agreements* or *redemption agreements*), in which the issuing corporation or partnership buys the interest from the withdrawing party or from the estate of the deceased party.
2. *Cross-purchase agreements,* in which one or more other individuals or entities buys the interest from the withdrawing party or from the estate of the deceased party.
3. *Hybrid agreements,* in which the issuer buys a portion of the interest and other stockholders or partners buy a portion. Such agreements can be drafted to allow both the company and the other shareholders the opportunity to wait until after the date of death to determine which is in the better tax and liquidity condition to purchase the shares.

Each type of agreement may be either mandatory—that is, binding on both parties—or optional on the part of one of the parties, usually the purchaser. Sometimes agreements are written to be optional during an owner's lifetime and mandatory for a decedent's estate.

---

[1]For an interesting discussion of the use of buy-sell agreements for divorce planning, see Stephen A. Landsman, "Divorce Planning in the Closely-Held Business Context," *Trusts & Estates*, May 1984, pp. 41–46.

It is not necessary that the same agreement apply to all the owners of a particular entity. One or a few owners may be subject to an agreement while others are not, or different owners may be subject to different agreements. For example, it is common to find minority owners of an enterprise subject to a buy-sell agreement while the controlling owner is not. In limited partnerships, provisions applicable to limited partners normally differ from those applicable to general partners.

The provisions of any buy-sell agreement should, of course, be designed to best carry out the objectives of all the parties. From a seller's viewpoint, an important objective is to provide liquidity in the event of withdrawal from the business or death. From a purchaser's viewpoint, an important objective typically is to provide continuity of ownership and management without possible interference from outside parties. From the viewpoints of both seller and purchaser, an additional purpose is to establish the circumstances under which the agreement will become effective and a means of determining the price and terms of the transaction. As one experienced attorney aptly put it:

> The particular method selected by the parties for the determination of the price to be paid for the interest will, of course, depend on their attitudes toward each other and their objectives with respect to survivors, their beneficiaries and the business entity.[2]

One consideration in the choice between the cross-purchase versus redemption form of buy-sell agreement is the number of shareholders or partners involved. The more there are, the more complicated the cross-purchase plan becomes relative to the redemption. In the cross-purchase arrangement, the number of party-to-party relationships, life insurance policies required if so funded, and so on rise exponentially with the number of parties involved. Also, the transfer of life insurance policies on other parties held in a decedent's estate could give rise to a taxable incident. One solution to these problems is to create an insurance trust agreement, but this would require drafting another complicated agreement. In the redemption type of agreement, the corporation owns the life insurance policies, so there are no administrative or tax problems arising from the necessity to transfer policies at the death of one party.

Naturally, the tax implications will be a major consideration in deciding which type of agreement to use. The tax implications, which are complicated and often subject to change, are beyond the scope of this book. Several references on tax implications appear in the bibliography at the end of this chapter, as well as in bibliography at the end of Chapter 19 on estate planning.[3]

---

[2]J. D. Hartwig, "Valuing an Interest in a Closely-Held Business for the Purpose of Buy/Sell Agreements and for Death Tax Purposes," University of Southern California Institute on Federal Taxation, 1974, p. 237.

[3]For a specific discussion of tax considerations involved in the choice between a cross-purchase agreement and a repurchase agreement, with extensive legal citations, see F. Hodge O'Neal and Robert B. Thompson, *Close Corporations*, 3rd ed. (Wilmette, Ill.: Callaghan & Company, 1987), pp. 172–94, §7.39. Reprinted with permission.

Valuation Provisions of the Buy-Sell Agreement

The provision for valuation is a critical element of the buy-sell agreement. The parties have a great deal of flexibility in structuring this provision, but often it is neglected or done hastily and thus eventually turns out to be unfair to one or the other party.

Need for Clear Direction

I cannot overstress the importance of having the valuation provisions of the buy-sell agreement thought through thoroughly by someone who understands valuation and understood by all parties before the agreement is signed. Attitudes and relationships change, and one cannot assume that any ambiguity in the buy-sell agreement will be resolved amicably when the time comes to consummate a transaction pursuant to the agreement. My own experience has demonstrated time and time again that most disputes relating to buy-sell agreements arise because one or several of the details of the agreement either were inadequately defined or were misunderstood by one or more of the parties.

For example, I testified as an expert witness in an arbitration case over the value of a business interest under a buy-sell agreement in which the document was so ambiguous about the applicable valuation date that the attorney required me to analyze and testify to the valuation of the interest for four different dates that the arbitration panel could conceivably select as being applicable in the circumstances. The value differences on the various dates were considerable, because the business was undergoing a series of significant and somewhat unpredictable changes during the relevant time period. The ambiguity as to the applicable valuation date substantially increased the time and cost involved for the analysis as well as the uncertainty of the outcome of the arbitration.

J. D. Hartwig, attorney, lecturer, and author, points out the typical lack of adequate definition even when the valuation criterion for the buy-sell agreement is simply book value:

> Rarely do the agreements define book value; identify whether the books kept for tax purposes or for business purposes are intended; or whether such book value shall be computed as of the date of death, as of the end of the month preceding death, as of the end of the last regular accounting period of the entity, as of the end of the fiscal year of the entity nearest the date of death, or as of some other date.[4]

Chapters 2 and 15 discussed the fact that the fair market value of a minority interest usually is less than a pro-rata share of the value of the entire enterprise. Many parties to buy-sell agreements have been unpleasantly surprised to learn that the fair market value of their interest (the standard of value specified in the agreement that

---

[4]Hartwig, "Valuing an Interest," pp. 238–39.

they hastily read and signed) was less than a proportionate share of the total enterprise value. Robert Blum, a CPA knowledgeable about both buy-sell agreements and closely held business valuations, notes that the "sum of the parts doesn't always equal the whole" and offers the following strong statement on this point:

> When stock ownership is divided among a number of shareholders, each being in a less than controlling ownership position, the application of a minority interest discount should be addressed in the agreement. Is each shareholder entitled to the proportionate value of the entire entity or is each interest to be reduced by the discount commonly applied to minority interests? Failure to address this question in the agreement will ensure litigation in the future.[5]

Buy-sell agreements may specify that the shares be valued strictly at their fair market value as minority interests, at a proportionate share of the enterprise value with no minority discount, or at a specified percentage discount (I have seen all the way from 10 to 50 percent) from a proportionate share of total enterprise value.

I suggest that the reader contemplating a buy-sell agreement read Chapter 1, "Defining the Appraisal Assignment," carefully and be sure that the agreement covers all the relevant points. In addition, the terms of payment should be specified. The payment terms may differ under various circumstances, and the agreement may allow the company some flexibility, making allowance for the company's ability to pay. *The key thing to keep in mind is that the buy-sell agreement is a legal document that will have to stand on its own at the time a triggering event occurs.*

One unique aspect of the price-fixing mechanism in a buy-sell agreement, as opposed to other valuation problems, is the extreme uncertainty concerning when a future event that triggers a transaction under the agreement will occur. This is one of the key reasons why there is no single approach to the problem of establishing the price for a buy-sell agreement that one can recommend as completely satisfactory for all situations. The valuation provision can be the same under all triggering events or it can differ in various circumstances, such as the owner's death or voluntary or involuntary termination of employment.

Most of the mechanisms for setting prices in buy-sell agreements generally fall into one or a combination of three categories:

1. Some type of formula based on the financial statements, such as book value, some type of adjusted book value, capitalization of earnings, or some combination of such variables.
2. Negotiation among the parties.
3. Independent outside appraisal.

Certain other approaches occasionally found in buy-sell agreements are in general disfavor with attorneys and other professionals

---

[5]Robert Blum, *Common Pitfalls to Avoid in Buy-Sell Agreements* (Milwaukee: CPA Services, 1985), p. 6. Reprinted with permission of the publisher, CPA Services, 16800 W. Greenfield Ave., Brookfield, WI 53005.

who frequently are involved with buy-sell agreements. Some agreements call for the value established for estate tax purposes to be determinative of the transaction price. This is exactly the opposite of the more typical logic, which would seek to establish a desired transaction price that is also determinative for estate and inheritance tax purposes. Besides, having the estate tax value determine the price has the obvious disadvantage of encouraging an upward bias in the negotiations between the executor and the IRS in setting the price, with the result that both the estate and the government will collect more money.

Another approach that is sometimes used but often disparaged in the literature written by practitioners is to have one party make an offer in an attempt to buy out the other with the provision that if the other party rejects it, the latter must buy out the offering party on the same terms. While some like this approach, others claim it does not seem to work well in practice and may even be quite unfair because each party probably lacks equal financial capability for buying out the other.

Formula Approaches

I am generally opposed to formula approaches for setting the price in a buy-sell agreement, because the result usually turns out to be unfair to one party or the other when the transaction eventually occurs. As this book indicates, the valuation process should reflect a complex set of factors—usually too complex to be adequately embodied in a formula. A formula that might produce an appropriate value in one year might not do so in another year when circumstances in the company and the economy differ. For example, in the case of *St. Louis County Bank* v. *United States,* the court refused to honor for estate tax purposes an agreement that gave a corporation the right to purchase the decedent's stock under a formula that produced a zero value, even though the formula may have originally produced an acceptable value.[6] Having made this point, we will consider some of the most common formulas for fixing the price in a buy-sell agreement.

The most popular basis for a formula approach is to use book value or some type of adjusted book value. Earlier chapters made the point that book value only occasionally coincides with fair market value or any other standard of value of a business or business interest. Book value tends to come closest to fair market value in a business that has a very high proportion of its total assets in current assets, such as receivables and inventories which can be liquidated at or near face value with little or no goodwill value.

One of the obvious attractions of using book value is its simplicity. Even so, however, it must be well defined. Some buy-sell agreements call for book value with certain adjustments, such as adding back the LIFO inventory reserve or adjusting certain assets to current market

---

[6]*St. Louis County Bank* v. *United States,* 674 F.2d 1207 (8th Cir. 1982).

value. Unless extremely carefully defined, such adjustments can be subjects of dispute among the parties. Some agreements specify that an independent appraiser or accountant make the adjustments in order to avoid disputes among the parties.

Of course, if a business is on a cash basis it is almost always necessary to make some adjustments to book value to reach a price that more nearly approximates an accrual basis book value, at least recognizing the receivables and payables.

If a net asset value approach is used in a repurchase agreement funded by life insurance, one must keep in mind that the company's net asset value will increase by the proceeds of the policy on the stockholder's death, a fact that the value should reflect.

If a capitalization of earnings formula is used, it seems almost essential to base it on an average or weighted average of several years' earnings to avoid aberrations in the result that could occur from one or two exceptionally good or poor years. Of course, as discussed elsewhere in this book, earnings should be adjusted to eliminate extraordinary items, although again such adjustments could be a source of disputes. The capitalization rate or multiplier is a critical variable, and a multiplier that is appropriate one year might not be so for another year because of changing economic conditions.

One common criticism of formula approaches that are based on the balance sheet or the income statement or both is that closely held companies have considerable latitude in reporting figures within the boundaries of generally accepted accounting principles, as well as control over such important variables as paying compensation to owner-employees versus retaining earnings. For this reason, controlling stockholders have the power to make decisions that could be detrimental to the minority stockholder whose value will be determined by a formula approach.

Negotiation among the Parties

Many practitioners believe that negotiation among the parties—usually annually—is the best approach to setting the buy-sell agreement price. The parties themselves usually have the most intimate knowledge of their own estate objectives as well as of their attitudes toward one another. They also may have a better idea than anyone else about how much the business is worth; in most cases, however, owners would benefit from professional outside guidance on that point.

The problems with this approach arise when the annual valuation is neglected or when the parties cannot agree. In my own and my staff's experience, the annual valuations seem to be neglected more often than not. The buy-sell agreement must provide for dealing with both of these eventualities.

The most common method of handling potential neglect of the annual valuation is to stipulate that if the price is not set annually on a timely basis, after some period (typically 12 to 24 months following the last price agreement) the price-fixing mechanism automatically reverts to either a formula approach or an independent appraisal. In the latter case, it is necessary to either name the appraisal firm or specify the method by which the appraiser will be selected. If a firm or person is named, provision must be made for an alternate selection procedure if the named appraiser is unable to serve.

O'Neal and Thompson offer the following guidance regarding provision for selecting appraisers in the buy-sell agreement. This guidance would apply whether appraisers are to be used in any case or to be used only in the event of inability to agree through negotiation:

> If the price of shares is to be fixed by appraisal, the names of the appraisers or a method of choosing them must be specified and a statement should be made that the decision of a majority of the appraisers will be binding. A typical appraisal provision states that the optionee or purchaser, as the case may be, shall select one appraiser, the offeror or vendor a second, and that the two appraisers shall choose a third. Occasionally an independent third party, such as a corporate fiduciary, is given the power to appoint the third appraiser; or the third appraiser is designated by office: e.g., the cashier of the bank with which the company does business may be named the third appraiser. Sometimes the appraisers are selected in advance and designated by name. If that is done, provision must be made for a method of appointing substitutes should the designated appraisers die, become incapacitated, or refuse to serve.[7]

Some buy-sell agreements provide for two or three appraisers to submit reports to an arbitration panel, which will make the final determination in case of a dispute, but this can get quite expensive.

One suggestion for avoiding the problem of neglecting the annual valuation is to ask one of the company's professional advisers, such as the attorney, accountant, insurance agent, or appraiser, to put a memo in his or her tickler file to remind the company to make its annual valuation.

Reversion to formula or outside appraisal approaches is also the most common type of provision for dealing with circumstances in which the parties cannot agree on a value through negotiation.

Exhibit 20–1 is a sample valuation article for a buy-sell agreement, providing for negotiation and for the price to be determined by an arbitration panel if negotiation fails.

Independent Outside Appraisal

An experienced stock appraiser presents a nine-point case for the advantage of having a formal, independent outside appraisal, kept current with periodic updates:

1. The Courts give great emphasis to formal appraisals and opinions of expert witnesses as to the valuation of interests in closely held businesses.
2. A professionally done, formal appraisal allows and promotes proper estate planning.

---

[7]O'Neal and Thompson, *Close Corporations*, p. 155.

EXHIBIT 20-1

Sample Valuation Provision for Buy-Sell Agreement
(Corporation Stock Redemption Example)

As soon as practical after the end of each fiscal year, the stockholders shall agree on the value per share of the stock that is applicable to this agreement. Such value will be set forth in Schedule A, which shall be dated, signed by each stockholder, and attached hereto. Such value shall be binding on both the corporation and the estate of any deceased stockholder whose date of death is within one year of the last dated and signed Schedule A.

If more than a year has elapsed between the date when Schedule A was last signed and the date of death of a deceased stockholder, then the value per share shall be determined, as of the date of death of the stockholder, by mutual agreement between the surviving stockholders and the personal representative or administrator of the deceased stockholder's estate.

If the surviving stockholders and the personal representative of the deceased stockholder's estate are unable to agree upon such a value within 90 days after such personal representative or administrator has qualified to administer the estate of the deceased stockholder, then such value shall be determined by binding arbitration. Either party may give written notice of such binding arbitration pursuant to this agreement to the other party. Within 30 days of such notice of arbitration, each party shall appoint one arbitrator. Within 30 days of the appointment of the two arbitrators, the arbitrators so appointed will select a third arbitrator. The first two arbitrators will have sole discretion in the selection of the third arbitrator, except that he must be an individual or qualified representative of a firm that regularly engages, as a primary occupation, in the professional appraisal of businesses or business in-

terests. In the event that the first two arbitrators are unable to agree on a third arbitrator within 30 days of their appointment, the Executive Director of the ABC Trade Association shall appoint the third arbitrator.

The standard of value to be used by the arbitrators shall be fair market value of the shares being valued as of the date of death, under the assumption that the stockholder is deceased and the corporation has collected the proceeds, if any, of insurance on the life of the deceased stockholder payable to the corporation.

Each arbitrator shall use his sole discretion in determining the amount of investigation he considers necessary in arriving at a determination of the value of the shares. The corporation shall make available on a timely basis all books and records requested by any arbitrator, and all material made available to any one arbitrator shall be made available to all arbitrators.

Concurrence by at least two of the three arbitrators shall constitute a binding determination of value. The value concluded by the arbitrators shall be reported to the corporation and to the personal representative or administrator of the estate of the deceased in writing, signed by the arbitrators concurring as to the concluded value, within 90 days of the appointment of the third arbitrator unless an extension of time has been agreed upon between the corporation and the personal representative of the estate.

The corporation and the estate shall each be responsible for the fees and expenses of the arbitrators they appoint. The fees and expenses of the third arbitrator shall be divided equally between the corporation and the estate.

---

3. A buy-sell agreement containing a professionally prepared formal appraisal may avoid costly litigation in the case of a dispute between owners of the stock or, for example, in a divorce action.
4. A formal, professionally prepared appraisal is more likely to assure fair treatment to all concerned.
5. Just as preventive medicine and preventive maintenance on machinery is usually less costly than emergency treatment or repairs, and is more effective (less downtime), so is an appraisal prepared for a buy-sell agreement likely to be better prepared and less costly than one done in an emergency atmosphere of a death, a divorce, etc.
6. As periodic updates are made, the appraiser becomes increasingly knowledgeable as to the economics of the individual business and the industry of which it is a part.
7. A professional appraisal provides not only an opinion as to the value of a closely held business, but also an analysis of that business from a management consultant's point of view.

8. Knowing the value of a closely held business allows proper planning of mergers, acquisitions, reorganizations, a sale of the business, a stock option plan, etc.
9. The underwriters generally have the last word as to the price at which a previously closely held stock will be offered to the public. In planning a public offering, however, it cannot fail to be helpful to the owners of a corporation to know the worth of their stock.[8]

The obvious disadvantage of the formal appraisal with regular updates is the cost. However, the appraisal does not necessarily have to result in quite as lengthy and detailed a report as an ESOP valuation, since there usually are fewer beneficiaries to be satisfied and the appraiser and the directors need not be concerned with meeting ERISA requirements.

Whether or not a complete, formal, written appraisal report is done when pricing the buy-sell agreement, some degree of guidance from an independent professional business appraiser usually is helpful in arriving at a value that will be equitable to all parties and will forestall subsequent disputes.

Philosophy: Should the Price Be High, Low, or in the Middle?

Since business valuations rarely can be made with undisputable precision, there usually will be some relevant range of reasonable prices that will be acceptable to the IRS and, possibly, to all the parties. In other words, as Jeffrey Matsen, a principal in a law firm and professor of law, gently states it, "In light of several available methods of valuing closely held shares and the notable subjectivity involved in such valuations, some flexibility in setting the price is possible."[9]

Appraisers of real estate, equipment, or other physical property frequently include statements that their appraisals are accurate to within plus or minus 10 percent. However, few business interests can be appraised within such tolerances. Just look at how widely the prices of many publicly traded stocks fluctuate over relatively short periods. For many closely held businesses, it is not unreasonable for the high end of a value range to be 50 percent above the low end. For highly dynamic or speculative businesses, the reasonable range may be much wider.

Considering this flexibility, if the buy-sell agreement price is to be determined by an independent outside appraiser, the appraiser can present the parties with a relevant price range, and they can make a decision based on their wishes. Of course, it is not uncommon for the various parties to the agreement to have differing circumstances and

[8]Orville B. Lefko, "Buy-Sell Agreements and Appraisals," *Michigan State Bar Journal*, February 1976, pp. 120–24.

[9]Jeffrey R. Matsen, "A New Look at Business Buy-Out Agreements," *Practical Lawyer*, July 1979, p. 57.

objectives that motivate them toward opposite pricing philosophies. In general, in arm's-length bargaining one would expect parties who anticipate withdrawing earlier to opt for a higher value and parties who expect to survive in the business the longest to choose a lower value. If the decision is left to the outside appraiser, it is, of course, incumbent on the appraiser to balance these conflicting self-interests in the fairest possible manner.

The consensus among the many articles that address this subject leans from the middle of the range to a somewhat conservative valuation. There are several valid arguments for inclining toward a conservative value. One, of course, is lesser tax consequences. Another is to reduce the burden of funding, however it is accomplished. Another is that recognizing that the valuation is an imprecise matter, the parties tend to feel that they will enhance their favorable working relationship by leaning over backwards (a little) to be fair to one another. I have encountered some feeling that if some benefit is to be gained in the pricing by one party or another, it most properly should accrue to those who will remain with the business, since they may need it and deserve it the most.

In a very close family situation, it is common to find the desire to minimize the price so as to lessen tax consequences. In these instances, it is especially important to have thoroughly documented justification of the price or basis selected, since the combination of a low price and a non–arm's-length family situation certainly will invite the scrutiny of the IRS and the state taxing authorities.

Finally, of course, there are a few mavericks who philosophize that the buy-sell agreement price should be maximized. This is the position Milton H. Stern takes:

> In essence I have abandoned the quest for the "true value" of the stock. Frankly, the disparities are so great in the valuation of stock of a closely held corporation made by the adversary parties' experts in contested cases, and the "willing buyer, willing seller" standard is so hypothetical that there need be no embarrassment in advising people to look for other approaches.
>
> I now urge clients to consider fixing the highest price they can afford to have their corporation fund through insurance, after taking into account pension and profit-sharing plan death benefits and other life insurance which the business pays for. If the grand total (susceptible of being readily financed by the corporation) is so great that it shocks the parties' sensibilities, it can always be reduced.[10]

Stern admits, however, "It is properly arguable that my approach is more of a plan of mutual insurance than a determination of stock value." One should keep in mind that, although Stern is an attorney, his article appeared in the *CLU Journal,* the official journal of the life insurance industry.

---

[10]Milton H. Stern, "A Different Approach to Price-Fixing in Stockholders' Stock Purchase Arrangements," *CLU Journal,* July 1974, pp. 22–23.

Terms and Funding

Two decisions that necessarily are integrally related in creating the buy-sell agreement are the provisions for payment terms and for funding.

Terms can run anywhere from immediate cash to payments spread out over several years, usually with interest. Funding can come from life insurance, from corporate funds in the case of a redemption, or from personal assets in the case of a cross-purchase. In some cases, borrowings may be used to fund either a redemption or a cross-purchase. In order for a buy-sell agreement to work, it is essential that funding adequate for carrying out its terms be available one way or another. Thus, provision for funding is an essential ingredient for a viable buy-sell agreement.

Term Payment Provisions

From the purchaser's viewpoint, the typical reason for preferring a term payment program to cash is to ease the funding burden. From the seller's viewpoint, the attraction of an installment payment program is the spreading out of the tax on the seller's gain over several of the seller's tax years.

If a term payment plan is used, careful consideration must be given to establishing the interest rate, because this is really an integral part of the pricing decision. Attention also should be given to the matter of collateral or other protection to ensure that the seller will receive the contractual payments in the full amount and on a timely basis.

As discussed elsewhere in this book, if the interest rate on a term contract is below the market interest rate for similar instruments at the time of the event that triggers the transaction, the cash equivalent value the seller receives will be less than the contract's face value. Similarly, if the interest rate is above the relevant market rate, the cash equivalent value will be greater than the face value. The arithmetic for computing the present value of a contract bearing interest above or below a comparable market rate is shown in Chapter 3, "The Discounted Future Returns Approach to Valuation" (see Exhibit 3–1).

However, in setting the interest rate in the buy-sell agreement, we face the problem that market interest rates fluctuate considerably over time, and we have no way of knowing at what time in the future the buy-sell transaction will be triggered nor what the market level of interest rates will be at that time. There are several possible approaches to dealing with this dilemma.

One approach is simply to agree on an interest rate despite these uncertainties and hope that it does not prove grossly off the mark in the future. If the price under the buy-sell agreement is set by annual negotiation or appraisal, the interest rate could be reviewed and adjusted annually at the same time. Another alternative is to set the interest rate by tying it to some index of interest rates at the time of the transaction. The interest rate index used should represent intermediate- to long-term rates, since such rates fluctuate less than short-term rates and would be more appropriate for a term payment contract. The yield on *Barron's* intermediate grade bonds or *Moody's* BBB bonds could provide appropriate guidelines for setting the interest rate. The agreement could specify that the index rate or some specified amount above or below it be used depending on the credit of the company involved, the degree of security provided, and the desires of the parties to the agreement.

It might be appropriate to use an interest rate index that represents securities whose maturities coincide with the payout terms of the buy-sell agreement. For example, an index representing five-year maturities can be used if the payout term is five years. The *Federal Reserve Bulletin* gives indexes of interest rates on U.S. Treasury bonds maturing in 1, 2, 3, 5, 7, 10, 20, and 30 years.

Income tax considerations could suggest the desirability of some trade-off between the price and the interest rate. The portion of the contract payments designated as interest will be a deductible expense to the buyer and income to the seller. The portion of the contract payments designated as principal will not be deductible to the buyer (unless there is an ESOP involved) and will be taxed as capital gains to the seller to the extent that they exceed the seller's basis.[11] Thus, if the seller is in a low tax bracket and the buyer in a high one, it may be advantageous to structure the program to increase the interest rate and lower the price. Conversely, if the seller is in a high tax bracket and the buyer in a low one, it may be advantageous to lower the interest rate and increase the price.

The buy-sell agreement should also provide for adequate collateral or security for the seller in a term payment agreement. Security could take the form of a mortgage or lien on physical assets, such as real estate or equipment. It is also common to require that certain financial criteria, such as some minimum level of working capital, specified minimum current ratio, and specified maximum debt-to-equity ratio, be met. A typical sanction for enforcing such protective standards would be to provide that the entire amount become due and payable immediately if any of the standards are violated. These are the types of protections that a bank would require in making a loan, and many people feel that a seller of a business interest should be no less protected.

Funding the Buy-Sell Agreement with Life Insurance

Life insurance can serve as an important source of funding for stock purchase agreements pertaining to deceased shareholders. The advantages of using life insurance for this purpose are several. First, deceased shareholders' estates get paid in cash, eliminating their need to rely on the corporation's continuing prosperity. Second, the corporation's investment in the cash value of an ordinary life policy is a

---

[11]The Tax Reform Act of 1986 provided attractive tax incentives for using ESOPs to buy out existing stockholders, including estates of deceased stockholders. For a discussion of these provisions, see Chapter 23, "Employee Stock Ownership Plans."

business asset. Third, any excess insurance the corporation carries over and above the value of the stock purchase agreement can be retained as earned surplus.

In general, the use of life insurance can fulfill three basic needs:

1. Liquidation of the stock of a departed or disabled stockholder, either by the corporation or by other stockholders.
2. Payment of estate taxes.
3. Provision for continuity of the business after loss of a key person.

The owner should constantly monitor the value of the business in order to know how much life insurance is needed to fulfill these needs and update the coverage accordingly. The owner should seek out and periodically consult with a professional who knows how to apply life insurance to businesses, especially the tax implications of the many types of policies and the various configurations of ownership and beneficiaries.

Liquidation of Departed or Disabled Owner's Stock. The beneficiary of life insurance purchased for the purpose of acquiring a departed owner's stock is logically determined by the buy-sell agreement: The corporation is the beneficiary in connection with a repurchase agreement, and the various stockholders are the beneficiaries in connection with a cross-purchase agreement. The repurchase agreement, with the corporation as the beneficiary of the life insurance policies, usually is simpler administratively if there are three or more stockholders involved, but tax and other considerations may outweigh this advantage.

Funding of the purchase of a stockholder's interest if the stockholder is terminated but not deceased can be accomplished through an annuity or through life insurance with a cash value feature. The matter of insurance for covering needs in the event of the stockholder's permanent disability often is overlooked, but such needs are a common occurrence.

Payment of Estate Taxes. Estate taxes become a problem only to the extent that the estate's value exceeds the amounts excluded from estate taxes, under the unified credit, as discussed in Chapter 19, "Estate Planning and Tax Valuations." Even then, the company can pay the estate taxes via a long-term payment plan through the use of an employee stock ownership plan (ESOP), as discussed in Chapter 23. If the value exceeds the amount eligible for exclusion, and if an ESOP is not used, the estate tax liability can be estimated from the estate and gift tax table in Chapter 19 (Exhibit 19–1). Provision for payment of the estimated amount of estate tax can be made with life insurance in that amount.

Providing for Business Continuity. Life insurance payable to the corporation also can provide funding to ensure continuity of the business following the loss of a key person. It is common to find a key person contributing far more to the business's annual cash flow than he or she is taking out in salary and benefits. The company can be protected against the financial impact of the loss of such a valuable person by estimating the potential earnings or cash flow shortfall to be compensated for until the key person can be replaced and the replacement brought up to speed. The company can then cover the estimated amount of that risk with life insurance on the key person.

Review of Prior Life Insurance Funding.   If funding of the foregoing requirements has been provided for through life insurance taken out in prior years, that insurance should be reviewed as to both amount and type.

The necessary amounts of insurance can change for several reasons. One, of course, is general inflation. Another likely reason is the increased value of the business due to its success. Still another could be changes in the makeup of the business's ownership. Finally, the value of a particular person in the role of a key person can change over time due to a variety of circumstances.

There has rarely, if ever, been as much change in the variety and costs of life insurance products as there has been during the 1980s, and important changes continue to occur at this writing. A review of the life insurance funding may very well reveal new products that are better suited to the owner's objectives and/or are more cost efficient.

Restrictions on Transfer

Most buy-sell agreements contain restrictions on the transfer of the shares. Generally, such restrictions require that before transferring shares to any outside party they first be offered to the corporation and/or to other stockholders. The price at which the shares must be offered to the company and/or other stockholders may be the price offered by the outside party. More often, however, the price is the one that would be determined by the buy-sell agreement price-fixing mechanism. Such restrictions often are determinative of, or at least useful evidence of value for, other purposes, since they limit both the shares' marketability and the potential amount received for them.

In a case where there is more than one class of stock, the buy-sell agreement may provide that the shares automatically be converted from one class to another if transferred, such as from voting to nonvoting. One result of this may be to keep two classes of stock at equal or nearly equal values.

If the parties to a buy-sell agreement desire to have restrictive transfer provisions apply to involuntary transfers, such as in the cases of divorces or foreclosures when the securities have been hypothecated and a loan defaulted, such extensions of the restrictions should be spelled out in the agreement. Otherwise, courts may rule that the restrictions do not apply to such involuntary transfers.[12]

---

[12]See, for example, *Castonguay* v. *Castonguay*, 306 NW2d 143 (Minn. 1981) and *Durkee* v. *Durkee-Mower, Inc.*, 428 NE2d 139 (Mass. 1981).

Relevance of Buy-Sell Agreement Values for Establishing Gift and Estate Tax Values

Generally speaking, the price as determined by a buy-sell agreement will be binding on the Internal Revenue Service for estate tax purposes if the value falls within the range of what would be determined under Revenue Ruling 59-60 at the time of death. Of course, that value would be binding even in the absence of a buy-sell agreement, but it usually is easier to substantiate—or at least usually more readily acceptable to the IRS—in the presence of a buy-sell agreement, especially to the extent that the agreement value was established by arm's-length negotiation.

However, a price established by a buy-sell agreement may be binding on the IRS for estate tax purposes even if it is lower than what would be established under Revenue Ruling 59-60 at the time of death under some circumstances. A review of the law, the literature, and the court cases indicates that the most important criterion is the extent to which the price was established on an arm's-length basis. Following is the complete text of Section 8 of Revenue Ruling 59-60, which addresses the effect of stockholder agreements on gift and estate tax values:

> Frequently, in the valuation of closely held stock for estate and gift tax purposes, it will be found that the stock is subject to an agreement restricting its sale or transfer. Where shares of stock were acquired by a decedent subject to an option reserved by the issuing corporation to repurchase at a certain price, the option price is usually accepted as the fair market value for estate tax purposes. See Rev. Rul. 54-76, C.B. 1954-1, 194. However, in such case the option price is not determinative of fair market value for gift tax purposes. Where the option, or buy and sell agreement, is the result of voluntary action by the stockholders and is binding during the life as well as at the death of the stockholders, such agreement may or may not, depending upon the circumstances of each case, fix the value for estate tax purposes. However, such agreement is a factor to be considered, with other relevant factors, in determining fair market value. Where the stockholder is free to dispose of his shares during life and the option is to become effective only upon his death, the fair market value is not limited to the option price. It is always necessary to consider the relationship of the parties, the relative number of shares held by the decedent, and other material facts, to determine whether the agreement represents a bona fide business arrangement or is a device to pass the decedent's shares to the natural objects of his bounty for less than an adequate and full consideration in money or money's worth. In this connection see Rev. Rul. 157 C.B. 1953-2, 255, and Rev. Rul. 189, C.B. 1953-2, 29.[13]

As can be seen, the buy-sell agreement price may be binding for estate tax purposes but not for gift tax purposes on the basis that the transaction price is binding on the estate but could be changed by negotiation among the parties to the agreement during their lifetime.

---

[13]Revenue Ruling 59-60, 1959-1 C.B. 237, Section 8.

One criterion considered is whether the price determined by the buy-sell agreement was reasonable when the agreement was executed, even if subsequent events resulted in an abnormally low price at the time of death. Matsen sums up the trend in court rulings regarding acceptability of buy-sell agreement prices for estate tax values as follows:

> . . . owners can no longer rely on an arbitrary valuation placed in an otherwise valid, enforceable, arm's-length buy-sell agreement, made for justifiable business purposes. It is becoming increasingly important that the valuation be one which can stand on its own merit as the actual worth of the shares represented, at least at the time the agreement is entered into.[14]

Matsen cites as an example the *Slocum* case,[15] in which the court upheld the buy-sell agreement price for estate tax purposes by holding that the facts existing at the time the agreement was entered into were controlling as to whether it had a valid business purpose rather than a tax avoidance purpose. One court case offers a useful summary sentence:

> It now seems well-established that the value of property may be limited for estate tax purposes by an enforceable agreement which fixes the price to be paid therefor, and where the seller if he desires to sell during his lifetime can receive only the price fixed by the contract and at his death his estate can receive only the price theretofore agreed on.[16]

It also should be pointed out that a value fixed by a buy-sell agreement may be legally binding on the estate for transaction purposes even if it is not binding on the IRS for estate tax purposes. This could result in a situation where the estate ends up paying taxes on a value substantially higher than the price the estate actually receives.

Matsen concludes his discussion of the potential acceptability (or lack of it) of the buy-sell agreement price for estate tax purposes as follows:

> A valuation made in consideration of all the factors set forth earlier in this article [covered in previous chapters of this book] is the first step in persuading the Service. . . .
>
> The second, and perhaps equally important step in persuading the IRS to accept the agreed valuation, is to make a record of the valuation process at the time when the valuation actually takes place. Although not expressly mentioned in any case, regulation, or ruling, it is inherently understandable that substantiation and justification documented at the time the transaction occurs, and long before the IRS becomes an interested party, will have significant probative and persuasive value.
>
> For maximum effectiveness, the record should contain at least a memorandum of the valuation procedure used, perhaps as an exhibit to the corporate minutes or to the agreement itself; or if the size and financial

---

[14]Jeffrey R. Matsen, "Establishing the Price for Closely-Held Business Buy-Sell Agreements," *Journal of Corporate Taxation*, Summer 1978, p. 150. Reprinted with permission. Copyright © Summer 1978, Warren, Gorham, & Lamont, Inc., 210 South St., Boston MA, 02111. All rights reserved.

[15]*Slocum* v. *United States*, 256 F.Supp. 763 (S.D.N.Y. 1966).

[16]*Wilson* v. *Bowers*, 57 F.2d 682.

position of the corporation so warrant, an independent appraisal should be considered.

In addition to bolstering and substantiating the value/price structure set up in the buy-sell agreement, a memorandum valuation or an independent appraisal will have several incidental benefits to the owner, and to the company itself. It will help the principals of the business to focus on the positive and negative aspects of their enterprise and perhaps assist them with short-term and long-range financial planning for the company. Moreover, it will assist the business owners in planning their estates and making personal financial decisions about the status of their business interests.[17]

It should be noted that, with the passage of the Revenue Act of 1987 and TAMRA 88, only buy-sell agreements that provide for a transaction price at fair market value as of the time of the exercise of the agreement will not be subject to the harsh tax effects of Section 2036(c).

Summary

Buy-sell agreements can be very useful tools for controlling ownership and liquidating the interests of deceased or departed shareholders or partners. They may take the form of cross-purchase agreements (among owners), repurchase agreements (between owner and company), or some combination of the two. Agreements may be funded in any of several ways, most commonly with some type of life insurance and/or annuity product. Under some circumstances, the buy-sell agreement value may determine estate taxes.

A key provision in any buy-sell agreement, and one that often receives inadequate attention in its drafting, is the provision for valuation. Aspects of the valuation provision that are not addressed, addressed in an unclear manner, and/or not understood in the same way by all the parties can lead to irreconcilable divisiveness and protracted litigation. It is extremely important that the implications of every aspect of the valuation provision be understood and considered in detail by all the parties. If independent appraisal is being contemplated, the procedure for selecting the appraiser(s) should be precise and complete. The agreement should give clear direction to the appraisers on all aspects of the appraisal assignment, including the valuation date and a clear definition of the applicable standard of value.

Care should also be taken in the planning stage to avoid the potentially disastrous estate tax consequences of transfers among family members or with others at less than full and adequate consideration.

---

[17]Matsen, *"Establishing the Price,"* pp. 150–51.

Bibliography

Articles

Antin, Michael. "Economics of Buy-Sell Planning: Putting the Package Together." University of Southern California Law Center Tax Institute, 1981, pp. 500–553.

Black, Louis E. "Partnership Buy-Sell Agreements." Institute on Federal Taxation, New York University, 1978, pp. 51–74.

Blau, Richard D.; Thomas P. Rohman; and Bruce N. Lemons. "Shareholder Agreements and the Single Class of Stock Requirement." *Journal of Taxation*, April 1988, pp. 238–40.

Block, Stanley. "Buy-Sell Agreements: Stockholder Liquidity in the Small Firm." *Journal of Small Business Management,* April 1986, pp. 51–57.

Blum, Robert. "Common Valuation Errors in Buy-Sell Agreements: How to Avoid Them." *Practical Accountant*, March 1986, pp. 27–37.

Bucholtz, H. R. "Using Restrictive Sales Agreements to Fix a Low Estate Tax Value for a Business Interest." *Estate Planning*, May 1981, pp. 146–52.

Christensen, Burke A. "Funding a Buy-Sell Agreement." *Trusts & Estates*, July 1984, pp. 57–58.

Denenberg, Howard M. "Stock Purchase Agreement: Redemption Usually, but Not Always, Preferable to Cross Purchase." *Taxation for Accountants*, August 1978, pp. 76–83.

Dickey, David H. "Buy-Sell Agreements Can Conclusively Limit Value without Recapitalization Problems." *Estate Planning*, September 1984, pp. 268–73.

Garrity, Vincent F., Jr. "Buy-Sell Agreements." *Pennsylvania Bar Association Quarterly*, March 1975, pp. 190–99.

Gorman, Joseph G. "The Buy-Sell Agreement as a Dispositionary Device: Tax and Valuation Problems in Transferring Corporate, Partnership and Real Estate Interests at Death." Institute on Federal Taxation, New York University, 1976, pp. 1591–1620.

Gray, David W., and Lorence L. Bravenec. "Buy-Sell Agreement of S Corporation Stock Affected by Corporation's Special Tax Status." *Journal of Taxation*, October 1985, pp. 202–7.

Greene, Richard L. "Tailoring Buy-Sell Agreements to Solve the Unique Problems of S Corporation." *Taxes*, December 1985, pp. 978–98.

Hartwig, Joesph D. "Valuing an Interest in a Closely-Held Business for the Purposes of Buy-Sell Agreements and for Death Tax Purposes." University of Southern California Law Center Tax Institute, 1974, pp. 215–75.

Kahn, Douglas A. "Mandatory Buy-Out Agreements for Stock of Closely-Held Corporations." *Michigan Law Review*, November 1969, pp. 1–64.

Kopple, Robert C. "An Introduction to Buy-Sell Agreements for Closely-Held Corporations." *ALI-ABA Course Materials Journal*, April 1980, pp. 5–24.

Kowalski, Lawrence L., and Brent B. Nicholson. "Buy-Sell Agreements Can Avoid Disputes as to the Value of a Minority Interest." *Taxation for Accountants*, June 1984, pp. 370–74.

Kozaczek, Kim Marie. "The Restrictive Stock Transfer Agreement: Still a Valid Means of Establishing the Value of Stock for Estate Tax Purposes after *St. Louis County Bank*?" *Syracuse Law Review*, 1986, p. 181 + .

Kuntz, Joel D. "Stock Redemptions Following Stock Transfers—An Expanding 'Safe Harbor' under Section 302(c)(2)(B)." *Taxes*, January 1980, pp. 29–42.

Landsman, Stephen A. "Divorce Planning in the Closely-Held Business Context." *Trusts & Estates*, May 1984, pp. 41–46.

Lefko, Orville B. "Buy-Sell Agreements and Appraisals." *Michigan State Bar Journal*, February 1976, pp. 116–27.

Linstroth, Paul J. "Stock Redemptions under Sections 302 and 306 of the 1954 Code and Tax Planning for Shareholders Terminating Their Interest in Closely-Held Corporations: Revenue Ruling 77-455." *Creighton Law Review*, 1978, pp. 1259–75.

Litvak, Lawrence. "The Use of Buy-Sell Agreements in Establishing the Value of Closely-Held Businesses." *Business Valuation News*, March 1984, pp. 3–16.

Lynch, W. B. "New Look at Buy-Sell Agreements." University of Southern California Law Center Tax Institute, 1978, pp. 775–99.

Martin, Mary Jill Lockwood. "Planning Options to Structure and Fund a Buy-Sell Agreement among Close Corporation Owners." *Taxation for Accountants*, July 1986, pp. 30–34.

Matsen, Jeffrey R. "A New Look at Business Buy-Out Agreements." *Practical Lawyer*, July 1979, pp. 443–64.

Matsen, Jeffrey R. "Establishing the Price for Closely-Held Business Buy-Sell Agreements." *Journal of Corporate Taxation*, Summer 1978, pp. 134–56.

Page, David Keith. "Setting the Price in a Close Corporation Buy-Sell Agreement." *Michigan Law Review*, 1958–1959, pp. 655-84.

Pratt, Shannon P. "Estate Planning, ESOPs, Buy-Sell Agreements, and Life Insurance for Closely Held Businesses." *Journal of the American Society of CLU*, September 1986, pp. 74–79.

Quinn, Jeff. "How to Get the Most Benefit from Buy-Sell Agreements in S Corporations." *Taxation for Accountants*, June 1983, pp. 364–69.

Russell, Walter J. "The New Impetus to Elect S Status Requires Prompt Review of Shareholder's Planning." *Estate Planning*, March–April 1987, pp. 98–102.

Schnur, Robert A. "How to Structure a Shareholder Agreement." *Practical Accountant*, August 1986, pp. 20–32.

Solberg, Thomas A. "Buy-Sell Agreements Can 'Freeze' Asset Values and in Some Cases Make Them Disappear." *Taxes*, July 1981, pp. 437–42.

Stechel, Ira. "Restrictive Buy-Sell Agreements Can Limit Estate Tax Value of Business Interest." *Journal of Taxation*, June 1976, pp. 360–66.

Tinio, Ferdinand S. "Valuation of Corporate Stock under Buy-Out or 'First Option' Agreement Giving Option to or Requiring Corporation or Other Stockholders to Purchase Stock of Deceased or Withdrawing Stockholders." 54 *A.L.R.* 3d 790 (1973, supplement 1979).

Tobisman, Stuart P. "Estate and Gift Tax Considerations in Buy-Sell Agreements." University of Southern California Law Center Tax Institute, 1983, pp. 17.1–17.26.

Treanor, Richard B. "Is the Eighth Circuit's *St. Louis Bank* Case the Death Knell for Restrictive Stock Agreements?" *Journal of Taxation*, October 1982, pp. 202–3.

Vogel, Nelson J. Jr., and Kenneth R. Petrini. "New Considerations in Drafting Buy-Sell Agreements for Estate Valuation Purposes: The Impact of *St. Louis County Bank*." Estate Planning Institute, University of Notre Dame Law School, 1982, pp. 615–41.

Wark, Jerry W. "Section 303 Stock Redemptions: A Post-1976 Tax Reform Act Appraisal." *Notre Dame Lawyer*, June 1978, pp. 913–33.

Wise, Richard M. "Some Valuation Concerns in Buy-Sell Agreements." *CA Magazine*, February 1985, pp. 52–58.

Zaritsky, Howard M. "Forgotten Provisions in Buy-Sell Agreements. " Philip E. Heckerling Institute on Estate Planning, University of Miami Law Center, 1985, pp. 6.1–6.95.

Zatt, Mark E. "Structuring Shareholder Buy-Out Agreements to Meet Business, Tax and Estate Planning Goals." *Taxation for Lawyers*, May–June 1985, pp. 360–64.

Books

Blum, Robert. *Common Pitfalls to Avoid in Buy-Sell Agreements* (Milwaukee, Wis.: CPA Services Inc., 1985).

Donald, Williamson P. 106-5th T.M. *Corporate Buy-Out Agreements* (Washington, D.C.: Tax Management, Inc., 1984).

Hull, Addis E. *Stock Purchase Agreements in Estate Planning—with Forms* 2nd ed. Englewood Cliffs, N.J.: Prentice-Hall, 1979.

Chapter 21

Analysis of the Central Trust Company Case—a Lesson in Federal Gift Tax Valuation

Despite the court's final opinion—almost exactly splitting the difference between the values posited by the opposing parties—I think the most informative court case for the student of business valuation is the *Central Trust Company* case,[1] primarily because of the judge's very thorough written opinion. The opinion outlines the testimony of five witnesses on the value of the stock in question, critiques many aspects of the testimony, and gives a detailed explanation of the rationale for the court's final decision.

Background

Heekin Can Company (Heekin), a well-established manufacturer of cans for the food industry, had 254,125 shares outstanding in 1954, of which 180,510 were owned by 79 persons who were related to James J. Heekin, the founder.

On August 3, 1954, Albert E. Heekin gifted 30,000 shares, composed of 5,000 shares each, to six trusts created for the benefit of his three sons, each of whom was the beneficiary under two trusts. Following his death on March 10, 1955, the executors of his estate filed a gift tax return in which the stock's value was fixed at $10 a share. On October 28, 1957, however, they filed an amended gift tax return and a claim for refund, contending that the correct value of the Heekin Can Company stock on August 3, 1954, was $7.50 per share.

On October 25, 1954, James J. Heekin and his wife, Alma, gifted 40,002 shares, consisting of 13,334 shares to each of three trusts created for the benefit of his three children and their families. Gift tax returns were filed in which the stock's value was similarly declared to be $10 per share. However, on January 21, 1958, James filed an amended gift tax return and a claim for refund, also contending that the correct value of the stock on October 25, 1954, was $7.50 a share. On the same day, the executor of Alma's estate (she had died on November 9, 1955) filed a similar amended return and claim for refund. The commissioner of the IRS subsequently determined that the stock was worth $24 per share on the gift dates, and gift taxes were paid on the deficiency on that basis. The Central Trust Company, as executor for the donors' estates, filed for a refund, claiming a value of $7.50 per share on the gift dates.

In 1951 and 1952, there were 44 transactions in the stock, totaling 13,359 shares, all at $7.50 per share. These transactions resulted from the desire of descendants of a partner of James Heekin, the founder, to liquidate their interests, and all the sales were made to Heekin family members, employees, or friends. In 1953, the only transaction in Heekin stock was a 100-share sale from one Heekin employee to another. In 1954, the only transaction in Heekin stock was a 200-share sale, also from one Heekin employee to another.

---

[1] *Central Trust Co. v. United States*, 305 F.2d 393 (1962).

Heekin's book value was $33.15 per share on June 30, 1954, and $33.55 on September 30, 1954. The company paid a cash dividend at the annual rate of $.50 per share, which it had paid each year from 1946 through 1954, except when the company had an extraordinary loss in 1950, when the dividend was omitted, and 1951, when it paid only $.25. The company was in a sound financial position, with a current ratio of better than 3 to 1 and current assets exceeding total liabilities by a ratio of almost 2 to 1.

The trial took place in the U.S. Court of Claims in 1962. At the trial, the taxpayers produced three independent expert witnesses and the government one. A spokesperson for the government also testified on the government's valuation. The court stated:

> Where, as in the present cases, the problem is the difficult one of ascertaining the fair market value of the stock of an unlisted closely held corporation, it is not surprising that, in assisting the court to arrive at an "informed judgment," the parties offer the testimony of experts. In such a situation, the opinions of experts are peculiarly appropriate.[2]

The court's opinion provides a thorough explanation of the positions of the different expert witnesses on various aspects of the valuation and the court's assessment of those positions.

Opposing Positions

Taxpayer's First Expert Witness

Taxpayer's first expert used $1.77 per share as an earning power base. He arrived at it using an unadjusted and unweighted average of the full years' 1952, 1953, and 1954 earnings, which he capitalized at a P/E ratio of 6.0. He capitalized the dividend at 7 percent. He discounted book value by 50 percent because of the age and "multi-storied inefficiency" of the company's two main plants. He assigned weights of 40 percent to capitalization of earnings, 20 percent to capitalization of dividends, 20 percent to the book value approach, and 20 percent to past sales of the stock. He then took a 25 percent discount for lack of marketability. The first expert did not utilize comparable publicly traded companies in his deliberations on the basis that he thought none could properly be compared with Heekin. This analysis produced the result as shown in Table 21–1.

Taxpayer's Second Expert Witness

Taxpayer's second expert used $1.68 as an earning power base. This figure represented an unadjusted and unweighted average of the full years' 1950 through 1954 earnings. He calculated that 11 publicly

---

[2]Ibid., p. 399.

TABLE 21-1

Earning Power							
$ 1.77	×	6	=	$10.62	×	.4	=	$ 4.25
Dividends							
$ .50	÷	.07	=	7.14	×	.2	=	1.43
Book value							
$33.20	×	50%	=	16.60	×	.2	=	3.32
Prior sales							
$ 7.50					×	.2	=	1.50
								$10.50
Less 25 percent discount for lack of marketability								2.62
Value per share								$ 7.88

traded companies in the container industry sold at an average price/ earnings ratio of 10 over the 5-year period and capitalized Heekin's earnings at 8 times, which he considered appropriate for a "marginal" company. From the result of this calculation, he took a 14.1 percent discount to move the price back to the August gift date, "derived by calculating the general rise in a relatively large group of certain other industry stocks between August 3 and December 31."[3]

Taxpayer's second expert used $.35 per share as the dividend base, the average for the 1950–1954 period. He capitalized it at 6 percent, noting a 5.1 percent average dividend yield for his 11 publicly traded companies and higher yields available on other general groups of industrial stocks.

The expert assigned weights of 40 percent to the capitalization of earnings, 40 percent to the capitalization of dividends, 10 percent to book value, and 10 percent to prior sales. He used a 15 percent discount for lack of marketability.

This analysis produced the following result:

TABLE 21-2

Earning Power							
$ 1.68	×	8	=	$13.44			
$13.44	−	14.1%	=	11.55	×	.4	=	$ 4.62
Dividends							
$ .35	÷	.06	=	5.83	×	.4	=	2.33
Book value							
$33.23					×	.1	=	3.32
Prior sales							
$ 7.50					×	.1	=	.75
								$11.02
Less 15% discount for lack of marketability								1.65
Value per share								$ 9.37

This witness then rounded the figure to $9.50. Using the same method, he valued the October gift at $9.65, based on a lesser downward adjustment in the earning power component of the valuation.

---

[3]Ibid., p. 400.

Taxpayer's Third Expert Witness

Taxpayer's third expert used the years 1949 to 1953 to compute an earnings base and adjusted the income statements to eliminate abnormal and nonrecurring items. He used eight companies in the container industry to derive a P/E ratio of 11.82. He also derived a value that he called the "earnings paid out" basis, which reflected both dividends and interest on long-term debt ("earnings paid out on capital invested"). He adjusted the book value to a "value based on invested capital."

The expert assigned weights of 33 1/3 percent to the capitalized earnings value, 33 1/3 percent to the "earnings paid out on capital invested" value, 16 2/3 percent to the value based on invested capital, and 16 2/3 percent to the prior stock sales. He used a 20 percent discount for lack of marketability.

This analysis produced the result:

TABLE 21-3

Earning power			
$13.78 ×	.3333	=	$ 4.59
"Earnings paid out on capital invested"			
$ 9.59 ×	.3333	=	3.20
Book value (or "value based on invested capital")			
$31.34 ×	.1667	=	5.22
Prior sales			
$ 7.50 ×	.1667	=	1.25
			$14.26
Less 20 percent discount for lack of marketability			2.85
Value per share			$11.41

The witness also noted that he would discount only 17.5 percent for lack of marketability if the transaction were viewed as one 30,000-share block and not three 10,000-share blocks, which would result in a price of $11.76 per share.

Using the same method, the witness derived a value of $9.40 per share for the October gifts, the sharp difference being attributable to drops in the market prices of the public companies used as comparables between the August and October valuation dates. He noted that he would use a price of $9.47 if the transaction were regarded as one block of 40,000 shares rather than three blocks of 13,334 shares each. No explanation was given in the case about why this differential was smaller than that used in the August gifts.

Government's Independent Expert Witness

The government's expert used earnings for 1950 through September 1954, with certain adjustments. He also computed earnings for the 12-month periods ended June 30 and September 30, 1954, the ends of the quarters immediately prior to the two valuation dates. He considered eight publicly traded container companies as possible comparables and ended up relying on two as the only ones comparable to Heekin. Based on these two comparables, he applied a P/E ratio of 7.24 to the adjusted earnings of $2.21 per share for the 12 months ended June 30 and a ratio of 8.29 times the $1.84 adjusted net profit per share for the 12 months ended September 30.

The witness evaluated the stock on a dividend yield basis by capitalizing dividends at 3.13 percent on the August valuation date and 3.28 percent on the October valuation date, which dividend yields he derived from the comparable companies. For a dividend figure, he used the average for the 4.5 years preceding the valuation dates, thus including the atypical period when no dividends were paid. The details of the weighting and computations are not given in the case opinion, but the witness finally took a discount of "almost 20 percent" for lack of marketability, resulting in a figure of $16.00 for the August date and $15.25 for the October date. He then noted that this final value also approximated the company's current assets less all of its liabilities giving no value at all to its plants, equipment, or other noncurrent assets.

Government's Staff Witness

The government staff witness computed "representative earnings" for Heekin at $1.89 per share, based on 1953 and 1954 adjusted earnings. He found an average P/E ratio of 13 on current earnings of 11 container companies. This ratio would produce a capitalized earnings value of $24.57 per share, which the government witness arbitrarily valued at $22.50.

The government staff witness noted that the average market-price/book value ratio was 1.4 and on this basis concluded that Heekin stock would not sell for less than its book value of about $33 per share.

Based on 7 of the 11 comparatives used in the earnings capitalization, the government staff witness capitalized Heekin's $.50 dividend at 3.75 percent. He ignored prior sales and denied the applicability of any discount for lack of marketability. He then assigned weights of 50 percent for capitalized earnings, 30 percent for capitalization of dividends, and 20 percent for book value.

This analysis produced the result as follows:

TABLE 21-4

Earning power			
$ 1.89 × 13	= $24.57		
Arbitrarily reduced to	22.50 × .5 =	$11.25	
Dividends			
$ .50 ÷ .0375	= 13.33 × .3 =	4.00	
Book value			
$33	× .2 =	6.60	
Value per share		$21.85	

Court's Positions

Comparative Appraisal Method

The court stated:

> [T]he comparative appraisal method is a sound and well-accepted technique. In employing it, however, every effort should be made to select as broad a base of comparative companies as is reasonably possible, as well as to give full consideration to every possible factor in order to make the comparison more meaningful.[4]

In discussing the study offered by the government's expert witness, the court observed, in part, that:

> [I]t has certain weaknesses . . . , the principal one being the limitation of the comparative companies to two, one of which Crown Cork & Seal, leaves much to be desired as a comparative because its principal business is the manufacture of bottle caps and bottling machinery, an entirely different business.[5]

In commenting on the government's own witness's use of comparatives, the court stated:

> [T]he selection of such companies as American Can and Continental Can as comparatives—companies held in esteem in the investment world—will obviously give an unduly high result. It simply is not fair to compare Heekin with such companies and to adopt their market ratios for application to Heekin's stock. Furthermore, defendant's use of comparatives is confusing. The employment of different comparatives for different purposes is unorthodox. When the comparative appraisal method is employed the comparatives should be clearly identified and consistently used for all purposes.[6]

Capitalization of Earnings

The court recognized that the capitalization of earnings should be the most important factor in the valuation of a manufacturing company. It also acknowledged that earnings should be adjusted to eliminate abnormalities and nonrecurring events. It further recognized that earnings (or any other factors) should be considered only to the extent of the information available up to the valuation date and be brought as current to the valuation date as reasonably possible. Finally, the court required that any trend in earnings be considered, which it did by using a weighted average rather than a simple average of past earning in deriving an earnings power base. All four of the foregoing principles are consistent with generally accepted business appraisal procedures.

---

[4]Ibid., p. 407.
[5]Ibid., p. 406.
[6]Ibid., p. 408.

Earnings Most Important Factor.   On earnings being the most important factor, the court stated:

> [I]t is generally conceded that, as stated in the Revenue Ruling, in evaluating stocks of manufacturing corporations such as Heekin, earnings are the most important factor to be considered.[7]

Adjustments to Earnings.   On elimination of abnormalities, the court stated:

> [I]t is accepted valuation practice, in ascertaining a company's past earnings, to attempt to detect abnormal or nonrecurring items and to make appropriate eliminations or adjustments.[8]

The court listed the adjustments it considered appropriate as:

> In these cases, this normalizing process should require (a) the elimination from the years 1950 to 1952 of the abnormal, nonrecurring losses incident to its financing subsidiary, which had been completely liquidated by 1952; (b) the elimination of the abnormally large 1951 profits due to the Korean war; (c) the redistribution of the expenses attributable to the establishment subsequent to 1951, of a retirement plan, which expenses, although borne in later years, were also applicable to 1950 and 1951, thereby overstating 1950 and 1951 profits and similarly depressing 1953 and 1954 profits; (d) the shift from 1954 to 1951 of the renegotiation refund paid with respect to excessive 1951 profits; (e) the elimination from 1954 of the abnormally large charge relating to the accrual in 1954 of certain expenses actually attributable to 1955, which resulted in the doubling up of 2 years of such expenses in 1954, as permitted by a then recent change in the tax laws.[9]

Use Only Data Available Up to Valuation Date.   The court criticized those witnesses who used data past the valuation date:

> [I]n using the Company's full 1954 financial data, and then working back from December 31, 1954, to the respective dates, data were being used which would not have been available to a prospective purchaser on the gift dates. The valuation of the stock must be made as of the relevant dates without regard to events occurring subsequent to the crucial dates.[10]

The court also criticized failure to utilize data available as close as possible to the valuation date:

> [T]he converse situation applies with respect to the data used by the third expert. His financial data only went to December 31, 1953, since the Company's last annual report prior to the gift dates was issued for the year 1953. But the Company also issued quarterly interim financial statements, and by the second gift date, the results of three-quarters of 1954 operations were available. In evaluating a stock, it is essential to obtain

---

[7]Ibid., p. 404.
[8]Ibid., p. 403.
[9]Ibid., p. 409.
[10]Ibid., p. 403.

as recent data as is possible as section 4 of the Revenue Ruling makes plain. Naturally, an investor would be more interested in how a corporation is currently performing than what it did last year or in even more remote periods. Although the use of interim reports reflecting only a part of a year's performance may not be satisfactory in a seasonal operation such as canning, it is possible here to obtain a full year's operation ending on either June 30 or September 30, 1954, which would bring the financial data up closer to the valuation dates.[11]

The court's solution was to consider the four full years 1950 through 1953, plus the 12 months ended June 30 for the August valuation date and the 12 months ended September 30 for the October valuation date.

It should be noted that the foregoing does not totally close the door on the use of some projections or forecasts, if available. For example, had the company had a budget for its full year 1954 earnings and had the budget been available to prospective stock purchasers on the valuation date, it could properly have been considered. Even so, as noted earlier in this book, courts usually rely far less on budgets or projections than on actual reported earnings and other data.

Recognition of Earnings Trend. The court criticized the expert witnesses for merely using average earnings in arriving at an earning power base rather than considering any trend in earnings. The court noted that an investor would be expected to pay more for a share of a company with a rising earnings trend than for a share of one with a declining earnings trend if the five-year average were the same for both companies. "Greater weight should fairly be given to the most recent years and periods."[12]

The court handled this matter by a weighted average, assigning a weight of 1 to the 1950 earnings, 2 to 1951, 3 to 1952, 4 to 1953, and 5 to the latest 12 months preceding each valuation date.

Capitalization of Dividends

Determination of Appropriate Dividend Rate. The court rejected using the past five years' average dividend as a base, making the point that the five-year period did not represent current dividend-paying capacity because it included an abnormal period when the dividend was temporarily suspended because of an extraordinary loss.

In accepting the current $.50-per-share rate as the dividend-paying capacity base, the court noted that the payment was a lower percentage of earnings than the industry average as demonstrated by the comparable public companies but that was justified because:

[N]o substantially larger payment, at least for some time to come, could reasonably have been anticipated. Heekin's equipment was, as shown, not modern and the Company was in need of relatively large sums for equip-

---

[11]Ibid., p. 403.
[12]Ibid., p. 409.

ment and plant modernization if it hoped to continue to be a competitive factor in the industry. For such a program, the Company would have to depend almost entirely on retained earnings. A further limitation on the Company's dividend-paying capacity was its repayment obligations on its long-term debt. Annual installments on principal of $150,000 had to be made through 1965, plus 20 percent of the net income (less $150,000) for the preceding year.[13]

Determination of Appropriate Rate at Which to Capitalize Dividend. The court basically took the position that the appropriate capitalization rate should be that shown by the marketplace for the publicly traded comparatives:

> [I]n capitalizing the dividend at 6 and 7 percent, as did two of the experts, rates of return were used which well exceeded those being paid at the time by comparable container company stocks.[14]

Use of Book Value

The government's independent expert witness characterized the consideration of book value as a defensive factor in the valuation, describing the net asset factor as "one which keeps a stock price from declining to zero when earnings become zero or even when losses are suffered and when a price-to-earnings ratio would therefore become meaningless."[15] In general the court seemed to agree with this assessment.

Prior Sales in the Stock

The court downplayed the importance of the record of prior stock sales in this case, primarily because the bulk of the prior sales took place too far in the past from the valuation date and when conditions were not comparable because the company was just recovering from its loss position. Less important (in this particular case), the court also questioned the extent to which the transactions actually were made on an arm's-length basis.

The court stated that the taxpayer's expert witnesses "all give undue weight as a factor to the $7.50 price of the prior stock sales."[16] The court explained the rationale for its position in this way:

> Almost all of these sales occurred in the relatively remote period of 1951 and early 1952. Only one small transaction occurred in each of the more recent years of 1953 and 1954. . . . Furthermore, the $7.50 price of the 1951 and 1952 sales evolved in early 1951 during a period when the Company was experiencing rather severe financial difficulties due to an unfortunate experience with a subsidiary which caused a loss of around $1 million, and when, consequently, the Company found itself in a de-

---

[13]Ibid., p. 409.
[14]Ibid., p. 404.
[15]Ibid., p. 405.
[16]Ibid., p. 402.

pleted working capital position and was paying no dividends. Further, there is no indication that the $7.50 sales price evolved as a result of the usual factors taken into consideration by informed sellers and buyers dealing at arm's length. Fair market value presupposes not only hypothetical willing buyers and sellers, but buyers and sellers who are informed and have "adequate knowledge of the material facts affecting the value." *Robertson* v. *Routzahn*, 75 F.2d 537, 539 (C.C.A.6th); Paul, Studies in Federal Taxation (1937), pp. 193–4. The sales were all made at a prearranged price to Heekin employees and family friends. The artificiality of the price is indicated by its being the same in 1951, 1952, 1953, and 1954, despite the varying fortunes of the Company during these years and with the price failing to reflect, as would normally be expected, such differences in any way.[17]

It should be clear from the foregoing explanation that the court was not downplaying the importance of prior sales as a valuation criterion in general if they were at arm's length and made under circumstances in which the economic factors determining the prices were comparable to those on the valuation date. The court simply thought that the prior sales generally failed to meet such standards. Even so, the court did not disregard the prior sales completely, as will be seen in the following summary section.

Discount for Lack of Marketability

The court recognized that a discount for lack of marketability must be used if valuing the stock with reference to publicly traded comparatives. Referring to the government's position on this issue, the court stated that "the refusal to make any allowance for lack of marketability contributes further to the unrealistic nature"[18] of the government's fair market value estimate.

However, all of the expert witnesses in this case approached the quantification of the appropriate marketability discount on the basis of the "cost of flotation," that is, how much it would cost to make a public offering of the shares involved. On this basis, the court found that the discounts for lack of marketability the experts offered were too high and accepted a discount of 12.17 percent based on a prior study of flotation costs, which it cited.

I believe this was a major conceptual error in the case and the only major procedure that subsequent cases generally have not followed, as we will see in the next chapter. The assumption implicit in using flotation cost as a basis for determining the discount for lack of marketability is that such a flotation is a viable possibility. Generally, that is not the case for minority stockholders. Depending on conditions, it might not even be a viable possibility for a controlling position.

Obviously, the adoption of the premise that flotation cost should be the basis for determining the marketability discount was not the

---

[17]Ibid., p. 402.
[18]Ibid., p. 408.

court's fault, since the expert witnesses were the ones who suggested it and the testimony did not refute the premise. Also, the data on discounts for lack of marketability discussed in Chapter 10 were not available at the time of this case. Subsequent cases have recognized that a public flotation normally is not a viable alternative, at least for minority stockholders, and, consequently, discounts for lack of marketability in most subsequent cases have been significantly higher.

Court's Final Summary

Earning Power.   The court used a weighted average of the latest five years' earnings for the earning power base. For both valuation dates the court gave a weight of 1 to the 1950 earnings, 2 to the 1951 earnings, 3 to the 1952 earnings, and 4 to the 1953 earnings, all adjusted as discussed earlier. For the August 3, 1954, valuation date, the court applied a weight of 5 to the earnings for the 12 months ended June 30, 1954. For the October 25, 1954, valuation date, the court applied a weight of 5 to the earnings for the 12 months ended September 30, 1954. This resulted in a weighted average earning power base of $1.93 for the August 3 valuation date and $1.79 for the October 25 valuation date.

Dividends.   The court said it could reasonably be anticipated that Heekin would continue its $.50 annual dividend. However, limitations on its dividend-paying capacity made it unlikely that it would increase the dividend, so that the current dividend rate appeared to approximate the firm's dividend-paying capacity.

Book Value.   The book value of Heekin stock was $33.15 at June 30, 1954, and $33.55 at September 30, 1954.

Comparable Public Companies.   The court selected five of the public companies submitted by the witnesses as suitable for use for the valuation. The court discussed this procedure:

> [I]t is . . . appropriate to select as closely comparable companies as is possible whose stocks are actively traded, and to ascertain what ratios their market prices bear to their earnings, dividends, and book values. The application of such ratios to Heekin would then give a reasonable approximation of what Heekin's stock would sell for if it too were actively traded. . . .
>
> [F]ive of them, are, while by no means perfect comparables, certainly at least reasonably satisfactory for the purpose in question. . . . In addition, five companies give a sufficiently broad base. . . .
>
> After similarly computing the earnings, as adjusted, of the comparatives for the same periods as Heekin. . . . and similarly weighting them to give effect to the trend factor. . . . the average ratio of their market prices to their adjusted earnings as of August 3 and October 25, 1954 (the "price-earnings" ratio) was 9.45 and 9.84 to 1, respectively. . . .

Similarly, the comparatives' dividend payments for the 12 months ending June 30 and September 30, 1954, show an average yield of 3.50 and 3.56, respectively. . . .

As to book value, the average market prices of the comparatives were 83.96 and 86.39 percent, respectively, of the book values of their common stocks on said dates. . . .[19]

Weighting of Factors. The court then accorded 50 percent weight to the capitalization of earnings, 30 percent weight to the capitalization of dividends, and 20 percent weight to the ratio of price to book value. This analysis produced these results:

TABLE 21-5

								August 3, 1954	October 25, 1954
Earning power									
$ 1.93	×	9.45	=	$18.24	×	.5	=	$ 9.12	
$ 1.79	×	9.84	=	$17.61	×	.5	=		$ 8.81
Dividends									
$ .50	÷	.0350	=	$14.29	×	.3	=	4.29	
$ .50	÷	.0356	=	$14.05	×	.3	=		4.22
Book Value									
$33.15	×	.8396	=	$27.83	×	.2	=	$ 5.57	
$33.55	×	.8639	=	$28.98	×	.2	=		$ 5.80
								$18.98	$18.83
Less 12.17% discount for lack of marketability								2.31	2.29
Value per share								$16.67	$16.54

Past Transactions, Other Factors, and Conclusion. The court concluded:

> . . . [W]hile the sales of Heekin stock at $7.50 warrant, as hereinabove pointed out, only minimal consideration, the figures derived from the above formula give them no cognizance whatsoever. Giving important weight to the figure of $16.67 produced by the application of the comparative appraisal method as applied herein, but viewing it in light of all the facts and circumstances involved in these cases, it is concluded that the fair market value of the 30,000 shares given on August 3, 1954, was $15.50 per share.[20]

The court went on to state that the company's prospects were no less bright as of October 25, 1954, and that the fair market value on that date also was $15.50 per share.

---

[19]Ibid., pp. 409–10.
[20]Ibid., p. 411.

Chapter 22

Other Federal Gift and Estate Tax Cases

We have now come full cycle and after weeks of preparation, days of trial, hundreds of pages of paper, thousands of dollars for lawyers, months of consideration by the court, and minutes reading the opinion, we are back where petitioner started on the Form 706.[1]

This chapter discusses several gift and estate tax cases that I think are worth noting because of the courts' statements of positions taken on various valuation issues. They illustrate such issues as primary reliance on capitalization of earnings versus asset values and several aspects of discounts for minority interest, lack of marketability, and other factors.

Kirkpatrick Case

Background

On the date of his death, April 17, 1968, Ernest E. Kirkpatrick owned minority interests in two closely held corporations. The decedent owned 1,091 out of 2,512 shares outstanding, or 43.43 percent, of French Tool & Supply Company (French Tool). Decedent's grandson owned 875.5 shares, or 34.85 percent, and decedent's daughter 545.5 shares, or 21.71 percent. The decedent also owned 130 out of 2,000 shares outstanding, or 6.5 percent, of French Oil Company (French Oil). L. R. French, Jr., owned 1,805 shares, or 90.25 percent. Decedent's daughter owned 65 shares, or 3.25 percent.

French Tool operated an International Truck dealership (and a related rig-up shop) and a Chrysler-Plymouth dealership and was engaged in oil production and ranching. The oil business consisted of some producing and some nonproducing properties. Ranching operations consisted of a 50 percent undivided ownership in two cattle and sheep ranches.

French Oil owned 22 producing oil leases. It also owned the other 50 percent undivided interest in the two cattle and sheep ranches referred to above, plus a 100 percent interest in a 1,280-acre ranch used occasionally for grazing. French Oil also sold oil field tubular goods.

Neither French Tool nor French Oil had ever paid dividends. There had never been an outside sale of either stock. In 1960, French bought 870 shares of French Oil for $287 per share from his former wife as part of a property settlement connected with a divorce.

French Tool Company

On the original tax return, the taxpayer had valued the French Tool stock at $353.63 per share. In the deficiency notice, government valued it at $600.34 per share, which was the book value on the latest interim

---

[1]*Estate of Martha B. Watts*, 51 T.C.M. 60 (1985), p. 63.

statement prior to the valuation date. At the trial, the taxpayer claimed a value of $216 per share for the French Tool stock, while government claimed $500 per share.

Taxpayer's Position.   Taxpayer's expert witness relied primarily on the capitalization of earnings approach for the valuation of the French Tool stock. The testimony is summarized as follows:

> He estimated that, based on numerous publicly-owned companies with financial prospects similar to French Tool's, decedent's stock, if it had been marketable, would have sold at eight times the company's earnings for the 12-month period ending March 31, 1968, or $432 per share. He then applied a 50-percent discount to this figure to reflect the nonmarketability of the stock, the lack of dividends, and the fact that a purchaser of decedent's interest would have no effective voice in the company's management. Thus, he concluded that, on April 17, 1978, decedent's 1,091 shares of French Tool stock had a fair market value of $216 per share.[2]

Government's Position.   Government's expert witness relied primarily on the value of the underlying assets for the valuation of the French Tool stock. He adjusted the book value upward to reflect an appraisal of the 50 percent owned ranch land in excess of the cost basis. He then discounted 50 percent from the resulting value to reflect the stock's lack of marketability and the decedent's minority interest.

Court's Position.   The court found the taxpayer's capitalization of earnings approach to the valuation of the shares more persuasive than the government's underlying asset value approach. The text of the court's opinion follows:

> On the date of the decedent's death, French Tool was actively engaged in three separate lines of business. Although it owned interests in large amounts of real estate, its land holding constituted an integral part of its ongoing ranching business. Thus, since French Tool was clearly an operating company actively engaged in selling products and services to the general public, we think that primary consideration should be given to its earnings and prospects for future profits as opposed to the value of its underlying assets. See *Levenson's Estate* v. *Commissioner* (60-2 USTC 969), 282 F.2d 581, 586 (3d Cir. 1960); Rev. Rul. 59-60, sec. 5(b), 1959-1 C.B. 237.
>
> From this perspective, we think that a prospective purchaser of decedent's French Tool stock, in examining the company's financial position on April 17, 1968, would discover a number of factors that would have a depressing influence on the value of decedent's shares.
>
> Such an examination would reveal that, for a number of years, French Tool's ratio of current assets to current liabilities had been about one-to-one. The company's net earnings had fluctuated widely for the past several years and, in fiscal year ending June 30, 1967, the company showed a net loss of approximately $3,000. It had a significant amount of long-

---

[2] *Estate of Ernest E. Kirkpatrick,* 34 T.C.M. 1490 (1975), p. 1499.

term debt that approximately equaled stockholder's equity. The company had never paid any dividends and had not been in a financial position to do so. Finally, the stock was not marketable, and a purchaser of decedent's 43.43 percent interest in French Tool would probably have had little or no voice in the company's management due to the fact that the majority interest was held by decedent's daughter and grandson.

However, we think these negative factors would be offset somewhat by the fact that the company's fiscal year ending June 30, 1968, was quite profitable in relation to past years.* Also, although the company's net earnings had been quite low for the past several years, its cash flow position (net income plus depreciation) had been much more favorable. Finally, even though the chances on April 17, 1968, were minimal that French Tool would be liquidated in the foreseeable future, we think the rather high adjusted book value of the company's underlying assets would have been an attractive feature to a prospective purchaser of decedent's stock.

After taking all of these factors into consideration and after adjusting the value of the underlying assets to reflect the $94 per acre value of the Ranch,** we find decedent's 1,091 shares of French Tool stock to have been worth $300 per share on April 17, 1968.[3]

---

*Although French Tool's June 30, 1968, financial data would not have been available to a prospective purchaser of decedent's stock on April 17, 1968, the company maintained monthly balance sheets and earnings statements. The financial data for the nine-month period ending March 31, 1968, would have been available and clearly forecasted the profitability of the 1967–68 fiscal year.

**We cannot accept [taxpayer's witness's] contention that the value of decedent's French Tool stock would not be increased if we found the Ranch to be worth more than $80 per acre. While we think that little weight should be given to the value of the company's underlying assets, to adopt [taxpayer's witness's] position is, in effect, to ignore their value altogether. This we cannot do. *See Estate of Lida R. Tompkins* (Dec. 15, 182(M)), T.C. Memo. 1961-338.

The foregoing opinion is instructive because it is generally is consistent with the lines of reasoning found in similar cases but perhaps articulated more clearly.

French Oil Company

On the original tax return, the taxpayer had valued the French Oil stock at $287.36 per share. In the deficiency notice, government valued it at $882.73 per share, which was the book value on the latest interim statement prior to the valuation date. At the trial, taxpayer claimed a value of $171 per share for the French Oil stock, while government claimed $650 per share.

Taxpayer's Position. Taxpayer's expert witness said that he could not approach the French Oil valuation on a capitalization of earnings basis because most of the recent earnings resulted from collection of

---

[3]Ibid., p. 1500.

old receivables, which previously had been written off, and from the sale of oil leases, neither of which was a continuing source of earnings and without which the company would have lost money. He therefore decided to estimate a liquidating value and proposed that a minority shareholder might "gamble" about a quarter of liquidating value to accept the risks involved.

Government's Position.   Government's expert witness approached French Oil the same way as he did French Tool—adjusting the book value upward to reflect increased value in the ranchland and then discounting 50 percent from the resulting adjusted asset value to reflect lack of marketability and minority interest.

Court's Position.   The text of the court's decision and rationale is:

> In making our determination that decedent's 130 shares of French Oil stock were worth $250 per share on the date of his death, we did not feel comfortable with either expert's method of valuation. We found [taxpayer's witness's] hypothetical amount that a purchaser would "gamble" in order to obtain a certain return on his investment to be too speculative to warrant our total reliance. With respect to the method utilized by [government's witness], we think the facts presented clearly show that French Oil, like French Tool, was an operating company on the date of decedent's death. Thus, we think [government's witness] gave excessive consideration to the value of the company's underlying assets in making his valuation.
>
> We think that a prospective investor would view French Oil primarily from the standpoint of its history and prospects as a profit-making corporation.
>
> An examination of its financial position as of April 17, 1968, reveals that the company was in rather poor shape. Its ratio of current assets to current liabilities had been about one-to-one for a number of years, and its long-term debt was quite high in relation to stockholder's equity. Its ranching business consistently operated at a loss and, although the company showed modest profits for its fiscal years ending August 31, 1965, 1966, and 1967, had it not been for the items of extraordinary income [collection of bad debts and sale of certain oil leases], the company would have lost money in each of these years.
>
> Surely a prospective purchaser would have taken into account the fact that, as of April 17, 1968, all of French Oil's bad debts had been collected and would have realized that the company could not continue to sell its oil and gas leases indefinitely.
>
> Moreover, French Oil had never paid any dividends in its 33 years of existence. Decedent's 130 shares were nonmarketable and represented a mere 6.5 percent of the company's issued and outstanding stock. A purchaser of decedent's interest would have had no voice in the company's management since the company was run by French, who owned approximately 90 percent of its stock and served as president and chief executive officer.
>
> As we found with French Tool, however, French Oil's cash flow position was more favorable than its net earnings position. Also, notwithstanding the minimal chances that the company would be liquidated, we think a

prospective purchaser would place some importance on the rather high adjusted book value of the underlying assets.

After taking all of these factors into account, we find that $250 per share would have been a fair price for decedent's 130 shares of French Oil stock.[4]

Gallun Case

Background

On September 29, 1969, Edwin A. Gallun (taxpayer) made a gift of 400 shares of common stock of A. F. Gallun & Sons Corporation to members of his family. This gift represented slightly more than 2.5 percent of the 15,722 shares of stock outstanding, of which Gallun owned 4,617.5 shares, or 28.7 percent.

The company owned a leather tanning operation, with related land, buildings, and equipment, plus an investment portfolio of stocks and bonds with a market value of $18,087,263 on September 30, 1969, the company's fiscal year-end.

Earnings per share were $30.89 in fiscal 1968 and $54.78 in 1969, much of which came from the investment portfolio. Dividends paid per share were $18 in fiscal 1968 and $23 in fiscal 1969. Book value at September 30, 1969, was $418.02 per share. Net asset value after adjusting the investment portfolio from cost to market value was $1,283.02 per share.

Taxpayer filed a gift tax return reporting the value of the 400 shares at $369.24 per share. Government filed a notice of deficiency, valuing the stock at $661.37 per share.

Points of Agreement and Issues Involved

The two expert witnesses for the taxpayer and the one for government all agreed that the company was a combined operating company and investment company and, therefore, the tannery operations should be valued as an operating company and the investment portfolio as an investment company.

They also agreed that an adjustment to the value of the investment portfolio for blockage was necessary for two large blocks of stock. This discount reduced the value of the investment portfolio from $18,087,263 to $16,204,439, which reduced the adjusted net asset value from $1,283.02 per share to $1,163.26 per share.

The main issues in the case were the determination of proper discounts for various factors, such as lack of marketability, retention of income not present in a publicly traded investment company, minority interest, and the potential capital gains tax if the stocks and bonds

---

[4]Ibid., p. 1501.

were to be liquidated by the corporation. At the time of the trial, government's expert witness was advocating only a 20 percent discount, while taxpayer's expert witnesses were advocating much greater discounts.

Court's Position

On the tannery operation, the court made these observations:

> The tannery operation is one of only a few remaining in the United States and represents an industry that is declining. . . . The performance of the tannery operation has been mediocre and it would be difficult to find an investor willing to invest in such an operation.[5]

The court valued the tannery operation at $900,000, or the equivalent of about $57 per share, a little less than half the portion of the company's book value that was attributable to the tannery.

The text of the conclusion of the court's opinion states:

> In arriving at our determination we have rejected the argument of [taxpayer] that a discount should be allowed for a potential capital gains tax that would result if the investment portfolio were to be liquidated. The record does not establish that the management of the portfolio had any immediate plans to liquidate the investment portfolio. Furthermore, it is possible that the management at some time in the future may dispose of certain or all of the investment assets without incurring a capital gains tax. Under these circumstances, such a discount is not appropriate. See *Estate of Frank A. Cruikshank,* 9 T.C. 162 (1947); *Estate of Alvin Thalheimer,* 33 T.C.M. 877 (1974).
>
> On the other hand, we believe that the [government's] witness erred in refusing to discount the value of the stock to account for a corporate entity intervening between the investment assets and the owner of Gallun stock. [Government's] witness reasoned that the Corporation could be compared to eight publicly-traded, closed-end investment companies and that accordingly no discount was in order because the stock in the closed-end investment companies was not selling at a discount at the time of the gift. We do not agree that such a comparison is valid, since the shares of the closed-end investment companies are readily marketable and the companies are entitled to certain tax benefits as regulated investment companies.
>
> Taking into account not only the arguments we have discussed but also the additional factors brought to our attention by the parties, we have concluded that the net asset value of the investment portfolio should be discounted by 55 percent. Thus, we find that the fair market value of the investment portion of the Corporation's business was $7,292,000. Adding the value of the tannery operation to this figure, dividing by the number of shares outstanding and rounding, we find the fair market value of the Corporation's stock was $520 on the date in issue.
>
> Based on the $23 dividend in 1969, the highest in a five-year period, the return on the Corporation's stock would be 4.4 percent at $520. Considering the declining state of the tannery industry and the nonmarket-

---

[5]*Edwin A. Gallun,* 33 T.C.M. 1316 (1974), p. 1320.

able nature of the Corporation's stock we do not believe that an investor would be willing to accept a lower return. This factor was an additional consideration in convincing us that a substantial discount of underlying net asset value was necessary.[6]

Commentary on Court's Opinion

I think that three observations on the above court opinion are important.

First, I do not interpret the court's opinion as a rejection of the validity of the general approach of using publicly traded, closed-end investment companies as useful comparables in valuing privately held investment companies. Indeed, many other cases have relied on that approach. The court's opinion merely is that there are at least two important differences between public and private investment companies—marketability and tax treatment—and it would not be valid to make the comparison without appropriate adjustments for those differences.

Second, the paragraph indicating that government erred in refusing to discount the stock's value to account for a corporate entity's intervention between the assets and the owner of the stock is extremely cogent. It is all too common for some people to jump to the conclusion that the value of a share of stock is its proportionate share of the value of the underlying assets, whereas the fact is that ownership of stock is not a legal claim on a proportionate share of the assets at all. This point was discussed in Chapter 2.

Third, the court's rejection of taxpayer's argument—that a discount should be allowed for a potential capital gains tax, which would result if the investment portfolio were liquidated—is inconsistent with many other cases. The courts are so inconsistent and, frequently, ambiguous on their treatment of this point that the appraiser cannot reliably predict which way it will be resolved in any particular case.

My own opinion is that the trapped-in capital gains tax on unrealized appreciation is clearly a deferred liability that requires recognition. Strong support for this position is found in the American Institute of Certified Public Accountants official guidelines for the preparation of personal financial statements, in which assets with unrealized appreciation are adjusted to market value. They unequivocally take the position that any upward adjustment to market value must be accompanied by a deduction for the related capital gains tax. The text of the AICPA position is:

> An accrual for income taxes on net unrealized appreciation [the difference between the tax basis of the net assets and estimated value] is required in the presentation of the estimated value column in personal financial statements. This accrual is necessary because the estimated values cannot generally be realized without incurring taxes.[7]

---

[6]Ibid., p. 1321.

[7]*Audits of Personal Financial Statements* (New York: American Institute of Certified Public Accountants, 1968), p. 5.

This may become especially true due to the repeal of the *General Utilities* doctrine (*General Utilities & Operating Comp.* v. *Helvering,* 296 U.S. 200 [1935]) in the Tax Reform Act of 1986.

Piper Case

Background

On January 8, 1969, William T. Piper, Sr., made gifts, to his son and to 11 trusts for the benefit of his grandchildren, of 100 percent of the outstanding stock of two investment companies, known as Piper Investment Company (Piper Investment) and Castanea Realty Company, Inc. (Castanea).

The two companies had somewhat similar asset portfolios, each consisting of unregistered shares of Piper Aircraft Corporation (PAC) common stock, whose shares were listed and traded on the New York Stock Exchange, plus some income-producing real estate. Piper Investment owned 37,500 (2.3 percent) shares of PAC, and Castanea owned 67,500 (4.1 percent), out of a total of 1,644,890 shares of PAC outstanding. The real estate had been purchased primarily to avoid the problem of having the two investment companies classified as personal holding companies.

No dividends were ever paid by either Piper Investment or Castanea, nor was any salary or other compensation ever paid to Piper, who, until the time of the gifts, was the only shareholder in both corporations.

Piper individually owned 73,920 (4.5 percent) shares of PAC separate from the two investment companies, and Piper family members collectively owned 28 percent of the outstanding PAC stock. Neither Piper nor any of his beneficiaries had any contractual rights to require the filing of a registration statement with the SEC covering the PAC shares nor to annex shares to a registration statement otherwise being filed by PAC. No SEC filing by PAC was contemplated at the time. On the basis of the then current NYSE-quoted price for PAC stock and fair market values of the various real estate holdings, Piper Investment's adjusted net asset value was about $178 per share and Castanea's about $370 per share.

On the gift tax return, taxpayer valued Piper Investment at $76.68 per share and Castanea at $158.59 per share; government's notice of deficiency valued Piper Investment at $101.89 per share and Castanea at $226.15 per share.

Discount for Unregistered Shares of Listed Stock

One of the issues in the case was the value of the unregistered shares of Piper Aircraft Company stock owned by the two investment companies. Government claimed that the stock was not restricted, even though unregistered, and that no discount from the NYSE-quoted price was appropriate. Taxpayer claimed that the stock was restricted and that there could be significant barriers to registering it and, hence, a full discount for lack of marketability, such as would be applied to letter stock, was appropriate.[8]

The court held that the stock was restricted, in the sense that it could not be sold without registration. However, it also noted that Piper was chairman of the board and three sons were included among the other seven directors. On the basis of these facts, along with the significant family ownership position, the court decided that Piper and his associates could force registration if they so desired. Therefore, the marketability discount to be applied directly to the value of the PAC stock should be only the costs of registration and sale. Noting that this would be less for unregistered shares of a company already trading on the NYSE than for a company with no public market, the court, on the basis of expert witness testimony submitted, determined the appropriate marketability discount for the PAC shares to be 12 percent.

With this marketability discount on the PAC shares, the adjusted net asset value of Piper Investment was $158.58 per share and that of Castanea was $327.71 per share.

"Portfolio Discount"

The parties agreed that the portfolios should be valued at some discount from their underlying net asset value but disagreed on the appropriate amount of "portfolio discount."

Both of the government's expert witnesses relied on prices of publicly traded, closed-end investment companies in arriving at their opinions on an appropriate portfolio discount. One witness proposed a discount of 7.7 percent from net asset value based on the market prices of 14 publicly traded, nondiversified investment companies. The other used a group of 24 closed-end investment companies, which he found ranged from a discount of 16.7 percent to a premium of 82.4 percent and concluded that because of Piper Investment's and Castanea's relatively unattractive portfolios the highest discount—approximately 17 percent—should be applied.

Taxpayer's witness did not present his evidence on this point. The text of the court's conclusion on the "portfolio discount" is:

> . . . [W]e are hampered in our evaluation of the testimony of [taxpayer's] valuation expert because [taxpayer] has failed to supply us with any data with which to analyze [taxpayer's witness's] statements. He stated that the only conclusion that could be drawn from the list of companies from which [government's witness] derived his discount was that an inverse correlation existed between the size of an investment company's assets and the size of the discount from net asset value, and that, because of their small size, Piper Investment and Castanea were comparable only to the three smallest companies considered by [government's witness], for which the discounts averaged over 40 percent. Since taxpayer has pre-

---

[8]The general concepts and typical discounts for lettered stock are discussed in Chapter 10, "Data on Discounts for Lack of Marketability."

sented no data to enable us to evaluate the validity of [taxpayer's witness's] statements, we can accord them little weight.

Taxpayer has also failed to introduce specific data to support his assertion that Piper Investment and Castanea were substantially inferior to the worst of the companies considered by [government's witness]. Taxpayer made no attempt to elicit evidence as to the portfolios of the companies considered by [government's witness], and taxpayer's expert witness commented only on [one government witness's] and not on [other government's witness's] report. We have only the fact that the companies considered by [government witness] were publicly-traded from which to infer that their portfolios were superior to those of Piper Investment and Castanea. We have taken account of the lack of a public market for the stock of Piper Investment and Castanea separately.

On the basis of the record before us, we conclude that the discount selected by [government's witness] was too low, but that there is insufficient evidence to support taxpayer's position that the discount should be higher than that proposed by [government's other witness]. Therefore, we find that 17 percent is an appropriate discount from net asset value to reflect the relatively unattractive nature of the investment portfolios of Piper Investment and Castanea.[9]

The language of the court's opinion leads me to believe that the court could have been persuaded to accept a larger discount in this aspect of the case had the taxpayer's witness presented more thorough evidence, such as comparative portfolio analysis, on why Piper Investment and Castanea should have been compared more closely with the investment companies selling at larger discounts. This is an excellent example of the necessity of having expert testimony to support every point, backed up by as much empirical evidence as possible.

Discount for Lack of Marketability

In addressing the discount for lack of marketability, one of the government's witnesses took the position that the discount should be based on the cost of a public flotation. The other government witness and the taxpayer's witness took the position that Piper Investment and Castanea would not make attractive public offerings and the marketability discount should be based on the difference between what stocks tend to sell for on the private placement market versus the publicly traded market. The text of the court's opinion on this issue is:

> We find this reasoning persuasive and reject the position of [government's witness] that a discount based on the costs of a secondary public offering should be employed since we find no support in the record for his premise that a public distribution would be an efficient method of disposing of the Piper Investment and Castanea stock. The situation in respect of the stock of these two companies stands in sharp contrast to the situation vis-à-vis the PAC stock where a previously registered and actively traded listed security was involved.
>
> Government argues that any further discount for the costs of disposing of the Piper Investment and Castanea stock beyond the costs of a regis-

---

[9]*Estate of William T. Piper, Sr.*, 72 T.C. 1062 (1979).

tration and public offering is rendered superfluous by the discounts for restrictions on the PAC stock and for the nondiversified nature of the investment companies' assets. However, because there was no established public market for the stock of Piper Investment and Castanea, and because the gifts were of minority interests in the investment companies, we believe that an investor would consider a purchase of the stock, which was the subject of the gifts, to involve risks and disadvantages which a direct investment in PAC stock would not entail and which are additional to the weaknesses in the investment companies' portfolios.[10]

Both the government witness who opted for the private placement market as a criterion for determining the discount and the taxpayer's witness agreed that the SEC *Institutional Investor Study*[11] provided an appropriate basis for quantifying the relevant discount.

Using various tables in the SEC *Institutional Investor Study* for discounts for private placement transactions, government's witness determined that a further 24 percent discount would be necessary, while taxpayer's witness claimed that the correct discount to be derived from the study should be 43.8 percent. The text of the court's position on this point and its final conclusion as to the value of the shares is:

> We have examined the *Institutional Investor Study* in light of the objections raised by taxpayer. The Study reveals an upward trend in the average discount throughout the period studied, January 1966 through June 1969, with a higher than average discount for the stock of companies with relatively low earnings. *Institutional Investor Study,* supra, at 2454, Table XIV-50. The Study also shows a preference for purchases direct from the issuer in private placements of stocks of closely-held companies rather than secondary securities. *Institutional Investor Study,* supra, at 2416 n. 86, and 2419. Furthermore, a stock with a less active public market tended to sell in private placements at a higher discount. *Institutional Investor Study,* supra, at 2445. The study also indicates that investment advisors were unlikely to be purchasers of stock like that of Piper Investment or Castanea, though it does not indicate, as [taxpayer] would have us believe, that only a venture capital company would purchase that stock since a considerable proportion of the private placements with banks and life insurance companies involved restricted common stocks of privately-held companies. *Institutional Investor Study,* supra, at 2419.
>
> After carefully reviewing the *Institutional Investor Study* and considering all the arguments raised by taxpayer and government, we conclude that a further discount of 35 percent would have been required in a private placement of the Piper Investment and Castanea stock, in view of conditions in the private placement market on the valuation date, the possible purchasers of the stock in a private placement, and the earnings and other attributes of Piper Investment and Castanea.
>
> After applying the discount for the weaknesses in Piper Investment's and Castanea's portfolios and the 35 percent discount required to market their stock in private placements, we arrive at a per share value of $85.55 for Piper Investment and $176.80 for Castanea.[12]

---

[10]Ibid.

[11]Use of this and subsequent related studies to quantify appropriate discounts for lack of marketability are discussed in Chapter 10.

[12]Ibid., p. 595.

Note that the above text refers to the fact that "the gifts were of minority interests." This is appropriate, because multiple gifts typically are each viewed as a minority interest even though the total amount given constitutes a controlling interest. The valuation was on a minority-interest basis, because it was made by comparison with sales of closed-end investment companies on the open market, which sales are, in fact, sales of minority interests.

Treatment of Trapped-in Capital Gain

Taxpayer proposed a discount for potential capital gains tax at the corporate level because Piper Investment and Castanea had a basis of less than $1 per share in their PAC stock. As in the Gallun case, the court rejected this position.

In one sense, however, some relief was indirectly granted the taxpayer on that point—that is, the portfolio discount was based on ratios of market prices to net asset values for closed-end investment companies. In the literature analyzing why such companies tend to sell at discounts from net asset value fairly regularly, the existence of trapped-in capital gains is consistently cited as one of the reasons. Thus, by granting a discount through reliance on closed-end investment company discounts, some relief from trapped-in capital gains tax liability is reflected. In this case, of course, it was rather nominal, since the average trapped-in capital gain for the public closed-end companies would have been only a small fraction of the value of the portfolio compared with the large amount in the Piper case.

Harwood Case[13]

The main issues in the Harwood gift tax case were minority interest and marketability discounts. The entity is a limited partnership buying timber and timberlands and cutting contracts for sale of the timber to affiliated companies for processing.

The court ruled for a combined discount from net asset value of 50 percent to reflect combined minority interest and lack of marketability, the latter influenced by a restrictive agreement. The court recognized that lack of marketability was the basis for a discount beyond that for minority interest, even though in the final decision the discount was given as a lump amount.

In support of the concept of a discount from net asset value for minority interest, the court accepted evidence of forest products stocks and closed-end investment companies selling at discounts from net asset values. The court noted that minority interests could not control disposal of assets.

One taxpayer witness testified to a 25 percent marketability discount, but the exact nature of that testimony is unclear—he was refer-

---

[13]*Virginia Z. Harwood*, 82 T.C. 239 (1984).

ring primarily to the effect of the restrictive agreement. Another witness said the marketability discount could be between 20 and 50 percent and chose 35 percent. The court said, "He failed to adequately substantiate the discount he chose to apply." This leads me to believe that the combined discount would have been higher had the 35 percent marketability discount been adequately substantiated.

On the minority-interest discount, a taxpayer witness testified to a 60 percent discount based on forest products companies. An IRS witness testified to 30 percent based on the fact that "non-diversified" closed-end investment companies sold at an average discount of 26.4 percent. The court said, "Data relied on in reaching a proposed discount of 60 percent is unfortunately incomplete, and we do not believe that he adequately substantiated his suggested 60 percent discount." This leads me to believe that the minority-interest portion of the total discount also would have been higher with proper documentation.

Because the partnership was primarily an asset-holding company buying timber for processing by affiliated companies, the court rejected a capitalization of earnings approach and relied 100 percent on the adjusted net asset value as the base from which to discount for minority interest and lack of marketability.

Bright, Propstra, and Andrews Cases

These three estate tax cases are discussed together because they have a common central issue: whether or not a minority interest discount is applicable when the controlling interest is held by immediate family members.

Bright Case[14]

During her lifetime, Mrs. Bright and her husband owned 55 percent of the stock of each of several affiliated corporations as their community property under the laws of the State of Texas. The district court issued a pretrial order that "no element of control can be attributed to the decedent in determining the value of the decedent's interest in the stock for estate tax purposes. The parties are hereby ordered to proceed with preparation for trial and trial of this case on that basis."

A panel of the court of appeals vacated the district court's judgment and remanded, holding that the district court had erred in entering the pretrial order relating to the element of control. The estate's petition for rehearing *en banc* (with all judges sitting) was granted, and the panel opinion was vacated. The district court's original judgment was affirmed.

The government argued that the property to be valued was an undivided one-half interest in a 55 percent control block. However, under Texas law, either the surviving spouse or the estate could exer-

---

[14]*Estate of Bright* v. *United States*, 658 F.2d 999 (1981).

cise its right to partition the stock. Thus, the estate had no means to prevent the conversion of its shares into a 27½ percent block. Therefore, the court concluded that the estate's interest was the equivalent of a 27½ percent block of the stock.

The government also argued that the block should be valued on a control basis based on the doctrine of family attribution. The court cited many prior cases in its rejection of the application to an estate's stock in the valuation process for estate tax purposes.

Propstra Case[15]

The Propstra case involved an undivided one-half interest in several parcels of real estate owned by the decedent and his wife as community property. The district court held that the estate was entitled to a 15 percent discount on the undivided one-half interest.[16] The government appealed, arguing that one could reasonably assume that the interest held by the estate ultimately would be sold with the other undivided interest and that the interests' proportionate shares of the market value of the whole would thereby be realized.

The court of appeals upheld the district court, citing Bright, and stating:

> After considering the language of sections 2031 and 2033 of the Internal Revenue Code of 1954 (I.R.C) and their accompanying regulations, we are unwilling to impute to Congress an intent to have "unity of ownership" principles apply to property valuations for estate tax purposes.[17]

Andrews Case[18]

In the Andrews case, the decedent owned approximately 20 percent of the total outstanding shares of each of four corporations; the remainder was owned by his four siblings in approximately equal proportions. All four corporations were involved primarily in the ownership, operation, and management of commercial real estate properties, although they also held some liquid assets such as stocks, bonds, and cash.

Control versus Minority Valuation Basis.   The government, citing the then recently issued Revenue Ruling 81-253, took the position that there should be no minority interest discount because the rest of the stock was all in the family. Citing both *Bright* and *Propstra,* the court rejected that position. The court summed up the willing-buyer, willing-seller standard with a reference to Propstra:

---

[15]*Propstra* v. *United States,* 680 F.2d 1248 (1981).

[16]I don't know what evidence was presented to quantify the discount for a one-half undivided interest in real estate at 15 percent. Very little empirical research has been done on discounts on transfers of fractional undivided interests in real estate, and none has been published. However, my staff and I have done some empirical research on this subject and believe that the decision is reasonably consistent with our findings for one-half undivided interests in real estate.

[17]*Propstra,* p. 1251.

[18]*Estate of Woodbury G. Andrews,* 79 T.C. 938 (1982).

. . . [T]he court emphasized the advantage of using an objective hypothetical willing-buyer, willing-seller standard, instead of a subjective inquiry into the feelings, attitudes, and anticipated behavior of heirs and legatees, which might well be boundless.[19]

Weighting of Factors. Another issue in the Andrews case was the relative weighting of factors, primarily between asset values and income-related approaches such as capitalization of earnings and dividends. The government took the position that the companies were investment companies and, therefore, all the weight should be accorded to the adjusted net asset value approach. Taxpayer characterized the companies as operating companies, and experts for taxpayers placed all or almost all the weight on capitalization of earnings and dividends.

The court accepted neither characterization, noting:

. . . [T]he corporations here cannot be characterized for valuation purposes as solely investment companies or solely operating companies. . . . [T]he corporations involved here were actively engaged in the real estate management business. . . . [However,] unlike many industrial companies, where the value of the manufacturing equipment and plant is tied to the nature of the manufacturing operation, here the value of the underlying real estate will retain most of its inherent value even if the corporation is not efficient in securing a stream of rental income.[20]

I think it is instructive to read the court's statement to the effect that taking only a single approach would not be appropriate even if the company were properly characterized as clearly an investment or holding company:

Furthermore, regardless of whether the corporation is seen as primarily an operating company, as opposed to an investment company, courts should not restrict consideration to only one approach to valuation, such as capitalization of earnings or net asst values. . . . Certainly, the degree to which the corporation is actively engaged in producing income rather than merely holding property for investment should influence the weight to be given to the values arrived at under the different approaches but it should not dictate the use of one approach to the exclusion of all others.

The regulations call for all relevant factors to be examined and, in a case such as this, we believe values arrived at under all the accepted valuation methods should be considered.[21]

Distinction between Marketability and Minority Interest Discounts. Finally, the Andrews decision specifically stated that discounts for *both* minority interest and lack of marketability were applicable and presented the clearest statement I can recall reading in any case that conceptually these are two distinct discounts. (The court's statement on this point was presented in Chapter 2, "Principles of Business Valuation—Theory and Practice.")

---

[19]Ibid., p. 955.
[20]Ibid., p. 944.
[21]Ibid., p. 945.

Watts Case[22]

On the taxpayer's return, decedent's 15 percent partnership interest in Rosboro, a forest products partnership with timber and processing facilities, was valued at $2,550,000. After an audit, the commissioner of the Internal Revenue Service determined that the fair market value of decedent's interest in the partnership was $20,006,000.

In an opinion that was short and to the point (see the quote that opens this chapter), the U.S. Tax Court refused to compromise and chose the taxpayer's reported value as the correct value for estate taxes. The Internal Revenue Service appealed.

Going-Concern versus Liquidation Value

The IRS argued that the appropriate valuation method was the calculation of the liquidation value of the decedent's interest. The Tax Court held that since the business was a going concern and that all partners intended to continue it, the going-concern value was the appropriate means of valuation analysis.

Fair Market Value before Marketability Discount

Even on a going-concern basis, there was considerable difference between the value presented by the taxpayer's (petitioner's) experts and the value presented by the IRS (respondent's) expert. I think it is instructive to note the factors that the Tax Court considered in deciding which expert testimony to accept:

> We have carefully considered the reports of the experts, their testimony, and the lengthy briefs of the parties in which they have dissected the other parties' evidence in the greatest detail. We have considered the experience and background of the experts, their particular experience in the lumber and timber industry, the comparables which they have used, the extent to which they have investigated the subject company and the comparables, the assumptions that they have made regarding the future of the lumber business, appropriate capitalization rates, reasonable expected earnings, valuation of assets, and all of the other factors which each considered in arriving at this conclusion. No useful purpose would be served in regurgitating, summarizing, and synthesizing all of the reports. None of this would have any bearing on any future case, and no new methods have evolved which call for comment by the Court. We would merely be reinventing the appraisal wheel and applying it to Rosboro Lumber Company. Suffice it to say that after lengthy and careful consideration of the entire record, we have found that the evidence of value by petitioner is more convincing than that of respondent.[23]

---

[22]*Estate of Martha B. Watts,* 51 T.C.M. 60 (1985), appealed and affirmed, U.S. Court of Appeals, Eleventh Circuit, August 4, 1987.

[23]Ibid., pp. 62–63.

Discount for Lack of Marketability

Since the values testified to by experts on both sides were based on comparative publicly traded companies, all experts agreed that there should be a discount for lack of marketability. Taxpayer's two experts testified to 35 and 45 percent and the IRS's expert to 20 percent. The Tax Court applied a 35 percent discount for lack of marketability.

Appellate Decision

There were two primary issues on appeal. The first was whether or not the Tax Court decision that the going-concern value was appropriate. The second was whether or not, even on a going-concern basis, the Tax Court decision adequately reflected the value of the underlying assets.

Going-Concern versus Liquidation Value. The court noted that the argument for liquidation value rested on the notion that the interest transferred entitled its holder to liquidate the business, but that was not the case. The court pointed out that the interest that passed was, by the terms of the partnership agreement, an interest in an undissolved partnership. Therefore, the Tax Court was correct in determining that "the value of Mrs. Watts' interest in Rosboro could not be ascertained by reference to the value of that interest upon the lumber company's liquidation."[24]

Adequate Reflection of Underlying Asset Values. The court noted that the timber Rosboro held was an inventory asset, used in the company's operations and not an investment asset. Thus, the portion of Revenue Ruling 59-60 saying that assets "of the investment type should be revalued on the basis of their market price and the book value adjusted accordingly" doesn't apply. Furthermore, the court noted that the experts used price/book value and price/adjusted book value ratios (based on comparative public companies) as one valuation factor. Therefore, the court concluded that asset values were adequately reflected.

Comment

This is a case in which a great deal of empirical evidence on the values of comparative company interests carried the day. However, the evidence was presented *before* the studies on private transactions prior to initial public offerings (discussed in the latter part of Chapter 10, "Data on Discounts for Lack of Marketability") became available. Therefore, the evidence presented on the discount for lack of marketability was based entirely on restricted stock studies.

---

[24]Ibid., p. 3933 of appeal.

Gallo Case[25]

In the Gallo case, the U.S. Tax Court clearly came down on the taxpayer's side—in fact, finding a per-share value lower than the value the taxpayer originally submitted in the estate tax return.

The estate held common shares (representing a minority interest) in a holding company, which held stock primarily in the privately held company E & J Gallo Winery. The taxpayer reported the value of the stock held at $290 per share. The IRS valued the stock at $1,043 per share.

At trial, the estate presented three expert witnesses. The primary valuation expert for the estate testified that the per-share value was $237. This value was derived by using a price/earnings multiple based on comparative publicly traded companies' price/earnings ratios and then discounting by 36 percent to recognize the stock's lack of marketability.

The Tax Court held for a value of $237 per share, holding (in addition to other findings) the following:

1. Comparative publicly traded company stock values (and market multiples) should be considered in arriving at the value of the privately held stock.
2. Operating companies should be valued primarily on earnings even though other valuation approaches should be considered.
3. A company's size and market dominance do not necessarily mean that a lack of marketability discount should necessarily be less than normal.

This case generally confirms the U.S. Tax Court's past positions on what must be considered in valuing closely held securities. It is a well-written decision that provides insights into proper and improper analysis and procedures that valuation experts use.

Summary

This chapter has presented estate and gift tax decisions involving some of the most important valuation issues that frequently arise, such as weighting of factors, discounts for minority interest, and discounts for lack of marketability. We can draw several conclusions:

1. It is imperative to demonstrate that appropriate consideration has been given to all relevant factors.
2. It is essential to be thorough in the empirical research used to substantiate numbers that bear on the valuation conclusion. It is especially important to do a thorough search for and analysis of

---

[25]*Estate of Mark S. Gallo* v. *Commissioner,* 50 T.C.M. 470 (1985).

comparative companies used to develop market data such as price/ earnings and price/book value ratios.

3. Courts are more willing to make uncompromising decisions on one side or the other when the values are clearly supported by the evidence presented.

4. Courts now distinguish more clearly between discounts for minority interest and discounts for lack of marketability and are receptive to empirical evidence on the quantification of each, when appropriate.

Although there are literally hundreds of cases worthy of study by the serious practitioner, those discussed in this chapter give a flavor of the courts' positions on some of the most important and frequent valuation issues.

Chapter 23

Employee Stock Ownership Plans

Employee stock ownership is one of the fastest-growing trends in America. Legislators, at both the federal and state levels, see employee ownership as a way to make the economy more efficient, more competitive, and more equitable. Many see it as not only a way to improve the workplace but also a way to hold out to our geopolitical adversaries an economic model they may be willing to emulate.[1]

Introduction to ESOPs

The Employee Retirement Income Security Act of 1974 (ERISA) elevated employee stock ownership plans (ESOPs) to the status of statutorily defined employee pension benefit plans.[2] An *ESOP* is defined as a *qualified retirement plan designed to invest primarily in the employer's securities, thus providing a means for employees to have an ownership interest in the company for which they work.*

The Tax Reform Acts of 1984 and 1986 provided major new income and estate tax incentives that greatly enhanced the attractiveness of ESOPs. Propelled by these incentives, the formation of new ESOPs accelerated in the late 1980s. As of 1988, it was estimated that there were over 8,000 ESOP companies, with the number continuing to grow.

The primary benefits of ESOPs are:

1. They provide a means for employees to share in the ownership of the company.
2. They provide liquidity for stockholders and their beneficiaries.
3. They are a valuable vehicle for corporate financing.
   a. For raising new capital.
   b. For financing a leveraged buyout (for either the entire company or a partial interest).
4. They offer the company income tax advantages.
5. They provide for estate tax savings and deferrals.
6. They promote improved employee relations and productivity.

Basic Features of an ESOP[3]

An ESOP is a qualified employee benefit plan designed to invest primarily in employer securities. The regulations do not define *primarily*. While most ESOPs are invested entirely in the employer's securities,

---

[1]Jeffrey R. Gates, counsel to the U.S. Senate Finance Committee, quoted in *Employee Ownership Plans: How 8,000 Companies and 8,000,000 Employees Invest in Their Futures* (Washington, D.C.: Bureau of National Affairs, 1987), p. 92.

[2]As used in practice, there is no distinction between the terms *ESOP* (employee stock ownership plan) and *ESOT* (employee stock ownership trust). An ESOP is, by definition, a trusteed plan, a trust is necessarily involved. For the purpose of this book, we will use the term *ESOP.*

[3]This and subsequent sections of this chapter present only broad generalities with respect to legal and tax aspects of ESOPs. More detail on these matters is available in the references provided in the bibliography at the end of the chapter. See especially Jared Kaplan, Gregory K. Brown, and Ronald L. Ludwig, 453-3rd T.M. *ESOPs* (Washington, D.C.: Tax Management, Inc., 1987).

various interpretations have suggested that the plan might need to be invested only to 50 percent or more in such securities.

Eligible Employer Securities.   The eligible employer securities can be either common stock or preferred stock that is convertible into common stock. While most ESOPs today are invested in common stock, the Tax Reform Act of 1986 made convertible preferred stock more attractive, as we will discuss later.

Contributions in Cash and/or Stock.   The ESOP can be used either separately or with other employee benefit plans. As in other such plans, there must be a nondiscriminatory definition of the group of employees who will be eligible to participate, along with a minimum vesting schedule similar to those in other plans.

The contribution can be made in either cash or the employer securities; it can also be some combination of the two. If the contribution is made in cash, all or part of it may be used to purchase stock from existing shareholders or, in the case of a leveraged ESOP, to make payments on ESOP debt. Both the cash and stock contributions are a tax-deductible expense to the company. If the contribution is made in securities, the value of the securities as of the contribution date is the amount considered to be a tax-deductible expense.

As in other employee benefit plans, the company usually can contribute up to 15 percent of the eligible payroll to the ESOP plan as a tax-deductible expense. In some circumstances, the tax-deductible contribution can be as high as 25 percent of the eligible payroll.[4]

Voting Rights.   In closely held companies, the voting rights that accrue to ESOP shares normally are exercised by the ESOP trustees. Voting rights need be "passed through" to the ESOP beneficiaries only on matters that, by either law or corporate articles, require more than a majority stockholder vote. In public companies, voting rights are passed through to plan participants.

Required Put Option Creates Repurchase Liability

Distribution of Stock.   In general, unless the participant elects otherwise, an ESOP must distribute any vested shares of stock to an employee within one year after the end of the plan year during which the participant's retirement, death, or disability occurred or one year after the end of the fifth plan year following the participant's termination for any other reason.

Right of First Refusal.   ESOP shares can be subject to a right of first refusal in favor of the ESOP itself or of the issuing corporation,

---

[4]A detailed explanation of these circumstances is beyond the scope of this book. See especially Kaplan, Brown, and Ludwig, *ESOPs.*

but not in favor of another shareholder or third party. The right of first refusal must lapse no later than 14 days after the security holder has given notice of a third-party offer to purchase.

Put Option.   An ESOP participant who receives a distribution of stock in a closely held firm must be given an option to sell the stock to the employer firm. This requirement became effective with the 1984 tax act. Such put rights are good for some limited period of time, depending on the plan's wording. The employer firm may redeem the stock for cash, or the plan may allow payments over a period of up to five years with a reasonable interest rate.

Repurchase Liability.   This mandatory distribution of the vested stock, along with the attendant put option, obviously creates a repurchase liability on the company's part. The company's potential ability to meet that liability is an important aspect of the ESOP's feasibility. Note also that the diversification-of-investments feature discussed in a subsequent section also adds to the company's obligation to repurchase stock. The company's financial strength with respect to meeting its repurchase obligation may also bear on whether or not the value of shares sold or contributed to the ESOP should reflect a discount for lack of marketability, as discussed later in the chapter.

Funding Repurchase Liability with Insurance.   Contributions to the ESOP—but not loan proceeds it receives—may be used to purchase key-person life insurance. The general rules that apply to the ESOP's purchase of key-person life insurance are similar to those applicable to other qualified employee benefit plans.

The insurance proceeds normally may be used to purchase stock for the ESOP from the estate of a deceased shareholder. The shareholder's estate may be contractually bound to offer the securities to the ESOP. However, the ESOP may not be contractually bound to buy the securities.

Also, the life insurance industry has developed certain annuity-type products designed to fund repurchase of retired or terminated ESOP participants' shares.[5]

Diversification of Investments

The Tax Reform Act of 1986 introduced a requirement to allow ESOP participants who so desire an opportunity to diversify their investments as they approach retirement age. Any employee who has attained age 55 and completed 10 years of service may elect to diversify up to 25 percent of his or her account into investments other than employer securities. The amount diversified can be up to 50 percent after age 60.

---

[5]The bibliography at the end of this chapter lists articles on these types of annuities.

Since the participant normally would exercise the option to sell shares of stock back to the employer in order to obtain funds with which to satisfy the diversification requirement, this requirement in effect accelerates the company's repurchase liability to an earlier point in time to the extent that employees elect to exercise their option to diversify.

ESOP Tax Incentives

As a result of the 1984 and 1986 tax reform acts, extremely attractive incentives are available to both companies and selling stockholders in connection with ESOPs. The primary tax incentives are the following (these points are discussed in more detail below):

1. Contributions are a tax-deductible expense to the company whether made in cash or in stock.
2. Selling stockholders can "roll over" proceeds of sales of stock to the ESOP tax free, deferring tax on the gain until the securities purchased with the proceeds ultimately are sold.
3. Estates can exclude 50 percent of the value of stock sold to the ESOP from the taxable estate.
4. Estates can have estate taxes paid by the company buying the stock on extended terms and at low interest rates.
5. Dividends paid on ESOP stock can be tax deductible to the paying company.
6. Lenders recognize only half the interest received on an ESOP loan as taxable income, which normally results in below-market interest loans to ESOPs.

Contributions to Plan Are Tax Deductible

Contributions to an ESOP are a tax-deductible expense to the company whether made in cash or in stock. Cash contributions can be used to buy stock from existing stockholders or, in the case of a leveraged ESOP, to make payments on ESOP debt. In the latter case, the effect is that the principal repayments, as well as the interest, become tax-deductible expenses to the company. If the contribution to the ESOP is made in stock (either treasury stock or authorized but unissued shares), there is some dilution to the existing stockholders but the effect on cash flow generally is positive. As the ESOP contribution is a deduction from taxable income, it thus results in a potentially lower tax bill with no cash outlay.

The contribution normally can be 15 percent of eligible payroll, but in some cases it may be 25 percent.[6]

---

[6]See Kaplan, Brown, and Ludwig, *ESOPs.*

Tax-Free Rollover on Sale of Stock to ESOP

A shareholder selling stock to an ESOP can reinvest the proceeds on a tax-free rollover if the ESOP owns at least 30 percent of the company's stock immediately after the sale. In order to qualify for the tax-free rollover, the shareholder must invest the proceeds in stock, debt, or options of one or more domestic operating corporations within a 15-month period beginning 3 months before the date of sale. Further, notice of the election must be filed on the appropriate form during the taxable year of the sale.

As long as the ESOP maintains 30 percent of the outstanding stock, additional sales of stock to the ESOP in any amounts are eligible for the tax-free rollover treatment.

Estates Exclude Half of Proceeds from Sale of Stock to ESOP

The Tax Reform Act of 1986 permits a deduction from the value of a decedent's gross estate of 50 percent of the proceeds of a sale by the executor of employer securities to an ESOP. The sale must be made before the due date for filing the estate tax return, including extensions. Also, the decedent must have owned the employer securities prior to death. There are still other requirements. Under the legislation as of this writing, this opportunity is scheduled to expire December 31, 1991.

Payment of Estate Taxes by ESOP on Extended Terms

Estates eligible for deferral of estate taxes under section 6166 of the Internal Revenue Code may transfer the estate tax liability to the ESOP to the extent of the value of employer securities sold to the ESOP.[7] The plan administrator and the employer must consent to the plan's payment of the tax, guaranteed by the employer.

There is an initial period during which payment of estate taxes may be deferred completely, followed by payments in 10 equal annual installments. A special interest rate of 4 percent applies to estate taxes on the first $1 million worth of stock in a closely held business; on the balance the interest rate set forth by the IRS is tied to the bank prime rate.

Dividends Tax Deductible to Company

Dividends Paid to Participants. Dividends paid on stock held by an ESOP are a tax-deductible expense to the corporation if they are paid directly to the plan participants or if paid to the ESOP and dis-

---

[7]For a complete discussion of section 6166, see Jane C. Bergner, "ESOPs and Other New Applications of Section 6166," *Estates, Gifts and Trusts Journal*, July–August 1985, pp. 111–24.

tributed to the participants or their beneficiaries no later than 90 days after the close of the plan year.

Dividends Used for Debt Service.   Dividends are also a deductible expense if they are used to make payments of principal and/or interest on a loan to the ESOP that was used to acquire ESOP stock. This, of course, greatly enhances the flexibility of leveraged ESOPs, since such tax-deductible dividends can be paid above and beyond the maximum contributions allowed on the basis of a percentage of eligible payroll. Also, the ability to use tax-deductible dividends to service ESOP debt enhances the attractiveness of using convertible preferred stock, which normally would carry a higher dividend rate than common stock, instead of common stock as the equity security in the ESOP.

ESOP Loan Interest Excluded from Taxes

Commercial lenders, such as banks, insurance companies, and regulated investment companies, may exclude from their taxable income 50 percent of the interest they receive on ESOP loans. Such loans may be made either directly to the ESOP or to the employer company, which in turn lends the loan proceeds to the ESOP.

As a result, many institutions are actively seeking ESOP loan business, and ESOP loans are available as a tool for either leveraged buyouts or raising capital for the company at rates below those it otherwise would have to pay for debt financing.

Leveraged ESOPs

A leveraged ESOP can be used to buy out an entire company or any portion of the total equity ownership of a company. A leveraged ESOP also can be used to raise capital for repayment of existing corporate debt, for expansion, or other corporate purposes.

The Basic Leveraged ESOP Transaction

The essence of the basic leveraged ESOP transaction is that the ESOP borrows money to buy employer securities, from a selling stockholder or stockholders and/or from the company. The company guarantees the loan, because the only collateral the ESOP is allowed to provide, even if it had anything else, is the employer securities.[8] The employer then makes annual cash contributions to the ESOP in an amount sufficient to amortize the loan. Normally, a vesting schedule is set up so that stock is allocated to employee accounts on approximately the same schedule by which the loan is amortized, and the securities pledged as collateral are released.

---

[8]Alternatively, the employer can borrow the money and lend it to the ESOP, but the substance of the transaction is the same.

The cash contributions to be used to amortize the loan may be based on the applicable percentage of eligible payroll, as discussed earlier. Provisions of the Tax Reform Act of 1986 enable the company to supplement the percentage of payroll contributions through dividends paid on the stock the ESOP holds in order to provide enough cash to amortize the loan. Both the contributions and the dividends are treated as expenses deductible from the corporation's taxable income.

A Leveraged ESOP Buyout Example

Adams Manufacturing Company has two 50% stockholders: the estate of Mr. Adams, who died two months ago, and Mr. Baker, who wishes to retire and diversify his investments. A committee of employees has been formed to consider a buyout of the entire company, possibly through an ESOP. The company has funded the committee's retention of an attorney, an administrative adviser, and a financial adviser, all well qualified and experienced in ESOP leveraged buyouts.

The financial adviser has given the committee a preliminary opinion that the value of the company's equity is between $11 million and $12 million. Based on the assumption that they would gain the estate tax and tax-free rollover advantages of a sale to an ESOP, both Mr. Adams' executor and Mr. Baker have agreed to sell on the basis of $11 million. The Adams estate would get $4.95 million cash and the assumption by the company of $550,000 of estate tax liability, and Mr. Baker would receive $5.5 million in cash.

In the meantime, a lender has made a tentative commitment for $10 million financing on a seven-year net level payment amortization schedule. Also, a group of key successor managers will buy the remaining $450,000 of the Adams estate stock. A summary of the salient facts follows:

Annual revenues	$20 million
Earning power before interest and taxes (EBIT)	$ 3 million
Payroll eligible for ESOP	$ 6 million
Combined federal and state income tax rate	40%
Loan interest rate without ESOP	10%
Loan interest rate with ESOP	8.5%

The first part of Exhibit 23–1 shows the first-year income statement assuming conventional financing and assuming financing through an ESOP. The second part shows the loan amortization schedule and the after-tax cost to the company of servicing the loan (1) assuming conventional financing and (2) assuming financing through an ESOP.

The committee's administrative adviser has analyzed the potential cash requirements of the liability to repurchase stock of ESOP participants under the mandatory put option triggered by retirements and participants' elections to diversify investments after age 55. It has been determined that the $628,000 cash available annually after debt service should be adequate to cover both the repurchase liability and the estate tax payments on the Adams estate.

EXHIBIT 23-1   **Conventional versus ESOP Financing
for Buyout of Adam Manufacturing Company**

First-Year Income Statements

Conventionally Financed Company		Leveraged ESOP Company	
Sales	20,000	Sales	20,000
Cost of sales	17,000	Cost of sales	17,000
Operating profit	3,000	Operating profit	3,000
Interest	1,000	ESOP contribution	1,954
Taxable income	2,000	Taxable income	1,046
Income taxes	800	Income taxes	418
Net income	1,200	Net income	628
Cash available after debt service	146	Cash available after debt service	628

Schedule of Loan Amortization

	Conventionally Financed Company					Leveraged ESOP Company				
Year	Total Payment	Principal	Interest	Value of Deductions	After-Tax Cost	Total Payment	Principal	Interest	Value of Deductions	After-Tax Cost
1	2054	1054	1000	400	1654	1954	1104	850	782	1172
2	2054	1159	895	358	1696	1954	1197	757	782	1172
3	2054	1275	779	311	1743	1954	1299	655	782	1172
4	2054	1403	651	260	1794	1954	1410	544	782	1172
5	2054	1543	511	204	1850	1954	1529	425	782	1172
6	2054	1698	356	143	1911	1954	1660	294	782	1172
7	2054	1868	186	75	1979	1954	1801	153	782	1172
Total	14378	10000	4378	1751	12627	13678	10000	3678	5474	8204

Assumptions:
1. $10 million loan amortized over seven years with net level payments
2. 10 percent interest rate with conventional financing
3. 8.5 percent interest rate on ESOP loan
4. 40 percent combined federal and state income tax rate
5. Amortization of the estate tax payments under IRC Section 6166 not shown

It has also been determined that the company could make tax-deductible contributions of up to 25 percent of the eligible payroll. That would amount to $1.5 million annually on the basis of a $6 million payroll—not enough to cover the $1,954,000 annual debt service. However, a modest annual tax-deductible dividend of between 4.5 and 5 percent of the stock's value will serve handily to make the full amount of the debt service, including the estate tax installments, tax deductible.

The deal has been made, and everybody has sent letters to their senators and representatives applauding their support of the incentives that made employee ownership a reality for Adams Manufacturing Company.

An analysis of the comparison between the conventional and ESOP financing reveals that the use of the ESOP provided the following benefits:

1. Mr. Baker got a tax-free rollover by selling his stock to the ESOP and reinvesting the proceeds in a diversified portfolio.
2. The Adams estate excluded $2.75 million (50 percent of the $5.5 million sale price of its stock) from the taxable estate.
3. By assuming $550,000 of estate tax liability, the company was able to finance $550,000 of the purchase price with no principal pay-

ments for a five-year period and the balance over nine years at a very attractive interest rate of 4 percent.

4. Because the lending institution could exclude 50 percent of the interest it received on the ESOP loan from its taxable income, the company got the loan at an 8.5 rather than 10 percent interest rate, resulting in a $100,000-per-year saving in annual debt service (principal and interest).

5. Because the contributions to the ESOP are tax deductible, both principal and interest on the loan payment are paid with pretax dollars.

6. Although the applicable percentage of payroll was not enough to cover the entire debt service, the company was able to pay tax-deductible dividends to the ESOP; thus, the *entire* principal and interest amount became tax deductible.

7. The employees were able to purchase the company at the bottom end of the range of appraisal values.

In this case, the ESOP not only facilitated the transaction; it made it feasible for the employee purchase. As is typical in such cases, financing of the transaction without the ESOP would have been extremely difficult to accomplish.

Multi-Investor Leveraged ESOPs

Often, companies using ESOPs for leveraged buyouts must structure several classes of securities in order to attract and satisfy all the desired participants. These participants typically include the party or parties supplying the bulk of the financing, a management group, and the ESOP.

Within the limitations of a fair allocation of the total value among the classes and ERISA regulations regarding the employee securities eligible for an ESOP, the structure of such classes of securities is bounded only by the imaginations of the parties involved in the ESOP, the company, other participants, and their respective financial advisers. Permissible securities can include one or more classes of common stock, straight and/or convertible debt or preferred stock, stock options, and various innovative junior securities. Voting rights may be assigned to the various classes in an almost limitless variety of configurations. In some cases, the amounts of certain securities allocated to a class of parties at interest and/or those securities' features may be a function of certain company performance measures over a given period.

Various chapters of this book address the valuation of classes of securities other than common stock, including debt securities (Chapter 16), preferred stock (Chapter 17), and options (Chapter 18). A convertible debt or preferred security is, in essence, a combination of a straight debt or preferred stock and an option. In many cases, it is impossible to find convertible securities in the public market that are comparable in characteristics to the convertible securities created for use in leveraged buyouts. Therefore, for valuation purposes, it may be useful to break down the convertibles into their components—straight debt or preferred stock plus an option—and value each component with the benefit of the guidance offered in the respective chapters.

Criteria for Establishing an ESOP

An ESOP can provide significant tax, liquidity, and other advantages for a company and its stockholders, as discussed in previous sections. However, I believe that these advantages are not compelling enough to establish an ESOP unless the company's stockholders have a genuine desire to have broad ownership of the company's securities by employees, since the "eligibility-to-participate" criterion must be nondiscriminatory.

If there is a genuine desire for employee ownership, the decision criteria turn toward weighing the costs versus the benefits. The primary costs are legal, administrative, and valuation. Most of the legal cost is in establishing the plan and can run anywhere from a few thousand dollars for a small, simple plan up to six figures for a large, complicated ESOP.

The administrative costs involve initial and ongoing recordkeeping duties to determine which employees are eligible to participate and to what extent, as well as to compute vested and forfeited interests and schedules of payments to those who have tendered stock to the company. These costs are similar to those in other employee benefit plans—probably in the low four figures per year for typical $1-million-to-$10-million-net-worth companies with 10 to 100 participants. The analysis of the repurchase liability may be done by the firm providing ESOP administrative services or by a company specializing in ESOP repurchase liability analysis.

If a leveraged ESOP is contemplated, typically an ESOP investment banker would be retained to arrange for the financing and be compensated based on performance.

Many practitioners suggest that a company should have at least $500,000 in eligible payroll to make the ESOP worthwhile, although many ESOPs have been established with less. It has also been suggested that a company must be reasonably well established, since the potential for employee disappointment or even total company failure certainly is greater with start-up companies.

Special Issues in Valuing ESOP Stock

In general, the valuation of ESOP stock must satisfy two government agencies: the IRS and the DOL. The IRS adheres to the standard of fair market value and the valuation guidelines of Revenue Ruling 59-60, shown in full in Exhibit 19–2 and discussed in Chapter 19, "Estate

Planning and Tax Valuations." As this book goes to press, the DOL has published a proposed regulation for guidance in valuing ESOP stock. The proposed DOL regulation is shown as Exhibit 23–2. Readers should obtain a copy of the final regulation, which is likely to contain some changes from the original proposed draft. The DOL valuation guidelines (Exhibit 23–2) embrace the standard of fair market value and the criteria set forth in Revenue Ruling 59-60. In addition, the DOL guidelines address certain issues peculiar to the value of ESOP stock and prescribe specific minimum content for inclusion in the valuation's written documentation.

There have been eight judicial decisions regarding ESOP valuation issues, all since the first edition of this book. The following chapter discusses the valuation issues addressed in each of those eight court decisions.

The following brief discussions of special considerations and controversies involved in the valuation of ESOP shares are based on my own reasoning, the considerable experience of my associates and myself in valuing and presenting expert testimony on the value of ESOP shares, a thorough study of the existing literature and court cases on ESOP stock valuation, and extensive discussions with ESOP valuation practitioners, especially my colleagues on the ESOP Association Valuation Advisory Committee. It is important to recognize that despite the judicial decisions to date, guidelines such as the new DOL regulation, and concerted efforts by responsible ESOP valuation practitioners, controversies regarding certain ESOP stock valuation issues are being resolved or narrowed only gradually. The following discussion attempts to address these issues objectively and clearly label my own opinions as such where they are offered.

Requirement of Independent Annual Stock Appraisal

The Tax Reform Act of 1986 made it mandatory that ESOP stock be appraised annually by a qualified, independent appraiser. A form stating the appraised value, signed by the independent appraiser, must be filed with the IRS.

The proposed Department of Labor (DOL) regulation providing guidelines as to what constitutes "adequate consideration" says that in order for fiduciaries to meet the requirement of determining fair market value in good faith, the valuation must be done by someone who is independent of all parties to the transaction. The DOL also requires a written valuation report and specifies minimum content. The relevant proposed DOL regulation is shown in full in Exhibit 23–2, and discussed further in the next section.

An appraisal is required:

1. When the ESOP makes its first acquisition of stock.
2. At least annually thereafter (some companies routinely have their stock appraisals updated semiannually or quarterly).

EXHIBIT 23-2

Tuesday
May 17, 1988

Part VI

Department of Labor

Pension and Welfare Benefits
Administration

29 CFR Part 2510
Regulation Relating to the Definition of
Adequate Consideration; Notice of
Proposed Rulemaking

17632 Federal Register / Vol. 53, No. 95 / Tuesday, May 17, 1988 / Proposed Rules

DEPARTMENT OF LABOR

Pension and Welfare Benefits Administration

29 CFR Part 2510

Proposed Regulation Relating to the Definition of Adequate Consideration

AGENCY: Pension and Welfare Benefits Administration, Department of Labor.

ACTION: Notice of proposed rulemaking.

SUMMARY: This document contains a notice of a proposed regulation under the Employee Retirement Income Security Act of 1974 (the Act or ERISA) and the Federal Employees' Retirement System Act of 1986 (FERSA). The proposal clarifies the definition of the term "adequate consideration" provided in section 3(18)(B) of the Act and section 8477(a)(2)(B) of FERSA for assets other than securities for which there is a generally recognized market. Section 3(18)(B) and section 8477(a)(2)(B) provide that the term "adequate consideration" for such assets means the fair market value of the asset as determined in good faith by the trustee or named fiduciary (or, in the case of FERSA, a fiduciary) pursuant to the terms of the plan and in accordance with regulations promulgated by the Secretary of Labor. Because valuation questions of this nature arise in a variety of contexts, the Department is proposing this regulation in order to provide the certainty necessary for plan fiduciaries to fulfill their statutory duties. If adopted, the regulation would affect plans investing in assets other than securities for which there is a generally recognized market.

DATES: Written comments on the proposed regulation must be received by July 18, 1988. If adopted, the regulation will be effective for transactions taking place after the date 30 days following publication of the regulation in final form.

ADDRESS: Written comments on the proposed regulation (preferably three copies) should be submitted to: Office of Regulations and Interpretations, Pension and Welfare Benefits Administration, Room N–5671, U.S. Department of Labor, 200 Constitution Avenue NW., Washington, DC 20216, Attention: Adequate Consideration Proposal. All written comments will be available for public inspection at the Public Disclosure Room, Pension and Welfare Benefits Administration, U.S. Department of Labor, Room N–5507, 200 Constitution Avenue NW., Washington, DC.

FOR FURTHER INFORMATION CONTACT: Daniel J. Maguire, Esq., Plan Benefits Security Division, Office of the Solicitor, U.S. Department of Labor, Washington, DC 20210, (202) 523–9596 (not a toll-free number) or Mark A. Greenstein, Office of Regulations and Interpretations, Pension and Welfare Benefits Administration, (202) 523–7901 (not a toll-free number).

SUPPLEMENTARY INFORMATION:

A. Background

Notice is hereby given of a proposed regulation under section 3(18)(B) of the Act and section 8477(a)(2)(B) of FERSA. Section 3(18) of the Act provides the definition for the term "adequate consideration," and states:

The term "adequate consideration" when used in part 4 of subtitle B means (A) in the case of a security for which there is a generally recognized market, either (i) the price of the security prevailing on a national securities exchange which is registered under section 6 of the Securities Exchange Act of 1934, or (ii) if the security is not traded on such a national securities exchange, a price not less favorable to the plan than the offering price for the security as established by the current bid and asked prices quoted by persons independent of the issuer and of any party in interest; and (B) in the case of an asset other than a security for which there is a generally recognized market, the fair market value of the asset as determined in good faith by the trustee or named fiduciary pursuant to the terms of the plan and in accordance with regulations promulgated by the Secretary.

The term "adequate consideration" appears four times in part 4 of subtitle B of Title I of the Act, and each time represents a central requirement for a statutory exemption from the prohibited transaction restrictions of the Act. Under section 408(b)(5), a plan may purchase insurance contracts from certain parties in interest if, among other conditions, the plan pays no more than adequate consideration. Section 408(b)(7) provides that the prohibited transaction provisions of section 406 shall not apply to the exercise of a privilege to convert securities, to the extent provided in regulations of the Secretary of Labor, only if the plan receives no less than adequate consideration pursuant to such conversion. Section 408(e) of the Act provides that the prohibitions in sections 406 and 407(a) of the Act shall not apply to the acquisition or sale by a plan of qualifying employer securities, or the acquisition, sale or lease by a plan of qualifying employer real property if, among other conditions, the acquisition, sale or lease is for adequate consideration. Section 414(c)(5) of the Act states that sections 406 and 407(a)

of the Act shall not apply to the sale, exchange, or other disposition of property which is owned by a plan on June 30, 1974, and all times thereafter, to a party in interest, if such plan is required to dispose of the property in order to comply with the provisions of section 407(a) (relating to the prohibition against holding excess employer securities and employer real property), and if the plan receives not less than adequate consideration.

Public utilization of these statutory exemptions requires a determination of "adequate consideration" in accordance with the definition contained in section 3(18) of the Act. Guidance is especially important in this area because many of the transactions covered by these statutory exemptions involve plan dealings with the plan sponsor. A fiduciary's determination of the adequacy of consideration paid under such circumstances represents a major safeguard for plans against the potential for abuse inherent in such transactions.

The Federal Employees' Retirement System Act of 1986 (FERSA) established the Federal Retirement Thrift Investment Board whose members act as fiduciaries with regard to the assets of the Thrift Savings Fund. In general, FERSA contains fiduciary obligation and prohibited transaction provisions similar to ERISA. However, unlike ERISA, FERSA prohibits party in interest transactions similar to those described in section 406(a) of ERISA only in those circumstances where adequate consideration is not exchanged between the Fund and the party in interest. Specifically, section 8477(c)(1) of FERSA provides that, except in exchange for adequate consideration, a fiduciary shall not permit the Thrift Savings Fund to engage in: transfers of its assets to, acquisition of property from or sales of property to, or transfers or exchanges of services with any person the fiduciary knows or should know to be a party in interest. Section 8477(a)(2) provides the FERSA definition for the term "adequate consideration" which is virtually identical to that contained in section 3(18) of ERISA. Thus, the proposal would apply to both section 3(18) of ERISA and section 8477(a)(2) of FERSA.

When the asset being valued is a security for which there is a generally recognized market, the plan fiduciary must determine "adequate consideration" by reference to the provisions of section 3(18)(A) of the Act (or with regard to FERSA, section 8477(a)(2)(A)). Section 3(18)(A) and section 8477(a)(2)(A) provide detailed reference points for the valuation of securities within its coverage, and in effect provides that adequate consideration for such securities is the prevailing market price. It is not the Department's intention to analyze the requirements of section 3(18)(A) or 8477(a)(2)(A) in this proposal. Fiduciaries must, however, determine whether a security is subject to the specific provisions of section 3(18)(A) (or section 8477(a)(2)(A) of FERSA) or the more general requirements of section 3(18)(B) (or section 8477(a)(2)(B)) as interpreted in this proposal. The question of whether a security is one for which there is a generally recognized market requires a factual determination in light of the character of the security and the nature and extent of market activity with regard to the security. Generally, the Department will examine whether a security is being actively traded so as to provide the benchmarks Congress intended. Isolated trading activity, or trades between related parties, generally will not be sufficient to show the existence of a generally recognized market for the purposes of section 3(18)(A) or section 8477(a)(2)(A).

In the case of all assets other than securities for which there is a generally recognized market, fiduciaries must determine adequate consideration pursuant to section 3(18)(B) of the Act (or, in the case of FERSA, section 8477(a)(2)(B)). Because it is designed to deal with all but a narrow class of assets, section 3(18)(B) and section 8477(a)(2)(B) are by their nature more general than section 3(18)(A) or section 8477(a)(2)(A). Although the Department has indicated that it will not issue advisory opinions stating whether certain stated consideration is "adequate consideration" for the purposes of section 3(18), ERISA Procedure 76–1, § 5.02(a) (41 FR 36281, 36282, August 27, 1976), the Department recognizes that plan fiduciaries have a need for guidance in valuing assets, and that standards to guide fiduciaries in this area may be particularly elusive with respect to assets other than securities for which there is a generally recognized market. *See*, for example, *Donovan v. Cunningham*, 716 F.2d 1455 (5th Cir. 1983) (court encourages the Department to adopt regulations under section 3(18)(B)). The Department has therefore determined to propose a regulation only under section 3(18)(B) and section 8477(a)(2)(B). This proposal is described more fully below.

It should be noted that it is not the Department's intention by this proposed regulation to relieve fiduciaries of the responsibility for making the required determinations of "adequate

consideration" where applicable under the Act or FERSA. Nothing in the proposal should be construed as justifying a fiduciary's failure to take into account all relevant facts and circumstances in determining adequate consideration. Rather, the proposal is designed to provide a framework within which fiduciaries can fulfill their statutory duties. Further, fiduciaries should be aware that, even where a determination of adequate consideration comports with the requirements of section 3(18)(B) (or section 8477(a)(2)(B) of FERSA) and any regulation adopted thereunder, the investment of plan assets made pursuant to such determination will still be subject to the fiduciary requirements of Part 4 of Subtitle B of Title I of the Act, including the provisions of sections 403 and 404 of the Act, or the fiduciary responsibility provisions of FERSA.

B. Description of the Proposal

Proposed regulation 29 CFR 2510.3–18(b) is divided into four major parts. Proposed § 2510.3–18(b)(1) states the general rule and delineates the scope of the regulation. Proposed § 2510.3–18(b)(2) addresses the concept of fair market value as it relates to a determination of "adequate consideration" under section 3(18)(B) of the Act. Proposed § 2510.3–18(b)(3) deals with the requirement in section 3(18)(B) that valuing fiduciary act in good faith, and specifically discusses the use of an independent appraisal in connection with the determination of good faith. Proposed § 2510.3–18(b)(4) sets forth the content requirements for written valuations used as the basis for a determination of fair market value, with a special rule for the valuation of securities other than securities for which there is a generally recognized market. Each subsection is discussed in detail below.

1. General Rule and Scope.

Proposed § 2510.3–18(b)(1)(i) essentially follows the language of section 3(18)(B) of the Act and section 8477(a)(2)(B) of FERSA and states that, in the case of a plan asset other than a security for which there is a generally recognized market, the term "adequate consideration" means the fair market value of the asset as determined in good faith by the trustee or named fiduciary (or, in the case of FERSA, a fiduciary) pursuant to the terms of the plan and in accordance with regulations promulgated by the Secretary of Labor. Proposed § 2510.3–18(b)(1)(ii) delineates the scope of this regulation by establishing two criteria, both of which must be met for a valid determination of

adequate consideration. First, the value assigned to an asset must reflect its fair market value as determined pursuant to proposed § 2510.3–18(b)(2). Second, the value assigned to an asset must be the product of a determination made by the fiduciary in good faith as defined in proposed § 2510.3–18(b)(3). The Department will consider that a fiduciary has determined adequate consideration in accordance with section 3(18)(B) of the Act or section 8477(a)(2)(B) of FERSA only if both of these requirements are satisfied.

The Department has proposed this two part test for several reasons. First, Congress incorporated the concept of fair market value into the definition of adequate consideration. As explained more fully below, fair market value is an often used concept having an established meaning in the field of asset valuation. By reference to this term, it would appear that Congress did not intend to allow parties to a transaction to set an arbitrary value for the assets involved. Therefore, a valuation determination which fails to reflect the market forces embodied in the concept of fair market value would also fail to meet the requirements of section 3(18)(B) of the Act or section 8477(a)(2)(B) of FERSA.

Second, it would appear that Congress intended to allow a fiduciary a limited degree of latitude so long as that fiduciary acted in good faith. However, a fiduciary would clearly fail to fulfill the fiduciary duties delineated in Part 4 of Subtitle B of Title I of the Act if that fiduciary acted solely on the basis of naive or uninformed good intentions. *See Donovan v. Cunningham, supra*, 716 F.2d at 1467 ("[A] pure heart and an empty head are not enough.") The Department has therefore proposed standards for a determination of a fiduciary's good faith which must be satisfied in order to meet the requirements of section 3(18)(B) or section 8477(a)(2)(B) of FERSA.

Third, even if a fiduciary were to meet the good faith standards contained in this proposed regulation, there may be circumstances in which good faith alone fails to insure an equitable result. For example, errors in calculation or honest failure to consider certain information could produce valuation figures outside of the range of acceptable valuations of a given asset. Because the determination of adequate consideration is a central requirement of the statutory exemptions discussed above, the Department believes it must assure that such exemptions are made available only for those transactions possessing all the external safeguards envisioned by

Congress. To achieve this end, the Department's proposed regulation links the fair market value and good faith requirements to assure that the resulting valuation reflects market considerations and is the product of a valuation process conducted in good faith.

2. Fair Market Value

The first part of the Department's proposed two part test under section 3(18)(B) and section 8477(a)(2)(B) requires that a determination of adequate consideration reflect the asset's fair market value. The term "fair market value" is defined in proposed § 2510.3–18(b)(2)(i) as the price at which an asset would change hands between a willing buyer and a willing seller when the former is not under any compulsion to buy and the latter is not under any compulsion to sell, and both parties are able, as well as willing, to trade and are well-informed about the asset and the market for that asset. This proposed definition essentially reflects the well-established meaning of this term in the area of asset valuation. *See,* for example, 26 CFR 20.2031–1 (estate tax regulations); Rev. Rul. 59–60, 1959–1 Cum. Bull. 237; *United States v. Cartwright,* 411 U.S. 546, 551 (1973); *Estate of Bright v. United States,* 658 F.2d 999, 1005 (5th Cir. 1981). It should specifically be noted that comparable valuations reflecting transactions resulting from other than free and equal negotiations (*e.g.,* a distress sale) will fail to establish fair market value. *See Hooker Industries, Inc. v. Commissioner,* 3 EBC 1849, 1854–55 (T.C. June 24, 1982). Similarly, the extent to which the Department will view a valuation as reflecting fair market value will be affected by an assessment of the level of expertise demonstrated by the parties making the valuation. *See Donovan v. Cunningham, supra,* 716 F.2d at 1468 (failure to apply sound business principles of evaluation, for whatever reason, may result in a valuation that does not reflect fair market value).[1]

The Department is aware that the fair market value of an asset will ordinarily be identified by a range of valuations rather than a specific, set figure. It is not the Department's intention that only one valuation figure will be acceptable as the fair market value of a specified asset. Rather, this proposal would require that the valuation assigned to an asset must reflect a figure within an acceptable range of valuations for that asset.

In addition to this general formulation of the definition of fair market value, the Department is proposing two specific requirements for the determination of fair market value for the purposes of section 3(18)(B) and section 8477(a)(2)(B). First, proposed § 2510.3–18(b)(2)(ii) requires that fair market value must be determined as of the date of the transaction involving that asset. This requirement is designed to prevent situations such as arose in *Donovan v. Cunningham, supra.* In that case, the plan fiduciaries relied on a 1975 appraisal to set the value of employer securities purchased by an ESOP during 1976 and thereafter, and failed to take into account significant changes in the company's business condition in the interim. The court found that this reliance was unwarranted, and therefore the fiduciaries' valuation failed to reflect adequate consideration under section 3(18)(B). *Id.* at 1468–69.

Second, proposed § 2510.3–18(b)(2)(iii) states that the determination of fair market value must be reflected in written documentation of valuation[2] meeting the content requirements set forth in § 2510.3–18(b)(4). (The valuation content requirements are discussed below.) The Department has proposed this requirement in light of the role the adequate consideration requirement plays in a number of statutory exemptions from the prohibited transaction provisions of the Act. In determining whether a statutory exemption applies to a particular transaction, the burden of proof is upon the party seeking to make use of the statutory exemption to show that all the requirements of the provision are met. *Donovan v. Cunningham, supra,* 716 F.2d

at 1467 n.27. In the Department's view, written documentation relating to the valuation is necessary for a determination of how, and on what basis, an asset was valued, and therefore whether that valuation reflected an asset's fair market value. In addition, the Department believes that it would be contrary to prudent business practices for a fiduciary to act in the absence of such written documentation of fair market value.

3. Good Faith

The second part of the Department's proposed two-part test under section 3(18)(B) and section 8477(a)(2)(B) requires that an assessment of adequate consideration be the product of a determination made in good faith by the plan trustee or named fiduciary (or under FERSA, a fiduciary). Proposed § 2510.3–18(b)(3)(i) states that as a general matter this good faith requirement establishes an objective standard of conduct, rather than mandating an inquiry into the intent or state of mind of the plan trustee or named fiduciary. In this regard, the proposal is consistent with the opinion in *Donovan v. Cunningham, supra,* where the court stated that the good faith requirement in section 3(18)(B):

is not a search for subjective good faith * * * The statutory reference to good faith in Section 3(18) must be read in light of the overriding duties of Section 404.

716 F.2d at 1467. The inquiry into good faith under the proposal therefore focuses on the fiduciary's conduct in determining fair market value. An examination of all relevant facts and circumstances is necessary for a determination of whether a fiduciary has met this objective good faith standard.

Proposed § 2510.3–18(b)(3)(ii) focuses on two factors which must be present in order for the Department to be satisfied that the fiduciary has acted in good faith. First, this section would require a fiduciary to apply sound business principles of evaluation and to conduct a prudent investigation of the circumstances prevailing at the time of the valuation. This requirement reflects the *Cunningham* court's emphasis on the use of prudent business practices in valuing plan assets.

Second, this section states that either the fiduciary making the valuation must itself be independent of all the parties to the transaction (other than the plan), or the fiduciary must rely on the report of an appraiser who is independent of all the parties to the transaction (other than the plan). (The criteria for determining

---

[1] Whether in any particular transaction a plan fiduciary is in fact well-informed about the asset in question and the market for that asset, including any specific circumstances which may affect the value of the asset, will be determined on a facts and circumstances basis. If, however, the fiduciary negotiating on behalf of the plan has or should have specific knowledge concerning either the particular asset or the market for that asset, it is the view of the Department that the fiduciary must take into account that specific knowledge in negotiating the price of the asset in order to meet the fair market value standard of this regulation. For example, a sale of plan-owned real estate at a negotiated price consistent with valuations of comparable property will not be a sale for adequate consideration if the negotiating fiduciary does not take into account any special knowledge which he has or should have about the asset or its market, *e.g.,* that the

property's value should reflect a premium due to a certain developer's specific land development plans.

[2] It should be noted that the written valuation required by this section of the proposal need not be a written report of an independent appraiser. Rather, it should be documentation sufficient to allow the Department to determine whether the content requirements of § 2510.3–18(b)(4) have been satisfied. The use of an independent appraiser may be relevant to a determination of good faith, as discussed with regard to proposed § 2510.3–18(b)(3), *infra,* but it is not required to satisfy the fair market value criterion in § 2510.3–18(b)(2)(i).

independence are discussed below.) As noted above, under ERISA, the determination of adequate consideration is a central safeguard in many statutory exemptions applicable to plan transactions with the plan sponsor. The close relationship between the plan and the plan sponsor in such situations raises a significant potential for conflicts of interest as the fiduciary values assets which are the subject of transactions between the plan and the plan sponsor. In light of this possibility, the Department believes that good faith may only be demonstrated when the valuation is made by persons independent of the parties to the transaction (other than the plan), i.e., a valuation made by an independent fiduciary or by a fiduciary acting pursuant to the report of an independent appraiser.

The Department emphasizes that the two requirements of proposed § 2510.3–18(b)(3)(ii) are designed to work in concert. For example, a plan fiduciary charged with valuation may be independent of all the parties to a transaction and may, in light of the requirement of proposed § 2510.3–18(b)(3)(ii)(B), decide to undertake the valuation process itself. However, if the independent fiduciary has neither the experience, facilities nor expertise to make the type of valuation under consideration, the decision by that fiduciary to make the valuation would fail to meet the prudent investigation and sound business principles requirement of proposed § 2510.3–18(b)(3)(ii)(A).

Proposed § 2510.3–18(b)(3)(iii) defines the circumstances under which a fiduciary or an appraiser will be deemed to be independent for the purposes of subparagraph (3)(ii)(B), above. The proposal notes that the fiduciary or the appraiser must in fact be independent of all parties participating in the transaction other than the plan. The proposal also notes that a determination of independence must be made in light of all relevant facts and circumstances, and then delineates certain circumstances under which this independence will be lacking. These circumstances reflect the definitions of the terms "affiliate" and "control" in Departmental regulation 29 CFR 2510.3–21(e) (defining the circumstances under which an investment adviser is a fiduciary). It should be noted that, under these proposed provisions, an appraiser will be considered independent of all parties to a transaction (other than the plan) only if a plan fiduciary has chosen the appraiser and has the right to terminate that appointment, and the

plan is thereby established as the appraiser's client.[3] Absent such circumstances, the appraiser may be unable to be completely neutral in the exercise of his function.[4]

4. Valuation Content—General

Proposed § 2510.3–18(b)(4)(i) sets the content requirements for the written documentation of valuation required for a determination of fair market value under proposed § 2510.3–18(b)(2)(iii). The proposal follows to a large extent the requirements of Rev. Proc. 66–49, 1966–2 C.B. 1257, which sets forth the format required by the IRS for the valuation of donated property. The Department believes that this format is a familiar one, and will therefore facilitate compliance. Several additions to the IRS requirements merit brief explanation.

First, proposed paragraph (b)(4)(i)(E) requires a statement of the purpose for which the valuation was made. A valuation undertaken, for example, for a yearly financial report may prove an inadequate basis for any sale of the asset in question. This requirement is intended to facilitate review of the valuation in the correct context.

Second, proposed paragraph (b)(4)(i)(F) requires a statement as to the relative weight accorded to relevant valuation methodologies. The Department's experience in this area indicates that there are a number of different methodologies used within the appraisal industry. By varying the treatment given and emphasis accorded relevant information, these methodologies directly affect the result of the appraiser's analysis. It is the Department's understanding that appraisers will often use different methodologies to cross-check their results. A statement of the method or methods used would allow for a more accurate assessment of the validity of the valuation.

---

[3] The independence of an appraiser will not be affected solely because the plan sponsor pays the appraiser's fee.

[4] With regard to this independence requirement the Department notes that new section 401(a)(28) of the Code (added by section 1175(a) of the Tax Reform Act of 1986) requires that, in the case of an employee stock ownership plan, employer securities which are not readily tradable on established securities markets must be valued by an independent appraiser. New section 401(a)(28)(C) states that the term "independent appraiser" means an appraiser meeting requirements similar to the requirements of regulations under section 170(a)(1) of the Code (relating to IRS verification of the value assigned for deduction purposes to assets donated to charitable organizations). The Department notes that the requirements of proposed regulation § 2510.3–18(b)(3)(iii) are not the same as the requirements of the regulations issued by the IRS under section 170(a)(1) of the Code. The IRS has not yet promulgated rules under Code section 401(a)(28).

Finally, proposed subparagraph (b)(4)(i)(G) requires a statement of the valuation's effective date. This reflects the requirement in proposed § 2510.3–18(b)(ii) that fair market value must be determined as of the date of the transaction in question.

5. Valuation Content—Special Rule

Proposed § 2510.3–18(b)(4)(ii) establishes additional content requirements for written documentation of valuation when the asset being appraised is a security other than a security for which there is a generally recognized market. In other words, the requirements of the proposed special rule supplement, rather than supplant, the requirements of paragraph (b)(4)(i). The proposed special rule establishes a nonexclusive list of factors to be considered when the asset being valued is a security not covered by section 3(18)(A) of the Act or section 8477(a)(2)(A) of FERSA. Such securities pose special valuation problems because they are not traded or are so thinly traded that it is difficult to assess the effect on such securities of the market forces usually considered in determining fair market value. The Internal Revenue Service has had occasion to address the valuation problems posed by one type of such securities—securities issued by closely held corporations. Rev. Rul. 59–60, 1959–1 Cum. Bull. 237, lists a variety of factors to be considered when valuing securities of closely held corporations for tax purposes.[5] The Department's experience indicates that Rev. Rul. 59–60 is familiar to plan fiduciaries, plan sponsors and the corporate community in general. The Department has, therefore, modeled this proposed special rule after Rev. Rul. 59–60 with certain additions and changes discussed below. It should be emphasized, however, that this is a non-exclusive list of factors to be considered. Certain of the factors listed may not be relevant to every valuation inquiry, although the fiduciary will bear the burden of demonstrating such irrelevance. Similarly, reliance on this list will not relieve fiduciaries from the duty to consider all relevant facts and circumstances when valuing such securities. The purpose of the proposed

---

[5] Rev. Rul. 59–60 was modified by Rev. Rul. 65–193 (1965–2 C.B. 370) regarding the valuation of tangible and intangible corporate assets. The provisions of Rev. Rul. 59–60, as modified, were extended to the valuation of corporate securities for income and other tax purposes by Rev. Rul. 68–609 (1968–2 C.B. 327). In addition, Rev. Rul. 77–287 (1977–2 C.B. 319). amplified. Rev. Rul. 59–60 by indicating the ways in which the factors listed in Rev. Rul. 59–60 should be applied when valuing restricted securities.

17636   Federal Register / Vol. 53, No. 95 / Tuesday, May 17, 1988 / Proposed Rules

list is to guide fiduciaries in the course of their inquiry.

Several of the factors listed in proposed § 2510.3–18(b)(4)(ii) merit special comment and explanation. Proposed subparagraph (G) states that the fair market value of securities other than those for which there is a generally recognized market may be established by reference to the market price of similar securities of corporations engaged in the same or a similar line of business whose securities are actively traded in a free and open market, either on an exchange or over the counter. The Department intends that the degree of comparability must be assessed in order to approximate as closely as possible the market forces at work with regard to the corporation issuing the securities in question.

Proposed subparagraph (H) requires an assessment of the effect of the securities' marketability or lack thereof. Rev. Rul. 59–60 does not explicitly require such an assessment, but the Department believes that the marketability of these types of securities will directly affect their price. In this regard, the Department is aware that, especially in situations involving employee stock ownership plans (ESOPs),[6] the employer securities held by the ESOP will provide a "put" option whereby individual participants may upon retirement sell their shares back to the employer.[7] It has been argued that some kinds of "put" options may diminish the need to discount the value of the securities due to lack of marketability. The Department believes that the existence of the "put" option should be considered for valuation purposes only to the extent it is enforceable and the employer has and may reasonably be expected to continue to have, adequate resources to meet its obligations. Thus, the Department proposes to require that the plan fiduciary assess whether these "put" rights are actually enforceable, and whether the employer will be able to pay for the securities when and if the "put" is exercised.

Finally, proposed subparagraph (I) deals with the role of control premiums in valuing securities other than those for which there is a generally recognized market. The Department proposes that a plan purchasing control may pay a control premium, and a plan selling control should receive a control premium. Specifically, the Department proposes that a plan may pay such a premium only to the extent a third party would pay a control premium. In this regard, the Department's position is that the payment of a control premium is unwarranted unless the plan obtains both voting control and control in fact. The Department will therefore carefully scrutinize situations to ascertain whether the transaction involving payment of such a premium actually results in the passing of control to the plan. For example, it may be difficult to determine that a plan paying a control premium has received control in fact where it is reasonable to assume at the time of acquisition that distribution of shares to plan participants will cause the plan's control of the company to be dissipated within a short period of time subsequent to acquisition.[8] In the Department's view, however, a plan would not fail to receive control merely because individuals who were previously officers, directors or shareholders of the corporation continue as plan fiduciaries or corporate officials after the plan has acquired the securities. Nonetheless, the retention of management and the utilization of corporate officials as plan fiduciaries, when viewed in conjunction with other facts, may indicate that actual control has not passed to the plan within the meaning of paragraph (b)(4)(ii)(I) of the proposed regulation. Similarly, if the plan purchases employer securities in small increments pursuant to an understanding with the employer that the employer will eventually sell a controlling portion of shares to the plan, a control premium would be warranted only to the extent that the understanding with the employer was actually a binding agreement obligating the employer to pass control within a reasonable time. *See Donovan* v. *Cunningham, supra,* 716 F.2d at 1472–74 (mere intention to transfer control not sufficient).

6. *Service Arrangements Subject to FERSA*

Section 8477(c)(1)(C) of FERSA permits the exchange of services between the Thrift Savings Fund and a party in interest only in exchange for adequate consideration. In this context, the proposal defines the term "adequate consideration as "reasonable compensation", as that term is described in sections 408(b)(2) and 408(c)(2) of ERISA and the regulations promulgated thereunder. By so doing, the proposal would establish a consistent standard of exemptive relief for both ERISA and FERSA with regard to what otherwise would be prohibited service arrangements.

Regulatory Flexibility Act

The Department has determined that this regulation would not have a significant economic effect on small plans. In conducting the analysis required under the Regulatory Flexibility Act, it was estimated that approximately 6,250 small plans may be affected by the regulation. The total additional cost to these plans, over and above the costs already being incurred under established valuation practices, are estimated not to exceed $875,000 per year, or $140 per plan for small plans choosing to engage in otherwise prohibited transactions that are exempted under the statute conditioned on a finding of adequate consideration.

Executive Order 12291

The Department has determined that the proposed regulatory action would not constitute a "major rule" as that term is used in Executive Order 12291 because the action would not result in: an annual effect on the economy of $100 million; a major increase in costs of prices for consumers, individual industries, government agencies, or geographical regions; or significant adverse effects on competition, employment, investment, productivity, innovation, or on the ability of United States based enterprises to compete with foreign based enterprises in domestic or export markets.

Paperwork Reduction Act

This proposed regulation contains several paperwork requirements. The regulation has been forwarded for approval to the Office of Management and Budget under the provisions of the Paperwork Reduction Act of 1980 (Pub. L. 96–511). A control number has not yet been assigned.

---

[6] The definition of the term "adequate consideration" under ERISA is of particular importance to the establishment and maintenance of ESOPs because, pursuant to section 408(e) of the Act, an ESOP may acquire employer securities from a party in interest only under certain conditions, including that the plan pay no more than adequate consideration for the securities.

[7] Regulation 29 CFR 2550.408b–(j) requires such a put option in order for a loan from a party in interest to the ESOP to qualify for the statutory exemption in section 408(b)(3) of ERISA from the prohibited transactions provisions of ERISA.

[8] However, the Department notes that the mere pass-through of voting rights to participants would not in itself affect a determination that a plan has received control in fact, notwithstanding the existence of participant voting rights. If the plan fiduciaries having control over plan assets ordinarily may resell the shares to a third party and command a control premium, without the need to secure the approval of the plan participants.

Statutory Authority

This regulation is proposed under section 3(18) and 505 of the Act (29 U.S.C. 1003(18) and 1135); Secretary of Labor's Order No. 1–87; and sections 8477(a)(2)(B) and 8477(f) of FERSA.

List of Subjects in 29 CFR Part 2510

Employee benefit plans, Employee Retirement Income Security Act, Pensions, Pension and Welfare Benefit Administration.

Proposed Regulation

For the reasons set out in the preamble, the Department proposes to amend Part 2510 of Chapter XXV of Title 29 of the Code of Federal Regulations as follows:

PART 2510—[AMENDED]

1. The authority for Part 2510 is revised to read as follows:

Authority: Sec. 3(2), 111(c), 505, Pub. L. 93–406, 88 Stat. 852, 894, (29 U.S.C. 1002(2), 1031, 1135); Secretary of Labor's Order No. 27–74, 1–86, 1–87, and Labor Management Services Administration Order No. 2–6.

Section 2510.3–18 is also issued under sec. 3(18) of the Act (29 U.S.C. 1003(18)) and secs. 8477(a)(2)(B) and (f) of FERSA (5 U.S.C. 8477)

Section 2510.3–101 is also issued under sec. 102 of Reorganization Plan No. 4 of 1978 (43 FR 47713, October 17, 1978), effective December 31, 1978 (44 FR 1065, January 3, 1978); 3 CFR 1978 Comp. 332, and sec. 11018(d) of Pub. L. 99–272, 100 Stat. 82.

Section 2510.3–102 is also issued under sec. 102 of Reorganization Plan No. 4 of 1978 (43 FR 47713, October 17, 1978), effective December 31, 1978 (44 FR 1065, January 3, 1978), and 3 CFR 1978 Comp. 332.

2. Section 2510.3–18 is added to read as follows:

§ 2510.3–18 Adequate Consideration

(a) [Reserved]

(b)(1)(i) *General.* (A) Section 3(18)(B) of the Employee Retirement Income Security Act of 1974 (the Act) provides that, in the case of a plan asset other than a security for which there is a generally recognized market, the term "adequate consideration" when used in Part 4 of Subtitle B of Title I of the Act means the fair market value of the asset as determined in good faith by the trustee or named fiduciary pursuant to the terms of the plan and in accordance with regulations promulgated by the Secretary of Labor.

(B) Section 8477(a)(2)(B) of the Federal Employees' Retirement System Act of 1986 (FERSA) provides that, in the case of an asset other than a security for which there is a generally recognized market, the term "adequate consideration" means the fair market value of the asset as determined in good

faith by a fiduciary or fiduciaries in accordance with regulations prescribed by the Secretary of Labor.

(ii) *Scope.* The requirements of section 3(18)(B) of the Act and section 8477(a)(2)(B) of FERSA will not be met unless the value assigned to a plan asset both reflects the asset's fair market value as defined in paragraph (b)(2) of this section and results from a determination made by the plan trustee or named fiduciary (or, in the case of FERSA, a fiduciary) in good faith as described in paragraph (b)(3) of this section. Paragraph (b)(5) of this section contains a special rule for service contracts subject to FERSA.

(2) *Fair Market Value.* (i) Except as otherwise specified in this section, the term "fair market value" as used in section 3(18)(B) of the Act and section 8477(a)(2)(B) of FERSA means the price at which an asset would change hands between a willing buyer and a willing seller when the former is not under any compulsion to buy and the latter is not under any compulsion to sell, and both parties are able, as well as willing, to trade and are well informed about the asset and the market for such asset.

(ii) The fair market value of an asset for the purposes of section 3(18)(B) of the Act and section 8477(a)(2)(B) of FERSA must be determined as of the date of the transaction involving that asset.

(iii) The fair market value of an asset for the purposes of section 3(18)(B) of the Act and section 8477(a)(2)(B) of FERSA must be reflected in written documentation of valuation meeting the requirements set forth in paragraph (b)(4), of this section.

(3) *Good Faith*—(i) *General Rule.* The requirement in section 3(18)(B) of the Act and section 8477(a)(2)(B) of FERSA that the fiduciary must determine fair market value in good faith establishes an objective, rather than a subjective, standard of conduct. Subject to the conditions in paragraphs (b)(3) (ii) and (iii) of this section, an assessment of whether the fiduciary has acted in good faith will be made in light of all relevant facts and circumstances.

(ii) In considering all relevant facts and circumstances, the Department will not view a fiduciary as having acted in good faith unless

(A) The fiduciary has arrived at a determination of fair market value by way of a prudent investigation of circumstances prevailing at the time of the valuation, and the application of sound business principles of evaluation; and

(B) The fiduciary making the valuation either,

(1) Is independent of all parties to the transaction (other than the plan), or

(2) Relies on the report of an appraiser who is independent of all parties to the transaction (other than the plan).

(iii) In order to satisfy the independence requirement of paragraph (b)(3)(ii)(B), of this section, a person must in fact be independent of all parties (other than the plan) participating in the transaction. For the purposes of this section, an assessment of independence will be made in light of all relevant facts and circumstances. However, a person will not be considered to be independent of all parties to the transaction if that person—

(1) Is directly or indirectly, through one or more intermediaries, controlling, controlled by, or under common control with any of the parties to the transaction (other than the plan);

(2) Is an officer, director, partner, employee, employer or relative (as defined in section 3(15) of the Act, and including siblings) of any such parties (other than the plan);

(3) Is a corporation or partnership of which any such party (other than the plan) is an officer, director or partner.

For the purposes of this subparagraph, the term "control," in connection with a person other than an individual, means the power to exercise a controlling influence over the management or policies of that person.

(4) *Valuation Content.* (i) In order to comply with the requirement in paragraph (b)(2)(iii), of this section, that the determination of fair market value be reflected in written documentation of valuation, such written documentation must contain, at a minimum, the following information:

(A) A summary of the qualifications to evaluate assets of the type being valued of the person or persons making the valuation;

(B) A statement of the asset's value, a statement of the methods used in determining that value, and the reasons for the valuation in light of those methods;

(C) A full description of the asset being valued;

(D) The factors taken into account in making the valuation, including any restrictions, understandings, agreements or obligations limiting the use or disposition of the property;

(E) The purpose for which the valuation was made;

(F) The relevance or significance accorded to the valuation methodologies taken into account;

(G) The effective date of the valuation; and

17638 Federal Register / Vol. 53, No. 95 / Tuesday, May 17, 1988 / Proposed Rules

(H) In cases where a valuation report has been prepared, the signature of the person making the valuation and the date the report was signed.

(ii) *Special Rule.* When the asset being valued is a security other than a security covered by section 3(18)(A) of the Act or section 8477(a)(2)(A) of FERSA, the written valuation required by paragraph (b)(2)(iii) of this section, must contain the information required in paragraph (b)(4)(i) of this section, and must include, in addition to an assessment of all other relevant factors, an assessment of the factors listed below:

(A) The nature of the business and the history of the enterprise from its inception;

(B) The economic outlook in general, and the condition and outlook of the specific industry in particular;

(C) The book value of the securities and the financial condition of the business;

(D) The earning capacity of the company;

(E) The dividend-paying capacity of the company;

(F) Whether or not the enterprise has goodwill or other intangible value;

(G) The market price of securities of corporations engaged in the same or a similar line of business, which are actively traded in a free and open market, either on an exchange or over-the-counter;

(H) The marketability, or lack thereof, of the securities. Where the plan is the purchaser of securities that are subject to "put" rights and such rights are taken into account in reducing the discount for lack of marketability, such assessment shall include consideration of the extent to which such rights are enforceable, as well as the company's ability to meet its obligations with respect to the "put" rights (taking into account the company's financial strength and liquidity);

(I) Whether or not the seller would be able to obtain a control premium from an unrelated third party with regard to the block of securities being valued, provided that in cases where a control premium is taken into account:

(*1*) Actual control (both in form and in substance) is passed to the purchaser with the sale, or will be passed to the purchaser within a reasonable time pursuant to a binding agreement in effect at the time of the sale, and

(*2*) It is reasonable to assume that the purchaser's control will not be dissipated within a short period of time subsequent to acquisition.

(5) *Service Arrangements Subject to FERSA.* For purposes of determinations pursuant to section 8477(c)(1)(C) of FERSA (relating to the provision of services) the term "adequate consideration" under section 8477(a)(2)(B) of FERSA means "reasonable compensation" as defined in sections 408(b)(2) and 408(c)(2) of the Act and §§ 2550.408b–2(d) and 2550.408c–2 of this chapter.

(6) *Effective Date.* This section will be effective for transactions taking place after the date 30 days following publication of the final regulation in the Federal Register.

Signed in Washington, DC, this 11th day of May 1988.

David M. Walker,

Assistant Secretary, Pension and Welfare Benefits Administration, U.S. Department of Labor.

[FR Doc. 88–10934 Filed 5–16–88; 8:45 am]

BILLING CODE 4510–29–M

3. Whenever there is a transaction with a controlling stockholder or member of a control group.
4. If the ESOP sells out its stock position.

The criteria as to who "qualifies" as an appraiser and what is required for satisfying the independence requirement are not thoroughly clarified as of the time of this writing. The Tax Management Portfolio on ESOPs referenced earlier makes the following observation:

A qualified appraiser is one who states on the appraisal form that he holds himself out to the public as an appraiser, is qualified to make appraisals of the property being valued, and understands that he may be subject to penalties for false or fraudulent overvaluations. Interested parties cannot act as independent appraisers, but it is not clear what degree of interest will disqualify an individual from acting as an independent appraiser.[9]

Proximity of Appraisal to Transaction Date

Appraisals for general ESOP purposes, such as repurchase of retired employees' shares, often remain in effect and are used for subsequent transactions for as much as a full year following the valuation date. However, a transaction with a control party requires an appraisal as

---

[9]Kaplan, Brown, and Ludwig, *ESOPs*, p. A-35.

of the time of the transaction. The question sometimes arises of how close to the time of the transaction is close enough for a closely held stock, lacking day-to-day market quotations.

There has been no regulation or court case on this point (except the extreme situation in *Donovan* v. *Cunningham,* saying that 14 months was too long, as discussed in the following chapter). I suggest, as a practical matter, that 90 days seems a reasonable rule of thumb, unless significant events that might affect the valuation have occurred in the interim. New comparative company data normally would become available on a quarterly basis, since most public companies issue quarterly reports to stockholders and are required to file a Form 10-Q with the SEC quarterly. Furthermore, 90 days is the period the SEC usually allows between the dates of financial reports in offering materials and the effective date of a public offering.

It may be a good safety measure to obtain a letter from the appraiser as of the transaction date stating that he or she is unaware of any significant events that would affect the value between the appraisal date and the transaction date (or stating the effect of significant events, if any have occurred). This is common practice, for example, when financial advisers issue fairness opinions in connection with going-private transactions.

Formula Appraisals

The 1985 booklet *Valuing ESOP Shares,* published by the ESOP Association, contains the following statement:

> Formula appraisals are totally unacceptable, because they will virtually always result in an unfair, if not absurd, appraisal at some future point in time. The variables that must be taken into consideration in the proper appraisal of a business or business interest are far too complex to be reduced to a formula that will continue to remain valid as changing economic, industry, and company circumstances evolve over time. While reasonable consistency of appraisal approaches is desirable as long as the approaches remain valid, the appraisal practitioner must use his informed judgment to evaluate the approaches at each appraisal date and institute any changes in approach that may be appropriate in light of changing circumstances.[10]

One approach that has been used successfully, albeit by a very limited number of companies, is a formula appraisal subject to review by a qualified appraisal firm to determine whether or not the value falls within a reasonable range. If not, the formula is adjusted so that the result falls within such a range of value as determined by the independent appraiser.

Accounting for Dilution

When the contribution to the ESOP is made in stock, more shares of stock will be outstanding, which will affect the value per share. After

---

[10]*Valuing ESOP Shares* (Washington, D.C.: The ESOP Association, 1985), pp. 7–8.

the issuance of additional treasury stock or authorized but previously unissued shares, the per share value will decrease because additional shares will be outstanding and no increase in the company's value will have occurred. This must be considered in computing the value per share. The following calculation will yield the appropriate value per share:

$$\frac{\text{Aggregate value of company stock} - \text{ESOP contribution}}{\text{Number of shares outstanding before contribution}}$$

Then one merely needs to divide the price per share thus derived into the dollar amount of the contribution to determine the number of shares to be contributed.

As an example, suppose there are 600,000 shares of stock outstanding prior to the ESOP contribution and the appraiser has appraised the stock at $10 per share. The aggregate value of the stock outstanding is $6 million (600,000 shares × $10 per share = $6,000,000). Since the issuance of additional shares will not increase the aggregate value of the shares outstanding, it will "dilute," or reduce, the value per share. If we assume that the value of the contribution is to be $300,000, the calculation for determining the value per share after the contribution is as follows:

Formula 23–1

$$\frac{\$6,000,000 - \$300,000}{600,000} = \$9.50 \text{ per share}$$

The numbers of new shares to be issued is then calculated as follows:

Formula 23–2

$$\frac{\$300,000}{\$9.50} = 31,579 \text{ shares}$$

This will, of course, result in 631,579 shares outstanding. As a check, multiplying the new number of shares by the new value per share results in the same aggregate value of shares outstanding as before the transaction (631,579 shares × $9.50 per share = $6,000,000).

Sometimes the appraiser's report must be rendered before the company has determined whether or how much new stock may be issued. In such a case, it would be proper for the company to adjust the appraiser's per share value in accordance with the above formula once the determination has been made. If the percentage dilution is quite small, the company may omit the adjustment altogether on the basis that the amount is immaterial.

Effect of ESOP on Earnings Base to Capitalize

One of the controversial issues in ESOP share valuation is the treatment of the ESOP contribution itself as it affects the measurement of the company's earning power base when a capitalization of earning power approach is used in the valuation procedure.

Cash Contribution.   If a cash contribution is made and the cash is used to buy stock from an existing stockholder, the cash goes out of the company and into another stockholder's pocket; thus, it would seem that no part of that deduction should be added back in determining the earning power base. In some situations, however, there could be justification for adjusting the cash contribution expense to the ESOP. For example, if the cash contribution is unusually large compared to what it is expected to be in future years, it may be appropriate to adjust the difference as one would normally adjust any nonrecurring expense item. For some companies, the cash contribution simply is an effective and legitimate way to distribute to owners company profits that a non-ESOP company might distribute as dividends.

An often-used approach to deciding whether or not to make an adjustment to ESOP cash contribution expense is to compare it, plus any other company employee benefit plan expenses, to the aggregate employee benefit plan expenses of comparative public companies or other firms for which data are available. The comparisons may be made as a percentage of revenues or pretax, prebenefit profit and an adjustment made to the earnings base to the extent that the contributions exceed comparative company averages.

For some small companies that are managed such that most of the pretax earnings are paid into the ESOP, the choice of how to treat the ESOP contribution can make a huge difference in the earning power base. There is no clear-cut answer on how to deal with this problem, and there have been no relevant judicial decisions. One way is to put relatively more reliance on asset-oriented or other approaches. The appraiser will have to rely on personal expert judgment in light of the facts in each case.

Stock Contribution.   If the contribution is made in stock, its value really remains within the company. The cash that would have been paid out stays in the cash account or is spent on other assets, and the capital account is increased by the stock's value. Thus, it would seem logical that the "expense" deducted as a result of this transaction be added back into net earnings in computing the earning power base. (Of course, the effect of this will be offset at least partially by the effect of dilution, discussed in the previous section.)

An argument against this reasoning would be that without the ESOP, the pre-ESOP earnings would be fully taxable and a buyer would consider only a fully taxed earnings base without the ESOP in deliberations concerning the price to pay in an acquisition. This argument, then, would lead one to add back to the earning power base the amount of the ESOP contribution, less the taxes that otherwise would have to be paid were there no ESOP contribution. It would seem that this is the minimum adjustment that should be made to net earnings in this case.

The argument becomes moot, of course, if cash flow or pretax earnings measures rather than aftertax earnings is capitalized. However, one still must take care to develop capitalization rates based on comparable measures of publicly traded companies' earnings.

Treatment of Excess Management Compensation

In Chapter 11, "Analyzing and Adjusting Financial Statements," it was suggested that an upward adjustment to earnings might be appropriate if management were drawing more compensation than would be necessary for replacing them. However, such an upward adjustment normally would be inappropriate for the valuation of ESOP shares if the compensation policy were expected to continue. The extent to which the compensation policy might be subject to change is an appropriate area of inquiry in the field interviews with the company's control persons.

Control versus Minority Basis for Valuation

As we have seen in previous chapters, for various reasons minority shares often change hands at a discount from a pro rata portion of the amount for which the entire company might be sold to an outside third party. Perhaps the greatest single controversy in the valuation of ESOP stock is the extent to which the valuation should be on a control or minority basis.

Two Yale professors address this issue as follows:

> In private companies, the control shareholder generally plans on initially transferring a noncontrolling interest at a control price. We think this practice is abusive unless:
> 1. A provision is made that control prices are to be used in all transactions with ESOP beneficiaries; or
> 2. There is a binding agreement that the sale of the balance of the shares to the company or the ESOP is to be at a fixed price or according to a fixed formula.
> Consistency in application of control or noncontrol prices is of paramount significance.[11]

Many companies that have used what might be considered control prices have addressed this matter by putting a provision in their ESOP plans to the effect that the control basis (or whatever basis is used) will be utilized in all transactions with ESOP beneficiaries. This certainly satisfies the criterion of consistency and forestalls any potentially disruptive effect on valuation if the plan assets move up or down along the line of constituting or not constituting a control position.

In the draft version of the DOL's new regulation shown in Exhibit 23–2, the section on required content for the written report refers to a "control premium" among factors to be considered as follows:

> (I) Whether or not the seller would be able to obtain a control premium from an unrelated third party with regard to the block of securities being valued, provided that in cases where a control premium is taken into

---

[11]Arthur N. Haut and William P. Lyons, "Issues in the Valuation of Control and Noncontrol Shares in Connection with the Acquisition of Stock by Employee Stock Ownership Plans," *Journal of Pension Planning and Compliance* 12, no. 4, p. 325. Reprinted with permission from *Journal of Pension Planning and Compliance.* Copyright 1986 by Panel Publishers, Inc., 14 Plaza Road, Greenvale, New York 11548 (516) 484–0006. All rights reserved.

account: (1) actual control (both in form and in substance) is passed to the plan with the sale, or will be passed to the plan within a reasonable time pursuant to a binding agreement in effect at the time of the sale, and (2) it is reasonable to assume that the plan's control will not be dissipated within a short period of time subsequent to acquisition.

Unless this language is changed in the final version, it may take years—and at least one court case—before the meaning of the term *control premium* in this context is fully interpreted. I would suggest, however, that one reasonable aspect of the interpretation would be that if the ESOP in fact lacks control, no premium should be reflected in the valuation for what an unrelated, third-party buyer might do differently with the company in the course of exercising his or her many prerogatives of control as enumerated in Chapter 2, "Principles of Business Valuation—Theory and Practice."

Discount for Lack of Marketability

Another controversy in ESOP share valuation is whether, or the extent to which, some discount should be applied for lack of marketability.

In Chapter 10, "Data on Discounts for Lack of Marketability," we saw that it frequently is reasonable to discount a minority interest in a closely held company with no market for its stock 35 percent or more compared to an otherwise comparable but freely tradable minority interest in a publicly held company. Some would take the position that an ESOP share should not be subject to a marketability discount because the ESOP's "put option" feature creates its own market. In the first edition of this book, I made the following statement on this issue:

> I think that the question has to be analyzed individually for each ESOP situation, and that the answer lies in how good the ESOP market is. Most of the answer will be found by analyzing the wording of the "put" feature of the ESOP agreement. The more favorable it is to the stockholder, the less the appropriate marketability discount, compared to the price that would be appropriate if the stock were publicly-traded. Other factors to consider are the company's financial strength and its past performance in ESOP stock redemptions.[12]

This is essentially the same as the position the DOL takes in its new valuation guidelines, as shown in Exhibit 23–2. In describing the content required in the written valuation report, it lists and discusses the marketability factor as follows:

> (H) The marketability, or lack thereof, of the securities. Where the plan is the purchaser of securities that are subject to "put" rights and such rights are taken into account in reducing the discount for lack of marketability, such assessment shall include consideration of the extent to which such rights are enforceable, as well as the company's ability to meet its obligations with respect to the "put" rights (taking into account the company's financial strength and liquidity); . . .

---

[12]Shannon P. Pratt, *Valuing a Business: The Analysis and Appraisal of Closely-Held Companies* (Homewood, Ill: Dow Jones-Irwin, 1981), p. 341.

In many of the ESOP valuations with which I have been associated, a marketability discount of between 5 and 20 percent was applied to reflect these factors. However, in others, it was determined after analyzing these factors that it was inappropriate to apply a discount for lack of marketability. Some companies have a policy of redeeming ESOP shares for cash when tendered and have established a track record of doing so, even though the ESOP document allows an extended redemption period at the directors' discretion. In such cases, where management indicates an intention to continue such a policy and where the company's financial position appears capable of supporting it, it would seem that a zero marketability discount is justifiable. Also, in some cases, as discussed earlier, companies have established funding programs for the repurchase liability, which would ameliorate or eliminate the applicability of a discount for lack of marketability.

Valuations in Leveraged ESOPs

Through utilizing many aspects of the favorable tax treatment of ESOPs discussed earlier, it has become common for ESOP companies to be able to obtain a very high degree of leverage, because their projected operating cash flows can support it. With such companies, it often is essential to use the debt-free approaches to valuation discussed in Chapter 4 in order to get meaningful valuation results. A discounted future earnings or cash flow approach, as discussed in Chapter 3, also may be appropriate.

Multi-investor ESOPs pose a further problem of allocating the total value among the classes of participants. As noted earlier, this would bring into play the approaches discussed in Part V, "Valuing Partial Interests," particularly Chapter 16, "Valuing Debt Securities"; Chapter 17, "Valuing Preferred Stocks"; and Chapter 18, "Valuing Stock Options." Multi-investor leveraged ESOPs cover such a variety of possibilities that no book could ever address all the combinations the appraiser is likely to encounter in his or her lifetime.

ESOP Valuation Problems

The subject of Chapter 24 is the court cases involving ESOP valuation issues that have been decided up to the time of this writing. However, these represent only a tiny fraction of all the possible ESOP valuation problems. Most have been resolved out of court but often at great expense to the company, even if the final outcome was in its favor. Many more are still somewhere in the litigation process, and undoubtedly several latent problems remain to be discovered.

Almost all of these problems can be categorized into one of two groups:

1. Actual overvaluations or undervaluations (the former being far more frequent).
2. Conclusion not necessarily resulting in over- or undervaluation, but valuation inadequately documented and supported.

Almost all of the problems with the IRS and DOL have resulted from appraisals that did not conform to the general principles of appraisal discussed in this book and suffered from one or more of the following shortcomings:

1. Appraisal done by a nonindependent person or firm.
2. Appraisal done by a person or firm not thoroughly experienced in ESOP appraisals.
   a. Unconventional procedures used that were unacceptable to IRS or DOL.
   b. Report insufficiently documented.
3. Appraisal out of date at time of transaction.

In order to avoid these problems, I suggest the following:

1. Retain a reputable independent appraisal firm with a proven track record with regulatory authorities and courts.
2. Bring the independent appraisal firm into the professional advisory team at the earliest possible time.
3. Allow adequate time and budget for doing the job right.
4. Do not expect to pressure the independent appraisal firm to reach some predetermined valuation conclusion.

Summary

This chapter has explained how the use of employee stock ownership plans can provide financial incentives for companies and stockholders that are unprecedented in the annals of American finance. However, in order to achieve these benefits, firms must follow strict and complex rules to protect the interests of employee participants and their beneficiaries. This chapter has focused on the valuation aspects of compliance, particularly those peculiar to ESOPs.

The stock valuation is one of the most critical aspects of ESOP compliance and the source of a large proportion of ESOP compliance problems. Most ESOP stock valuation problems have arisen because the appraisal was lacking in independence, objectivity, understanding of appraisal principles and/or regulatory or legal guidelines, or lack of adequate written documentation of the appraisal process and conclusion. Hopefully, the principles and practices espoused in this book will help many companies to enjoy a prosperous ESOP experience based on sound valuation criteria.

Often appraisal firms are engaged by the ESOP Trust, Administrative Committee, or Trustee to act as a financial adviser to the Trust.

This financial advisory role encompasses responsibilities and expertise beyond that of business valuation. Such responsibilities may include expressing opinions as to the fairness of a transaction from a financial point of view, adequacy of consideration, and capital adequacy. In addition, the financial adviser should be expected to represent the Trust's best interests in any active negotiations among prospective investors in the transaction. This financial advisory activity, while within the capabilities of business valuation experts, embodies responsibilities and representations beyond the intended purpose of this book.

Bibliography

Articles

Baker, Pamela. "Pension Fund Investing: Enhanced Incentives for Leveraged ESOPs after the 1984 Tax Reform Act." *Journal of Taxation of Investments,* Winter 1985, pp. 178–92.

Bergner, Jane C. "ESOPs and Other New Applications of Section 6166." *Estates, Gifts and Trusts Journal,* July–August 1985, pp. 111–24.

Bonovitz, Sheldon M. "Leveraged Buyouts under the Tax Reform Act of 1984." Tulane Tax Institute, September 12–14, 1984, pp. 1–24.

Brown, Karen W. "After the ESOP Leveraged Buy-Out." *ESOP Report,* March 1987, pp. 4–5.

Burck, Charles G. "There's More to ESOP Than Meets the Eye." *Fortune,* March 1976, pp. 128–33.

Buxton, Dickson C. "ESOP: A Beginner's Manual." *Supply House Times,* October 1985, pp. 135–55.

Buxton, Dickson C. "The ESOP: Business Perpetuation through an Employee Benefit Plan." *Journal of the American Society of CLU,* July 1987, pp. 40–58.

Case, John. "Every Worker an Owner?" *Inc.,* May 1987, pp. 14–16.

Cohen, Alan, and Michael Quarrey. "Performance of Employee-Owned Small Companies: a Preliminary Study." *Journal of Small Business Management,* April 1986, pp. 58–63.

Connor, J. Michael. "ESOPs and Sec. 401(k) Plans—a Marriage Made in Heaven?" *Tax Adviser,* October 1985, pp. 640–44.

Edlund, Taina E., and Lynn K. Pearle. "Favorable Tax Treatment to ESOPs Used in Estate Planning Extended by New Law." *Estate Planning,* January–February 1987, pp. 20–24.

Elinski, Peter I. "The Use of ESOPs." Annual Conference on Employee Benefits and Executive Compensation, Institute on Federal Taxation, New York University, Spring 1984, pp. 7–41.

"Employee Stock Ownership Plans: Part 1, Financial and Motivational Tools." *Small Business Report,* June 1987, pp. 70–76. (Prepared with assistance of The ESOP Association.)

"Employee Stock Ownership Plans: Part 2, Framework for Implementation." *Small Business Report,* July 1987, pp. 66–72. (Prepared with assistance of The ESOP Association.)

"ESOPs: Revolution or Ripoff?" *Business Week,* April 15, 1985, pp. 94–108.

"ESOPs Tables: A Survey of Companies with Employee Stock Ownership Plans." *Journal of Corporation Law,* Spring 1981, pp. 551–623.

Esterces, Howard M., and Steven Glaser. "ESOPs Even More Attractive to Major Shareholders after Tax Reform Act of 1986." *Journal of Taxation,* May 1987, pp. 273–78.

Goodman, Barry R. "A Long Look at the Leveraged ESOP Transaction and Valuation Issues That It Brings Up." *Business Valuation News,* June 1986, pp. 20–32.

Haut, Arthur N., and William P. Lyons. "Issues in the Valuation of Control and Noncontrol Shares in Connection with the Acquisition of Stock by Employee Stock Ownership Plans." *Journal of Pension Planning & Compliance,* 12, no. 4 Winter 1986, pp. 319–26.

Horwood, Richard M. "The ABCs of ESOP/LBOs—Past, Present, and Future." *Journal of Corporate Taxation,* Spring 1986, pp. 233–63.

Jaffer, David, and Michael Sanchez. "The Tax Reform Act Favors ESOPs." *Colorado Lawyer,* November 1984, pp. 1981–87.

Kaplan, Jared. "Is ESOP a Fable? Fabulous Uses and Benefits Or Phenomenal Pitfalls?" *Taxes,* December 1987, pp. 788–95.

Lee, M. Mark. "Valuing Closely-Held Stock for ESOP Purposes Is No Simple Matter, Part I." *Pension and Profit Sharing Tax Journal,* 1975, pp. 310–19.

Lee, M. Mark. "Valuing Closely-Held Stock for ESOP Purposes Is No Simple Matter, Part II." *Pension and Profit Sharing Tax Journal,* 1975, pp. 29–45.

Lipkin, Lawrence. "The Theory of Minority Discount in Regard to ESOP Shares of Closely-Held Corporations." *ASA Valuation,* November 1980, pp. 130–34.

Ludwig, Ronald L., and Anna Jeans. "Estate Tax Deduction for Sales to an ESOP." *The Employee Ownership Report,* January–February 1987, p. 5.

Maldonado, Kirk F. "Employee Stock Ownership Plans under the Tax Reform Act of 1986." *Tax Management Memorandum,* January 19, 1987, pp. 15–26.

Marsh, Thomas R., and Dale E. McAllister. "ESOPs Tables: A Survey of Companies with Employee Stock Ownership Plans." *Journal of Corporation Law,* Spring 1981, pp. 551–623.

Mattingly, William E., and Zarina O'Hagin. "Planning for ESOPs under the Tax Reform Act of 1984." *Taxes,* May 1985, pp. 323–32.

McCarter, Mary, and Shannon P. Pratt. "A Primer to the Appraisal Process." *The Employee Ownership Report,* July–August 1987, pp. 1, 6.

Midkiff, Robert R., and Luis Granados. "Choosing an ESOP Trustee." *Journal of the American Society of CLU,* November 1987, pp. 94–99.

Much, Paul J. "ESOP Valuation Considerations." *The Tax Times* (Prentice-Hall, February 1987), pp. 10, 26.

Much, Paul J., and Scott L. Beiser. "ESOPs Offer Corporate Financing Pluses." *The Tax Times* (Prentice-Hall, March 1987), pp. 16–17.

Pratt, Shannon P. "Estate Planning, ESOPs, Buy-Sell Agreements, and Life Insurance for Closely Held Businesses." *Journal of the American Society of CLU,* September 1986, pp. 74–79.

Pratt, Shannon P. "ESOPs: Fables, Foibles and Facts." *Midway* 2, no. 1 (January 1987), pp. 32–33, 56, 60.

Raby, William L. "How to Use a Leveraged ESOP for a Small Company Buy-out." *The Tax Times* (Prentice-Hall, May 1987), pp. 1, 27.

Racusin, Warren. "The Benefits of Employee Stock Ownership Plans." *Trusts & Estates,* August 1985, pp. 42–46.

Reichler, Richard. "Deficit Reduction Act Makes Significant Changes to Rules Governing ESOPs." *Journal of Taxation,* February 1985, pp. 70–75.

Reilly, Robert F. "ESOP Formation and Valuation Procedures." *Business Valuation News,* March 1986, pp. 23–35.

Reilly, Robert F. "Owners of Closely Held Corporations Can Reap Special Benefits from ESOPs." *Taxation for Accountants,* June 1986, pp. 362–67.

Rice, Bob. "Fabled ESOPs: Tax Reform Makes Them Even More Attractive." *Barron's,* November 3, 1986, pp. 70–71.

Rosen, Corey. "Using an ESOP for Business Continuity." *Journal of the American Society of CLU,* July 1986, pp. 54–58.

Rosen, Corey; Katherine J. Klein; and Karen M. Young. "When Employees Share the Profits." *Psychology Today,* January 1986, pp. 30–36.

Rudin, Brad. "Fiduciary Duty in Mergers Eyed." *Pensions and Investment Age,* December 28, 1987.

Smiley, Robert W., Jr. "How to Plan for an ESOP's Repurchase Liability." *Pension and Profit Sharing Service* (Prentice-Hall Information Services, 1987), pp. 1215–29.

Spero, Peter. "ESOP or Stock Bonus Plan Can Provide Tax Benefits on Sale of Closely Held Business." *Taxation for Lawyers,* March–April 1984, pp. 290–96.

Stokes, Robert J., and Eva A. Rasmussen. "TRA Has New Limits on Plan Benefits, Allocations and Covered Compensation, as Well as ESOP Changes." *Taxation for Lawyers,* May–June 1987, pp. 368–75.

Swad, R. G., and B. P. Hartman. "Financial Accounting and Reporting of ESOPs." *CPA Journal,* January 1980, pp. 37–42.

Books

Blasi, Joseph R. *Employee Ownership: Revolution or Ripoff?* Cambridge, Mass.: Ballinger, 1988.

Employee Benefit Plans in Mergers and Acquisitions. Chicago: American Bar Association, 1987.

Employee Ownership Plans: How 8,000 and 8,000,000 Employees Invest in Their Futures. Washington, D.C.: Bureau of National Affairs, 1987.

Employee Stock Ownership Plans: Interim Report on a Survey and Related Economic Trends. Washington D.C.: U.S. General Accounting Office, 1986.

ESOP Survey 1985. Washington, D.C.: The ESOP Association, 1985.

Frisch, Robert A. *The Magic of ESOPs and LBOs.* Rockville Centre, N.Y.: Farnsworth, 1985.

Kaplan Jared; Gregory K. Brown; and Ronald L. Ludwig. 453-3rd T.M. *ESOPs* (Washington, D.C.: Tax Management, Inc., 1987).

Proceedings of The 1987 ESOP Association Convention (Tenth Annual Convention). Washington, D.C.: The ESOP Association, 1987. Includes texts and/or outlines of speakers' presentations.

Proceedings of The 1988 ESOP Association Convention (Eleventh Annual Convention). Washington, D.C.: The ESOP Association, 1988. Includes texts and/or outlines of speakers' presentations.

Quarrey, Michael. *Employee Ownership and Corporate Performance* (Research Papers in Employee Ownership). Oakland, Calif.: National Center for Employee Ownership, 1986.

Quarrey, Michael; Joseph R. Blasi; and Corey Rosen. *Taking Stock: Employee Ownership at Work*. Cambridge, Mass.: Ballinger, 1986.

Rosen, Corey; Katherine J. Klein; and Karen M. Young. *Employee Ownership in America: The Equity Solution*. Lexington, Mass.: D.C. Heath, 1986.

Valuing ESOP Shares. Washington D.C.: The ESOP Association, 1985.

Chapter 24

Court Cases Involving ESOP Valuation Issues

A pure heart and an empty head are not sufficient . . .[1]

This chapter presents a synopsis of all the court cases decided through mid-1988 that I know of in which the value of a closely held employer stock owned by an employee benefit plan was a major issue. Of the eight cases reported in this chapter, four were brought by the IRS, one by the Department of Labor, and three by beneficiaries. The cases are presented in the order in which the decisions were published. Although some of the cases also involved other issues, this chapter discusses only valuation-related issues for the most part.

The fact that there have not been more court cases involving valuation issues decided up to this point should not be interpreted as indicating a paucity of legal challenges to valuations of employer stock held in employee benefit plans. In fact, quite the opposite is true. I personally have been involved in the settlement of many such challenges brought by the IRS, Department of Labor, and beneficiaries. Furthermore, all cases reported in this chapter involve valuations for the years 1973 through 1981. There are many existing and potential cases for valuations for years throughout the 1980s at various stages of adjudication.

Hopefully the presentation of the valuation issues discussed in these cases will help readers forestall or cope successfully with challenges to employee plan stock valuation issues.

Lanson Industrial, Inc. v. U.S.[2]

For fiscal 1975, Lanson Industrial, Inc. claimed an income tax deduction of $266,955, or $97.50 per share on 2,738 shares of Class B (nonvoting) stock contributed to its ESOP. For fiscal 1976 (apparently following a stock split), Lanson claimed a deduction of $447,074.89, or $17.0283 per share on 26,255 Class B shares contributed to the ESOP.

The commissioner of the Internal Revenue Service determined that the allowable deduction for 1975 was only $36,457.20, based on a fair market value of $15.99 per share. For 1976 the commissioner allowed a deduction of only $187,255.20, or $6.56 per share.

The appraiser Lanson retained had considerable experience in valuing closely held corporate stock. In making this appraisal, he visited the facilities and interviewed management at various levels and plant workers. The court noted that "he appears to have thoroughly studied, considered, and evaluated every facet and aspect of Lanson Industries."

The expert witnesses who testified on behalf of the IRS did not visit the plant and did not interview Lanson management. The only

---

[1]Judge Gee in *Donovan v. Cunningham*, 716 F.2d 1455 (C.A. 1983), affirming in part, vacating in part, remanding 541 F. Supp. 276 (D.C. Texas 1981).

[2]*Lanson Industrial, Inc. v. U.S.*, U.S. District Court for the Northern District of Alabama, Southern Division, Civil Action No. 78-x-5206-5. Numbers do not coincide, apparently because of interim transactions which do not appear in the court case. Above are the numbers as they appear in the case.

financial records they examined were the financial statements. They were unaware of several factors that had a material bearing on the shares' value.

Lanson had stated to its employees that it would redeem ESOP shares at retirement and had established a record of consistently doing so.

The price Lanson's appraiser placed on the stock reflected a 10 percent discount for the shares' nonvoting status. In the capitalization of earnings approach, Lanson's appraiser adjusted the income statements for nonrecurring items and also added back to the income base the value of shares contributed, since that expense did not constitute a cash outlay on the statements. The court said of this approach, "Its methodology in these respects is held to be soundly based." The court noted that Lanson's valuations "were based on objective standards" and that "the basic factors listed in Revenue Ruling 59-60 were closely followed." It also stated that Lanson's appraiser "had no business or other relationship with Lanson prior to his employment for the initial appraisal."

Contrary to the IRS position in the case, the court found that "a marketability discount is not applicable under the facts of this case."

However, the court found that a total discount of 20 percent should be applied for minority interest and nonvoting status rather than the 10 percent Lanson's appraiser used. Applying the 20 percent discount, the court found values of $86.66 and $15.14 per share for fiscal years 1975 and 1976, respectively.

Hooker Industries, Inc. v. Commissioner[3]

For fiscal 1974, Hooker Industries, Inc., claimed an income tax deduction of $720,000, or $4.78 per share on 150,727 shares of common stock contributed to its ESOP. For fiscal 1975, Hooker claimed a deduction of $186,300, or $4.14 per share on 45,000 shares contributed to the ESOP.

The IRS claimed that the deduction for 1974 should have been only $327,078, or $2.17 per share. For 1975, the IRS allowed only $85,950, or $1.91 per share.

The court considered actual transactions in the stock, the report, and testimony presented by Hooker's appraiser. With respect to the expert witness, the court was impressed with the "thorough report" and the fact that it gave "adequate consideration to the many factors affecting the value of petitioner's stock."

With respect to the 1974 valuation, the court noted that it was reasonable to consider the earnings projections made by Hooker's vice president of finance, especially in light of Hooker's earnings record in

---

[3]*Hooker Industries, Inc. v. Commissioner,* 44 T.C.M. 259 (1982).

the early 1970s, even though his "expectations as to future earnings were never fulfilled." Also, the court supported Hooker's position that the earnings base to be considered should be the earnings *before* the ESOP contribution, since the contribution was in stock instead of cash.[4]

The court criticized the valuation procedures used by the IRS witness on several grounds. One was for relying exclusively on a price/ earnings approach, thereby failing to consider other factors affecting the value of petitioner's stock. Also, the court stated that the IRS witness had erred in considering only two years of operating income (the second year of which had been a down year) in arriving at an earnings base to capitalize while a five-year period would have been more representative. The court went on to say:

> . . . [the IRS witness's] lack of understanding of the issues involved in valuing ESOP stock is further emphasized by his failure to consider several factors which, were we to accept [the witness's] earning base as accurate, would have *decreased* his value per share. [The witness] took no discount for lack of marketability. We believe that one is appropriate. Although petitioner in 1975 and 1976 purchased stock from terminating ESOP participants, it was under no obligation to do so. The ESOP did not give terminating participants a put option, but only gave the company a right to grant one if so desired. . . . Additionally, [the witness], in arriving at a value per share, divided the earnings base by the number of shares outstanding *before* the ESOP contribution. The proper method is to divide the number of shares outstanding *after* the ESOP contribution. . . . The report of petitioner's expert witness adequately considered these various factors.
>
> In sum, we conclude that because of the weaknesses in the [IRS witness's] report we cannot rely on its conclusion as to the stock's fair market value.

The court also rejected an IRS argument that a buy-sell agreement between two stockholders at $2.83 per share should be considered. On that point, the court stated:

> The buy-sell prices were calculated pursuant to a formula designed for a specific company purpose and there is no evidence that they reflect the prices at which a willing buyer would buy, or a willing seller sell, petitioner's stock.

The court concluded:

> Contrary to what we suspect was each party's expectation when this dispute was submitted to us, we have not reached a middle-of-the-road compromise. . . . Rather, we conclude that the fair market value of petitioner's stock was $4.138375 at June 30, 1975, and $4.35 on June 30, 1974.

---

[4]In supporting this position, the court stated, "For an argument that no deduction is appropriate if the ESOP contribution is made in stock," see S. Pratt, *Valuing a Business: The Analysis and Appraisal of Closely-Held Companies* 340–41 (1981).

Donovan v. *Cunningham*[5]

Court of Appeals Decision on Fiduciary Duty

In *Donovan* v. *Cunningham,* brought by Secretary of Labor Raymond Donovan, it was found that the ESOP fiduciaries had breached their duties under the section of ERISA governing fiduciary duties in connection with the valuation of ESOP stock. The action was in connection with ESOP stock transactions that occurred in August 1976 and February 1977.

The crux of the secretary's case was that the ESOP had purchased stock from Cunningham (the 100 percent shareholder prior to the first ESOP transaction) for more than adequate consideration.

Before commenting on the respective positions of the secretary and the defendants, the court offered the following prefatory remarks:

> Until the present case, no court has had occasion to interpret or apply Section 3(18). It is with some trepidation that we undertake to be the first to do so, unaided by the views of others, for we must satisfy the demands of the Congressional policies that seemed destined to collide. On the one hand, Congress has repeatedly expressed its intent to encourage the formation of ESOPs by passing legislation granting such plans favorable treatment and has warned against judicial and administrative action that would thwart that goal. Competing with Congress' expressed policy to foster the formation of ESOPs is the policy expressed in equally forceful terms in ERISA: that of safeguarding the interest of participants in employee benefit plans by vigorously enforcing standards of fiduciary responsibility.

The ESOP fiduciaries relied on an independent appraisal report that had undertaken to estimate the fair market value of a 100 percent block of the company's stock as of June 30, 1975. All parties and their expert witnesses agreed that the independent appraisal report's estimate was a reasonable approximation of the fair market value of 100 percent of the company's stock as of that appraisal's valuation date.

The secretary mounted a two-pronged attack on the fiduciaries' decision-making process. First, the appraisal was out of date by the time of the ESOP transactions—13 and 22 months later—and the factual assumptions on which it was based were no longer valid. In addition, he urged that failure to discount the value ascribed to a 100 percent controlling block of shares when setting the price to be paid for a minority block of shares (14 percent in the first transaction) violated general valuation principles.

The appraisal had been based partly on management's projections, which had not been met as of the time of the ESOP transactions 13 and 22 months later. Furthermore, the appraiser had not contemplated an ESOP, with the attendant cash drains from the company for purchasing stock from the controlling shareholder. Further still, the

---

[5]*Donovan* v. *Cunningham,* 716 F.2d 1455 (U.S.C.A. 1983), affirming in part, vacating in part, remanding 541 F. Supp. 276 (D.C. Texas 1981).

ESOP had leveraged the second transaction by borrowing to buy the stock; thus, future cash contributions to the ESOP were no longer discretionary but were necessary for repaying the loan.

The secretary urged that ESOP valuation procedures follow Revenue Ruling 59-60. With the following language, the court scolded the secretary for not promulgating any valuation directives:

> Judicial adoption of this Revenue Ruling is no substitute for the regulations the Secretary has never promulgated: we are unwilling to hold that ERISA fiduciaries who fail to follow it jot and tittle have breached their duties. Appraisal of closely-held stock is a very inexact science; given the level of uncertainty inherent in the process and the variety of potential fact patterns, we do not think a court should require fiduciaries to follow a specific valuation approach as a matter of law under Section 3(18). The standard they must follow remains one of prudence. If more specific rules are needed, the better—and fairer—approach is to inform fiduciaries of them beforehand by regulation.

The court concluded that the ESOP fiduciaries had breached their responsibility by relying on an appraisal that was both out of date and done for a different purpose. Following is the text of the court's concluding comments:

> To sum up, we hold that appellees failed to conduct an investigation sufficient to determine if the Rotan Mosle appraisal remained a reasonable approximation of the fair market value of MCS stock at the times they relied on it. Two critical assumptions made by Rotan Mosle—the growth projections and the absence of an ESOP—no longer were valid. Had the appellees compared the 17-page Rotan Mosle report and its exhibits with the information at their disposal when they bought MCS stock for the ESOP, they should have realized this. In these circumstances, it was not enough for fiduciaries simply to rely on their generalized notions that the company's prospects were good. Their appraisal represented a quantitative analysis of specific facts and assumptions. Prudent fiduciaries would have sought to analyze the effect of obvious changes in those facts and assumptions—either by their own efforts or with the help of advisors. An independent appraisal is not a magic wand that fiduciaries may simply wave over a transaction to ensure that their responsibilities are fulfilled. It is a tool and, like all tools, is useful only if used properly. To use an independent appraisal properly, ERISA fiduciaries need not become experts in the valuation of closely-held stock—they are entitled to rely on the expertise of others. However, as the source of the information upon which the expert's opinions are based, the fiduciaries are responsible for ensuring that the information is complete and up-to-date. In failing to do so, the appellees breached their duties of prudence under Section 404 and likewise cannot establish that they paid adequate consideration.

Final Damage Judgment

Late in 1986, a final judgment and order of injunction was filed, pursuant to a settlement agreed to between the U.S. Department of Labor, plaintiff, and trustees Cunningham, Hairell, and Robertson, defendants.[6]

---

[6]*Brock* v. *Cunningham*, Civil Action No. H-80-87 (S.D. Texas, November 14, 1986).

Cunningham, also the selling stockholder, agreed to pay to former participants in the ESOP $400,000 and was enjoined from serving as a fiduciary of any employee benefit plan covered by ERISA for five years. Hairell and Robertson were also enjoined from violating ERISA. In the event that beneficiaries identified cannot be located, damages attributable to such beneficiaries shall be reallocated among those located.

Capital City Excavating Co., Inc. v. Commissioner[7]

For each of the years 1975 and 1976, Capital City Excavating Company, Inc., claimed a deduction of $100,000, or $100 per share of nonvoting common stock purchased from the company by the ESOP. The ESOP's total holdings represented a minority interest.

For each of those years, the IRS allowed only $70,000, or $70 per share.

The initial calculations leading to the $100-per-share figure used in the ESOP transaction were done by the company's treasurer. Essentially, he calculated an adjusted book value of $111.92 per share (versus actual book value of $88.98 per share) by removing the effect of accelerated depreciation.

At the trial, the company presented testimony supporting an adjusted book value of $151.40 per share. The witness calculated this figure by valuing the equipment on the basis of an equipment pricing manual and relying on an outside appraiser and a savings and loan association to revalue the land and improvements. The witness who presented the adjusted net asset value also presented a valuation of $164.08 per share based on an excess earnings approach, demonstrating the existence of goodwill value over and above net tangible asset value. He took the average of the foregoing two approaches and then discounted 10 percent for lack of marketability, resulting in a value of $142 per share.

The Internal Revenue Service witness, described as "a financial analyst in the Valuation Analysis Section of the Internal Revenue Service," valued the stock at $70 per share, based on five comparative public companies and using regression analysis. No detail is offered as to exactly which calculations he made for the comparative public companies. The taxpayer's witness criticized on several grounds the lack of comparability of the public companies selected.

The court stated that the taxpayer "closely followed the parameters of Revenue Ruling 59-60 in determining the price of the shares." The court also stated that "the intangible assets of petitioner did have value, and the adjustment taken therefore was warranted in theory and reasonable in amount."

The court made the following comments, in part with respect to the comparable sales method as presented by the IRS witness:

---

[7]*Capital City Excavating Co., Inc. v. Commissioner*, 47 T.C.M. 1527 (1984).

This method is an accepted practice of valuation. . . . It is, however, only one of many factors to be used . . . petitioner challenges the corporations selected for comparison by respondent's expert in several respects. . . . We have considered such objections by petitioner and, while not without flaws, we find they have some merit. In any event, the comparable sales data relied on by respondent is not so persuasive as to rebut the evidence of value set forth by petitioner.

Simultaneously with the ESOP transaction, the company sold 97 shares of voting common stock to six directors at the same price of $100 per share. Other than the voting-versus-nonvoting difference, the stock sold to the directors was identical to that sold to the ESOP. The court said that the distinction between voting and nonvoting should be taken into consideration. It said, however, "in any event, the appropriate discount for nonvoting shares would not be so large as to reduce the valuation estimate of $151.40 (the company witness's average of adjusted book and excess earnings approach values) below $100."

The court concluded:

. . . we hold that the price of $100 per share . . . constituted adequate consideration. . . . We recognize that additional steps such as the employment by petitioner of an outside appraiser prior to this controversy might have aided the valuation process and ameliorated the need for litigation. Nonetheless, we do not find that petitioner's methods were impermissible nor that the price of $100 per share was unreflective of fair market value.

Las Vegas Dodge, Inc. v. *U.S.*[8]

Las Vegas Dodge, Inc., filed income tax returns for 1973 reflecting deductions for its contributions to the employee stock ownership trust at $61.35 per share based on the fair market value arrived at by an independent appraising firm. The IRS asserted that the value was between $5.36 and $8.00 per share. The independent appraisal gave heavy emphasis to earning power and dividend-paying capacity, while the IRS stressed net asset value (book value was $7.05 per share).

The court found itself in agreement with the emphasis placed on the earning power and dividend-paying capacity. The court was somewhat concerned "that the appraisal took into account a 20-year earnings projection" but thought it was "not unreasonable in light of past earnings increases." The court concluded that "the only reasonable appraisal presented to it was the one at $61.35 per share."

The court said that it found persuasive the discussion in *Donovan* v. *Cunningham* that "a pure heart and an empty head are not sufficient," but in this case not only had the company exercised good faith, but the value reached in good faith was found to be reasonable.

---

[8]*Las Vegas Dodge, Inc.* v. *U.S.*, 85-2 U.S.T.C. Paragraph 9546 (1985).

Sommers Drug Stores Co. v. *Corrigan Enterprises, Inc.*[9]

In December 1977, trustees of the Sommers Drug Stores Company employee profit-sharing trust accepted an offer to sell the trust's holdings of stock in the company, then representing about 20 percent of the outstanding stock, back to the company for $10,000 per share. Prior to the time of the stock sale, the company had sold its drug store operations, leaving it primarily as a holding company owning cash and real estate.

In December 1980, the trust sued the company and its principal stockholder for breach of fiduciary duty under ERISA and common law in connection with the stock sale. The trust's expert witness testified that the stock was worth $27,171 per share. Defendant's expert testified that the stock was worth only $8,500 per share.

The jury found that both the principal stockholder and the company had breached their fiduciary duty under ERISA. It found that the stock was worth $27,171 per share. After granting defendant's motion for a remittitur,[10] the effect of which was to reduce the damages the jury had assessed, the district court entered judgment in favor of the trust for $552,612 actual damages and $1,250,000 punitive damages, $500,000 against the principal stockholder and $750,000 against the company.

The principal stockholder and the company appealed. The U.S. Court of Appeals remanded the case for further proceedings. The court held that "there is insufficient evidence in the record to support the jury's finding of fair market value, upon which the district court's judgment of actual damages was based." The court also held that the trust could not recover punitive damages under the applicable section of ERISA.

The plaintiff's expert's method of determining fair market value per share had been to sum all the company's net assets, including the discounted present value of a 10-year employment contract received by the principal stockholder in connection with the sale of the drug store operations, and divide by the number of shares outstanding.

Appellants' principal contention was that plaintiff's expert's testimony lacked probative value because his valuation was based on liquidation or asset value rather than on fair market value. The court of appeals agreed, stating:

> On cross-examination [the witness] acknowledged that market value and asset value were different measures, but he asserted that in this case they were the same. We conclude that [the witness's] testimony was so conclusory and lacking in analysis that no jury could reasonably have relied on it in determining the fair market value of the Trust's stock.

---

[9]*Sommers Drug Stores Co.* v. *Corrigan Enterprises, Inc.*, 793 F.2d 1456 (5th Cir. 1986).
[10]A *remittitur* is a remission to a defendent by a plaintiff of the portion of a verdict for damages considered excessive by trial or appellate court.

It seems to me that the particularly instructive part of this case, from a valuation point of view, is what the court said the expert *should have* considered in determining the fair market value of the trust's shares of stock for purposes of ERISA, as detailed in the following excerpts from the opinion:

> Although ERISA does not define the term "fair market value," it is defined in other contexts as the price that a willing buyer would pay a willing seller, both having reasonable knowledge of the pertinent facts. . . . We conclude that this definition is appropriate for purposes of ERISA.
>
> Determining fair market value for the stock of a closely held company can be difficult; typically no readily available market exists in which to determine what willing buyers are prepared to pay. This problem has arisen most frequently in the estate tax context, and it is to that area of law that we turn for guidance. The Internal Revenue Service's estate tax regulations provide that closely held stock for which there is no available market price should be valued according to "the company's net worth, prospective earning power and dividend-paying capacity, and other relevant factors." 26 C.F.R. & 2012031-2(f)(2)(1985).
>
> Among the "other relevant factors" are
>
> > The good will of the business; the economic outlook in the particular industry; the company's position in the industry and its management; the degree of control of the business represented by the block of stock to be valued; and the values of securities of corporations engaged in the same or similar lines of business which are listed on a stock exchange.
>
> Id.; see also Rev. Rul. 59-60, & 4.01, 1959-1 C.B. 237, 238-39 (offering a similar list of factors to be weighed in valuing closely held stock).
>
> [The witness's] valuation ignored most of these factors. Of particular significance, he failed to consider that the Trust's stock represented a minority position in [the company]. He also neglected to consider the prices at which shares of comparable companies were traded on the national exchanges. He did not take account of the prices at which Sommers' stock had changed hands in a series of tender offers between 1970 and 1977, one of the factors mentioned in Rev. Rul. 59-60. See Rev. Rul. 59-60 & 4.02(g), 1959-1 C.G. 237, 241-42; see also *Fitts' Estate* v. *Commissioner,* 237 F.2d 729, 731 (8th Cir. 1956). ("In determining the value of unlisted stocks, actual sales made in reasonable amount at arm's length, in the normal course of business, within a reasonable time before or after the basic date, are the best criterion of market value."); *Duncan Industries, Inc.* v. *Commissioner,* 73 T.C. 266, 276 (1979) (same). Nor did [the witness] consider whether a discount for lack of marketability should be applied to the Trust's stock. See *Estate of Andrews* v. *Commissioner,* 79 T.C. 938, 953, 957 (1982).
>
> We do not suggest that consideration of these factors would necessarily have changed [the witness's] valuation of the Trust's shares. Indeed, in support of his apparent approach, we note that under Rev. Rul. 59-60, "[t]he value of the stock of a closely held investment or real estate holding company [which (the company) arguably was] . . . is closely related to the value of the assets underlying the stock." Rev. Rul. 59-60, & 5(b), 1959 1 C.B. 237, 243. But [the witness's] utter failure to consider other relevant factors, or to explain his reasons for disregarding them, renders his testimony unworthy of credit.

Martin Hines et al. v. *Frederick P. Schlimgen, Mark C. Rowley, and Rowley & Schlimgen, Inc.*[11]

In the *Martin Hines* case, brought by a beneficiary, both the trustees and the company were held liable for overvaluation.

On August 15, 1980, the Rowley & Schlimgen, Inc., employee stock ownership plan purchased 740 newly issued shares of common stock from the company for $125 per share on the basis of an appraisal by an individual who subsequently became controller of the company. The court found the value to be $56 per share.

The court determined that there had been a breach of fiduciary duty by the ESOP trustees. It found that the trustees had purchased stock from the company at a price determined by an individual who was not independent and that the valuation "was flawed in several respects." The court held both the trustees and the company liable for the difference in the amount plus costs and attorneys' fees.

In determining the $56-per-share value, the court made frequent reference to Revenue Ruling 59-60. Among the respects in which the court considered the valuation flawed were the following:

1. A loss year was ignored without explanation in calculating the earnings base.
2. All relevant facts were not considered, including management voids and weaknesses, lack of diversification, lack of computerization, and undercapitalization.
3. An inappropriate multiplier factor of earnings was used.
4. There was no recognition that the stock was a minority interest.

The court found the minority interest discount to be 20 percent, noting that "such discounts are often in the range of 20 to 30 percent and may go as high as 50 percent."

The court concluded that the trustees' business judgment "was not in any way directed to the best and sole interests of the participants, which the law requires."

U.S. News & World Report, Inc.[12]

Although U.S. News & World Report, Inc. concerned a profit-sharing plan and a stock bonus plan, the issues were similar to those that might have been involved had there been an ESOP. The case was followed with great interest by ESOP valuation practitioners.

---

[11]*Martin Hines et al.* v. *Frederick P. Schlimgen, Mark C. Rowley, and Rowley & Schlimgen, Inc.*, U.S. District Court, Western District of Wisconsin, Civil Case 85-C-1037-S, October 10, 1986.

[12]*Charles S. Foltz, et al.,* v. *U.S. News & World Report, Inc., et al., and David B. Richardson, et al.,* v. *U.S. News & World Report, Inc., et al.* U.S. District Court, District of Columbia, Civil Actions No. 84-0447 and 85-2195, June 22, 1987. (The Foltz case, a class action, dealt with the years 1973 through 1980; the Richardson case, not a class action, covered 1981.)

Background

Suits were brought by retirees who claimed they were underpaid at retirement because the closely held stock of U.S. News & World Report, Inc. (U.S. News), was undervalued by independent appraisers in the years 1973 through 1981. Defendants included U.S. News, certain directors, the U.S. News Profit-Sharing Plan (the plan), and the independent appraisal company. During their employment, the plaintiffs had participated in the plan. They were also beneficial owners of stock in the company under its stock bonus plan. Upon retirement or separation, they liquidated their plan accounts and redeemed their stock interests. Plaintiffs sought recovery of benefits they claimed were owed them by virtue of an alleged undervaluation of the company's stock during the class period.

In 1962, U.S. News' stock was sold to various parties associated with the company, including the plan, for a total consideration of $15 million, based on an independent appraisal. In 1975, the stock was appraised at $69 per share. By 1980 the appraised price had risen to $152 per share, and in 1981 it was appraised at $470 per share. From 1962 until the company was sold in 1984, at $2,842 a share, the same independent appraisal firm appraised the stock annually. The amount of plan benefits distributed to retirees was based on the annual appraisal, and the company exercised its option to purchase stock from certain stockholders who left the firm, at a price based on the annual appraisal.

Early in the 1970s, the plan's stock holdings increased to the point of constituting a majority of the outstanding stock. The plan stock, as well as most of the nonplan stock, was voted by a voting trust. After 1977, the voting trust could have been dissolved by a vote of the stock held by the plan, although there was never any movement to do so.

The company owned real estate at its headquarters location in Washington, D.C. During the 1970s, real estate values in the area increased significantly. There were discussions about developing the real estate for alternative uses, but nothing definite was done about it until 1981, when an agreement was reached with Boston Properties for development of the property.

Issues

In a 106-page memorandum opinion, Judge Barrington D. Parker stated that "the central issue requiring resolution in this litigation has always been the propriety of the methodology employed in appraising the U.S. News stock." The primary valuation issues in the case were as follows.

Control versus Minority Valuation Basis. The annual appraisals valued the stock on a minority basis. Plaintiffs contended that the stock should have been valued on a control basis.

Discount for Lack of Marketability.   Most of the annual appraisals applied a 10 percent discount for lack of marketability. The plaintiffs contended that no discount for lack of marketability should have been taken. (The stock had no put option. The company had a call option at the appraised price, which it exercised consistently to retire stock from the stock bonus plan when employees left. Most such calls were for cash, but on certain occasions the company exercised its option to purchase the stock on extended terms and at a low interest rate, which the call option permitted.)

Importance of Real Estate and Other Assets.   The annual appraisals placed various weights on the real estate values in different years depending on the circumstances at the time. In all years, however, the appraisals' primary emphasis was on the company's earning power. Plaintiffs contended that considerably more weight should have been accorded to the analysis and values of the real estate and certain other assets.

Subsequent Events.   The annual appraisals valued the stock on a going-concern basis, taking into consideration only facts and circumstances as they were known or perceived as of the appraisal date. Plaintiffs contended that prospects for future changes, such as those that arguably might be instituted by a buyer of the company (and thus impounded into the price that a buyer might be willing to pay for the company), should have been considered and reflected in the annual appraisals. As noted earlier, U.S. News was sold in 1984 at a price of $2,842 per share.

Other Issues.   There were a variety of other contentions as to adjustments that the appraisers should or should not have made to the company's income statements and balance sheets in the course of the appraisals.

Findings

Judge Parker's decision is worthwhile reading for students of valuation. This very brief abstract can highlight only a few of the salient points. The court concluded, "After consideration of the expert testimony presented, the Court is not persuaded that the per-share price arrived at each year by American Appraisal did not fall within a reasonable range of acceptable values."

Control versus Minority.   Regarding the stock held by the plan, the court stated:

> [S]ince the terms of the U.S. News plan did not contemplate anything other than a series of minority-interest transactions . . . the valuation of its stock on a minority basis does not offend ERISA. . . .
>
> [V]arious individuals concurrently held undivided, minority interests in a control block of stock. . . . The mere fact that Plan members' inter-

ests, if added together, amounted to a majority of the outstanding shares in the company does not, standing alone, entitle them to pro rata control value.

The following language not only speaks to the control-versus-minority issue but, in a broader sense, strongly supports the acceptance of appraisers' judgment when reasonable alternatives exist:

> Clearly, in the absence of any statutory, administrative, or judicial authority for the proposition that a control value might have been indicated, defendants cannot be faulted for employing a minority valuation. . . . ERISA does not require plan fiduciaries to maximize the benefits of departing employees . . .; it only requires them to make a reasonable choice from among possible alternatives.

The court also noted that the minority interest valuation was consistent with the appraisal methodology used when the plan purchased its stock in 1962 and 1966.

With respect to the voting trust, the court noted:

> [I]t is well recognized that, not only does the existence of a voting trust fail to make the underlying stock more valuable, it most often decreases the value of those shares. . . . [D]efendants would have been justified in reducing the value of the company's stock to reflect the impediment that the trust placed against the full enjoyment of the rights that would ordinarily have attached to the stock.

As to bonus stock, the court stated, "There is no basis for plaintiffs' assertion that their common stock should have been valued on a majority-interest basis."

Discount for Lack of Marketability.   The Court noted that:

> [T]he company was under no obligation to repurchase the stock. It has, rather, an option to call the stock. . . . Moreover, . . . the company could— and from time to time did—exercise its option . . . to pay for the stock on terms that would not have been accepted gladly by an outside investor. . . . [T]he modest 10 percent marketability discount that American Appraisal applied generally to the U.S. News stock in the aggregate was perfectly appropriate.

Real Estate and Other Assets.   The court stated:

> In a minority valuation . . . assets may or may not play an important part in arriving at a per-share figure, because a minority shareholder cannot reach those assets. . . . Generally speaking, if the valuation being undertaken is of a business, such as U.S. News, that produces goods or services, primary consideration will be given to the earnings of the company and the resultant return on a shareholder's investment.

Subsequent Events.   The court stated:

> [T]he approach to be used is not retrospective, but prospective. One must look at the situation as of the time that each employee separated from the company. Therefore, the appropriate inquiry is whether the company was properly valued during the class period, not whether former employ-

ees become eligible for a greater share of benefits upon the contingency of a subsequent sale.

With respect to possible future development of the real estate holdings, the court cited testimony that

> Any realizable value should be attributed to the real estate only if it was evident that the controlling interest had a firm and clear intent to dispose of the real estate within a very short or reasonable period of time [, that is,] absolute evidence . . . not mere development plans.

The decision explores the facts and issues quite thoroughly. However, immediately following its release, the attorney for the Foltz plaintiffs was quoted as saying that the plaintiffs will probably appeal on the basis that an appellate court's interpretation of the law might be very different from Judge Parker's view of things. As of this writing, an appeal has been filed.

Summary

Valuation of employer closely held stock held in an employee benefit plan is subject to challenge from three sources: the IRS, the Department of Labor, and the beneficiaries. This chapter has presented results of court cases based on challenges from all three sources. All eight of these cases involved valuations for years sometime between 1973 and 1981, so undoubtedly there are more cases in the pipeline involving valuations done in the 1980s.

In general, in those cases where the plaintiffs prevailed, the valuation that was found wanting was arrived at by someone who was not independent of the employer company and/or did not fully and adequately reflect all the factors relevant to the valuation of the subject stock. It is hoped that these problems will be alleviated to some extent by the requirement in the Tax Reform Act of 1986 that all ESOPs have the stock appraised at least annually by an independent, qualified appraiser of such stock. Certainly, however, we will hear of many additional employee plan stock valuation challenges over the next few years.

Chapter 25

Divorces, Dissolutions, Dissenting-Stockholder Suits, and Damages

Frequently litigation follows a dispute over the value of a business or an interest in one. Following are the most common reasons why closely held companies become involved in litigation concerning the value of holdings: (1) divorces, (2) corporate and partnership dissolutions, (3) damages, and (4) dissenting-stockholder suits.

Imminent or potential litigation requires that the appraiser understand the legal context within which the appraisal is being made. The appraiser must tailor the valuation methods and criteria to relevant statutory and case law, which often varies considerably from one valuation purpose to another and among jurisdictions. This chapter offers some general guidance regarding the most common situations in which the value of a business or a partial interest is a litigation issue.

The Legal Context

When a valuation involves existing or potential litigation, a thorough understanding of the legal context is essential. The appraiser and the attorney must work very closely together so they both are fully cognizant of how the legal context may influence certain aspects of the valuation procedures and conclusion.

The primary aspects of the legal context are:

1. Statutes.
2. Regulations and administrative rulings.
3. Case law.
4. Court directives and preferences.

Statutes

Federal law governs valuation issues in some types of cases, such as gift and estate tax matters, and damages in antitrust actions. State statutes apply to many other valuation issues, such as divorces, corporate and partnership dissolutions, damages resulting from condemnation, dissenting-stockholder suits, and values for ad valorem taxation. Statutes governing these issues vary considerably from state to state, and states occasionally change their statutes. If there is a chance that litigation involving a valuation issue will arise, the appraiser (or the attorney) should look into the legal jurisdiction and the relevant statutes.

Regulations and Administrative Rulings

Statutes may be supplemented by regulations and administrative rulings, some of which have the force of law and some not. For example, to implement the federal tax laws, the U.S. Treasury Department issues regulations with the force of law. However, the Internal Revenue Service issues Revenue Rulings representing its opinion on various issues, which do not have the force of law. The appraiser should know what regulations and rulings exist and their potential impact on the matter at hand.

Case Law

Case law is defined as past judicial cases to which courts may look for established precedent on a particular issue. Since most courts follow precedents set down by other cases within their jurisdictions, it behooves the appraiser to be familiar with the relevant case law. Courts may also consider precedents established in the decisions of courts in other jurisdictions, but they would not accept those decisions as binding.

Because courts rely heavily on case law, it plays an important part in valuations involving litigation. Some appraisers have studied case law in depth and maintain extensive files of court cases involving the valuation of businesses and professional practices. Others rely on the attorney involved in the case to research the case law and provide them with the relevant cases for their study. Either way, promoting the necessary understanding of relevant case law is an important area of cooperation between the appraiser and the attorney in any valuation situation involving imminent or potential litigation.

Court Directives and Preferences

Most courts prefer not to hear valuation cases at all and will try to encourage a settlement, if possible. Some courts exercise considerable discretion in the handling of valuation cases, determining such matters as when or whether the retention of experts must be disclosed to the opposing side, rules for discovery, and whether or not written appraisal reports must be prepared and exchanged.

Some of the foregoing items are standing matters of law or policy in certain jurisdictions; others are left to the discretion of the judge in the particular case. When litigation is involved, the appraiser should learn from the attorney at the outset the known ground rules and the court's preferences about the procedures of the case so that the appraiser may plan accordingly.

Divorces

Of all the types of litigated cases in which a business value can be a primary issue, divorce cases tend to be the most acrimonious and are most often the ones that go all the way to trial.

One primary reason for this situation probably is an outgrowth of the emotions leading up to the divorce itself. Obviously the appraiser should not be caught up in these emotions or allow his or her opinion of value to be influenced by the client's wish to "punish" the other spouse with the business value ruling.

Another primary reason why many divorce valuation cases go to court is the more ambiguous appraisal guidelines available to the appraiser, such as the standard of value to use or the appraisal date or dates to consider. While it is paramount that the appraiser request answers to these questions from the attorney handling the case, in many instances the attorney will look to the appraiser to make these decisions. Although the appraiser is not normally the person to make the final determination of the standard of value or appraisal date to be used, he or she should be able to explain to the attorney how a change in assumption will impact on the value. Also, the appraiser must be aware of the relevant laws governing these issues in order to understand what factors to consider in the appraisal report so that it conforms with the case law relevant for the state in which the divorce is being sought. It is ultimately the attorney's responsibility to instruct the appraiser as to the valuation date and standard of value to use, but the appraiser usually will be consulted in making these decisions.

Another difficulty in appraisals of businesses in divorce proceedings arises when the operating spouse resists disclosure of the information that the other spouse's appraiser needs. In some situations, court orders are necessary for obtaining the information. Often this means that essential information is unavailable until just before trial.

Standard of Value

The family law court is a court of equity. Because of that, the standards of value generally are not defined but are very elusive. One court may hold that fair market value should be used in the valuation of a business interest, and another may decide that the intrinsic value (to the spouse retaining the business) should be used.[1]

Generally, commercial businesses and salable service businesses and practices are valued using a fair market value standard. However, this is not universally true.

I have seen situations in which the court ignored a minority interest discount, even though the marital estate consisted of minority shares in the family business. The judge reasoned that because the operating spouse would continue to work in the business and still receive a large salary and perquisites, the business interest should be valued based on what it was worth to that particular shareholder.

---

[1] A classic example of differing standards of value occurred in California on May 10, 1983, when the California Court of Appeals, Second District, Division 7, held that the standard of valuation in a divorce proceeding should be the business's "investment value as distinguished from its market value" (*In re Marriage of Hewitson*, 142 Cal.App. 3d 874). Less than one month later, the California Court of Appeals, Fourth District, Division 1, held that the proper standard of valuation in divorce proceedings should be the business's "market value" and not "going concern value" (*In re Marriage of Sharp*, 192 Cal. Rptr. 97).

The value of a medical doctor's or lawyer's professional goodwill is considered marital property in many states, even though it cannot be sold.[2]

Another issue being confronted in some states involves the valuation of educational degrees and professional licenses. The New York Court of Appeals held that under the Domestic Relations Law of New York, a medical license is marital property that can be valued and allocated in the distribution of properties.[3] Although the court did not specifically comment on the standard of value to be used, it is obvious that a fair market value standard was not its choice.

Valuation Date

In most states, the valuation date generally is the date of trial. In some, however, the date of separation can be the relevant valuation date. In others, the valuation date may be the date the complaint was filed or the date of the commencement of the action.

One of the more complex situations that can arise results in community property states, which generally consider the valuation date to be as of the date of trial but also hold that earnings after the separation date are the distinct property of the party making those earnings. Therefore, in a situation in which a business value increases or decreases from date of separation to date of trial as a result of the operating spouse's efforts (which are separate property efforts), the matter of the proper date of value becomes more complex.

The appraiser often must walk into the courtroom prepared with opinions of values for several different dates. Obviously the appraiser needs direction from the attorney handling the case as to the valuation date or dates to use.

Discovery

The animosity and emotions that sometimes accompany a divorce frequently interfere with the appraiser's job, usually by the opposing spouse's refusal to provide the business records necessary for completing the appraisal. In such situations, the attorney for the spouse requesting the documents may need a declaration or affidavit from the appraiser listing the items needed and why each item is relevant to the appraisal. Often, the operating spouse objects to providing information because of legitimate concerns about keeping records confidential. As an example, a psychiatrist, not wanting to disclose the names of patients, may be unwilling to give a listing of the practice's accounts receivable. In such a case, the appraiser should strive to reach an accord in which the psychiatrist supplies only the information needed to actually value the business. If formal discovery is necessary, the appraiser should ask for all existing information that may have a bear-

---

[2] For a more complete discussion on professional goodwill value, see Shannon P. Pratt, *Valuing Small Businesses and Professional Practices* (Homewood, Ill.: Dow Jones-Irwin, 1986), Chapter 25.
[3] *O'Brien* v. *O'Brien*, 66 N.Y.2d 576.

ing on value. Often only one document request is allowed, which means that the appraiser should request all documents conceivably related to the valuation.

Other Issues

Clients, attorneys, and judges will ask the appraiser many questions in areas that are related to the appraisal but are not part of the appraisal itself. Such questions may relate to the potential tax consequences of a proposed settlement or the advisability of a split of the business stock. Generally, splitting the business's stock between the two parties is not advisable and will merely cause a marital dispute to become a shareholder dispute.

The complexity of taxes and their potential impact on a divorce requires the expertise of a tax attorney or certified public accountant familiar with these issues. The appraiser should avoid giving tax advice unless he or she has specific knowledge in this area.

One of the most important functions of the appraiser in a divorce case is to review and critique the appraisal report the opposing party submits. This usually means educating the attorney as to what the report says and where it is weak or in error. The importance and time spent on this phase should never be minimized, because the weaknesses of an appraisal report usually are disclosed only in the cross-examination of the expert.

The appraiser must be forthright with the client and the client's attorney as to the relative risk of going to trial versus accepting a settlement offer in regard to a business valuation. This might involve calculating the present value of an offer to pay proceeds over a period of time and comparing the result to the business values opined. Also, the appraiser must be careful not to lose sight of the fact that the entire divorce settlement proposal is more important than the parts— including the business value.

Corporate and Partnership Dissolutions

Corporate and partnership dissolutions have many characteristics in common with divorces—specifically, people who are terminating a relationship, frequently under antagonistic circumstances.

Corporate and partnership dissolutions are regulated by state statute. Generally, approval by at least a majority of the shares entitled to vote is required in order to effect a corporate dissolution. However, almost 50 percent of the states require approval by an affirmative vote of at least two thirds of all shares outstanding. Generally speaking, in most states there is little statutory or case law providing guidance on the issue of valuation. California Corporation Code Section 2000, however, does address this matter.

California Corporation Code Section 2000 authorizes the purchase by the other shareholders of the shares of the "moving parties" in a dissolution action. (*Moving parties* refers to the parties seeking dissolution of the corporation.) This code section specifies "fair value" as the standard of value and states, "The fair value shall be determined on the basis of the liquidation value but taking into account the possibility, if any, of sale of the entire business as a going concern in a liquidation."[4] The rationale behind this standard of value is explained by Harold Marsh, Jr., principal draftsman of the California General Corporation Law of 1977, as follows:

> Since the moving parties have initiated a dissolution proceeding pursuant to which the corporation will be liquidated unless the other shareholders buy them out or otherwise defeat their objective of having a liquidation of the corporation, the Drafting Committees believed that the moving parties should not be entitled to more than the liquidation value of their shares, i.e., what they would receive if their objective is obtained.[5]

The case law pursuant to California Corporation Code Section 2000 generally has interpreted the language "sale of the entire business as a going concern in a liquidation" to mean the value as if the entire enterprise were sold to a third party. Note that this is a different interpretation of the term "fair value" than that often encountered in the case law relating to dissenting stockholder statutes, as discussed in the next section.

In many instances, a buy-sell agreement that may specify a standard of value exists. In other cases, the parties may draw a document specifically for the purpose of providing guidance on the valuation of the interest and other aspects of the dissolution. Arbitration often can be a useful way to resolve valuation differences in conjunction with a corporate or partnership dissolution.

Dissenting-Stockholder Suits

In all states, current corporate statutes grant minority shareholders the right to dissent from certain fundamental corporate actions, such as merger, consolidation, or sale or exchange of a large portion of the corporations' assets. A minority shareholder who exercises the right to dissent can demand that his or her stock be appraised and can file suit requesting the corporation to purchase the stock at its appraised value.

Origin of Dissenting-Stockholder Statutes

Dissenting-stockholder statutes originated early in the twentieth century. Prior to that time, under common law mergers or similar corporate transactions required unanimous shareholder approval. This requirement often impeded corporate reorganization and became a

---

[4] California Corporation Code Section 2000(a).
[5] Harold Marsh Jr., *California Corporation Law,* Section 20.22 at 638 (1983).

contentious issue as the tremendous expansion of commerce in the last half of the nineteenth century created a need for larger and more complex corporate entities.

"Recognizing a need for corporate flexibility, courts proceeded to temper the rule of unanimity by allowing dissenters to recover the value of their shares in cash from the corporation in situations where the costs of upsetting the transaction would be excessive."[6] When, in the early twentieth century, the state legislatures began enacting statutes to allow corporations to effect changes by a simple majority vote, they also developed "the appraisal concept, which granted dissenters the right to receive the cash value of their stock as compensation for the elimination of the common-law rule that a single shareholder could block a corporate action."[7]

Squeeze-Out Mergers

In all states, stockholders who control some percentage of the stock, ranging from 50 percent plus one share up to 90 percent (depending on the state) can force out minority stockholders by effecting a *statutory merger,* often referred to colloquially as a *squeeze-out merger.* Such a merger can be effected either with an already existing company or with a new company created by the controlling stockholders for the purpose of the merger. This and other corporate actions can give rise to dissenting-stockholder actions requiring appraisal of, and cash payment for, shares held. Some common reasons for squeeze-out mergers include the cost or nuisance of having minority stockholders, disagreements with minority stockholders, and the need for additional capital infusion into a company that minority stockholders are not willing or able to share on a pro rata basis.

Dissenting-Stockholder Appraisal Rights

Stockholder appraisal rights are defined by state statute. The state statutes also designate the standard of value to be applied. A recent review of the state statutes relating to dissenting-stockholder rights indicates that all states except California designate *fair value* or *fair cash value* as the standard of value. (California's statute specifies *fair market value.*) Most states have modeled their dissenting-stockholder statutes after the Model Business Corporation Act. This act, which was revised in 1984, defines *fair value* as follows:

> "Fair value," with respect to a dissenter's shares, means the value of the shares immediately before the effectuation of the corporate action to which the dissenter objects, excluding any appreciation or depreciation in anticipation of the corporate action unless exclusion would be inequitable.[8]

---

[6] "Reconsideration of the Stock Market Exception to the Dissenting Shareholder's Right of Appraisal." *Michigan Law Review* 74 (April 1976), pp. 1023–66.
[7] Ibid., p. 1023.
[8] Model Business Corporation Act, Section 13.01(3).

According to the official comment of the Model Business Corporation Act, the definition of *fair value* leaves to the parties (and, ultimately, to the courts) the details by which *fair value* is to be determined within the broad outlines of the definition. As a result, interpretations of *fair value* vary somewhat from state to state. Although some courts have explicitly considered the fact that the valuation was for a minority interest,[9] others are less clear about their definition of *fair value*.

The Delaware courts in particular historically have been vague in their interpretation of *fair value*.

This is due in part to the development of the "Delaware Block Rule," which holds that various weightings should be given to each of four relevant factors: (1) earnings, (2) asset values, (3) dividends, and (4) market value. Historically, the earnings and dividends approaches generally have been based on comparative publicly traded companies and the market value on some measure of the market price for the company's stock (if it was publicly traded). *Fair value* would then be determined by weighting these approaches along with some measure of the company's asset value or ratio of price to asset value. As a result, depending on the weighting used, *fair value* often ends up somewhere between the minority value approaches and a proportionate share of net asset value.

However, a landmark case in 1983 said that the traditional factors considered under the Delaware Block Rule alone were not necessarily sufficient; instead, all relevant factors must be considered. In that particular case, the court specifically made the point that projections of future earnings were available and should be considered. The court also made the point that a determination of *fair value* "must include proof of value by any techniques or methods which are generally considered acceptable in the financial community."[10]

The interpretation of *fair value* is a subject of continued debate and is difficult to generalize. Several recent court decisions indicate that many courts will consider the size of the interest being valued in their decision regarding fair value. However, in certain situations, particularly those involving fraud, different interpretations appear. Therefore, it is important for the appraiser to confirm the appropriate definition of *fair value* with the client's attorney in each case.

Damages

The most common types of damage cases involving valuation of a business are the following:

1. Breach of contract.
2. Condemnation.

---

[9] Several recent court decisions have commented on the appropriateness of minority interest discounts, including *Perlman* v. *Permonite Manufacturing Co.*, 568 F.Supp. 222 (1983) *affirmed* 734 F.2d 1283 (7th Cir. 1984) and *Atlantic States Const., Inc.* v. *Beavers*, 314 S.E.2d 245 (Ga. App. 1984).

[10] *Weinberger* v. *UOP, Inc.*, 457 A.2d 701 (Del. Supr.1983).

3. Lost business opportunity.
4. Antitrust actions.
5. Personal injury.
6. Insurance casualty claims.

Except for breach of contract that denies someone a right to a business interest, all of the above have at least one common characteristic: The result of the damage is that the business did not operate as it would have had the event not caused the damage. This characteristic means that damage cases usually result in a hypothetical valuation—that is, a valuation of what would have been had the damage not occurred. The loss may be either lost profits for some period of time or the total loss of the business.

One other factor that often differentiates damage cases from other litigation involving business valuations is the fact that damage cases usually are tried before a jury, while most other valuation-related litigation, such as divorce cases, dissenting-stockholder suits, and tax cases, usually are tried before a judge without a jury. Preparation for a jury trial requires every possible effort to simplify the presentation of the complex subject of business or professional practice valuation, along with graphic exhibits to illustrate major points.

Breach of Contract

A variety of breach of contract actions can give rise to a lawsuit requiring a valuation of a business or a fractional interest in a business as a measure of damages. Perhaps a stockholder or partner was squeezed out in a manner that breached provisions of a contract between the parties, or maybe a prospective stockholder or partner was denied stock or a partnership interest that he or she had a contractual right to receive. In a totally different context, a supplier company could be damaged or even destroyed if a customer canceled a major contract that it had awarded and that the supplier company had positioned itself to fulfill.

Denial of a right to a business interest usually is a normal, straightforward valuation problem involving the value of whatever interest in the entity was denied as a result of the breach of contract. When the business itself is damaged by a breach of contract, however, the valuation problem is to determine the value of the lost profits or possibly the total value of the business as it would have been had the damage not occurred. It is axiomatic that the present value of lost future profits can be equal to, but not greater than, the total value of the enterprise had the damaging event not occurred. However, I have seen "experts" testify to damage sums many times any reasonable value for the entire entity.

Condemnation

A frequent cause of damages is the taking of business premises through eminent-domain or expropriation proceedings. Condemnation may result in the total loss of the business if relocation is not feasible or in a temporary loss of profits plus relocation costs. These temporary costs may also be combined with some permanent loss of locational goodwill, since it is unlikely that all patrons will follow a business or practice to a new location. Ideally, one would like to be able to document the loss of locational goodwill by the use of customer lists before and after the condemnation, but few businesses are likely to have such records.

The *Uniform Eminent Domain Code,* paragraph 1016(a), (1974), provides:

> In addition to fair market value determined under Section 1004, the owner of a business conducted on the property taken, or on the remainder if there is a partial taking, shall be compensated for loss of goodwill only if the owner proves that the loss (1) is caused by the taking of the property or the injury to the remainder; (2) cannot reasonably be prevented by a relocation of the business or by taking steps and adopting procedures that a reasonably prudent person would take and adopt in preserving the goodwill; (3) will not be included in relocation payments under Article XIV; and (4) will not be duplicated in the compensation awarded to the owner.

The above language places the burden of proving loss of business goodwill due to condemnation on the business owner and the appraiser.

Lost Business Opportunity

The most common scenario leading to a damage claim for lost business opportunity arises when an employee comes upon an opportunity through contacts made through the employer company and then exploits the opportunity personally or through another company without offering it to the initial employer. In this case, the measure of damages usually is the value lost to the initial employer as a result of not being offered the business opportunity.

Antitrust Actions

Perhaps the most complicated of all categories of business damage cases is antitrust. The stakes can be very high, because damages resulting from antitrust violations can be trebled.

The valuation problem is difficult because the appraiser must develop evidence to demonstrate the difference between the profit the business would have made had it not been for the antitrust violations and the profit it actually earned. Obviously, that requires hypothetical analysis.

Antitrust actions are tried in federal court, and each circuit of the federal court system develops its own case law. Courts usually take cognizance of case law developed in other circuits, but they are not bound by these precedents, some of which may conflict with the local circuit. Therefore, the appraiser should be aware of the local circuit case law as it affects the determination of damages in antitrust matters.

Personal Injury

Sometimes an injury impairs a person's ability to carry on his or her business or practice. In such cases, the amount of the economic loss normally is the measure of damages, usually estimated by the discounted future returns method discussed in Chapter 3.

Insurance Casualty Claims

It is not uncommon for a business to be interrupted or destroyed by a casualty loss, such as that from a fire or storm. Again the discounted future returns method commonly comes into play in estimating the loss, offset by whatever value is salvaged.

Summary

This chapter has discussed the four most commonly encountered categories of disputes over values of businesses and business interests other than valuations for tax purposes. Perhaps the most important fact that the appraiser, business owner, or attorney can gain from this chapter is that the applicable standard of value, and the many nuances thereof, for the resolution of many disputed business valuations can be elusive. Appraisals for the purpose of attempting to resolve such disputes should start with an understanding of the relevant statutory and case law, and proceed accordingly.

Chapter 26

Going Public

The purpose of including a chapter on going public is threefold:

1. When valuing any company or its shares of stock, it is helpful for the appraiser to think in terms of who the buyers for the company or its shares may be and to try to view it as a buyer would.
2. Since going public is a viable option for many companies, the price that a public offering could be expected to bring may be one indication of the shares' value whether or not a public offering is under active consideration.
3. Many users of this book may consider and/or be involved in a public offering at one time or another and thus wish some guidance on both the pricing and the process.

This chapter offers a brief primer on the process and pricing of initial public offerings. The material is offered only as a broad guide rather than a technical treatise on legal requirements. Securities regulation is one of the most specialized and complex areas of U.S. law. Anyone contemplating a public securities offering should consult with competent counsel experienced in working with securities law. Also, firms contemplating a public offering often retain independent financial advisers familiar with public markets to provide guidance on the timing, structure, and pricing of a public offering.

Market Acceptance of Initial Public Offerings (IPOs)

The market acceptance of initial public offerings has been much wider in the 1980s than in the late 1970s. This trend is demonstrated in Exhibit 26–1, which gives the number and dollar amounts of initial public offerings each year from 1978 through 1987.

EXHIBIT 26-1

Initial Public Offerings 1978-1987[a]

Year	No. of Issues	Amount $ Million
1978	18	214
1979	61	408
1980	152	1,400
1981	355	3,180
1982	124	1,350
1983	688	12,510
1984	354	3,890
1985	359	8,600
1986	719	22,380
1987	541	24,150

[a] Firm-commitment IPOs; excludes best-efforts and self-underwriting.

SOURCE: *Going Public: The IPO Reporter*

The capital markets have been awash with available funds in the late 1980s, and public offerings of all sizes have been readily accepted. Other factors that have enhanced the feasibility of public stock offerings by small and medium-size companies include:

1. Passage of legislation simplifying legal registration requirements for public offerings up to $7.5 million (e.g., the S-18 registration, discussed later in this chapter).
2. Development of a much more efficient national over-the-counter trading market through the NASDAQ (National Association of Security Dealers Automated Quotations) system.
3. Emergence of a network of regional investment banking firms actively promoting initial public offerings (IPOs) of small and medium-size companies.

Advantages of Going Public

A company may gain the following advantages by going public:

1. A public offering raises capital.
2. It provides liquidity for stockholders.
3. It facilitates acquisitions of other companies or interests for stock.
4. It provides exposure and prestige for the company.
5. In some cases, it may facilitate the sale of the entire company.

Access to Capital Markets

The most dominant reason for most companies to go public is to raise capital. As noted in Part I, it is common to find companies that would realize good growth if they were supported by additional capital. Many such companies have no people directly associated with them who have the means to provide that capital. Some companies' needs for increased capital may be ongoing over several years, and tapping the public equity markets may be the most feasible way to meet those needs.

Liquidity for Stockholders

For some companies, gaining liquidity for stockholders is the dominant reason for going public, and in most cases it is a major consideration. As the data in Chapter 10 show, the capital markets place a high premium on liquidity, or, conversely, levy a high discount for lack of it.

As discussed further in subsequent sections, proceeds from an IPO may go entirely to the company, entirely to selling stockholders, or to any combination of the two. Stock held by insiders that is not registered for sale in a public offering is still subject to restrictions on its sale, but, depending on those restrictions, there is an established market into which it eventually can be sold. Consequently, as demonstrated in Chapter 10, the discount for lack of marketability for restricted shares of a public company typically is less than that for shares of an otherwise comparable private company.

Means of Financing Acquisitions

Having a publicly traded stock provides a form of currency that the company may use for acquisitions. The primary advantage to the acquirer is the ability to acquire other companies, or interests in other companies, by paying in securities instead of cash. The primary advantage to the seller is the ability to structure the sale as a tax-free exchange so that taxes are not triggered on any gain from the transaction.

The public company stock the seller receives usually is restricted from immediate resale in the public market. However, as noted earlier, even restricted shares of a public company generally are a step closer to being readily marketable than are shares of a privately held company.

Exposure and Prestige

A public stock listed on a national exchange or quoted on the NASDAQ system has its name and stock price quoted daily in national and local newspapers throughout the country. In addition, its press releases are picked up and published or quoted far more often than those of a private company, because they are of greater interest to the financial community. Some public companies structure their annual reports to be an effective marketing tool as well as a necessary financial reporting mechanism. This public spotlight is, of course, of greater interest and benefit to some companies than to others.

Facilitation of Sale of Company

Many investment bankers believe that a public company is a more likely acquisition candidate and will command a higher price when sold than an otherwise comparable closely held company. One reason that a public company may get a better price than a closely held company relative to earnings, asset values, and other fundamental factors is the extent and credibility of its financial reporting. Compliance with regulations for disclosure of financial information goes well beyond the minimum requirements for audited financial statements. Also, potential acquirers almost surely know of public companies through various public information sources, which is not necessarily true of private companies, especially if acquirers are not in the same industry. Further, the acquirer can make a first-pass evaluation of the prospective acquiree on the basis of publicly available information.

Still another reason why a public company often achieves some premium in its price is that some private companies in effect "go public" by acquiring a public company and structuring a merger to provide public market liquidity for themselves by preserving the acquiree's registration and public trading market.

Disadvantages of Going Public

The primary disadvantages of going public, of varying significance to different companies, are the cost, the need for public disclosure, compliance and fiduciary requirements and restrictions, price volatility, and possible exposure to an unfriendly raid.

Costs of Going Public

There are two distinct aspects of the costs of going public: the out-of-pocket cash costs and, in the case of new securities sold by the company, the dilution resulting from additional shares owned by outside investors. These costs can be further divided into initial costs and ongoing costs.

The major initial costs of going public, sometimes called *flotation costs,* usually are underwriting, legal, accounting, and printing. These costs are discussed in some detail in Chapter 10, "Data on Discounts for Lack of Marketability." The major ongoing costs are the SEC filings, described in Chapter 9, "Comparative Transaction Data," and the costs of printing and mailing annual and quarterly reports and proxy materials to shareholders.

In addition to whatever dilution occurs as a direct result of the stock's sale to the public, the underwriters usually receive some warrants to compensate them over and above their cash commissions. The warrants may be at—or, perhaps more typically, a little above—the public offering price and will be good for some negotiated period of time, often five years.

Public Disclosure

Many people consider confidentiality of financial and other information an important advantage of being a closely held rather than a publicly traded company. Each company must evaluate this factor in light of its own circumstances and perspectives. In addition to the material discussed in Chapter 9, the bibliography at the end of this chapter includes many references covering public disclosure requirements. One of the most comprehensive of these publications is the *Securities Regulation Handbook.*[1]

---

[1]*Securities Regulations Handbook* (Los Angeles: Ticor Print Network/Jeffries Banknote Company, 1983).

Regulatory and Fiduciary Compliance and Restrictions

Going public (unless through an intrastate-only offering) makes the company subject to the Securities Act of 1933 and all the subsequent legislation and regulations, which are far beyond the scope of this book (see the bibliography at the end of this chapter). Actual or alleged breaches of fiduciary responsibility by public company directors and officers have led to a plethora of lawsuits in this litigious society, some generated by regulatory authorities and others by disgruntled stockholders. This has caused many well-qualified people to be reluctant to serve on boards of directors of public companies and led to an increasing trend toward public companies acquiring directors' liability insurance, an additional indirect cost of going public.

Stock Price Volatility

The price of a public company's stock can be subject to volatile (and not necessarily rational) price swings. As demonstrated in Chapter 2, "Principles of Business Valuation—Theory and Practice," P/E ratios and other fundamental indicators of current fair market value are much more volatile in the public stock market than in the merger and acquisition market. An exorbitant market price can render new stock options nearly useless as a form of management compensation. An unduly depressed price, which can persist for extended periods, can impose a hardship on those who need or desire to sell and can cause a high cost of equity capital in terms of a high degree of dilution when a company needs to go into the equity market during times of depressed prices.

As a result of discussions with hundreds of owners of closely held company shares over many years, it is my perception that owners of private company shares both expect and desire that the prices of those shares, to the extent that they are bought and sold from time to time, be less volatile than would be the case if the stock were traded in the public market. I believe that the negotiated prices of the shares of the majority of closely held companies that do occasionally transfer shares have been largely consistent with this expectation.

Unfriendly Raids

If a majority of the stock is in the hands of the general public, the company could be the target of an unfriendly raid, a prospect that does not threaten a closely held company.

Preparing for an IPO

Much of the preparation for an initial public offering is no different than what should be done if a sale of the entire company were contemplated, such as cleaning up the company, maintaining excellent records, and so forth. As with selling out, companies considering public offerings often are well served by starting their preparations several years in advance.

Audited Financial Statements

Depending on the form of registration, audited financial statements covering some number of years are necessary for most public offerings. It usually is much easier and cheaper to do these year by year in contemplation of an offering than to attempt to audit retroactively when the company decides it is ready to try a public offering.

In this respect, there is some advantage in using a C.P.A. firm that has experience in auditing public companies. Such a firm may enhance the company's credibility with prospective underwriters. Also, the firm's experience in preparing financial statements for meeting SEC requirements may help prevent delays in obtaining regulatory approval of the offering's registration.

Preparing a Business Plan

Preparing a business plan in contemplation of a public offering is much like preparing a business plan in conjunction with raising capital from other sources in that it reflects the expected effects of the proceeds of the new capital. In many cases, the plan should account for two or even more possible infusions of capital over a period of two to five years. One of the most common shortcomings encountered in business plans is underestimation of the amount of capital required for achieving the company's objectives.

The business plan should be prepared carefully and realistically. Many so-called business plans tend to be what investment bankers call "hockeystick projections"—starting with a low base and going straight up. Anybody with computer spreadsheet software can make a fairly detailed-looking projection. What is important to an investment banker, however, is how well the company has thought out how it is going to get there, including consideration of all the many things that can go wrong.

Legal and Other Advisers

Public securities registration and compliance is an extremely specialized area of law. It is absolutely essential for any company involved in a public offering to have legal counsel that is experienced in and knowledgeable about securities law. Either an investment banking firm or a business valuation firm should be able to refer the company to attorneys with the requisite expertise. Conversations with such an attorney should take place well in advance of any contemplated offering in order for the company to learn what to expect in terms of registration, ongoing reporting, and other compliance requirements.

As noted earlier, the company may also wish to engage a business valuation firm knowledgeable about the public markets as financial adviser in the years or months prior to a possible public offering. Financial advisory services could include any or all of the following:

1. Assistance in preparing a business plan.
2. Advice regarding realistic timing, price, and structure of the offering.
3. Introduction or referral to underwriters, counsel, and/or other professionals related to the public offering process.
4. Advice regarding interim financing alternatives.
5. Valuation guidance for various possible stock transfers, issuance of options, and other possible transactions prior to the offering.

Transfers of Stock Prior to IPO

The vast majority of transfers of minority ownership interests within three years or so prior to an IPO occur for one of three reasons: (1) to liquidate an investor's interest, (2) to raise interim capital, or (3) to provide a growth opportunity for family members and or employees.

These transactions usually (though certainly not always) take place at prices far below the eventual public offering price—typically half the public offering price or less. This has been demonstrated in studies by Willamette Management Associates, Inc., and Baird & Company., Inc., the results of which are presented in Chapter 10, "Data on Discounts for Lack of Marketability." The largest single reason for such price differences is the lack of marketability of the securities prior to the public offering recognizing that even if a public offering is contemplated, there is no assurance that it will be successfully accomplished or, if it is, at what price.

Another reason for price differences, of course, may be differences in the company's fundamental position between the time of the private transaction and the time of the public offering.

Many companies that hope to go public never make it. Sometimes, because of either market conditions or internal company problems, offerings are withdrawn even after the preliminary prospectus has been printed and distributed, never again to appear in the public market eye. Offering prices may be revised substantially from prices discussed during negotiations. For example, after the October 19, 1987, record single-day stock market drop of 508 points on the Dow Jones Industrial Average, many offerings were withdrawn and others adjusted downward in price as much as 25 percent. Furthermore, stock not actually sold in the initial public offering may not even be included in the stock registration and thus may still be subject to a substantial discount for lack of marketability from the public trading price.

Liquidation of Investors' Interests

It is not unusual for some investors to sell all or part of their interest in a company prior to a public offering even if they know that an offering is contemplated, because they want or need to convert the interest to cash for one reason or another. They may not want to endure the waiting period or the uncertainty as to whether, when, and at what price the offering will actually occur. In such cases the buyer may be the company, another stockholder, or a third party.

Raising Interim Capital

There can be several reasons why a company may want or need to take an intermediate step of one or more private placements to raise some capital prior to a public offering. The lead time and costs may be considerably less than for a public offering of the size needed at the interim point. The company may not be sufficiently developed for the market to be ready to accept its stock in a public offering.

Today there are many investment groups in the business of supplying such interim funding. Be forewarned, however, that the expected rate of return on such venture capital investments is very high—expected annually compounded returns in excess of 30 percent are more the rule than the exception.[2] Furthermore, such venture capitalists expect downside protection, or at least a preferred position. They rarely buy straight common stock; rather they usually take some type of debt or preferred stock position with warrants or conversion rights.

Equity Interests for Family Members or Employees

In many cases, owners of a company contemplating a public offering may want to sell or gift stock or other equity interests to family members and/or employees in order to provide them with an opportunity to participate in the company's future growth.

If stock is gifted, or if an owner dies, a gift or estate tax return showing the stock's fair market value should be filed, supported by a competent appraisal. In numerous instances, the IRS has attempted to collect substantial amounts of gift or estate tax based on a public offering a few weeks or months after the gift or death at a price considerably higher than the value reported on the tax return. Court decisions on such cases generally have tended toward favoring the taxpayer because of value factors already discussed in this chapter and elsewhere in the book, but only when such factors have been presented convincingly through credible expert testimony.[3]

Employee incentives can be provided through issuance of the same class of shares that will be sold to the public, through creation of a separate class of shares especially designed for management incentive, or through options. In most cases, incentive stock or options will not exceed 10 to 15 percent of total stock outstanding. The design of management compensation securities is a complex and fascinating spe-

---

[2]For an excellent primer on venture capital, see Arthur Lipper III, *Venture's Guide to Investing in Private Companies* (Homewood, Ill.: Dow Jones-Irwin, 1983).

[3]See, for example, *Cecilia A. Tallichet*, 33 T.C.M. 1133 (1974); *Morris M. Messing*, 48 T.C. 502 (1967); and *Minette Hermelin*, 36 T.C.M. 426 (1977).

cialty within the broader field of business valuation, but it is beyond the scope of this book. The main thing the company should be cautious about is that such incentive stock or other participation not be issued at a price or on a basis that the IRS might construe as being subject to income tax at the time of issue. In order to avoid this, it must be clear that it was not issued for consideration at less than fair market value of the stock or option received; otherwise, it may be considered taxable compensation for services as an employee.

Legal Forms of Registration

Registration requirements for going public fall under two broad sets of jurisdictions—federal and state. In some states, registration with the SEC automatically qualifies the securities for sale in the particular state. However, the majority of states require registration if securities are to be offered in the state even if they are also registered with the SEC.

Some states impose criteria that are in some respects more stringent than the federal standards. The point of SEC registration is to require full disclosure of material information. Some states, for example, require not only full disclosure but that the offering meet some standard such as "fair, just, and equitable." It is up to the respective state's corporation commission or comparable body to determine whether each proposed offering meets such a standard. Many offerings that the SEC and other states have approved have been rejected in certain states for failing to meet such standards.

S-1 Registration

The most comprehensive securities registration form is the S-1. There is no limit to the amount of capital a company can raise under an S-1 registration form. The securities may be offered by the issuer, by one or more existing stockholders, or by any combination thereof. Once an S-1 registration has been approved by the SEC, it can be offered in any or all states in which it also has been approved or that automatically allow federally registered offerings.

The S-1 normally entails the greatest legal, accounting, and printing costs. It must be filed with the SEC headquarters in Washington, D.C. Besides being the most costly, the S-1 filing tends to require the most lead time for completion and gaining SEC approval. It is not uncommon to require six months or more to prepare and amend the document to the SEC's satisfaction.

S-18 Registration

On April 23, 1979, the SEC adopted the Form S-18 registration statement. This may be used for offerings of up to $7.5 million, of which not more than $1.5 million may be for the account of selling shareholders. It may be used by most types of companies; exceptions are natural resource companies, investment companies, and certain other types of firms.

The S-18 is somewhat easier to prepare than the S-1. In particular, it does not require historical audited financial statements for as long a period of time. Also, it may be filed at any of the regional offices of the SEC rather than at the headquarters in Washington, D.C., if the issuer so desires. Usually processing through the regional offices is a little quicker than through the national office. However, the reverse can be true if the registration has some unusual features that cause the regional office to call on the national office for advice or approval.

The Form S-18 registration has gained increasing use in recent years and has helped make it more feasible for smaller companies to complete successful offerings.

Reg A Registration

Congress has authorized the SEC to allow the more abbreviated "Reg A" registration to be used for offerings of up to $2 million. At the time of this writing, the SEC has implemented this authority to the extent of allowing Reg A filings for offerings of up to $1.5 million. The securities may be offered by the issuing corporation, by existing stockholders, or any combination thereof. The Reg A may be filed at the regional SEC offices and is less costly and time consuming than the S-1 or S-18. In recent years, however, since the S-18 filing has become more developed, Reg A filings have become increasingly rare.

Regulation D

Federal regulations regarding exemptions to the above registration requirements are now contained in Regulation D, primarily Rules 504, 505, and 506. Rule 504 allows issuance of up to $500,000 worth of securities per year with no limitation on the number of investors or their qualifications, and the issuer may sell the securities through brokers and pay commissions. Rule 505 (replacing old Rule 242) covers offerings of between $500,000 and $5 million and has restrictions as to purchasers's qualifications. Rule 506 allows an unlimited dollar amount of securities to be sold to 35 or fewer buyers who meet specified standards.

All sales of securities pursuant to Regulation D require a series of filings on Form D. Also, all are subject to restriction from resale for a period of two years.

Intrastate Offering

If all of the securities in a public offering are offered and sold only to the residents of a particular state, the offering need be registered only with that state and not with the SEC. There is no limit on the number of dollars the company can raise or on the number of people to whom it may offer the securities. The costs and time required run substantially lower than those for an S-1 registration—more in line with a Reg A offering. Many companies have successfully used intrastate offerings to raise millions of dollars.

However, intrastate offerings have some serious disadvantages. First, the seller may inadvertently violate the securities laws by selling to someone who is not a bona fide resident of the state in which the offering is registered. Second, the purchaser may not resell to other buyers outside the state for a considerable period of time. This restriction severely limits the offering's after-market liquidity, thus reducing its attractiveness. Broker-dealers in the stock market do not like to deal in securities that are subject to intrastate restrictions, because they are afraid of inadvertently violating the securities laws by selling to a non–bona-fide resident of the state of the offering. An intrastate offering thus tends to suffer considerably from lack of marketability compared with an offering registered with the SEC under the S-1, S-18, or Reg A registration provisions.

Arranging the Public Stock Sale

Selecting an Investment Banker

The investment banking firm selected to handle the offering should be large enough to be able to get the entire offering sold and, preferably, should be well represented in the areas in which the issuing company is best known.

If the offering is relatively small, a regional investment banking firm usually is the best choice—in fact, most S-18 offerings sold by brokers are made through regional investment bankers rather than national houses. One should inquire as to which investment bankers have established a successful track record in selling offerings of the size and type contemplated. An outside independent valuation consultant or corporate finance consultant usually can be quite helpful to the company in this respect. Such a consultant also can inform the issuing company of a reasonable level of underwriting fees for a given size and type of issue.

The best market for the company's securities often is where the company is located or where it is most visible. For this reason, it is desirable to choose an investment banker that is well represented in the issuing company's area, either directly or through other brokerage firms that would participate in the selling group.

Firm Underwriting versus Best-Efforts Offering

Firm Underwriting. The term *firm underwriting* means that the underwriting firm guarantees the issuer of the securities that the issuer will receive the agreed-upon proceeds of the offering. In other words, the underwriter is obligated to pay the issuer the net proceeds that have been contracted for whether or not it succeeds in selling the entire issue at the public offering price.

However, it is important for prospective offerors to understand that the investment banker does not make the firm underwriting commitment until virtually the moment the registration becomes effective and the stock is about to be sold to the public. Up until that time the price, terms, and size of the offering are still subject to negotiation and the entire offering can be withdrawn.

Best-Efforts Offering.   Smaller companies, especially those going to the public market for the first time and those of a somewhat speculative nature, frequently have to settle for a *best-efforts offering*. This means that the underwriting firm will use its best efforts to sell the entire offering but does not guarantee that all or even any part of it will be sold.

A best-efforts offering can prescribe that a certain amount be sold and, if not sold, have the money returned to the purchasers. Alternatively it may prescribe that whatever amount has been sold by a predetermined date subsequently be turned over to the issuer, with the offering closed at that point. Exactly what arrangement will be appropriate depends to some extent on the purpose of the offering. If the purpose is to build a new plant, which will require some minimum amount of capital, there usually will be a minimum amount of proceeds that will be acceptable. If the offering is for another purpose, such as repayment of debt or building up working capital, it might not be necessary to set any minimum amount.

Most best-efforts issues are sold out in full, but certainly not all. When it is necessary to do an offering on a best-efforts basis, it is especially important to thoroughly assess the ability of the investment banking firm to sell the full amount of the offering.

Pricing IPOs

Pricing initial public offerings is a classic exercise in estimating fair market value. The pricing of public offerings relies very heavily on the analysis of prices at which other comparable publicly traded securities are selling in the marketplace. The underwriter's analysts will consider all the standard value indicators discussed in Chapter 4, such as price/earnings ratios, price/revenues ratios, and price/book value ratios.

Underwriters also consider the discounted future returns method discussed in Chapter 3. Chester Paulson, president of Paulson Investment Company, an active underwriter of offerings from $1 million to $10 million, says, "For young companies, investors need to see the possibility of realizing five to ten times their investment in three to five years, if projections are fully met, since few companies fully meet their projections."

Companies hoping to go public generally tend to be overoptimistic in their earnings projections and also to have an inflated expectation of a realistic offering price. The underwriter's analysts must weight the probability of achieving projected results. They will be less interested in the numbers in the company's projections as in exactly how the company expects to achieve them.

Regarding excessively high price expectations, Paulson comments, "The classic mistake is for the company president to expect to price his stock by taking current market price/earnings ratios of existing public companies and multiplying them times projected earnings that his company hopes to achieve at some time in the future."

Most practitioners agree that it is a good idea to price the initial offering a little on the conservative side in the hope that the market will establish and maintain a rising price trend. This generally is considered preferable to setting the price as high as possible, which increases the risk that investors will suffer losses either if the company has a bit of misfortune or if bad market conditions are encountered, thus jeopardizing the viability of future offerings.

Structuring IPOs

Decisions to be made in structuring the public offering include the offering's size, the amount of proceeds going to the company and to selling stockholders, and whether the offering will consist of straight common stock or some other security or combination of securities.

Size of Offering

The size of the offering will depend on the company's capital needs, the underwriter's ability to sell the stock, and the percentage of the company's equity that the owners are willing to give up. The percentage of the equity sold on initial public offerings varies greatly, but 30 to 45 percent is quite typical. Often a company plans the initial offering with the intent of having another offering within a year or two, optimally at a higher price if it is successful in its use of the proceeds from the first offering.

Allocation of Proceeds between Company and Stockholders

Generally, but not always, most or all of the proceeds from an initial public offering go to the company rather than to selling shareholders. Occasionally a company with little or no need for capital will go public primarily for the purpose of providing liquidity for the owners, in which case most or even all of the proceeds may go to selling shareholders.

Decision to Offer Stock and/or Other Securities

Sometimes an initial offering can be made more attractive to the investing public by structuring it in some way other than straight common stock. For example, a convertible bond offers the investor some interest income, plus a security that is senior to the common stock. Another popular technique is to issue units, which can consist of either debt or equity-type securities with warrants attached. There is almost no limit to the possible ramifications in the creative structuring of an offering. The investment banker's experience should be very helpful in analyzing the alternatives.

Convertible debentures may be feasible if the company will have enough cash flow to cover the interest payments and the balance sheet can stand the added debt. Convertible preferred stock is also a possibility. Conversion prices typically are set somewhat above the common stock's offering price.

More typical than the use of convertibles is the use of warrants, which often are an attractive sweetener for inducing investors to buy the offering. Warrants can be useful as a vehicle for facilitating a second round of financing. They can be made callable so that the company effectively can force exercise if the stock price is above the strike price, thus bringing in new capital without incurring the delays and costs of a new underwriting.

The exercise price of warrants may be fixed or variable depending on some factor such as earnings, revenues, or stock's market price. A variable price provides a performance incentive to the insiders running the company, since a higher exercise price based on good performance would mean a lower percentage of the equity that would have to be given up as a result of the warrants' exercise.

After the Public Offering

Following a public securities offering, a company is subject to ongoing legal requirements to report financial and other information to the SEC and to stockholders. It also is desirable to have an ongoing program of communications with existing and prospective stockholders and brokers beyond the minimum reporting and information distribution required by law. Insiders are subject to various restrictions on stock that they continue to hold.

Legal Reporting Requirements

A public company must report regularly to stockholders and also must comply with the additional requirements of the annual 10-K, quarterly 10-Q, and special-events 8-K reports that must be filed with the SEC. (The various required forms and their contents are summarized in Exhibit 9–2.) If a company goes public using an S-18 registration, its annual reporting requirements on Form 10-K are ameliorated for two years to the extent that the company need only update the disclosures required in Form S-18. From time to time, the SEC makes changes in its reporting requirements, so companies should check the latest regulations in any case.

Investor Communications and Relations

There are many good reasons to maintain an active investor relations program beyond the minimum required by law. For one thing, a consistent investor relations program can help maintain an active trading market in the stock at a reasonable price. Also, the company very likely will want to go to the public market with an additional offering at some future time. The better appreciated the company is in the financial markets, the easier it will be to make an additional offering at a reasonable price.

At any given time, there are thousands of public securities competing for a limited amount of public interest in their ownership. A company contemplating a public offering should plan to commit to a budget for an ongoing investor relations program to maintain public interest in the stock once it has made the initial offering.

Insider Trading Restrictions

Once the company is public, the sale of stock still held by insiders is subject to a variety of legal restrictions. The restrictions are contained primarily in Section 16(b) of the 1934 Securities Exchange Act and SEC Rules 10b-5 and 144. Limited amounts of stock may be sold to the public when certain conditions are met. Such sales should be governed by advice of counsel. Large blocks, unless registered for sale to the public through a secondary offering, can be sold only in private transactions to certain categories of investors. Because of this limited marketability, such sales of unregistered stock usually take place at prices somewhat below the public market trading price of the otherwise exactly equal but registered and freely tradable shares. Data on such discounts for lack of marketability are discussed in Chapter 10.

Summary

This chapter has provided brief insight into the process of going public, including preparation, registration, structuring, and pricing the offering. The price that a public offering might bring can be one indication of the value of a private company's stock if a public offering is a viable alternative for that company. However, the public market's willingness to accept various types of offerings, as well as the pricing, tends to be quite volatile, even within a very short time frame. It is also important to recognize that minority stockholders do not have the right to register a company's stock for a public offering.

Due to the availability of capital, regulatory encouragement of smaller-company offerings, and the development of underwriting groups and a more efficient secondary market, going public is a viable alternative for more companies than ever before. However, attempting to go public can be a costly process and one that ultimately may fail for many companies. Once public, a company has ongoing compliance and other costs, as well as certain restrictions on its activities, with which closely held companies are not burdened.

Bibliography

Articles

Bekey, Michelle. "How Not to Get Taken." *Venture,* April 1987, pp. 53, 55, 57.

Feinberg, Andrew. "The Push Is On." *Venture,* April 1987, pp. 47–50.

Henning, Harry L. "So Your Client Wants to Go Public." *ABA Journal,* March 1, 1986, pp. 58–62.

James, Ellen. "How Not to Get Sued." *Venture,* April 1987, pp. 52, 54, 56.

Laderman, Jeffrey M. "Timing Is Everything When You Go Public." *Business Week,* November 3, 1986, pp. 120, 124.

Mamis, Robert A. "All Shares Are Not Created Equal." *Inc.,* March 1987, pp. 99–100, 102.

Schneider, Carl W., and Jason M. Shargel. "Now That You Are Publicly Owned . . ." *Business Lawyer,* July 1981, p. 1631.

Sutton, David P. and Tom Post. "The Cost of Going Public." *Venture,* April 1986, pp. 30–34, 38, 40.

Books and Booklets

A Guide to Going Public in the U.K. London: Peat, Marwick, Mitchell & Co., 1985.

Deciding to Go Public: Understanding the Process and the Alternatives. New York: Ernst & Whinney, 1984.

Going Public in Canada. Vancouver, British Columbia: Peat, Marwick, 1985.

Going Public on the Vancouver Stock Exchange. Vancouver, British Columbia: Peat, Marwick, 1987.

Going Public: What the CEO Needs to Know. New York: Peat, Marwick, Mitchell & Co., 1985.

Going Public: What the High Technology CEO Needs to Know: Guidebook & Executive Summary. New York: Peat, Marwick, Main & Co., 1987.

Halloran, Michael J. *Going Public.* 5th ed. New York: Arthur Andersen & Co. and Sorg Printing Co., Inc., 1983.

O'Flaherty, Joseph H. *Going Public: The Entrepreneur's Guide.* New York: John Wiley & Sons, 1984.

Taking Your Company Public. New York: Price Waterhouse, 1987.

The Going-Public Decision. New York: Arthur Young, 1984.

Wat, Leslie. *Strategies for Going Public*. New York: Deloitte, Haskins & Sells, 1983.

Periodicals

Going Public: The IPO Reporter. New York: The Dealers' Digest, Inc., weekly newsletter.

Investment Dealers' Digest. New York: The Dealers' Digest, Inc., weekly magazine.

New Companies. Menlo Park, Calif.: Data Financial Press, annual and quarterly volumes supplemented by weekly fact sheets.

Part VII

Litigation

Chapter 27

Litigation Support

This chapter consists largely of observations based on my own experience with some 600 or so litigated valuation cases in which my staff and I were involved over the past 20 years. Many of the experiences and opinions in this chapter are stated in the first person, hopefully making it clear that they represent my own views and not necessarily a consensus of any group of either legal or valuation practitioners.

I strongly believe that when an attorney takes on a case in which the value of a business is or may be an issue, the client's interest usually is best served by retaining a competent business appraisal firm at the outset. That is why this chapter on litigation support precedes the chapter on expert testimony.

I have found that most business valuation disputes can be resolved and that the odds of resolution in the client's best interest are substantially increased by working closely from the very beginning with a business valuation expert who is experienced in litigation. A well-grounded expert can be very helpful in assessing the case, both in determining a reasonable range of value and in weighing the risks involved in going to court. If the case cannot be resolved outside the courtroom, the decision to go to court will be based on a sound assessment of the situation from a valuation viewpoint, and the preparation for court will be orderly and thorough.

On the negative side, I know of scores of instances in which clients were shortchanged because they or their attorneys tried to "wing it" without an expert, retained an expert who was less than competent, or brought the expert in too late to get the full benefit of his or her expertise. These situations usually arose because someone tried to eliminate or minimize the expert's fees, not fully understanding the expert's benefits and services, not knowing how to locate and evaluate the best expert for the particular situation, or just from plain inertia. I can't count the times our firm has been contacted for litigation support by attorneys for one side of a case literally *months* after having already been retained by the opposite side. Also, we have declined assignments on a number of occasions because we were contacted too late to get the necessary work done in the time remaining.

At the outset, I wish to comment on the importance of integrating preparation for expert testimony with other litigation support services. On the one hand, many of the litigation support services discussed in this chapter are a logical by-product of thorough preparation for expert testimony; also, many such services contribute to the strength of preparation for expert testimony. I just mention a word of caution expressed several times elsewhere. The expert is not practicing law by providing litigation support. The expert is an advocate for his or her position, not for the client. The appraiser may assist both the client and the lawyer in preparing the best possible case, but when it comes to the appraiser's opinions, the appraiser must present an unbiased, nonadvocate position on all substantive issues on which he or she has been asked for an opinion. The expert must remain free from both bias and the taint of bias. If the attorney thinks that any litigation support functions that the expert otherwise might logically perform would create bias, or even an appearance of bias, the attorney might wish to have them done by another valuation analyst on the expert's professional staff or even by a different business valuation firm.

This chapter deals with locating and engaging business valuation experts and the use of experts for a broad range of litigation support services. The following two chapters deal with expert testimony and arbitration.

Litigation Support Services

Exhibit 27–1 lists some of the most common litigation support services that business appraisal experts provide. Although the quality of expert testimony is undeniably critical, often the scope and quality of related litigation support that business valuation experts provide is just as important to the case, or even more so.

The vast majority of litigated business valuation disputes never reach the stage of requiring testimony before a judge or jury. Well-focused and top-quality business valuation support services contribute significantly to successful settlements. The same support services that typically lead to successful settlements also provide the underpinnings for proper trial preparation. Conversely, the surest way to facilitate a successful settlement is to begin preparing to go to court right at the outset.

Evaluating Experts

Most business valuation analysts have a business-school pragmatism and would recoil at the idea of being perceived as college-of-liberal-arts economists. Nevertheless, a business valuation expert providing expertise in a litigated valuation case is a "forensic economist" in the very best sense of that expression—that is, he or she is using expertise in the microeconomics of the firm as translated into present value in a legal proceeding. For litigation, it is important to retain experts who not only can use their education and experience to develop and support a sound position but can communicate that position in terms that a

EXHIBIT 27-1

Litigation Support Services
Available from Business Valuation Experts

Assessing the case
Framing and focusing valuation issues
Reasonable range of value
Risks and uncertainties
Benefit/cost relationship of pursuing
litigation

Discovery
Documents request list
Interrogatories
Preparation for meaningful depositions
Facility visits and interviews

Research
Authority for positions on valuation
issues (books, articles, court cases,
and other sources)
Economic and industry data
Comparative transaction data

Consultation on procedural matters
Scheduling
Content and wording of agreements with
opposing parties

Written reports
Valuation reports
Reports and/or affidavits on various
valuation-related matters

Assistance with other experts
Selection of supporting experts
Supervision and preparation of
supporting experts
Review of other experts' reports and/or
presentations

Critique of opposition
Critique of opposing experts' reports
Comment on opposing experts' depositions
Preparation of rebuttal information

Preparing for court
Preparing exhibits
Outlining direct examination
Preparing cross examination questions
for opposing expert

Expert testimony

Briefs
Assistance in preparing briefs
Critique of opposing briefs

---

judge and/or jury can understand. One can evaluate such experts' ability through examination of their credentials and experience, their reputations, their references, and/or personal interviews.

At this writing, there are no legally recognized criteria by which to qualify as an "expert" in business valuation. There are a few hundred full-time professionals in the discipline of business valuation and thousands of part-time participants, the latter usually in conjunction with some related activity. Furthermore, courts are extremely reluctant to deny the right to testify to almost anyone offered as an expert in the field, regardless of how meager or tangential his or her qualifications may seem. Unfortunately, the result has been a plethora of self-made but ill-qualified "experts" who provide litigation support and expert testimony in the field of business valuation but often to the detriment of the client's interests. Consequently, when evaluating experts for litigation support, it is extremely important to thoroughly understand and investigate relevant qualifications.

Litigation and Other Related Experience

One of the most important factors to evaluate in selecting experts for litigation support is the scope and success of the firm's (or individual's) experience in related litigation. The firm should be willing to provide information on its experience, names of specific cases that have gone to court and thus are a matter of public record, and references.

Although litigation experience is important, it is equally crucial that the expert have had considerable experience in appraisals for the purpose of actual purchase and sale decisions and thus the benefit of "real-world" exposure along with the experience of doing battle in a courtroom.

Experience in a particular industry also can be important. Appraisal of a forest products company for example, will differ dramatically from that of a telecommunications firm. Industry-specific knowledge often can be essential.

Knowledge of Valuation Law

Valuation issues are affected by a wide variety of legal mandates and precedents. Such mandates and precedents differ significantly in their application to various valuation purposes, such as federal gift and estate taxes, ESOPs, dissenting-stockholder suits, involuntary dissolution cases, damage cases, divorces, and ad valorem tax matters. Even for valuations for similar purposes, both statutory law and case law are subject to considerable variation from one jurisdiction to another. Many statutes and court decisions contain vague or ambiquous wording so that an understanding of different interpretations from one jurisdiction to another may require study of several cases. Ignorance of these variations can result in woeful misdirection in litigation-related valuation work. Of course, the attorney must finally decide any legal matter; nevertheless, such decisions can be greatly enhanced by experts with a good working knowledge of valuation law.

Litigation Support Resources

An important but sometimes underrated issue is the extent to which the firm under consideration has the resources to provide the litigation support the particular case demands. These resources include a staff with both the appropriate qualifications and a size sufficient to meet the required deadlines, many types of relevant information, and the ability to put it all together to produce persuasive written reports, graphic exhibits, and testimony.

It is hard to generalize about the number and training of people needed for litigation, since case requirements vary substantially. Some situations require a cadre of expert researchers to do various tasks in order to meet a schedule, while others require very specialized knowledge and expertise.

Library resources are time-consuming and expensive to develop. This is due less to the cost of acquiring the library materials themselves than to the need to index and organize articles, statistical data, court cases, and miscellaneous economic, industry, and corporate reports. Vast storehouses of information are becoming increasingly available through computer-accessible data bases. Having the relevant material well organized and indexed can spell the difference between an unsubstantiated assertion and a documented fact or weight of authority in the eyes of a judge or jury.

Computer capabilities are important in cases involving complex analyses of masses of statistical data. Examples would include the types of income models typically used in the valuation of utilities and railroads for ad valorem taxation and some of the complex models used in valuing stock options.

Professional and Academic Credentials

The two most relevant professional credentials are the ASA (accredited senior appraiser) and CFA (chartered financial analyst), both discussed in the Introduction. Since the ASA is multidisciplinary, the expert's accreditation should be in a relevant discipline, in this case business valuation, or possibly in a technical valuation specialty if the subject relates to public utilities, mineral interests, or certain other specialized industrial companies.

The most relevant academic degrees are those in business administration, preferably with a major in finance or a major in accounting with a dual major or strong minor in finance. Graduate degrees certainly can be helpful in many cases, but there are outstanding experts with undergraduate degrees bolstered by professional designations and relevant litigation support experience.

Professional Involvement

I believe that ongoing involvement in professional organizations and activities increases an expert's ability to provide effective litigation support. These activities include attending seminars sponsored by leading professional organizations involved in business valuation, speaking at such programs, serving as officers and committee persons, and writing for well-recognized professional publications. These activities help keep experts current on the thinking and developments in the mainstream of the profession and expose their own thinking to the scrutiny of their peers.

Unbiased Approach

My own opinion is that the client is best served by unbiased experts. In tax cases, for example, the appraiser's impartiality can be evidenced by prior retention by both the government and taxpayers on various assignments. In damage cases or dissenting stockholder actions, the expert may have been retained by plaintiffs as well as by defendants on various occasions. Likewise, in business valuations for divorces, the expert may have been retained nearly as often by the spouse remaining in the business as by the spouse whose interest in the business will be terminated.

In order to provide credible and effective litigation support, the expert must be able to appreciate the merits of the situation from both sides' viewpoints. Experts tarred with the brush of advocacy may lack not only credibility but perspective, which, in turn, may hinder his or her ability to assess the merits, or lack thereof, of particular position when the client requests guidance.

Engaging Experts

It is wise to interview prospective experts by telephone and/or in person to determine whether they are adequately qualified to provide effective litigation support. One might learn even more about prospective experts by corresponding with them and, especially, discussing their services with their references. It is also appropriate to discuss valuation philosophy, possible conflicts of interest, compensation basis and payment terms, and scheduling.

Concurrence of Valuation Philosophy

The client, attorney, or both may be neither tentatively nor irrevocably committed to preconceived notions about value but may rely on the independent business appraiser's guidance. This situation is probably ideal, especially since an open-minded client relying on an expert is more likely to arrive at a settlement short of a trial. However, in the real world few participants are without preconceived ideas; some are more than others receptive to change in light of new evidence.

To establish whether there is a concurrence of valuation philosophy, the attorney may wish to approach the prospective witness with a hypothetical scenario. In this way, the attorney can get some idea of the methods and parameters the witness would use in reaching the value conclusion without revealing the client's name or identifying the business interest to be valued.

One of the nuances of this exercise is that the establishment of valuation parameters should be left to the prospective witness rather than determined by the attorney or client. In other words, the witness should establish valuation parameters independently, not led by the a priori thinking of the attorney or client. A witness generally will have more credibility in court if it can be established that he or she was hired to ascertain a value independently, not to testify to some value predetermined by the interested party.

This comparison of valuation philosophies is as important to the witness as it is to the client, since no reputable appraiser wants to be under pressure to testify to a value that cannot be professionally supported. If that appears to be the situation, the witness should decline the assignment. Usually, a brief dialog between an experienced attorney and an experienced appraiser is all that is necessary to determine whether the appraiser can be useful as a witness.

Of course, if the attorney trusts the prospective witness's expertise and finds that person taking a more realistic position on the value than the client, the attorney may enlist the appraiser's aid in dissuading the client from an untenable position, thus perhaps facilitating an otherwise impossible settlement. The attorney must use his or her best judgment in advising the client whether to get the prospective appraiser involved under such circumstances.

Conflicts of Interest

Very early in the proceedings, the attorney must disclose the names of both (all) parties in the case to the prospective witness to ascertain that there is no conflict of interest. The witness should be independent of the parties on both sides of the case. The most common conflict of interest (apart from having already been retained by the opposing party) would be having a financial interest in the entity that would call the witness's independence into question. Nevertheless, it is also possible that the prospective witness has some personal or business relationship with some party to the action that would cause him or her to decline the assignment even if the relationship would not challenge the witness's independence or credibility.

In general, it is not a disqualifying conflict that the appraiser has performed services for the opposing party. It is never a disqualifying conflict that the appraiser has been retained on unrelated assignments by the opposing party's law firm. On the contrary, that may be viewed as a sign of professional integrity and independence. One common problem is the expert who is interviewed by one side and not retained, and then is contacted by the other side. A problem can be avoided if the expert makes clear to the attorney in the initial interview that no confidential information or analysis should be shared until after the expert has been retained.

If the prospective witness is willing to accept the assignment but questions whether there could be any conflict of interest, the witness should disclose all the relevant facts to the attorney. The attorney should then decide whether the expert's credibility could be impeached on the grounds of conflict of interest.

Compensation

The expert witness must be compensated on a flat-fee or hourly basis, or some combination of the two, regardless of the outcome of the case. Any compensation agreement based on who wins the case or by how much will absolutely destroy the expert witness's independence in testimony, and is considered unethical by most professional societies as well.

If the appraiser knows enough about the property to be appraised to estimate the time required, the appraisal itself may be done for a fixed fee or within a reasonably narrow estimated fee range. However, the amount of time to be spent in depositions, preparation with attorneys for court, observing and testifying in court, and other aspects of litigation support normally is beyond the expert's control. For that reason, the compensation usually is made on an hourly basis, at a specific hourly rate for each member of the professional valuation staff. The attorney and the experts must cooperate to structure the compensation to be flexible enough to accommodate the many uncertainties involved in litigation but rigid enough that the expert witness will not become a party at interest to the outcome of the case.

I have seen attorneys on cross-examination leave the impression that the expert's fees not yet paid were contingent even though the expert insisted that was not the case. The safest course of action, albeit perhaps self-serving to the appraiser, is to have the expert's fees paid in full for all services prior to court testimony and have a designated daily or hourly fee for court time to be billed against a deposited retainer. Dan Poynter speaks from his experience in the *Expert Witness Handbook* as follows:

> Make sure you receive the check for your air fare, estimated hotel expenses and three days of your time before you leave home for a trial. . . . If it comes out in court that you have not been paid lately, the jury may think the outcome of the case is very important to you. Your objectivity may be suspect. . . .
>
> Q. *Does your client owe you any money?*
> A. *No. My bills have been paid to date and my expenses for this trip were paid in advance. My being paid does not depend on the outcome of this case.*[1]

Engagement Agreement

To the greatest extent possible, the engagement agreement should include all the elements of the appraisal assignment discussed in Chapter 1 plus whatever additional information is appropriate regarding desired litigation support services. However, in many cases engagement agreements for litigation support services give very little detail, often because the attorneys must determine just what services they will need from experts as the case evolves. It is not uncommon for the expert to assist the attorney materially in focusing the valuation issues, the scope of the engagement, and the wording of the engagement agreement, either at the outset of the engagement or at one or more points in its progress. In drafting the initial engagement agreement and any modifications to it, both the attorney and the expert should keep in mind that the agreement may become discoverable by the other side. Most appraisal firms have a standard engagement letter that can be modified as necessary to suit the particular assignment.

---

[1]Daniel F. Poynter, *Expert Witness Handbook* (Santa Barbara, Calif.: Para Publishing, 1987).

Assessing the Case

Frequently the valuation expert can materially aid the attorney at the very outset of potential litigation by helping to assess the valuation aspects of the case. The appraiser's insights can be important in deciding whether and/or how to proceed with litigation.

Framing and Focusing Valuation Issues

Matters such as the applicable standard of value and the relevant valuation date or dates are not always as obvious as they might appear on the surface. Lack of focus can waste time and money at the beginning of a case and, ultimately, can result in going to court with useless testimony.

Consider the time that Larry Litigator hired Alan Analyst to testify in the defense of a dissenting-stockholder suit resulting from a merger that squeezed out the minority stockholders of a Delaware corporation. Litigator instructed Analyst to express an opinion as to the fair market value of the stock as of the date the proxy statement was mailed to stockholders. Analyst, a self-proclaimed "expert" who was unfamiliar with valuation law, did as instructed without question. When on cross-examination the opposing attorney correctly pointed out that the statutory standard of value was "fair value" and not "fair market value" and the statutory valuation date was the day before the effective date of the merger rather than the date of the proxy several months earlier, it became apparent that Analyst's testimony was of little consequence. Analyst presented his bill and was paid in full, as he should have been. He had carried out the assignment for which he had been retained to the best of his ability. But the next time Litigator had a case involving a valuation issue, he hired the expert who had testified for the plaintiffs, and that expert's engagement included participation in defining the valuation assignment.

Most litigation situations involving valuation issues are not as simple as the foregoing illustration. In many cases, there is no statutorily defined standard of value or applicable valuation date. Sometimes the relative rights of various parties at interest are very complex and careful definition of the property and its relevant rights and restrictions is a crucial prerequisite to the appraisal itself. Ultimately, the attorney must decide the question or questions to ask the appraiser to address. Often, however, the expert's knowledge and experience can be very helpful in focusing the relevant questions.

Reasonable Range of Value

Once the basic valuation issue is framed, the appraiser may be asked to do some preliminary work to suggest a reasonable range of value within which the appraisal might be expected to fall. It usually is possible to perform a range of value appraisal on a preliminary basis. However, in certain cases where the value is heavily influenced by factors that only come to light after significant investigation, the appraiser will conclude that a preliminary range of value study is not feasible. The preliminary range of value can help the attorney decide on the litigation posture. Sometimes the most valuable thing to do for clients is to tell them what they don't want to hear—that the value is not what they suspected and, at least from a monetary viewpoint, they appear to have no case. Heading off financially unproductive litigation can save the client tens of thousands of dollars. In one damage case for which my staff and I provided litigation support services for the defense and in which I was scheduled to testify, the court granted a defense motion for involuntary dismissal at the end of the plaintiff's case, because the plaintiff had failed to establish damages. Thus, the question of whether there was liability became moot, and the jury was sent home without ever having addressed it. The case was appealed and upheld. Each side spent well up into six figures. The case struck me as one of many that should never have gone to trial.

It has been my experience in disputed valuations that if each side gets an opinion as to a reasonable range of value from a genuinely competent expert, the groundwork for a settlement often is laid, although the experts may need to complete their work before an actual settlement. On the other hand, if a settlement cannot be reached, the preliminary range of value the expert provides lends some confidence to a decision to proceed with litigation.

Risks and Uncertainties

In some instances, the level of risk affects litigation posture. In one case, an estimate of value (or damages or whatever financial matter is being estimated) may be $10 million, with a range of $8 million to $12 million; in another, the estimate may be $10 million, with a range of zero to $20 million. It often helps to try to quantify the risk that arises from various uncertainties. Sometimes reasonable people will reach different conclusions of value because of different assessments of the economic or industry factors affecting the subject company. Sometimes there may be contingent assets or liabilities whose assessment may have a substantial impact on a court's determination of value. Other cases may involve legal issues about which the court's interpretation will significantly affect value.

Often the expert can facilitate the identification and quantification of areas of financial uncertainty so that the attorney can better assess the risks of litigation.

Benefits and Costs of Pursuing Litigation

The process of framing the valuation issues, estimating a preliminary range of possible values, and identifying areas of uncertainty logically lead to the attorney's assessment of the relationship between the litigation's potential benefits and costs. In making this analysis, the attorney usually will want the experts to estimate some range of likely or possible costs for their services. Once familiar with the case, the expert usually can make a fairly close estimate of the cost of developing direct testimony. Other factors affecting the cost of experts, however, are uncertain and largely beyond the experts' control, such as depositions (including related preparation), work with the attorney to prepare for court, court time, and any work necessary in order to respond to the other side's positions. The last can be both the biggest cost variable and one of the most important factors in the case.

It seems to me that in the heat of litigation, costs tend to run over expectations more often than under. I suggest that when assessing the potential cost/benefit relationship of litigation, attorneys and clients fully consider the difficulty of controlling deposition and court time and, especially, the costs of responding to possible unknown material the opposition may present.

Discovery

Experts should have an opportunity to participate in the discovery process from the outset in order to ensure that they obtain, preferably on a timely basis, all the information necessary for doing their assignment properly.

The Discovery Process

It is my opinion that in most cases the more cooperative and less formalized the discovery process, the better both parties are served. If all parties are willing to cooperate, it often is easiest for experts to gather sufficient information for a thorough understanding by directly contacting the information sources rather than by working through the attorneys. For example, in a sizable tax case in which we were retained by the government, the parties agreed that we could contact the company directly for information. The company attorney produced all the documents we requested and arranged for and accompanied me on field visits and management interviews literally all across the country. By the time we completed our report, both sides had an excellent perspective on the facts and valuation issues, and the case settled.

When the parties are unwilling to cooperate, the experts must, of course, rely on the attorneys to enforce discovery of the necessary information. If the information is delayed or documents do not arrive on a timely basis, the attorneys must follow up immediately and vigorously. Futher, it is up to the experts to keep the attorneys informed about whether the requested information is arriving in a timely manner. Keeping the attorneys apprised in this way will facilitate their follow-up and make it possible for them to accurately report to the court about the receipt of information. I suggest that all documents be date-stamped upon receipt and logged in indicating the source from which received, so that if questions arise later they need not be answered from memory.

Documents Request List

A checklist for use as a starting point for a documents request list is shown in Exhibit 5–1 in Chapter 5. Most situations do not require everything on that list, but most do require documents applicable only to a particular industry or company that are not included. The expert should compose a list tailored as specifically as possible to the particular situation given what is known about it at the time and provide for one or more follow-up requests, since it usually is impossible to know what every relevant document will be until the appraiser has reviewed the initial batch of data and knows more about the company.

If the expert can expect to receive the parties' cooperation, the initial documents request need cover only the known essentials, and the expert can inspect additional documents during a facilities visit and/or include them in a supplementary request as necessary. If the parties refuse to cooperate, the initial documents list must be as comprehensive as possible. Even so, lists that demand voluminous material of little or no direct relevance serve no useful purpose and often delay discovery on the grounds that the demand is unreasonably burdensome. The expert's experience and judgment can help generate a reasonable and manageable documents list for the specific circumstances.

Interrogatories

Interrogatories are far more cumbersome than interactive questions and answers. For one thing, the next logical question often depends on the answer to the prior question. Moreover, in an interactive situation the respondent has the opportunity to clarify and perhaps narrow the scope of a broad inquiry, which may save considerable time and expense in complying with the inquiry. As with the documents request list, the burden of the initial interrogatories can be eased for both parties if they provide for follow-up interrogatories. In developing suggested questions, the expert must keep in mind both the scope of the inquiry and the clarity of wording in order to elicit what is intended and relevant. Also, as with the documents request list, the expert's experience and judgment can be invaluable in developing relevant and incisive interrogatories. (In some cases, of course, the documents request list is an integral part of the interrogatories.) Unfortunately, interrogatories that seek other than simple objective data (such as identification of witnesses) often lead to circumspect and largely useless answers.

Preparation for Meaningful Depositions

In business valuation cases, depositions usually fall into two categories: depositions of people who can provide information and depositions of opposing experts. The valuation analyst can help the attorney prepare for both categories of deposition. The expert should be consulted in preparing for depositions of people related to the case in order to be able to suggest areas of questioning that will enhance the information on which to base his or her expert opinion. The purpose of deposing the fact witness is to get information and to ensure as far as possible that the witness is committed to whatever the factual testimony will be.

The purpose of deposing opposing experts usually is to understand what they have done, what they have concluded, and the basis for their conclusions. In some cases, where settlement is the object, the deposition can be a powerful tool of persuasion by exposing weaknesses in the expert's analysis. Most depositions of experts that I have observed have not accomplished these objectives as well as I think they could have. No one can look into an expert's mind and work with the same insight as his or her peers. Attorneys can widen their perspective by calling on their own experts for some guidance in deposing opposing experts. The attorney may have his or her own expert, or a member of the expert's staff, on hand when deposing the opponent's experts. The appraiser can thus point out lines of questioning that might elude the attorney but are perfectly logical to one with specific knowledge of information sources, various valuation techniques, and all the calculations and jargon current in the business appraisal field. Unfortunately, valuation experts frequently go into court still wondering exactly what the opposing experts did in developing their opinions; a meaningful deposition, however, would prevent that. In many cases, information and insights gained through an incisive deposition can lead the parties to a settlement.

Facility Visits and Interviews

The expert should be allowed to visit company facilities and interview company management and other parties to the extent considered necessary in developing an opinion. At the same time, company personnel should have an opportunity to present their views to experts on both sides. Attorneys may wish to ask their experts to evaluate the various parties' positions. Thoroughly airing and evaluating others' viewpoints may facilitate a settlement; even if it does not, it may eliminate or narrow some points of disagreement or at least refine and focus the dispute.

Research

Business valuation experts and their staffs can support litigation by providing research on such topics as economic and industry data, comparative transaction data, authority for positions on valuation issues, and many others. Specific research assignments may be tailored to the needs of a particular case. Results of this research may eventually be incorporated into expert testimony or brought into evidence in other ways. Such information may also be used by attorneys in cross-examination, arguments, and briefs.

Economic and Industry Data

Often the outlook for certain economic or industry variables have an important bearing on the value of a business at a particular time. Different assumptions about these outlooks often lead to widely differing opinions about value. The better both the experts and the attorneys understand these factors, the more likely they will be to reach a settlement or to prevail in their positions if the case goes to trial. Business valuation firms normally are well positioned by both experience and resources to research these factors.

Comparative Transaction Data

Good comparative transaction data can provide some of the most compelling evidence in support of an opinion as to value. Nevertheless, I continually see disputed valuation cases in which one side or the other, and sometimes both, have failed to collect and analyze available comparative transactions, either because they didn't realize their importance or didn't know how to find them. The attorney is aided in evaluating the case by knowing what comparative transaction data are available. If there are many very comparable transactions, the risk involved in the litigation is lower (provided, of course, that the transactions support the attorney's expert's opinion—and if not, the attorney should know that, too). If there are few or no comparative transactions, the risk of an undesired or unexpected outcome increases. Good business valuation firms usually are good at ferreting out and analyzing relevant comparative transaction data.

Authority for Positions on Valuation Issues

Often the court is persuaded by seeing authoritative support for experts' opinions that goes beyond the experts' mere assertions of validity, particularly if the situation seems to be merely one expert's word against another's. Some of the most common controversies are appropriate capitalization or discount rates, the applicability and extent of various discounts and premiums, the impact on value of various rights and restrictions attaching to the interest, and the relative weight to be accorded various valuation factors. The rules in many courts allow for the expert's position on these and similar issues to be substantiated by citing books, articles, court cases, and a variety of other sources. The division of the research labor between the law firm and the business valuation firm may depend on the extent and availability of their respective library resources and research personnel.

Consultation on Procedures

Appraisal experts frequently are able to help attorneys with some kinds of procedural matters, such as deciding whether to go to court or to arbitration, determining the content and wording of agreements with opposing parties, and setting schedules and other miscellaneous matters.

To Court or to Arbitration

Agreeing to arbitration rather than going to court can save time and money for both parties (see Chapter 29). Business valuation experts with arbitration experience can provide useful consultation on the relative merits of arbitration versus court for a particular case and can suggest an efficient arbitration procedure. On the other hand, if there is a significant legal issue affecting the valuation case, it should be recognized that an authoritative appellate decision can usually be obtained only after a court trial and not after arbitration.

Content and Wording of Agreements

Valuation experts can provide special insights into the valuation impact of any agreement with opposing parties being contemplated. Thus, they can help protect both the client and the attorney from entering into an agreement that could be interpreted other than intended from a valuation viewpoint. In several cases, clients have entered into agreements stating a procedure for determining the "fair market value" of minority shares of closely held corporate stock without realizing that, as discussed in Chapter 15, "Valuing Minority Interests," the term usually implies some discount from a pro rata portion of the value of the entire company. Their shock at being awarded an amount reflecting a minority interest discount has resulted in additional lawsuits, sometimes against the attorneys who drew up the documents.

Scheduling and Miscellaneous Matters

The valuation consultant can help guide the progress of the case so that it is expedient while allowing adequate time to prepare for depositions and court. Without such consultation, it is easy to underestimate the lead time necessary for preparing fully and, consequently, the expert may have to go into trial inadequately prepared or the trial may have to be continued to a date far later than what would have been available on the court calendar had the initial planning been better. (Of course, this problem often arises when the appraiser is called in late rather than at the beginning of the litigation proceedings.) Experts can also help develop realistic schedules for depositions and other steps in the litigation. Their experience and knowledge can be useful in a wide variety of other procedural decisions as well.

Written Reports

Written reports that the experts may provide can range from a single-page letter addressing a single fact or conclusion to a fully detailed valuation report. The two most common forms of written reports are affidavits and standard valuation reports.

Affidavits

An *affidavit* is "a written declaration made under oath before a notary public or other authorized official."[2] A sample of a typical affidavit format is shown in Exhibit 27–2. Note that the affidavit may need to be notarized.

The purpose of an affidavit is to put something official before the court without the author's physical presence. Affidavits are most commonly used in connection with pretrial matters, but sometimes they are introduced as evidence in a trial. The subject matter of an affidavit can be anything from scheduling information, such as the days on which an expert is and is not available for testimony, to a statement of an expert's opinion with a summary of the supporting reasons. The most lengthy affidavit I ever wrote was for a government agency in a case in which an appellate court had found certain parties liable for violation of fiduciary duties and had remanded the case to the lower court for valuation. Our firm performed the valuation for the agency, and the affidavit summarized our qualifications, the work done, the valuation approaches used, and our conclusion as to value. The agency filed the affidavit and used it as a basis for their position in settlement negotiations, which ultimately succeeded.

Valuation Reports

For valuation cases in some jurisdictions, such as the U.S. Tax Court, it is mandatory to exchange written valuation reports at least two weeks before trial. In other jurisdictions, whether or not there will be a written report at all is left totally to the respective attorneys' discretion. In such jurisdictions, some attorneys always want a written report, others never use a written report, and still others decide whether to have a written report prepared on a case-by-case basis. A written report gives the court a document for reference when reviewing the case. Some attorneys, however, think that the knowledge that a written report is available detracts from the court's attention to the expert's testimony during the trial. If a written report is to be prepared for litigation support, it normally will follow the same format as reports for other purposes, as discussed in Chapter 13, "Writing an Appraisal Report."

Assistance with Other Experts

A business valuation firm may help select and supervise supporting experts. Its staff also can review and critique the material of other experts the attorney considers using.

---

[2] *The American Heritage Dictionary,* 2nd College Edition (Boston: Houghton Mifflin, 1985).

EXHIBIT 27-2

Sample Affidavit Format

1   **In the Circuit Court of the State of Oregon**

2   **for the County of Multnomah**

3   JOHN A. DOE,   )

4   Plaintiff,   )
)   A88-01-0100
5   v.   )
)   AFFIDAVIT OF JACKSON P. SMITH
6   JANE B. DOE,   )

7   Defendant.   )

8   STATE OF OREGON   )
)   ss.
9   County of Multnomah   )

10   I, JACKSON P. SMITH, being first duly sworn, depose, and say:

11

12   I am an expert on business valuation in the above-entitled case. Etc.

13

14

15

16

17   DATED this _____ day of _____, 1989.

18

19   _____
                                             JACKSON P. SMITH
20

21   SUBSCRIBED AND SWORN to before me this _____ day of _____, 1989.

22

23   _____
                                             NOTARY PUBLIC FOR OREGON
24   My Commission Expires: _____

25

Page   AFFIDAVIT OF JACKSON P. SMITH

Selection of Supporting Experts

Specialized experts may be needed to address certain elements that may bear on the value of a business, such as the value of real estate, machinery and equipment, or timber. Business valuation firms usually maintain files of such experts because they need to call on them from time to time for litigation or other valuation purposes.

For various reasons, the attorney may call in more than one business valuation expert: to get more than one expert's opinion of the value; to have an expert address in depth certain especially controversial or critical aspects of the case, such as the appropriateness of a certain methodology or the quantification of some premium or discount; or to have an expert for rebuttal other than the one for the case in chief, either because some aspect of the rebuttal begs some specialized expertise or to avoid any implication of advocacy on the part of the primary witness. Business valuation experts experienced in litigation usually can suggest other experts suitable for the particular assignment.

Supervision and Preparation of Supporting Experts

The relationship between the primary business valuation experts and the supporting experts can vary widely depending on the attorney's preferences, the primary expert's capabilities, and the circumstances of the case. At one extreme, the business valuation firm may select and subcontract the supporting experts and use them as though they were members of the primary firm. At the other, the attorney may select and hire the supporting experts and ask them to have no contact with the primary witness. The most common situation is something in between: The attorney hires the supporting experts after consultation with the primary witness, and the experts are in contact with one another and with the attorney, the primary supervision of the supporting experts being the responsibility of either the attorney or the lead witness.

While in trial, attorneys put in long hours under intense pressure. A knowledgeable expert can provide some welcome relief by doing much of the preparation of support witnesses for court. In one fast-paced case during which the attorneys were getting little sleep, I prepared the entire set of questions for one morning's witness and reviewed the questions with him the night before. The attorney saw both the questions and my summaries of the witness's answers for the first time a few minutes before court and had no direct preparation with the witness himself. I am happy to say that the testimony went superbly.

Review of Other Experts' Reports and/or Presentations

One extremely valuable litigation support service of an experienced expert is to review and critique material prepared by other experts on the same side of the case. In some situations, for a variety of reasons, the review can be part of the input an attorney needs in order to decide whether to call in a particular expert to testify. In other cases, the review may help focus and buttress the testimony to be presented by a particular expert.

Critique of the Opposition

In many litigated valuations, I have considered the process of critiquing the opposition's position as important to reaching a satisfactory resolution as preparing our own valuation or direct testimony—or even more so. After all, if the opposition's position were sound and acceptable, there probably would be no case (unless, of course, your side was not sound and reasonable).

Critique of Opposing Experts' Reports

The critique of an opposing expert's report or presentation may take place at any time from the outset of possible litigation through the trial itself. If an expert's report is available at the beginning stage of assessing the case, it is helpful to review it at that time. It may be an entirely sound piece of work, and an early review may result in a recommendation to accept it or possibly to negotiate some minor modifications, thus forestalling thousands of dollars of futile litigation costs.

If the opposition's expert is off base, it is good to know why as soon as possible. I have found that the more sophisticated the valuation expert on the other side, the more likely it is that a settlement can be reached through narrowing and compromising on valuation issues that are genuinely arguable. If the other side has utilized as an expert someone who is untrained in business valuation, it is usually much more difficult to engage in a constructive exchange leading to a resolution short of the courtroom. In any case, the valuation expert must provide the attorney with an understanding of the strengths and weaknesses of the opposing expert's position.

Preparation of Rebuttal Information

The type of rebuttal information needed largely depends, of course, on what is wrong with the other expert's work. If the expert has made a mathematical error, that should be brought to the court's attention, along with its impact on the value, if significant. If the expert has taken a position unsupported by the preponderance of authority on an issue, evidence as to the preponderance of authority must be researched and developed. For example, if the opposition takes the position that there should be no discount from enterprise value when determining the fair market value of a minority stock interest, the rebuttal must cite authoritative regulations, texts, articles, and other sources that make it clear that such a discount should be taken. If the expert's approaches are basically sound but the expert has reached a poor conclusion because of inadequate and/or erroneous data, the best rebuttal approach may be to recalculate the results with his or her own methodology, but using complete and accurate data.

The latter approach to rebuttal is effective far more often than one might imagine. As noted earlier, comparative transactions are not always easy to find, and the opposing expert may not have searched for comparative transactions as exhaustively as was necessary. Furthermore, financial data are extremely complex and difficult to work with and often are not uniform in one or more respects from company to company. There is a very large potential for error in the use of financial data, and a thorough review may uncover one or more significant mistakes. The most striking example of such an error in my own experience occurred many years ago when an expert relied on a single comparative public company in reaching his value but failed to adjust the financial data for a two-for-one split of the company's stock. The expert was quite surprised when the trial attorney brought the error to his attention on cross-examination (after the expert had thoroughly reaffirmed the soundness of his methodology), and the court immediately recognized that the valuation conclusion should have been twice what had been proclaimed.

Court Preparation

Experts can assist in preparation for court by preparing exhibits, outlining testimony, and composing possible cross-examination questions for opposing experts.

Preparing Exhibits

Some business valuation firms maintain graphic arts departments to augment their written material with various charts and illustrations. These illustrations can be useful in any trial, but they are especially so in a jury trial, when complex issues must be presented as graphically as possible.

Outlining Direct Examination

Attorneys have different preferences for various processes of preparing the plan for direct examination. Some prefer to outline the sequence of all testimony topics themselves; others prefer that the expert prepare the initial outline of the presentation of his or her work and opinion. The attorney knows how the testimony fits in with the overall case, and the expert has the best insight into the details needed to make his or her opinion supportable. Which one has the better perspective on making the expert's opinion *understandable* to a judge and/or jury depends on the individuals.

If the expert is both well experienced in court and articulate in expressing his or her opinion, I tend to lean toward asking the expert to make the first cut at shaping the testimony, either in outline or question-and-answer format. In any case, the attorney and the expert must discuss the testimony thoroughly enough to understand each other completely.

Preparing Cross-Examination Questions for Opposing Experts

Since the expert is retained for specialized knowledge of the subject area, he or she should be able to contribute questions that will probe the soundness of the opposing expert's opinion and expose its weaknesses. These questions may cover such topics as the opposing expert's specific qualifications, methodology, sources of authority, comprehensiveness and accuracy of data, and anything else that will serve to emphasize the differences between the experts. Focusing on the differences will lay the groundwork for arguments as to which expert's position is the more persuasive.

Expert Testimony

Obviously, one of the most important litigation support services available from business valuation experts is expert testimony, whether by affidavit, deposition testimony, court testimony, or testimony presented to an arbitration panel. We have already discussed affidavits; deposition and court testimony are the subjects of the next chapter.

Assistance with Briefs

Another way in which the valuation analyst often can contribute is by providing input into the preparation of briefs and replies to opponents' briefs.

Assistance in Preparing Briefs

Experts who have testified and either listened to or read the testimony of an opposing expert tend to have a sharp sense of the difference between their and their opponents' positions on the important valuation issues. Briefs in a case are enriched by a good expert's insights; the expert can help bring these differences into sharp focus, particularly as they apply to issues that have the greatest monetary impact, and can express clear, concise reasons why his or her position is superior. The attorney may want to take advantage of the expert's insights by discussing the briefs before preparing them or by having the expert review the briefs in draft form.

Critique of Opposing Briefs

Similarly, the expert often can provide a special understanding of the opponent's briefs. One thing to look for is any mischaracterization of the expert's own evidence or testimony; another is any unjustifiable conclusions or implications made on the basis of the opposing expert's testimony. Sometimes the expert reviewing the opposing briefs will notice a clearly erroneous factual statement on some valuation matter that the attorney reading the brief might not realize is an error. A review by the expert is a good safety check for ensuring that any unwarranted contentions do not go unnoticed but are treated with a firm and convincing reply.

Keeping Records

Depending on the nature of the case, all notes, correspondence, working papers, and other materials used in conjunction with litigation support may become discoverable by the other side. The safest course is to assume from the outset that files will become discoverable and that the attorney on the other side will be an advocate who will try to find a damaging way to use them.

The date of engagement and basis for fees should be clear from the engagement agreement. If fees are based on hours worked, the expert should keep accurate time records.

The sources of all documents and notes should be identified. As mentioned above, it is important to indicate the date that each document was received, especially if this date may become critical at some point in the proceeding. Notes should be dated and initialed by the person making them. In taking notes of meetings and telephone calls, it is important to keep a record of who said what. Such records may be kept fairly easily by listing the parties to the conversation at the top of the page and indicating the speaker by his or her initials at the left of each item. If a written report goes through several drafts, it may be wise to date them to avoid confusion if the prior drafts are maintained in the files. However, many experts do not retain early drafts. A favorite tactic of many opposing attorneys is to seek production of earlier drafts and then infer that any change was manipulative. If several people participated in drafting written material, the file should contain a copy with preparers' initials on their respective contributed portions.

On the positive side, the objective is to make the file clear and complete so that it can be used constructively to refresh a witness's memory and provide well-documented support of details when needed. On the negative side, the objective is to avoid ambiguous or abstruse material that an opposing attorney could use to imply some conclusion other than what was intended.

Another tactic used by some cross examining attorneys is to try to infer some lack of objectivity on the part of the witness on the basis of something in correspondence or telephone notes between the expert and the attorney. For this reason, most communications between the expert and the attorney who retained the expert are verbal rather than written prior to the final report. An expert's communication to an attorney generally is not covered by either the attorney-client or the attorney-work product privileges. After all, it is the expert's work product, not that of the attorney. If production of the document is resisted on the grounds of attorney work-product that argument may itself constitute a significant adverse admission.

Summary

This chapter has presented a brief discussion of many of the important litigation support services that a business appraisal firm can provide in addition to expert testimony. It is extremely important to engage expert's assistance at an early point in the litigation proceedings so that such services, particularly as they relate to the discovery process, can be fully integrated with the anticipated expert testimony. Very often, the expert's services may facilitate a settlement rather than culminate in expert testimony in the court.

Although the expert may be of great assistance in many ways in preparing and administrating the case, it is essential that the attorney and the client fully respect the expert's independence in arriving at any opinion or opinions. The expert not only must avoid any taint of bias, but also must avoid any appearance of taint of bias. For this reason, it may be preferable to have certain litigation support services performed by another appraiser in the expert's firm or even by another business appraisal firm. In any case, full utilization of the business appraiser's expertise in providing litigation support services can facilitate an expeditious and satisfactory outcome in litigation situations.

Chapter 28

Expert Testimony

*"Give your evidence," said the King; "and don't be nervous, or I'll have
you executed on the spot."*[1]

Court testimony challenges an expert witness because it is part of an adversary proceeding. If the opposite side were willing to accept the witness's valuation, there probably would be a settlement instead of a trial. Indeed, most valuation cases settle before they reach the courtroom, especially if the witness has prepared the case thoroughly and the attorney has drawn on the expert's research in negotiating with the opposition. Thus, if the case goes to court, it's because of sharp disagreement. Competent, thorough preparation must culminate in a clear and convincing presentation.

It is essential that a business appraiser be objective and unbiased when legal testimony is involved. One school of thought holds that since courts in some situations tend to split the difference between opposing positions an appraiser must take an extreme position, because that is the only strategy that will lead to a fair court result. I do not adhere to this philosophy; rather, I believe that the expert witness should arrive at a figure that he or she expects to present and defend without compromise on cross-examination. Usually a rigorously prepared, convincingly presented, objective case will prevail over an extreme position, which a competent judge will tend to discredit. Fortunately, in the 1980s courts have tended to adopt the well-supported position of one side of a case without compromise.[2]

Background Preparation

When legal controversy is involved, there is no substitute for thorough homework and preparation. The appraiser virtually must prepare not only his or her own case but the other side's as well. The expert valuation witness must attempt to anticipate any apparent weaknesses that the opposing attorney may seize upon in cross-examination and be prepared to defend against attacks on them. Also, the expert witness should be prepared to critique the case the opposing side presents.

Basic Preparation and Documentation

The basic research itself should follow the principles and procedures outlined in Parts I, II, and III of this book. As discussed in Part I, in legal testimony one must rely as much as possible on facts, not on conjecture. Documentation is the undergirding of every step. It makes no difference how thoroughly the witness is personally convinced of

---

[1]Lewis Carroll, *Alice's Adventures in Wonderland* (Middlesex, England: Puffin Books, Penguin Books, Ltd., 1946).

[2]See, for example, *Buffalo Tool and Die Manufacturing Co., Inc.,* v. *Commissioner,* 74 T.C. 441 (1980); *Donald Strutz, et al.,* v. *Commissioner,* 40 T.C.M. 928 (1980); *Hooker Industries, Inc.,* v. *Commissioner,* 47 T.C.M. 1527 (1984); *Estate of Mark S. Gallo,* 50 T.C.M. 470 (1985); *Estate of Martha B. Watts,* 51 T.C.M. 60 (1985).

the validity of the facts and conclusions if he or she is unable to convince the court.

If the witness were presenting the company in question to a prospective buyer, it might be valid to presume that the buyer knows something about the business or industry involved. However, an appraiser cannot presume that the court can have the prospective buyer's sophistication about every business brought before it. Every fact on which the witness intends to rely in reaching his or her conclusion must be presented, along with whatever supporting documentation is necessary for convincing the court that the fact should indeed be relied upon.

Moreover, unlike the situation of presenting the company to a prospective buyer, in which the appraiser would have an opportunity, at the buyer's request, to research and provide supplementary information, the expert has no such chance in court. The appraiser cannot take a couple of weeks to do additional homework and come back for another audience. The court, however concerned it may be with reaching an equitable decision, will make its determination based on the initial presentation, however inadequate. Thus, the research had better be thorough the first time around.

Discovery

If the managers of the business being valued are unwilling to cooperate with the witness, they can make it difficult to get the information necessary for doing the job. The appraiser must keep the attorney apprised of what documents need to be reviewed, what facilities should be visited, and who need to be interviewed. The expert witness must provide this information as early as possible so that if the opposition parties decide to drag their feet they will not succeed in preventing the appraiser from completing a thorough valuation study. As noted in the previous chapter, the expert witness also should keep the attorney informed of the timeliness and adequacy of the information received. That way, the attorney can follow up on missing data and report accurately to the court on how promptly and completely the information was supplied.

Reading Prior Cases and Articles

Part of the homework for testifying on a valuation issue is to read relevant prior court cases. I specifically recommend reading the full texts of the cases rather than only the digests various services provide. Although the digests help keep one abreast of day-to-day developments in the field, they are no substitute for the detail of the full text when addressing a specific case. It also can help to read articles analyzing particular cases or categories of cases.

This book offers a fairly detailed analysis of a few tax cases; these were selected to represent some of the most frequently occurring valuation issues. Several of the most significant court cases on valuations for other purposes are cited throughout the book.

Use of Hearsay Evidence

The opposing attorney probably will object to any testimony the expert witness offers that might be classified as hearsay. The term *hearsay* refers broadly to any information obtained from third parties without personal verification. The expert witness should not, however, avoid collecting information and opinions from other people if they are relevant. The judge has a great deal of latitude in deciding what evidence to consider and usually wants to hear anything that might help reach an equitable decision. Most judges are reluctant to disallow any potentially relevant testimony on technical grounds, especially if there is no jury. Once the witness has been qualified to testify as an expert before the court, judges tend to want to hear what he or she has to say. They want to know how the witness reached his or her opinion, even if portions of the testimony would be disallowed as hearsay in certain other legal proceedings. The judge can then determine what weight, if any, to accord any statements in the testimony. Rule 703 of the Federal Rules of Evidence states:

> The facts or data in the particular case upon which an expert bases an opinion or inference may be those perceived by or made known to him at or before the hearing. If of a type reasonably relied upon by experts in the particular field in forming opinions or inferences upon the subject, the facts or data need not be admissible in evidence.[3]

Correctly analyzed, it is the opinion of the expert that is the evidence, not the hearsay information that supports it. The key phrase in the above quotation from the Federal Rules is *"reasonably relied upon by experts in the particular field in forming opinions."* Particularly in business valuation, the expert often derives important portions of information from conversations with other people. The expert may conduct some interviews personally, and members of his or her support staff may conduct others. If the use of such information may provoke controversy, the attorney should ask the expert a question, or a series of questions, on the stand to ensure that the court understands that appraisers typically rely on such information in the course of valuing businesses.

Nevertheless, the witness runs the risk that anything that could be considered hearsay may be disallowed or accorded little or no weight in the court's deliberations. Therefore, the expert should take all feasible steps to make any research that might be considered hearsay both admissible and convincing. If the expert is surveying customers, suppliers, or competitors to obtain information on industry practices, the larger the sample, the better. Using specific names and companies to identify who said what will tend to make the testimony more acceptable than using confidential sources.

To be on the safe side, though, the expert should structure the research and conclusion so that anything that could be considered hearsay is not essential to the conclusion even if it may lend considerable support to the conclusion if accepted.

---

[3]Michael Graham, *Handbook of Federal Evidence*, 2nd ed. (St. Paul, Minn.: West Publishing, 1987).

Depositions

The term *depose* means to *state under oath but not in open court*. It is common practice for the opposing attorney to take an expert witness's deposition some time before the trial, for several reasons. One is to help the attorney assess the relative strengths of the opponent's case for guidance on whether to offer or accept a settlement and, if so, on what basis. Another reason is to try to learn enough about the witness and his or her testimony in advance to prepare a cross-examination that will damage the testimony's credibility. Still another reason is that an attorney can sometimes embarrass or discredit a witness by bringing out inconsistencies between deposition testimony and trial testimony.

Scheduling Depositions

The time and place of the deposition is determined by the attorneys subject to the expert's availability. Some attorneys like to take depositions of experts well in advance of trial, but also expect the experts to complete trial preparation prior to the deposition. Unless there is some unusual pretrial order, the other side cannot force the expert to complete the entire research and preparation of the testimony ahead of the trial date. Obviously, a witness cannot disclose the results of research not yet completed. Therefore, there is an inherent conflict between the desire for an early deposition and the desire for the work to be as complete as possible.

When scheduling the deposition, the expert should advise the attorney how complete the preparation can be expected to be as of various dates. If the attorney wants the expert to be thoroughly prepared at the deposition—perhaps because he considers a settlement possible—the need to finish the work should be taken into account when setting the schedule. The attorney should give the expert adequate notice and lead time and confirm the expert's ability to be prepared on time.

What to Take to the Deposition

The expert should ask the attorney what to take to the deposition. The necessary materials will vary greatly from one situation to another. My instructions for depositions have varied all the way from taking absolutely nothing to taking every document and working paper in my file.

Keep in mind that everything taken to a deposition must be made available to opposing counsel if demanded. The federal rule (Rule 612), and many state rules, also entitle the adverse party to demand production of any document used by a witness before a deposition or trial to refresh his memory for purposes of his testimony.[4]

---

[4]Federal Rules of Evidence, 28 U.S.C.A. 759 (1984).

If there is any question, the expert's attorney should advise the expert as to which items opposing counsel are entitled to see and which they are not. Obviously, before the deposition the attorney and the appraiser should review all workpapers, correspondence, memos, and any other material in the appraiser's case file. By doing so, the attorney will gain a thorough knowledge of the information used and also get a chance to review the material for items, if any, that are not subject to discovery by the opposing attorney because of attorney-client privilege. The attorney should have this opportunity even when the deposition is pursuant to a subpoena that specifies what is to be brought.

Deposition Testimony

The witness will be sworn in, and the deposing attorney will introduce himself or herself and state a few basic ground rules, which include the witness's right to have any question repeated or clarified.

The opposing attorney will ask most, if not all, of the questions. The scope of allowable questions varies considerably from one situation to another, but often it is quite broad. It usually starts with the expert's background. Attorneys often ask about the expert's past valuation work, other testimony, and work on past cases of a similar nature in the hope of finding something that will appear to contradict the witness's positions in the current case.

The question of work done for other clients is sensitive, because much of the information may be confidential. The expert must advise the attorney that he or she cannot divulge confidential information without the client's permission. If uncertain about how to handle this or any other matter, the witness may request a recess in order to consult with his or her attorney.

For the most part, the general rules applicable to courtroom testimony, discussed later in this chapter, also apply in deposition testimony. The expert is not required to provide any more information than the question specifically calls for—and normally should not. The two worst faults of some expert witnesses are unresponsiveness and over-responsiveness, that is, giving answers beyond the scope of the question. Once certain that he or she understands the question, the expert should answer forthrightly, to the point, and as briefly as possible. It is not the witness's responsibility to assist examining counsel by re-phrasing questions the way they should have been asked or to volunteer information, no matter how pertinent, that the question did not address.

The attorney often tries to fence in the witness with a question such as "Is that *everything* you considered in forming your opinion?" The witness usually should insist on leaving the gate open with something like "That's everything I can recall at this time."

The expert should remember that although the deposition results in a written transcript, pauses generally do not appear in the text. Before starting to talk, the witness should take time to frame a concise answer that will read well in the transcript. A good rule is to answer questions as though you were dictating your testimony—which will make you think before you speak.

After the Deposition

The witness has the right to receive, read, and make any corrections to the transcript of the deposition, or he or she may waive that right. I recommend exercising it. For one thing, although court reporters generally are incredibly fast and accurate, they do make mistakes—and occasionally the mistakes can change the sense of a point. Also, reading over the transcript of the deposition is a constructive exercise for the witness, because it helps call attention to any weakness or disorganization, which the witness can correct before the trial.

Further, the witness has the right to check and recheck data as thoroughly as desired. Any errors found at any time between the deposition date and the court date should be corrected. If the opposing attorney tries to embarrass the witness with the inconsistency in court, the witness should state frankly that the material was preliminary at the time of the deposition and that the process of checking the material disclosed an error that subsequently was corrected.

Outlining Courtroom Testimony

In preparing for courtroom testimony, it is important to know what the format of the trial will be. Whether a judge or a jury will be making the decision can affect how detailed the testimony must be, the nature and size of exhibits, and much of the style of testimony. Most business valuation cases are tried before a judge without a jury. Even if the parties have a right to a jury trial, attorneys on both sides usually opt to waive that right in business valuation cases, partly because of the extra time and cost of dealing with a jury. Moreover, it is very difficult to educate laypeople about the complexities of business valuation within the tight time frame and structured format of a jury trial. Consequently, regardless of how conscientious and well intentioned the jury may be, they could be hard-pressed to reach an equitable decision in a business valuation case.

Regardless of the format, the expert witness and the attorney must spend time together preparing the presentation. The witness should know what areas of questions to expect in order to prepare direct and complete answers. The attorney needs to know what evidence the expert witness has prepared to be sure of getting all of it presented. Some attorneys like to put the expert witness on the stand and ask one broad question, such as, "Will you please describe your investigation and findings as to the value of XYZ Company?" Most attorneys prefer to develop the case logically and point by point in a format of questions and short answers between the attorney and the witness.

In some instances, the judge issues a pretrial order requiring each side of the case to prepare and exchange formal, written reports and then find areas of agreement and disagreement among themselves, limiting the verbal testimony to the unresolved issues. I think it is harder to convey to the court the full context of a case in this way. Unless the court requires a written report, I prefer to prepare only the tables and exhibits in written form and to present the text of the case verbally in the attorney/witness question-and-answer format.[5]

It is up to the attorney to decide whether he/she or the witness should prepare the first draft of the question list. Either way, the direct testimony usually proceeds in more or less the following sequence:

1. Identification and qualifications of witness.
2. Description of the assignment.
3. Conclusion.
4. Steps taken in carrying out the assignment.
5. Findings.
6. Restatement of the conclusion.

Qualifying the Witness

Qualifying the witness as an expert is an essential first step in establishing the witness's credibility in the court's eyes. This step usually establishes not only the witness's expertise on the subject of business valuation but his or her position and affiliations, making it clear that the witness is independent of the company being valued and the parties to the suit.

Frequently, opposing counsel gratuitously offers to stipulate that the witness qualifies as an expert. This offer should be rejected. The attorney calling the expert wants to acquaint the judge and/or jury firsthand with the expert and his or her qualifications relevant to the forthcoming testimony. The extent of the qualifying process varies considerably from one case to another, but it usually proceeds approximately along the following sequence and format.

Education.   The qualifications usually start with academic degrees and relevant nondegree programs.

Professional Credentials.   Professional credentials are the expert's professional designations and affiliations. Since appraisal and financial analysis designations (such as ASA and CFA) are less known to most courts than accounting designations such as CPA, it often is appropriate to explain to the court the nature of these designations

---

[5]Some of my professional peers disagree on this point, and prefer going into court with a full written report. One reviewer of the manuscript stated that "some will not testify unless a full written report has been prepared."

and the qualifications required for attaining them. Professional involvements such as holding office and/or serving on committees may also be covered at this point, as well as special honors or recognition.

Publications and Teaching. Books and/or articles written, appraisal courses taught, and a summary of relevant professional appraisal lectures given usually logically follow professional credentials.

Employment History. The focus should be on the portion of the witness's employment history that bears on his or her qualifications as an appraiser. It may focus on the scope of the appraisal work of the firm that employs the analyst and on the analyst's involvement in that work.

Experience Particularly Relevant to the Case at Bench. The expert's relevant experience may be past appraisal work on companies in the same industry and/or may focus on past experience with appraisals involving similar issues.

Description of the Assignment

The description of the assignment usually includes such information as when the witness was retained, by whom, and what the assignment was, including the standard of value to be used. This information is similar to that included in the description of the assignment section of a written report as discussed in Chapter 1, "Defining the Appraisal Assignment."

The matter of the witness's compensation may or may not be raised, either by the attorney on direct examination or by the opposing attorney on cross-examination. Whether the compensation is a flat fee or on an hourly basis, it is a good idea for the witness to come to court prepared to answer the question of how many hours have been spent in preparation. If the witness has carried out all the steps in the valuation process suggested in this book, he or she will have spent a good many hours, and testimony to that effect will lend further support to the thoroughness of the preparation.

Summary of Conclusion

Once the witness has been qualified and the assignment defined, most attorneys ask the witness to state his or her valuation conclusion, before describing the research undertaken to reach it, very much as the introduction to a written appraisal report summarizes the ultimate conclusion. Some attorneys prefer to wait until the entire research project has been described before having the witness present the conclusion. In this, as in all other procedural matters in testimony, the attorney's judgment should prevail.

Description of Steps Taken

The description of the steps taken in reaching the valuation conclusion should include the sources of information, such as those that appear in the written report, plus brief statements of what was obtained from the various sources. For example, in listing persons interviewed the witness might relate at this point in the testimony which subjects were discussed. In listing written information sources, the witness also might discuss which pieces of information were obtained from each source.

Findings

The oral testimony about the research findings should cover the remainder of the information discussed in Chapter 13, "Writing an Appraisal Report." Findings include pertinent aspects of the economic outlook, the industry in which the company operates and the company's position in that industry, a description of the company, and the analysis leading to the valuation conclusion.

Final Conclusion

Even though in valuing the company at issue the appraiser probably has used several valuation approaches and has come up with a reasonable range of possible values, the concluding statement usually should be a single figure and a restatement of the standard of value. The attorney probably will ask the witness to state the conclusion in a manner similar to this: "It is my opinion that the fair market value of Ace Widget is $167 per share." The attorney usually will also ask whether all the procedures followed in the valuation have been in accordance with generally accepted business valuation principles and procedures.

Exhibits

Naturally, an important part of preparing for court testimony is creating exhibits that will help communicate the thoroughness and credibility of the valuation. Such exhibits usually include the witness's qualifications, in a format such as that used as an appendix to a written report, all the tabular statistical data for the written report, and any charts, pictures, or other supporting material that may assist the court in understanding the business and how it should be valued.

In courtroom testimony, the old adage "A picture is worth a thousand words" is particularly true. The witness probably has seen and toured the company's facilities; the judge very likely has not. Since the court usually can't go to the facilities, the next best thing is to bring the facilities to the court. Through photographs, the witness can give a "walking tour" of the business, giving the court a better understanding of what is being valued and, one would hope, making the financial analysis more meaningful. The pictures used in the courtroom usually can be prints that the judge can see and that can be entered as official exhibits. If the proceeding is a jury trial, the attorney and witness may wish to present the pictures as slides so that all parties in the courtroom can see the same thing while the witness is describing the company's operations. If slides are used, copies should be prepared for possible submission as exhibits.

For exhibits of a size and format that can be readily copied, such as 8½-by-11-inch or 11-by-17-inch pages, such as would be included in a written report, it is convenient to prepare an extra set for the judge in addition to the set to be labeled by the clerk and entered as the official exhibit in the court record. Doing so will make it convenient for the judge to look at the tables and other exhibits while the witness is discussing them in direct testimony, as well as during cross-examination. It is also a courtesy, and in some cases a requirement, to provide a set of copies for the opposing attorney.

The exhibits the witness proposes to use should be reviewed with the attorney who will conduct the examination to ensure that all are appropriate and are legally admissible. A sample list of exhibits appropriate for a simple, basic case is shown in Exhibit 28–1.

Preparation with the Attorney

Once the testimony outline and exhibits have been drafted, the attorney should review them thoroughly with the expert. The attorney should understand the significance of the major points in the expert's work in order to be able to phrase questions most meaningfully, spend

EXHIBIT 28-1

**Typical List of Exhibits
to Be Submitted with Court Testimony
on Business Valuation**

Qualifications of witness

Pictures of business facilities

Latest five years' financial statements for the subject company

Five-year summary of the subject company's balance sheets

Five-year summary of the subject company's income statements

Subject company's financial ratios compared with industry norms

Market price data for comparative publicly traded companies

Summary statistics of valuation approaches used and conclusion

NOTE: The above list applies to a simple, basic case and should be expanded to include whatever additional material may be relevant in each specific case.

the most time on the most salient points, and know what topics, if any, to revisit on redirect examination. The expert should be sure to understand any legal issues that bear on the testimony and how his testimony fits into the overall case. Even though the trial attorney is busy and under pressure, both he/she and the appraiser must understand how important it is to work together to prepare a well-focused and persuasive presentation of the expert's work. All too often the attorney fails to gain the full impact of the expert's knowledge and research because of inadequate preparation.

In the Courtroom

The expert should appear in court as rested, alert, and neatly groomed as possible. Whether a man or a woman, the expert should wear a business suit, perhaps one appropriate for an initial meeting with a new client.

What to Have on the Stand

In general, the witness should take what he or she expects to have to refer to, a calculator, perhaps a note pad, and no more. If asked questions about any document the witness has not brought along; the witness is entitled to request a copy of it and examine it. Documents should be sufficiently organized that the witness will have little trouble finding references.

The witness should not plan to read the testimony except quotations from documents when it is important to have the record reflect the document's exact wording. An outline of testimony points might help ensure that the witness overlooks no important point. The expert should keep in mind, however, that opposing counsel may examine and copy all materials brought to or referred to on the witness stand.

General Guidelines for Testimony

Perhaps the most critical thing for the witness to keep in mind in the courtroom is the need to be objective and unbiased, not an advocate. An advocate is defined as "one who pleads the cause of another" or "one who supports something as a cause." Pleading and supporting the client's cause is the attorney's role. The expert witness's role is to present the facts as they are and to use his or her professional expertise to interpret those facts to reach an objective conclusion.

Another key resonsibility on the witness stand is to respond to the questions asked. The witness first must pay attention to the question and be sure of understanding it and should pause long enough before answering to be *sure* that the answer will satisfy the question. If unsure whether he or she understands the question, the witness should ask for clarification.

Although answers should be concise but complete, how far to go is a matter of judgment. However, the witness definitely should avoid introducing material or ideas irrelevant to the question. Nevertheless, there is a fine line of judgment. A question may be worded such that a direct answer without clarification could leave a misleading impression. Naturally, in such cases the witness should volunteer the necessary clarification. (Of course, such questions are more likely to come from the opposing attorney during cross-examination, because he or she either doesn't understand the material or wishes to lead the witness into creating a false impression.)

The witness should speak distinctly and slowly enough for the judge and attorneys to understand the ideas and for the court reporter to type the words into the record. If it is necessary to use proper names or esoteric terminology, the appraiser should spell them so that the court reporter can enter them into the record correctly.

The witness should make enough eye contact with the judge and/or jury to ensure that they are following the testimony and understanding the ideas. If not sure whether the judge and/or jury understands, the witness should pause and rephrase the point more clearly. The key point is that the person you are trying to communicate to is the trier of fact, either judge or jury, *not* your client's counsel or opposing counsel.

In general, the expert witness should avoid technical language and jargon. Usually there is no reason to believe that the judge and/or jurors are trained in the very technical discipline of business valuation or in the specifics of the industry in which the subject business operates. If a technical term is necessary for making a point, it should be defined or explained in terms intelligible to a layperson.

In referring to an exhibit, the witness should say something like "I direct your attention to Exhibit 10" and give the judge time to find Exhibit 10 before proceeding.

The witness should avoid distracting mannerisms and utterances such as "well," "ummm," and "uhhh." Unconscious habits, such as clicking a ballpoint pen or tapping a pencil, should be eliminated.

Otherwise, the witness should be his or her natural self, exuding competence and confidence but never arrogance.

Direct Examination

The expert witness must be careful not to omit any material facts, even (or especially) if their implications do not support the client's case. One should always assume that the opposing attorney and expert witness are properly prepared (even if one suspects they are not) and will not allow any adverse facts to be overlooked. If the expert witness omits material facts, whether because of incompetence or of advocacy, his or her credibility with the court will be in question. It is also essential that the expert witness not distort any facts or their interpretations. "Straightforward" is a good keyword to go by.

Whether the expert enters all exhibits in one batch at the beginning of the testimony or one by one as they become relevant is a matter of preference. Many attorneys think the latter approach helps keep the court's attention focused on the subject at hand, and I generally concur. After the oral qualification of the expert witness, his or her written credentials may be entered as an exhibit. From that point forward, each exhibit can be introduced immediately before the witness discusses it so that the judge can view it as the witness describes and interprets it.

Exhibits are numbered by the court as they are entered, and usually other exhibits have been entered earlier in the case; therefore, the witness's Table II may be the court's Exhibit 15. As the exhibits are entered, the witness should write the court's exhibit number at the top of his or her own copy, since that usually is how the exhibit will be identified when the witness is called to discuss it in cross-examination.

The witness should not be surprised if the opposing attorney raises frequent objections. He or she may object to the form or substance of a question, an answer given by a witness, or the introduction of an exhibit. When an objection is raised, the witness must pause while the attorneys fight it out, then proceed when so instructed by the judge or by the attorney conducting the examination.

Cross-Examination

It is the opposing attorney's job to expose to the court any weaknesses in the expert witness's testimony. The witness should not take it personally. The attorney may attempt to discredit the witness in various ways; such as asking questions designed to attack the witness's competence to present expert testimony on the valuation issue at hand or to bring out possible conflicts of interest that would impugn the witness's independence. If the witness has testified in previous cases, he or she should assume that the opposing attorney has read the transcripts of such cases and will ask questions to bring out any apparent inconsistencies between previous and present testimony. The witness also should assume that the attorney has reviewed all the books and articles that he or she has written.

As discussed earlier, in preparing for direct testimony the witness also must prepare for cross-examination. If the witness did not use a particular approach that may seem reasonable on the surface, he or she should be prepared to explain why. If the witness did not use a company as a comparative, he or she should be prepared to explain why the company was disqualified. (This particular problem will be taken care of almost automatically if the procedures outlined in Chapter 9, "Comparative Transaction Data," are followed and documented.)

Some attorneys use a cross-examination technique of asking questions in a manner designed to leave the court with an impression that they might like to convey but may be misleading. A favorite ploy is to carefully frame a complicated question so as to leave a certain impression and then demand a yes or no answer. The witness should realize that he or she cannot be compelled to limit the answer to yes or no if it would not be completely appropriate. The witness has the right to clarify the answer and should demand to be allowed to do so if failure to clarify would leave a misimpression. The witness should first answer yes or no if it is possible to do so and then give the clarification. If it is a compound question and the answer is yes to one or more parts and no to others, the witness should make clear to which part or parts each response refers. If the question simply cannot be answered yes or no, the witness should explain why. The witness also may request the attorney to rephrase a question, either for clarification or to "unbundle" a compound question.

Another cross-examination ploy is to ask a question that contains a misleading presumption. In such a case, the witness must correct the false presumption in the answer; otherwise, he or she will risk leaving the impression of accepting the false premise.

It also is common for cross-examining attorneys to mischaracterize a witness's prior testimony, reading into it some impression that was never intended. In replying to such a misrepresentation, the witness may need to preface the answer with wording such as "To put the answer to your question in proper context, I need to correct the misunderstanding of my prior testimony that was implied in your paraphrasing of it."

The hardest questions to deal with are those that are so abstruse that they are unintelligible. Usually the expert should not heroically attempt to interpret such questions but admit not understanding them and request clarification.

Through all of this, the witness should try to remain courteous. Nevertheless, he or she must also be firm and not feel intimidated by an overbearing attorney.

One thing that a witness absolutely must avoid is attempting to bluff if he or she does not know an answer. Any suspicion of bluffing could cast doubt on the credibility of the witness's entire testimony. If the witness does not know the answer, he or she must say so. Also, if there is some error in the data, the witness should admit it and correct it, making whatever adjustment to the conclusion the correction would indicate.

If the expert witness has done his or her homework thoroughly, the cross-examination actually can help the case. In one case, the attorney conducting the cross-examination asked a series of questions on why I had not used certain valuation approaches or specific comparable companies. To each question I replied that I had considered using the approach or the comparable company and explained why it was inappropriate for the case at hand. Finally, I overheard a colleague of the examining attorney sitting next to him whisper, not too discreetly, "Let's get this guy off the stand. He's hurting us." As it turned out, the attorney was destroying his own case. The approaches and the prospective comparable companies in question were ones that the opposition's expert witness had researched and planned to use. With each answer explaining why I had rejected the particular approach or company, I was rebutting the opposition's expert witness's testimony—which hadn't even been presented yet!

Redirect Examination

Even when the cross-examination has been completed, it is not time for the witness to breathe a sigh of relief. The attorney who conducted the original examination usually will want to keep the witness on the stand to ask redirect examination questions. The general purpose of redirect is to expand any points brought out in the cross-examination that the attorney thinks should be elaborated on. It is the attorney's opportunity to counter possible misimpressions that might have been left with the court during the cross-examination and to reinforce any positions about which the cross-examination may have raised doubts.

If there is a recess between cross- and redirect examinations and the witness feels the need to clarify any points further, he or she should inform the attorney so the attorney can ask the appropriate questions. If the witness feels strongly that something should be brought out on redirect examination and there is no scheduled recess, he or she usually can request a conference with the attorney.[6] The redirect and recross examinations can go back and forth indefinitely, limited only by the attorneys' restraint and the judge's patience.

The judge may break in at any time during the direct examination, cross-examination, or any part of the proceedings to ask questions. Some judges are more apt to do so than others. Questions from the judge usually are a good sign—at least the judge is paying attention, and judges often ask penetrating and perceptive questions. Also, the witness should prefer that the judge ask for clarification of something the witness has left unclear or omitted rather than just leaving the issue alone.

Rebuttal Testimony

Attorneys often ask experts to present testimony for the purpose of rebutting testimony presented by the opposition's expert. Such testimony can take a wide variety of forms. In my experience, rebuttal testimony is most often presented to correct factual errors or errors in appraisal procedure committed by the opposing expert. Of course, if factual errors are to be corrected, it is important to present complete documentation for the correction. If procedural errors are to be corrected, the appraiser must present as strong authority as is possible for the correct procedures.

As discussed at more length in the previous chapter, in many cases rebuttal testimony is at least as important as the basic testimony and it should be presented as constructively as possible. Often, when the errors are corrected, the different approaches of the opposing experts ultimately may lead to similar conclusions.

---

[6]In British jurisprudence, it is common to not allow any communication between the witness and the attorney after cross-examination has started, and I have encountered that rule occasionally in American jurisprudence.

Segal's Rules of Testimony

A few years ago, I had the privilege of testifying for a well-known and very effective veteran Philadelphia trial lawyer by the name of Irwin "Buddy" Segal. Part of Buddy's standard preparation of his expert witnesses included viewing his videotape entitled "Segal's Five Rules of Testifying." Exhibit 28–2 is a summary outline of my notes on that tape.

EXHIBIT 28-2

Segal's Rules for Testifying

1. Listen
⇒To everything--anyone who talks in the room--including anyone who interrupts
⇒Listen hard at all times
⇒Listen with ears and with eyes--for most of us, if we listen without looking, we miss up to half of what is being said
⇒Do nothing else but listen when you're listening--don't wonder what's coming next
⇒Sit up in front portion of chair--head forward
⇒Listen to question in full

2. Hear
⇒Hear the question
⇒Ask to repeat if you don't hear

3. Understand the question
⇒All of it
⇒Totally
⇒You can't be doubtful as to any part of the question
⇒Note any assumption inserted in the question
⇒If you don't understand, say "I don't under- stand the question," or ask to rephrase-- nine times out of ten a difficult question becomes easier if it is rephrased

4. Answer the question
⇒Directly
⇒If you don't know, say "I don't know"
⇒If you don't remember, say "I don't remember"
⇒Always tell the truth
⇒If the question has more than one part (including assumptions), answer every part of the question
⇒ If possible, start with "yes" or "no"

5. Stick to the answer
⇒The same question should elicit the same answer no matter how often or how it is presented
⇒The objective of good cross examiners is to try to get you to change your answer if it's a good one--to attempt to find some fallibility or flaw in your answer--to try to reverse the effect of your answer--don't fall for it

SOURCE: Irving R. Segal, law firm of Schnader, Harrison, Segal & Lewis, Philadelphia, Pennsylvania.

Chapter 29

Arbitration

Disputes over the values of businesses and business interests arise from a variety of circumstances, including divorces, corporate or partnership dissolutions, dissenting-stockholder actions, and assorted damage cases. In recent years, there has been a growing trend to resolve such disputes through arbitration rather than taking them through a court trial.

There is potential for grief, however, for both the principals (parties at interest) and the arbitrators if they do not understand the arbitration process and therefore fail to anticipate and agree upon the essential elements. I hope that the following pages, which are based heavily on my experiences and those of my associates as arbitrators and as consultants in arbitration situations, will assist principals, their attorneys and other advisers, and those who may act as arbitrators to use the arbitration process efficiently and with results that are fair to all. Not all situations are suitable for arbitration, and a decision to arbitrate should be cleared by the principal's attorney in each case.

To ensure the most efficient and effective arbitration of a disputed business valuation matter, I recommend careful consideration of the following two points:

1. *Start with an unambiguous arbitration agreement that all parties understand.*
2. *Engage competent, independent arbitrators with a high degree of relevant business valuation expertise.*

I have participated in many very satisfactory arbitrations in which these two rules were closely followed. Conversely, I have encountered numerous horror stories in which they were not.

Advantages of Arbitration over Court Trial

The primary advantages of arbitration over a court trial are the following:

1. Arbitration usually takes less elapsed time from start to finish.
2. Scheduling normally can be made more convenient for all parties involved.
3. Arbitration usually costs less. Attorneys' time and experts' fees frequently are considerably reduced. The appraisal process itself may not be less expensive than a court trial, but the amount of time required for preparing for cross-examination and rebuttal to an opposing expert in court can be substantial.
4. Arbitration usually is less formal and less taxing on all participants, especially the principals in the disputed issue.
5. The hearings are private rather than public, and in many cases are not recorded by a court reporter, a compelling advantage in many circumstances.

6. There is less likelihood of an outlandish result in favor of one side over the other, provided the arbitrators are qualified, professional business appraisers. In cases where the issue is a dispute over the value of a business or a business interest, an arbitrator, if properly chosen, is usually in a better position as a result of experience and knowledge to assess the value of a business or business interest than either a judge or jury.

7. In most states, the decision (assuming there is no fraud) cannot be reviewed by a court. Thus, the arbitration decision usually is a *final* one.

Situations Suitable for Arbitration

Almost any dispute over the value of a business or a partial interest in one can lend itself to resolution by arbitration instead of trial. If the parties in divorce and corporate or partnership dissolutions decide ahead of time to resolve any valuation issues by arbitration, they may never reach the point of dispute. The following have been the major categories in my own experience.

Divorces

Of all situations involving disputed valuations of businesses or professional practices, I believe that those arising from divorces are the most difficult for the parties to resolve by amicable negotiation. Although divorces are only a small part of my staff's valuation practice, they account for a large proportion of the occasions on which we prepare for, and appear on, the witness stand in court to present expert testimony.

Disputed valuation issues can become a major element in the already intense emotional strain accompanying divorce proceedings. Frequently, the valuation for the property settlement is the major, if not the only, disputed issue. Besides the time and cost advantages, arbitration spares the parties the tension and added antagonism of fighting it out in court.

Corporate and Partnership Dissolutions; Buyouts of Minority Interests

Akin to a divorce situation is a corporate or partnership dissolution. I would also include in this general category the buyout of a minority stockholder or partner pursuant to (or in the absence of) a buy-sell agreement. By arbitrating the valuation issue, the principals can part on as friendly a basis as possible regardless of the circumstances of the dissolution.

Dissenting-Stockholder Actions

As discussed in Chapter 25 a merger, sale, or other major corporate action can give rise to dissenting stockholders' appraisal rights under the statutes of all states except West Virginia. The expediency and lower cost make the arbitration process an attractive alternative to a trial in such cases, especially smaller ones for which prolonged and expensive court proceedings can result in a no-win situation for everyone.

Damage Cases

Damage cases, in which the valuation of a business or practice often is the central issue in determining the amount of relief, include the following:

1. Breach of contract.
2. Condemnation.
3. Antitrust.
4. Lost profits.
5. Lost business opportunity.
6. Amount of casualty insurance proceeds or allocation of proceeds among parties at interest.

I have observed that the risk of the court reaching an outlandish determination of value is greater in damage cases—especially those involving breach of contract and antitrust—than in any other major category of disputed valuation cases. The reason for such extreme decisions may be that some juries or courts allow the damages that a party is liable for to affect their objectivity about the valuation issue; similarly, they may be swayed by some sentiment toward the parties involved. This risk can be significantly reduced through the use of an arbitration process using qualified appraisers as arbitrators.

The Arbitration Agreement

The ground rules by which the arbitration will proceed are critical. They start with a document mandating certain elements of the arbitrators' assignment. This document may be a buy-sell agreement, a prenuptial agreement, or an agreement or court order drawn up specifically for the arbitration's purpose. Sometimes an agreement such as a buy-sell agreement will be supplemented by written instructions agreed upon by the attorneys involved. It is important that the written agreement directing the arbitration specify which factors the agreement mandates and which are left to the arbitrators' discretion. It is also critical that the agreement be complete, clear, and unambiguous.

I have seen incredible amounts of unnecessary frustration and wasted time and energy expended as a result of parties' and arbitrators' disagreements as to the interpretation of the arbitration document.

Factors Specified in the Arbitration Agreement

Factors that should be mandated by the agreement include the following:

1. Procedure for selection of arbitrators.
2. Definition of the property to be appraised.
3. Date as of which the property is to be valued.
4. Standard of value to be used (as discussed in Chapter 1 and elsewhere in the book).
5. What constitutes a conclusion by the arbitrators, such as:
   a. Agreement by at least two out of three.
   b. Average of the two closest to each other.
   c. Conclusion of the third (neutral) arbitrator, such as in a "special master" situation.
6. Format and procedure for the arbitrators' rendering of their conclusion.
7. Terms of payment of the amount determined by the arbitrators, including interest, if any.
8. Time schedule for the various steps in the arbitration process, at least the selection of arbitrators and some outside time limit for the total process.
9. Arrangements for compensation of arbitrators.[1]

Failure to specify any of the above factors may leave the door open for costly and extensive legal battles. Most state statutes specify that the standard of value for dissenting-stockholders' appraisal rights is fair value, although a minority of states specify fair market value. In other cases, the arbitrators usually must look to the arbitration document to establish the standard of value.

Some buy-sell agreements specify fair market value as the standard of value. For minority interests, of course, this standard of value implies a discount from a proportionate share of the fair market value of the total entity, a fact that many owners (and even some attorneys) may overlook when drafting the agreement. Some buy-sell agreements specify that the valuation is to be a proportionate share of the fair market value of the total enterprise, with no minority interest discount. I recommend that whoever drafts the agreement discuss the minority-interest discount, or lack of it, with the parties to the agreement (see Chapter 20, "Buy-Sell Agreements," for sample wording).

---

[1] The most typical arrangement that I have seen calls for payment of party-appointed arbitrators by the party that appointed them with payments to a third arbitrator split between the parties. Sometimes fee arrangements are specified by statute, such as in dissenter stockholder appraisal statutes. Sometimes attorneys agree on special arrangements for payment of a neutral arbitrator which are contingent on the outcome of the arbitration in which case such arrangements may not be disclosed to the arbitrator (but the funds may be placed in trust or the fees otherwise guaranteed).

The agreement may specify a reporting deadline, or a schedule may be worked out in conjunction with the process of engaging the arbitrators.

The wording of the arbitration agreement carries many far-reaching ramifications. An apparently insignificant omission can cause someone an unpleasant surprise, and if the agreement is not carefully worded, unintended implications can crop up later that make it an agreement to which no one really agreed. Even the standard of value can be called into question if not everyone has the same understanding of its definition within the given context. Because of all the contingencies, I recommend that an appraiser experienced in arbitration be consulted when drafting the agreement.

Factors Left to the Arbitrators' Discretion

Factors that can—and in most cases I believe should—be left to the arbitrators' discretion include the following:

1. Whether or not each arbitrator is expected or required to make a complete, independent appraisal or the extent to which each arbitrator considers it necessary to do independent work as opposed to relying on certain data or analyses furnished by other arbitrators and/or appraisers.
2. Procedures for the arbitrators to communicate with one another (writing, telephone calls, personal meetings) and the rules for sharing information.
3. Scheduling of the arbitrators' work and meetings within the constraint of the agreed-upon reporting schedule.
4. Valuation approaches and criteria to be considered within the constraints of any legally mandated criteria.
5. Facts, documents, and other data on which to rely (although the principals may agree to stipulate certain facts or assumptions, which could make the arbitrators' job easier with respect to some matters of possible uncertainty).

Other Factors to Address

As a generality, the arbitration agreement may specify rules on various matters, or, in the absence of specific rules should contain some broad language giving the arbitrators authority to make rules on points not addressed in the agreement. An example would be rules regarding contacts between parties and the arbitrators. Often participants in arbitrations are given no rules as to whether ex parte contact is permitted, and arbitration statutes provide little or no guidance.

Another topic often not addressed is rules specifying whether the arbitrators are free to obtain property-specific information independent of the parties, or should rely soley on information presented to them by the parties and made part of the arbitration record.

Procedure for Selecting Arbitrators

The most typical procedure for selecting arbitrators is to have each party select one arbitrator and the two arbitrators select the third. I think it is preferable for the two arbitrators appointed by the parties to have complete authority to select the third rather than leaving that selection subject to the approval of the principals. This avoids delays and the necessity of dealing with pressures arising from the principals' biases, which are almost sure to be injected.

It is important that there be an alternative procedure for selecting a third arbitrator in case of a deadlock. This contingency procedure should be planned in advance or in conjunction with entering into the arbitration agreement. The procedure in the event of a deadlock should call for the appointment of the third arbitrator by some predetermined party, such as a court or a responsible (and totally neutral) official in the industry or profession. This procedure will almost ensure that at least two of the three arbitrators will be professional appraisers if one side already has chosen one. If one side insists that the third arbitrator be a qualified professional appraiser and presents a list of people who are totally independent of the principals involved, it is unlikely that an independent party charged with making the appointment would select someone not so qualified over someone who was.

There should be a deadline after which the alternate selection process takes effect if the first two arbitrators have failed to agree on the third arbitrator.

Another possibility is to establish the procedure such that the two arbitrators attempt to reach agreement between themselves, bringing in the third arbitrator only if they are unable to do so. In that case, I recommend that the two agree on the prospective third arbitrator at the outset, before they get involved in other types of interaction with each other in the arbitration process. This procedure could be established as part of the language in a buy-sell agreement.

If appointed by a court, the third arbitrator may be an equal part of a three-member arbitration panel or a *special master*, that is, one whose conclusion does not require the concurrence of any other arbitrator, although he or she normally is expected to take their positions into consideration.

Criteria for Selecting Arbitrators

The selection of competent and unbiased arbitrators usually is the most critical step in assuring the disputants an equitable arbitration result.

Qualifications

Although it may seem self-serving to the appraisal profession for me to espouse the utilization of expert business appraisers as arbitrators in business valuation disputes, my experience has led me to conclude that this course gives the highest probability of an equitable result. Anyone reading this book must realize that business appraisal is a highly technical subject. In-depth schooling in business valuation should help to avoid pitfalls and errors that otherwise might be committed even by people of indisputable integrity, business experience, and other professional qualifications. I suggest that the qualifications desired in an arbitrator would not significantly differ from those one would seek in an expert witness, as discussed in Chapter 27, "Litigation Support."[2]

In some cases, if the business is highly specialized, it may be desirable to seek as arbitrators one or more appraisers who have experience in appraising the specific line of business. Nevertheless, it generally is *not* advisable to gain the desired industry expertise by utilizing as an arbitrator someone who is an active or retired participant in the industry or profession involved or who has performed ancillary functions such as accounting or economic analysis in the industry or profession but is not experienced in matters directly related to valuation. Many such people lack the requisite training for dealing professionally with the specific issue of valuation. Further, there is the risk that such people's biases toward the industry or profession could preclude objective valuation. If specialized knowledge of industry people is required, their expertise can instead be drawn on through informal discussion with the arbitrator(s) or by formal testimony presented to the arbitrator(s).

I have observed sound valuation conclusions reached by arbitration panels composed of industry people knowledgeable in finance, along with attorneys versed in both industry and valuation matters. However, in these instances the parties incurred costs not only for the three arbitrators but for expert testimony for presentation to the arbitration panel by at least two appraisers. I have also seen panels of arbitrators who were not business valuation experts reach conclusions that I believe a consensus of responsible professional appraisers would have considered outrageously beyond a reasonable range of value.

Independence

The arbitrators should be independent of any party to the dispute, and any relationship that would call a prospective arbitrator's independence into question should be disclosed to all parties. The arbitrators should view the arbitration process not as an adversarial proceeding

---

[2]A list of senior members of the American Society of Appraisers who are certified in business valuation may be obtained from the American Society of Appraisers, P.O. Box 17265, Washington, D.C. 20041 (703) 478-2228.

but as a cooperative effort to reach an equitable conclusion. All the parties should realize that each arbitrator, regardless of who appointed him or her, is not an agent of any principal (as might be the case in a negotiation for a sale); rather, each arbitrator is acting independently in using his or her expertise and judgment to reach a conclusion that will be fair to all parties.

This attitude of cooperation is especially significant in the way expert appraisers appointed as arbitrators normally interact during the arbitration process compared to their interaction when presenting expert testimony in a court proceeding. In a court proceeding, there normally is no direct communication whatsoever among experts. Expert testimony is limited to answering the questions posed by attorneys on direct or cross-examination or questions posed by the court. In an arbitration proceeding, on the other hand, maximum communication among arbitrators normally is expected from the outset; discussion is expected to cover all points thoroughly and impartially and need not be limited to answering questions posed by opposing attorneys, each acting from the perspective of advocacy.[3]

Availability and Compensation

Obviously, one criterion for selection is the availability of the desired arbitrator(s) within a reasonable time frame so that the effectiveness of the arbitration will not be significantly diminished.

The amount of compensation usually is based on each arbitrator's normal professional hourly or daily billing rate (or some mutually agreed-upon rate), plus out-of-pocket expenses. It is much less common for an arbitrator's compensation to be based on a fixed fee, because it is very difficult to determine in advance just how much time the total appraisal and arbitration process will require. However, it is reasonable to expect to discuss some estimate of probable fees and to know the daily rate or other fee basis. Hourly rates for business appraisal experts are similar to those for other professionals with comparable academic and professional credentials, experience, and skills.

Engagement of Arbitrators

Once the arbitrators have been appointed, the engagement should be committed to writing. The description of the engagement may take the form of an engagement letter initiated by one or more attorneys and/or principals, a standard professional services agreement initiated by an appraiser serving as arbitrator, or both. Either the letter or the professional services agreement is satisfactory as long as all aspects of the engagement are adequately covered (see Chapter 1, "Defining

---

[3]Although the arbitrators' role espoused above is the role normally assumed by most professional appraisers with whom I have worked, I have encountered party-appointed arbitrators who understood their role to be one of advocacy. It would seem desirable that the arbitation agreement address this matter.

the Appraisal Assignment"). Sometimes addenda to the initial engagement document(s) may be necessary, since decisions on some items, such as schedules and certain expenses, may be made or changed as the engagement progresses.

The engagement document(s) should include reference to the document(s) giving rise to the arbitration (e.g., a buy-sell agreement) and should cover compensation of the arbitrator and all necessary instructions not addressed or clarified in the arbitration document(s).

All documents relating to the engagement of an arbitrator should be signed by the arbitrator and whoever is responsible for compensation for his or her services. The most common compensation arrangement is one in which each party assumes responsibility for the compensation and expenses of the arbitrator that that party has nominated or appointed and the parties share equally the compensation and expenses of the third arbitrator. Such arrangements vary, however, from case to case.

The Arbitration Process

I have been involved in many arbitrations and have never seen any two that were alike, so it is difficult to offer general guidance about the arbitration process. Both arbitration documents and arbitrators' requirements vary widely, and procedures that are practical in some circumstances are rendered impractical in others. One major variable is the extent of the appraisal required of the arbitrators. Some arbitration documents require each member of the arbitration panel to carry out a complete, independent appraisal. More commonly, however (and I think preferably in most cases), the extent of independent appraisal work is left to the judgment of the individual arbitrators or to the arbitration panel as a whole.

Review of the Arbitration Document

Each arbitrator should begin by carefully reviewing the document(s) giving rise to the arbitration. If the arbitrators do not understand any details of the assignment, such as the specification of the property, or disagree as to their interpretation, they should seek clarification immediately. Furthermore, they should make these requests in writing to preclude possible future disputes.

Initial Communication among Arbitrators

I recommend that the arbitrators establish communication among themselves as soon after their appointment as possible. A face-to-face meeting is ideal if their geographic proximity makes that feasible, but a conference call or series of conference calls, perhaps supplemented by correspondence, usually is sufficient. Each case is unique, but the following is a generalized list of points to try to establish early:

1. Status of work already accomplished, if any (who has done what work up to that point).
2. An agreement about sharing information. (My preference is to agree that all information gathered or developed by one arbitrator will be shared with the other arbitrators as quickly as possible.)
3. An agreement as to the relevant valuation approaches to consider, if possible.
4. A list of documents and data needed and assignment of responsibility for obtaining each and seeing that they are distributed to other arbitrators.
5. Any other possible division of the research effort, such as searches for comparative transactions, development of economic and/or industry data, and routine financial statement analysis (spreadsheets, ratio analysis, comparison with industry averages, and so on). Division of research effort, of course, must depend on each arbitrator's willingness to accept certain efforts of another, which must be based on a judgment of professional ability and unbiased presentation of data and analyses.
6. Scheduling.

Field Visit

In most cases, arbitrators will want to visit the operating premises and interview relevant principals and/or management. I think it works out best if the arbitrators can conduct this field trip together rather than separately. That way, they can all see the same things at the same time and all can benefit from hearing the others' questions and answers first hand. A joint field trip also gives the arbitrators an opportunity to address any items not fully covered in their previous communications. Also, it gives arbitrators who previously did not know one another an opportunity to get acquainted and form a basis for working together.

Hearings

The arbitrators should offer each party the opportunity to present oral and written information and opinions if they so desire. It frequently is convenient to hold a meeting in conjunction with the field trip to accommodate such input.

Arbitration hearings are tantamount to court hearings but usually are somewhat less formal. The parties and the arbitrators have some latitude in the hearings to observe courtroom-type procedures more or less strictly according to the situation. A court reporter may or may not attend and make a transcript of the hearing. Although testimony presented at an arbitration hearing is considered to be under oath and subject to the laws of perjury, the parties may either have witnesses formally sworn in by a notary public or other authorized official or waive that procedure and simply have the chairperson of the hearing inform witnesses that they are obligated to provide truthful testimony.

The same latitude applies to the matter and format of testimony. Attorneys may conduct the interviews in a formal question-and-answer structure, or the arbitrators may interview the witnesses without counsel. As in a courtroom, the exhibits are numbered in the order of their appearance in the hearing. Unlike in a courtroom, though, there generally are no rules of evidence, and arbitrators try to be as lenient as is reasonable in allowing all parties to present whatever evidence and arguments they wish. Typically arbitrators ask witnesses more questions for themselves than do judges from the bench. At or following the conclusion of arbitration hearings, attorneys may or may not offer closing arguments and may or may not file written briefs with the arbitrators.

Unlike most courtroom proceedings, arbitration hearings generally are not open to the public. Frequently, however, there is a limited audience of people related to or affiliated with the disputing parties. This aspect of privacy is a major factor in some parties' decisions to go to arbitration rather than to court when they have the opportunity to choose between the two.

The Valuation Meeting

Usually the arbitrators meet in person to reach the valuation conclusion, although in some instances this meeting may be replaced by a conference call. In either case, all the arbitrators should be thoroughly prepared, having exchanged and assimilated as much information as possible prior to the meeting.

The valuation meeting is most productive if it is structured so that the arbitrators can discuss each issue in turn, identifying and monitoring each point of agreement and disagreement. To that end, they should make sure that someone is keeping notes of the proceedings, covering both the points of agreement and the points on which agreement has yet to be reached. Each arbitrator must be receptive to the others' information and willing to compromise on issues on which reasonable judgments might differ.

It is best to reach a conclusion that all members of the arbitration panel can endorse as fair. In my experience, this agreement usually is possible if all the arbitrators are qualified professional business appraisers. If the arbitrators cannot reach unanimity, the arbitrator in the minority position may render a dissenting opinion for the record, if he or she so desires.

Reporting the Results of the Arbitration

The formal report of the arbitrators' valuation conclusion usually is contained in a very brief letter that does no more than refer to the arbitration agreement, state that the arbitrators have completed their assignment in accordance with the agreement, and state the conclusion reached. The letter is signed by the arbitrators concurring in the conclusion.

In a significant proportion of cases, the principals on both sides request a brief report explaining how the valuation conclusion was reached. In these situations, I suggest that such an advisory report be the responsibility solely of the third appraiser. To make such a report a joint task of two or more arbitrators, each of whom probably judged various factors slightly differently—though they were able to agree on a conclusion—usually would be an unnecessarily complicated and costly exercise, although it is done this way in a number of arbitrations.

If the valuation conclusion is reached unilaterally by a special master, normally that person will be the only one to prepare and sign the report. In such cases, an explanation of the procedures and criteria usually is included.

Summary: The Most Critical Elements

The two most critical elements for an expeditious and successful arbitration are (1) a definitive arbitration agreement that provides the arbitrators with unambiguous instructions on the key matters described above and (2) the appointment of independent arbitrators who will be both fair and competent in reaching a conclusion about the subject property's value. If these two elements are properly addressed, the arbitration process can be a very efficient and fair way of resolving business valuation matters.

Appendix A

Present Value Tables

APPENDIX TABLE A-1
Present Value of One Dollar Due at the End of _n_ Periods

$$PV = \frac{\$1}{(1+r)^n}$$

PV = present value; r = discount rate; n = number of periods until payment.

n	1%	2%	3%	4%	5%	6%	7%	8%	9%	10%
1	.99010	.98039	.97007	.96154	.95238	.94340	.93458	.92593	.91743	.90909
2	.98030	.96117	.94260	.92456	.90703	.89000	.87344	.85734	.84168	.82645
3	.97059	.94232	.91514	.88900	.86384	.83962	.81630	.79383	.77218	.75131
4	.96098	.92385	.88849	.85480	.82270	.79209	.76290	.73503	.70843	.68301
5	.95147	.90573	.86261	.82193	.78353	.74726	.71299	.68058	.64993	.62092
6	.94204	.88797	.83748	.79031	.74622	.70496	.66634	.63017	.59627	.56447
7	.93272	.87056	.81309	.75992	.71068	.66506	.62275	.58349	.54703	.51316
8	.92348	.85349	.78941	.73069	.67684	.62741	.58201	.54027	.50187	.46651
9	.91434	.83675	.76642	.70259	.64461	.59190	.54393	.50025	.46043	.42410
10	.90529	.82035	.74409	.67556	.61391	.55839	.50835	.46319	.42241	.38554
11	.89632	.80426	.72242	.64958	.58468	.52679	.47509	.42888	.38753	.35049
12	.88745	.78849	.70138	.62460	.55684	.49697	.44401	.39711	.35553	.31863
13	.87866	.77303	.68095	.60057	.53032	.46884	.41496	.36770	.32618	.28966
14	.86996	.75787	.66112	.57747	.50507	.44230	.38782	.34046	.29925	.26333
15	.86135	.74301	.64186	.55526	.48102	.41726	.36245	.31524	.27454	.23939
16	.85282	.72845	.62317	.53391	.45811	.39365	.33873	.29189	.25187	.21763
17	.84438	.71416	.60502	.51337	.43630	.37136	.31657	.27027	.23107	.19784
18	.83602	.70016	.58739	.49363	.41552	.35034	.29586	.25025	.21199	.17986
19	.82774	.68643	.57029	.47464	.39573	.33051	.27651	.23171	.19449	.16351
20	.81954	.67297	.55367	.45639	.37689	.31180	.25842	.21455	.17843	.14864
21	.81143	.65978	.53755	.43883	.35894	.29415	.24151	.19866	.16370	.13513
22	.80340	.64684	.52189	.42195	.34185	.27750	.22571	.18394	.15018	.12285
23	.79544	.63414	.50669	.40573	.32557	.26180	.21095	.17031	.13778	.11168
24	.78757	.62172	.49193	.39012	.31007	.24698	.19715	.15770	.12640	.10153
25	.77977	.60953	.47760	.37512	.29530	.23300	.18425	.14602	.11597	.09230

APPENDIX TABLE A-1 (Continued)
Present Value of One Dollar Due at the End of *n* Periods

n	11%	12%	13%	14%	15%	16%	17%	18%	19%	20%
1	.90090	.89286	.88496	.87719	.86957	.86207	.85470	.84746	.84034	.83333
2	.81162	.79719	.78315	.76947	.75614	.74316	.73051	.71818	.70616	.69444
3	.73119	.71178	.69305	.67497	.65752	.64066	.62437	.60863	.59342	.57870
4	.65873	.63552	.61332	.59208	.57175	.55229	.53365	.51579	.49867	.48225
5	.59345	.56743	.54276	.51937	.49718	.47611	.45611	.43711	.41905	.40188
6	.53464	.50663	.48032	.45559	.43233	.41044	.38984	.37043	.35214	.33490
7	.48166	.45235	.42506	.39964	.37594	.35383	.33320	.31392	.29592	.27908
8	.43393	.40388	.37616	.35056	.32690	.30503	.28478	.26604	.24867	.23257
9	.39092	.36061	.33288	.30751	.28426	.26295	.24340	.22546	.20897	.19381
10	.35218	.32197	.29459	.26974	.24718	.22668	.20804	.19106	.17560	.16151
11	.31728	.28748	.26070	.23662	.21494	.19542	.17781	.16192	.14756	.13459
12	.28584	.25667	.23071	.20756	.18691	.16846	.15197	.13722	.12400	.11216
13	.25751	.22917	.20416	.18207	.16253	.14523	.12989	.11629	.10420	.09346
14	.23199	.20462	.18068	.15971	.14133	.12520	.11102	.09855	.08757	.07789
15	.20900	.18270	.15989	.14010	.12289	.10793	.09489	.08352	.07359	.06491
16	.18829	.16312	.14150	.12289	.10686	.09304	.08110	.07078	.06184	.05409
17	.16963	.14564	.12522	.10780	.09293	.08021	.06932	.05998	.05196	.04507
18	.15282	.13004	.11081	.09456	.08080	.06914	.05925	.05083	.04367	.03756
19	.13768	.11611	.09806	.08295	.07026	.05961	.05064	.04308	.03669	.03130
20	.12403	.10367	.08678	.07276	.06110	.05139	.04328	.03651	.03084	.02608
21	.11174	.09256	.07680	.06383	.05313	.04430	.03699	.03094	.02591	.02174
22	.10067	.08264	.06796	.05599	.04620	.03819	.03162	.02622	.02178	.01811
23	.09069	.07379	.06014	.04911	.04017	.03292	.02702	.02222	.01830	.01509
24	.08170	.06588	.05322	.04308	.03493	.02838	.02310	.01883	.01538	.01258
25	.07361	.05882	.04710	.03779	.03038	.02447	.01974	.01596	.01292	.01048

APPENDIX TABLE A-1 (Continued)
Present Value of One Dollar Due at the End of *n* Periods

n	21%	22%	23%	24%	25%	26%	27%	28%	29%	30%	n
1	.82645	.81967	.81301	.80645	.80000	.79365	.78740	.78125	.77519	.76923	1
2	.68301	.67186	.66098	.65036	.64000	.62988	.62000	.61035	.60093	.59172	2
3	.56447	.55071	.53738	.52449	.51200	.49991	.48819	.47684	.46583	.45517	3
4	.46651	.45140	.43690	.42297	.40960	.39675	.38440	.37253	.36111	.35013	4
5	.38554	.37000	.35520	.34111	.32768	.31488	.30268	.29104	.27993	.26933	5
6	.31863	.30328	.28878	.27509	.26214	.24991	.23833	.22737	.21700	.20718	6
7	.26333	.24859	.23478	.22184	.20972	.19834	.18766	.17764	.16822	.15937	7
8	.21763	.20376	.19088	.17891	.16777	.15741	.14776	.13878	.13040	.12259	8
9	.17986	.16702	.15519	.14428	.13422	.12493	.11635	.10842	.10109	.09430	9
10	.14864	.13690	.12617	.11635	.10737	.09915	.09161	.08470	.07836	.07254	10
11	.12285	.11221	.10258	.09383	.08590	.07869	.07214	.06617	.06075	.05580	11
12	.10153	.09198	.08339	.07567	.06872	.06245	.05680	.05170	.04709	.04292	12
13	.08391	.07539	.06780	.06103	.05498	.04957	.04472	.04039	.03650	.03302	13
14	.06934	.06180	.05512	.04921	.04398	.03934	.03522	.03155	.02830	.02540	14
15	.05731	.05065	.04481	.03969	.03518	.03122	.02773	.02465	.02194	.01954	15
16	.04736	.04152	.03643	.03201	.02815	.02478	.02183	.01926	.01700	.01503	16
17	.03914	.03403	.02962	.02581	.02252	.01967	.01719	.01505	.01318	.01156	17
18	.03235	.02789	.02408	.02082	.01801	.01561	.01354	.01175	.01022	.00889	18
19	.02673	.02286	.01958	.01679	.01441	.01239	.01066	.00918	.00792	.00684	19
20	.02209	.01874	.01592	.01354	.01153	.00983	.00839	.00717	.00614	.00526	20
21	.01826	.01536	.01294	.01092	.00922	.00780	.00661	.00561	.00476	.00405	21
22	.01509	.01259	.01052	.00880	.00738	.00619	.00520	.00438	.00369	.00311	22
23	.01247	.01032	.00855	.00710	.00590	.00491	.00410	.00342	.00286	.00239	23
24	.01031	.00846	.00695	.00573	.00472	.00390	.00323	.00267	.00222	.00184	24
25	.00852	.00693	.00565	.00462	.00378	.00310	.00254	.00209	.00172	.00142	25

APPENDIX TABLE A-2
Present Value of an Annuity of One Dollar for n Periods

$$PV = \frac{\$1}{r} - \frac{\$1}{r(1+r)^n}$$

PV = present value; r = discount rate; n = number of periods until payment.

n	1%	2%	3%	4%	5%	6%	7%	8%	9%	10%	n
1	.9901	.9804	.9709	.9615	.9524	.9434	.9346	.9259	.9174	.9091	1
2	1.9704	1.9416	1.9135	1.8861	1.8594	1.8334	1.8080	1.7833	1.7591	1.7355	2
3	2.9410	2.8839	2.8286	2.7751	2.7232	2.6730	2.6243	2.5771	2.5313	2.4868	3
4	3.9020	3.8077	3.7171	3.6299	3.5459	3.4651	3.3872	3.3121	3.2397	3.1699	4
5	4.8535	4.7134	4.5797	4.4518	4.3295	4.2123	4.1002	3.9927	3.8896	3.7908	5
6	5.7955	5.6014	5.4172	5.2421	5.0757	4.9173	4.7665	4.6229	4.4859	4.3553	6
7	6.7282	6.4720	6.2302	6.0020	5.7863	5.5824	5.3893	5.2064	5.0329	4.8684	7
8	7.6517	7.3254	7.0196	6.7327	6.4632	6.2098	5.9713	5.7466	5.5348	5.3349	8
9	8.5661	8.1622	7.7861	7.4353	7.1078	6.8017	6.5152	6.2469	5.9852	5.7590	9
10	9.4714	8.9825	8.5302	8.1109	7.7217	7.3601	7.0236	6.7101	6.4176	6.1446	10
11	10.3677	9.7868	9.2526	8.7604	8.3064	7.8868	7.4987	7.1389	6.8052	6.4951	11
12	11.2552	10.5753	9.9539	9.3850	8.8632	8.3838	7.9427	7.5361	7.1607	6.8137	12
13	12.1338	11.3483	10.6349	9.9856	9.3935	8.8527	8.3576	7.9038	7.4869	7.1034	13
14	13.0038	12.1062	11.2960	10.5631	9.8986	9.2950	8.7454	8.2442	7.7861	7.3667	14
15	13.8651	12.8492	11.9379	11.1183	10.3796	9.7122	9.1079	8.5595	8.0607	7.6061	15
16	14.7180	13.5777	12.5610	11.6522	10.8377	10.1059	9.4466	8.8514	8.3125	7.8237	16
17	15.5624	14.2918	13.1660	12.1656	11.2740	10.4772	9.7632	9.1216	8.5436	8.0215	17
18	16.3984	14.9920	13.7534	12.6592	11.6895	10.8276	10.0591	9.3719	8.7556	8.2014	18
19	17.2261	15.6784	14.3237	13.1339	12.0853	11.1581	10.3356	9.6036	8.9501	8.3649	19
20	18.0457	16.3514	14.8774	13.5903	12.4622	11.4699	10.5940	9.8181	9.1285	8.5136	20
21	18.8571	17.0111	15.4149	14.0291	12.8211	11.7640	10.8355	10.0168	9.2922	8.6487	21
22	19.6605	17.6580	15.9368	14.4511	13.1630	12.0416	11.0612	10.2007	9.4424	8.7715	22
23	20.4559	18.2921	16.4435	14.8568	13.4885	12.3033	11.2722	10.3710	9.5802	8.8832	23
24	21.2435	18.9139	16.9355	15.2469	13.7986	12.5503	11.4693	10.5287	9.7066	8.9847	24
25	22.0233	19.5234	17.4131	15.6220	14.0939	12.7833	11.6536	10.6748	9.8226	9.0770	25

APPENDIX TABLE A-2 (Continued)
Present Value of an Annuity of One Dollar for n Periods

n	11%	12%	13%	14%	15%	16%	17%	18%	19%	20%
1	.9009	.8929	.8850	.3772	.8696	.8621	.8547	.8475	.8403	.8333
2	1.7125	1.6901	1.6681	1.6467	1.6257	1.6052	1.5852	1.5656	1.5465	1.5278
3	2.4437	2.4018	2.3612	2.3216	2.2832	2.2459	2.2096	2.1743	2.1399	2.1065
4	3.1024	3.0373	2.9745	2.9137	2.8550	2.7982	2.7432	2.6901	2.6386	2.5887
5	3.6959	3.6048	3.5172	3.4331	3.3522	3.2743	3.1993	3.1272	3.0576	2.9906
6	4.2305	4.1114	3.9976	3.8887	3.7845	3.6847	3.5892	3.4976	3.4098	3.3255
7	4.7122	4.5638	4.4226	4.2883	4.1604	4.0386	3.9224	3.8115	3.7057	3.6046
8	5.1461	4.9676	4.7988	4.6389	4.4873	4.3436	4.2072	4.0776	3.9544	3.8372
9	5.5370	5.3282	5.1317	4.9464	4.7716	4.6065	4.4506	4.3030	4.1633	4.0310
10	5.8892	5.6502	5.4262	5.2161	5.0188	4.8332	4.6586	4.4941	4.3389	4.1925
11	6.2065	5.9377	5.6869	5.4527	5.2337	5.0286	4.8364	4.6560	4.4865	4.3271
12	6.4924	6.1944	5.9176	5.6603	5.4206	5.1971	4.9884	4.7932	4.6105	4.4392
13	6.7499	6.4235	6.1218	5.8424	5.5831	5.3423	5.1183	4.9095	4.7147	4.5327
14	6.9819	6.6282	6.3025	6.0021	5.7245	5.4675	5.2293	5.0081	4.8023	4.6106
15	7.1909	6.8109	6.4624	6.1422	5.8474	5.5755	5.3242	5.0916	4.8759	4.6755
16	7.3792	6.9740	6.6039	6.2651	5.9542	5.6685	5.4053	5.1624	4.9377	4.7296
17	7.5488	7.1196	6.7291	6.3729	6.0472	5.7487	5.4746	5.2223	4.9897	4.7746
18	7.7016	7.2497	6.8399	6.4674	6.1280	5.8178	5.5339	5.2732	5.0333	4.8122
19	7.8393	7.3658	6.9380	6.5504	6.1982	5.8775	5.5845	5.3162	5.0700	4.8435
20	7.9633	7.4694	7.0248	6.6231	6.2593	5.9288	5.6278	5.3527	5.1009	4.8696
21	8.0751	7.5620	7.1016	6.6870	6.3125	5.9731	5.6648	5.3837	5.1268	4.8913
22	8.1757	7.6446	7.1695	6.7429	6.3587	6.0113	5.6964	5.4099	5.1486	4.9094
23	8.2664	7.7184	7.2297	6.7921	6.3988	6.0442	5.7234	5.4321	5.1668	4.9245
24	8.3481	7.7843	7.2829	6.8351	6.4338	6.0726	5.7465	5.4509	5.1822	4.9371
25	8.4217	7.8431	7.3300	6.8729	6.4641	6.0971	5.7662	5.4669	5.1951	4.9476

APPENDIX TABLE A-2 (Continued)
Present Value of an Annuity of One Dollar for *n* Periods

n	21%	22%	23%	24%	25%	26%	27%	28%	29%	30%
1	.8264	.8197	.8130	.8065	.8000	.7937	.7874	.7813	.7752	.7692
2	1.5095	1.4915	1.4740	1.4568	1.4400	1.4235	1.4074	1.3916	1.3761	1.3609
3	2.0739	2.0422	2.0114	1.9813	1.9520	1.9234	1.8956	1.8684	1.8420	1.8161
4	2.5404	2.4936	2.4483	2.4043	2.3616	2.3202	2.2800	2.2410	2.2031	2.1662
5	2.9260	2.8636	2.8035	2.7454	2.6893	2.6351	2.5827	2.5320	2.4830	2.4356
6	3.2446	3.1669	3.0923	3.0205	2.9514	2.8850	2.8210	2.7594	2.7000	2.6427
7	3.5079	3.4155	3.3270	3.2423	3.1611	3.0833	3.0087	2.9370	2.8682	2.8021
8	3.7256	3.6193	3.5179	3.4212	3.3289	3.2407	3.1564	3.0758	2.9986	2.9247
9	3.9054	3.7863	3.6731	3.5655	3.4631	3.3657	3.2728	3.1842	3.0997	3.0190
10	4.0541	3.9232	3.7993	3.6819	3.5705	3.4648	3.3644	3.2689	3.1781	3.0915
11	4.1769	4.0354	3.9018	3.7757	3.6564	3.5435	3.4365	3.3351	3.2388	3.1473
12	4.2785	4.1274	3.9852	3.8514	3.7251	3.6060	3.4933	3.3868	3.2859	3.1903
13	4.3624	4.2028	4.0530	3.9124	3.7801	3.6555	3.5381	3.4272	3.3224	3.2233
14	4.4317	4.2646	4.1082	3.9616	3.8241	3.6949	3.5733	3.4587	3.3507	3.2487
15	4.4890	4.3152	4.1530	4.0013	3.8593	3.7261	3.6010	3.4834	3.3726	3.2682
16	4.5364	4.3567	4.1894	4.0333	3.8874	3.7509	3.6228	3.5026	3.3896	3.2832
17	4.5755	4.3908	4.2190	4.0591	3.9099	3.7705	3.6400	3.5177	3.4028	3.2948
18	4.6079	4.4187	4.2431	4.0799	3.9279	3.7861	3.6536	3.5294	3.4130	3.3037
19	4.6346	4.4415	4.2627	4.0967	3.9424	3.7985	3.6642	3.5386	3.4210	3.3105
20	4.6567	4.4603	4.2786	4.1103	3.9539	3.8083	3.6726	3.5458	3.4271	3.3158
21	4.6750	4.4756	4.2916	4.1212	3.9631	3.8161	3.6792	3.5514	3.4319	3.3198
22	4.6900	4.4882	4.3021	4.1300	3.9705	3.8223	3.6844	3.5558	3.4356	3.3230
23	4.7025	4.4985	4.3106	4.1371	3.9764	3.8273	3.6885	3.5592	3.4384	3.3254
24	4.7128	4.5070	4.3176	4.1428	3.9811	3.8312	3.6918	3.5619	3.4406	3.3272
25	4.7213	4.5139	4.3232	4.1474	3.9849	3.8342	3.6943	3.5640	3.4423	3.3286

Appendix B

UNIFORM STANDARDS OF PROFESSIONAL APPRAISAL PRACTICE

694

UNIFORM STANDARDS OF PROFESSIONAL APPRAISAL PRACTICE

PREAMBLE

It is essential that a professional appraiser arrive at and communicate his or her analyses, opinions, and advice in a manner that will be meaningful to the client and will not be misleading in the marketplace. These Uniform Standards of Professional Appraisal Practice reflect the current standards of the appraisal profession.

These standards include a Competency Provision which places an immediate responsibility on the appraiser prior to acceptance of an assignment. The standards contain binding requirements, as well as specific guidelines to which a Departure Provision applies under certain conditions. Definitions applicable to these standards are also included.

These standards deal with the procedures to be followed in developing an appraisal, analysis, or opinion and the manner in which an appraisal, analysis, or opinion is communicated. Standards 1 and 2 relate to the development and communication of a real estate appraisal. Standard 3 establishes guidelines for reviewing an appraisal and reporting on that review. Standards 4 and 5 address the development and communication of various real estate analysis functions. Standard 6 sets forth criteria for the development and reporting of mass appraisals for ad valorem tax purposes. Standards 7 and 8 establish guidelines for developing and communicating personal property appraisals. Standards 9 and 10 establish guidelines for developing and communicating business appraisals.

These standards are developed for appraisers and the users of appraisal services. To maintain the highest level of professional practice, appraisers will observe these standards. The users of appraisal services should demand work performed in conformance with these standards.

EXPLANATORY COMMENTS RELATING TO THE UNIFORM STANDARDS OF PROFESSIONAL APPRAISAL PRACTICE

PREFACE

To provide additional information concerning the background, interpretation, or application of a Standards Rule, these Explanatory Comments Relating to the Uniform Standards of Professional Appraisal Practice are adopted.

Explanatory Comments have been developed for Standards Rules for which additional explanation and interpretation might prove to be helpful. There are no Explanatory Comments for Standards Rules that are axiomatic or have not yet required further explanation; however, additional Explanatory Comments will be developed and others supplemented or revised as the need arises.

COMPETENCY PROVISION

Prior to entering into an agreement to perform any assignment, an appraiser must carefully consider the knowledge and experience that will be required to complete the assignment competently and either:

1. have the knowledge and experience necessary to complete the assignment competently; or

2. with regard to appraisal, review, and analysis as defined herein, immediately disclose the lack of knowledge or experience to the client, and take all steps necessary or appropriate to complete the assignment competently; or

3. with regard to mass appraisal as defined herein, immediately take all necessary or appropriate steps to ensure the mass appraisal is developed under the supervision of an appraiser who has the qualifications referred to in Standard 6.

COMPETENCY PROVISION

Comment on Competency Provision

Since the background and experience of appraisers varies widely and a lack of knowledge or experience can lead to inaccurate or inappropriate appraisals, the competency provision requires an appraiser to have both the knowledge and the experience required to perform a specific appraisal service competently. If an appraiser is offered the opportunity to perform an appraisal service but lacks the necessary knowledge or experience to complete it competently, the appraiser must disclose his or her lack of knowledge or experience to the client prior to accepting the assignment and then take the necessary or appropriate steps to complete the appraisal service competently. This may be accomplished in various ways including, but not limited to, personal study by the appraiser; association with an appraiser reasonably believed to have the necessary knowledge or experience; or retention of others who possess the required knowledge or experience. If, in the course of performing an appraisal service, an appraiser discovers that he or she lacks the required knowledge or experience, the appraiser must immediately take all appropriate steps to remedy the deficiency.

The concept of competency also extends to appraisers who are requested or required to travel to geographic areas wherein they have no recent appraisal experience. An appraiser preparing an appraisal in an unfamiliar location must spend sufficient time to understand the nuances of the local market and the supply and demand factors relating to the specific property type and the location involved. Such understanding will not be imparted solely from a consideration of hard data such as demographics, costs, sales and rentals. The necessary understanding of local market conditions provides the bridge between a sale and a comparable sale or a rental and a comparable rental. If an appraiser is not in a position to spend the necessary amount of time in a market area to obtain this understanding, affiliation with a qualified local appraiser may be the appropriate response to ensure the development of a competent appraisal.

DEPARTURE PROVISION

An appraiser may enter into an agreement to perform an assignment that calls for something less than, or different from, the work that would otherwise be required by the specific guidelines, provided that prior to entering into such agreement:

1. the appraiser has determined that the assignment to be performed is not so limited in scope that the resulting appraisal, review, or analysis would tend to mislead or confuse the client, the users of the report, or the public; and

2. the appraiser has advised the client that the assignment calls for something less than, or different from, the work required by the specific guidelines, and therefore the report will include a qualification that reflects the limited or differing scope of the appraisal, review, or analysis.

In the context of this departure provision, exceptions to the following binding requirements are not permitted: S.R. 1-1, S.R. 1-5, S.R. 2-1, S.R. 2-3, S.R. 2-5, S.R. 3-3, S.R. 4-1, S.R. 5-1, S.R. 5-3, S.R. 6-1, S.R. 6-5, S.R. 6-6, S.R. 7-1, S.R. 8-1, S.R. 8-3, S.R. 9-1, S.R. 9-3, S.R. 9-5, S.R. 10-1, S.R. 10-3 and S.R. 10-5.

DEPARTURE PROVISION

Comment on Departure Provision

Before making a decision to enter into an agreement for appraisal services calling for a departure from a specific appraisal guideline, an appraiser must use extreme care to determine whether the scope of the appraisal service to be performed is so limited that the resulting analysis, opinion, or conclusion would tend to mislead or confuse the client, the users of the report, or the public. For the purpose of this provision, users of the report might include parties such as lenders, employees of government agencies, limited partners of a client, and a client's attorney and accountant. In this context the purpose of the appraisal and the anticipated or possible use of the report are critical.

If an appraiser enters into an agreement to perform an appraisal service that calls for something less than, or different from, the work that would otherwise be required by the specific appraisal guidelines, S.R. 2-2(k), 5-2(i), 8-2(h), and 10-2(h) require that this fact be clearly and accurately set forth in the report.

An appraiser must use extreme care in determining whether to enter into an agreement calling for a report that is something less than, or different from, the complete report that would otherwise be required by the specific reporting guidelines. If the limited scope of the report would tend to mislead or confuse the client, the users of the report, or the public, the appraiser must not enter into such agreement.

The requirements of the departure provision may be satisfied by the technique of incorporating by reference. For example, if an appraiser's complete file was introduced into evidence at a public hearing or public trial and the appraiser subsequently prepared a one-page report that (1) identified the property, (2) stated the value, and (3) stated that the value conclusion could not be properly understood without reference to his or her complete file and directed the reader to the complete file, the requirements of the departure provision would be satisfied if the appraiser's complete file contained, in coherent form, all the data and statements that are required by the Uniform Standards of Professional Appraisal Practice. Another example would be an updated report that expressly incorporated by reference all the background data, market conditions, assumptions, and limiting conditions that were contained in the original report prepared for the same client.

JURISDICTIONAL EXCEPTION

If any part of these standards is contrary to the law or public policy of any jurisdiction, only that part shall be void and of no force or effect in that jurisdiction.

DEFINITIONS

For the purpose of these standards, the following definitions apply:

ANALYSIS: the act or process of providing information recommendations and/or conclusions on diversified problems in real estate other than estimating value.

APPRAISAL: the act or process of estimating value.

CASH FLOW ANALYSIS: a study of the anticipated movement of cash in or out of real estate.

CLIENT: any party for whom an appraiser performs a service.

FEASIBILITY ANALYSIS: a study of the cost-benefit relationship of an economic endeavor.

INVESTMENT ANALYSIS: a study that reflects the relationship between acquisition price and anticipated future benefits of a real estate investment.

MARKET ANALYSIS: a study of real estate market conditions for a specific type of property.

MASS APPRAISAL: the process of valuing a universe of properties as of a given date utilizing standard methodology, employing common data, and allowing for statistical testing.

MASS APPRAISAL MODEL: a mathematical expression of how supply and demand factors interact in a market.

PERSONAL PROPERTY: identifiable portable and tangible objects which are considered by the general public as being ''personal,'' e.g., furnishings, artwork, antiques, gems and jewelry, collectibles, machinery and equipment.

REAL ESTATE: an identified parcel or tract of land, including improvements, if any.

REAL PROPERTY: the interests, benefits, and rights inherent in the ownership of real estate.

REPORT: any communication, written or oral, of an appraisal, review, or analysis; the document that is transmitted to the client upon completion of an assignment.

REVIEW: the act or process of critically studying a report prepared by another.

DEFINITIONS

Comment on Definitions

In the Definitions adopted for the Uniform Standards of Professional Appraisal Practice, three terms are used to encompass the work performed by appraisers in the marketplace: analysis, appraisal, and review. These terms are intentionally generic. These standards are intended to apply to all appraisal practice, and the use of other nomenclature by an appraiser (e.g., counseling, evaluation, study, submission, valuation) does not exempt an appraiser from adherence to these standards.

NOTE: The Uniform Standards of Professional Appraisal Practices includes ten Standards. Because Standards 9 and 10 establish the guidelines for developing and communicating business appraisals, they are the only ones included in this Appendix.

STANDARD 9 & STANDARDS RULES

EXPLANATORY COMMENTS

ADDITIONAL DEFINITIONS APPLICABLE TO STANDARDS 9 & 10

BUSINESS ASSETS: tangible and intangible resources other than personal property and real estate that are employed by a business enterprise in its operations.

BUSINESS ENTERPRISE: a commercial, industrial or service organization pursuing an economic activity.

BUSINESS EQUITY: the interests, benefits, and rights inherent in the ownership of a business enterprise or a part thereof.

ADDITIONAL DEFINITIONS
APPLICABLE TO STANDARDS 9 & 10

Comment on Additional Definitions

To the extent that several of the definitions cited on Page V of these standards apply to business appraisal and include a direct reference to real estate, they are modified for the purpose of Standards 9 & 10.

STANDARD 9

In developing a business appraisal, an appraiser must be aware of, understand, and correctly employ those recognized methods and techniques that are necessary to produce a credible appraisal.

STANDARD 9

In developing a business appraisal, an appraiser must be aware of, understand, and correctly employ those recognized methods and techniques that are necessary to produce a credible appraisal.

STANDARD 9 & STANDARDS RULES

EXPLANATORY COMMENTS

STANDARDS RULES RELATING TO STANDARD 9

S.R. 9-1

In developing a business appraisal, an appraiser must:

(a) be aware of, understand, and correctly employ those recognized methods and techniques that are necessary to produce a credible appraisal;

(b) not commit a substantial error of omission or commission that significantly affects an appraisal;

(c) not render appraisal services in a careless or negligent manner, such as a series of errors that, considered individually, may not significantly affect the results of an appraisal, but which, when considered in the aggregate, would be misleading.

S.R. 9-2

In developing a business appraisal, an appraiser must observe the following specific appraisal guidelines:

(a) adequately identify the business enterprise, assets, or equity under consideration, define the purpose and the intended use of the appraisal, consider the scope of the appraisal, describe any special limiting conditions, and identify the effective date of the appraisal;

(b) define the value being considered.
  (i) if the appraisal concerns a business enterprise or equity interests, consider any buy-sell agreements, investment letter stock restrictions, restrictive corporate charter or partnership agreement clauses, and any similar features or factors that may have an influence on value.
  (ii) if the appraisal concerns assets, the appraiser must consider whether the assets are:
  (1) appraised independently; or
  (2) appraised as parts of a going concern.

  (iii) if the appraisal concerns equity interests in a business enterprise, consider whether the interests are appraised on a majority or minority basis.

S.R. 9-3

In developing a business appraisal relating to a majority interest in a business enterprise, an appraiser must investigate the possibility that the business enterprise may have a higher value in liquidation than for continued operation as a going concern. If liquidation is the indicated basis of valuation, any real estate or personal property to be liquidated must be valued under the appropriate standard.

General Comment

Standard 9 is directed toward the same substantive aspects set forth in Standard 1, but addresses business appraisal.

EXPLANATORY COMMENTS RELATING TO STANDARD 9

Comment S.R. 9-1(a)

S.R. 9-1(a) is identical in scope and purpose to S.R. 1-1(a). Changes and developments in the economy and in investment theory have a substantial impact on the business appraisal profession. Important changes in the financial arena, securities regulation, tax law and major new court decisions may result in corresponding changes in business appraisal theory and practice.

Comment S.R. 9-1(b)

S.R. 9-1(b) is identical in scope and purpose to S.R. 1-1(b).

Comment S.R. 9-1(c)

S.R. 9-1(c) is identical in scope and purpose to S.R. 1-1(c).

Comment S.R. 9-2(b)

S.R. 9-2(b) is identical in scope and purpose to S.R. 1-2(b).

Comment S.R. 9-2(b)(ii)

The value of assets held by a business enterprise may change significantly depending on whether the basis of valuation is acquisition or replacement, continued use in place, or liquidation.

Comment S.R. 9-2(b)(iii)

S.R. 9-2(b)(iii) is identical in scope and purpose to S.R. 1-2(d).

Comment S.R. 9-3

This rule requires the appraiser to recognize that continued operation of a marginally profitable business is not always the best approach as liquidation may result in a higher value. It should be noted, however, that this should be considered only when the business equity being appraised is in a position to cause liquidation. If liquidation is the appropriate basis of value, then assets such as real estate and personal property must be appraised under Standard 1 and Standard 7, respectively.

STANDARD 10 & STANDARDS RULES

S.R. 9-4

In developing a business appraisal, an appraiser must observe the following specific appraisal guidelines when applicable:

(a) value the business enterprise, assets or equity by an appropriate method or technique.

(b) collect and analyze relevant data regarding:

(i) the nature and history of the business;

(ii) financial and economic conditions affecting the business enterprise, its industry, and the general economy;

(iii) past results, current operations, and future prospects of the business enterprise;

(iv) past sales of capital stock or partnership interests in the business enterprise being appraised;

(v) sales of similar businesses or capital stock of publicly held similar businesses;

(vi) prices, terms, and conditions affecting past sales of similar business assets;

(vii) physical condition, remaining life expectancy, and functional and economic utility or obsolescence.

No pertinent information shall be withheld.

Comment S.R. 9-4(b)

This guideline directs the appraiser to study the prospective and retrospective aspects of the business enterprise and to study it in terms of the economic and industrial environment within which it operates. Further, sales of securities of the business itself or similar businesses for which sufficient information is available should also be considered.

This guideline also requires the appraiser to investigate and take into account not only that loss of value that results from deterioration due to age but also loss of value due to functional and economic obsolescence. Economic obsolescence is a major consideration when assets are considered as parts of a going concern. It is also the criterion in deciding that liquidation is the appropriate basis for valuation.

S.R. 9-5

In developing a business appraisal, an appraiser must:

(a) select one or more approaches that apply to the specific appraisal assignments;

(b) consider and reconcile the quality and quantity of data available for analysis within the approaches that are applicable.

Comment S.R. 9-5

This rule requires the appraiser to use all approaches for which sufficient reliable data are available. However, it does not mean that the appraiser must use all approaches in order to comply with the rule if certain approaches are not applicable.

STANDARD 10

In reporting the results of a business appraisal, an appraiser must communicate each analysis, opinion, and conclusion in a manner that is not misleading.

STANDARDS RULES RELATING TO STANDARD 10

S.R. 10-1

Each written or oral business appraisal report must:

(a) clearly and accurately set forth the appraisal in a manner that will not be misleading;

(b) contain sufficient information to enable the person(s) who receives or relies on the report to understand it properly;

STANDARD 10

In reporting the results of a business appraisal, an appraiser must communicate each analysis, opinion, and conclusion in a manner that is not misleading.

General Comment

Standard 10 is identical in scope and purpose to the appraisal reporting requirements in Standard 2.

EXPLANATORY COMMENTS RELATING TO STANDARD 10

Comment S.R. 10-1(a)

S.R. 10-1(a) is identical in scope and purpose to S.R. 2-1(a).

Comment S.R. 10-1(b)

S.R. 10-1(b) is identical in scope and purpose to S.R. 2-1(b).

STANDARD 10 & STANDARDS RULES

(c) clearly and accurately disclose any extraordinary assumption or limiting condition that directly affects the appraisal and indicate its impact on value.

S.R. 10-2

Each written business appraisal report must comply with the following specific reporting guidelines:

(a) identify and describe the business enterprise, assets or equity being appraised;

(b) state the purpose of the appraisal;

(c) define the value to be estimated;

(d) set forth the effective date of the appraisal and the date of the report;

(e) describe the scope of the appraisal;

(f) set forth all assumptions and limiting conditions that affect the analyses, opinions, and conclusions;

(g) set forth the information considered, the appraisal procedures followed, and the reasoning that supports the analyses, opinions, and conclusions;

(h) set forth any additional information that may be appropriate to show compliance with, or clearly identify and explain permitted departures from, the requirements of Standard 9;

(i) include a certification in accordance with S.R. 10-3;

(j) include a letter of transmittal signed by the person assuming technical responsibility for the appraisal.

EXPLANATORY COMMENTS

Comment S.R. 10-1(c)

This rule requires a clear and accurate disclosure of any extraordinary assumptions or conditions that directly affect an analysis, opinion, or conclusion. Examples of such extraordinary assumptions or conditions might include items such as the execution of a pending lease agreement, atypical financing, infusion of additional working capital or making other capital additions, or compliance with regulatory authority rules.

Comment S.R. 10-2(a), (b), (c) and (d)

Every business appraisal report must include information sufficient to identify what is being appraised, for what purpose, what type of value is being sought and the date as of which that value applies. If the appraisal concerns equity, it is not enough to identify the entity in which the equity is being appraised but also the nature of the equity, for example: how many shares of common or preferred stock. The purpose may be to express an opinion of value but the intended use of the appraisal must also be stated.

Not only the type of value being sought—fair market value, value in use, etc.—must be stated but it must also be defined clearly. The report date is when the report is submitted; the appraisal date or date of value is the effective date of the value conclusion. This date cannot be later than the report date.

Comment S.R. 10-2(e), (f), (g) and (h)

S.R. 10-2(e), (f), (g) and (h) are identical in scope and purpose to S.R. 2-2(f), (g), (h) and (i).

Comment S.R. 10-2(j)

An appraisal report cannot be anonymous. The appraiser or the person assuming technical responsibility for the appraisal must sign the report. The person assuming technical responsibility for the appraisal must be the person under whose direct supervision the appraisal investigation was conducted and who had final responsibility for the conclusions and opinions of value in the appraisal report. Reports issued by a firm may be signed by the person authorized to sign on behalf of the firm, only if the person assuming technical responsibility for the appraisal also signs.

STANDARD 10 & STANDARDS RULES

EXPLANATORY COMMENTS

S.R. 10-3

Each written business appraisal report must contain a certification that is similar in content to the following:

I certify that, to the best of my knowledge and belief:

— the statements of fact contained in this report are true and correct.

— the reported analyses, opinions, and conclusions are limited only by the reported assumptions and limiting conditions, and are my personal, unbiased professional analyses, opinions, and conclusions.

— I have no (or the specified) present or prospective interest in the property that is the subject of this report, and I have no (or the specified) personal interest or bias with respect to the parties involved.

— my compensation is not contingent on an action or event resulting from the analyses, opinions, or conclusions in, or the use of, this report.

— my analyses, opinions, and conclusions were developed, and this report has been prepared, in conformity with the Uniform Standards of Professional Appraisal Practice.

— no one provided significant professional assistance to the person signing this report. (If there are exceptions, the name of each individual providing significant professional assistance must be stated.)

S.R. 10-4

To the extent that it is both possible and appropriate, each oral business appraisal report (including expert testimony) must address the substantive matters set forth in S.R. 10-2.

Comment S.R. 10-4

S.R. 10-4 is identical in scope and purpose to S.R. 2-4.

S.R. 10-5

An appraiser who signs a business appraisal report prepared by another, even under the label "review appraiser," must accept full responsibility for the contents of this report.

Comment S.R. 10-5

S.R. 10-5 is identical in scope and purpose to S.R. 2-5.

In anticipation of the formation of the Foundation, nine appraisal organizations in 1986 formed the Ad Hoc Committee on Uniform Standards of Professional Appraisal Practice. The document developed by the Ad Hoc Committee, Uniform Standards of Professional Appraisal Practice, contains 10 Standards as follows:

Standard 1 - Real Estate Appraisal

Standard 2 - Real Estate Appraisal, Reporting

Standard 3 - Review Appraisal

Standard 4 - Real Estate Analysis

Standard 5 - Real Estate Analysis, Reporting

Standard 6 - Mass Appraisal

Standard 7 - Personal Property Appraisal

Standard 8 - Personal Property Appraisal, Reporting

Standard 9 - Business Appraisal

Standard 10 - Business Appraisal, Reporting

The nine appraisal organizations represented on the Ad Hoc Committee are listed below. The eight United States organizations have adopted the Uniform Standards.

- American Institute of Real Estate Appraisers
- American Society of Appraisers
- American Society of Farm Managers and Rural Appraisers
- Appraisal Institute of Canada
- International Association of Assessing Officers
- International Right of Way Association
- National Association of Independent Fee Appraisers
- National Society of Real Estate Appraisers
- Society of Real Estate Appraisers

Appendix C

Definitions of Terms Adopted by
the Business Valuation
Committee of the American
Society of Appraisers

Adjusted Book Value: The book value which results after one or more asset or liability amounts are added, deleted, or changed from the respective book amounts.

Appraisal: The act or process of determining value. It is synonymous with valuation.

Appraisal Date: The date as of which the appraiser's opinion of value applies.

Appraisal Method: A specific procedure applied to determine value.

Appraised Value: The appraiser's opinion or determination of value.

Book Value:
1. With respect to assets, the capitalized cost of an asset less accumulated depreciation, depletion or amortization as it appears on the books of account of the enterprise.
2. With respect to a business enterprise, the difference between total assets (net of depreciation, depletion and amortization) and total liabilities of an enterprise as they appear on the balance sheet. It is synonymous with net book value, net worth and shareholders' equity.

Business Appraiser: A person who by education, training and experience is qualified to make an appraisal of a business enterprise and/or its intangible assets.

Business Enterprise: A commercial, industrial or service organization pursuing an economic activity.

Business Valuation: The act or process of arriving at an opinion or determination of the value of a business enterprise or an interest therein.

Capitalization:
1. The conversion of income into value.
2. The capital structure of a business enterprise.
3. The recognition of an expenditure as a capital asset rather than a period expense.

Capitalization Factor: Any multiple or divisor used to convert income into value.

Majority: Ownership position greater than 50% of the voting interest in an enterprise.

Majority Control: The degree of control provided by a majority position.

Marketability Discount: An amount or percentage deducted from an equity interest to reflect lack of marketability.

Minority Discount: The reduction, from the pro rata share of the value of the entire business, to reflect the absence of the power of control.

Minority Interest: Ownership position less than 50% of the voting interest in an enterprise.

Net Assets: Total assets less total liabilities.

Capitalization Rate: Any divisor (usually expressed as a percentage) that is used to convert income into value.

Capital Structure: The composition of the invested capital.

Cash Flow: Net income plus depreciation and other non-cash charges.

Control: The power to direct the management and policies of an enterprise.

Control Premium: The additional value inherent in the control interest, as contrasted to a minority interest, that reflects its power of control.

Discount Rate: A rate of return used to convert a monetary sum, payable or receivable in the future, into present value.

Economic Life: The period over which property may be profitably used.

Enterprise: See **Business Enterprise.**

Equity: The owners' interest in property after deduction of all liabilities.

Fair Market Value: The amount at which property would change hands between a willing seller and a willing buyer when neither is acting under compulsion and when both have reasonable knowledge of the relevant facts.

Going Concern: An operating business enterprise.

Going Concern Value:
1. The value of an enterprise, or an interest therein, as a going concern.
2. Intangible elements of value in a business enterprise resulting from factors such as having a trained workforce, an operational plant, and the necessary licenses, systems and procedures in place.

Goodwill: That intangible asset that arises as a result of name, reputation, customer patronage, location, products and similar factors that have not been separately identified and/or valued but which generate economic benefits.

Invested Capital: The sum of the debt and equity in an enterprise on a long term basis.

Net Income: Revenues less expenses, including taxes.

Rate of Return: An amount of income realized or expected on an investment, expressed as a percentage of that investment.

Replacement Cost New: The current cost of a similar new item having the nearest equivalent utility as the item being appraised.

Reproduction Cost New: The current cost of an identical new item.

Valuation: See **Appraisal.**

Working Capital: The amount by which current assets exceed current liabilities.

Appendix D

Bibliography

General Valuation Issues
    Articles
    Books
Dissenting-Stockholders' Actions
    Articles
Goodwill and Other Intangibles
    Articles
Marketability and Minority Interests
    Articles
Mergers and Acquisitions
    Articles
    Books

Separate subject bibliographies relevant to certain chapters have been appended to these chapters:

General Valuation Issues

Articles

Albo, Wayne P. "Special Purchasers." *Journal of Business Valuation,* 1987 (Proceedings of the First Joint Institute of Chartered Business Valuators and The American Society of Appraisers, October 1986), pp. 139–61.

Alderman, David. "Evaluating a Company's Management Team." *Journal of Business Valuation,* 1987 (Proceedings of the First Joint Institute of Chartered Business Valuators and The American Society of Appraisers, October 1986), pp. 129–37.

Alvarez, Edward M. "The Deductibility of Reasonable Compensation in the Close Corporation." *Santa Clara Lawyer* 11 (1971), pp. 20–36.

Arneson, George S. "Accounting for Inflation in Valuing Closely Held Companies." *Taxes* (June 1981), pp. 391–98.

Arneson, George S. "Dividend Paying Capacity Has Little or No Relevance in Valuing Closely Held Corporations." *Taxes* (April 1981), pp. 251–57.

Bakken, John E. "Professional Negligence and Liability of the Appraiser." *Journal of Business Valuation,* 1987 (Proceedings of the First Joint Institute of Chartered Business Valuators and The American Society of Appraisers, October 1986), pp. 257–64.

Banks, Warren E. "Measuring the Value of Corporate Stock." *California Western Law Review* 11 (Fall 1974), pp. 1–59.

Banks, Warren E. "The Accounting Balance Sheet as a Guide to Stock Value." *Detroit College of Law Review* (1978), pp. 241–59.

Bannen, John T. "Valuation of Closely Held Corporations." *Wisconsin Bar Bulletin* (February 1982), pp. 15–17, 53.

Barenbaum, Lester. "Utilizing the Gordon Model: Discounting Net Income vs. Available Cash Flow." *Journal of Business Valuation,* 1987 (Proceedings of the First Joint Institute of Chartered Business Valuators and The American Society of Appraisers, October 1986), pp. 119–27.

Barenbaum, Lester, and Thomas F. Monahan, "Revenue Ruling 59-60: Valuation Theory and Practice in Conflict." *ASA Valuation* (December 1984), pp. 2–7.

Bielinski, Daniel W. "The ERI Equity Risk Premium Selection Method." *Business Valuation Review* (September 1987), pp. 124–27.

Blair, Vernon A. "Valuation Terms and Concepts: Canadian vs. U.S." *Journal of Business Valuation,* 1987 (Proceedings of the First Joint Institute of Chartered Business Valuators and The American Society of Appraisers, October 1986), pp. 7–15.

Bonovitz, Sheldon M. "Impact of the TRA Repeal of *General Utilities.*" *Journal of Taxation* (December 1986), pp. 388–97.

Brinig, Brian P., and Michael W. Prairie. "Expert Testimony: The Business Appraiser as a Valuation Expert Witness." *Business Valuation News* (March 1985), p. 8.

Brock, Thomas. "More on Capitalization Rates." *ASA Valuation* (June 1986), pp. 68–71. Also in *Business Valuation News* (December 1985), pp. 5–8.

Brown, Ralph J., and Dennis A. Johnson. "Inflation Valuation and the Discount Rate." *Appraisal Journal* (October 1980), pp. 549–55.

Butala, John H., Jr. "Valuation of Closely Held Corporations." Philip E. Heckerling Institute on Estate Planning, University of Miami Law Center, 1973, pp. 1400–1434.

Cantor, Gilbert M. "New Warnings on Stock Valuation." *Journal of the American Society of CLU* (May 1985), pp. 60–63.

Carn, Neil; Joseph Rabianski; and James D. Vernor. "Trial Techniques of Expert Witnesses." *Real Estate Review* (Spring 1986), pp. 66–74.

Casey, Cornelius J., and Norman J. Bartczak, "Cash Flow—It's Not the Bottom Line." *Harvard Business Review* (July–August 1984), pp. 61–66.

"Compilation and Review of Financial Statements." American Institute of Certified Public Accountants, Accounting and Review Services Committee. *Statement on Standards for Accounting and Review Services, No. 1* (1979).

Cooper, Glen. "How Much Is Your Business Worth?" In *Business* (September–October 1984), pp. 50–54.

Craig, Darryl; Glenn Johnson; and Maurice Joy. "Accounting Methods and P/E Ratios." *Financial Analysts Journal* (March–April 1987), pp. 41–45.

Cushing, James E., Jr. "The Valuation of a Close Corporation: Glimpses of Objectivity In an Inflationary Period." *Loyola University of Chicago Law Journal* 13 (Fall 1981), pp. 107–33.

Czumak, Michael. "The Appraiser Goes to Court." *ASA Valuation* (June 1988), pp. 34–40.

Dickerson, F. Gregg. "The Appraisal of Public Utilities and Railroads for Ad Valorem Taxation: Application of the Unit Rule. " *Property Tax Journal* (June 1988), pp. 145–55.

Dietrich, William C. "A Risk Premium/Growth Model to Determine the Earnings Multiple." *Business Valuation News* (March 1986), pp. 10–17.

Donias, Claire H. "Valuation Terms and Concepts: Canadian vs. U.S." *Journal of Business Valuation,* 1987 (Proceedings of the First Joint Institute of Chartered Business Valuators and The American Society of Appraisers, October 1986), pp. 1–5.

Donohue, Matthew J. "Closely Held Stock Valuation—in Support of General Guidelines and in Defense of the Courts." *Taxes* (June 1982), pp. 455–58.

Drymalski, Raymond, Jr. "Valuation of Stock of a Subchapter S Corporation—a New Form of Business Organization." *Illinois Bar Journal* (April 1968), pp. 672–89.

Faris, John P.; Walter R. Holman; and Patrick A. Martinelli. "Valuing the Closely Held Business." *Mergers & Acquisitions* (Fall 1983), pp. 53–59.

Feakins, Nicholas L. "Relevance of Financial Analysis to Standard Appraisal Methodology." *Business Valuation Review* (September 1987), pp. 105–15.

Fearon, Richard H., and Mitchell R. Julis. "The Role of Modern Finance in Bankruptcy Reorganizations." *Temple Law Quarterly* 56, no. 1 (1983), pp. 1–48.

Feinberg, Andrew. "What's It Worth?" *Venture* (January 1988), pp. 27–31.

Field, Irving M. "A Review of the Principles of Valuation." *ASA Valuation* (June 1986), pp. 2–10.

Fishbein, Mark. "Valuation—An Ozymandian Task." *Corporate Finance* (July 1988), pp. 37–39.

Fishman, Jay E. "The 'Key Man' Concept in Business Valuation upon Divorce." *FAIR$HARE* (June 1982), pp. 3–4.

Fishman, Jay E. "The Problem with Rules of Thumb in the Valuation of Closely Held Entities." *FAIR$HARE* (December 1984), pp. 13–15.

Forbes, Wallace F. "Putting a Value on a Closely Held Company." *Family Advocate* (Summer 1984), pp. 28–30.

Fortang, Chaim J., and Thomas Moers Mayer. "Valuation in Bankruptcy." *UCLA Law Review* 32 (1985), pp. 1061–1132.

Fox, Jeffery D. "Closely Held Business Valuations: The Uninformed Use of the 'Excess Earnings/Formula' Method." *Taxes* (November 1982), pp. 832–36.

Gilbert, Gregory A. "Price/Sales Ratios." *Business Valuation News* (June 1986), pp. 7–15.

Goff, Gary A. "Fair Market Value: A Primer for Texas Legal Practice." *Texas Tech Law Review* 15 (May 1984), pp. 637–71.

Goldberg, Daniel S. "Fair Market Value in the Tax Law: Replacement Value or Liquidation Value." *Texas Law Review* 60 (May 1982), pp. 833–73.

Goodman, Barry R. "Valuing Investment Limited Partnerships." *Business Valuation News* (September 1986), pp. 8–15.

Goodman, Wolfe D. "Development in Valuation Principles, As Reflected in Some Recent Judicial Decisions." *Journal of Business Valuation,* 1987 (Proceedings of the First Joint Business Valuation Conference of The Canadian Institute of Chartered Business Valuators and The American Society of Appraisers, October 1986), pp. 17–29.

Goodwin, Michael W. "Use and Misuse of the Income Approach." *Property Tax Journal* (June 1986), pp. 85–96.

Gordon, Myron J., and Paul J. Halpern. "Cost of Capital for a Division of a Firm." *Journal of Finance* (September 1974), pp. 1153–63.

Graham, Gale. "Use 'Equivalency': Keep Your Friendly Lender Solvent." *The Real Estate Appraiser and Analyst* (Winter 1985), pp. 19–22.

Gray, Gerald. "When Is Fair Market Value Unfair?" *ASA Valuation* (June 1984), pp. 2–7.

Haynsworth, Harry J., IV. "Valuation of Business Interests." *Mercer Law Review* 33 (Winter 1982), pp. 457–517.

Heaton, Hal. "A Reply to 'Use and Misuse of the Income Approach.'" *Property Tax Journal* (June 1988), pp. 199–209.

Howard, J. "What's It Worth to You?" *Inc.* (July 1982), pp. 75–80.

Howe, Rex C., and Lee A. Kamp. "Appraisers as Expert Witnesses Before the IRS." *The Real Estate Appraiser and Analyst* (Summer 1984), pp. 52–55.

Janata, Jerrold F. "Appraisals—Use to Determine Fair Market Value in Tax-Oriented Partnerships and Other Transactions." New York University Institute on Federal Taxation, 1985, pp. 57.1–57.37.

Jensen, Herbert L. "Valuing Actively Traded Securities Involves More Than Researching Daily Price Quotations." *Taxation for Accountants* (July 1976), pp. 36–40.

Johnson, Lyle R.; Eli Shapiro; and Joseph O'Meara, Jr. "Valuation of Closely-Held Stock for Federal Tax Purposes: Approach to an Objective Method." *Pennsylvania Law Review* 166 (1951), pp. 166–95.

Jones, D. A. "Update on Valuation Issues and Policies." *Journal of Business Valuation,* 1979 (Proceedings of the Fourth Biennial Conference of the Canadian Association of Business Valuators, October 1978), pp. 121–36.

Jones, Jeffrey. "The Spouse Loses Out if *Rathmell* Stands." *ASA Valuation* (June 1988), pp. 60–65.

Joyce, Allyn A. "Valuation of Nonpublic Companies." In *Accountants' Handbook,* 6th ed. (1981), pp. 38.1–38.28.

King, Alfred M. "Fair Value Reporting." *Management Accounting* (March 1985), pp. 25–30.

Kingston, John P. R. "Damages—Lost Profits." *Journal of Business Valuation,* 1987 (Proceedings of the First Joint Institute of Chartered Business Valuators and The American Society of Appraisers, October 1986), pp. 111–18.

Kinsman, Michael D., and Bruce Samuelson. "Personal Financial Statements: Key Thorny Issues for CPAs: Closely Held Businesses, Trust Interests, Estimated Taxes." *Journal of Accountancy* (September 1987), pp. 138–48.

Klein, Ronald. "The Role of the Expert in Divorce Valuation." *FAIR$HARE* (May 1986), pp. 3–6.

Landsman, Stephen A. "Handling the Control Problems When Close Corporation Stock Is Transferred in a Divorce." *Taxation for Accountants* (July 1983), pp. 26–31.

Largay, James A., III, and Clyde P. Stickney. "Cash Flows, Ratio Analysis and the W. T. Grant Company Bankruptcy." *Financial Analysts Journal* (July–August 1980), pp. 51–54.

Lembke, Valdean C. "Determination of Reporting Basis for Long-Term Intercorporate Investment." *Mergers and Acquisitions* (Fall 1979), pp. 14–17.

Leung, T. S. Tony. "Myths about Capitalization Rate and Risk Premium." *Business Valuation News* (March 1986), pp. 6–10.

Leung, T. S. Tony. "Tax Reform Act of 1986: Considerations for Business Valuations." *Business Valuation Review* (June 1987), pp. 60–63.

Leung, T. S. Tony. "Understanding Fair Market Value." *Business Valuation News* (December 1982), pp. 4–6.

Litzenberger, Robert H., and Krishna Ramaswamy. "The Effect of Personal Taxes and Dividends on Capital Asset Prices." *Journal of Financial Economics* (June 1979), pp. 163–95.

Longenecker, Ruth R. "A Practical Guide to Valuation of Closely Held Stock." *Trusts & Estates* (January 1983), pp. 32–41.

Looney, Steve R. "Using LIFO to Value Costs under the Completed Contract Method: A Tale of Two Accounting Methods." *Tax Lawyer* (Winter 1986), pp. 235–83.

Loudon, Colin H., and John M. Davison. "The Law of Damages—A Valuator's Perspective." Journal of Business Valuation, 1987 (Proceedings of the First Joint Business Valuation Conference of The Canadian Institute of Chartered Business Valuators and The American Society of Appraisers, October 1986), pp. 97–110.

Lusht, Kenneth M. "Most Probable Selling Price." Appraisal Journal (July 1983), pp. 346–54.

Maughan, G. B. "The Defence of Professional Liability Claims against Valuators in Canada." *Journal of Business Valuation,* 1987 (Proceedings of the First Joint Business Valuation Conference of the First Canadian Institute of Chartered Business Valuators and The American Society of Appraisers, October 1986), pp. 251–55.

McDaniel, William R. "Sinking Fund Preferred Stock." *Journal of the Financial Management Association* 13, no. 1 (Spring 1984), pp. 45–52.

McMullin, Scott G. "Discount Rate Selection." *Business Valuation News* (September 1986), pp. 16–19.

Meyers, Robert M. "United States Experience in Valuating Closely-Held Corporations." *Journal of Business Valuation,* 1983 (Proceedings of the Sixth Biennial Conference of the Canadian Association of Business Valuators, November 1982), pp. 195–207.

Miller, Paul B. W. "The New Pension Accounting (Part 1): If Pensions Weren't Broke, How Come the FASB Fixed 'Em?" *Journal of Accountancy* (January 1987), pp. 90–108.

Miller, Paul B. W. "The New Pension Accounting (Part 2): Putting It into Practice." *Journal of Accountancy* (February 1987) pp. 86–94.

Mollica, Anthony F. "Evaluating the Stock of a Closely Held Corporation." *Case & Comment* (January 1982), pp. 12–15.

Moskowitz, Jerald I. "What's Your Business Worth?" *Management Accounting* (March 1988), pp. 30–34.

Nevers, Thomas J. "Capitalization Rates." *Business Valuation News* (June 1985), pp. 3–6.

Newton, Grant W., and James J. Ward, Jr. "Valuation of a Business in Bankruptcy." *CPA Journal* (August 1976), pp. 26–32.

Office of the Chief Economist. "The Effects of Dual-Class Recapitalizations on the Wealth of Shareholders." Securities and Exchange Commission, June 1, 1987, pp. 1–34.

Oliver, Robert P. "Moving Beyond the Real Estate Appraisal: Valuing Fractional Interests in Closely Held Real Estate Companies." *Business Valuation News* (June 1986), pp. 16–19.

Parker, George G. C., and Samuel S. Stewart, Jr. "Risk and Investment Performance." *Financial Analysts Journal* (May–June 1974), pp. 49+.

Patterson, R., and W. Albo. "What's It Worth? Business Valuations and the Banker (Canada)." *Canadian Banker* (June 1984), pp. 18–23.

Paulsen, James Walter. "Closely Held Corporations in the Wake of *Vallone:* Enhancement of Stock Value by Community, Time, Talent, and Labor." *Baylor Law Review* 35 (1983), pp. 47–96.

Pratt, Shannon P. "A Note on Developing a Capitalization Rate Using the Capital Asset Pricing Model." *Business Valuation News* (March 1985), p. 24.

Pratt, Shannon P. "Closely Held Company Valuation Techniques Differ by Size and Purpose of Appraisal." Parts I and II. *The Oregon Certified Public Accountant* (January–February 1986).

Pratt, Shannon P. "Developing the Valuation Model—Comparisons, Approaches, and Sources." *Journal of Business Valuation* (Proceedings of the Seventh Biennial Conference of the Canadian Association of Business Valuators, 1985), pp. 7–18.

Pratt, Shannon P. "Rates of Return as an Influence on Value." New York University Proceedings of the Third Annual Institute on State and Local Taxation and Conference on Property Taxation (1985), pp. 21.1–21.15.

Pratt, Shannon P. "Understanding Capitalization Rates." *ASA Valuation* (June 1986), pp. 12–29.

Pratt, Shannon P. "Valuing a Practice: Choosing the Right Capitalization Rates." *CA Magazine* (April 1987), pp. 49–52.

Pratt, Shannon P., and Philip M. Smith. "Valuing Stock Options, with Applications to Closely Held Companies." *Journal of Business Valuation,* 1987 (Proceedings of the First Joint Business Valuation Conference of The Canadian Institute of Chartered Business Valuators and The American Society of Appraisers, October 1986), pp. 227–49.

Rappaport, Alfred. "Converting Merger Benefits to Shareholder Value." *Mergers & Acquisitions* (March–April 1987), pp. 49–55.

Rappaport, Alfred. "Do You Know the Value of Your Company?" *Mergers and Acquisitions* (Spring 1979), pp. 12–21.

Reiff, Wallace W., and Arthur E. Gimmy. "Assigning Values to Management Contracts." *Mergers & Acquisitions* (January–February 1986), pp. 77–81.

Reilly, Raymond R. "Business Valuation Using the Stock and Debt Method." *ASA Valuation* (December 1984), pp. 28–34.

Rennie, Richard; Jack G. Vico; and George T. Murphy. "Factors in the Determination of the Valuation of Private Business Interests." *Osgood Hall Law Journal* (June 1982), pp. 261–73.

Roll, Richard, and Stephen A. Ross. "An Empirical Investigation of the Arbitrage Pricing Theory." *Journal of Finance* 35 (December 1980), pp. 1073–1103.

Rosen, Arthur R.; Joan S. Faber; and Jeffrey Tutnauer. "The Effect of Federal Tax Reform and Accounting Changes on the Valuation of Utilities." *Property Tax Journal* (June 1988), pp. 181–98.

Rosenbloom, Arthur H. "How to Determine the Value of a Business: A Case Study." *Practical Accountant* (March 1983), pp. 28–34.

Rubinstein, William S., and Nancy R. London. "Sales and Leasebacks: Some Valuation Problems." *Tax Lawyer* (Spring 1984), pp. 481–507.

Sammons, Donna. "Evaluating the Valuators." *Inc.* (May 1983), pp. 186–88.

Schilt, James H. "A Rational Approach to Capitalization Rates for Discontinuing the Future Income Stream of a Closely Held Company." *Financial Planner* (January 1982), pp. 56–57.

Schilt, James H. "A Review of the Standard Methods of Evaluating Closely Held Companies." *ASA Valuation* (November 1981), pp. 2–9.

Schilt, James H. "A Short Essay on Intrinsic Value." *Business Valuation News* (March 1984), pp. 23–26.

Schilt, James H. "An Objection to the Excess Earnings Method of Business Appraisal." *Taxes* (February 1980), pp. 123–26.

Schilt, James H. "Appraisal under California Corporations Code Section 2000." *Business Law News* (State Bar of California, Summer 1985). Also in *Business Valuation News* (December 1985), pp. 9–16.

Schilt, James H. "Appraising the Close Corporation, *Lotz, Hewitson* and *Ronald* Not Withstanding." *Business Valuation Review* (December 1986), pp. 25–34. Also in *Business Law News* (State Bar of California, Summer 1986).

Schilt, James H. "Challenging Standard Business Appraisal Methods." *Business Valuation News* (December 1984), pp. 4–14. Also in *Business Law News* (State Bar of California, Winter 1985), and *ASA Valuation* (June 1985), pp. 2–10.

Schilt, James H. "Pitfalls in the Valuation of Closely Held Companies." *Trusts & Estates* (June 1980), pp. 44–47.

Schilt, James H. "Selection of Capitalization Rates for Valuing a Closely Held Business." *Business Law News* (Spring 1982), pp. 35–37.

Schmehl, John W. "How Liquidations and S Elections May Avoid the Impact of TRA '86." *Journal of Taxation* (July 1987), pp. 30–38.

Schneider, Willys H., and Sarah G. Austrian. "Widespread Changes for Corporations in 1987 Act." *Journal of Taxation* (April 1988), pp. 196–202.

Schreier, W. T., and O. Maurice Joy. "Judicial Valuation of 'Close' Corporation Stock: Alice in Wonderland Revisited." *Oklahoma Law Review* 31 (Fall 1978), pp. 853–85.

Siegel, Joel G. "The 'Quality of Earnings' Concept—A Survey." *Financial Analysts Journal* (March–April 1982), pp. 60–68.

Singleton, Margaret "What's It Worth to You?" *Inc.* (September 1986), pp. 113–14.

Sirmans, C. F.; G. Stacy Sirmans; and Ben T. Beasley. "Income Property Valuation and the Use of Market Extracted Overall Capitalization Rates." *The Real Estate Appraiser and Analyst* (Summer 1986), pp. 64–68.

Stockdale, John J. "Comparison of Publicly-Held Companies with Closely-Held Business Entities." *Business Valuation Review* (December 1986), pp. 3–11.

"The Use of Appraisals in SEC Documents." *University of Pennsylvania Law Review* (November 1973), pp. 138–61.

Thompson, Donald J., IV. "Sources of Systematic Risk in Common Stock." *Journal of Business* (April 1976), pp. 173–88.

Thompson, Mark S. "How to Value Real Estate Limited Partnership Interests." *Trusts & Estates* (December 1984), pp. 35–41.

Thompson, Mark S. "Valuing Interests in Real Estate Partnerships." *Real Estate Review* (Winter 1987), pp. 36–40.

Treanor, Richard B., and Jack Johnson. "Valuation of Community Property Minority Interests Reflect Judicial Inconsistencies." *Journal of Taxation* (June 1980), pp. 356–60.

"Valuing a Closely-Held Business: What a Buyer Will Pay." *Small Business Report* (November 1986), pp. 30–35.

Vinso, Joseph D., and Burton H. Marcus. "Valuing the Closely Held Company: The Implications of the *Hewitson* Case." *Business Valuation News* (June 1985), pp. 7–10.

Weberman, Bernard H. "Current Approaches to Findings of Overvaluations in Tax Shelter Cases." *Journal of Taxation of Investments* (Winter 1986), pp. 99–127.

Weiss, Arthur A. "S Election Can Mitigate Effect of *General Utilities* Repeal." *Journal of Taxation* (December 1986), pp. 414–16.

Weiss, Stuart. "Business Appraising: Beware of Amateur Hour." Business Week (February 9, 1987), p. 74.

Wilcox, Jarred W. "The P/B-ROE Valuation Model." *Financial Analysts Journal* (January–February 1984), pp. 58–66.

Wise, Richard M., ed. "More Laws—More Valuations." *CA Magazine* (October 1987), pp. 52–57.

Wise, Richard M. "Valuing Business For Foreign Investors." *CA Magazine* (May 1987), pp. 89–94.

Yaney, J. P.; D. G. Seamans; and J. D. Crawford, Jr. "Going-Concern Value: An Elusive Intangible Asset That Can Upset Allocations in Business Transfers." *Taxation for Lawyers* (May–June 1985), pp. 366–70.

Books

Appraisal of Utilities and Railroad Property for Ad Valorem Taxation. Seventeenth Annual Program Proceedings of the Public Utilities Workshop. Wichita Kan.: Wichita State University, 1987. (Program proceedings are published annually from 1971 to present.)

Babcock, Henry A. *Appraisal Principles and Procedures.* Washington, D.C.: American Society of Appraisers, 1980.

Baron, Paul B. *When You Buy or Sell a Company.* Meriden, Conn.: The Center for Business Information, Inc., 1983.

Bernstein, Leopold A. *Financial Statement Analysis: Theory, Application and Interpretation.* 4th ed. Homewood, Ill.: Richard D. Irwin, 1989.

Bienenstock, Martin J. *Bankruptcy Reorganization.* New York: Practicing Law Institute, 1987.

Bierman, Harold, Jr., and Seymour Smidt. *The Capital Budgeting Decision: Economic Analysis of Investment Projects.* 6th ed. New York: Macmillan, 1984.

Blackman, Irving L. *The Valuation of Privately Held Businesses.* Chicago: Probus Publishing, 1986.

Bonbright, James C. *The Valuation of Property,* vols. 1 and 2. Charlottesville, Va.: The Miche Company, 1965. (Reprint of 1937 ed.)

Borden, Arthur M. *Going Private.* New York: Law Journal Seminars Press, 1986.

Brown, Ronald L., ed. *Valuing Professional Practices and Licenses: A Guide for the Matrimonial Practitioner.* Clifton, N.J.: Prentice Hall Law & Business, 1987.

Burke, Frank M., Jr. *Valuation and Valuation Planning for Closely Held Businesses.* Englewood Cliffs, N.J.: Prentice-Hall, 1981.

Cohen, Jerome B.; Edward D. Zinbarg; and Arthur Zeikel. *Investment Analysis and Portfolio Management.* 4th ed. Homewood, Ill.: Richard D. Irwin, 1982.

Cottle, Sidney; Roger F. Murray; and Frank E. Block. *Graham and Dodd's Security Analysis.* 5th ed. New York: McGraw-Hill, 1988.

Crandall, Arthur L. *Valuing Businesses and Professional Practices with Revenues under $20 million.* New York: American Institute of Certified Public Accountants, 1988.

Desmond, Glenn M., and Richard E. Kelley. *Business Valuation Handbook.* Los Angeles, Calif.: Valuation Press, 1980.

Desmond, Glenn M., and John Marcello. *Handbook of Small Business Valuation Formulas.* Los Angeles, Calif.: Valuation Press, 1987.

Dewing, Arthur Stone. *The Financial Policy of Corporations.* 5th ed., vols. 1 and 2. New York: Ronald Press, 1953.

Diamond, Stephen C. *Leveraged Buyouts.* Homewood, Ill.: Dow Jones-Irwin, 1985.

Dunn, Robert L. *Recovery of Damages for Lost Profits.* 3rd ed. Kentfield, Calif.: Lawpress Corporation, 1987.

Fisher, Irving. *The Theory of Interest.* New York: Macmillan, 1930. (Reprinted Augustus M. Kelley, 1961.)

Fisher, Kenneth L. *Super Stocks.* Homewood, Ill.: Dow Jones-Irwin, 1984.

Foster, Henry H., Jr., and Ronald L. Brown, eds. *Contemporary Matrimonial Law Issues: A Guide to Divorce Economics and Practice.* New York: Law & Business, Inc./Harcourt Brace Jovanovich, 1985.

Fuller, Russell J. *Capital Asset Pricing Theories: Evolution and New Frontiers.* Charlottesville, Va.: The Financial Analysts Research Foundation, 1981.

Goldberg, Barth H. *Valuation of Divorce Assets.* St. Paul, Minn.: West Publishing, 1984.

Goldstein, Arnold S. *The Complete Guide to Buying and Selling a Business.* New York: New American Library, 1983.

Graham, Benjamin; David L. Dodd; and Sidney Cottle. *Security Analysis: Principles and Techniques.* 4th ed. New York: McGraw-Hill, 1962.

Grimes, John Alden, and William Horace Craigue. *Principles of Valuation.* New York: Prentice-Hall, 1928.

Gurney, Roland. *Share Valuation Manual.* Brookfield, Vt.: Gower Publishing Company, 1987.

Hampton, John J. *Financial Decision Making: Concepts, Problems, and Cases.* 3rd ed. Reston, Va.: Reston Publishing, 1983.

Ibbotson, Roger G., and Gary P. Brinson. *Investment Markets: Gaining the Performance Advantage.* New York: McGraw-Hill, 1987.

Krahmer, Johannes R. *Valuation of Shares of Closely Held Corporations.*

Washington, D.C.: Tax Management Inc., 1985 (Estates, Gifts, and Trusts, 221-2d T.M.).

Kramer, Yale. *Valuing a Closely Held Business,* Accountant's Workbook Series. New York: Matthew Bender, 1987.

Lane, Marc J. *Purchase and Sale of Small Businesses: Tax and Legal Aspects.* New York: John Wiley & Sons, 1985.

Levine, Sumner N., ed. *The Financial Analyst's Handbook.* 2nd ed. Homewood, Ill.: Dow Jones-Irwin, 1988.

Lipper, Arthur, III. *Venture's Guide to Investing in Private Companies.* Homewood, Ill.: Dow Jones-Irwin, 1984.

Martin, Thomas J., and Mark R. Gustafson. *Valuing Your Business.* New York: Holt, Rinehart & Winston, 1980.

McCarthy, George D., and Robert E. Healy. *Valuing a Company: Practices and Procedures.* New York: John Wiley & Sons, 1971.

Miles, Raymond C. *Basic Business Appraisal.* New York: John Wiley & Sons, 1984.

Ness, Theodore, and William F. Indoe. *Tax Planning for Disposition of Business Interests.* Boston: Warren, Gorham & Lamont, 1985.

O'Neal, F. Hodge, and Robert B. Thompson. *O'Neal's Close Corporations.* 3rd ed., vols. 1 and 2. Wilmette, Ill.: Callaghan & Company, 1958, 1963, 1965–1987.

O'Neal, F. Hodge, and Robert B. Thompson. *O'Neal's Oppression of Minority Shareholders.* 2nd ed., vols. 1 and 2. Wilmette, Ill.: Callaghan & Company, 1975–1985.

Poynter, Daniel F. *The Expert Witness Handbook: Tips and Techniques for the Litigation Consultant.* Santa Barbara, Calif.: Para Publishing, 1987.

Pratt, Shannon P., ed. *Readings in Business Valuation.* Washington, D.C.: American Society of Appraisers Educational Foundation, 1986.

Pratt, Shannon P. *Valuing Property Management Companies* (A Study). Chicago: Institute of Real Estate Management Foundation, 1988.

Pratt Shannon P. *Valuing Small Businesses and Professional Practices.* Homewood, Ill.: Dow Jones-Irwin, 1986.

Reilly, Frank M. *Investment Analysis and Portfolio Management.* 2nd ed. Hinsdale, Ill.: Dryden Press, 1985.

Schnepper, Jeff A. *The Professional Handbook of Business Valuation.* Reading, Mass.: Addison-Wesley Publishing, 1982.

Shank, Steven J., and Richard K. Olson. *Practical Divorce Valuation and Financial Analysis.* Eau Claire, Wis.: Professional Education Systems, Inc., 1986.

Siegel, Joel G. *How to Analyze Businesses, Financial Statements, and the Quality of Earnings.* Englewood Cliffs, N.J.: Prentice-Hall, 1982.

Sokoloff, Kiril, ed. *The Paine Webber Handbook of Stock and Bond Analysis.* New York: McGraw-Hill, 1979.

Speedy, Squire L. *Financial Appraisal.* Wellington, New Zealand: New Zealand Institute of Valuers, 1982.

Williams, John Burr. *The Theory of Investment Value.* Cambridge, Mass.: Harvard University Press, 1938. (Reprinted in Amsterdam by North Holland Publishing, 1956.)

Dissenting-Stockholders' Actions

Articles

"Achieving Fairness in Corporate Cash Mergers: *Weinberger v. UOP.*" *Connecticut Law Review* 16 (Fall 1983), pp. 95–119.

Allred, William S. "Corporate Law—Chipping Away at the Delaware Block: A Critique of the Delaware Block Approach to the Valuation of Dissenters' Shares in Appraisal Proceedings." *Western New England Law Review* 8 (Spring 1986), pp. 191–227.

Banks, Warren E. "A Selective Inquiry into Judicial Stock Valuation." *Indiana Law Review* 6 (1972), pp. 19–44.

Birk, David R. "Shareholders' Appraisal Process: Need for Reform." *New York State Bar Journal* (June 1979), pp. 274–77, 314–21.

Booth, Richard A. "The New Law of Freeze-Out Mergers." *Missouri Law Review* 49 (1984), pp. 517–69.

Brudney, Victor. "Standards of Fairness and the Limits of Preferred Stock Modifications." *Rutgers Law Review* 26 (1973), pp. 445–87.

Brudney, Victor, and Marvin A. Chirelstein, "Fair Shares in Corporate Mergers and Takeovers." *Harvard Law Review* 88 (December 1974), pp. 297–346.

Chazen, Leonard. "Fairness from a Financial Point of View in Acquisitions of Public Companies: Is 'Third-Party Sale Value' the Appropriate Standard?" *Business Lawyer* (July 1981), pp. 1439–81.

Cohen, Shlomo. "*Bell v. Kirby Lumber Corp.:* Ascertaining 'Fair Value' under the Delaware Appraisal Statute." *Columbia Law Review* 81 (March 1981), pp. 426–40.

Coleman, Joseph M. "The Appraisal Remedy in Corporate Freeze-Outs: Questions of Valuation and Exclusivity." *Southwestern Law Journal* 38 (1984), pp. 775–98.

Dennis, Roger J. "Valuing the Firm and the Development of Delaware Corporate Law." *Rutgers Law Journal* 17 (Fall 1985), pp. 1–49.

Deutsch, Jan G. "The Mysteries of Corporate Law: A Response to Brudney and Chirelstein." *Yale Law Journal* 88 (1978), pp. 235–41.

Easterbrook, Frank H., and Daniel R. Fischel. "Corporate Control Transactions." *Yale Law Journal* 91 (1982), pp. 698–737.

Gray, Gerald. "When Is Fair Market Value Unfair?" *ASA Valuation* (June 1984), pp. 2–7.

Haight, Carol B. "The Standard of Care Required of an Investment Banker to Minority Shareholders in a Cash-Out Merger: *Weinberger v. UOP, Inc.*" *Investment Banker* 8 (1983), pp. 98–121.

Herzel, Leo, and Jesse A. Finklestein. "Fairness: Majority vs. Minority." *National Law Journal* (July 16, 1984), pp. 15–19.

Hobart, Geoffrey A. "Delaware Improves Its Treatment of Freezeout Mergers: *Weinberger v. UOP, Inc.*" *Boston College Law Review* 25 (May 1984), pp. 685–723.

Hotchkiss, David L. "Corporations—Fair Value for Dissenting Shareholders under the Pennsylvania Appraisal Statute." *Dickinson Law Review* 78 (Spring 1974), pp. 582–96.

Johnson, W. A. "Dissenter Shareholder Valuations: A Study of Cases and References." *Business Valuation Review* (March 1988), pp. 9–17.

Kanda, Hideki, and Saul Levmore. "The Appraisal Remedy and the Goals of Corporate Law." *UCLA Law Review* 32 (Fall 1985), pp. 429–73.

Lorne, Simon M. "A Reappraisal of Fair Shares in Controlled Mergers." *University of Pennsylvania Law Review* 126 (May 1978), pp. 955–88.

McLean, John T. "Minority Shareholders and Cashout Mergers: The Delaware Court Offers Plaintiffs Greater Protection and a Procedural Dilemma— *Weinberger v. UOP, Inc.*" *Washington Law Review* 59 (1983), pp. 119–40.

Mirvis, Theodore N. "Two-Tier Pricing: Some Appraisal and 'Entire Fairness' Valuation Issues." *Business Lawyer* (February 1983), pp. 485–501.

Nathan, Charles M., and K. L. Shapiro. "Legal Standard of Fairness of Merger Terms under Delaware Law." *Delaware Journal of Corporate Law* 2 (1977), pp. 44–64.

Payson, Robert K., and Gregory A. Inskip. "*Weinberger v. UOP, Inc.:* Its Practical Significance in the Planning and Defense of Cash-Out Mergers." *Delaware Journal of Corporate Law* 8 (1983), pp. 83–97.

Prickett, William, and Michael Hanrahan. "*Weinberger v. UOP:* Delaware's Effort to Preserve a Level Playing Field for Cash-Out Mergers." *Delaware Journal of Corporate Law* 8 (1983), pp. 59–82.

Rams, Edwin M. "Judicial Valuation of Dissenting Shareholder Interests." *Lincoln Law Review* 8 (1973), pp. 74–89.

Roberts, William M. "The Status of Minority Shareholders' Remedies for Oppression after *Santa Fe* and *Singer* and the Question of 'Reasonable Investment Expectation' Valuation." *Delaware Journal of Corporate Law* 6 (1981), pp. 16–53.

Rogers, J. Steven. "The Dissenting Shareholder's Appraisal Remedy." *Oklahoma Law Review* 30 (Summer 1977), pp. 629–43.

Schaefer, Elmer J. "The Fallacy of Weighting Asset Value and Earnings Value in the Appraisal of Corporate Stock." *Southern California Law Review* 55 (July 1982), pp. 1031–96.

Schilt, James H. "*Weinberger v. UOP, Inc.:* Challenge for the Business Appraiser." *Trusts & Estates* (August 1984), pp. 87–90.

Seligman, Joel G. "Reappraising the Appraisal Remedy." *George Washington Law Review* 52 (May 1984), pp. 829–71.

Steinberg, Marc I., and Evalyn Lindahl. "The New Law of Squeeze-Out Mergers." *Washington University Law Quarterly* 62 (Fall 1984), pp. 352–414.

Thompson, Robert B. "Squeeze-Out Mergers and the 'New' Appraisal Remedy." *Washington University Law Quarterly* 62 (1984), pp. 415–34.

Tinio, Ferdinand S. "Valuation of Stock of Dissenting Stockholders in Case of Consolidation or Merger of Corporation, Sale of Its Assets, or the Like." 48 *A.L.R.* 3d 430 (1973, Supplements 1979, 1986).

"Valuation of Dissenter's Stock under Appraisal Statutes." *Harvard Law Review* 30 (May 1966) pp. 1453–74.

Van Nuis, Rosalie P. "Delaware's Solution to the Problem of the Minority Stockholders in a Cash-Out Merger—*Weinberger v. UOP, Inc.*" *Northern Kentucky Law Review* 11 (1984), pp. 575–611.

Ward, David A. "The Appraisal Remedy." *Journal of Business Valuation,* 1983 (Proceedings of the Sixth Biennial Conference of the Canadian Association of Business Valuators, November 1982), pp. 117–32.

Ward Rodman, Jr., and John G. Day. "Finding Fair Value: The Delaware Block Method Revisited." *Journal of Business Valuation,* 1987 (Proceedings of the First Joint Business Valuation Conference of The Canadian Institute of Chartered Business Valuators and The American Society of Appraisers, October 1986), pp. 87–96.

Weiss, Elliott J. "Balancing Interests in Cash-Out Mergers: The Promise of *Weinberger v. UOP, Inc." Delaware Journal of Corporate Law* 3 (1983), pp. 1–58.

Weston, Mark G. "Delaware's Appraisal Statute: The Courts' Artificial Ceiling on Asset Valuation Weighting." *Notre Dame Law Review* 58 (December 1982), pp. 410–28.

Wise, Richard M. " 'Fair Value' and the Appraisal Remedy." *Journal of Business Valuation,* 1987 (Proceedings of the First Joint Business Valuation Conference of The Canadian Institute of Chartered Business Valuators and The American Society of Appraisers, October 1986), pp. 77–86.

Goodwill and Other Intangibles

Articles

Ackerman, Alan T. "Just Compensation for Condemnation of Going Concern Value." *ASA Valuation* (June 1986), pp. 42–55.

Adams, Fred M. "Professional Goodwill as Community Property: How Should Idaho Rule?" *Idaho Law Review* 14 (Spring 1978), pp. 473–91.

Arnold, Ralph. "Putting a Value on Future Interests." *Family Advocate* (Summer 1984), pp. 32–36, 42.

Baker, Glenn A. "Goodwill, Going Concern Become Harder to Avoid." *Mergers & Acquisitions* (Summer 1984), pp. 58–62.

Bergman, Gregory M. "Valuation of Goodwill." *Los Angeles Bar Journal* (August 1977), pp. 87–98.

Blaine, Davis R. "Valuation of Goodwill and Going Concern Value." *Mergers & Acquisitions* (Spring 1979), pp. 4–11.

Blum, Marc P. "Valuing Intangibles: What Are the Choices for Valuing Professional Sports Teams?" *Journal of Taxation* (November 1976), pp. 286–88.

Boehm, Ted. "'Hoskold's Formula' for the Valuation of Intangibles." *Capital University Law Review* 10 (Winter 1980), pp. 293–307.

Davis, Michael E. "Valuation of Professional Goodwill upon Marital Dissolution." *Southwestern University Law Review* 7 (Spring 1975), pp. 186–205.

Doernberg, Richard U., and Thomas D. Hall. "The Tax Treatment of Going-Concern Value." *George Washington Law Review* 52, no. 3 (March 1984), pp. 353–94.

Dostart, Thomas J. "Professional Education as a Divisible Asset in Marriage Dissolutions." *Iowa Law Review* 64 (March 1979), pp. 705–21.

Florio, Nicholas, and Frank J. LaGreca. "Valuing Amortizable Intangible Assets: Are They Being Wasted?" *Tax Adviser* (September 1986), pp. 544–49.

Ganier, Patricia K. "Treatment of Goodwill: Allocating a Lump Sum Purchase Price among Mixed Assets of a Going Business." *Journal of Corporate Taxation* (Summer 1980), pp. 111–36.

"Going Concern Value Can Exist Even without Goodwill." *Taxation for Lawyers* (January–February 1977), pp. 229–30.

"Goodwill." 5 *American Jurisprudence Proof of Facts* 505 (1960, Supplement 1979).

"Goodwill." 38 *American Jurisprudence* 2d 911 (1968, Supplement 1979).

"Goodwill." 38 *Corpus Juris Secundum* 948 (1943, Supplement 1979).

Gross, Paul H. "Establishing Fair Market Value of Intangible Assets." *Journal of Business Valuation* 4 (July 1977), pp. 5–17.

Hauserman, Nancy R., and Carol Fethke. "Valuation of a Homemaker's Services." *Trial Lawyer's Guide* (Fall 1978), pp. 249–66.

Henszey, Benjamin N. "Going Concern Value after *Concord Control, Inc.*" *Taxes* (November 1983), pp. 699–705.

Hocker, Jerry W. "Methods of Valuing Intangibles in Leveraged Buyouts." *Journal of Buyouts & Acquisitions* (August–September 1984), pp. 33–37.

King, Roger T. "The Valuation of Goodwill: An Approach for the Appraiser." *Appraisal Review Journal* (Summer 1984), pp. 77–79.

Locke, Dennis H. "A Systematic Approach to Patent Valuation." *Business Valuation News* (September 1986), pp. 23–27.

McMullin, Scott G. "The Valuation of Patents." *Business Valuation News* (September 1983), pp. 5–13.

Osborne, Kent L. "Recent Decision Invalidates Second Tier Allocation and Favors Residual Method for Valuing Goodwill and Going Concern Value—A Note." *Business Valuation News* (June 1985), pp. 11–13.

Paulsen, Jon. "Measuring Rods for Intangible Assets." *Mergers & Acquisitions* (Spring 1984), pp. 45–49.

Pinnell, Robert E. "Divorce after Professional School: Education and Future Earning Capacity May Be Marital Property." *Missouri Law Review* 44 (Spring 1979), pp. 329–40.

Projector, Murray. "Valuation of Retirement Benefits in Marriage Dissolutions." *Los Angeles Bar Bulletin* 50 (April 1975), pp. 229–38.

Rosenstein, Barnard Lapointe Pierre. "The Valuation of Intangibles: Legal and Tax Aspects." *Journal of Business Valuation*, 1983 (Proceedings of the Sixth Biennial Conference of the Canadian Association of Business Valuators, November 1982), pp. 67–84.

Schilt, James H. "Goodwill and Excess Earnings." *Business Law News* (Winter 1982), pp. 18–20.

Schnee, Edward J., and Barney R. Cargile. "Going Concern Value—a New Intangible?" *Tax Adviser* (July 1984), pp. 386–92.

Shipley, W. E. "Accountability for Good Will on Dissolution of Partnership." 65 *A.L.R.* 2d 521 (1959, Supplements 1978, 1979).

Udinsky, Jerald H. "The Microeconomics of Goodwill with an Application to Law." *Business Valuation News* (June 1983), pp. 3–10.

Udinsky, Jerald H. "Putting a Value on Goodwill." *Family Advocate* (Fall 1986), pp. 37–40.

Vinso, Joseph D. "Excess Earnings Estimation of Intangibles—a Note." *Business Valuation News* (December 1984), pp. 15–17.

Vinso, Joseph D. "Valuing Professional Goodwill: The *Slivka* Case Revisited." *Business Valuation Review* (December 1987), pp. 156–63.

Wiener, Hilton M. "Going Concern Value: Goodwill by Any Other Name?" *Tax Lawyer* (Fall 1979), pp. 183–97.

Marketability and Minority Interests

Articles

Amihud, Yakov, and Haim Mandelson. "Liquidity and Stock Returns." *Financial Analysts Journal* (May–June 1986), pp. 43 +.

Arneson, George S. "Minority Discounts beyond Fifty Percent Can Be Supported." *Taxes* (February 1981), pp. 97–102.

Arneson, George S. "Nonmarketability Discounts Should Exceed Fifty Percent." *Taxes* (January 1981), pp. 25–31.

Arneson, George S. "The Case for No Majority-Control Premium." *Taxes* (March 1981), pp. 190–93.

Austin, Douglas V., and Michael J. Jackson. "Tender Offer Update." *Mergers & Acquisitions* (updated article appears annually).

Bolten, Steven E. "Discounts for Stocks of Closely Held Corporations." *Trusts & Estates* (December 1984), pp. 22–23.

Coolidge, H. Calvin. "Discount for Minority Interest: Rev. Rul. 79-7's Denial of Discount Is Erroneous." *Illinois Bar Journal* 68 (July 1980), pp. 744–49.

Coolidge, H. Calvin. "Fixing Value of Minority Interest in a Business; Actual Sales Suggest Discount as High as 70%." *Estate Planning* (Spring 1975), pp. 138–40.

"Cost of Flotation of Registered Issues, 1971–72." Washington, D.C.: Securities and Exchange Commission, 1974.

Cummins, J. R.; M. S. Weinberg; and D. M. Roth. "Current Attitudes towards Estate Tax Discounts for Restricted Securities and Underwriting Fees." *Estate Planning* (September 1983), pp. 276–81.

Dant, Thomas W., Jr. "Courts Increasing Amount of Discount for a Minority Interest in a Business." *Journal of Taxation* (August 1975), pp. 104–9.

"Discounts Involved in Purchases of Common Stock (1966–1969)." *Institutional Investor Study Report of the Securities and Exchange Commission.* H. R. Doc. No. 64, Part 5, 92d Cong., 1st Sess. (1971), pp. 2444–56.

Emory, John D. "The Value of Marketability as Illustrated in Initial Public Offerings of Common Stock: January 1985 through June 1986." *Business Valuation Review* (December 1986) pp. 12–14.

Emory, John D. "The Value of Marketability as Illustrated by Initial Public Offerings of Common Stock: January 1980 through June 1981." *Business Valuation Review* (September 1985), pp. 21–24.

Featherston, Thomas M., Jr., and William R. Trail. "Enhanced Value of Closely-Held Stock, Community or Separate: Closer to a Solution." *Texas Bar Journal* 47 (February 1984), pp. 128–44.

Gampel, Peter. "Recent Thoughts When Valuing a Minority Interest in a Closely Held Company." *Business Valuation Review* (June 1987), pp. 64–85.

Gauthier, Andre P. "Valuation of Minority Shares of Publicly Held Companies." *Journal of Business Valuation,* 1981 (Proceedings of the Fifth Biennial Conference of the Canadian Association of Business Valuators, October 1980), pp. 201–22.

Gelman, Milton. "An Economist–Financial Analyst's Approach to Valuing Stock of a Closely-Held Company." *Journal of Taxation* (June 1972), pp. 353–54.

Harper, John S., Jr., and Peter J. Lindquist. "Quantitative Support for Large Minority Discounts in Closely Held Corporations." *The Appraisal Journal* (April 1983), pp. 270–77.

Johnson, Richard D., and George A. Racette. "Discounts on Letter Stock Do Not Appear to Be a Good Base on Which to Estimate Discounts for Lack of Marketability on Closely Held Stock." *Taxes* (August 1981), pp. 574–81.

Lease, Ronald C.; John J. McConnell; and Wayne H. Mikkelson. "The Market Value of Control in Publicly-Traded Corporations." *Journal of Financial Economics* 11 (1983), pp. 439–71.

Lease, Ronald C.; John J. McConnell; and Wayne H. Mikkelson. "The Market Value of Differential Voting Rights in Closely Held Corporations." *Journal of Business* (October 1984), pp. 443–67.

Lipkin, Laurence. "The Theory of Minority Discount in Regard to ESOP Shares of Closely-Held Corporations." *ASA Valuation* (November 1980), pp. 130–34.

Lyons, William P., and Martin J. Whitman. "Valuing Closely-Held Corporations and Publicly-Traded Securities with Limited Marketability: Approaches to Allowable Discounts from Gross Values." *Business Lawyer* (July 1978), pp. 2213–29.

Maher, J. Michael. "An Objective Measure for a Discount for a Minority Interest and a Premium for a Controlling Interest." *Taxes* (July 1979), pp. 449–54.

Maher, J. Michael. "Application of Key Man Discount in the Valuation of Closely-Held Businesses." *Taxes* (June 1977), pp. 377–80.

Maher, J. Michael. "Discounts for Lack of Marketability for Closely Held Business Interests." *Taxes* (September 1976), pp. 562–71.

Moore, Philip. "Valuation Revisited." *Trusts & Estates* (February 1987), pp. 40–52.

Moreland, E. R. "The Control Value of Noncontrolling Shares." *Review of Taxation of Individuals* 8 (Fall 1984), pp. 291–348.

Moroney, Robert E. "Most Courts Overvalue Closely Held Stocks." *Taxes* (March 1973), pp. 144–54.

Moroney, Robert E. "Why 25 Percent Discount for Nonmarketability in One Valuation, 100 Percent in Another?" *Taxes* (May 1977), pp. 316–20.

Obstler, David M. "The Investment Company Discount: *Estate of Folks* and Beyond." *Taxes* (January 1983), pp. 47–50.

Penn, Thomas A. "Premiums: What Do They Really Measure?" *Mergers & Acquisitions* (Fall 1981), pp. 30–34.

Pratt, Shannon P. "Valuing a Minority Interest in a Closely Held Company." *Practical Accountant* (June 1986), pp. 60–68.

Solberg, Thomas A. "Valuing Restricted Securities: What Factors Do the Courts and the Service Look For?" *Journal of Taxation* (September 1979), pp. 150–54.

"Survey Shows Trend toward Larger Minority Discounts." *Estate Planning* (September 1983), pp. 281–82.

Trout, Robert R. "Estimation of the Discount Associated with the Transfer of Restricted Securities." *Taxes* (June 1977), pp. 381–85.

"Valuation of Corporate Stock for Purposes of Succession, Inheritance, or Estate Tax, as Affected by Quantity Involved." 23 *A.L.R.* 2d 775 (1952, Supplements 1970, 1979).

"Valuing Closely Held Stock: Control Premiums and Minority Discounts." *Emory Law Journal* 31 (Winter 1982), pp. 139–99.

Vaughan, Jack M.; Chris B. Parsons; and Thomas J. Featherston, Jr. "Valuation of Community Property Interests in Closely Held Stock: The Minority Interest Discount Controversy Continues." *Community Property Journal* (Winter 1982), pp. 3–14.

Vincent, Gordon S. "*Estate of Bright* and *Propstra:* Rejection of Family Attribution in Estate Valuation." *Virginia Tax Review* 2 (Spring 1982), pp. 357–69.

Wiley, Thomas W. "Valuing Large Holdings of Publicly-Traded Stock: The 'Blockage' Problem." Philip E. Heckerling Institute on Estate Planning, University of Miami Law Center, 1974, pp. 800–819.

Mergers and Acquisitions

Articles

Alberts, William W., and James M. McTaggart. "The Short-Term Earnings per Share Standard for Evaluating Prospective Acquisitions." *Mergers & Acquisitions* (Winter 1978), pp. 4–18.

Anderson, Charles M. "1 + 1 = 3." *Management Accounting* (April 1987), pp. 28–31.

Asquith, Paul. "Merger Bids, Uncertainty, and Stockholder Returns." *Journal of Financial Economics* 11 (1983), pp. 51–83.

Asquith, Paul; Robert F. Bruner; and David W. Mullins, Jr. "The Gains to Bidding Firms from Merger." *Journal of Financial Economics* 11 (1983), pp. 121–39.

Bierman, Harold, Jr. "Valuing an Acquisition." *Financial Executive* (July 1980), pp. 20–23.

Blaising, James S., and John R. Gasiorowski. "Beyond Tire-Kicking: The Appraiser's New M & A Role." *Mergers & Acquisitions* (Summer 1983), pp. 34–40.

Bradley, James W., and Donald H. Korn. "Bargains in Valuation Disparities: Corporate Acquirer versus Passive Investor." *Sloan Management Review* 20 (Winter 1979), pp. 51–64.

Brown, Paul B., and John A. Byrne. "Let's Do a Deal." *Business Week* (April 18, 1986), p. 265.

Brudney, Victor. "Efficient Markets and Fair Values in Parent Subsidiary Mergers." *Journal of Corporation Law* (Fall 1978), pp. 63–86.

Brudney, Victor, and Marvin A. Chirelstein. "Fair Shares in Corporate Mergers & Takeovers." *Harvard Law Review* (December 1974), pp. 297–346.

Chambers, John C., and Satinder K. Mullick. "Determining the Acquisition Value of a Company." *Management Accounting* (April 1970), pp. 24–31, 39.

Chazen, Leonard. "Fairness from a Financial Point of View in Acquisitions of Public Companies: Is 'Third-Party Sale Value' the Appropriate Standard?" *Business Lawyer* (July 1981), pp. 1439–81.

Chirelstein, Marvin A.; Ernest J. Sargeant; and Martin Liptin. "'Fairness' in Mergers between Parents and Partly-Owned Subsidiaries." New York: Practising Law Institute, Institute on Securities Regulation, 1977, pp. 273–308.

Einhorn, Stephen. "Notes on the Decision to Keep or to Sell a Small Business." *Mergers & Acquisitions* (Summer 1977), pp. 29–31.

Faber, Peter L. "Acquisitions and Liquidations Involving S Corporations after Tax Reform." *Practical Accountant* (September 1987), pp. 98–114.

Faris, John R.; Walter R. Holman; and Patrick A. Martinelli. "Valuing the Closely Held Business." *Mergers and Acquisitions* (Fall 1983), pp. 53–59.

Fiflis, Ted J. "Accounting for Mergers, Acquisitions and Investments in a Nutshell." *Business Lawyer* (November 1981), pp. 89–140.

Ginsburg, Martin D. "Special Topics in the Acquisitions Area." *San Diego Law Review* 22 (1985), pp. 159–69.

Gooch, Lawrence B., and Roger J. Grabowski. "Advanced Valuation Methods in Mergers and Acquisitions." *Mergers & Acquisitions* (Summer 1976), pp. 15–29.

Heath, John, Jr. "Appraisal Processes in Mergers and Acquisitions." *Mergers & Acquisitions* (Fall 1974), pp. 4–21.

Levinton, Howard, and Robert A. Snyder, Jr. "Negotiating Strategies When a Client Wants to Sell a Closely Held Corporation." *Taxation for Lawyers* (January–February 1986), pp. 204–11.

Loomis, Carol J. "LBOs Are Taking Their Lumps." *Fortune* (December 7, 1987), pp. 63–68.

Lorne, Simon M. "A Reappraisal of Fair Shares in Controlled Mergers." *University of Pennsylvania Law Review* 126 (May 1978), pp. 955–88.

Mullaney, Michael D., and Richard W. Bailine. "Corporate Acquisitions after the Tax Reform Act of 1986." *Tax Adviser* (April 1987), pp. 212–25.

Penn, Thomas A. "Premiums: What Do They Really Measure?" *Mergers & Acquisitions* (Fall 1981), pp. 30–34.

Rappaport, Alfred. "Financial Analysis for Mergers and Acquisitions." *Mergers & Acquisitions* (Winter 1976), pp. 18–36.

Reilly, Robert F. "Pricing an Acquisition: A 15-Step Methodology." *Mergers & Acquisitions* (Summer 1979), pp. 14–31.

Ritchey, James S. "Acquisition Valuation: DCF Can Be Misleading." *Management Accounting* (January 1983), pp. 24–28.

Roche, James M.; Lonn W. Myers; and Daniel M. Sucker. "Price Allocation on Acquisitions and Basis Step-Up: Tilting at Windmills?" *Taxes* (December 1987), pp. 833–45.

Rock, Milton L., and Martin Sikora. "Accounting for Merger Mania." *Management Accounting* (April 1987), pp. 20–27.

Rosenbloom, Arthur H., and Alex W. Howard. "'Bootstrap' Acquisitions and How to Value Them." *Mergers & Acquisitions* (Winter 1977), pp. 18–26.

Saffer, Brian H. "Touching All Bases in Setting Merger Prices." *Mergers & Acquisitions* (Fall 1984), pp. 42–48.

Schipper, Katherine, and Rex Thompson. "Evidence on the Capitalized Value of Merger Activity for Acquiring Firms." *Journal of Financial Economics* 11 (1983), pp. 85–119.

Vernick, Mitchell F. "Business Value Lending in a Leveraged Acquisition." *Mergers & Acquisitions* (November–December 1987), pp. 73–77.

Whitmarsh, Duane R. "How to Investigate a Potential Acquisition." *Practical Accountant* (June 1981), pp. 37–43.

Books

Douglas, F. Gordon. *How to Profitably Sell or Buy a Company or Business.* New York: Van Nostrand-Reinhold, 1981.

Grimm, W. T. & Company. *Mergerstat Review.* Chicago: W. T. Grimm & Company, annual.

Jenkins, James W. *Mergers and Acquisitions: A Financial Approach,* 2nd ed. New York: American Management Association, 1986.

Jurek, Walter. *Merger & Acquisition Sourcebook,* vols. 1 and 2. Santa Barbara, Calif.: Quality Services Company, annual.

Lee, Steven J., and Robert P. Colman, eds. *Handbook of Mergers, Acquisitions and Buyouts.* Englewood Cliffs, N.J.: Prentice-Hall, 1985.

Lorne, Simon M. *Acquisitions and Mergers: Negotiated and Contested Transactions.* New York: Clark Boardman Company, Ltd., 1986.

Marren, Joseph H. *Mergers and Acquisitions: Will You Overpay?* Homewood, Ill.: Dow Jones-Irwin, 1985.

Morris, Joseph M. *Acquisitions, Divestitures, and Corporate Joint Ventures.* New York: John Wiley & Sons, 1984.

Pritchett, Price. *Making Mergers Work: A Guide to Managing Mergers and Acquisitions.* Homewood, Ill.: Dow Jones-Irwin, 1987.

Pritchett, Price. *After the Merger: Managing the Shockwaves.* Homewood, Ill.: Dow Jones-Irwin, 1985.

Rock, Milton R., ed. *The Mergers & Acquisitions Handbook.* New York: McGraw-Hill, 1987.

Scharf, Charles A.; Edward E. Shea; and George C. Beck. *Acquisitions, Mergers, Sales, Buyouts and Takeovers: A Handbook with Forms.* 3rd ed. Englewood Cliffs, N.J.: Prentice-Hall, 1985.

Smith, William K. *Handbook of Strategic Growth through Mergers and Acquisitions.* Englewood Cliffs, N.J.: Prentice-Hall, 1985.

Index

NOTE: Boldface numbers indicate primary references; ex. following a page number indicates an exhibit.